COLORADO'S ROCK CHRONICLES

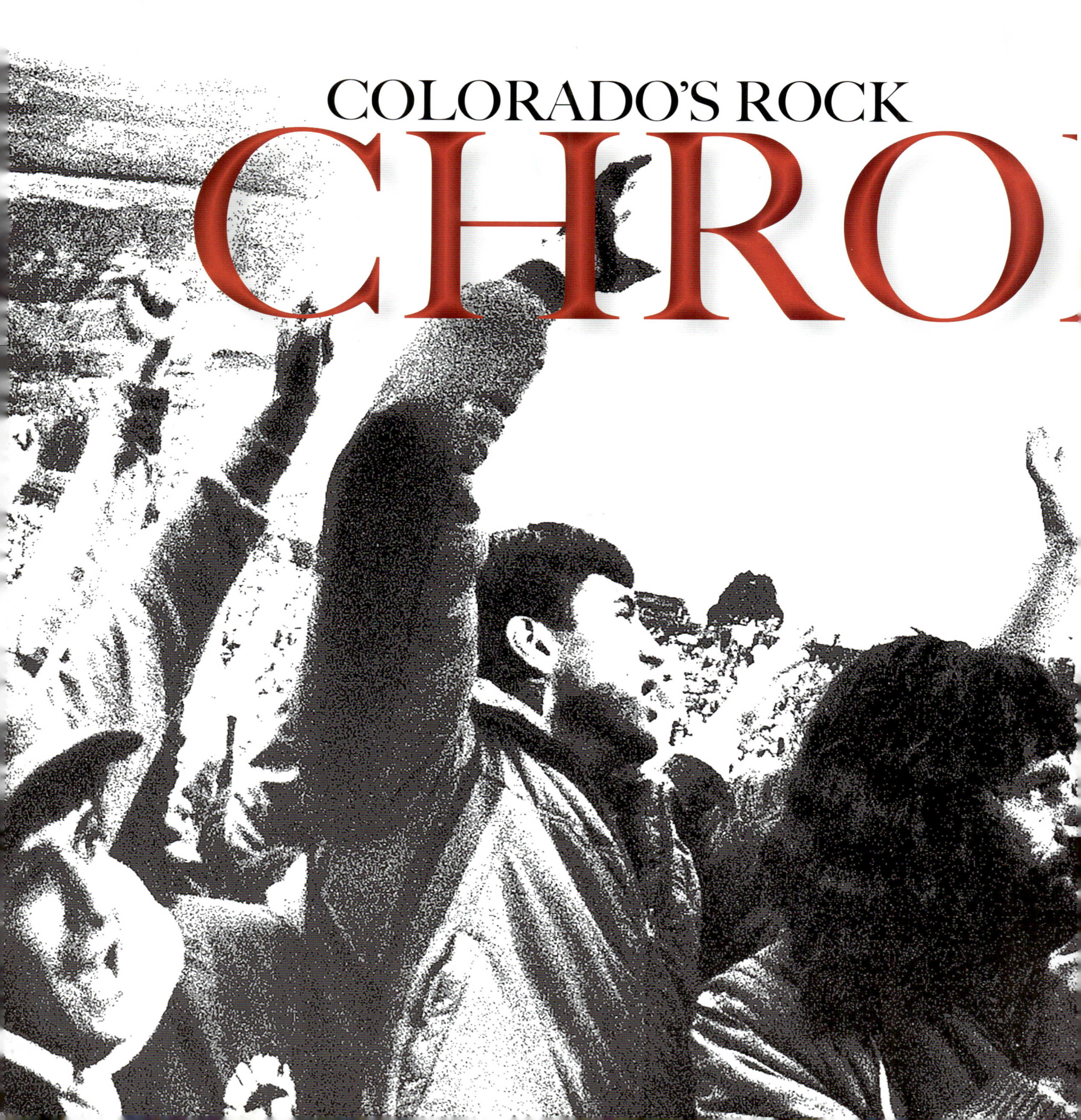
COLORADO'S ROCK
CHRO

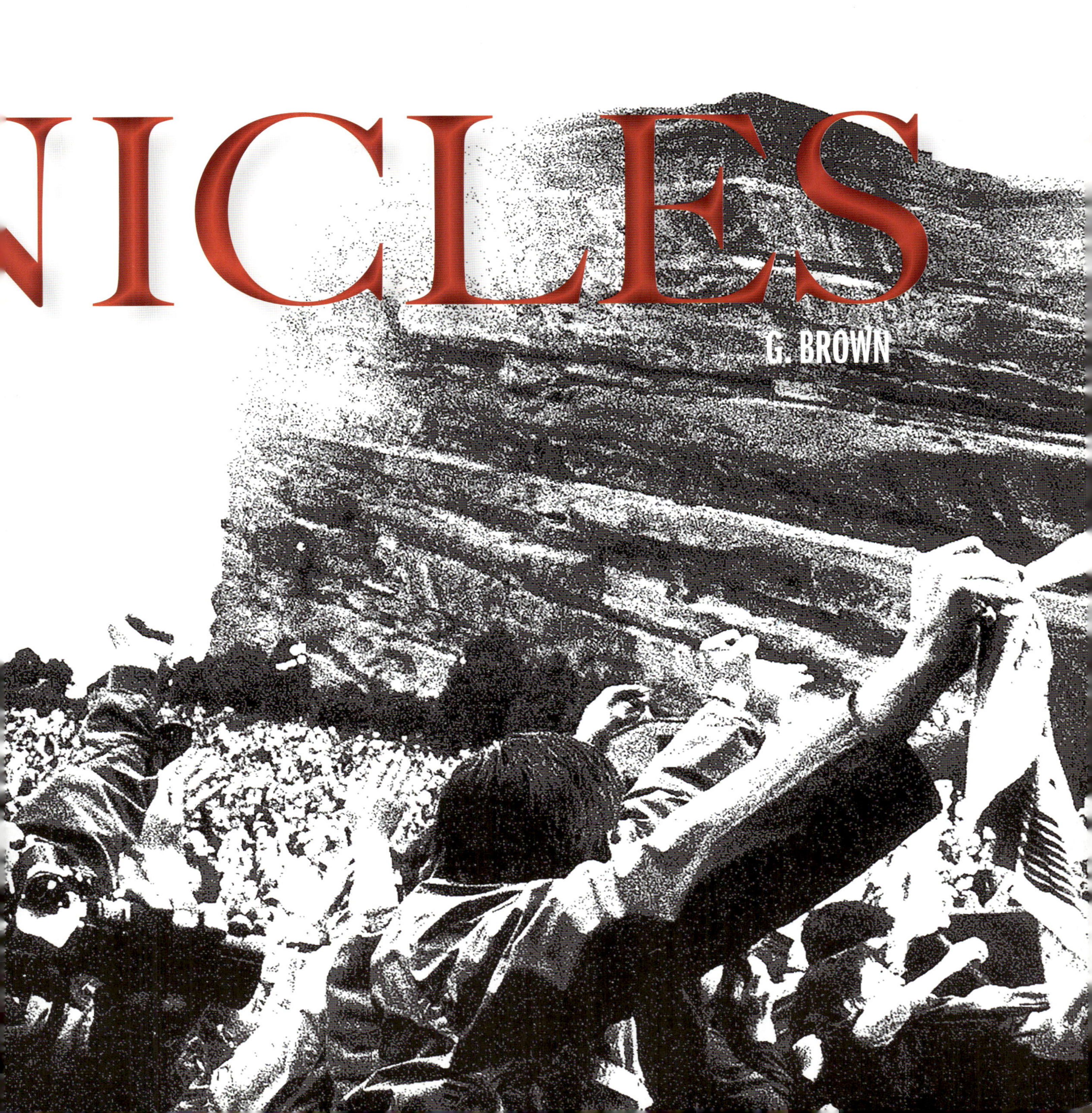
NICLES
G. BROWN

TABLE OF CONTENTS

1988 - 1995

1996 - 2003

2004 - 2015ww

INTRODUCTION

COLORADO IS A STATE OF MUSIC LOVERS. Born here in 1965, I have been shaped, for better or worse, by the musical love affairs of those I have encountered in life. My earliest memories are of my mother listening to the radio. More than anything, I remember how strongly she sometimes felt about a song, how it really moved her—this more distinctly than the music itself. How and what people feel about a piece of music are what gives it its first and most important life. It is a shared experience, a social experience and, in Colorado, I would say (partly with a chuckle) nearly a miraculous experience.

My childhood years were graced by a remarkable era in music, not just for Colorado, but globally. It has since been an evolution where we are always trying to recapture that very first high, serendipitously going on some great adventures of our own without realizing it. Rock 'n' roll is the attempt to retake that first virgin "blues moment"—every well-meaning rock guitarist wants to sit squarely at Robert Johnson's crossroads. Music conjures a secret link to the past, but in a way that is explosive, vital, and forward reaching. It's about living in the present, being present, being turned on.

You could say that Colorado has had an identity crisis of sorts. Denver isn't Chicago or New York City or Los Angeles, a "music town." The West is so new; it lacks the regionalism that some older cities gave to music, like New Orleans-style jazz or Detroit soul. But in Colorado there definitely exists a rare affection and love for music that isn't found in many other places.

There has always been a stream of concerts of all kinds, in some of the most beautiful settings found anywhere. Anyone who has been to Red Rocks Amphitheatre or the Telluride Bluegrass Festival will find it hard to do better. Colorado has a history of progressive-minded radio stations, including KFML, KBCO, KTCL, KBPI, KAZY, KQMT and KCUV.

I can cite major developments in Colorado music from my own experience. When we first started playing, there weren't many roofs for an "original" band to play under. The accepted notion was that if you were from Denver, you played covers. Everyone told us that we needed to move if we wanted to make it big. Yet as we performed around the country, I found that the "music towns" were not so musical after all. Of course, no one in the band ever found a good reason to leave Colorado. And, as it happened, we made it big anyway.

Which brings me to a point worth considering. It is always worth building your culture where you are, to be yourself. There are few things more valuable to a society than "folk culture." Always regional and personal, it grows out of artists having the courage to be individuals and reaching out to the neighbors. Folk culture is about making the apartment floor shake, so to speak, and about people being brought together. It is about taking risks, enough of them to get lucky. Every great movement in art has its origins in a supernatural or super-funky folk event—a local breakthrough. This happens all the time, everywhere.

But especially in Colorado.

—**TODD PARK MOHR**
Big Head Todd & the Monsters

1957-1971

IN THE early 1960s, most Americans still regarded Denver as an Old West cowtown in the Rocky Mountains, a blip on the national radar screen. Pop music crackled on AM airwaves, and every Colorado kid had a transistor radio tuned to KIMN, the Top 40 giant. The Denver Folklore Center became a pivotal stop for the national folk revival. As the counterculture movement took hold, Barry Fey opened the Family Dog, a hippie club, and promoted a rock festival that predated Woodstock by months. Once a venue for classical music, the stunning outdoor Red Rocks Amphitheatre regularly began to host rock acts—including the Beatles—with no roof over the stage and only nails on which to hang clothes in the dressing room. In 1971, a riot resulted in a ban on rock shows on the Rocks.

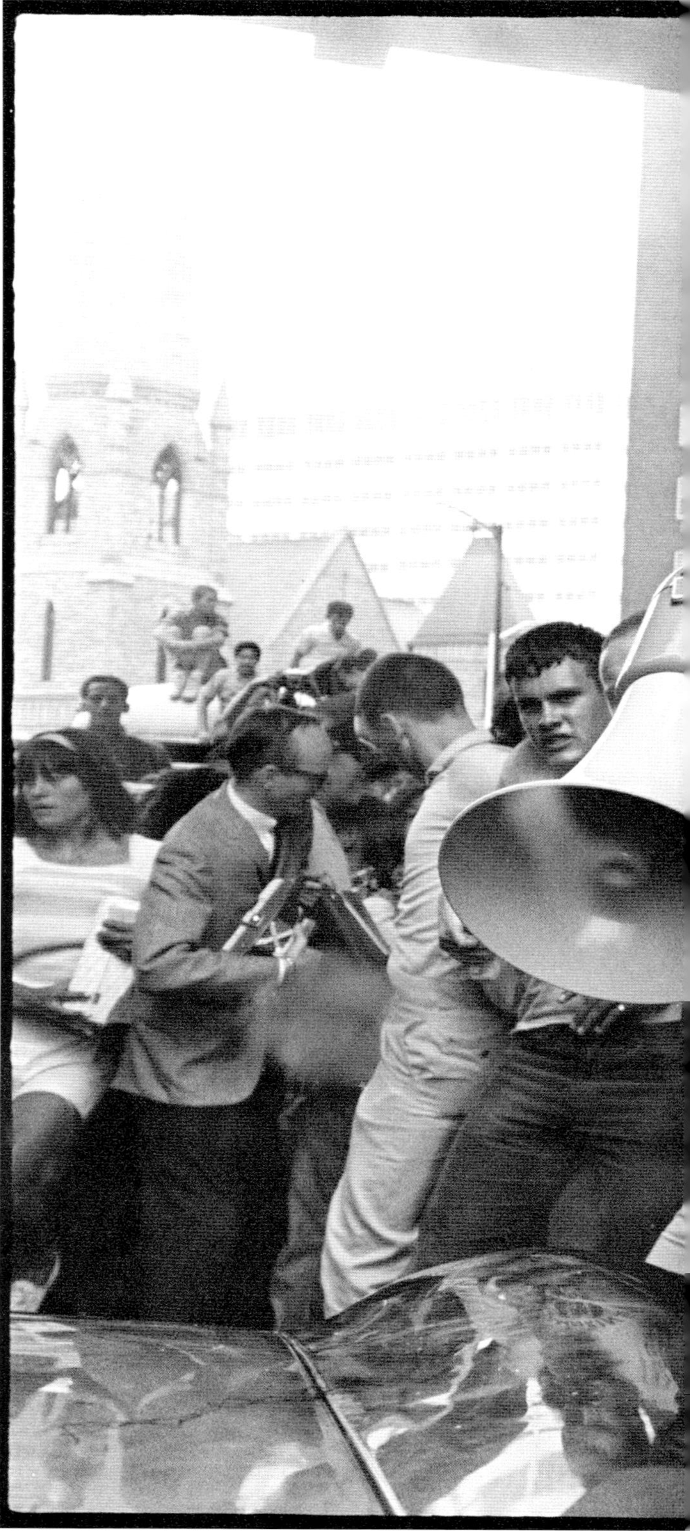

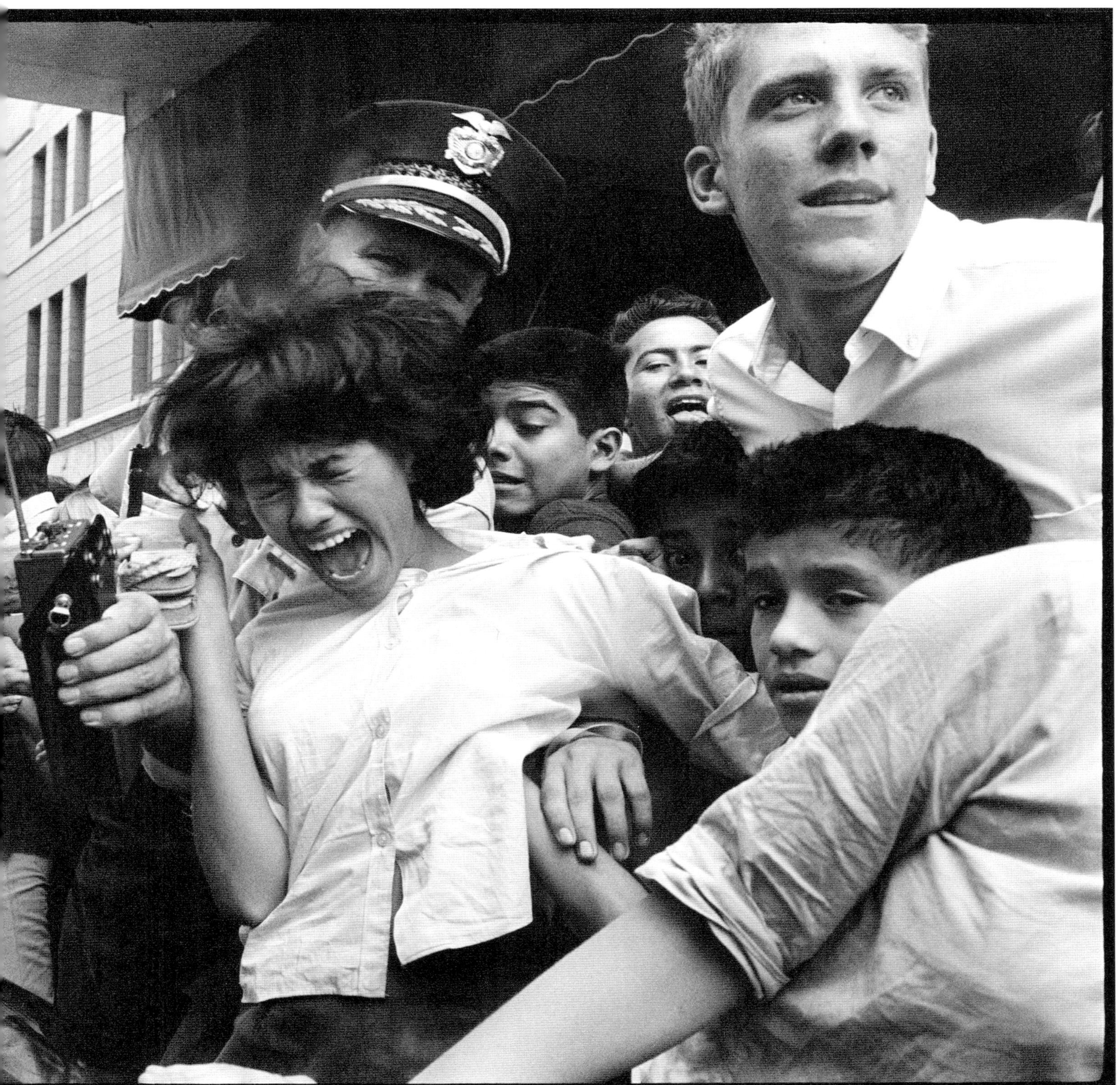

Beatles fans at Denver's Brown Palace, 1964

CHUCK BERRY }

AS A songwriter, Chuck Berry stood head and shoulders above rock 'n' roll's early stars. The majority of his output was self-penned, and during the second half of the 1950s he added new hits to his repertoire with almost every tour—compositions that gave the explosive new music genre a good deal of its language and style.

Several tunes were written from true-life experiences. "Sweet Little Sixteen," Berry's highest-ranking hit of the decade, was inspired after a Denver concert.

"I wasn't sweet little sixteen when I wrote it, of course," Berry said.

Berry had embarked on impresario Irving Feld's "Greatest Show of 1957" package tour, with Fats Domino, Clyde McPhatter, the Five Satins, LaVern Baker and others. The event went through every region of the United States, including some—such as the northern Rocky Mountain states—which had never witnessed live rock 'n' roll.

"I happened to open the show this particular date at the Denver Coliseum, and while the other acts were performing, I walked around and signed autographs," Berry said.

"I noticed that there was this little girl wearing a big, flowery yellow dress running around and around the oval-shaped auditorium. I passed her six or seven times—she was searching for autographs a mile a minute, waving her wallet high in her hand.

"She never saw one complete act fully, and she didn't seem to care about who was on stage—she only cared about when they came off so she could get her autographs. And this made me think that she wanted things to remember."

Berry never got around to speaking with the girl who would serve as the muse for his classic celebration of everything beautiful about fandom. "I wish I could have gotten her name," he said. "I was writing as I was looking at this kid, and I got several lines of 'Sweet Little Sixteen' that night."

"Sweet Little Sixteen," with pianist Johnny Johnson rocking at top form, sold more than one million copies. It reached #2 on the *Billboard* pop charts in March 1958 and topped the R&B chart for three weeks. In July 1958, Berry sang "Sweet Little Sixteen" at the Newport Jazz Festival, demonstrating his trademark duck walk, which he had developed two years prior. Playing a pattern on his guitar, he flashed across the stage, knees bent, without missing a beat. It left the audience breathless, and the fluid grace of his workout was later seen in *Jazz on a Summer's Day*, Bert Stern's classic 1960 documentary film. ●

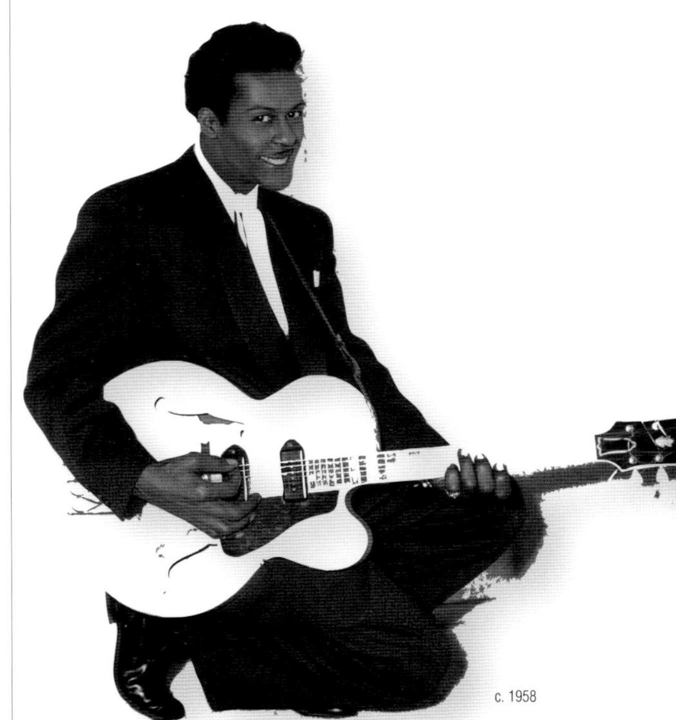

c. 1958

DEAN REED }

HE NEVER attained eminence in America. Even in Colorado, where he was born and raised, he was a virtual unknown.

But in the Soviet Union and other Communist bloc countries, Dean Reed was bigger than Elvis Presley—a superstar so famous that shops sold his image alongside Joseph Stalin's.

Reed graduated from Wheat Ridge High in 1956. He briefly took meteorology classes at the University of Colorado in Boulder and performed locally. He dropped out to become a guitar-slinging folk hero. Capitol Records was fishing for fresh talent and signed him to a recording contract in 1958.

Reed made a few marginally successful folk-pop singles—"The Search" reached #96 on *Billboard*'s Hot 100 in March 1959—and he boasted a Colorado fan club of 6,000. By 1960, the good-looking innocent had gone to Hollywood for a screen test.

He played some bit parts in television and movies, but he was impatient with his lack of wealth, position and fame. He heard that his song, "Our Summer Romance," had hit the top of the charts in Chile and Argentina. He took off for South America in 1962, and his boyish, blue-eyed looks made him a teen idol. A 1962 South American *Hit Parade* poll showed Reed trouncing Elvis Presley, 29,330 votes to 20,805.

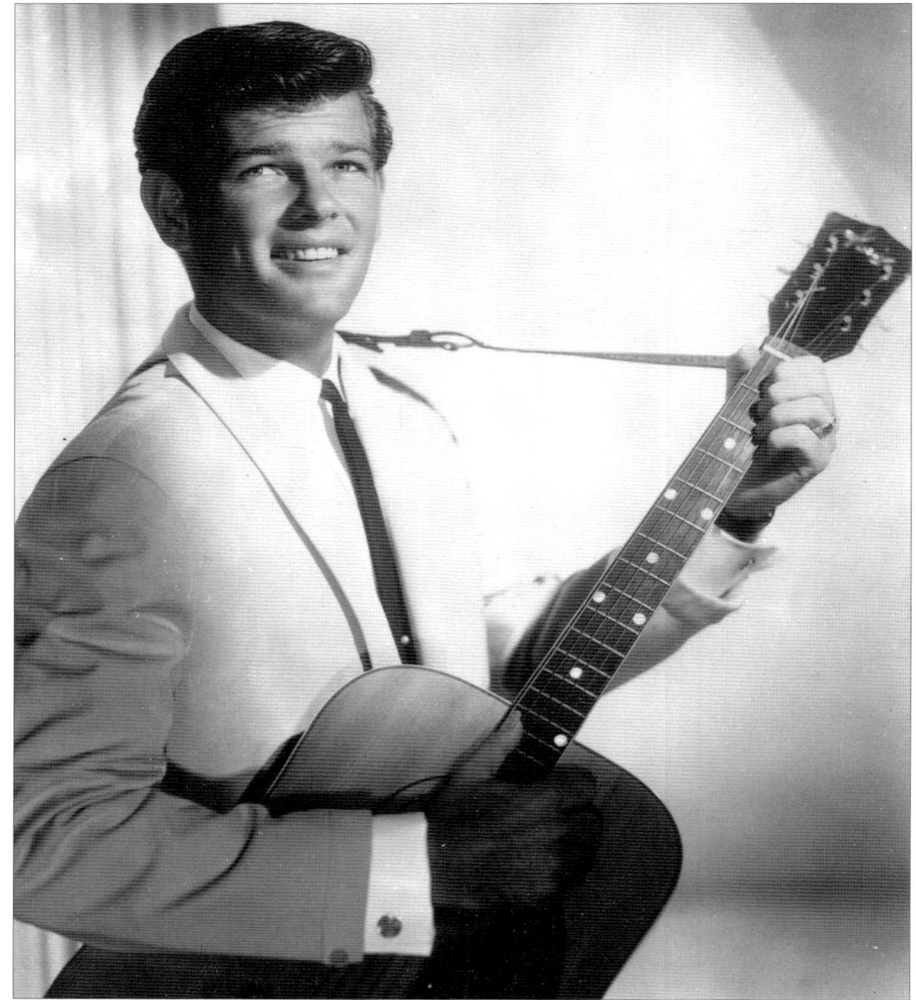

c. 1959

But Reed was falling in love with leftist politics, and he became converted to the international peace movement. He traveled with his guitar and cast himself as a political good guy, picketing embassies and singing for the workers, who bought the slogans he stitched in between the songs.

The head of Komosol, the Soviet youth organization, stumbled upon Reed. Komosol was looking for something that could stop the mass defection of young Communists to the decadent music of the West. Melodiya, the state recording company, had never before released a rock 'n' roll record, but the handsome, honey-voiced Reed got a recording contract.

Hits in Soviet Union followed—his signature tune was "Ghost Riders in the Sky"—and his albums sold

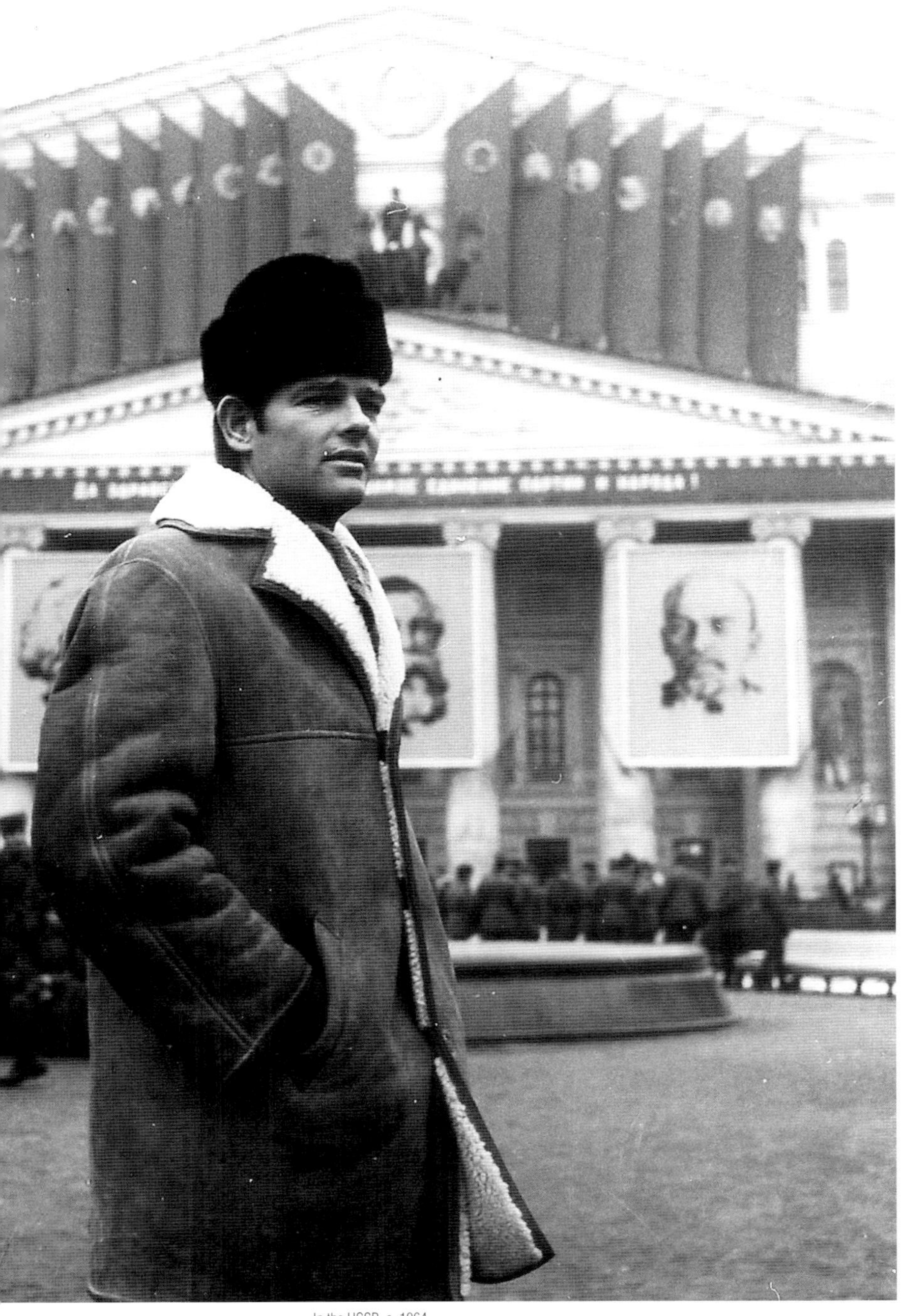

In the USSR, c. 1964

in the hundreds of thousands across the Eastern bloc. The first Dean Reed tour of the Soviet Union in 1966 was like Beatlemania. His voice was light and he couldn't play the guitar very well, but the American singer electrified the Soviet kids by singing show tunes, wearing silky clothes and moving like a star. One of his concerts drew 60,000 fans.

The propaganda stories said Reed was a sensation in his native land but that he had been brutally rejected for his politics. Dubbed "the Red Elvis," he was the only American to receive the Lenin Prize for art.

Reed played the global radical circuit, becoming friends with Salvador Allende in Chile and meeting with Daniel Ortega in Nicaragua, and he was frequently pictured in freedom fighter garb. Reed liked telling the story of crooning "Ghost Riders in the Sky" for a grinning Palestinian Liberation Organization chief Yasser Arafat in Lebanon. "His men danced around the table, their guns aloft. I said, 'Yasser, I always include "My Yiddish Momma" in my repertoire.' He said, 'That's okay, Dean—I have nothing against the Jewish people.'"

The entertainer settled in East Berlin and was adored and mobbed when he appeared in public throughout the 1970s. He began making movies and starred in dozens of foreign-language spaghetti westerns. A million East Germans saw *Sing Cowboy Sing*.

But Reed missed his friends in Colorado. He wrote them long tracts about how the Communist system would improve people's lives. "Yet we lack certain things in East Germany—hamburgers, for example," he joked wistfully.

The Communist world changed in the 1980s, and Reed's time passed. In the age of glasnost, he was no more than a curiosity from the Cold War. He had kept his U.S. passport and remained an American citizen. In the fall of 1985, he returned to the States for the Denver International Film Festival's showing of *American Rebel*, an American-produced documentary of his life.

It wasn't 1962 anymore. Rural Wheat Ridge had been eaten by Denver's urban sprawl. "The only buildings I recognize are those I've seen on *Dynasty*," he said, referencing the TV series.

Mike Wallace interviewed Reed in East Berlin for *60 Minutes*. Reed thought it would be his ticket back to America, but he made a mistake by defending the Berlin Wall. His long-standing sympathies left him reviled by many in his home country.

In June 1986, the 47-year-old Reed was found dead in an East German lake near his home. Accidental death by drowning was the official verdict. Reed's daughter later alleged that East German agents had killed him. His mother moved his remains to Green Mountain Cemetery in Boulder. ●

GARY STITES }

BORN AND bred in Colorado, Gary Stites had a big hit in April 1959 when "Lonely for You" peaked at #24 on the *Billboard* singles chart.

"I grew up in Wheat Ridge, where my father owned a Gulf service station," Stites said. "He always wanted me to go into the business, but I hated working on cars, getting my hands dirty. I found that I could make more money playing music than I could in a real job."

When he turned 15, Stites got his start with the Rocking Rhythm Kings.

"Elvis Presley and Carl Perkins were starting to hit, and the rockabilly 'Blue Suede Shoes' sound was coming out. We played on a second-floor ledge at the Grubstake Saloon in Central City, which is now a casino. Every time we'd play a song, we'd ring a cowbell and drop a bucket with a rope on it down to the floor, and people would put quarter tips in.

"There was only one other rock 'n' roll band in Denver at the time, Del Toro & the Rockers. They were Mexican and had their own following on the east side of town. So I ran into some of the guys and we formed Gary Stites & the Satellites. The group took off like a rocket. We got bookings four, five months ahead. We played a lot of teen dances, sock hops, Elks Clubs, 3.2 beer joints.

"Because things got to poppin' so much with the band, I quit school in the eleventh grade. Stupid me—I was making money and said, 'Hell, I don't need an education, I'll just be a rebel on the road.'"

Stites met the program director at KIMN, the Denver AM radio giant and friend of every teenager in town.

"He said, 'I really think you could get a contract to go national. You come down to the studio tonight.' He made a call to Joe Carlton in New York."

Carlton had been head of RCA Records' A&R (Artists & Repertoire), a group of old guard rock 'n' roll haters who no doubt believed they would wake up one morning to find Elvis Presley had been a bad dream. But Carlton was dismissed, and he subsequently started Carlton Records. He no doubt thought, "Who could be my Elvis?"

"I sang a song for him over the phone," Stites said. "It was on a Friday. He said, 'Can you be in New York by Monday?' I said, 'I certainly can.' They didn't want the band. I was 18 years old, with my white socks and high-rising pants.

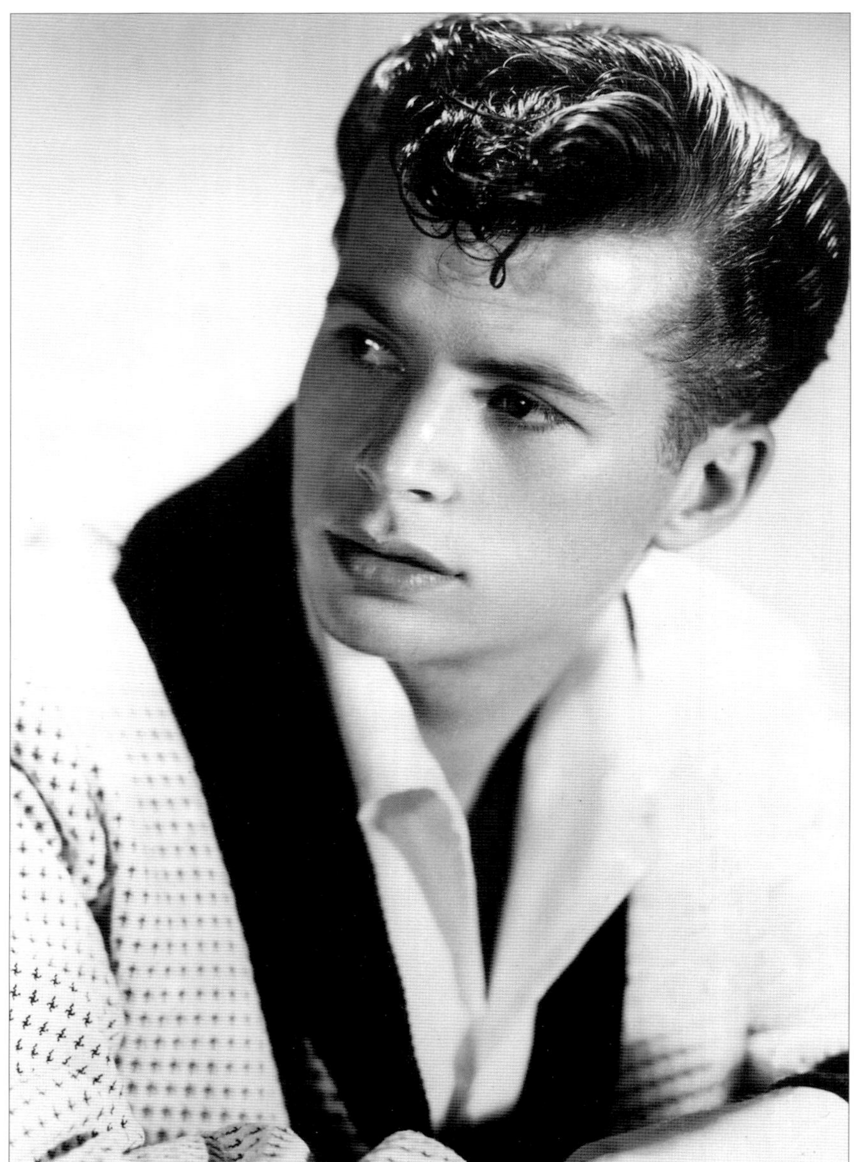

c. 1959

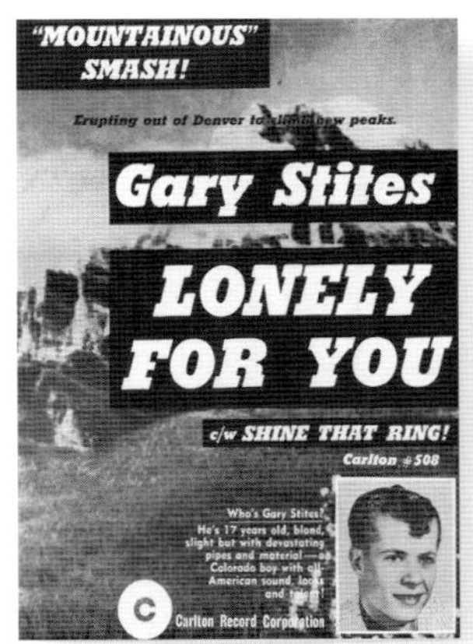

Trade ad

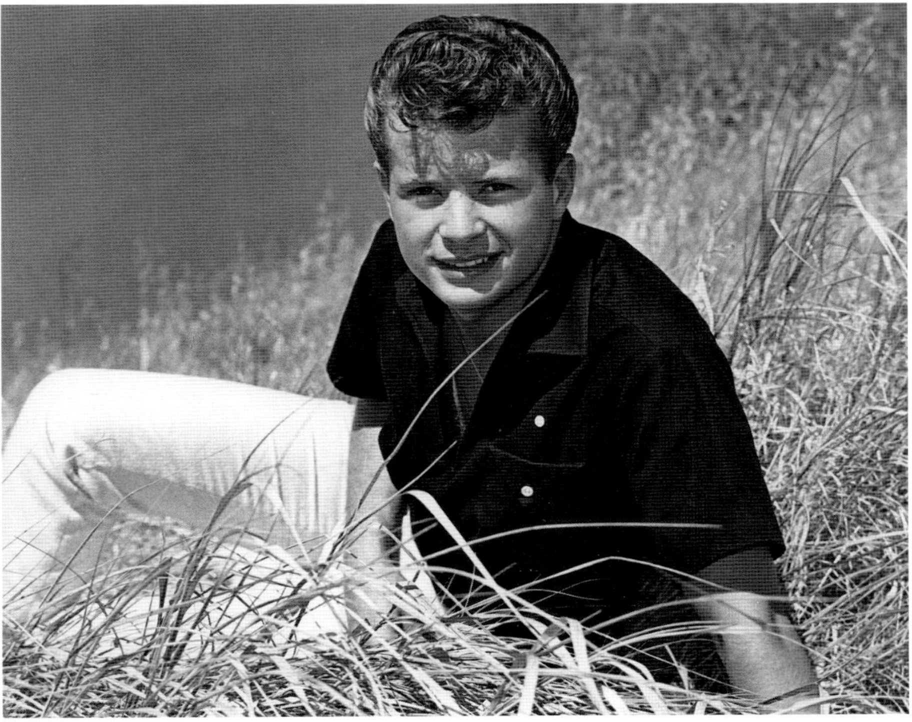
c. 1960

I didn't know anything about the big time."

At that point, the song was called "The Diary of Love."

"Carlton said, 'I love the song, but I don't like the title. I want you to change the lyrics.' If you listen to 'Lonely for You' real close, in the last half I say something about 'Help me write chapter four.' Well, when I was in the studio doing it, I got the lyrics on 'Diary of Love' and 'Lonely for You' confused, and I ended up putting in 'Help me write chapter four.'

"Everyone in the control room was going 'What the hell...?' But they liked the way it came out and they said they'd better not redo it because I had strep throat and my tonsils were swollen completely out of my head. They said, 'We'll just keep it; nobody will ever notice.'"

Stites' "Lonely for You'" had the same type of gradually-scaled lyrics that Conway Twitty had made famous with "It's Only Make Believe." He sang the song on *The Dick Clark Show*, the Saturday night extension of *American Bandstand* televised from New York.

"'Lonely for You' sold, but there was also a lot of hype—this was in the days of payola, whereby record companies won plugs and influenced disc jockeys. You could get an awful lot done."

Stites followed with several minor hits—"A Girl Like You" (#80, July 1959), "Starry Eyed" (#77, November 1959) and a cover of Lloyd Price's rhythm & blues classic, "Lawdy Miss Clawdy" (#47, February 1960)—and he toured everywhere. But he could never build on the success of "Lonely for You."

"My brief little existence in the record business was not major by any sense of the word. But for a kid who grew up lower-middle-class, I thought I had the world by the tail until the bottom fell out—I went from $40-50,000 a year down to absolutely nothing. I wasn't smart enough. I didn't have people around me saying, 'You've got to put it away, you're going to want to do something else one of these days.'

"When you're a has-been at 20 years old, that's pretty hard to take."

Stites wasn't heard from again until his 1992 cassette, *The Old Racetracker*, recorded under the singular name Cloud and saluting his first love—horse racing. ●

JUDY COLLINS }

INEXTRICABLY TIED to the rise in the populist song movement that first swept the music scene during the 1960s, Judy Collins claims Colorado as her home state. In 1949, her family moved from Seattle to Denver, where her discovery of folk music at age 15 set her on a path that brought international fame.

Her early years in music gave her a taste for variety. At the age of ten, she began the study of classical piano with Dr. Antonia Brico, a woman teacher and conductor who had studied with the legendary Finnish composer Jean Sibelius and had visited celebrated Austrian musician and physician Albert Schweitzer every summer. Collins' father was a singer, composer and broadcasting personality in Denver during the golden days of radio, and she appeared as a youngster on his KOA radio program, *Chuck Collins Calling*. She debuted with the Denver Businessmen's Orchestra when she was just a teenager.

By the time she was a Denver East High School student, Collins had traded the classical piano for a second-hand guitar, a gift from her father. "I'd never heard of folk music until listening to Jo Stafford and the Kingston Trio and Harry Belafonte sing it on the radio in '57. But I really got interested through Lingo the Drifter," an enigmatic Lookout Mountain resident who taught her the songs of Woody Guthrie and Josh White. She started her singing career in the late 1950s, performing at various clubs. Even at the age of 19, Collins had gained her social conscience and the special gift of turning folk songs into art songs.

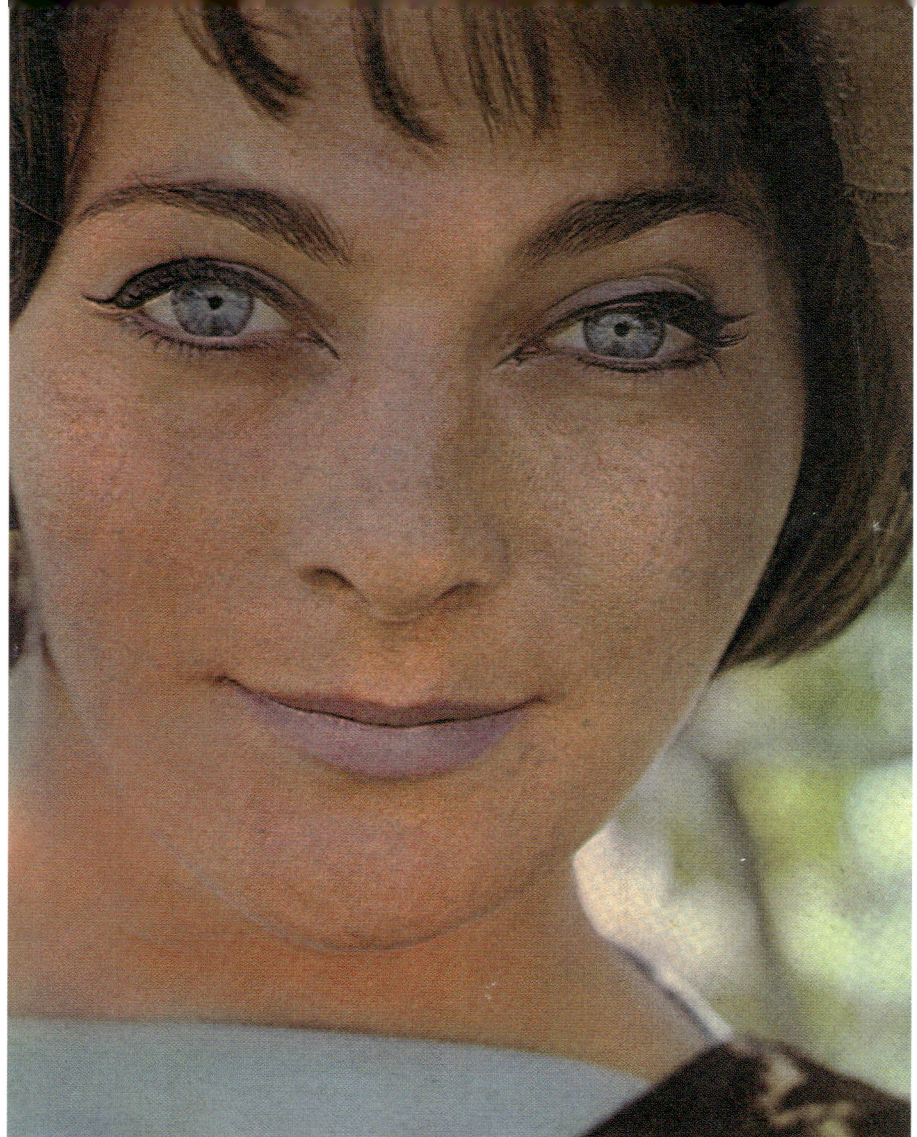

c. 1963

"By the time I was discovered to be a folk singer, I already had a trail of Mozart, Cole Porter and Frank Sinatra," she said.

At 20, the new mother and wife won an audition for a job at Michael's Pub, a Boulder hangout where all the college students went to eat pizza and guzzle gallons of "horse-piss," which is what they called the 3.2 percent beer you had to drink in Colorado if you were under 21. At Michael's, you could sometimes hear a barbershop quartet or one of the pop acts from Denver, but never a folk singer.

"I was with my guitar

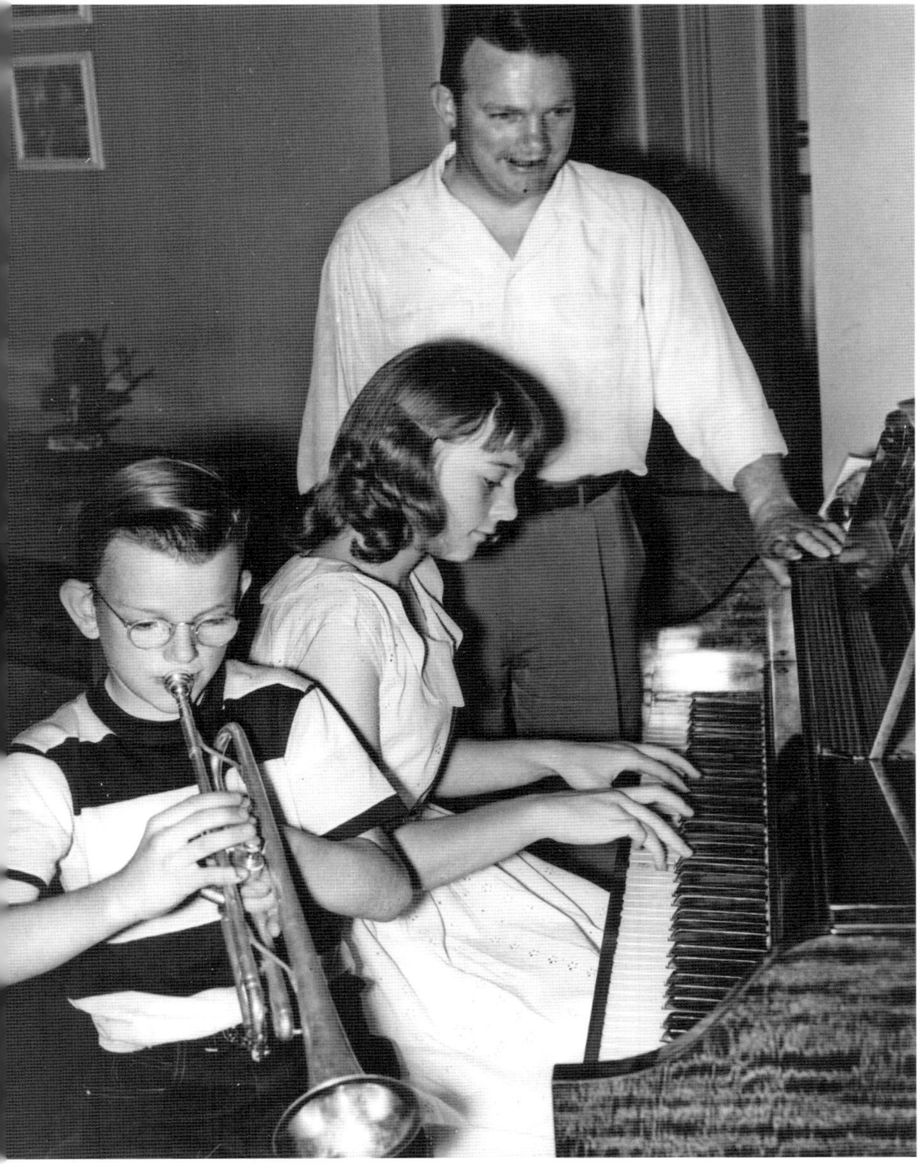

Practicing with brother Denver for father Chuck Collins.

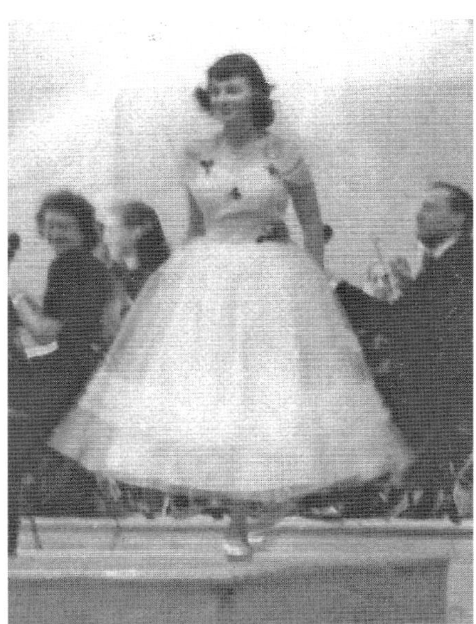

Performing with the Denver Businessmen's Orchestra, c. 1955

case, my hair cut short in a pixie. The room was filled with a noisy crowd, half of them a little drunk. The microphone sputtered and coughed, gave a high-pitched squeal. I climbed up onto the partially raised platform that served as a stage. There was some sparse clapping. I sat down on a chair, my guitar in my lap, and waited. The smoke rose from the dark, and lights were dim. Slowly people put down their beer glasses and looked at me. I looked out at them. It was a mutual dare—they dared me to show them what I could do, and I dared them to give me a chance.

"I sang everything I knew. When I finished singing, they started clapping and calling for more as soon as I stood up."

The folk craze, as it was named, was an entertainment distraction that caught America's fancy. In coffeehouses, folk music displaced the experimental arts of the 1950s. Teenagers congregated and sang along with and harmonized to intelligent lyrics. They behaved in a civilized manner and searched for an equitable link between music and the past. Collins performed at the Satire Lounge and the Green Spider and mountain bistros such as the Gilded Garter in Central City and the Limelite in Aspen. In Denver, the place to play was the Exodus, the focal point for local beats, artists and poets and a sprinkling of button-down college kids. Denver's trendies gravitated there for art shows, poetry readings and folk sessions; Collins was asked to be an opening act.

"There was a dissatisfaction with popular music," she said. "People wanted to hear a story and a lyric they could understand. There was a throwing-off of all show business glitter. It was very important for people to get down to the idea of just a person with an instrument talking about issues or telling his or her own story."

Collins subsequently moved to New York's Greenwich Village, which propelled her to stardom. With a voice that could electrify audiences with its crystal purity and wide range, she easily progressed to a record contract and major concerts. On her first albums in the early 1960s, she stayed mainly with readings of traditional material, as well as a sprinkling of folk-oriented writers (such as Tom Paxton, Eric Andersen and Richard Farina).

But Collins began to make a transition, singing more and more of the music of her contemporaries. She was often the artist who was first to recognize the talent of new composers and introduce them to their audiences—Leonard Cohen ("Suzanne"), Randy Newman ("I Think It's Going to Rain Today") and Joni Mitchell ("Chelsea Morning" and "Both Sides Now," Collins' first commercial hit in 1967).

And she became the foremost American interpreter of the emotionally and musically expressive French composer, Jacques Brel. In addition, Collins slowly began to write her own songs. The 1960s closed with her scoring a hit single in the Ian Tyson-written "Someday Soon," singing about a cowboy from Colorado, and her piercing blue eyes inspired Stephen Stills to write the Crosby, Stills & Nash classic "Suite: Judy Blue Eyes." Collins enjoyed more commercial success with the 1975 Grammy-award winner "Send In the Clowns" from the Broadway play *A Little Night Music* and an a cappella cover of "Amazing Grace."

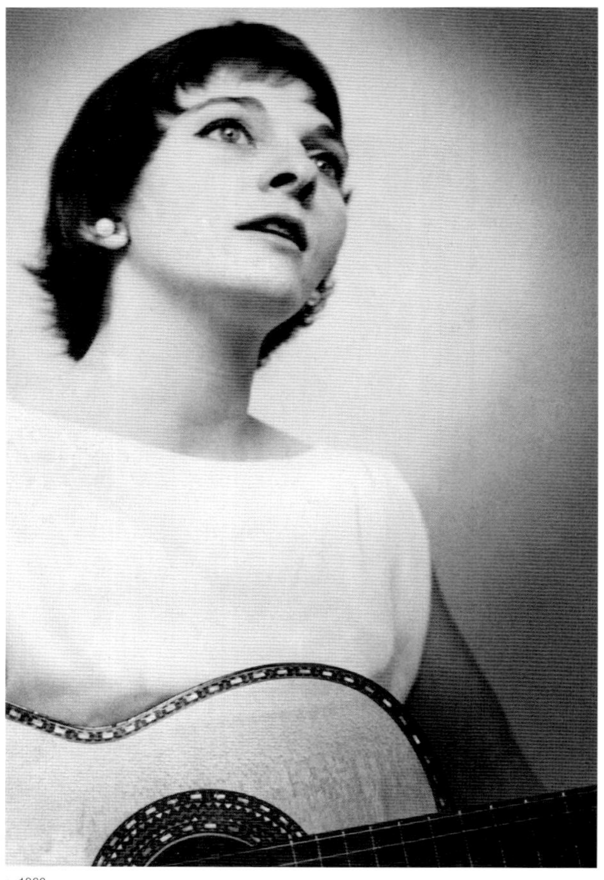

c. 1960

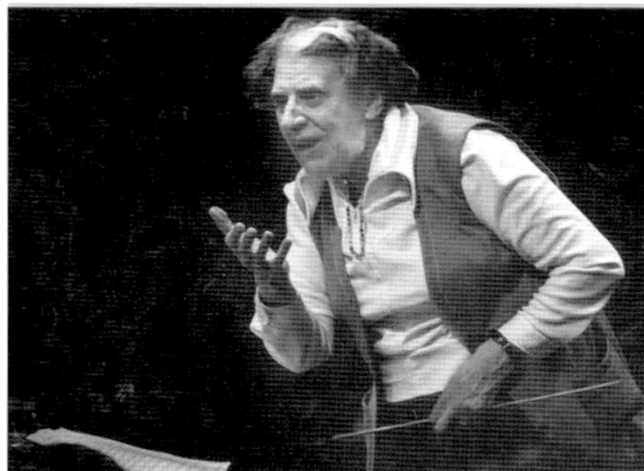

Dr. Antonia Brico

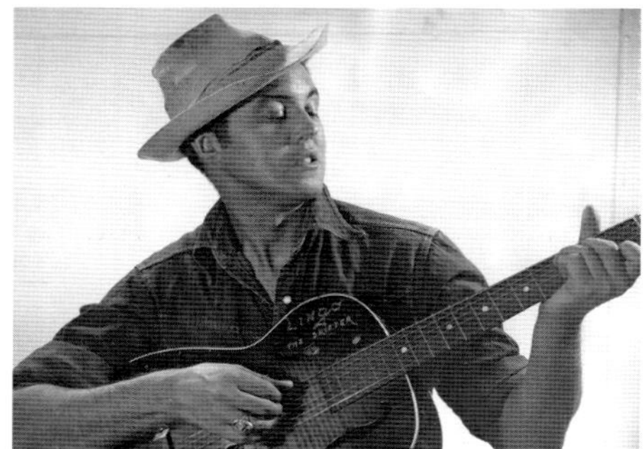

Lingo the Drifter

Simply linking the prolific Collins to the folk music tradition would be too limited a platform for her talent. She produced a documentary with director Jill Godmillow about Dr. Brico's life entitled *Antonia: A Portrait of the Woman* (which earned an Academy Award nomination), wrote several autobiographical books and a novel, and received numerous humanitarian awards for her work with UNICEF and alcohol abuse and suicide prevention programs. She continued to record and perform music worldwide.

"I'm in Colorado from time to time, but I don't ever spend enough time in the place that's really important to me. I think Colorado is a metaphor for special, almost mythological places where we feel safe." ●

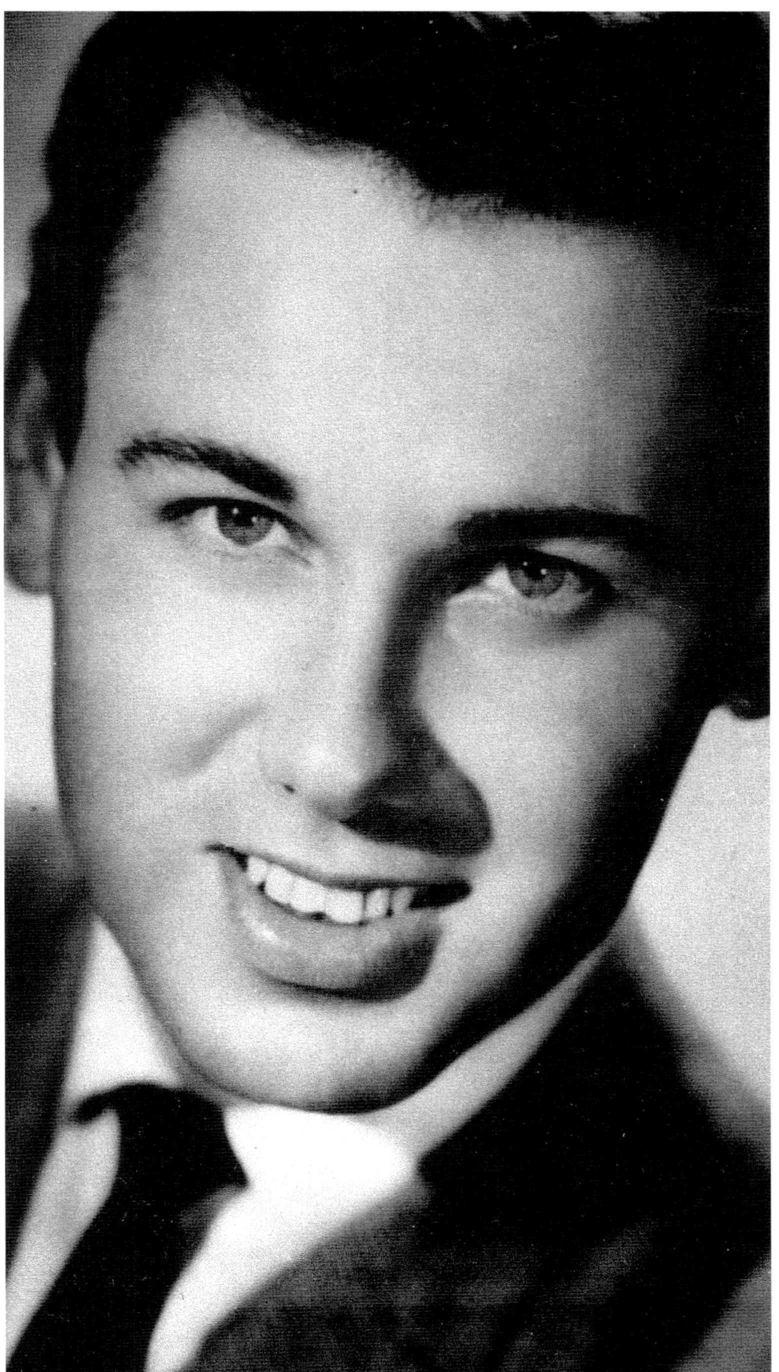

c. 1959

TOMMY FACENDA }

WITH ONE of the most unusual—and difficult—novelty discs of all time, Tommy Facenda made the national charts in 1959.

Atlantic Records released "High School U.S.A." in 28 local versions across America, each mentioning the names of specific major high schools in a particular city. Facenda, who hailed from Virginia, sang the verse over each time in the studio to add the name changes.

The effort picked up grass roots appeal, as kids in all the major markets listened to Facenda singing about their schools. The Colorado version crammed in 15 high school names. It refered to "Fort Morgan leading the band/Denver High was clapping their hand/Englewood was doing the crawl/Alamosa was having a ball/Walsenburg was hopping, too/Well, I want to do the high school bop with you..."

"I remember looking up the schools in the New York library," Facenda said. "I did most of the research, because I was the one that had to sing it. I had to put them to a rhyme and a beat in the song. It was an nightmare!"

Atlantic gave each version of the song its own individual record number—from 51 to 78. The Colorado single was Atlantic 77.

"On tour, I often got confused what version to sing in the town I was going to at the time. Back then we didn't have what were called concerts, we did rock 'n' roll shows—there might have been 20 of us on one tour package, and we all traveled together on a bus. Everybody else could just sing the same hit recordings all the time. While they were sleeping, I'd have a little pen light to study the upcoming town's high school name list."

"High School U.S.A." peaked at #28 on the pop chart. "I was real fortunate and lucky because it was just the idea of the song—it sure wasn't me," Facenda said. "Anybody could have made it a hit." ●

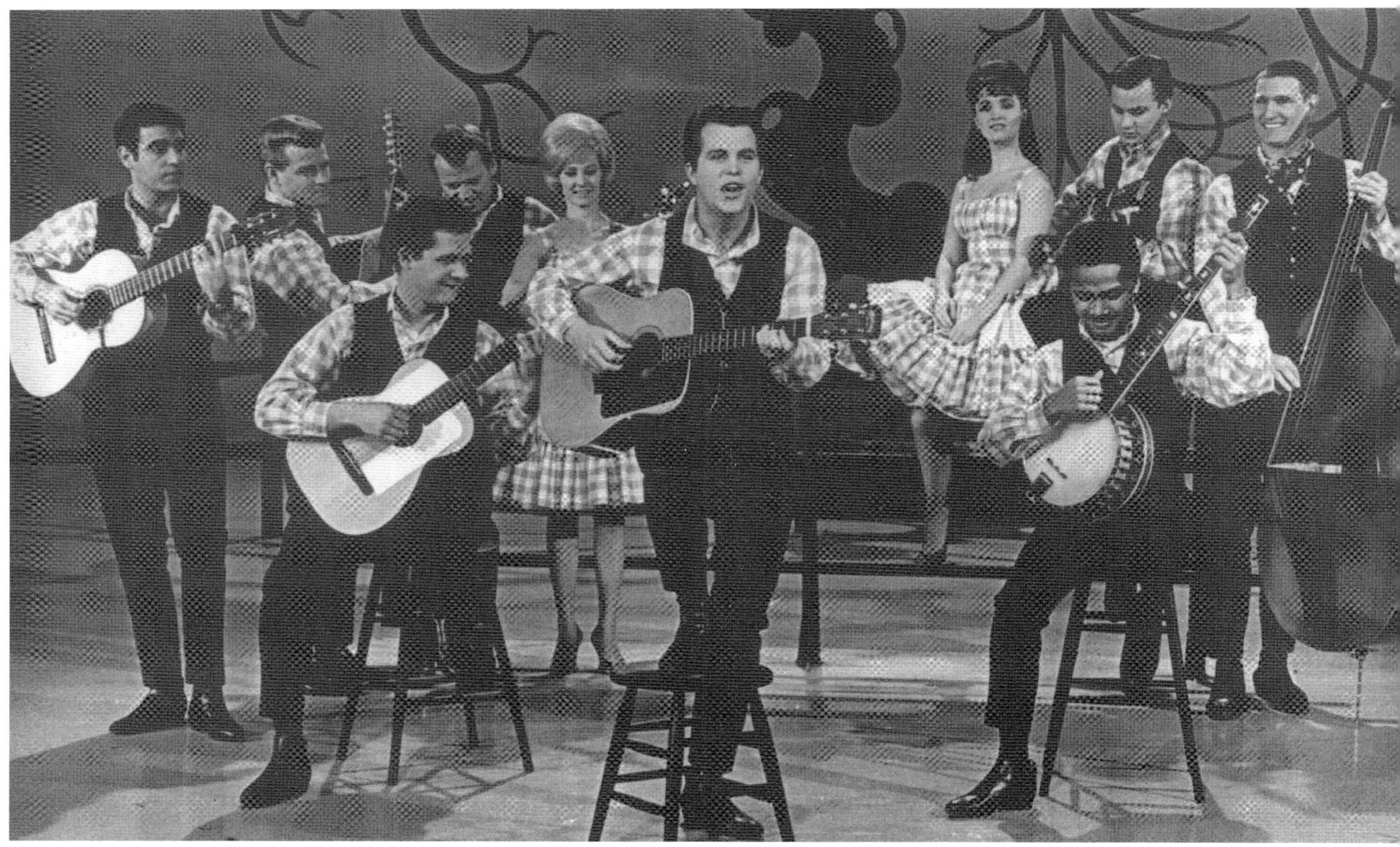

c. 1963

THE NEW CHRISTY MINSTRELS }

BEFORE THE Beatles emerged as pop's dominant power, Denver was a bastion of slick, commercial folk-pop—the soul and inspiration for groups like the New Christy Minstrels.

Randy Sparks founded the New Christy Minstrels in 1961. The act was unlike any group on the folk scene, starting out as a large ensemble of singers and instrumentalists. Named after E. P. Christy's minstrel troupe of the 1800s (which introduced many Stephen Foster songs), the New Christy Minstrels were a barrage of starched petticoats, color-coordinated blazers, choreographed grins and stage makeup.

Their success was immediate. Lined up across the stage, the group was a spectrum of ten colorful personalities. The arrangements creatively spotlighted the players in various "step outs" as duos, trios and soloists.

"Everybody sang. Everybody played," the Kansas-born Sparks said. It was an idea many inside and outside the group thought was crazy. They were successful because their big sound was refreshing at the time and because members contributed original material. Their Top 40 hits were "Green Green," "Saturday Night" and "Today."

"Denver"—the first single from the New Christy Minstrels' second album, *In Person*, recorded live at the Troubadour in Los Angeles circa September 1962—was bubbling under the *Billboard* Hot 100 in March 1963, at #127. But it was No. 1 on Denver's KIMN radio station for three weeks.

"It was one of our first records, and it immediately became a big hit in Denver," Sparks said. "I was really the man in Denver. They played everything that I put out. My phone rang constantly—

'Will you come to Denver?' The Back Porch Majority (a sort of farm club for the group) was huge there—I put them in Taylor's Supper Club. It was a love affair."

Sparks successfully used the traditional melody "Old Rosin the Beau" for "Denver." "It probably came out of the music halls of Ireland or England," he said. "It's part of our heritage. We all own it together."

His reasoning was simple: "If you did not have music that was old, nobody wanted to hear it in the folk tradition. If you wrote a new song, people were suspect of what you were doing and they rejected it out of hand. Very few new songs made it in. I looked at it very logically. 'Okay, we'll play a little game with them. I'll snag a public domain melody, people know they've heard it before, so they'll accept it. And I'll put new words to it and I won't violate any tradition. I'll make it chronologically correct.'

"At the time, one of the top songs in the country was 'Kansas City.' I said, 'That's neat, you can write a song about any location and it will become successful there, and if you're good enough with it, it'll spread.' I started looking at the map for places I could write about.

"'Denver' was an instant thing: 'Driving a rig out of Texas, full loaded and bound for Cheyenne.' I couldn't violate the timeline—it had to be as possible in 1880 as it was in 1960. And it worked. It was a good, up-tempo song, with Barry McGuire doing the 'Yeah!'s. It was a smash, but only in a few places."

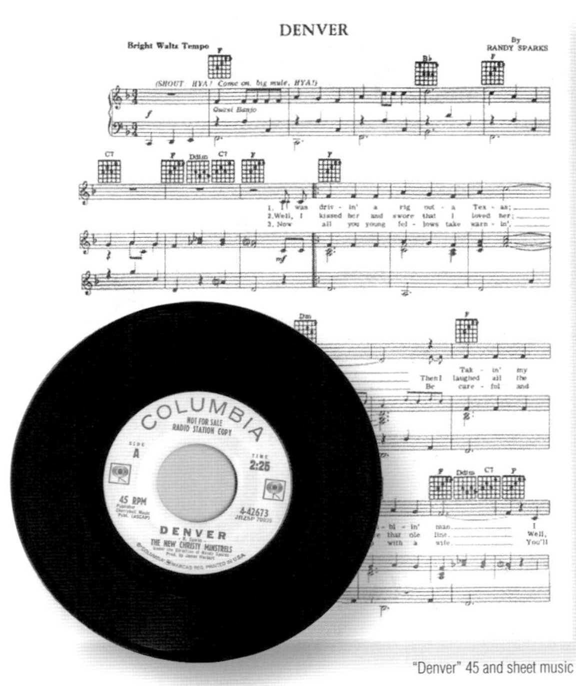

"Denver" 45 and sheet music

The New Christy Minstrels radiated a contagious spirit that charmed their audience and the show-biz press alike. Andy Williams booked them for his television show throughout the 1962-1963 season, and in 1964, the Grammy-winning group hosted its own summer television series.

The New Christy Minstrels provided an early training ground for Kenny Rogers & the First Edition, some members of the Association, actress Karen Black, future Byrd Gene Clark and Kim Carnes, as well as John Denver.

"I was the one who changed his name, and he fought it all the way," Sparks said. "He wasn't named after the city, or after his love for the Rocky Mountains. He was named after my song 'Denver.'

"This corny new kid named Little Johnny Deutschendorf came into my place. I said, 'I don't have room to put that on my marquee.' He said, 'Well, I'm not changing my name—I love my father, and he'd be really disappointed in me if I did.' I said, 'You'd better get used to it, because you can't market yourself with the name Little Johnny Deutschendorf.' You had to have a handle that people could spell and pronounce. I said, 'I'll give you a job beginning this weekend, but I need another name from you.' I gave him three days to think of one.

"Mike Crowley, a Back Porch Majority man, said to John, 'Let me give you a piece of advice that worked for me—if you keep the same initials, you won't have to buy new luggage.' So we were all looking for a name beginning with 'D.' 'Denver' was the first song I had sheet music done for. I had a piece of it above my desk. I looked up and said, 'What about John Denver?' He said, 'No, it's too close to Bob Denver (known to many as the title character on television's *Gilligan's Island*; he also played beatnik Maynard G. Krebs on *The Many Loves of Dobie Gillis* from 1959 to 1963).' I said, 'Young man, if you play your cards right, nobody will remember Bob Denver.' And that's the way it worked out."

After the New Christy Minstrels, Sparks spent the next three decades with folk icon Burl Ives, as well as having his hands in a variety of businesses both in and out of the entertainment arena. ●

THE SERENDIPITY SINGERS }

WHEN PETER, Paul & Mary's 1963 recording of Bob Dylan's "Blowin' in the Wind" became an unofficial civil rights anthem, the identification of the folkies with the politics of progress was cemented. Though the music industry continued trying to capitalize on the folk boom, the music's implicit and explicit politics made many major corporations nervous, and a lot of effort went into developing purveyors of well-scrubbed folk-pop. The Serendipity Singers, organized at the University of Colorado, were one of the most popular ensembles to emerge.

"Folk music, of course, had been arouind forever," member Bryan Sennett said. "It still is. But that was the big commercial era for it."

Sennett and Brooks Hatch worked in the Harlin Trio, formed at the Delta Tau Delta house. When Sennett was inspired to expand the group, they recruited another trio of Delts, the Mark III—John Madden, Jon Arbenz and Mike Brovsky—and two other CU students, Bob Young and Lynne Weintraub. The group, then called the Newport Singers, proved popular in Denver through stage performances and radio commercials. They created a unique sound with the use of several guitars, banjos, bass fiddles and drums. Virtually everyone also sang.

"We should have put it together earlier," Sennett said. "I had signed the Newport Singers with William Morris while we were still in Colorado. Seven of us borrowed $1,500 and we took it all to New York in the summer of '63, hoping to land a recording contract."

Expanding again with the addition of Texas-born folksingers Diane Decker and Tommy Tiemann, the nonet performed at the Bitter End, one of the top clubs in Greenwich Village, and gained the management expertise of its owner, Fred Weintraub.

"We changed our name and that's where we got started," Sennett said. "We were at the Bitter End night and day the first two months with a musical director. It was my last go-round by that time. I thought, 'If something doesn't happen, I'm going to law school.'"

Billing themselves as the Serendipity Singers, they passed an audition to alternate as the headline act on *Hootenanny*, the weekly ABC-TV folk music showcase taped at different college campuses, the audience consisting of students. Shows ran for a half-hour on Saturday night and featured four acts. *Hootenanny* was the network's second-rated program for a while. Many of America's most important and popular folk-singers initiated a boycott when ABC announced that it would not allow performers associated with "radical causes" to appear on its program.

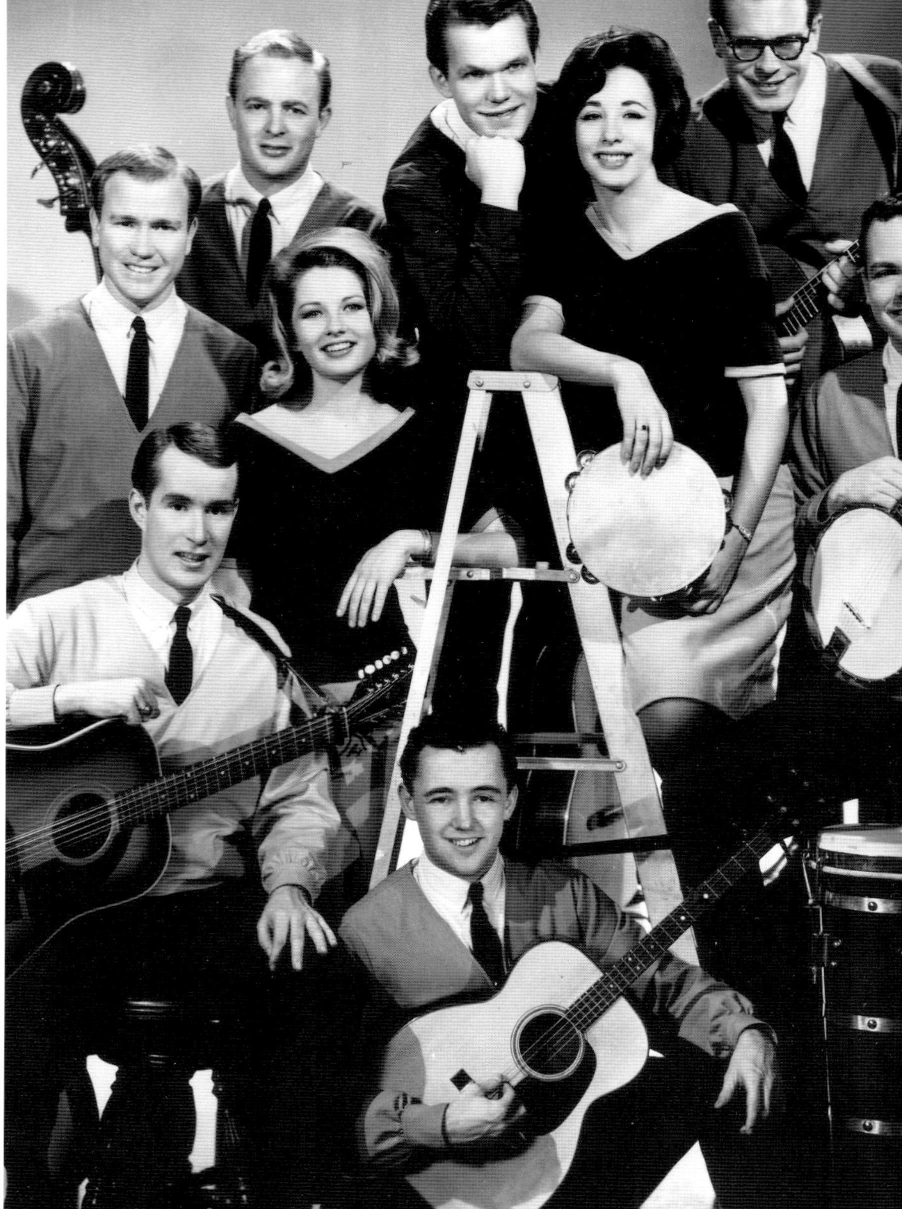

c. 1964

"The whole college concert business grew up around folk music, where you sat there and listened, and *Hootenanny* helped that explode," Sennett said. "It was a more rustic form of music, but it became more show business. It was a hard thing to do a

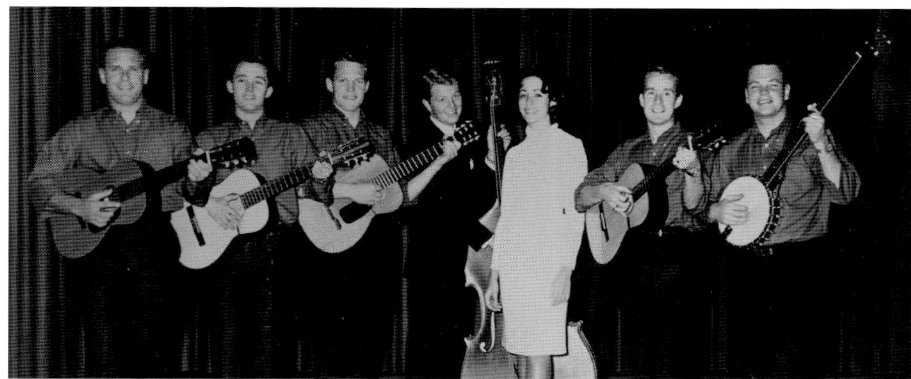

The Newport Singers, c. 1962

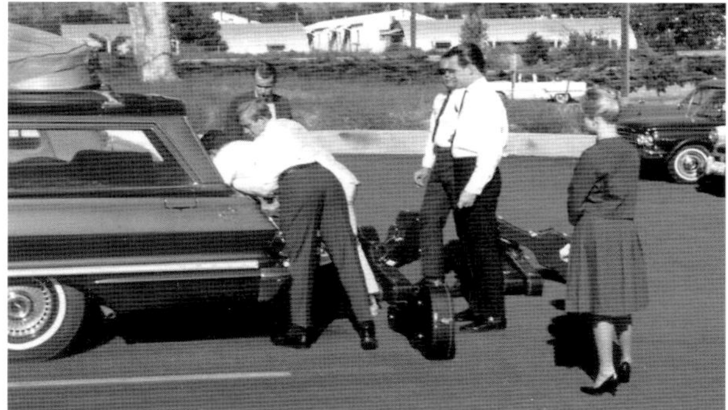

Heading to New York, c. 1962

remote broadcast from some college facility—technology wasn't as great, and there would be mishaps. But it was right in the thick of when folk music was popular. We were real fortunate to be on it."

Signed to the Philips label, the Serendipity Singers reached the national Top 10 with "Don't Let the Rain Come Down (Crooked Little Man)"—#6 in February 1964, written by Ersel Hickey of "Bluebirds over the Mountain" fame.

"Before that, it had been a traditional English nursery rhyme. We played with it and added things."

The song was nominated at the 7th Grammy Awards in 1965 for Best Performance by a Chorus. The follow-up, "Beans in My Ears" hit #30 in June 1964.

"It was banned in Boston, which always seemed to be the first place to take a song off. Some televisions shows asked us to do something different. Understandably so—it was dangerous, trying to do that if you took it literally. Obviously, it was a statement about adults not listening to children," Sennett said.

"We did a bigger variety of music—the folk center was there, but we were doing Broadway things. We were trying to do a different sound. We mixed it up a lot. We had a very visual act, a lot of talk and blackouts along with it—everybody had some theater background.

"The main thing was instrumentation. People had all done different things—classical, jazz—and they brought all that together. A lot of times, folk music was new to a lot of people. When they first heard it, they would say, 'You're country & western!' The background of that music was interesting, and we did a lot of adaption and arrangements of traditional things, to the point of not being recognizable sometimes."

Charting albums were *The Serendipity Singers* (#11 in March 1964), *The Many Sides of the Serendipity Singers* (#68 in June 1964) and *Take Off Your Shoes with the Serendipity Singers* (#149 in January 1965). The group appeared on such network television shows as *The Ed Sullivan Show*, *The Dean Martin Show*, *The Tonight Show*, *Shindig!* and *Hullabaloo*.

"There was a huge amount of variety television, and that was a big, big boost, especially if you were fortunate enough to get started," Sennett said. "We played to millions.

"We were also pretty active politically. We did barbeques all over the country with young Democrats in '64. Hey, it was the 1960s."

The Serendipity Singers' upbeat, massed vocal sound broke on the charts just as the continued impact of the Beatles and the British Invasion was about to sweep the music landscape. New member Patti Davis succeeded Lynne Weintraub, and the group performed at the White House with President Lyndon B. Johnson in attendance. The last original members had moved on by 1970; the name was sold and the Serendipity Singers continued with new lineups as a concert attraction into the 1990s. ●

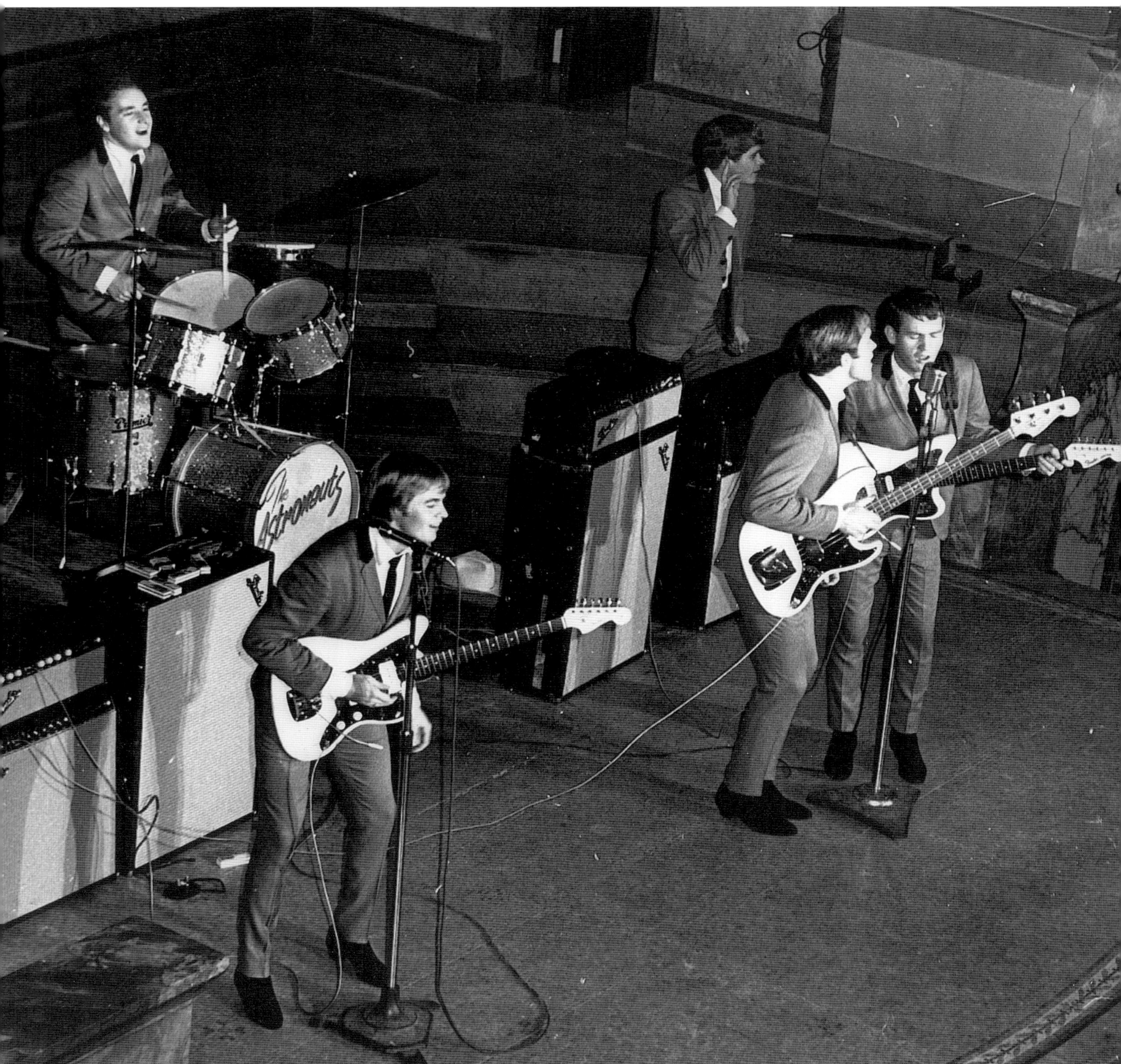

At West Point, c. 1964

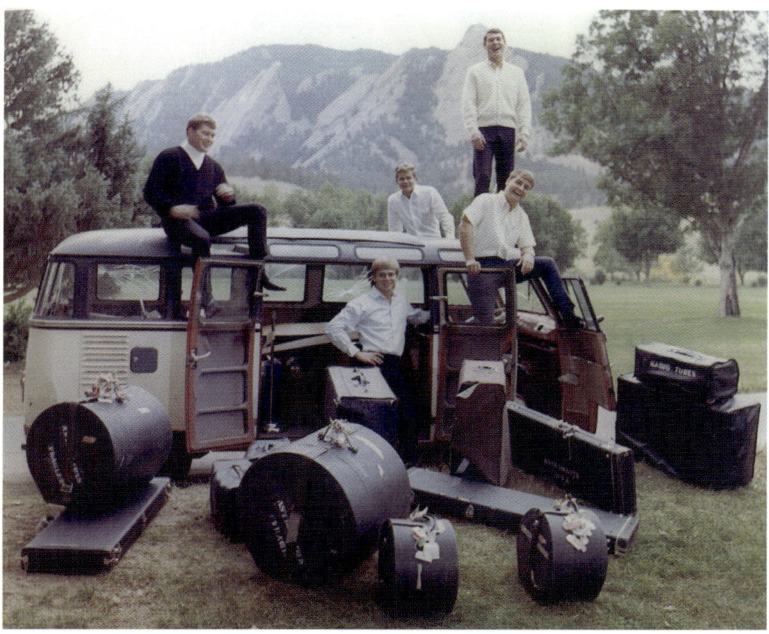

c. 1964

THE ASTRONAUTS }

IN THE early 1960s, most surf bands were big California concert acts. But the Astronauts caught the sun, sand and summer fun from Boulder, Colorado—a remarkable feat in that they were 1,000 miles away from the nearest ocean.

The Astronauts originally formed in 1960 as a trio, the Stormtroupers (named after bassist Jon Storm Patterson). But concern over the name's fascist connotations from Boulder's Jewish community necessitated a change. The guys opted for the Astronauts in honor of Boulderite Scott Carpenter, one of NASA's first spacemen.

The classic Astronauts lineup—Rich Fifield (the only member who hadn't graduated from Boulder High), Dennis Lindsey and Bob Demmon on guitars, drummer Jim Gallagher and Patterson—played rock 'n' roll and R&B hits of the day to pre-hippie crowds around the University of Colorado campus circa 1962.

"We bought matching amplifiers and guitars, wore tuxedos and patent-leather shoes," Fifield said. "We did that whole pre-Beatles bit."

At the time, RCA Records was looking for an act to compete with Capitol Records' enormously successful Beach Boys, a West Coast surfing group scoring big on the national charts with songs like "Surfin' Safari." Even though they had never played surf music (or even surfed, for that matter), the landlocked Astronauts wound up with a long-term recording contract.

Amazingly enough, the ruse actually worked for a while.

"It was the strangest marketing scheme I'd ever heard of, and I've heard of a lot," Gallagher confessed.

The liner notes from the group's first album, *Surfin' with the Astronauts*, released in May 1963, explained it this way: "Fact is, they call themselves the Astronauts because they are the HIGHEST surfing group in the United States. And we mean like their home base is Boulder, Colorado, way up in the Rockies, just around the corner from the Air Force Academy and real live astronauts."

The Astronauts were the first Boulder band to make *Billboard*'s national charts—*Surfin' with the Astronauts* rose to a respectable #61. The album included "Baja," penned by Lee Hazlewood (better known as the writer of Nancy Sinatra's big hits). The single—a typical surf instrumental with a reverberation-heavy twangy guitar and driving drum beat—occupied #94 on *Billboard*'s Hot 100 for one week in the summer of 1963.

On Denver radio, however, "Baja" reached No. 1 and earned the Astronauts a much bigger regional following. The group returned to their frat rock roots for two live albums, one recorded at their own Club Baja in Denver. The other, 1964's *Astronauts Orbit Kampus*, was recorded at Boulder's famous Tulagi and featured a cover shot with a snowy Boulder in the background.

A local group of Astronauts devotees formed a fan club and petitioned to get the group on *The Ed Sullivan Show* to no avail. But the band appeared on television's *Hullabaloo* several times and also had cameo roles in the teen movies *Wild on the Beach* (also featuring Sonny & Cher), *Wild Wild Winter*, *Out of Sight* and *Surf Party*.

Like hundreds of other bands around the country, the Astronauts achieved a sort of working success, constantly touring a mind-numbing blur of colleges, gyms and bars. Ironically, the Astronauts enjoyed their greatest success overseas—in 1964, RCA discovered that the Japanese were mad for the band. They outsold the rival Beach Boys, and five albums and three singles made the Japanese Top 10. "Movin'," titled "Over the Sun" for the

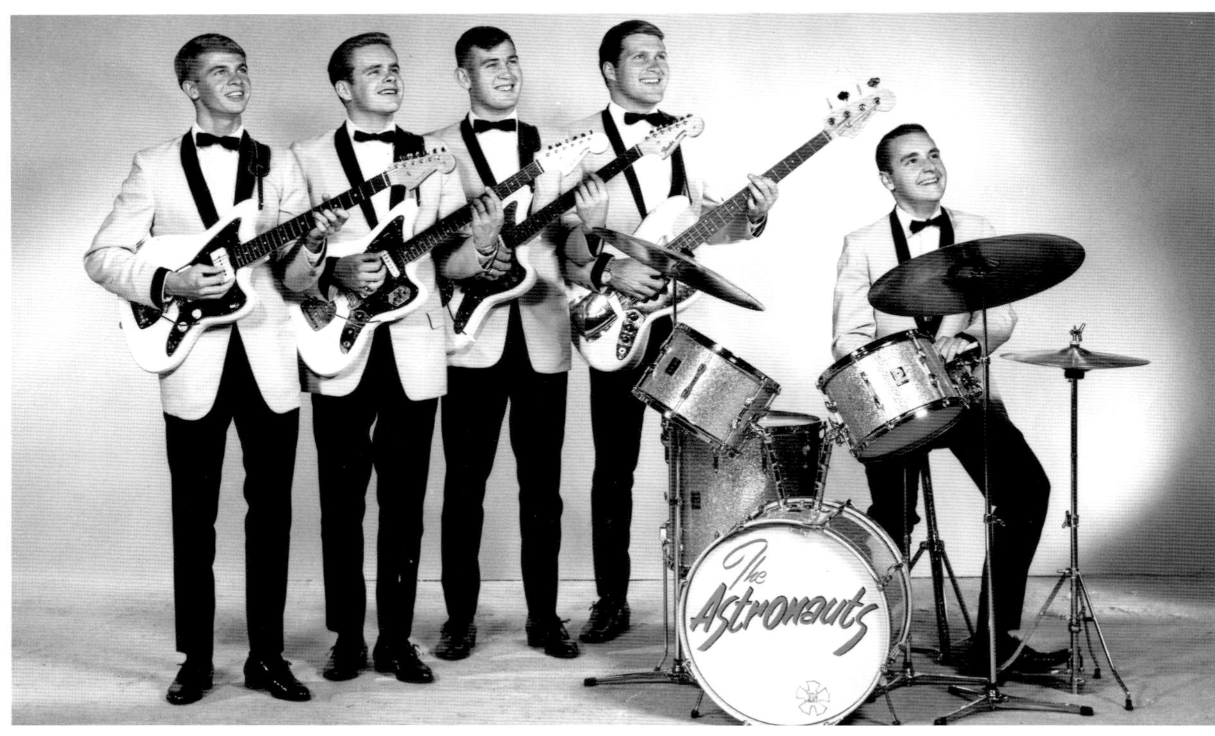

c. 1962

Japanese market, hit No. 1. Five 50-foot billboard statues in their likeness were hoisted in Sapporo.

"When we went to Japan for two tours, it was earth-shattering," Gallagher said. "We'd played the Midwest and done pretty well, but nothing spectacular. *Surfin' with the Astronauts* came out here in 1963, but didn't break in Japan until later. We had no idea how popular we were over there, or why.

"Then when we arrived at the Tokyo airport, 8,000 screaming kids were there. We kept wondering who they were waiting for. Then we found out it was us.

"One morning we woke up early and decided to go look around outside our hotel. We were accustomed to going where we wanted to go. We got about eight blocks and realized that there were 40 kids following us at six in the morning. Pretty soon we were pressed up against shop windows signing autographs."

Unfortunately, the Astronauts' conquest of the Rockies and Asia meant little to the rest of America, where the group could never build on the initial chart success. Subsequent albums like *Competition Coupe* found the Astronauts trying on other styles like hot-rod songs. What really doomed them as a recording act was the 1964 British Invasion.

"I heard the Beatles' 'I Wanna Hold Your Hand' on the radio and thought, 'That's it, we've had it—maybe I'd better dig out that dental-school manual again,'" Gallagher recalled. "They were so good and I was so elated to hear what they were doing—I loved it, it was the sound we wanted to get. That's what made it so hard on us."

The Astronauts continued touring through 1966, but immediately after recording their final album (1967's *Travelin' Men*), the draft struck. Gallagher and Lindsey both wound up serving in Vietnam. The Astronauts were essentially done until a triumphant 1989 reunion at the Boulder Theater, which would prove to be their last with the passing of Lindsey in 1991 and Demmon in 2010. ●

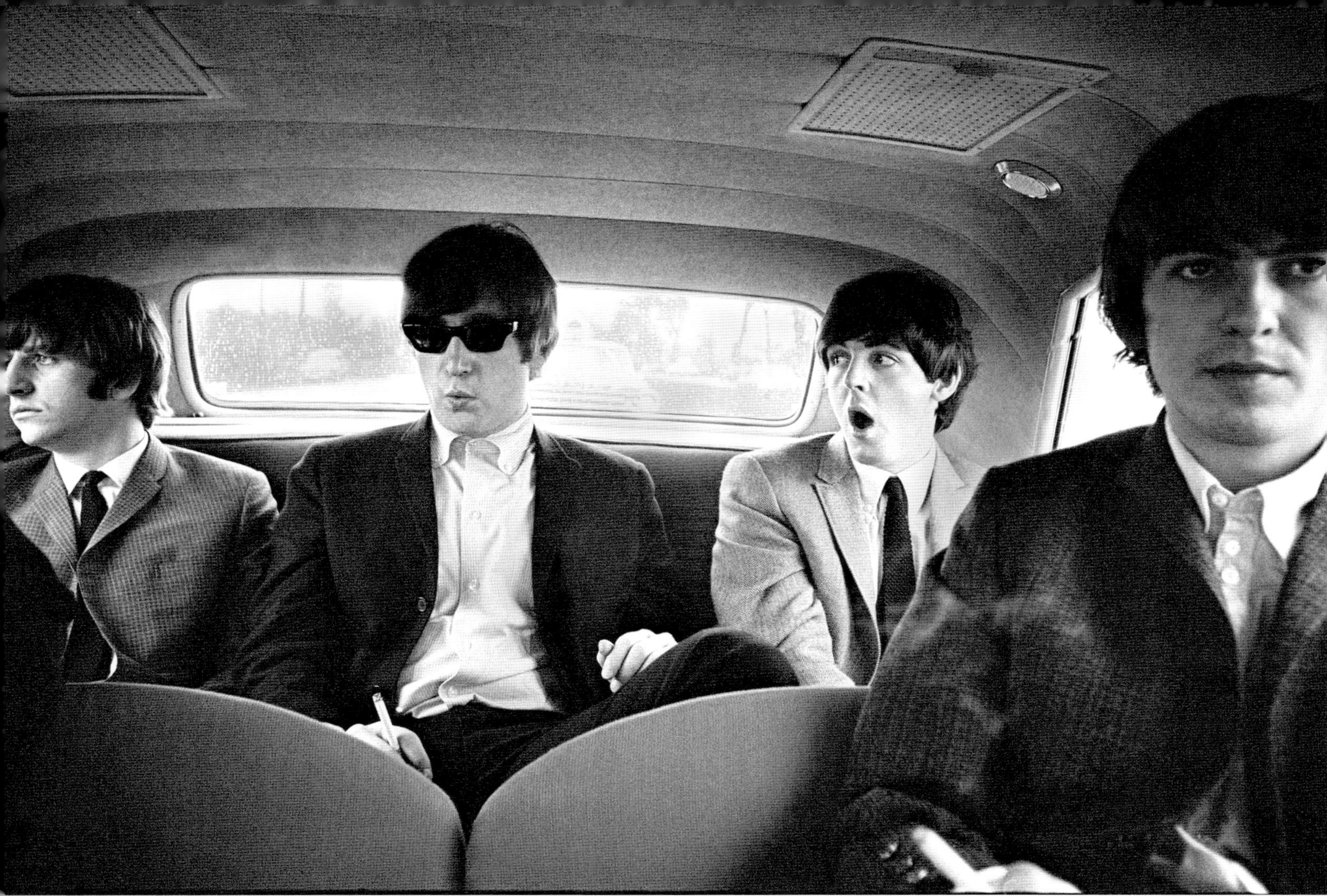

Ringo, John, Paul and George in Denver, August 26, 1964

THE BEATLES }

THE LONGEST concert swing the Beatles ever undertook was their first American tour, a 32-day visit. The sixth stop was a performance at Red Rocks Amphitheatre in Morrison, Colorado.

Verne Byers, the promoter, said he had never even heard of the group before the booking, noting that they used their bowl-shaped haircuts as a "gimmick" to separate themselves from similar acts that were touring that summer, such as Peter & Gordon and the Beach Boys. It was the only performance on the itinerary that didn't sell out—only 7,000 fans bought tickets to the Beatles' one show in the famed 9,000-capacity natural amphitheater. At the time, the distance of Red Rocks from Denver, coupled with no public transportation, was blamed for the unsold tickets.

But in 1964, Red Rocks was viewed more as a National Park than an outdoor music venue. It was well known in Denver that there were a lot of ways to get into Red Rocks, and having a ticket was only one of them. Some theorize that there was well over a capacity crowd there—photographs and news clips of the crowd showed no empty seats—but only 7,000 actually shelled out for tickets.

Nevertheless, Denver, like the rest of the country, succumbed to Beatlemania in a tidal wave of sheer exuberance. At least 250 Denver policemen and auxiliary recruits were briefed on "Beatle Invasion" strategies.

On the morning of August 26, 1964, a crowd bearing "I Love the Beatles" signs, Beatles hats and Beatles pins began to gather for the group's anticipated arrival at Stapleton Airport. By noon, nearly 10,000 had blanketed a fenced area on an adjoining boulevard. At 1:35 p.m., the Beatles' chartered 707 touched down from Los Angeles, and 24 hours of pandemonium ensued.

Huge numbers of teens also descended on Red Rocks Park and the venerable Brown Palace Hotel. At 10 a.m., an estimated 1,000 were camped around Red Rocks, listening to transistor radios. Weather predictions called for rain, and emergency plans were made to transfer the show to the Denver Coliseum if necessary.

Nearly 5,000 sobbing and fainting fans mobbed the sedate Brown Palace's front entrance. Six girls and one harried policeman (who had been bitten on the wrist) were taken to Denver General Hospital for treatment.

At $6.60, general admission tickets for the Beatles' show at Red Rocks were nearly $3 more than ducats for a recent concert by Igor Stravinsky, who was con-

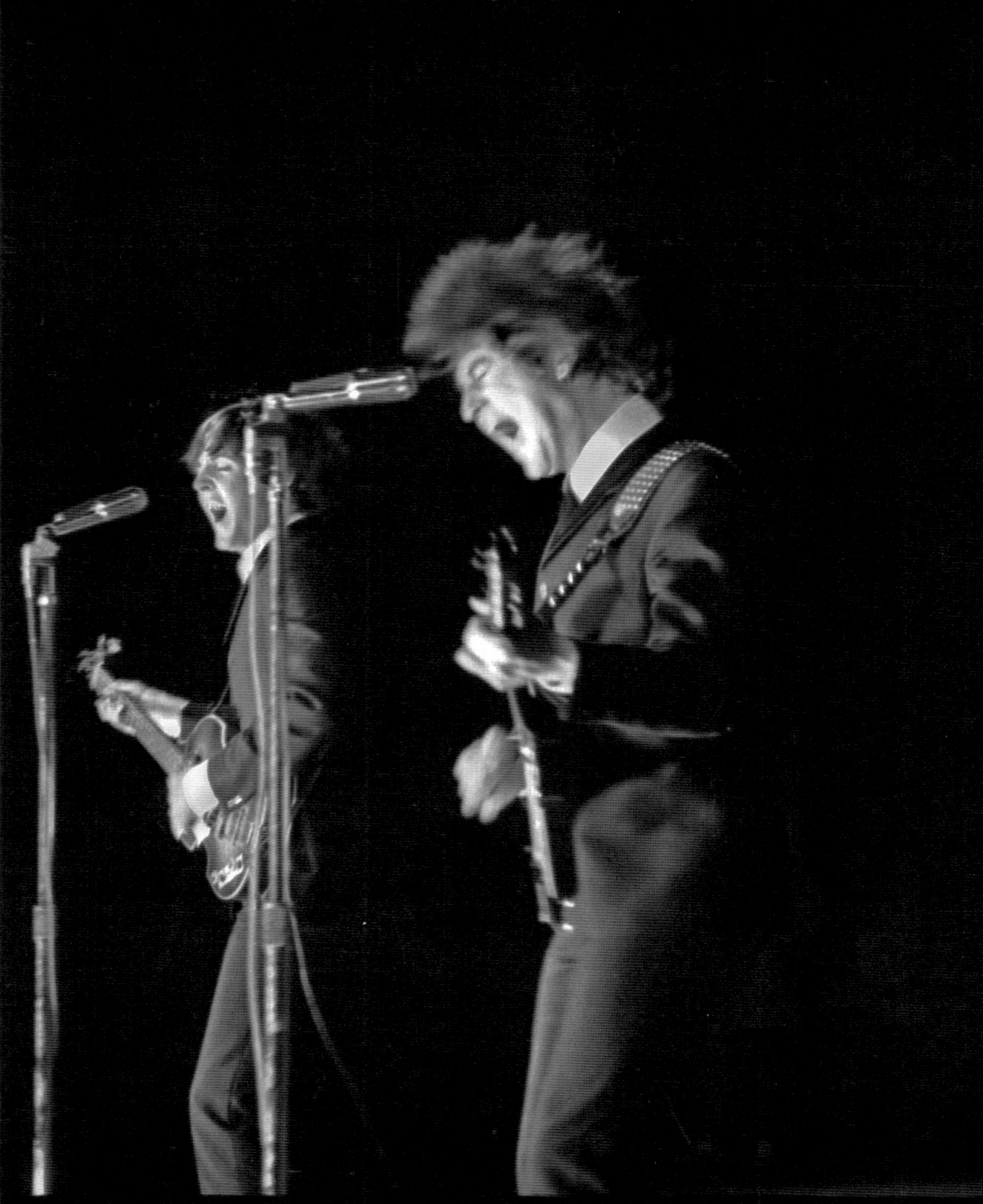

Red Rocks Amphitheatre, August 26, 1964

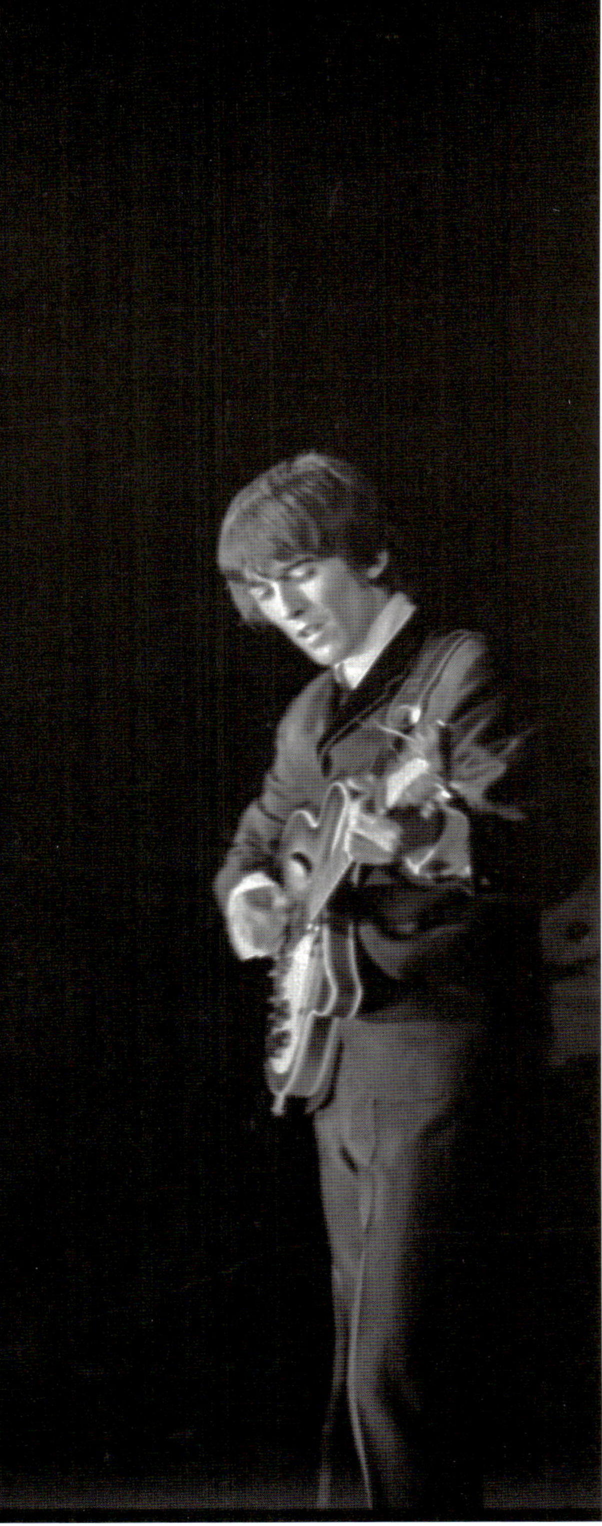

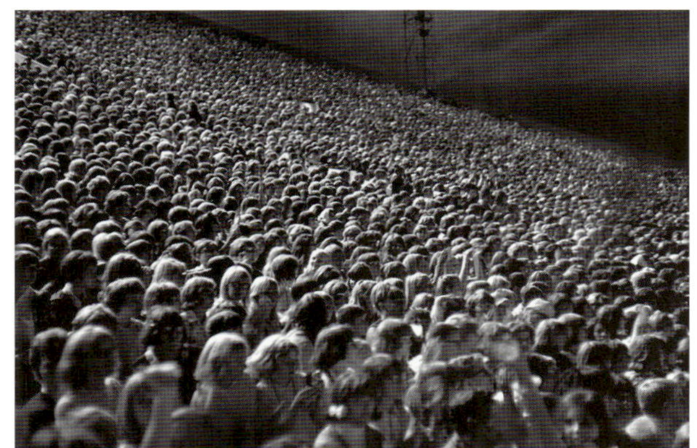

The SRO crowd of only 7,000 ticket holders

— ADMIT ONE —
Admission.......6.09
Federal Tax.......51
6.60

In case of rain event may be moved to Denver Coliseum on the same date. Listen for radio announcements.

KIMN presents
THE BEATLES
IN CONCERT
Red Rocks Amphitheater
Wed., August 26, 1964
8:30 p.m.

NO REFUND
NO SEATS RESERVED

Nº 9810

Ticket to the Red Rocks concert

sidered the world's greatest living composer. The 100-minute show featured the Bill Black Combo, the Righteous Brothers, Jackie DeShannon, the Exciters and, finally, a set by the Beatles. Unbeknownst to the band, the Red Rocks concert was used to test a new ordinance banning alcoholic beverages, cans and bottles in the park. Two years earlier, rowdies had hurled beer cans at Ray Charles, and other incidents had followed. The ordinance was passed after a 1963 Peter, Paul & Mary concert.

At 9:30 p.m., the Beatles took the stage, and the quartet was indeed pelted—with jellybeans (reportedly their favorite candy), not beer cans. The audience was loud to the point of drowning out all the performers, but polite.

The altitude was the only factor that proved troublesome throughout the Beatles' 35-minute performance. Halfway through the first song, they were out of breath.

"We were all told it was high above sea water, altitude. We thought, 'Well, so? What's the difference?' We got there, and we started finding it a little hard to breathe, because we weren't used to it," Paul McCartney said. "I remember singing 'Long Tall Sally' and thinking, 'Hey, this is great—hyperventilation of the highest order!' 'Well, Long Tall Sally, wheeze, wheeze...' I was sweating, but I got through it. It was an interesting experience, physically.

"It was a lovely arena—it looked beautiful at night."

After the show, the Fab Four retired to Suite 840 at the Brown Palace and visited for a while with Joan Baez, who would appear at Red Rocks two nights later.

"Joan used to hang out with us a lot back then," drummer Ringo Starr recalled. "She would go on the road with us for a few days at a time."

The predicted rain finally arrived as the Beatles headed for the airport the following day. An estimated 3,500 people waited at Stapleton. Shortly after noon, the plane took off for Cincinnati, where the group was to perform next. ●

BOB LIND }

A COLORADO "folkie," Bob Lind found pop music success recording "Elusive Butterfly," a #5 national hit in March 1966.

While not a Colorado native, Lind called the state home. He graduated from high school in Aurora and attended Western State College in Gunnison, where he focused on playing guitar to the exclusion of academics. He dropped out circa 1964 and moved to Denver, where he became immersed in the folk music scene and took

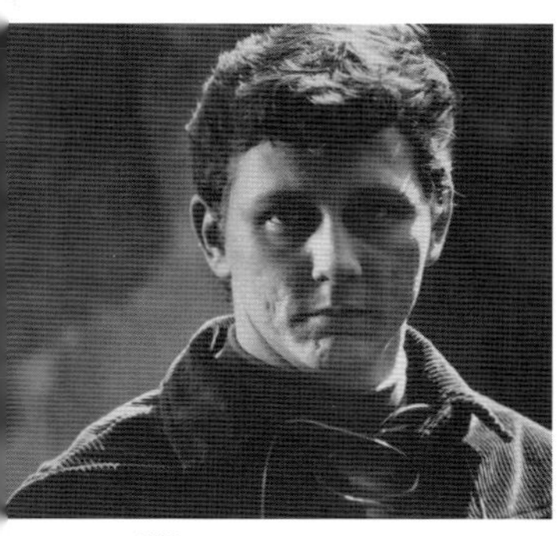

c. 1966

coffeehouses such as the Exodus, the Green Spider and especially the Analyst by storm.

"It didn't last long—I'm talking about months. People think the folk boom of the early 1960s was an era like rock 'n' roll. It was really closer to the hula hoop fad—it just dried up," Lind said.

"But during that time, other strains of music were formed. There was a great split between ethnic or commercial. You either wore a striped shirt or you were funky. There were people in Denver who would learn a Blind Lemon Jefferson song lick-for-lick from a record—nice Jewish kids singing black music. They did it well, but they frowned upon anybody applying any individuality to this music.

"And that's where it lost a lot of us. We wanted to express ourselves in these folk forms. So I began to write.

"Here's my day in the summer of 1964. I'd get up at 10 a.m., put on a pot of coffee, take some uppers for some energy, sit down at the kitchen table with a pad of paper and a guitar, and write songs all day smoking cigarettes and drinking coffee. At six, I'd fall into the shower, get something to eat, and then usually I'd have a gig or go listen to somebody else."

Late one night, Lind wrote a song called "Elusive Butterfly." It had vivid imagery and an extended, metaphoric narrative—"Don't be concerned/It will not harm you/It's only me pursuing something I'm not sure of/Across my dreams/With nets of wonder/I chase the bright elusive butterfly of love."

"There was a poem I loved by William Butler Yeats called 'The Wandering Angus.' I wanted to write something that felt that way, that had the sense of being alive most when we're searching or chasing after something. That expectation is more life-affirming than getting the thing you're after. Other people call it the thrill of the hunt.

"It was originally five verses long, and I'd leave a lot of space in—it took ten minutes to play it. I played it for everybody I knew, but I didn't say, 'Man, this is my best song. It's going to be a hit. Millions of people are going to hear it.' It was just another song. I was thrilled by everything I wrote. I didn't know how crummy some of them were."

Al Chapman, the owner of the Analyst, had made a tape of Lind and suggested he take it to record labels. In early 1965, the singer-songwriter left for California and shopped it.

"The absolute first thing that happened, I took it to World Pacific (a jazz and international-oriented subsidiary of Liberty Records). The president of the label listened to it and they signed me. I said to myself, 'Gee, this is easy. That's all there is to it—you go to the record company and get a deal!' I had no idea that people struggled for years to get signed."

Lind's first session with noted arranger Jack Nitzsche yielded a single, "Cheryl's Going Home." It had been out for about a month during the Christmas season of 1965 when a disc jockey at the Florida station WQAM flipped it over to the B-side. Listeners flipped, too. With "Elusive Butterfly," his first, biggest and only hit, Lind helped define the folk-rock ferment. His groundbreaking combination of emotionally literate lyrics with lush yet tasteful orchestration was the kind of delicate song that until then had been thought to be too breathy, wispy and lyrical to be commercial.

"It was my last choice as a single," Lind admitted. "I didn't have the slightest inkling of what would tickle the public's fancy."

Chart momentum was gone by the summer of 1966. Out of his own pocket, Lind had recorded an acoustic demo tape during his Denver days at Band Box studios; Verve Folkways Records overdubbed new accompaniment without his input and released it as *The Elusive Bob Lind*. Follow-up singles charted on Denver's KIMN radio but barely cracked the national charts. During the 1970s, Lind began easing out of the music business, concentrating on writing screenplays, novels, plays and short stories. Over the years, more than 200 artists recorded his songs. In 2004, he resumed performing worldwide. ●

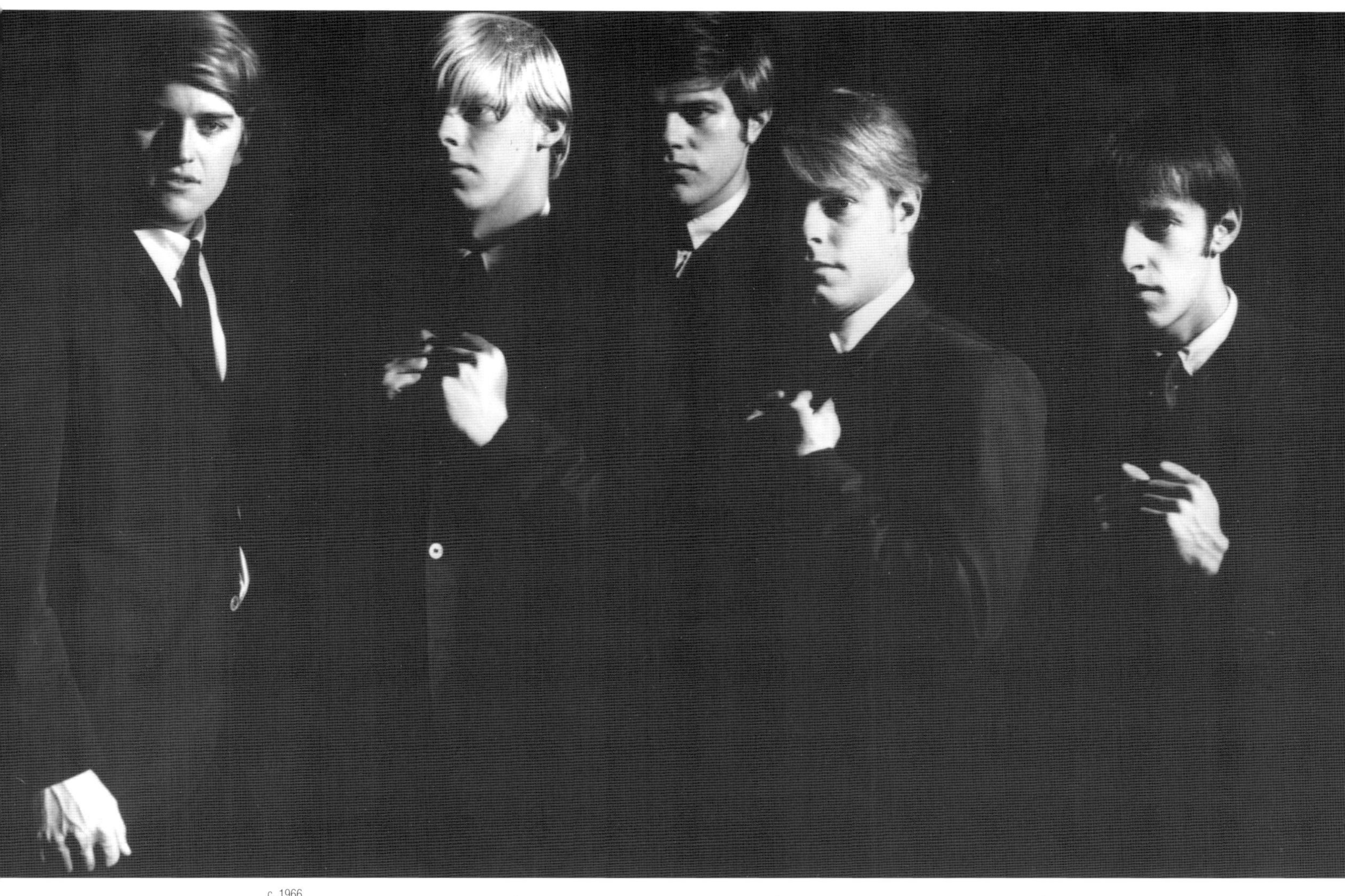

c. 1966

THE RAINY DAZE }

ONE OF the biggest Colorado-based hits of the 1960s, "That Acapulco Gold" by the Rainy Daze was an ode to marijuana crooned in Roaring Twenties vaudeville style.

Formed in 1963, the Rainy Daze played six nights a week at the Galaxy, a Denver club.

"We were a working band," lead singer Tim Gilbert said. "The idea wasn't to get rich and famous, although the availability of young women was way up on the list of reasons to do it. The whole idea was to play and make money, $350 to $500 a night.

"A band's identity was more determined by the covers you played than anything else. You had to play some Beatles, but we were more Stones, Yardbirds and Who, so people thought we were 'edgy.' We would periodically go into the studio and try to record an original song and become stars so that the pool of available women would grow!"

Originals were written by Gilbert and fellow Denver South High School student and lyricist John Carter.

"Everybody was going to the University of Colorado," Gilbert said. "John was a roommate, a guy who hung around. It was a long time before I took him seriously. He had a great musical sense, but he couldn't carry a tune. When it became important to write original music, with people in Hollywood saying, 'If you're going to be anything, you've got to write your own music,' we looked at each other and said, 'Shit, who can do that?' John insinuated himself into that process. I had a micro-talent for writing melodies, and John was quite a talented lyricist."

In 1966, the Denver quintet—Gilbert, his brother Kip Gilbert (drums), Sam Fuller (bass), Bob Heckendorf (organ) and Mac Ferris (guitar)—issued "That Acapulco Gold" on the Chicory label.

"There was a song out at the time called 'Winchester Cathedral' (a No. 1 hit by the New Vaudeville Band, sung through a megaphone). A lot of what we did on 'Acapulco Gold' was reflective of that. It was 180 degrees from all the music we were playing."

The group was then signed to Uni, which distributed "That Acapulco Gold" nationally. The song continued to dominate Denver radio in early 1967 and peaked at #70 on the *Billboard* pop singles charts. However, national sales and airplay went up in smoke once word got around about the song's real inspiration. It was unceremoniously yanked from playlists.

According to Gilbert, "KHJ was the 'boss' radio station in Los Angeles at that point. Every week, they'd print the Top 30 weekly survey. At one point, 'That Acapulco Gold' was No. 1 with an asterisk next to it that said, 'Not suitable for airplay.'

"Stations didn't think it was inappropriate until (radio performer and publisher of the *Gavin Report*) Bill Gavin wrote in his tip sheet that if you played this record on the air, you did stand a chance of losing your license, because it did proselytize drug use. Which was fairly obvious...

"Carter and I found ourselves in Los Angeles in the spring of '67. I figured, 'Hey, how often in your life are you going to have a record on the charts?' I went back and got my degree later. We were sitting in a restaurant one day and George Carlin came up and shook our hands and said, 'You're the most courageous people in the United States.' There was a moment when we were at the head of the parade, all over this little song."

Gilbert and Carter were asked to write a song for another Uni act. They scored a national No. 1 hit with "Incense and Peppermints" by the Strawberry Alarm Clock.

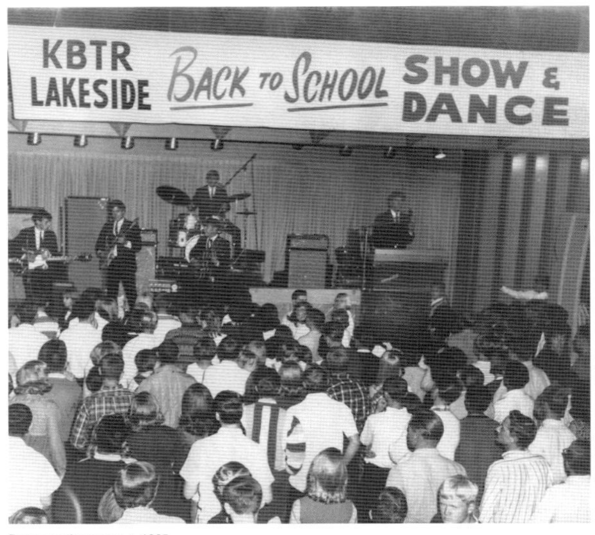

Denver performance, c. 1965

During the early 1970s, Spiro Agnew led a Nixon administration strike against rock lyrics. In a much-reported speech, he explained that "Puff the Magic Dragon" was code for marijuana and the "friends" the Beatles were getting a little help from were illegal narcotics. His blacklist of 22 songs, compiled by a core of "concerned" generals of the Department of the Army, included "That Acapulco Gold."

"We had our 15 minutes of fame," Gilbert said. "It was a happy accident, or an unhappy accident—ultimately, the song broke up the band. We got pigeonholed into that kind of a sound, and nobody wanted to play that music."

Carter went on to spend a dozen years as an artists and repertoire (A&R) representative at Capitol Records, serving as a kind of staff producer and overseeing more than 20 albums, including hit records by Sammy Hagar, Bob Welch and Tina Turner. ●

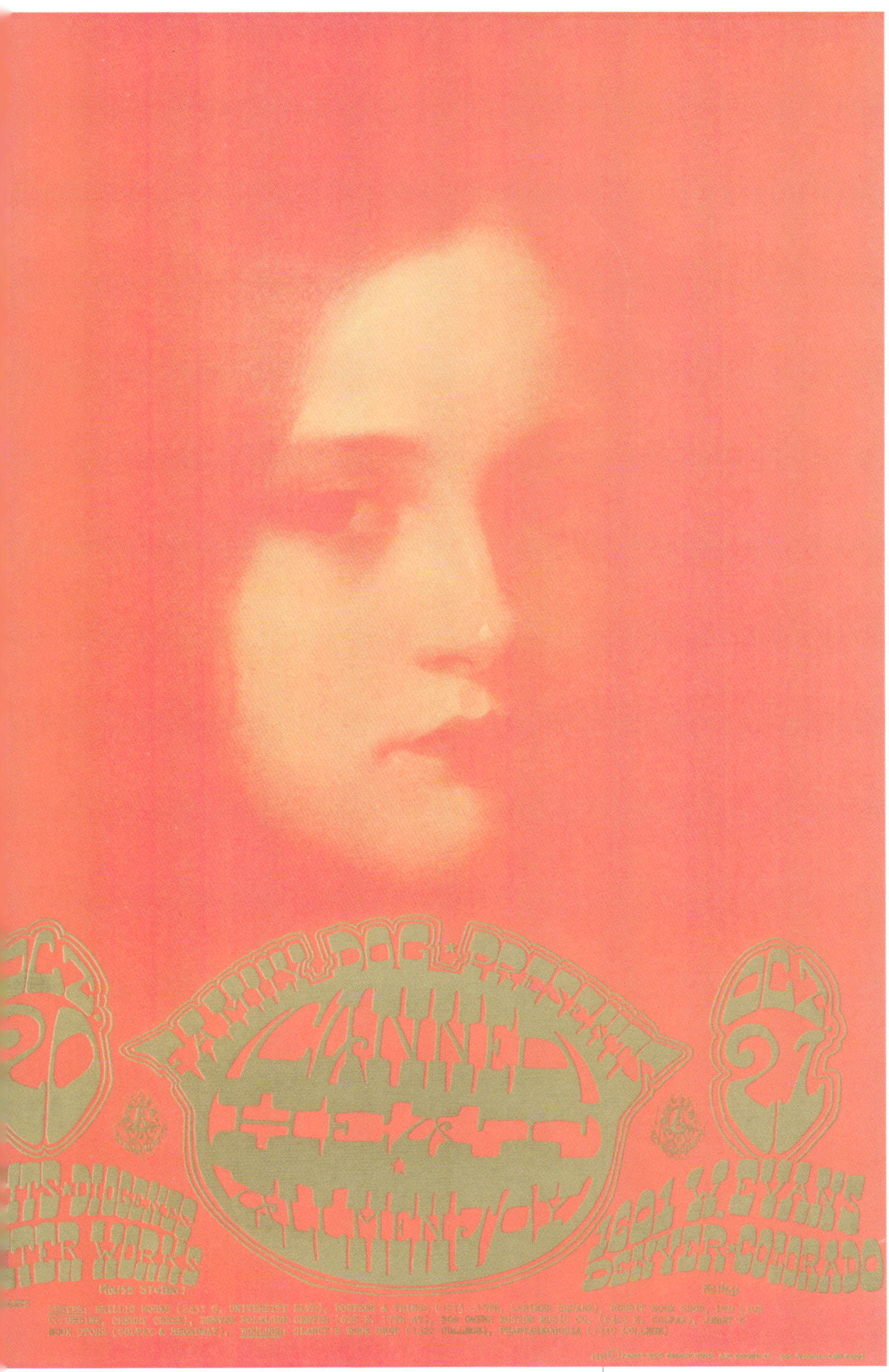

Family Dog concert poster, October 21, 1967

CANNED HEAT }

PROMOTER BARRY Fey was one of the most influential people to emerge from the 1960s Colorado music scene. He moved to Denver from Illinois in early 1967 and, after a trip to San Francisco's Haight Ashbury district, contacted Chet Helms, manager of Janis Joplin's band, Big Brother & the Holding Company, to discuss bringing a bit of the "Summer of Love" scene to Denver. Joe Neddo of the band Böenzee Cryque informed Fey of a recently closed nightspot in Denver, a rectangular stucco building in an industrial stretch of Evans Avenue.

It became the Family Dog, named after the San Francisco collective that sponsored dances at the Fillmore and the Avalon Ballroom.

Fey became the local booking agent for the 2,500-seat concert hall, which opened on September 8, 1967, with a show featuring Joplin and Big Brother plus the heavy sounds of Blue Cheer. For ten glorious months, the Family Dog prospered, hosting an amazing roster of talent—the Grateful Dead, the Byrds, Buffalo Springfield, Van Morrison, Jefferson Airplane, Frank Zappa, Cream and more.

Psychedelic images were hand-painted on the floor. Colorful posters and handbills prepared by San Francisco artists such as Rick Griffin, Stanley Mouse and Alton Kelley promoted the shows. The most expensive ticket ever at the venue, for the Doors on New Year's Eve 1967, cost $4.50.

But the club struggled to stay open, both financially and with mounting police pressure. The Denver police hated the idea of having a hippie club in their city and had done all they could to stop the Family Dog from opening. Helms and his people endured a barrage of harassment and illegal searches.

It was Canned Heat's bad luck to show up on a Saturday night, October 21, 1967, just as the police figured they'd bust one of the bands and the bad press and legal troubles would carry over to Helms. Officers followed the members of Canned Heat, a seminal influence on white urban blues, to a nearby motel at Santa Fe and Florida.

"The band didn't have any dope in Denver—everyone knew that things were tough there—so the guys showed up clean to play that gig," said drummer Fito De La Parra, who joined Canned Heat a few months later. "But the police dispatched a stool pigeon with some weed to the hotel to socialize and turn us on."

It turned out the stool pigeon was an old friend of Bob "The Bear" Hite, the band's singer.

According to De La Parra, "Bear was raised in Denver before his family moved to Los Angeles, so he had made some friends there when he was a kid. So he trusted the guy, until he suddenly disappeared out the door and the cops came barging in to 'discover' a package of weed under the cushion of the chair where the 'friend' had been sitting. They busted everybody on charges of marijuana possession—still a big offense in those days. A judge wasn't available until Monday, so the band spent the weekend in the can.

"It was a terrible thing. To pay the fines and court costs, the band had to sell its publishing."

The drama was immortalized in "My Crime," from the album *Boogie with Canned Heat*:

I went to Denver late last fall
I went to do my job, I didn't break any law
We worked in a hippie place
Like many in our land
They couldn't bust the place, and so they got the band
Cause the police in Denver
No they don't want long hairs hanging around
And that's the reason why
They want to tear Canned Heat's reputation down

At the time of the Family Dog bust, Hite said to a reporter, "To sing the blues, you have to be an outlaw. Blacks are born outlaws, but we white people have to work for that distinction."

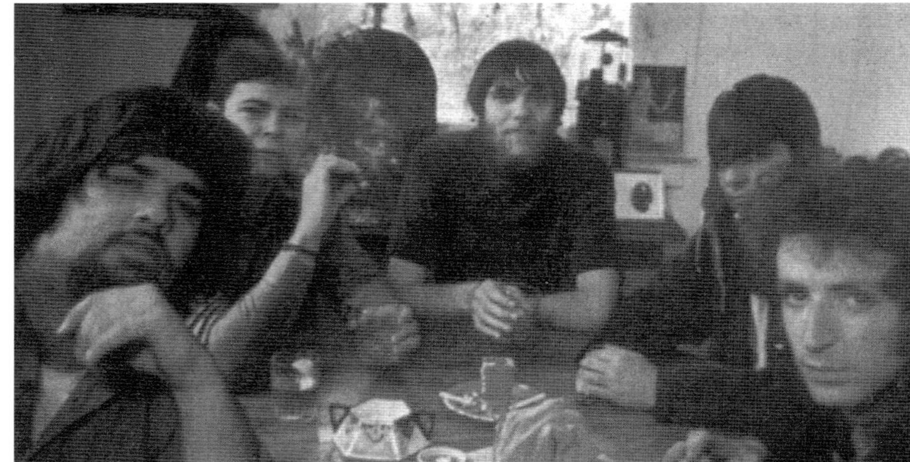
c. 1968

The Family Dog began to falter when the club obtained an injunction forbidding police presence on its premises. Rather than benefitting the venue, news of the injunction resulted in diminishing patronage. After a short stint as the Dog, the club closed in July 1968. It enjoyed a much longer and successful run as a gentlemen's club. ●

STEVE ALAIMO }

A PURVEYOR of so-called "blue-eyed soul," Steve Alaimo offered a good glimpse into the R&B rock style of the day with his best-known hit, "Every Day I Have to Cry."

Alaimo, who hailed from New York, eventually found his niche as a pop vocalist on Dick Clark's late-afternoon *Where the Action Is*, a popular show of the mid to late 1960s. It made stars of Paul Revere & the Raiders, the clean-cut house band, and younger teens could see "teen idols" like Alaimo, a regular on the program.

"Denver," written by Dan Penn & Spooner Oldham (who were responsible for the Box Tops' "Cry Like a Baby"), was a minor hit in March 1968, making *Billboard*'s "Bubbling Under the Hot 100" charts at #118.

"It was at the end of *Where the Action Is*—we did one of those big Dick Clark tours up in Colorado—and I met the woman that I ended up marrying later, in '71," Alaimo recalled. "Candy was going to Colorado Women's College. That's the reason I recorded 'Denver.' Mark Lindsay of Paul Revere & the Raiders was my closest friend at the time, so I ended up naming my daughter Lindsey after him."

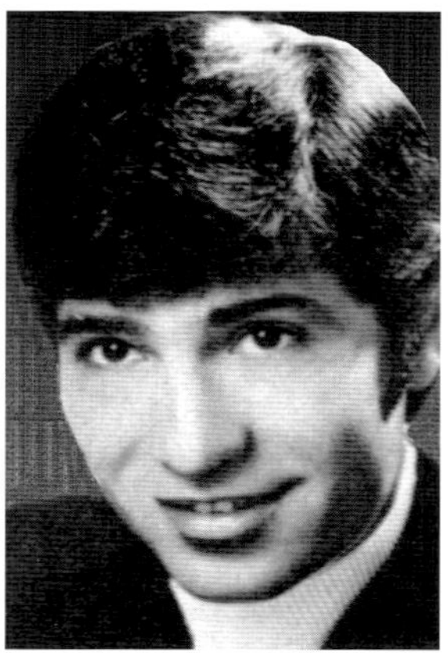
c. 1966

Country singer Ronnie Milsap's version of "Denver" reached #123 in May 1969.

During the 1970s, Alaimo became Henry Stone's right-hand man at Florida-based TK Records and helped to guide the careers of George McCrae, KC & the Sunshine Band and many others. ●

PAUL REVERE & THE RAIDERS }

A POP-ROCK group formed in Portland, Oregon, circa 1960, Paul Revere & the Raiders centered around keyboardist Revere and lead singer Mark Lindsay. Their guitarist, Drake Levin, had grown up in Boise, Idaho, playing in Revere's teenage nightclub, Crazy Horse, in a band with Phillip "Fang" Volk, who in 1963 would go on to attend the University of Colorado on a scholarship. Intending to be a music major, he studied opera and classical music. In the meantime, he kept playing guitar in a fraternity band.

While Volk headed to Boulder, Levin joined Revere's band. A year and a half later, after Levin had become a road warrior with the Raiders, he eventually talked Revere into inviting his old friend into the band. "Drake and I could do dance routines together," Volk said. "Paul had seen us at his club every weekend. They needed a bass player, and I was a guitar player. Paul called me in college and said, 'You'd better start learning the bass.' I wasn't very good at first."

Volk would replace Mike "Doc" Holliday on bass, the final piece in what would come to be considered the "classic" Raider lineup. His toothy grin earned him the nickname "Fang."

"I went right from the University of Colorado with my wing-tip oxfords and my blue blazer and my grey slacks and short hair, looking like Joe College, to Las Vegas, and joined Paul Revere & the Raiders at the Pussycat à Go-Go on the Strip. You talk about two worlds colliding. It was an amazing metamorphosis.

"My fraternity brothers took me to the airplane and got me a little bit soused. The airline almost didn't let me on the plane. In those days, you walked up a stairway off the tarmac to the airplane, and I jumped off that onto the wing, doing a little boogaloo. People didn't appreciate that..."

Paul Revere & the Raiders went to Los Angeles in 1965 and got on a daily ABC-TV show called *Where the Action Is.*

"It ran five days a week for two years, which is a phenomenal thing for any band, to be in front of a national audience every day," Volk remembered.

"Even Columbia Records didn't realize the kind of popularity the show had given us. They said, 'Well, let's take the boys on a promotional tour, set up appearances at supermarkets and amusement parks.' They were shocked at the response. Every city we went to around the country, there were massive crowds gathered, riots. A couple of vehicles were destroyed when kids would jump on them trying to get a peek at us. They weren't ready for that."

Top 40 hits included "Steppin' Out," "Just Like Me," "Kicks," "Hungry," "Good Thing" and "Ups and Downs"; Volk's bass lines helped to revolutionize how the bass guitar was used in rock music.

"We had a really hard-edged sound, and we were a viable rock band," Fang said. "We played our own instruments during (those) years. Yeah, we had a couple of extra friends come into the sessions to augment the sound, but we were always there playing the chops."

On leaving the Raiders, Volk formed a new band called Brotherhood with Raider bandmates Levin and Mike "Smitty" Smith. Following the breakup of Brotherhood, Volk headed several groups of his own. ●

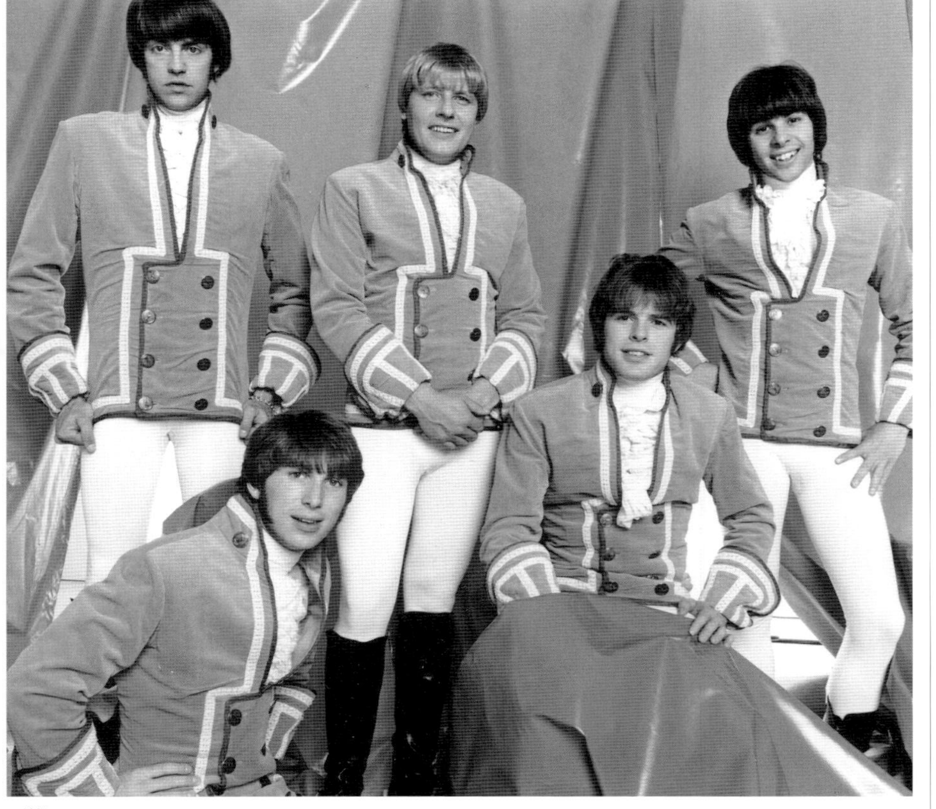

c. 1965

LED ZEPPELIN }

IN LEAVING London to come to America in 1968, Led Zeppelin took a calculated risk. The band had no album out yet, response from the press in England was mild, and three of the group had never been to America before and didn't know what to expect.

But manager Peter Grant's strategy was simple—it was still worth the gamble to go out and play, to see if they could create some excitement that might snowball into an avalanche. Grant had five years of experience in the United States with bands like the Yardbirds and the Animals. He felt he knew which American cities would maximize Zeppelin's exposure.

He saw an opportunity when the Jeff Beck Group, managed out of the same office, cancelled an American tour with Vanilla Fudge. He called the upset promoters and talked them into a new group.

"The agent said, 'Do you want to add another act, Led Zeppelin, for $1,500?'" Denver promoter Barry Fey recalled. "It was a sold-out show. I said, 'Why pay $1,500 for another act?' We settled on $500."

Then Grant had to convince the members of Led Zeppelin to leave their warm homes during Christmastime for parts unknown.

"I was 20 years old, and Christmas away from home for the English is the end of the world," singer Robert Plant explained.

But Led Zeppelin packed its bags, ready to test America's waters. The band's flight from London departed for the Los Angeles airport on December 23. Plant was incredulous.

"L.A. was absolutely devastating for me," he said. "I was too young to go into any bars—not that that was the first thing I thought about. I had no idea what to expect—American TV in England was *Dragnet* or a U.S. cop thing. It was the first time I saw a 20-foot-long car."

The morning after Christmas, Led Zeppelin headed back to LAX, boarding a TWA flight for Denver. That night they met up with bass player John Paul Jones, who had arrived on a separate flight from New Jersey, where he and his wife had spent the holidays.

They assembled downtown at the Auditorium Arena and began their first U.S. tour. They paced nervously, biting their fingernails. Plant and drummer John Bonham tried to stay calm backstage.

"Colorado was so beautiful and gentle compared to L.A., but I was petrified by the hugeness of the venue," Plant said.

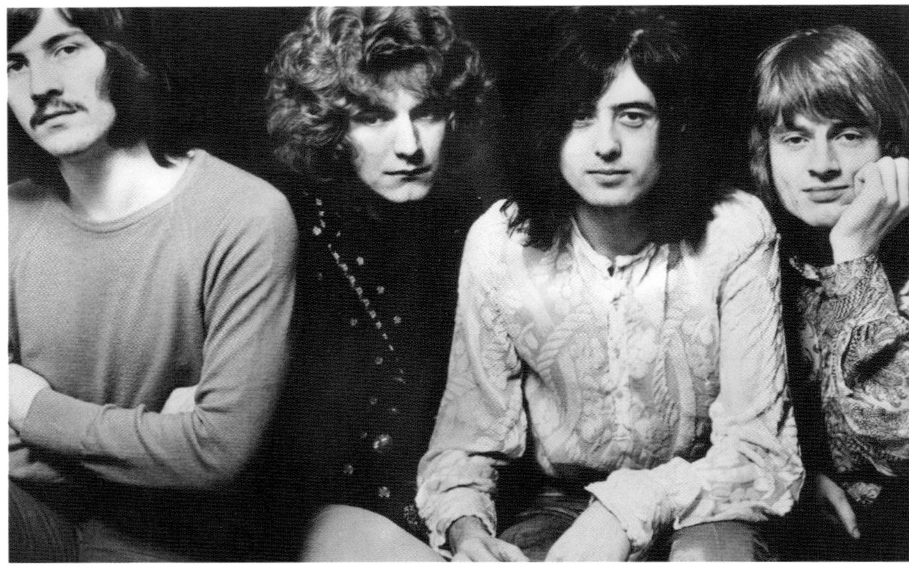

c. 1968

"Neither Robert nor John nor John Paul had played in a really big hall like that first performance," guitarist Jimmy Page recalled. "Since I'd toured with the Yardbirds, I was the only one who knew how big the places would be, even though we were only opening the show. I just tried to boost morale."

Led Zeppelin wasn't even listed in advertisements for its first U.S. concert—the bill was Vanilla Fudge and Spirit. The band performed an hour-long set on a revolving platform that night, introducing their powerful personalities and unprecedented sound—"Good Times Bad Times," "Dazed and Confused," "Communication Breakdown," "I Can't Quit You Babe," "You Shook Me," "Your Time Is Gonna Come."

After Led Zeppelin sprinted from the stage, Plant reached into a cardboard container filled with spareribs from a local restaurant.

"I couldn't believe that the promoter could charge for food backstage," he laughed.

Denver was only the beginning. Led Zeppelin spent the next year and a half on the road, including six separate tours of American that featured the band as headliners on most nights, earning its fortune and a reputation for bawdy mayhem and excess. Between 1969 and 1980, the Zep released nine multi-million-selling albums and reigned as the No. 1 hard-rock band in the world. ●

DOUG LUBAHN | THE DOORS }

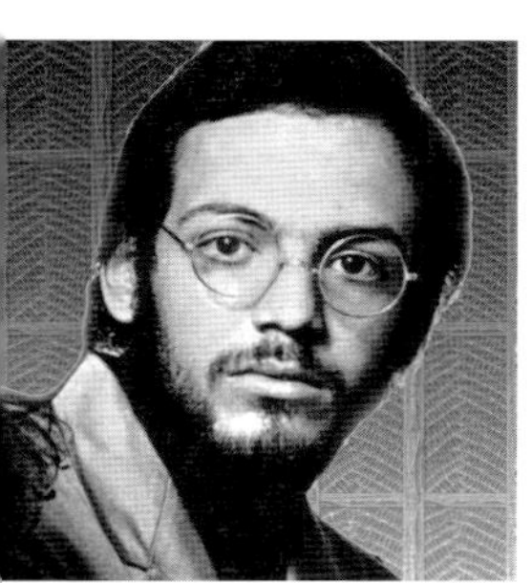

1967

BECAUSE THEIR instrumental chemistry was driven by a keyboard, rather than by all guitars, the Doors distinguished themselves from virtually every other rock band of the late 1960s.

John Densmore (drums), Robby Krieger (guitar), Ray Manzarek (electric organ) and Jim Morrison (lead singer) had looked for a bassist, but most of the players they rehearsed gave them a sound that was too full. The solution came when Manzarek discovered the 32-note Fender Rhodes keyboard bass. He could control the compact model with his left hand while playing chords and solos with his right on the Vox organ. It became the bass sound for the Doors.

"The piano bass was okay for live work, but in the studio, it didn't record well—it just didn't have any definition," Manzarek said. "It had a soft sound on the first album, so that's why I didn't use it after that.

"When we did *Strange Days*, we said, 'Let's get some bass players in here.'"

The Doors used Doug Lubahn, who hailed from Colorado—a Golden High School graduate, class of 1965.

"In school, I got the gig as the bass player in the hottest band, the Carpetbaggers. But they didn't want me to stay because I had bad breath," Lubahn laughed. "I was going to be a ski instructor. I was 17, a fanatic. I hitchhiked up to Aspen for the summer, and a friend and I started skiing the glaciers. I knew some of the local bands, and every night I'd sit in and play bass. A group called the Candy Store came to Aspen to play, and with them came Mama Cass. She heard me and said, 'What are you doing here? You should come with me back to L.A. You should be playing for real.' I jumped on a plane in the spring of '66."

Lubahn joined Clear Light, a Los Angeles rock band. *Clear Light* peaked at #126 on the *Billboard* album chart in November 1967.

"All the musicians looking for stuff to do would hang out at a delicatessen called Canter's at night. These guys came walking through with a sign on their shirts saying 'We need a bass player.' I'd been staying in a basement somewhere. They took me to pick up my stuff, drove me to their community house and I ended up staying," Lubahn said.

"We had the same producer as the Doors, Paul Rothchild. He said they needed a bass player for their records. He drove me up to Laurel Canyon, I played with them for a half-hour and got the job. The first album hadn't come out yet. When it did, they were huge."

Lubahn played bass on the hit albums *Strange Days*, *Waiting for the Sun* and *The Soft Parade*.

"Ray Manzarek would show me the bass part and then I would play it adding my own little filigrees. I admired him so much, because he would come up with the most interesting bass lines, then he'd let me go have fun with it."

But Lubahn never played live. "Paul felt it was better that they remain a quartet, visually and fan-wise. They didn't want to add or subtract anything, just keep it the way it was. I was happy to do it. It was great music, great fun."

Harvey Brooks, another bass player, came in about midway through *The Soft Parade*.

"Dumb me—they did that song 'Touch Me,' and I hated it," Lubahn said. "And I didn't think they were paying me enough money to do it, now that they were all millionaires. I got tired of the whole thing, so I told them I was leaving. They were nice about it, and they were anxious to get Harvey in anyway. It was amicable."

Lubahn moved to New York and played in Dreams, a jazz-rock group formed by Michael and Randy Brecker. In the early 1980s, he co-wrote "Treat Me Right" with Pat Benatar. He also played bass on albums by Billy Squier and Ted Nugent. ●

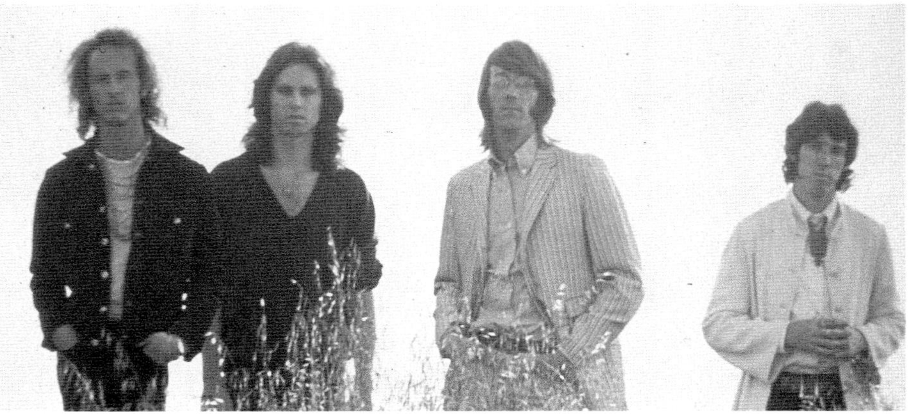

c. 1968

BEAST }

BASED FOR a time in Colorado Springs, Beast premiered at the Kelker Junction nightclub in 1968. Members included Bob Yeazel on lead guitar and Kenny Passarelli on bass for the first of its two albums, *Beast*, which charted for two weeks in late 1969, peaking at #195.

"I graduated early from East High School, then went to the University of Denver on a trumpet performance scholarship," Passarelli said. "I quit DU after a year when the Beast got a record deal.

"David Raines was an R&B singer, like Mitch Ryder. He had that kind of throaty voice, and he did the splits. The instrumentation had an R&B texture to it—Gerry Fike played a Hammond B-3 organ with Leslie speakers—and part of it was funky, part of it was Motown-ish. But we weren't a straight-ahead soul band. We were doing original material, the majority of it Yeazel's, and it was more psychedelic. It was a real odd mixture."

A few members of the septet connected with a rough crowd fom Denver, which was nicknamed "Crystal City" because of the speed laboratories that were proliferating.

"We settled in the Black Forest, an area northeast of Colorado Springs, and lived on a farm, almost like a commune—a couple of guys had their old ladies," Passarelli said. "Word got out that these speed guys were going to use our farm to set up a drug lab. The feds grilled us on that."

Passarelli started hanging out more in Boulder, where he got introduced to Stephen Stills, who was putting together a new group and looking for a bass player. "He'd broken up with Judy Collins and was clearing out his head in Gold Hill. It was the first time in my life that I thought, 'Maybe I have a chance to do this—someone's given me the green light to make it.'"

But the bassist contracted hepatitis B. "I was down for six months. I freaked out. At 19, I thought I'd been offered the gig of my life and didn't get it. When I got well, I left Beast. They made a second record, continued playing through the Midwest, then fell apart."

Beast made both of its albums with Norman Petty in the Clovis, New Mexico studio that recorded all of Buddy Holly's songs.

Passarelli went on to bigger success with Joe Walsh, Elton John and studio sessions. Yeazel and drummer Larry Ferris put in an appearance with Sugarloaf in the 1970s. ●

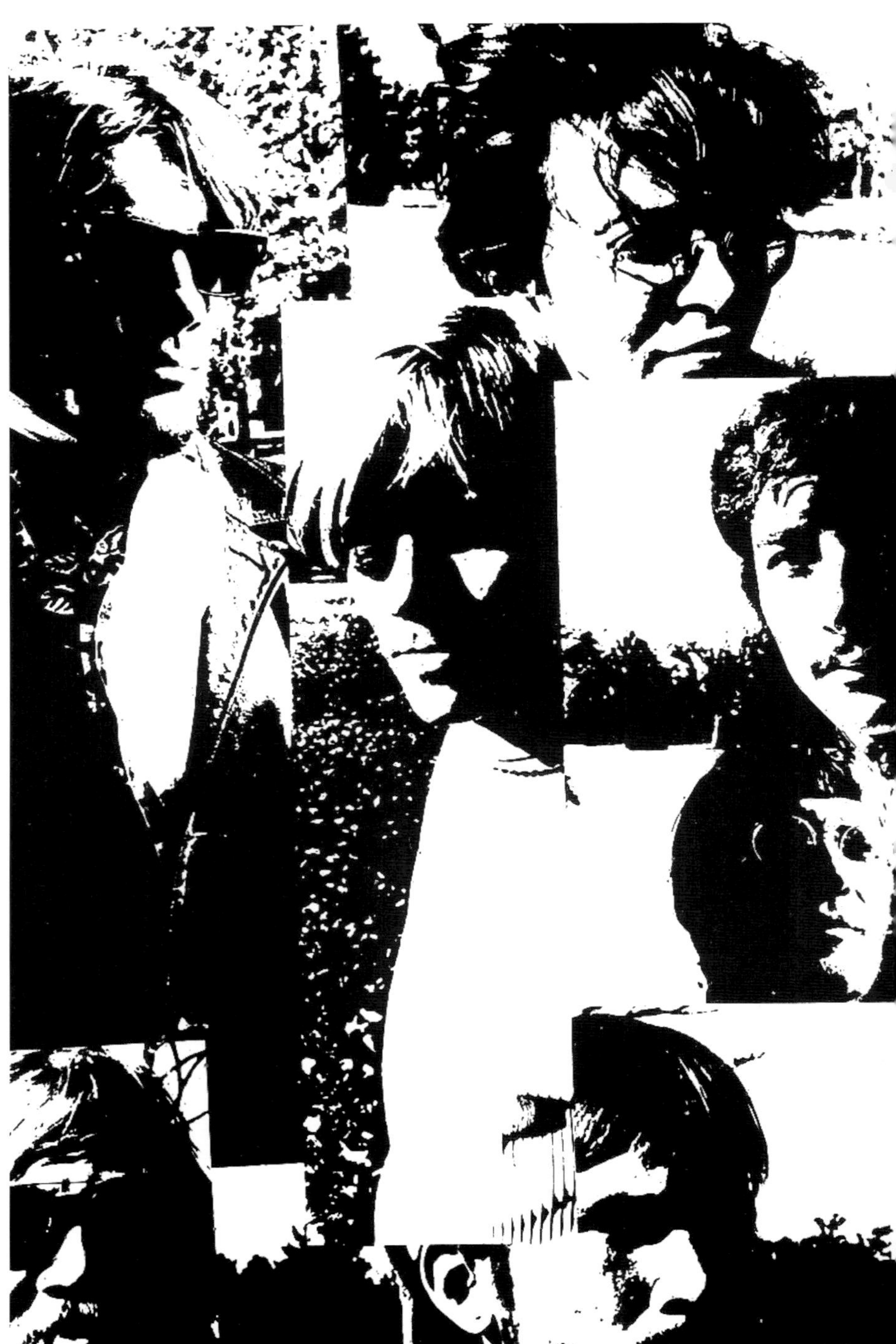

c. 1969

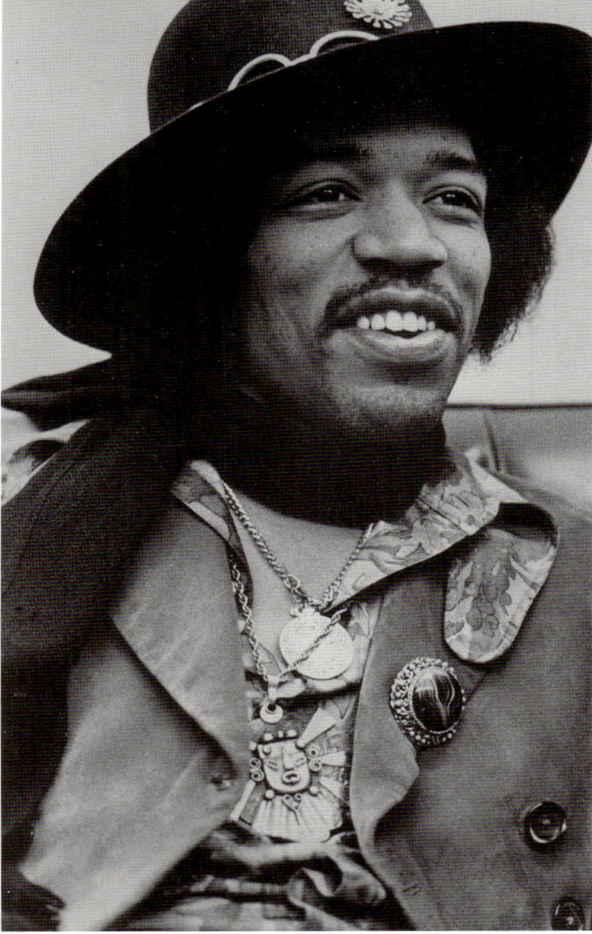

c. 1969

JIMI HENDRIX }

BY 1968, THE counterculture's idea of rock—as opposed to the latest Top 40 hit—started to dominate in Denver. During this period, the city generally objected to rock music at Red Rocks Amphitheatre, which wasn't good news for Barry Fey, a fledgling promoter whose career would span more than three decades.

Fey had founded his promotions firm, Feyline, and he had grown ambitious enough to book Red Rocks to close the summer season, his first concert using a city facility—a billing with the Jimi Hendrix Experience, Soft Machine and headliner Vanilla Fudge. Tickets were $4.50.

By all accounts, Hendrix didn't stack up to the competition at Red Rocks. His flight was delayed, and the trucks carrying equipment had been late. When he finally took the stage, one of his Marshall amplifiers blew. There was a delay while roadies replaced tubes in the back of the amp; when that didn't work, they swapped it out all together. "I'm really sorry," an upset Hendrix apologized. "I don't know what the hell we are trying to do up here."

Hendrix later said, "I had a lot of fun at Red Rocks. That was groovy and nice, 'cause people are on top of you there, or at least they can hear something. That's where it should be, natural-theater type things."

Noel Redding, bass player for the Experience, said that Red Rocks "was a really flashy gig. We were taken to and from the concert by a police escort. The park is so big, and we'd drawn 9,000 people. Unfortunately, Jimi didn't play very well that night, and afterwards Denver had nothing to offer in after-gig entertainment. Or even daytime entertainment, for there was nothing to do the next day either, so we all took acid and went into the mountains."

Something positive did ultimately result from Hendrix's sole appearance at Red Rocks. After the gig, he returned to his Cosmopolitan hotel room in downtown Denver and wrote the liner notes to his *Electric Ladyland* album.

The following year, the first and only Denver Pop Festival opened at Mile High Stadium on Friday, June 27. The event was Fey's shot at the big time; Woodstock didn't happen until three months later. Admission for each day was $6, or concertgoers could buy a three-day ticket for $15. The festival ended up with 60,000 admissions.

The lineup:

FRIDAY: Flock, Big Mama Thornton, Mothers of Invention, Three Dog Night, Iron Butterfly.

SATURDAY: Aorta, Zephyr, Poco, Tim Buckley, Johnny Winter, Creedence Clearwater Revival.

SUNDAY: Aum, Rev. Cleophus Robinson, Sweetwater, Joe Cocker, the Jimi Hendrix Experience.

1969 was a time for drawing hard lines. Civil rights demonstrations, antiwar protests and student strikes were loose in the land, but it was the Denver Pop Festival that brought home to Coloradans that, ready or not, the rock revolution was on.

In the late afternoon of

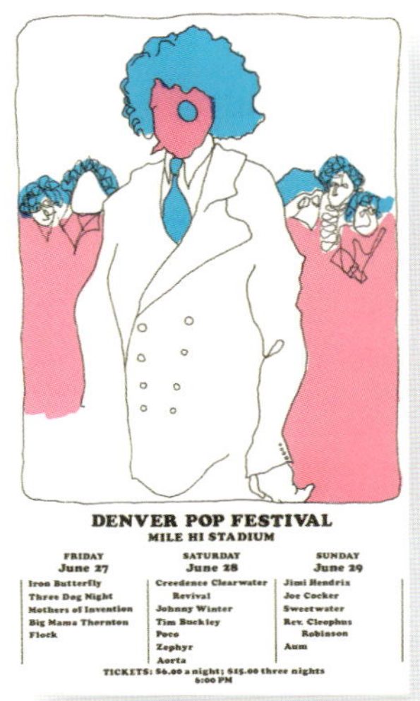

Official poster, 1969

the second day, the event changed from a musical episode to a panic. Tear gas intended for gate-crashers outside the stadium swept over the west stands, blinding and gagging many of the 21,000 fans seated inside listening to Zephyr. Violence erupted in the audience, and police moved in with clubs and more tear gas.

On the festival's final day, the Jimi Hendrix Experience played its last concert. Rumors of an imminent split in the band had been supported by the announcement that Redding had formed his own band, Fat Mattress.

At a press conference in the afternoon, Hendrix announced a new bassist, his old Army buddy Billy Cox, and a new approach: "A sky church sort of thing...I want to get the whole Buddy Miles group and call them the Freedom Express..." He added that Redding and drummer Mitch Mitchell weren't necessarily out of the band.

During the gig, Mile High Stadium was in an uproar. The stage was located on the infield dirt, and fans were bursting forth from the stands, desperate to get close to the music. Hendrix clambered onto the stage and launched into "Bold as Love."

Meanwhile, some 2,500 kids outside the stadium lobbed beer bottles, firecrackers and rocks at police, who responded with clouds of tear gas. The battle raged for two hours, ending only when the gates were opened to allow anyone to hear the music.

"We were just finishing our set when suddenly they let tear gas off and people started to panic," Mitchell recalled. "The road crew found us one of those two-ton panel vans, with aluminum sides and a top. The band got into the back, this huge cavernous space, and they locked us in."

To avoid the gas, people immediately swarmed onto the roof of the van, which started to cave in.

"Suddenly we were very scared—we thought it was just a matter of moments before we were going to be crushed," Mitchell said. "We only had to drive about a quarter of a mile back to the hotel, but it took us nearly an hour—and there were still people on top of the van and hanging on the sides.

"We really still felt like a band, no animosity—we had all linked arms and shook hands, feeling that if we were going to go, we'd all go together. But Noel did fly back to England the next day to announce that he'd left the band."

Soon after the Denver Pop Festival, Hendrix went into virtual seclusion, and the Jimi Hendrix Experience

Page 1. USE on L.P. Jimi Hendrix Electric Lady land -

the Cosmopolitan
DENVER, COLORADO 80202 • BROADWAY AT EAST EIGHTEENTH AVE. • PHONE

TITLE: Letter to the room full of mirrorS. 4:30 – 6:00am Denver Colo Sept 2nd. 1968 ... alone

4:30 to 6:00Am Denver Colo. Sept 2nd 1968

let's see now.... "It wasn't too long ago, but it feels like, yearS ago, since I've felt the warm hello of the Sun... lately thingS...." and then he was interrupted by the Slow motion Speeded up Sound that sometimeS cut so deep, that sound waS from those chellophane typwriterS... Excatly. Constantly from the South Side of those carpets and Sweet Rome was on my mind. "She gave So Sweetly...." And on he walked until after crowning Ethel the dog, the Only Queen of ears, The sky cracked wide open and split many of his BrotherS and SisterS headS all over the world apart still the approximate same) ....

WESTERN INTERNATIONAL HOTELS

Handwritten liner notes for *Electric Ladyland*

name was no longer used. He delved further into experimentalism, recording an immense quantity of unfinished music before his sudden death in 1970. The only other full-scale album project released in his lifetime was with his all-black Band of Gypsys; Cox and drummer Miles were basically a jam-rhythm section for Hendrix.

Rock concerts in city facilities were limited to the Denver Coliseum until 1974, when the first Colorado Sun Day was staged at Mile High Stadium. ●

THE ROLLING STONES }

BY 1969, IT was beginning to dawn on people that most of the decade's rock icons weren't functioning. The Beatles hated each other. Bob Dylan had become a recluse. Jim Morrison's encounters with the law were stacking up against him.

The Rolling Stones were the only ones left, putting their talent on stage for the first time since 1966.

When the Stones had last toured and made their reputation, it was still basically as a pop group—they were obliged to do little more than fill theaters with shrieking teens (in Colorado, Gov. John Love had declared Rolling Stones Day on November 29, 1966).

But in those three years, pop had evolved into rock culture and consciousness. The music was not only a thousand watts louder; it was also a thousand times weightier. The Stones had been portrayed as both heroes and villains. There was public controversy over their drug busts, censorship battles and their reportedly unconventional sex lives.

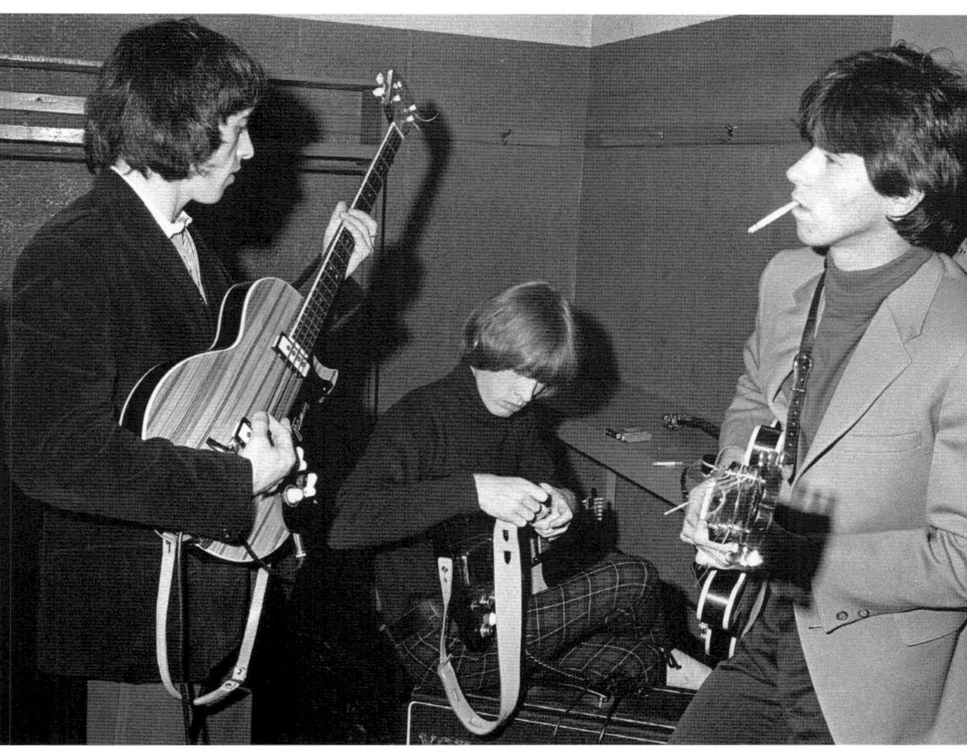

Bill Wyman, Brian Jones, Keith Richards at Denver Coliseum, November 29, 1966

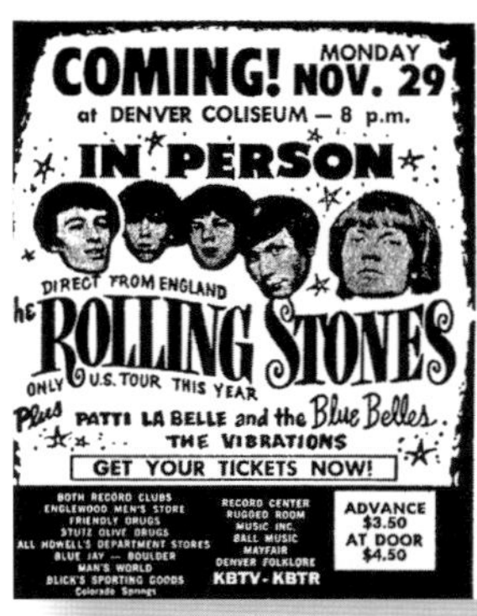

Official poster

Jittery at the prospect of moving into arenas, "the greatest rock 'n' roll band in the world" assembled a traveling rock 'n' roll circus with the lighting and sound equipment that the venues demanded. They even booked their own maintenance, publicity and security staffs and their own supporting act, Ike & Tina Turner.

The opening gig was scheduled at the Forum in Los Angeles. But the tour actually started the day before, on Friday, November 7, when the Stones flew to Colorado to perform at Colorado State University's Moby Gym in Fort Collins, about sixty miles north of Denver. It was a "break-in" concert—a rehearsal, though no one called it that. The performance had been advertised for three weeks, but no one outside of Colorado seemed to know of it. The Stones had asked that details of the concert go untold, in case something went wrong.

At sunset, the Stones got dressed in the Letterman's Lounge. And then Mick Jagger danced onstage and Keith Richards pumped out the opening chords to "Jumpin' Jack Flash."

Founding member Brian Jones had died in July 1969, and the tour showcased new guitarist Mick Taylor, who was instrumental in revitalizing the Stones. They concocted a brutal, salacious onstage sound. The set included "Stray Cat Blues," "Carol," "Love in Vain" and "Little Queenie." "Street Fighting Man" closed the show.

Fans weren't familiar with "Midnight Rambler,"

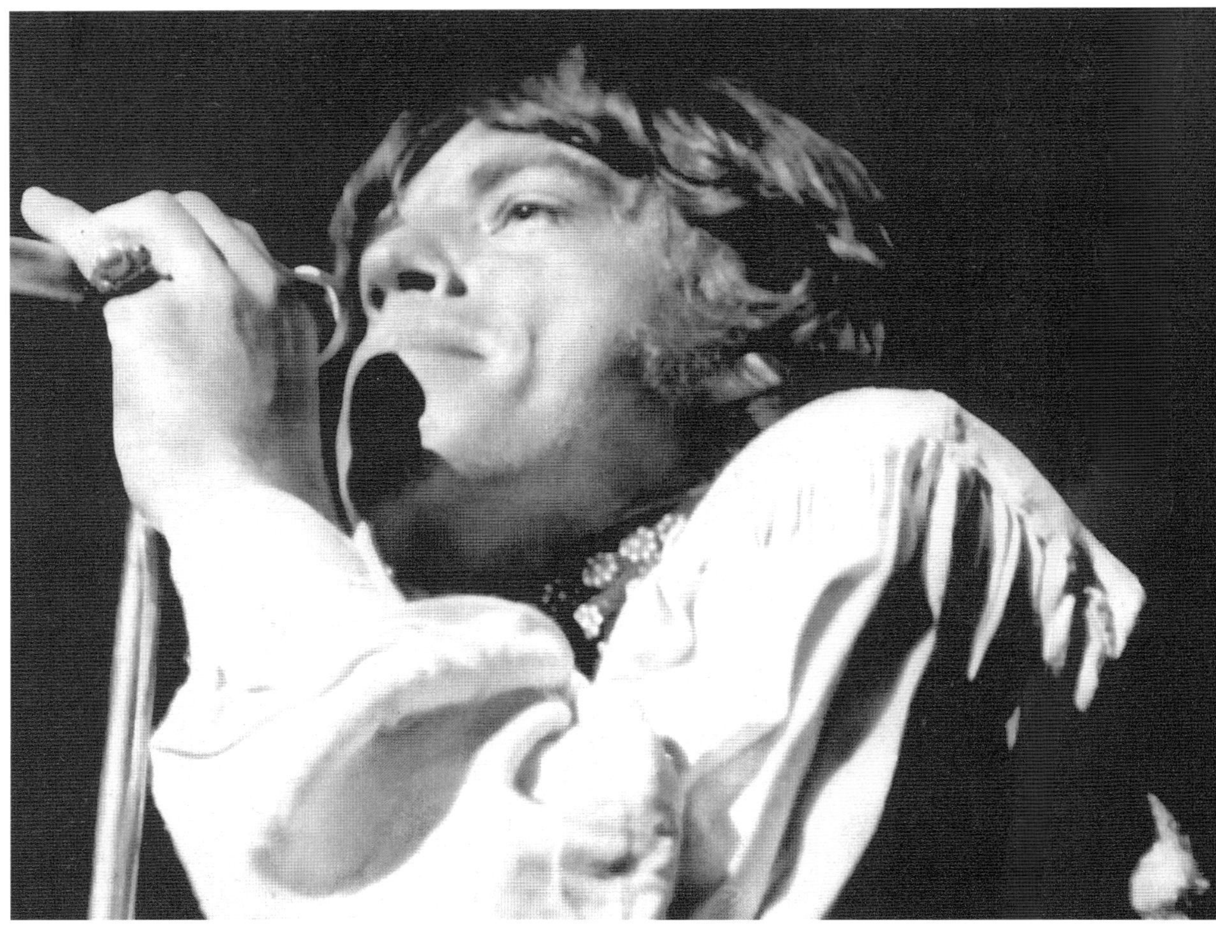

Mick Jagger at Moby Gym, Fort Collins, November 7, 1969

Jagger's eulogy to the Boston Strangler. The singer pranced around the stage, posing maliciously. He lashed the stage with his belt and thrust his crotch into the audience's faces.

The audience response? "They just sat there," Jagger later said. "They were, I think, too stoned to move."

Drummer Charlie Watts found 1969 America to be a radically different country than the one the Stones had entertained three years earlier.

"People didn't scream anymore—the music was taken seriously," he recalled. "And you had proper amplification—suddenly you could hear everybody. Nobody had heard drums before. We must have sounded a joke before that. But in '69, you really had to be on top of it to play. That's how Hendrix and bands like Led Zeppelin came about."

The tour was a media event, but the Stones' satanic image came home to roost in December at California's Altamont Speedway. Prodded by the summer's Woodstock gathering, the band chose to stage a free thank-you-America concert, which also included performances by the Flying Burrito Brothers and Jefferson Airplane. The Stones appointed members of the Hell's Angels motorcycle gang to work security for the day-long event. Their "protection" resulted in numerous violent altercations—the most infamous of which was the fatal stabbing of a young black man in front of the stage. It was a fitting end to one of the most dynamic and dysfunctional decades in American history.

During their 1972 tour, the Rolling Stones stayed at the Warwick Hotel in downtown Denver when the place was part of the Radisson chain. Keith Richards and sax player Bobby Keys got bored and started smashing up televisions with room service trolleys and throwing them out of the window. It was captured on *Cocksucker Blues*, an unreleased movie in which Richards elucidated about sending explosives through the plumbing to see if anything got blown up. ●

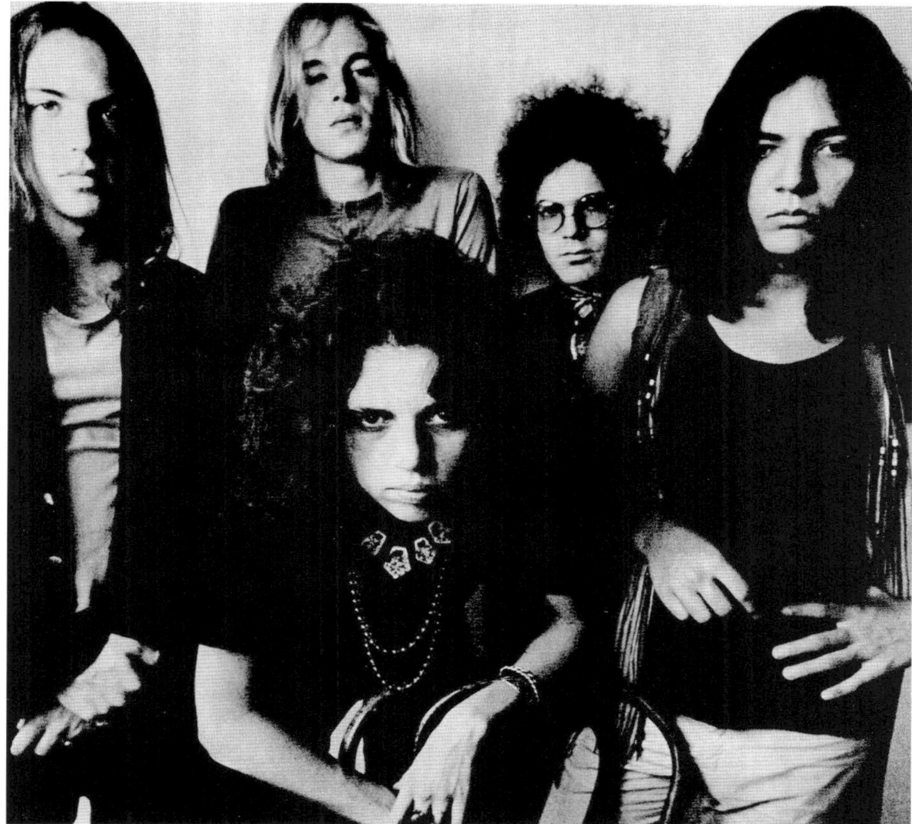

c. 1969

ZEPHYR }

JANIS JOPLIN, with her band Big Brother & the Holding Company, popularized a style of music recalling the days of great black soul singers such as Bessie Smith and Billie Holiday—only with a much harder edge. In Boulder, a feisty little singer named Candy Givens, a Golden High School graduate, and her husband, bassist David Givens, recruited drummer Robbie Chamberlin, keyboardist John Faris and a special young Iowa guitar player named Tommy Bolin to play this same style in a band called Zephyr.

"Our first performance was at a nightclub called the Sink back in an alley near the University of Colorado," David Givens said. "This may sound immodest, but it's the truth—we had no competition in Colorado. Right from the start, people treated us as if we were extraordinary."

Zephyr's music quickly developed as a curious mix of heavy jazz-inflected blues-rock, underpinned by a strong keyboard sound. Candy Givens' harmonica and vocals—from lusty growls to lacquer-thin highs—and Bolin's guitar raised the roof in Boulder and Denver clubs and college haunts. The group lived the typical late 1960s lifestyle, headquartering at Candy Givens' mother's house until Bolin wrangled an audition with concert promoter Barry Fey.

Fey liked the band (and especially Bolin, who was the hottest young guitarist on the scene) and set up a showcase in Los Angeles. After playing the legendary Whisky a Go Go nightclub, Zephyr was signed by ABC's Probe Records. *Zephyr*, also known as the "rainbow in the bathtub" record for its cover, reached the Top 50 in 1969. It was a fairly hesitant affair with a primitive studio sound, but it established Bolin as one of the premier guitarists in the country.

"The first record was recorded in two days," David Givens recalled. "Then a producer came in and wrecked it. I liked the basic tracks—it was real spontaneous, especially Tommy's guitar work."

One of David Givens' fondest memories of Candy Givens' performing days was at the riot-filled Denver Pop Festival in August 1969: "The cops were tear-gassing people at the gate and the performers were getting gassed. Candy took charge. She said, 'We're crying anyway. We may as well do some blues.'"

Zephyr gigged solidly through 1970 and 1971. The act performed at such noted rock emporiums as the Fillmore, the Fillmore East and the Whisky a Go Go, and opened for such luminaries as Jimi Hendrix, Led Zeppelin, Mountain and Fleetwood Mac. But their recording career was held up after Probe folded. When they did venture back into the studio, it was for the Warner Brothers label. Eddie Kramer, who had produced successful albums for Led Zeppelin and Hendrix, had heard the group in Colorado and put them on Warners. The sessions for 1971's *Going Back to Colorado* took place in the prestigious Electric Ladyland Studios in New York.

"We'd been there a couple

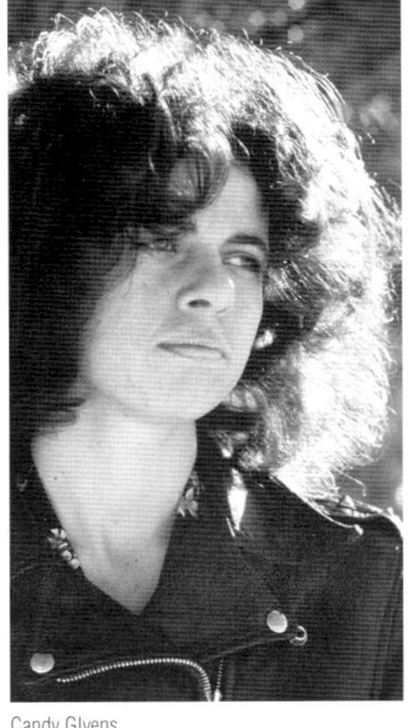
Candy Givens

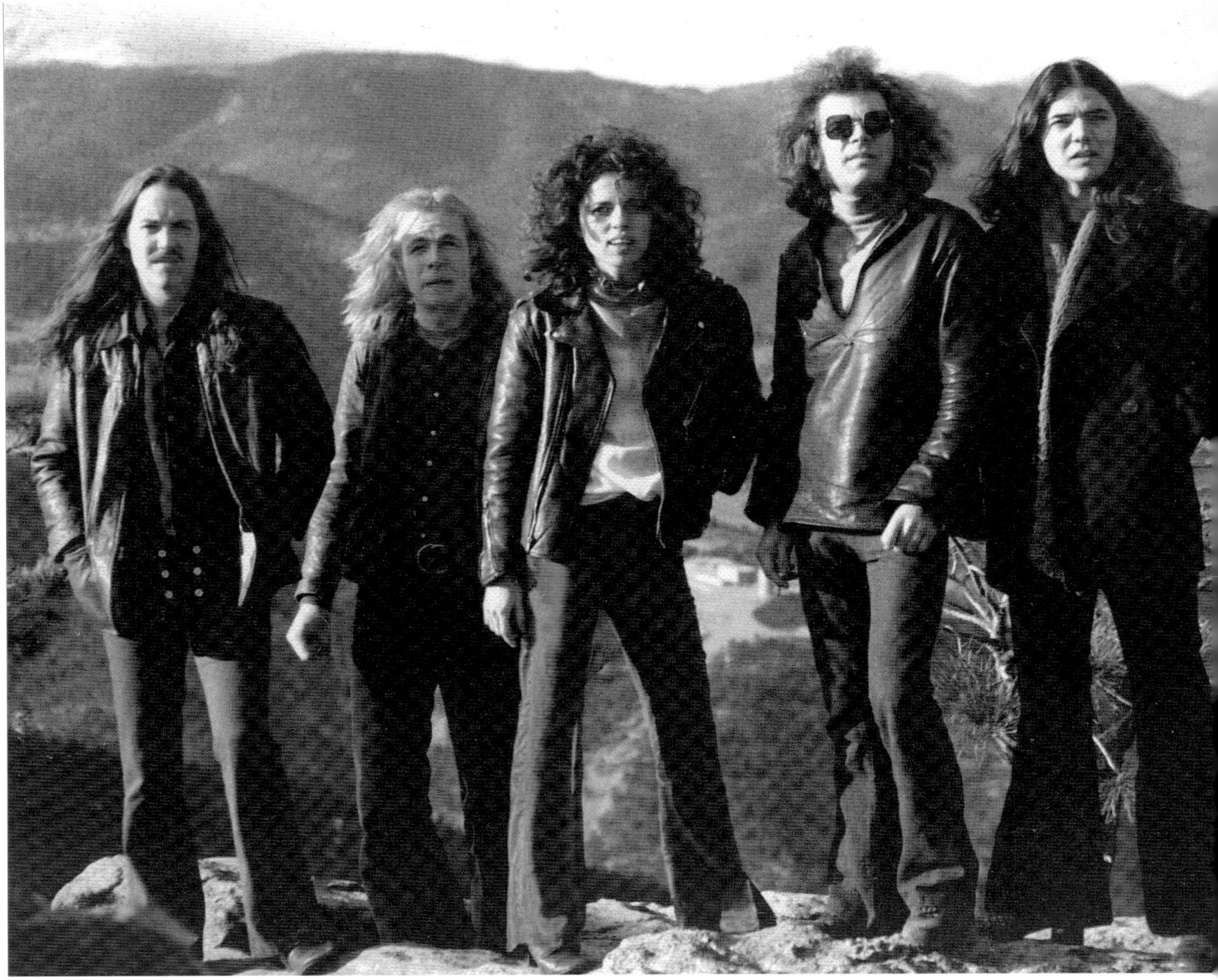

c. 1970

of weeks when Jimi Hendrix died. It fell to Eddie Kramer to try and make Hendrix's *Cry of Love* album sound finished. He felt the weight of trying to complete it. We were pushed aside right when we needed him to help us," Givens said.

Zephyr learned the music business through painful mistakes. Sad tales of managerial hang-ups and broken promises ensued.

"The hassles started," Givens recalled. "Tommy fought with the drummer, then the drummer came back, so Tommy quit, blah, blah."

Bolin and drummer Bobby Berge quit Zephyr in early 1972 for new pastures. Bolin formed a new band called Energy before leaving town to play with the James Gang. Zephyr persevered with a third album, *Sunset Ride*, featuring guitarist Jock Bartley.

In 1973, Candy and David Givens, Bolin and Faris joined up with Harold Fielden and Mick Manresa from Flash Cadillac, as the Legendary 4-Nikators, playing oldies every Monday night at Art's Bar & Grill in north Boulder. They packed the place and made more money than they ever had as Zephyr.

In 1976, four years after leaving Zephyr, Bolin died of a drug overdose.

Candy Givens drowned in her hot tub after overdosing on Quaaludes and alcohol in 1984.

"Candy was unique, the first female lead singer who could hang with the guys that I was aware of," her widower said. "Over the years, Candy was accused of copying Janis Joplin, but she was an entirely different kind of duck. True, she was brash and sang hard sometimes, and our records didn't often capture her at her best. But she was never a Janis clone to anyone with eyes or ears." ●

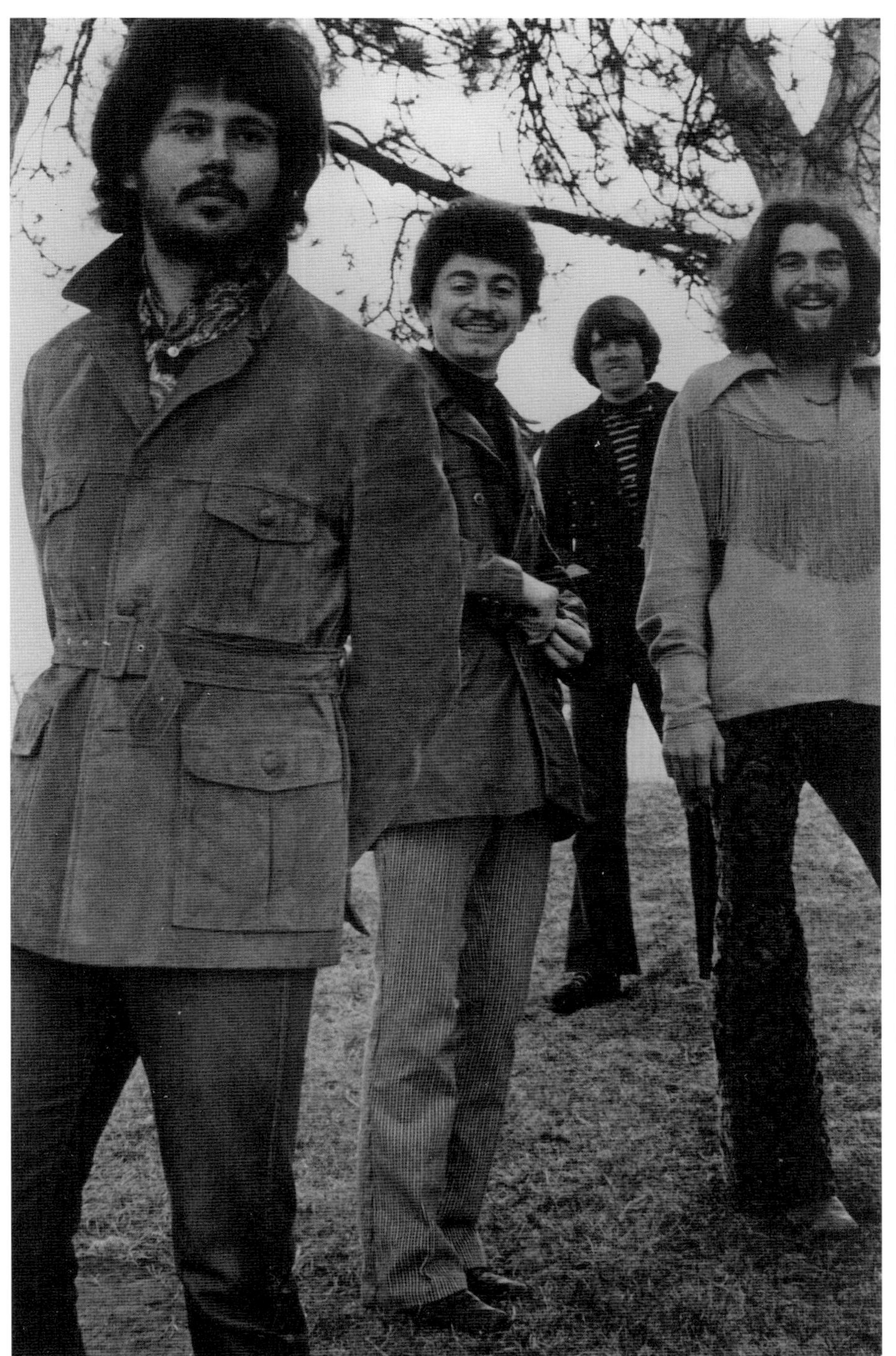

c. 1970

SUGARLOAF }

THE MOONRAKERS were the most popular group in Denver during the mid-1960s, with four singles hitting the local charts (the biggest being "You'll Come Back"). But Joel Brandes, Denny Flannigan, Bob MacVittie, Bob Webber and Veeder Van Dorn couldn't break out nationally.

After several membership changes, the Moonrakers returned in 1969 with the Christian rock album *Together with Him*. The drummer on half the songs was Jerry Corbetta, who as a teenager had played keyboards in the Half Dozen't and the Brambles.

"The Moonrakers and the Half Dozen't were seasoned bands. Musicians were lucky—Denver had nightclubs where you could drink 3.2 beer when you were 18. We played six nights a week for years. I had a Corvette bought and paid for before I could drive. You honed your chops—you could play the songs in your sleep, with a shower or without a shower," Corbetta said.

"Bob Webber was the Moonrakers' guitarist, and he and I were fire and ice personality-wise. He's a real linear thinker—an aerospace engineer, 4.0 student. I was

Italian, from North Denver—I played the accordion.

"But I knew music theory and harmony, and he respected me on that. I sat him down one night and said, 'If the Moonrakers can get a deal, I'm convinced that you and I could start a band and get twice as good a deal.' That was my simple, straight logic."

With Webber, Bob Raymond (bass), Myron Pollock (drums) and Corbetta returning to keyboards, the four players transformed into Chocolate Hair, recording a seven-song demo that got them signed to Liberty Records. There was also a name change.

"When we didn't have a name, we wrote down a bunch of nouns and adjectives, put them in a bowl and drew the name Chocolate Hair," Corbetta explained. "When we signed our record deal, the legal department met with us and said, 'You can't call yourself Chocolate Hair because it has racial overtones.' We didn't care. We just wanted to play."

The band took the name of a mountain summit in the foothills above Boulder where Webber lived, transforming into Sugarloaf. The demo, a mix of rock, R&B and jazz licks, became the basis for the debut LP, but only after new drummer Bob MacVittie came on board to record the last song for the album, which scored the group a big national hit—"Green-Eyed Lady" peaked at #3 in October 1970.

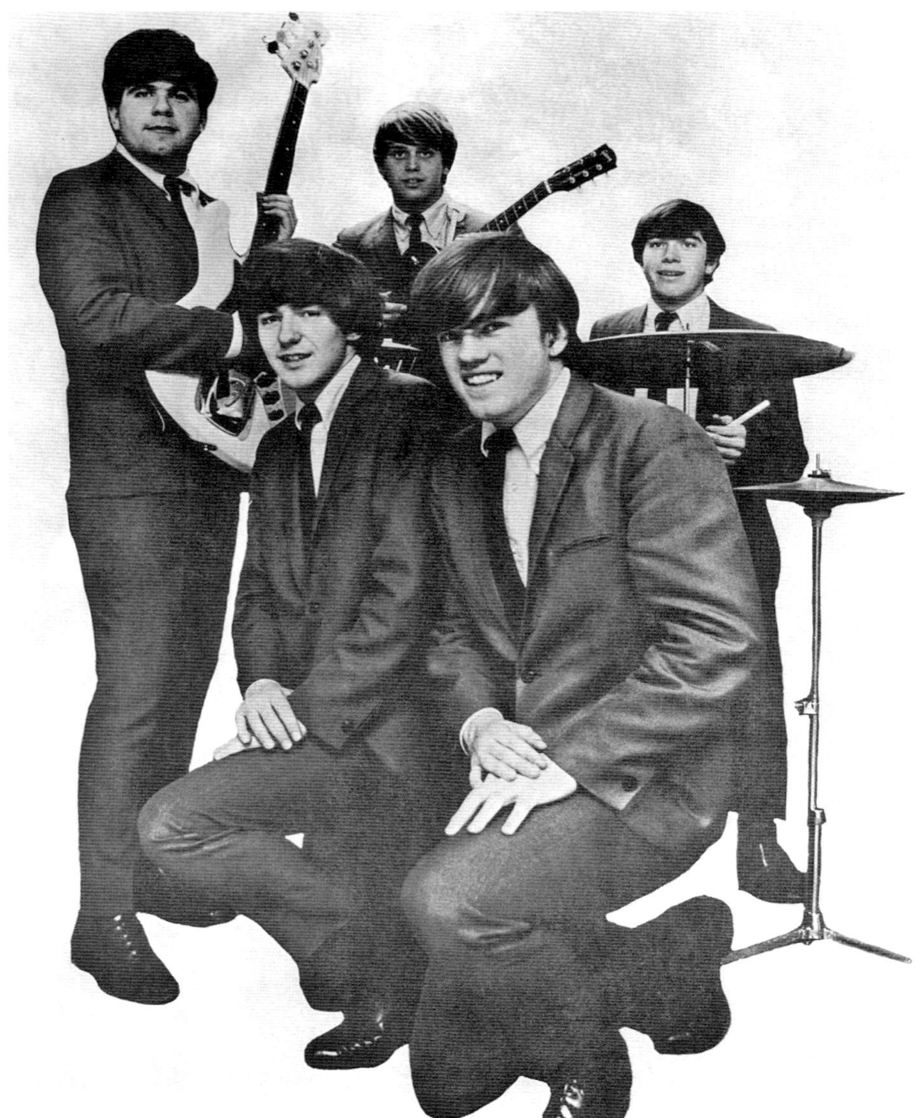

The Moonrakers, c. 1965

"We went out to Hollywood to record, but the record company said the demo was going to be our first album—'Don't make waves.' I said we needed one more song. I thought I'd write better if I knew we were doing it for real.

"So I went back in my room and wrote the melody. It wasn't called 'Green-Eyed Lady' at the time—I wasn't a lyricist. The guys in my band used to call my girlfriend from Denver, Kathy Peacock, the green-eyed lady. We wrote the words on a taco bag.

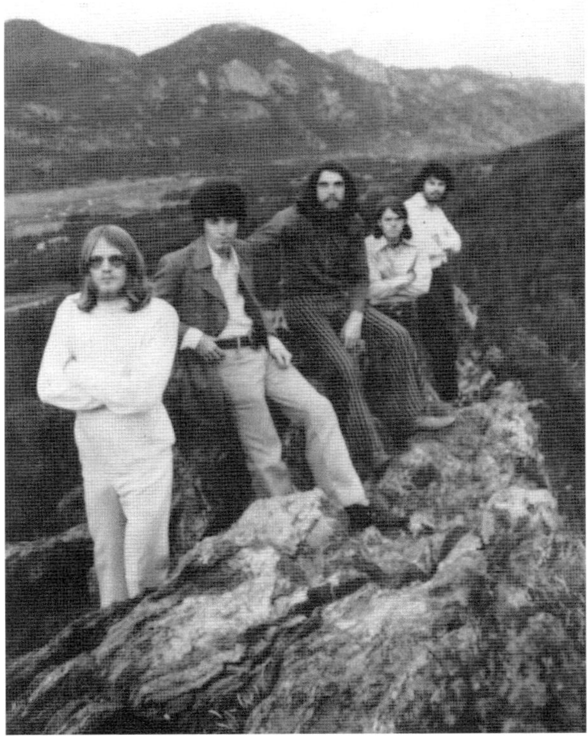

Sugarloaf, c. 1971

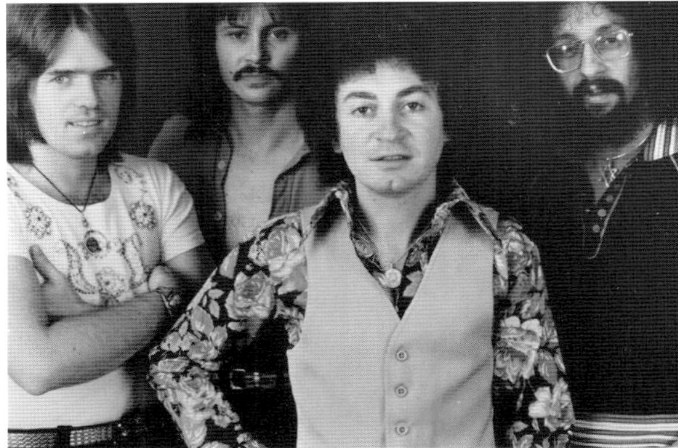

c. 1975

"The singer never showed up that day in the studio. I sang the funky stuff in Chocolate Hair—I was trying to emulate Bobby Darin. So I ended up on the record."

Corbetta's organ solo in "Green-Eyed Lady" is regarded as a classic.

"(Jazz organist) Jimmy Smith was my idol. I knew all of his songs, every lick he played. 'Green-Eyed Lady' was a combination of his jazz and my rock influence. It's truly a jazz-rock song.

"I was taking private piano lessons, I was giving lessons, I was in the college jazz band and I was playing six nights a week. I was right in the middle of the music—my fingers were in shape, flying. So, boy, I just had the juice."

Non-stop touring gave the band little time for songwriting, so they invited Robert Yeazel from the Colorado band Beast to join on guitar and vocals. An edit of his "Tongue in Cheek," a track on the second Sugarloaf album, *Spaceship Earth*, became a minor hit in 1971.

In trying to regain a recording deal, Corbetta was spurned rather imperiously, which resulted in an amusing song about the fickle music industry. Recorded with initial drummer Pollock back in the fold, the dance-friendly new track spelled out the CBS Records phone number and a general White House number—touch-tone style—for the world.

"It was an attitude song," Corbetta explained. "'You got my number?' 'Yeah, don't hold your breath.'

"CBS changed its number. But three months later we got this letter from the White House saying a gentleman from the State Department wanted to meet with us.

"This official-looking guy said, 'Look, we get over 50,000 phone calls a day, and we've heard this name "Sugarloaf."' I said, 'Well, that's the name of my band.' He had to see the albums. I told him I was going to call my lawyers. I was really a cocky kid."

"Don't Call Us, We'll Call You" by Jerry Corbetta/Sugarloaf peaked at #9 in March 1975. But the band quickly dropped from sight anyway.

Life after Sugarloaf was artistically lucrative for Corbetta. He co-wrote the Grace Jones hit "On Your Knees" and the Peabo Bryson/Roberta Flack number "You're Looking Like Love to Me." He also was asked to join the Four Seasons for their 20th Anniversary Tour and continued to write, perform and tour as a full member for four years. He toured with the Classic Rock All-Stars until retirement.

"Colorado has always been the little sister of Los Angeles, not Seattle or anywhere else," Corbetta said. "That's why all of the rockers came here—'Hey, this is only a two-hour flight, it's beautiful and you're a mile high already. What's not to like?'" ●

JETHRO TULL }

IN ONE of the most infamous events in Denver concert history, Jethro Tull appeared at Red Rocks Amphitheatre on June 10, 1971. Police fired tear gas canisters to disperse a mob of 2,000 fans who were attempting to climb the barricades and get into Tull's sold-out gig for free.

Undaunted, the venerable British rock act played anyway.

"It was so polarized it was ridiculous," singer Ian Anderson recalled. "Those who disrupted things outside were just as much to blame as police for overreacting."

Rumors on impending trouble had flown in the days before the show.

"Some of the blame belonged on me," promoter Barry Fey admitted. "Tull was so big, I should have booked them for two shows.

"As it turned out, there was an unhealthy combination of people. Outside there were maybe 50 punks who wanted to start trouble, mixed in with 2,000 people holding cash, saying, 'Hey, take my money, let me in.' Then it came to, 'Okay, if you won't take my money, I'm coming in anyway.'"

The disorderly throng swarmed around the perimeter of the outdoor venue, walking over the bluffs and into the top parking lot. The first volley of tear gas was dropped by a police helicopter. Livingston Taylor, the opening act, was onstage, and once he got a whiff he began crying, "This is supposed to be music! What's going on here?"

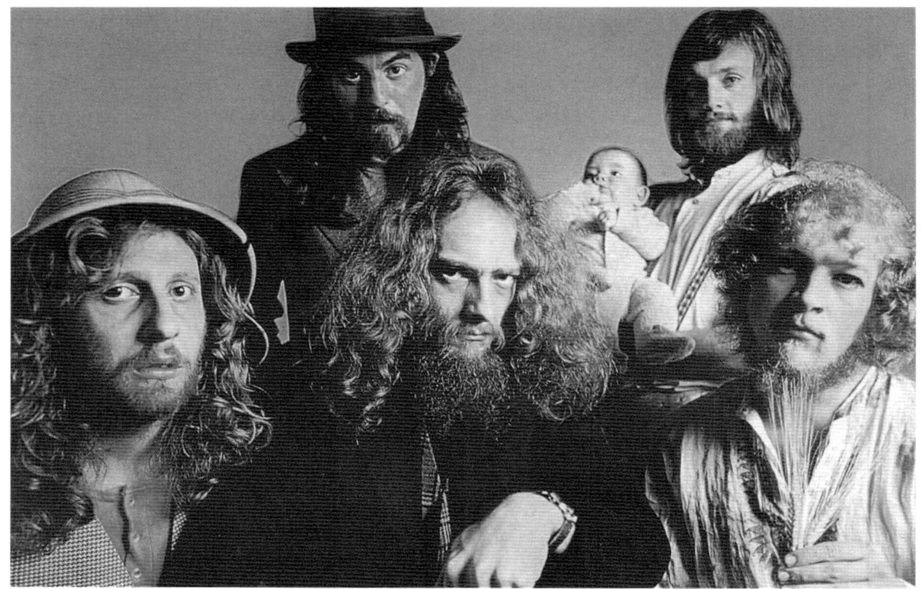

c. 1971; (opposite) Scene outside Red Rocks Amphitheatre, June 10, 1971

At that point the encounter between the gatecrashers and police erupted into a full-scale riot. Police cars were set on fire and hundreds of arrests were made.

"We were leaving our hotel to go up to the show when we received word that there was a problem," Anderson said. "We set off in our rented station wagons and were met by a police roadblock that tried to turn us back. We said, 'We're the band,' and we were told, 'There's not going to be a show. Go away.'

"We thought that was ridiculous, so we managed to find a back route on a dirt road. We still had to make a fairly aggressive effort to get to the site—we wound up running a roadblock—and when we got there, we realized there was trouble going on outside.

"I said, 'Look, if you don't let us go onstage, not only are there going to be 2,000 people outside rioting, but 9,000 people inside are going to go crazy as well.'"

Reluctantly, the authorities allowed Tull to take the stage, even though keyboardist John Evan couldn't see his piano through the tear gas. Anderson was magnificent, stalking the stage and playing his flute like a man possessed despite the circumstances.

"The gas made life very difficult in the amphitheatre itself," he said. "The wind blew a cloud of it over the audience to the stage. We had to stop several times. I saw babies being passed down through the crowd so they wouldn't be affected by the gas. It was a horrifying sight."

The Red Rocks show was drummer Barriemore Barlow's first date with the band. "Having slightly upset the police on the way up there, we had to be careful going down again," Anderson said. "We were hiding under blankets in the back of a station wagon, licking our wounds. Our eyes were streaming; we were coughing. Barrie turned to me and asked, 'Is it going to be like this every night?'"

The rest of that summer's Red Rocks shows were cancelled, and the debacle convinced Denver officials to ban rock concerts from the site until 1975. ●

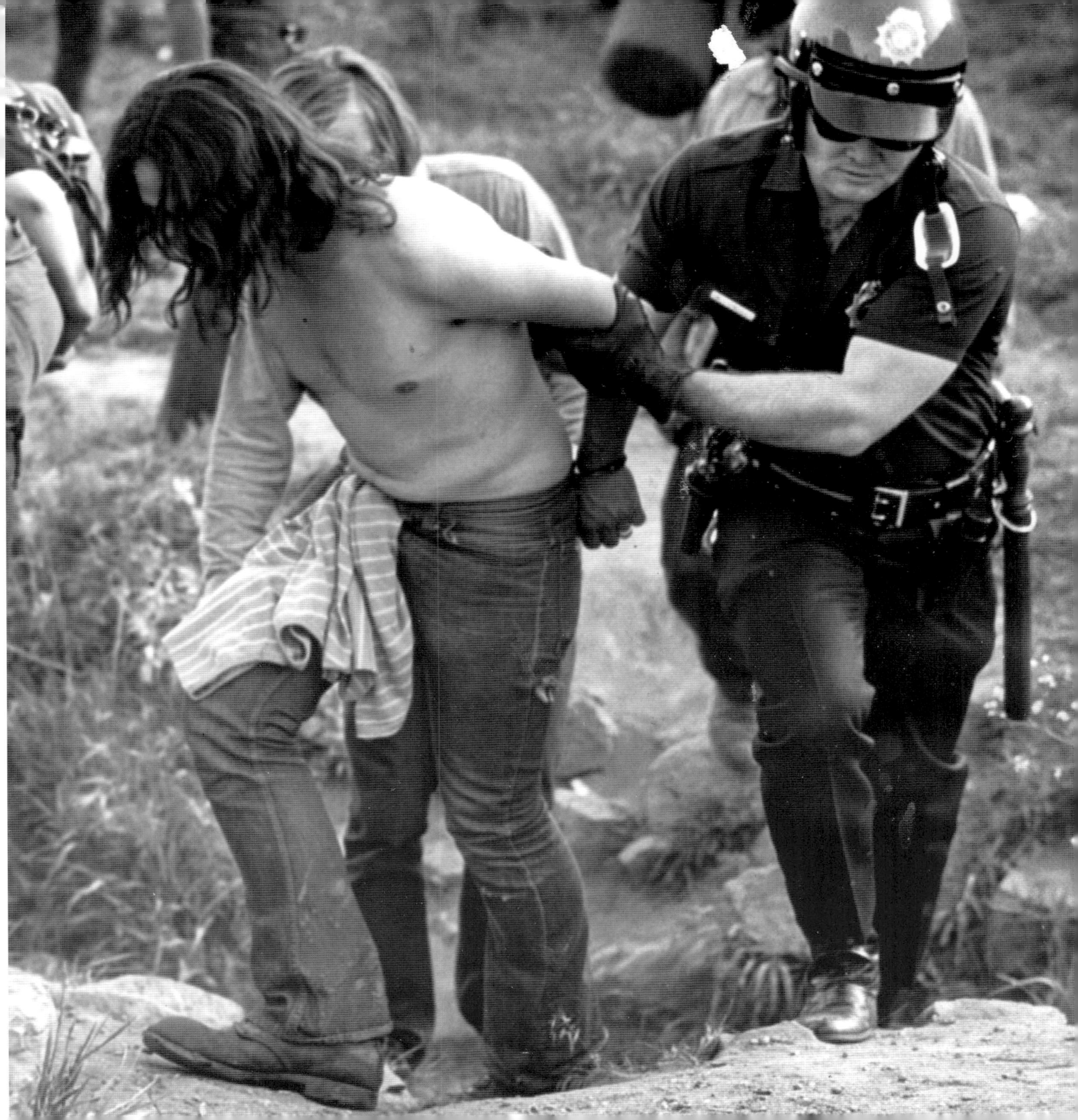

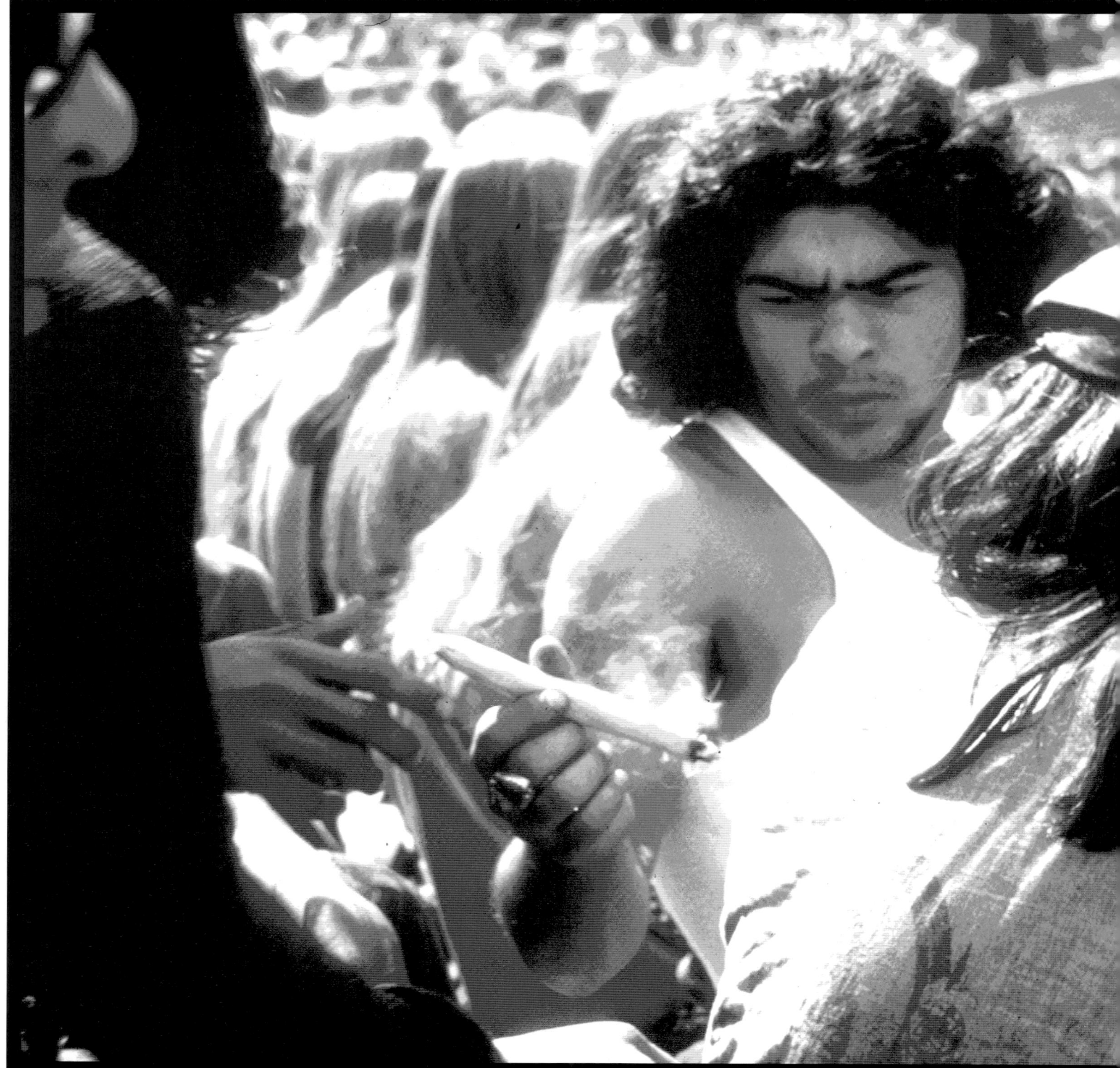

Grateful Dead fans at a concert at Boulder's Folsom Field, 1972

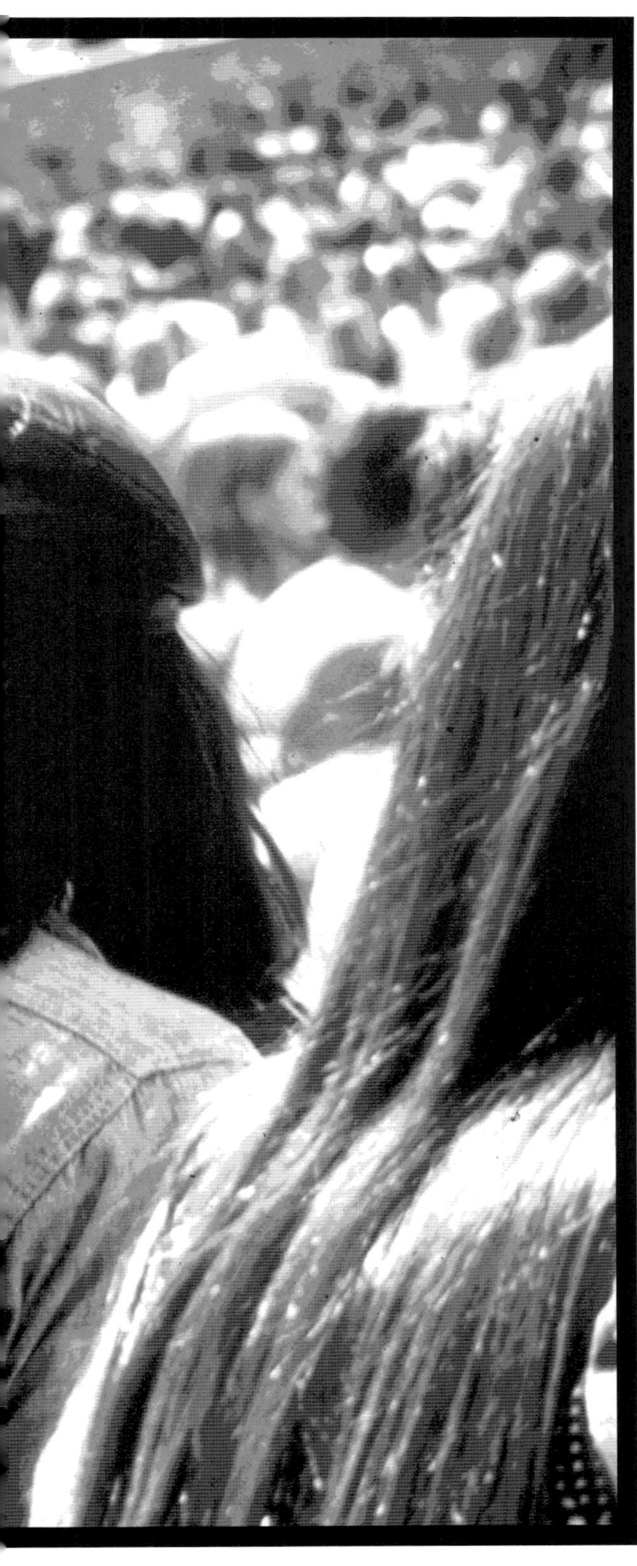

1972-1975

BY THE early 1970s, it was cooler to listen to FM album rock station KFML than to an AM Top 40 station. Colorado had earned its status as a prime skiing destination, and the state mushroomed on a surge of oil and energy revenues. The Eagles incubated their sound in Aspen and Boulder, the home of Tulagi night club and a burgeoning country-rock scene. Many folks claimed John Denver's "Rocky Mountain High" inspired them to move to Colorado and enjoy the great outdoors. Nobody closed the door behind them. Ebbets Field in Denver, which sat only 238 patrons, was a stopping point for nearly every musical up-and-comer of the decade, and a veritable who's who of rock music's elite—from Elton John to Michael Jackson—came to Colorado to record at Caribou Ranch.

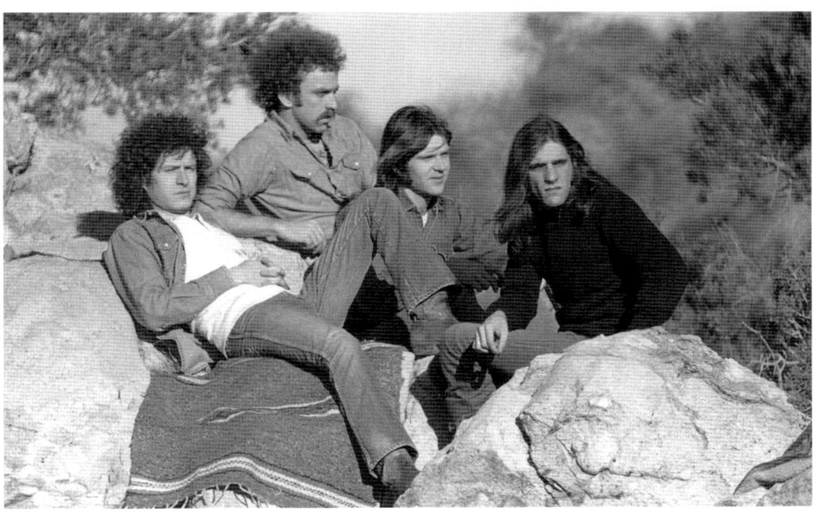

c. 1972

THE EAGLES }

THE ARCHETYPAL California band of the 1970s, the Eagles were synonymous with the country-rock movement that sprang up in Los Angeles.

In the summer of 1970, Linda Ronstadt's manager had an idea for a supergroup to back up his star singer, coming up with the combination of Glenn Frey (a guitarist and singer from Detroit), Don Henley (a singer and drummer from Texas), multi-instrumentalist Bernie Leadon (previously in the Flying Burrito Brothers and Dillard & Clark) and Randy Meisner (formerly the bassist in Poco and Rick Nelson's Stone Canyon Band).

They eventually left Ronstadt and took shape as the original Eagles. In 1971, David Geffen (the head of Asylum Records, home of Jackson Browne and Joni Mitchell) got involved as manager. He provided expense money for the guys to leave Hollywood and get their act together so that they could come back and blow minds rather than develop in front of everyone's eyes.

They went to Colorado and got gigs in local bars. In Aspen, "Eagle" played two stints at the Gallery.

Eagle was then scheduled to perform December 11-15 at Tulagi, the nationally famed 3.2 beer nightclub on Boulder's University Hill. It was finals week at the University of Colorado, limiting attendance to 15 to 50 people a night. The band got paid $500 for the five nights.

Yet Henley and Frey were confident to the point of insisting that they were going to be huge stars.

"Oh, yeah, we were cocky little bastards," Henley said. "Those gigs were our coming-out party."

Frey said they were matter-of-fact over the inevitability of success.

"We had it all planned. We had watched landmark country-rock bands like Poco and the Flying Burrito Brothers lose their initial momentum. We were determined not to make the same mistakes. This was going to be our best shot. Everybody had to look good, sing good, play good and write good. We wanted it all. Peer respect. AM and FM success. No. 1 singles and albums. Great music. And a lot of money."

The members dressed in the fashion of the time, ripped jeans with paisley patches. One cold night at Tulagi, the heat went out and Leadon played with gloves on. The crowds were small but voluble. A beered-up patron kept screaming, "Play some Burritos, ma-a-a-an!"

"We're a new group with our own songs," Frey earnestly explained from the stage.

Those songs served as an audition for British producer Glyn Johns, whose work with the Beatles, the Rolling Stones and other music giants had made him a legend.

"He was this superstar producer who none of us had ever met," Henley noted. "He agreed to fly over from England and listen to us when we played Tulagi. I got designated to drive to the airport to pick him up.

"It was a horrible, snowy night, and nobody was at the concert. We were nervous and not very good, and Glyn passed. Later, he came to Los Angeles on a more casual scale when we weren't so keyed up about performing. He listened to us rehearse, singing harmonies with acoustic guitars, and that's what got him."

Within weeks, Eagle became the Eagles. The band went to London to record its first album, produced by Johns. *Eagles*, released in 1972, was a huge success, helped by the hit singles "Take It Easy" and "Peaceful Easy Feeling." The Eagles went on to become the most successful American music act of the 1970s with sales of more than 50 million albums worldwide.

Henley lived near Aspen for decades. "I fell in love with the place. Colorado was great back then, but it's changed a lot now. It's getting a little glitzy up there."

Frey maintained a residence in Aspen. "After the shows at the Gallery, I swore if I ever made a dime in the music business, I wanted to have a house there. It's a good place to practice. If you can sing in Aspen's thin air, you can sing anywhere." ●

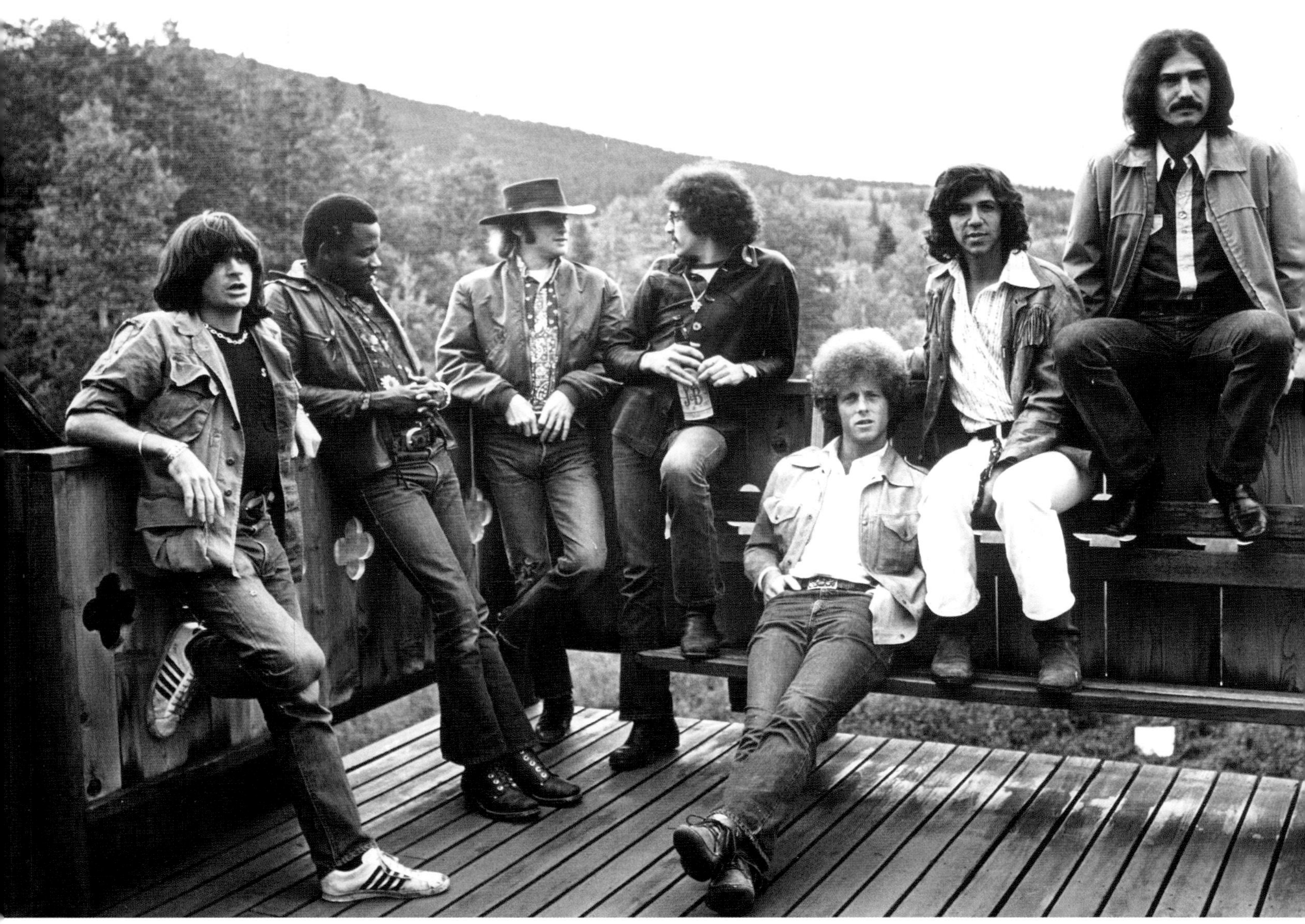

Stills (in hat) with Manassas at his Gold Hill home, c. 1972

STEPHEN STILLS | MANASSAS }

SEARCHING FOR some peace from the supergroup Crosby, Stills, Nash & Young in the early 1970s, Stephen Stills would fly in a Lear jet to airports in Boulder County that were close to his cabin near Gold Hill, Colorado. Locals always knew when Stills was in town because he had a Mercedes truck, one of the few in the country.

"It was as far away as I could think of to get," Stills recalled. "Basically, nobody up on that mountain gave a shit about who I was or what I did."

On September 20, 1970, snow fell in the Rockies. Stills, at dawn, walked outside his cabin, guitar in hand, and posed for his first solo album cover photo. He wrote many of the songs for his second solo album that winter while in Colorado. He also named his publishing company after the town of Gold Hill.

Chris Hillman, then the Flying Burrito Brothers' lead singer and driving force, was bored and broke. He got a call from Stills to meet him in Miami. Stills wanted Hillman to bring along Burrito guitarist Al Perkins and fiddler Byron Berline.

He had been visualizing a group that would bring together rock, folk, Latin, country and blues. He also retained Dallas Taylor on drums, bass player Fuzzy Samuels, Paul Harris and a young percussionist named Joe Lala.

When the Stills-Burritos amalgam—dubbed Manassas—congregated in the studio, something clicked. Rehearsals flowed right into marathon recording sessions that went round-the-clock and then some. According to engineer Howard Albert, the longest stretch lasted 106 straight hours.

"Manassas was such a terrific band—it had some structure and could play anything," Stills said. "I had a house in Colorado, and we based the band there, but I took the band over to England to get good. We all lived at this little house out in Surrey."

The debut album *Manassas*, featuring the song "Colorado," peaked at #4 on the charts. On stage, Manassas shows generally ran close to three hours and built off the Burritos format, with an opening rock set, then Stills playing solo acoustic followed by Hillman and Perkins playing bluegrass, then Manassas country, more Manassas rock and an acoustic finish.

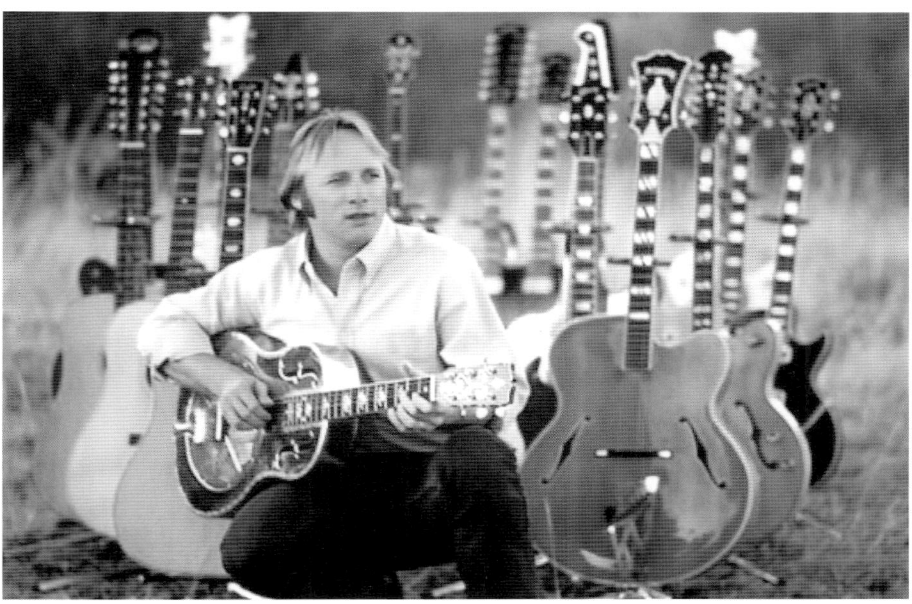
At Caribou Ranch, c. 1975

Down the Road, which peaked at #26 on the *Billboard* album charts in May 1973, was completed at Caribou Ranch Studios in Nederland, Colorado.

"But I short-circuited there for a while," Stills admitted. "Things were moving too fast. I got a little crazed. Too much drinkin', too many drugs. What can I say?"

In 1972, Stills had married French singer-songwriter Veronique Sanson. Their son, Chris, was born in April 1974 in Boulder Community Hospital.

"When I was growing up in the Southeast, I hated the humidity and was totally addicted to air conditioning. I discovered that in Colorado there was (natural) air conditioning all the time, and I loved it," Stills reflected.

"Also, in Colorado, I met some real down-home people who had no particular illusions about who I was. To them, I was just Stephen. I liked that. It helped me sort out a few things and bought me back to an understanding that there's more to this life than just rock 'n' roll. I began to paint. I was a Rocky Mountain Rescue volunteer, as well as an auxiliary fireman.

"But the high and dry does not agree with my throat, and I never did ski worth a shit, and now I'm paying for it. Both of my knees are completely trashed. I can't dance anywhere near the way I'd like to." ●

RICK NELSON & THE STONE CANYON BAND }

AS A way to promote records, Rick Nelson was the first teen idol to use television. In 1948, he joined his parents' radio show, *The Adventures of Ozzie and Harriet*, which moved to television in 1952 for a 14-year run. Eight years into the show, Nelson became an "overnight success" when he released his first single, "A Teenager's Romance"/"I'm Walking." Television's commercial power was unrealized at that time, and almost as an afterthought, a Ricky-sings-at-the-party sequence was aired. "A Teenager's Romance" sold a million copies the following week.

Nelson released an endless stream of hit singles, such as "Stood Up," "Poor Little Fool," "Lonesome Town," "Travelin' Man" and "Teen Age Idol," to name but a few. By the mid-1960s, when *The Adventures of Ozzie and Harriet* went off the air, his hits began to dry up and his music was eclipsed by the British Invasion.

Determined to establish an adult identity and gain the respect he deserved as a musician, Nelson put together the Stone Canyon Band with Poco bassist Randy Meisner.

"The Stone Canyon Band came together almost from a negative standpont," Nelson said. "I didn't know what kind of music I wanted to do. I couldn't verbalize it, really, so I just got to thinking about how I started, the kind of music I liked. I was really fortunate in getting a unique type of style and then clicking with musicians who played along those lines. The first guy I found was Randy."

Meisner grew up on a farm near Scottsbluff, Nebraska. He travelled throughout the Midwest working the road and pursuing his musical ambitions. An affable, easygoing sort with a sweet, high voice, he cut his teeth playing with the Driving Dynamics and arrived in Denver in 1966 to play a battle of the bands.

He linked up with one of the competing groups, the Soul Survivors—not the New York-based white soul group of "Expressway to Your Heart" fame, but a well-produced pop-rock act that scored two No. 1 hits on Denver's Top 40 giant KIMN ("Can't Stand to Be in Love with You" and "Hung Up on Losing").

"When they lost their bass player, they asked me if I wanted to jump ship and move to Los Angeles with them," Meisner said. The name of his new band was changed to the Poor. Meisner and lead guitarist Allen Kemp slept on the living room floor of a one-bedroom apartment in East Los Angeles for $85 a month. Gigs were few and far between.

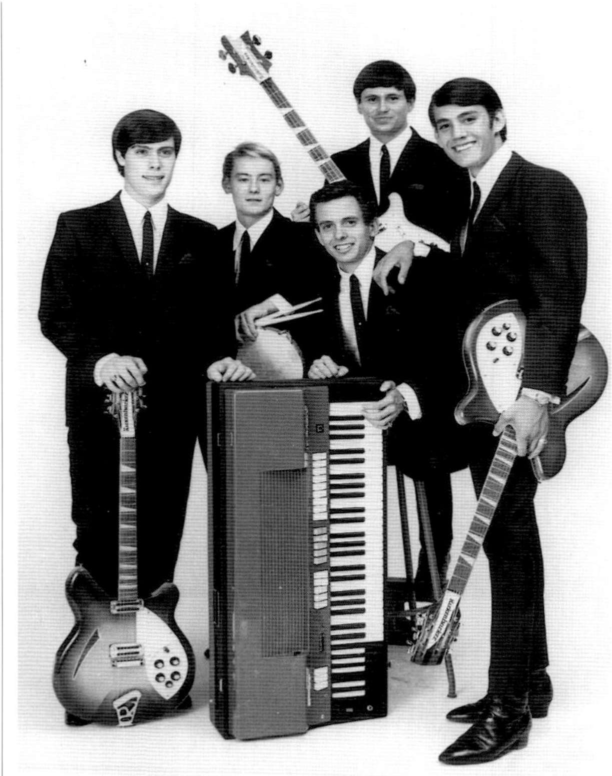

The Soul Survivors, c. 1966

"We didn't realize how much competition was out there," Meisner said. "My jacket was my first pillow. We really had nothing at all."

When Meisner took the job with Poco, the Poor broke up. With drummer Patrick Shanahan, Kemp moved to a cheaper three-bedroom house in Sherman Oaks and got a job washing cars. Meisner left Poco in a dispute over the final mixes to the country-rock group's first album. Upon leaving the band, Meisner was reached about working with Nelson.

Meisner contacted Kemp and Shanahan, his buddies from the band that first brought him from Denver. Nelson got the Stone Canyon Band's name from a remote area of the Los Angeles hills he used to drive by. The sound was crisp and clear—Meisner and Kemp stacked

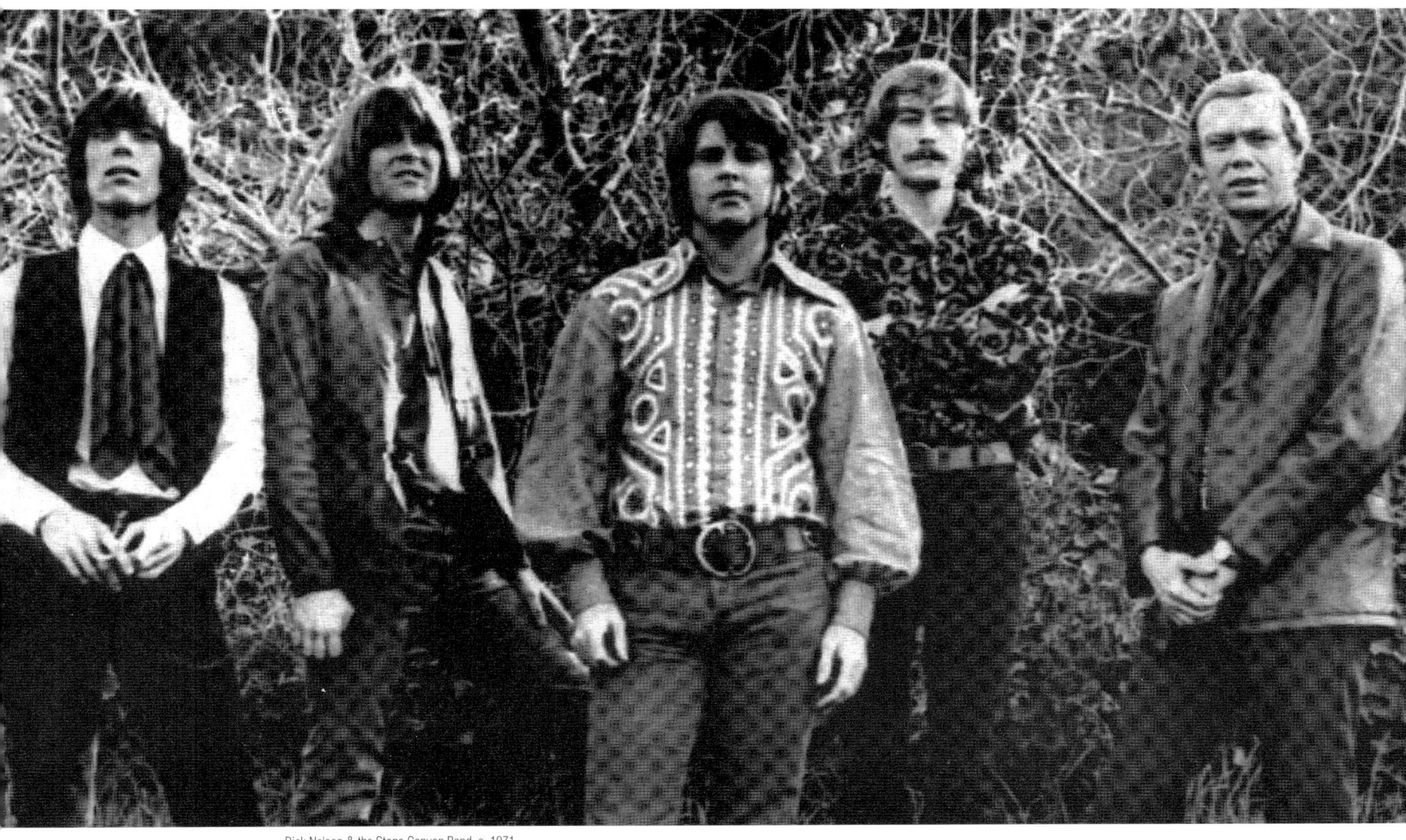

Rick Nelson & the Stone Canyon Band, c. 1971

their vocals in angelic harmonies on top of Nelson's.

Meisner quit and rejoined, then quit again to form a band with Glenn Frey and Don Henley. They hit it off so well, he decided to fly with the Eagles.

On October 15, 1971, Rick Nelson & the Stone Canyon Band were special guest stars at the Richard Nader Rock & Roll Revival at New York City's Madison Square Garden. The concert program acquired an integral place in Nelson's own legend.

"At sound check, everybody else was looking out of the '50s and doing just their strict old hits. Rick refused to do that. He wanted to do something different," Kemp said.

Nelson fed the Garden crowd pure nostalgia. But when he sat down at the piano and performed new material, he was booed off the stage for departing from the rigid oldies program, for having long hair and for his band's drugstore cowboy appearance.

The experience inspired Nelson to pen a song six months later featuring a mildly scornful mood and the resolute conclusion: "If memories are all I sing, I'd rather drive a truck." "Garden Party" climbed all the way to #6 on the *Billboard* pop singles charts, one of the most extraordinary comeback hits in rock history.

Rick Nelson & the Stone Canyon Band went through several personnel changes. Kemp and Shanahan went on to play with the New Riders of the Purple Sage in the 1980s. Nelson died in a plane crash in 1985 at the age of 45. ●

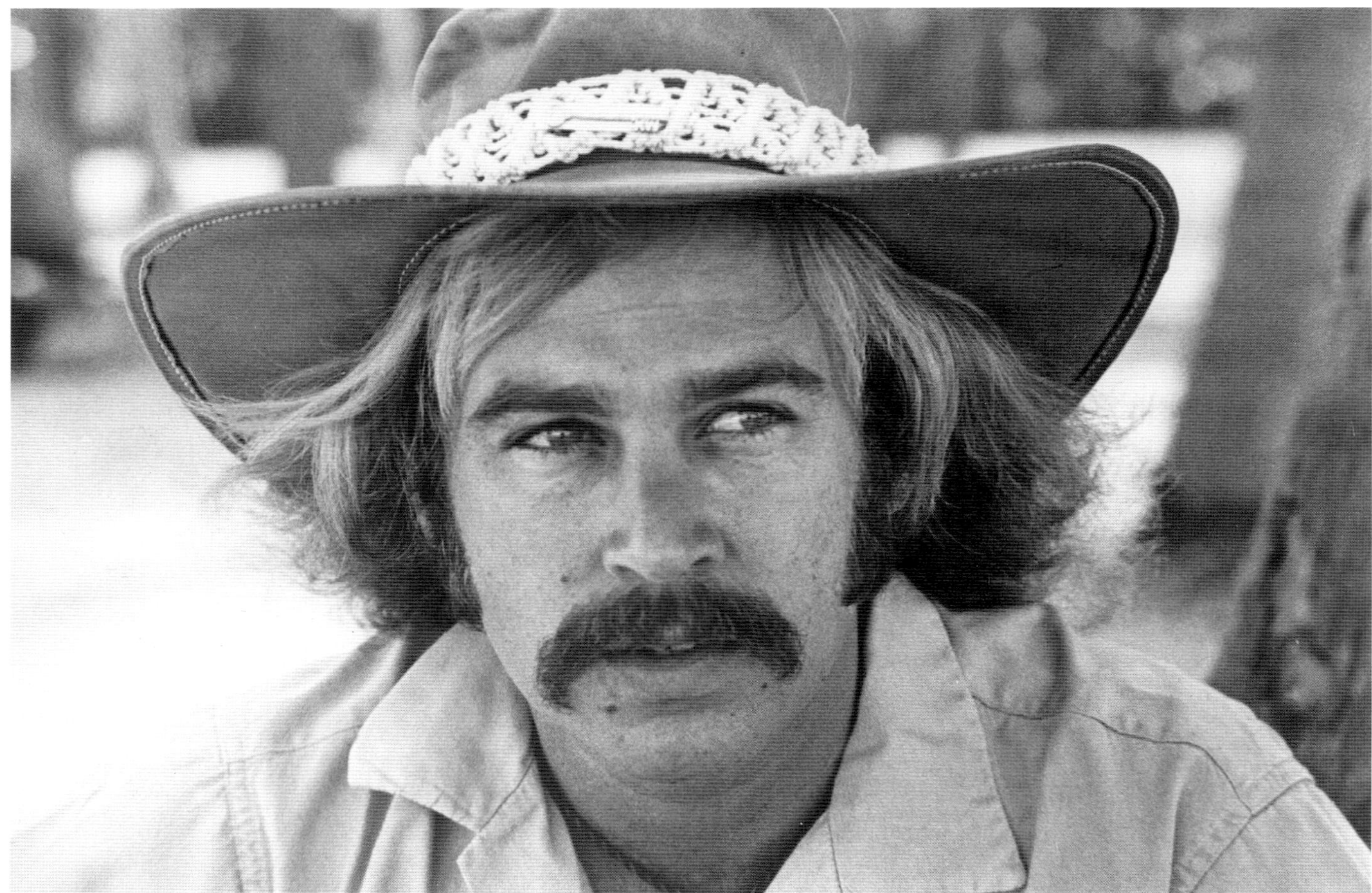

c. 1973

JIMMY BUFFETT }

RAISED IN Alabama, Jimmy Buffett had never seen the mountains until a friend from Colorado's Timberline Rose turned him on to the Rockies.

"I was a preacher of living in that swamp gas environment. I had been up to Montana to visit people, but I hadn't spent a long period of time out West," Buffett said.

"Denver was the first place I went on tour. I got out of humidity and came to the mountains to play. The Cafe York on Colfax was my first gig in Colorado."

Dressed in Levis and a cowboy shirt, his hair long, Buffett carried his two Martin guitars from the small coffeehouses to college campuses. There, with a distinctive southern-flavored accent, he entertained. "No flashing diamond rings, no skin-tight tuxedo, no Las Vegas marquees," he said—just sharing an honest talent with his audiences.

"I lived in a little sleazy hotel in metropolitan Denver, and then I did the summer mountain circuit up in Evergreen, Bailey and Breckenridge, having a glorious time.

"I wound up the tour in downtown Pueblo, not known as the most beautiful spot in Colorado. But seeing every side of the state eventually led to me settling there for a while.

"Circa 1971, I'd gone out to San Francisco and was staying in a Howard Johnson's in Marin County. I had left my girlfriend, who later became my wife, in Aspen. I was thinking about her and I wrote 'Come Monday.'"

The song became Buffett's first hit single in 1974.

Buffett became an Aspen resident for many years. "Most people always consider going to Colorado for the winter, but my attachment was a summertime thing," Buffett testified, having made yet another survey of Aspen's bars. "There's so much to do."

The song "A Mile High in Denver" appeared on Buffett's *Before the Beach* album. ●

RICK ROBERTS | THE FLYING BURRITO BROTHERS }

WHEN GRAM Parsons left the Flying Burrito Brothers to begin a solo career in 1970, the band continued without replacing him for four months, gigging around the West Coast as a four-piece. In late summer, Rick Roberts, a newcomer to the Los Angeles scene, was chosen to fill Parsons' role.

"I'm a Floridian. I left college in South Carolina in July 1969 and was living in Colorado for a while," Roberts said. "I arrived in Los Angeles on my mother's birthday, September 14. I was telling her and everyone else I was going to L.A. to become famous. Through every step of joining the Burritos, I would get discouraged and think about going back to Colorado."

Though they had virtually invented the blueprint for country-rock, morale of the remaining original members was low. In 1971, Bernie Leadon left to join members of Linda Ronstadt's backing group to form the Eagles. Michael Clarke went to Hawaii, while Chris Hillman and Al Perkins left for Stephen Stills' band Manassas. Roberts reorganized the band and finished all the Burritos' performing commitments, including a tour of Europe.

Roberts recalled, "Gram had drug problems—he eventually OD'ed—and they parted ways on not-so-cordial terms. I was a raw rookie. Here I was given the opportunity to play with some of the people that I had grown up idolizing."

Roberts' stay with the Burritos was mildly profitable, very productive and an exceptionally valuable experience. Playing on the final pair of albums by the group, he contributed several songs to the repertoire, including his best-known composition—"Colorado," from *Last of the Red-Hot Burritos*.

"I wrote that song in California. I'd been out there for four or five months. I was 19 years old. When I got to Colorado on my way out to L.A., I stopped in order to see some friends of mine, but it turned out they had moved on. I ended up coming up to Boulder looking for a place to stay for a couple of days, to catch my breath. I ended up staying for three months and fell in love with Colorado.

"When I got out to California, that song came out of sitting around one night—'Boy, I wish the hell I'd never left Colorado.' Those were the days when the Hill in Boulder was really happening. I would run into the guys in Zephyr."

By June 1972, the group was no more. Roberts stayed with A&M Records as a solo artist. "I made my second solo album in Colorado for $12,500 with Joe Walsh, some Poco people, Kenny Passarelli." Roberts would later form Firefall.

Linda Ronstadt's version of Roberts' "Colorado" bubbled under *Billboard*'s Hot 100 in 1974, reaching #108. ●

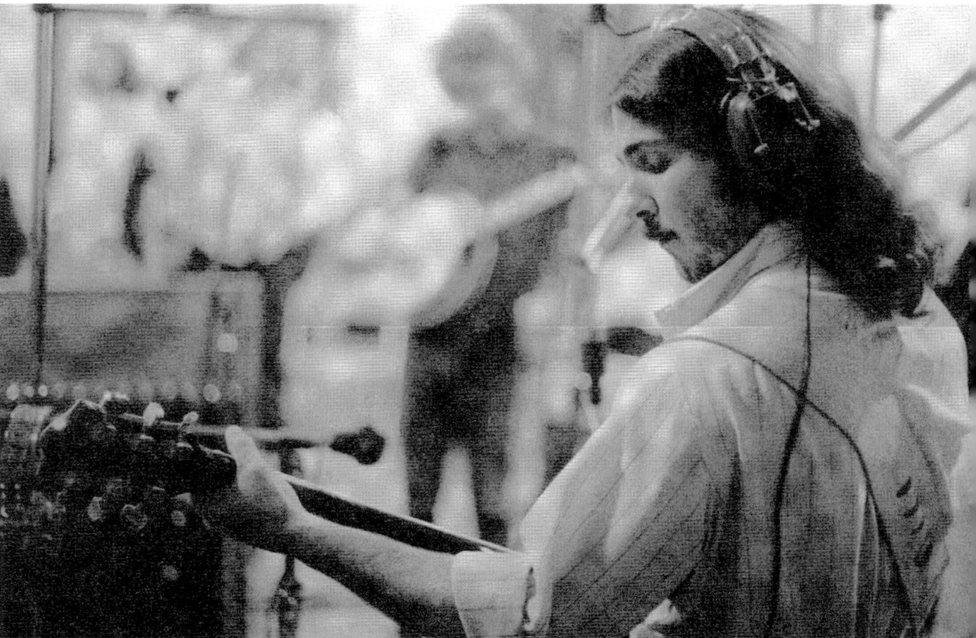

c. 1973

DANNY HOLIEN }

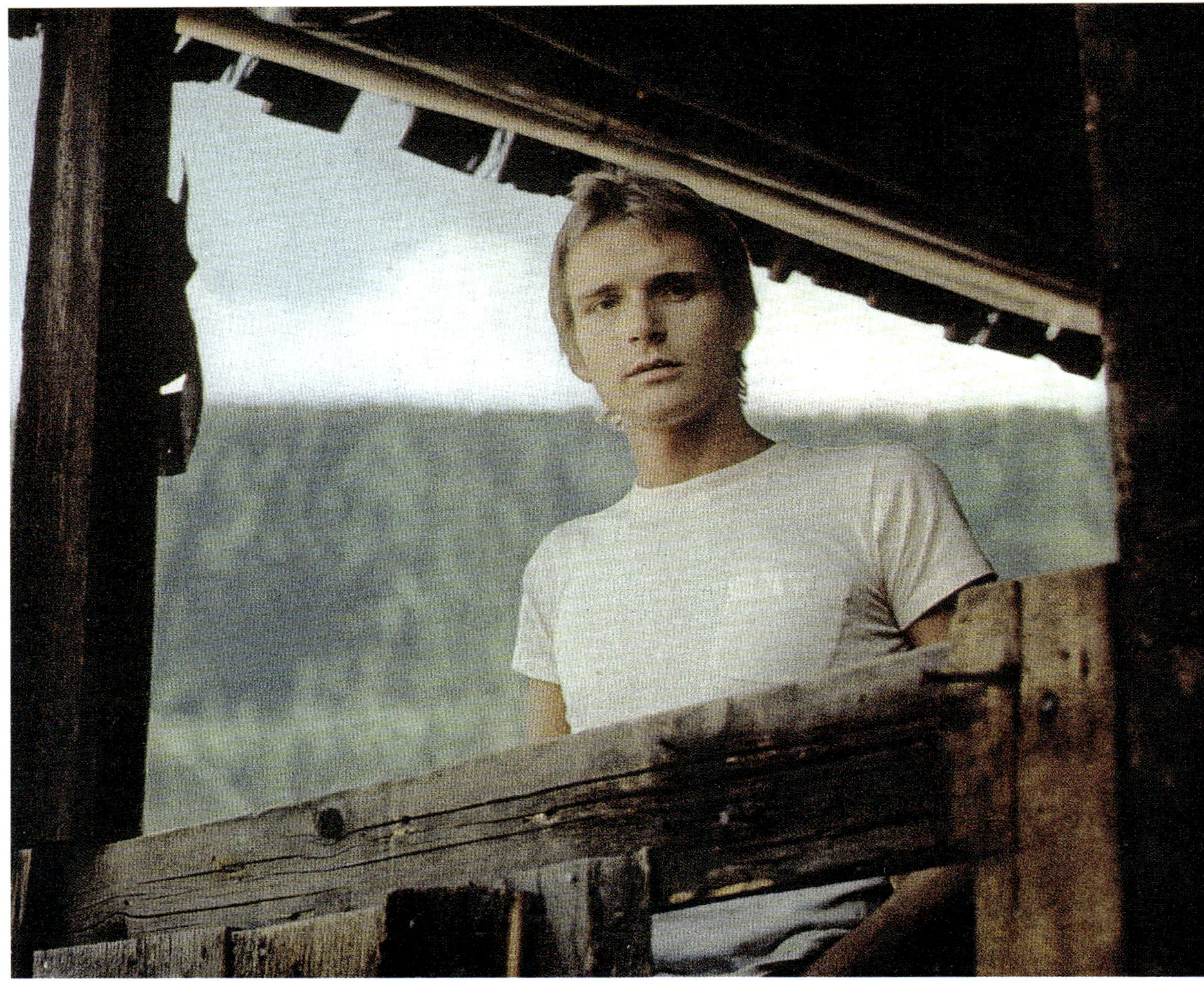

c. 1972

RAISED IN rural Minnesota, guitarist and vocalist Danny Holien came to Colorado and wrote songs that moved Denver's Tumbleweed Records to produce *Danny Holien* in 1972.

"A friend of mine had moved out to Colorado," Holien remembered. "He said there was all kinds of work, so we moved to the ghetto and starved for quite a while! We played some ski resorts, but it wasn't the big hotshot clubs; it was on the edge. The whole band lived in a house together."

Tumbleweed Records was a small independent label owned by Bill Szymczyk, whose first major success had come when he convinced blues legend B.B. King to cut contemporary-sounding albums. The result was King's first major pop crossover, "The Thrill is Gone," a hit in 1971. The producer went on to have great success in the 1970s, both as an A&R man and behind the board, signing and producing the James Gang.

"I decided to leave Los Angeles after a big earthquake," Szymczyk recalled. "A few of us record-company people had bandied about the idea of starting our own label. Back in the early '70s, you'd get two hit records and you could do that."

Tumbleweed Records was based out of a funky old house just east of downtown Denver on Gilpin Street, with Szymczyk running the show.

"Gulf + Western owned Famous Music, which bankrolled us," Szymczyk said. "The reason we went to Denver was that my partner Larry Ray's wife was from there. I had visited two times for a total of six days, but both trips, I had an incredibly good time! Colorado was happening in a lot of ways back then."

Indeed, thousands of suntanned, blue-jeaned artists, poets and just ordinary people had instinctively come to the state from New York, Chicago, San Francisco and Boston for basically the same reason Szymczyk left L.A.—the big city just didn't make it.

"Everything was self-contained in that house," Holien said of Tumbleweed. "They had a lot of money behind them. Most of it was blown partying. That's what it takes to make money—spend a lot

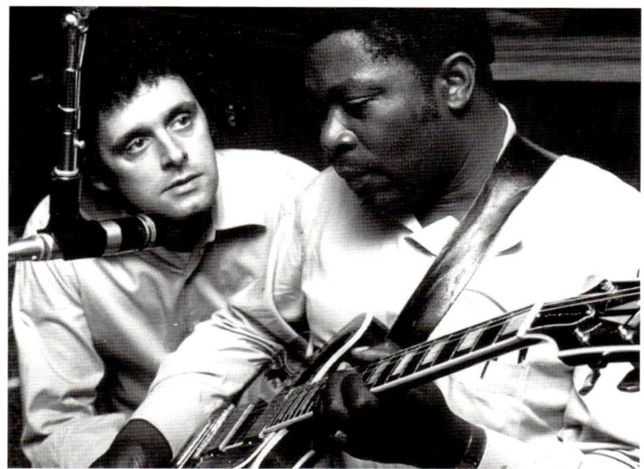
Bill Szymczyk and B.B. King, c. 1971

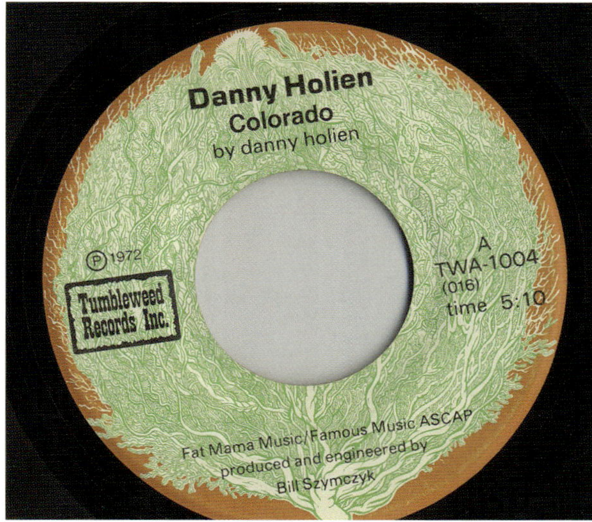

"Colorado" 45

of money to impress a lot of people. But I saw the inner workings and didn't care for it too much. Nice people, but I thought everyone was trying to be big time. Boy, did they spend a lot."

Tumbleweed released some very good albums featuring expensive covers. *Danny Holien* came housed in a luxurious die-cut jacket with a 16-page songbook.

"It was the first bunch of songs I'd written, for the most part. I was naïve and green. It was a fluke. I wasn't an aggressive self-promoter, but I just happened to meet a person who introduced me to Bill Szymczyk. I sat down and played a couple of songs for him acoustically, and he slapped his knee and said, 'Hot damn, let's do an album.' I said okay. It was that funny."

Holien's music was that of a poet, not a philosopher. "I don't want people to hear what I have to say," he said at the time. "I want them to hear what I'm saying."

Holien almost hit with a single called "Colorado," a quiet protest against the rape of the land. Very popular on FM stations, "Colorado" reached #66 on the *Billboard* charts in September 1972.

"I hate to be a protest singer. Things just come up. In Denver, I was in a house a block from the busy intersection of Colorado Boulevard and Colfax Avenue. I wrote it in a few minutes one day, a feeling—it's a nice little tune. 'Colorado' did better in Northern California—Salinas, Monterey—than it did in Denver. I was not very well known in Colorado. I was playing around the fringes."

On another Tumbleweed recording, Joe Walsh, Joe Vitale, Rick Derringer and Todd Rundgren played for Michael Stanley, whose self-titled album included "Rosewood Bitters," a song that became a concert mainstay throughout his career, and "Denver Rain," an introspective ballad.

Holien and Steve Swenson played on *Chief*, the solo album by Dewey Terry (of Don & Dewey fame), on Tumbleweed. Holien didn't want to tour, so Swenson teamed up with Don DeBacker from 60,000,000 Buffalo, Dan McCorison and others and formed Dusty Drapes & the Dusters—in essence, Boulder's first alt-country band.

But Tumbleweed was short-lived. The label folded in 1973.

"We lacked for nothing," Szymczyk said. "The Gulf + Western corporate structure went along with it for the first year, anyway, until we ran through a million and a half dollars—a lot of bucks back then!"

When the Eagles wanted a more rock 'n' roll sound, they hired Szymczyk, and the unprecedented chart success of the 1974 *On the Border* and 1975 *One of These Nights* albums made both parties millions.

Holien eventually moved back to Minnesota, then to Estes Park, Colorado, in the late 1970s and early 1980s with a band called Hoi Polloi. He then moved back to Minnesota and dropped out of the music business. ●

JOE WALSH | BARNSTORM }

A PERFECT vehicle for his soaring guitar work and odd strangled voice, "Rocky Mountain Way" was Joe Walsh's signature tune.

"It's about living in Colorado and having no regrets at all," Walsh said of the classic-rock nugget.

Before going out on his own in 1971, Walsh had made a considerable reputation as lead guitarist and lead vocalist for the James Gang, based in Cleveland. The success of the band's first three albums brought wide popularity for such Walsh tunes as "The Bomber," "Funk #49," "Tend My Garden" and "Walk Away"—and endless touring.

As the James Gang became bigger and the big bucks beckoned, Walsh turned the other way. Encouraged by the Who's Peter Townshend (who admired Walsh's fretboard talent and asked the James Gang to open the Who's 1971 European tour), the Kent State alumnus made the difficult decision to go it alone, moving to the open air of Boulder County in Colorado. For months he lived in the mountains and practiced ham radio operations.

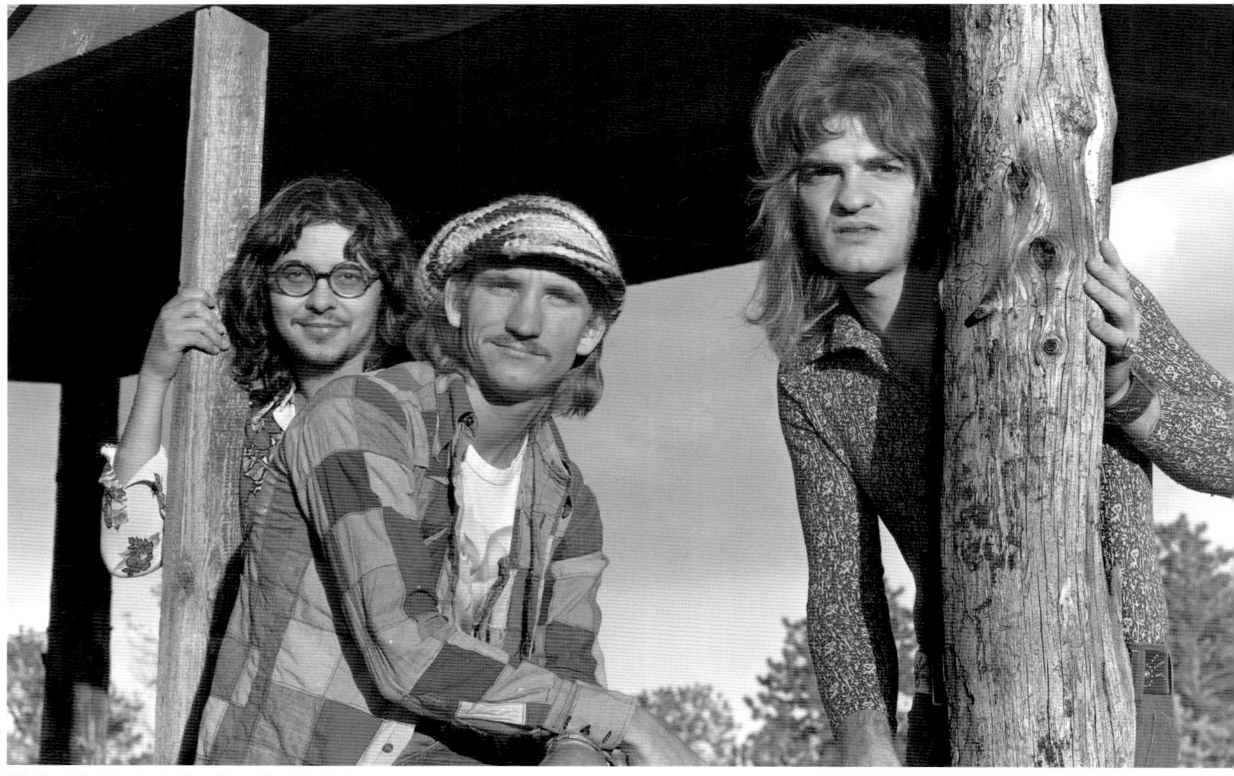

Walsh (center) with bandmates Kenny Passarelli and Joe Vitale, c. 1972

"I didn't get much help from my management or record company at the start of pursuing a solo career," Walsh said. "Moving to Colorado had a lot to do with my friendship with Bill Szymczyk, who at that point was an advisor helping me feel confident—because I was scared to death."

"The James Gang was on tour and played Denver," Szymczyk recalled, "and Joe hung out with me and saw the Tumbleweed Records offices on Gilpin Street and what we were doing and said, 'This is kinda nice here.' He was making noises about quitting the band and starting his own solo career. I said, 'Well, if you do, move here.' He said, 'Okay!'"

Walsh found an easygoing lifestyle in perfect accord with the music he was bent on making. At a time when he needed encouragement, Colorado challenged him and seeded a new perspective. Full-time exposure to the rural landscape and rustic lifestyle in the small towns of the Rockies was almost therapeutic.

"I took an amount of time off and began forming an arrangement of players conceived in a way to express what I was hearing and what I thought a band should be," he said. "They were strange times and it was hard, but it took me back to basic survival, which is always very positive in terms of creative energy. When you have to get yourself together, you play differently from when you're rich."

In 1972, Walsh emerged from a long winter and spring in the studio with an album called *Barnstorm*, accompanied by drummer Joe Vitale, an old colleague, and bassist Kenny Passarelli, a newfound friend. The album—which included "Mother Says," "Turn to Stone" and "Here We Go"—showcased Walsh as not only an innovative, distinctive guitarist, but as a competent keyboardist and songwriter with impressive scope.

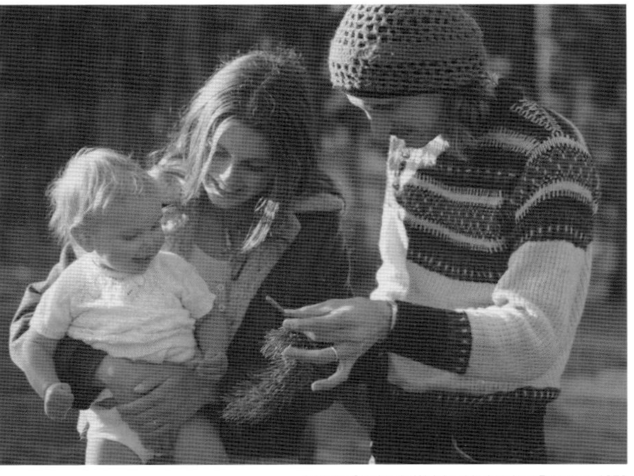

Joe and Stephanie Walsh with daughter Emma, c. 1972

"When Joe and I were getting ready to do his first solo record, I had heard rumors of Jimmy Guercio's Caribou Ranch," Szymczyk said. "So of course I wanted to suss him out and see what was going on."

Guercio, producer of the band Chicago, bought Caribou, near Nederland, for a reported $1 million in 1971 and installed a studio by 1973. But Caribou served Walsh and Szymczyk before it gained fame as a destination studio.

"Guercio was going to direct a movie, *Electra Glide in Blue*, starring Robert Blake," Szymczyk explained. "He said, 'I'm not going to finish the studio because I'm not going to be here for six months.' We begged and pleaded with him. We definitely wanted to record there because it was only three miles from Joe's house. We thought it would be good if we could break it in for Guercio while he was off making a movie, so he finished the room for us.

"But the downstairs was still dirt floors, there was no bathroom, and upstairs was two-by-fours. We used the studio, but it was a lot of DIY stuff."

For the road, Walsh built a larger version of the *Barnstorm* band, also called Barnstorm (with Rocke Grace on keyboards). He officially went solo with 1973's *The Smoker You Drink, the Player You Get*—its title growing evidence of his comic persona—which became the first Top 10 album of his career and went on to sell more than a million copies. Two songs, the radio hit "Rocky Mountain Way" and the memorable "Meadows," opened up an enormous audience for Walsh and the group.

"I always felt 'Rocky Mountain Way' was special, even before it was complete," Walsh said. "We had recorded that before I knew what the words were going to be, but I was very proud of it. That was pretty much one shot at it, all playing at the same time.

"I got kind of fed up with feeling sorry for myself, and I wanted to justify and feel good about leaving the James Gang, relocating and going for it. I wanted to say, 'Hey, whatever this is, I'm positive and I'm proud,' and the words just came out of feeling that way, rather than writing a song out of remorse. It turned out to be a special song for a lot of people.

"It's the attitude and the statement. It's a positive song, and it's basic rock 'n' roll, which is what I really do."

Barnstorm parted amicably in 1975, allowing Walsh to produce Dan Fogelberg's first hit album, *Souvenirs*. The Eagles invited Walsh aboard as guitarist-writer-vocalist-keyboardist, and he gave the country-rock band a much-needed harder edge. It gave him enhanced visibility, and along the way he continued his solo career.

Colorado was where Walsh experienced some of his greatest musical triumphs—and a great personal tragedy.

A simple plaque adorns the water fountain in North Boulder Park: "This fountain is given in loving memory of Emma Walsh. April 29, 1971 to April 1, 1974." Walsh and former wife Stephanie donated the water fountain to the park in 1976 because it was a favorite playspot of their daughter, who died in a car accident. Walsh's 1974 *So What?* album also included another tribute, "Song for Emma."

"Joe was on the road constantly, and when he'd get off he'd spend more time in L.A. than he would in Colorado," Szymczyk said.

"When Emma died, that put the period on the whole deal. Stephanie went to pieces, and so did he, and so did I—I was her godfather, in the hospital when they had to take her off life support. That was a very dark time.

"Very shortly after that, Joe was permanently gone from Colorado." ●

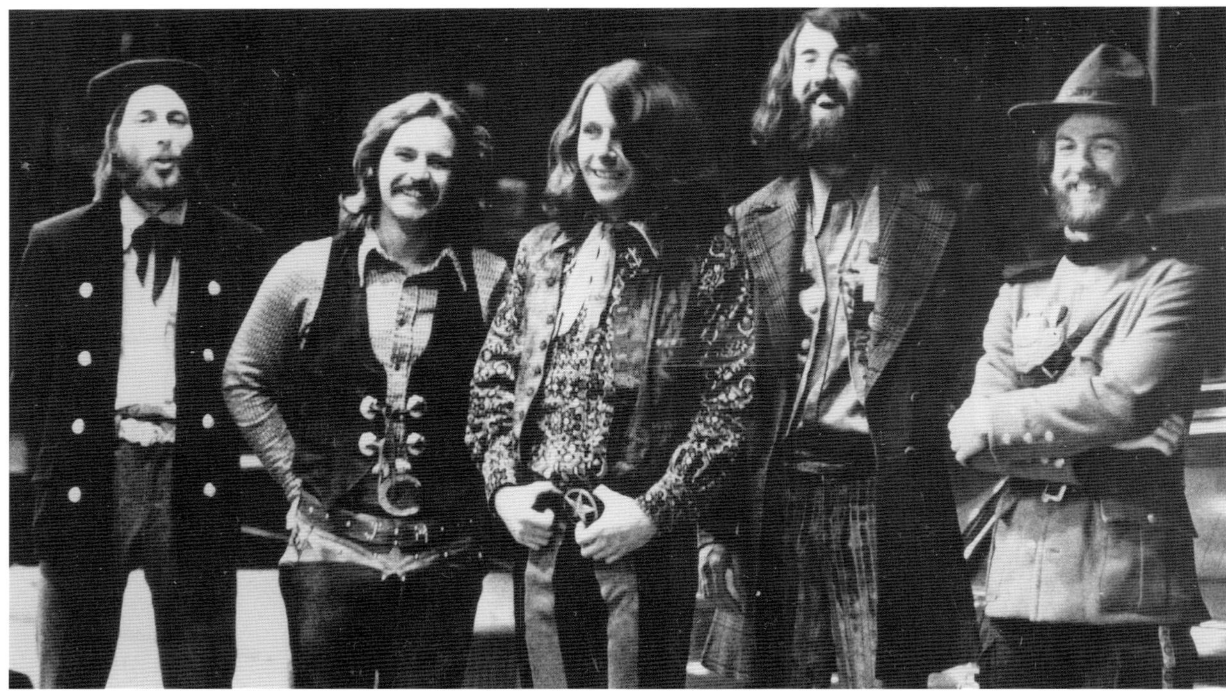

c. 1970

THE NITTY GRITTY DIRT BAND }

MOVING TO Colorado from Los Angeles in 1971 was perhaps the singular most important element contributing to the Nitty Gritty Dirt Band's rise in stature, both commercially and creatively.

To attempt to chronicle the various manifestations of the group is a bewildering task. Jim Ibbotson, Jeff Hanna, John McEuen, Jimmie Fadden and Les Thompson came together as the Nitty Gritty Dirt Band in 1969. There had been four iterations of the lineup before that. It was part of the very fluid California scene that flowered with the careers of Jackson Browne, Linda Ronstadt and the like. NGDB was in at the beginning of it all.

They had some pop singles ("Buy for Me the Rain" and "House at Pooh Corner") and one massive hit (a 1971 cover of Jerry Jeff Walker's "Mr. Bojangles") and had been a pioneering band, straddling diverse styles.

"There was a country-rock movement born out of that big folk music scare of the '60s," Hanna said. "And all of a sudden, they were going, 'Hmm, let's see where we can go with this,' and coming up with this weird hybrid."

The Nitty Gritty Dirt Band was trying to decide whether to maintain one foot in pop or to go with tradition. The band had played to enthusiastic crowds in Denver and Boulder during early tours. When the San Fernando earthquake hit in 1971, the band members, most of them California natives, got spooked and looked for safer ground. They left Los Angeles to relocate in the Colorado mountains, settling into their respective wooded communities—Evergreen, Golden and Aspen.

Then, at the suggestion of manager Bill McEuen, the Dirt Band outlined plans for recording a selection of traditional country numbers to be performed in conjunction with the original musicians. The band went to see the Earl Scruggs Revue at Tulagi in Boulder in 1972.

It was Scruggs' picking that had made the banjo a lead instrument over two decades prior and given bluegrass a distinctive style. Scruggs was still innovating, but it wasn't always easy. His Revue—featuring his hip-looking sons, Gary and Randy, and Vassar Clements, the middle-aged fiddler—used electric instruments and drums, and traditionalists at bluegrass festivals often booed the band.

"He had come to see us at a concert we did at Vanderbilt University," Hanna said. "Before he left the room, we said, 'Would you think about playing banjo on one of our records?' And then months later, he played Tulagi. And we had come up with this idea...

"The catalyst? Randy and Gary had been listening to our records—they were into this country-rock aspect. And having grown up in Nashville under the tutelage of the greats—their Sunday dinners with Merle Travis coming over—they saw the potential for something as well. And they nurtured this along with their father. Earl was our liaison."

The Nitty Gritty Dirt Band went to Nashville, gathering a cross-section of country music stalwarts—Scruggs, Travis, Clements, Doc Watson, Mother Maybelle Carter, Roy Acuff, Jimmy Martin (of Bill Monroe's Bluegrass Boys) and Norman Blake. Some of the stars were skeptical at first of the Dirt Band members and their amplified instruments. The longhairs had their own preconceptions. Common ground was found when the traditional musicians saw how respectful the Nitty Gritty Dirt Band was toward them and their work, as well as how serious the members were about their own music. In a modest and self-effacing manner, the band allowed the spotlight to fall on the old masters.

Recorded live on a two-track machine, the amazing results changed the direction of popular music—*Will the Circle Be Unbroken* brought a new appreciation for unadulterated folk and roots-country stars to rock listeners' ears. The ambitious three-record set elicited positive reviews from both the rock and country music press. *Circle* even sold well, an amazing achievement that produced the first gold album for Scruggs, Carter, Watson, Acuff and others.

The geographical transition to Colorado had brought an immediate host of fresh, attentive new faces to the front of stages, the personification of all the things the band stood for conceptually. The Nitty Gritty Dirt Band reflected the locals' consciousness, and it wasn't long before the new citizens of Idaho Springs and Castle Rock claimed the group for their own. Keyboardist and vocalist Bob Carpenter had been based in Aspen during the 1970s with the band Starwood. He joined the Nitty Gritty Dirt Band in 1977.

"There was a general feeling of unity, of having a home base, working in Colorado," John McEuen said. "It was hard to feel that way in Los Angeles, even though that's where most of us came from. Colorado in the 1970s was where a lot of people were finding a new direction. That effect was felt in the song 'Ripplin' Waters,' which became a Dirt Band standard."

Subsequent album releases were peppered with country-flavored material, but still the Nitty Gritty Dirt Band was seen as more of a rock act than a country outfit. Because of its impressive history and outstanding live shows, the band was able to continue working. A couple of pop singles made the charts—1980's "Make a Little Magic" and "An American Dream" with Linda Ronstadt, both released under the name the Dirt Band.

The band didn't make any inroads into the contemporary country music world until Chuck Morris, whose attention had been steered to concert promotion in Denver, entered the management picture. In 1983, the band gradually forced its way onto country radio with a slew of Top 10 hits—"High Horse," "I Only Love You," "Partners, Brothers and Friends," "Soldier of Love," "Long Hard Road," "Fishin' in the Dark," "Modern Day Romance" and more. Originally recorded in 1983 for a compilation album, "Colorado Christmas" remained a radio staple around the holidays.

"But in the 1980s, our focus was Nashville, in terms of making albums," John McEuen said. "Things change. It was difficult to work flying in and out of Apsen."

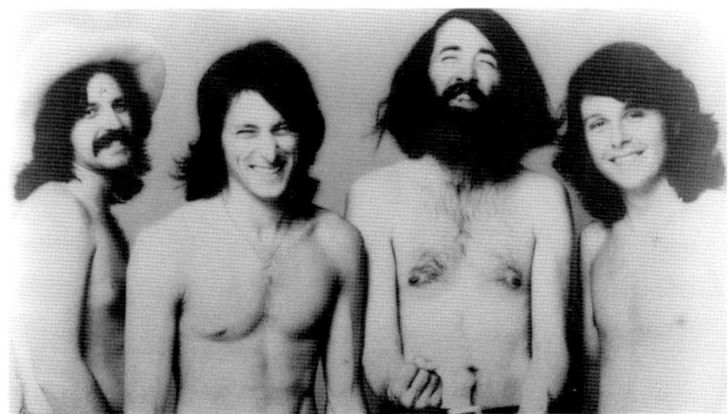

c. 1974

When Ibbotson was taking a hiatus from the Nitty Gritty Dirt Band in the 1970s, he linked up with Jim Ratts and Jim Salestrom, and they played the Colorado ski circuit. Ratts had recorded and toured with his Denver-based band Runaway Express. Salestrom had spent a number of years as lead guitarist and singer in Dolly

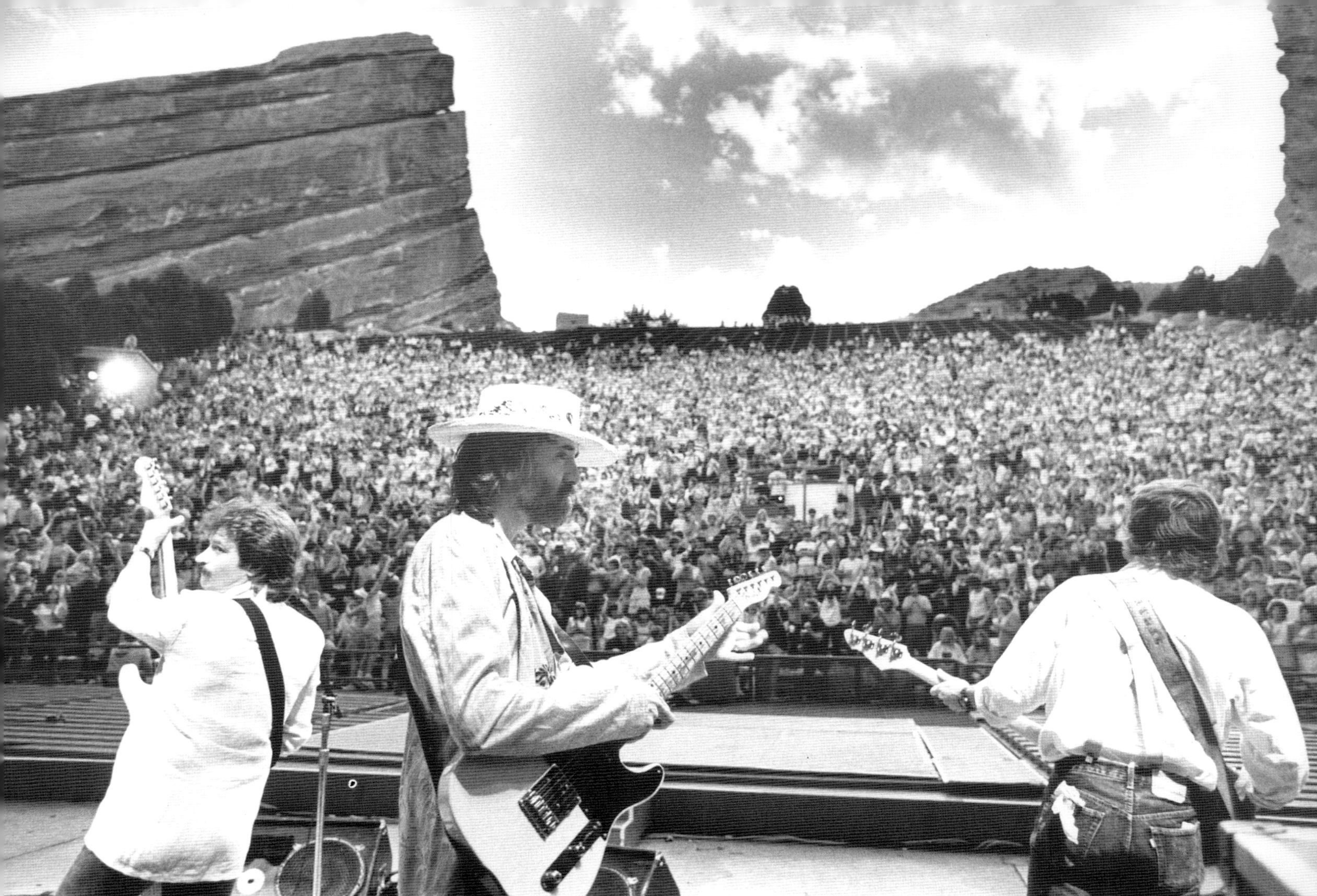

The Nitty Gritty Dirt Band at Red Rocks Amphitheatre, c. 1982

Parton's band.

Even after Ibbotson returned to the Dirt Band, Wild Jimbos continued to get together to have some cheap fun and to give him another outlet for recording some of his folk-ish songs that didn't fit the NGDB's country repertoire. In 1991, mandolinist Sam Bush, a founding member of New Grass Revival, produced the free-spirited *Wild Jimbos* album. A cover of John Prine's philosophical ditty "Let's Talk Dirty in Hawaiian" got novelty record airplay nationally, and the funny low-budget video received heavy rotation on CMT.

"My marriage to the Dirt Band will not be put asunder by the Jimbos, but it's nice to have a fling," Ibbotson said. "These guys are a joy—Salestrom's got a great undiscovered voice, and Ratts is the hardest-working guy on the Denver scene."

The Nitty Gritty Dirt Band continued to record a new album every year or so, but the members had raised their families by the 1990s. Ibbotson was the only member who remained in Colorado. He left after the tour in support of the album *Welcome to Woody Creek* in 2004, having had enough of the road. Hanna, Fadden, Carpenter and McEuen continued to record and tour. ●

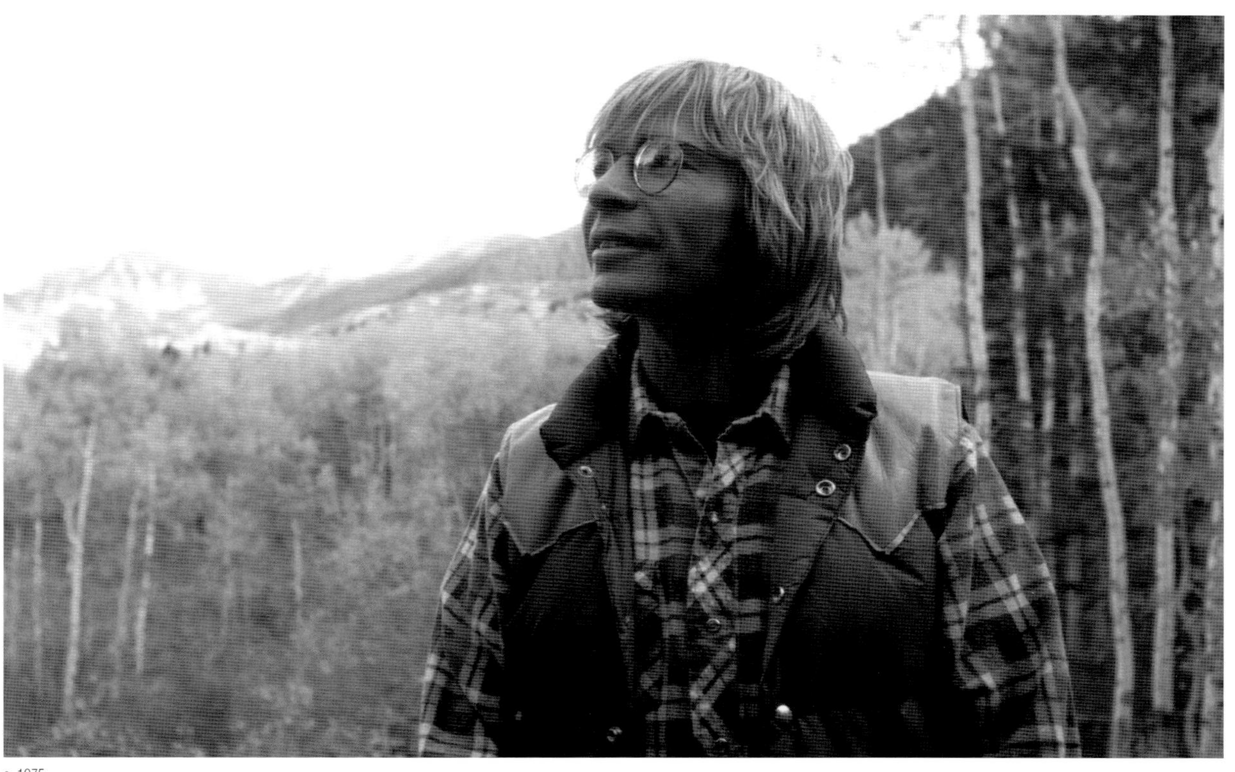

c. 1975

JOHN DENVER }

ONCE ONE of the five top-selling recording artists in the history of the music industry, John Denver will always be associated with the Rocky Mountains and the city from which he took his name.

In 1974, Colorado Governor John Vanderhoof proclaimed Denver the state's poet laureate. Concern for the mountains and the environment at large spurred him to found the Windstar Foundation in 1976 as a research facility to study alternative solutions to food production, energy and land education. Every year prior to his death in 1997, he returned to his Aspen home to host his own Celebrity Pro/Am Ski Tournament.

His explanation for the attraction? "When I get to the mountains, I'm happy," he said. "That's all there is to it."

Henry John Deutschendorf, Jr. was born New Year's Eve, 1943, in Roswell, New Mexico. An Air Force brat, his childhood was spent all over the Southwest, but his favorite times were spent on his grandmother's Oklahoma farm. The guitar his other grandmother had given him at age eight accompanied him everywhere.

He took one year of lessons "to learn the basic chords," then joined a rock band in high school. Architecture was his official major at Texas Tech, but he spent more time playing than drawing. Folk music clubs drew him to Los Angeles midway through his junior year, where he renamed himself John Denver after his favorite city.

"I liked it because my heart longed to live in the mountains," he said.

In 1965, Denver was selected out of 250 candidates to replace Chad Mitchell in the Chad Mitchell Trio. During his three-year tenure as the new lead singer with the popular trio, he began writing songs. Meanwhile, other performers were discovering his talents. In 1969, Peter, Paul & Mary, the most popular folk group of that decade, had their first and only No. 1 hit with a cover of Denver's "Leaving on a Jet Plane." Less than two years later, Denver was zooming up the pop charts with "Take Me Home, Country Roads," the first of many hits.

Denver insinuated himself into the public's consciousness with "Rocky Mountain High," which scaled to #9 in March 1973.

"It's very much an autobiographical song," he said. "It came out of several things. One was finally moving to Colorado, that first summer of my 27th year, and making it my home. I'd been to Colorado several times. It was the Rocky Mountains, man—I wanted to live there.

"I did a lot of camping that summer, which had me getting back to the things I love most—the beauty of the land and the quiet of the wilderness—and just how precious it is to me. There was a trip during the Perseid meteor shower, which happens August 12 through 15—a really spectacular night. I'm an amateur astronomer, and there's never been a better one.

"And there was all this stuff going on then about having an Olympics in Colorado. With the experience I'd had seeing some of the other places around the world, I was very much opposed to it.

"So those questions were going on in my mind—the experience of feeling like I'd found home, this glorious night under the stars and then the problems that face any place where tourism is the primary industry, keeping development and growth under control and guided wisely. Out of all that came the song.

"I've never burnt out on it. It's fun to think of coining a phrase that gets into the language, and 'Rocky Mountain High' is in the language now."

A cheerfully optimistic image marked Denver's 1970s heyday; he was a grinning sprite known for saying "Far out!" Between 1974 and 1975 he produced five No. 1 songs ("Sunshine on My Shoulders," "Annie's Song," "Thank God I'm a Country Boy," "I'm Sorry" and "Calypso"). The strength of Denver's popularity was measured in record sales that few other artists have achieved, including eight platinum albums in the U.S. alone.

Windsong (1975) was probably Denver's most nature-inspired album. It lent its name to his newly established record label—formed, he said, to further Colorado musicians and his own self-taught knowledge of his craft. The first act signed to Windsong was the Starland Vocal Band, which featured Bill Danoff and his wife, Taffy Nivert.

Danoff had been a folksinger working nights as the light and sound man at a club in Washington, D.C.,

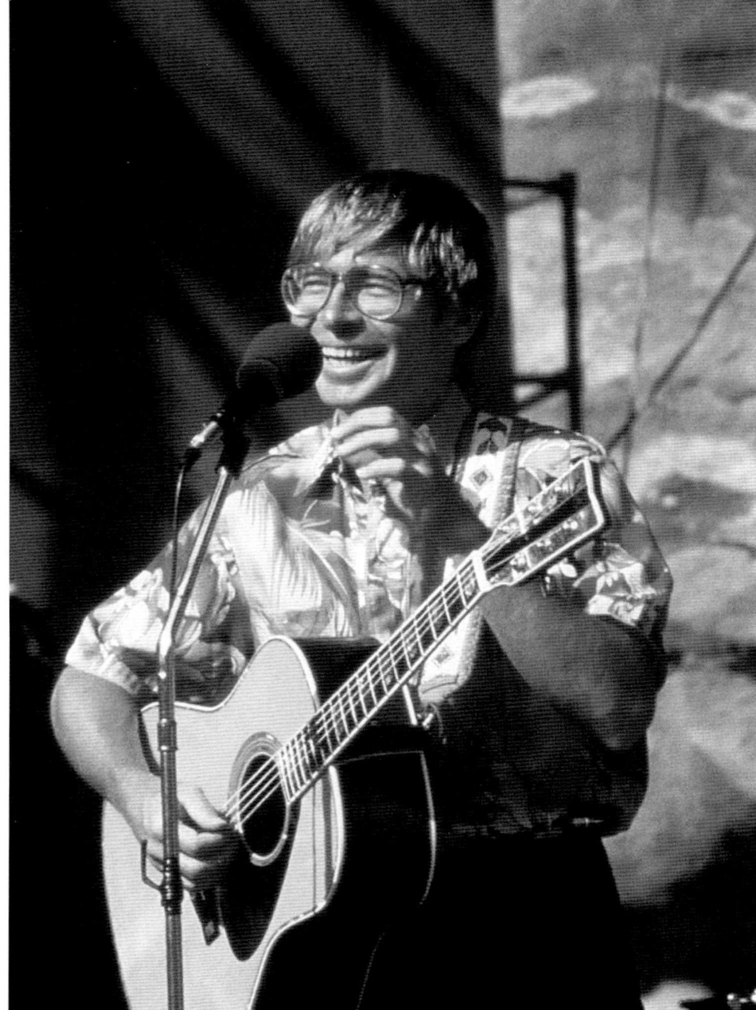

Denver at Red Rocks Amphitheatre, July 5, 1982

where he met Denver, who was near the end of his stretch fronting the Chad Mitchell Trio. Soon Denver recorded Danoff's "I Guess I'd Rather Be in Colorado." The friendship between them was cemented when they co-wrote Denver's first smash hit, "Take Me Home, Country Roads."

Formerly members of the band Fat City, Danoff and Nivert created the Starland Vocal Band, fine-tuning the clean-cut, all-American quartet's rich pop harmony sound before signing on with Windsong. The band's first single, "Afternoon Delight," was released in late April 1976, and nine weeks later, the Starland Vocal Band and the label had their first and only No. 1 single.

Denver starred alongside celebrities as diverse as opera singer Beverly Sills, violinist Itzhak Perlman and flautist James Galway. Frank Sinatra was the "Friend" in Denver's *John Denver and Friend* television special, and their

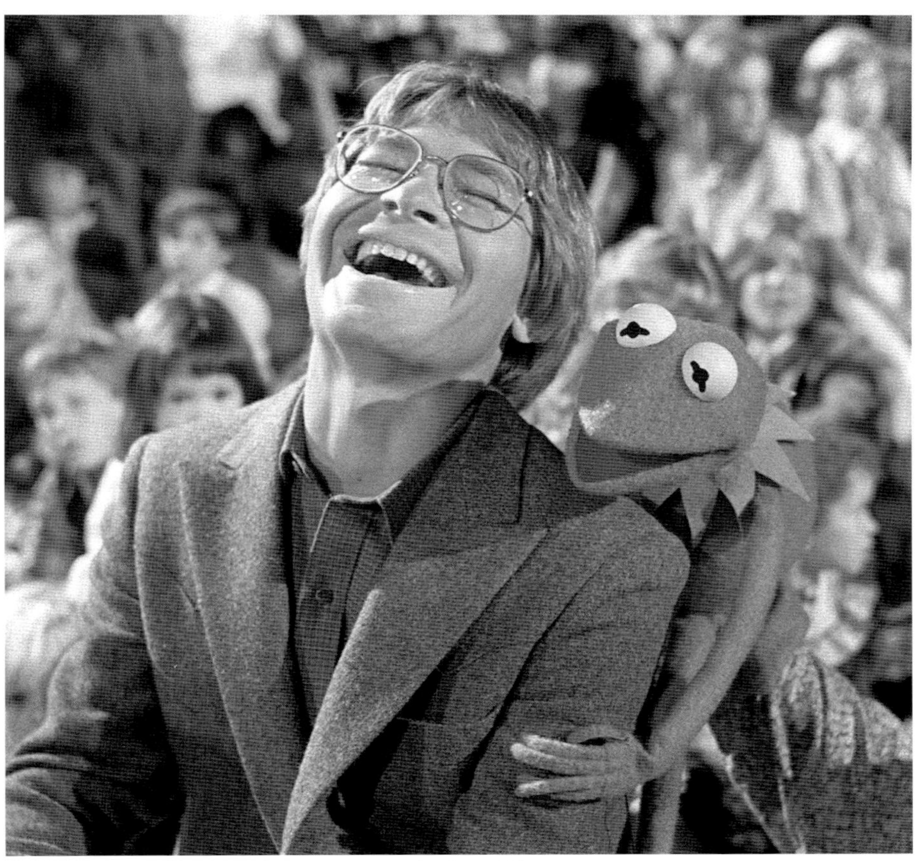

Denver with Kermit the Frog, c. 1979

"back-to-back" co-billing at Harrah's Tahoe was one of the most sought-after tickets in the casino hotel's history. Denver and Placido Domingo recorded "Perhaps Love," a song written by Denver, as a duet, earning the Spanish tenor considerable recognition outside of the opera world.

Denver used his popularity to promote his favorite cause: the environment. His concern spurred him to found the Windstar Foundation as an education and demonstration center dedicated to the creation of a sustainable future. Many of his songs incorporated environmental themes. He was known for his close friendship with Jacques Cousteau, the most famous undersea explorer of the 20th century, and he wrote "Calypso" in 1975 as a tribute to Cousteau and his research boat of the same name that sailed around the world for oceanic conservation.

Denver took his music beyond American shores, traveling to mainland China (where he was the first Western artist to do a multi-city tour) and the Soviet Union (the first time an artist had been invited to give public performances since the cultural exchange agreement expired in 1980), as well as Europe, the Far East, Australia, New Zealand and Latin America. His charitable activities encompassed a trip to Africa to publicize the food crisis there and act as spokesman for UNICEF's fundraising drive.

When Denver guest-starred on *The Muppet Show*, it was the beginning of a life-long friendship between him and Jim Henson that spawned two television specials with the Muppets ensemble; *A Christmas Together* and *Rocky Mountain Holiday* are considered classics. Denver's movie debut in the comedy *Oh God!* alongside George Burns was a solid hit. He also starred and guest-starred in many television productions, including *Higher Ground* and *Foxfire*, and the seasonal special *A Christmas Gift* filmed in the Rocky Mountains in 1986. He guest-hosted *The Tonight Show* on multiple occasions and hosted the Grammy Awards five times in the 1970s and 1980s.

Absent from the top of the charts in the 1990s, Denver focused his output on a mature interest in the range of human experience. "I look back at some of my old album cover pictures and I wonder who that guy is," he said. "I just don't feel like that anymore. I guess I've gotten past the picture that people had of long hair and the granny glasses, and I'm glad about that. The worst things that have ever happened to me have been what people said about my music—'the Mickey Mouse of pop,' or 'the Ronald Reagan of rock.'

"That's aimed at diminishing not only me, but all the folks whose lives have been touched by my music. I still meet people who use my songs in their weddings, who have played them while they're going through labor. But I know that it took going through all of those former years to get where I am."

Denver's father, a U.S. Air Force test pilot nicknamed "Dutch," taught him how to fly, and his love for flying became a passion to bring them closer together. Denver, a licensed pilot, died at age 53 when his experimental aircraft crashed into the Pacific Ocean in October 1997. ●

RICHIE FURAY }

WHILE WALKING down a road to his house near Nederland, Richie Furay wrote Poco's most distinctive composition—1973's "A Good Feeling to Know."

"It's that opening line—'Colorado mountains, I can see your distant sky.' When we were away on the road, flying from east to west and seeing the mountains, it was like, 'Oh, boy, this is home,'" Furay said.

"But that song devastated me. I thought it was going to catapult Poco into another realm of acceptance, yet we had a lot of trouble getting played on the radio at the time. We were too country for the rock stations and too rock for the country stations."

In the spring of 1966, Furay had formed Buffalo Springfield with Stephen Stills and Neil Young. The West Coast group had only one major hit (Stills' ominous protest song, "For What It's Worth"), but Furay's songs made the rock band perhaps the first to experiment with a country sound. His best-known track with Springfield was "Kind Woman," which he wrote for his wife, Nancy.

The volatile outfit broke up in 1969, and Furay formed Poco with Jim Messina (Buffalo Springfield's recording engineer who took over as the bass player) and Randy Meisner, along with ex-Coloradans Rusty Young and George Grantham, who left Böenzee Cryque. Meisner left Poco to join Rick Nelson's Stone Canyon Band and later the Eagles; Messina departed after three albums to form Loggins & Messina.

In the fall of 1970, the remaining band members moved to Colorado, and Furay provided Poco with the rugged toughness of "A Good Feeling to Know." The parent album reached #69 on *Billboard*'s pop album chart, but the title track failed to make the singles chart.

"We were thinking we had to write a Top 40 hit," Furay allowed. "At the very same time our album was released, I heard 'Take It Easy' by the Eagles on the radio, and I knew it wasn't going to happen with Poco. Glenn Frey had sat on my living room couch when I was rehearsing Poco. I guess he took a lot of notes!"

Frustrated by the record's failure to generate the expected commercial success, in September 1973 Furay left Poco to form the Souther-Hillman-Furay Band, a ready-made supergroup put together by record mogul David Geffen. By all indications, success was inevitable. J.D. Souther was a masterful songwriter in the Eagles mold. Furay's roots were Buffalo Springfield and Poco, and Chris Hillman's utilitarian prowess supposedly clinched it.

"I was consumed with wanting to be a big rock 'n' roll star," Furay mused. "David seemed to be the guy who could put his hand on anything—Jackson Browne, Linda Ronstadt, Joni Mitchell, the Eagles. So why not us? But what looks good on paper doesn't always translate in real life."

Furay wrote "Fallin' in Love," the group's sole hit. It peaked at #27 on *Billboard*'s pop singles chart in 1974. But the band never jelled and it evaporated after two years. Yet while recording the second Souther-Hillman-Furay album at Caribou Ranch in Nederland, steel guitarist Al Perkins—a former Flying Burrito Brother and a member of Manassas—suggested Furay consider Christianity.

"When Chris wanted Al in the band, I said, 'No way—I know this guy's reputation. He's one of those born-again Christians with a Jesus sticker on his guitar,'" Furay remembered. "I didn't want anything to get in the way of my personal success.

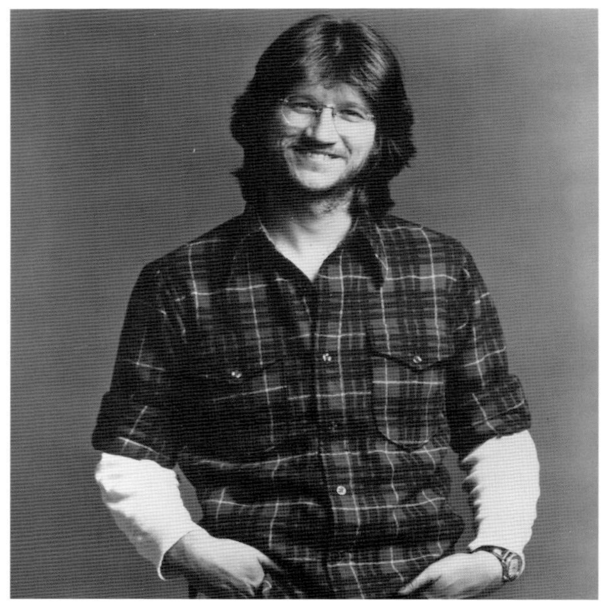

c. 1976

"But I couldn't deny his musicianship. And I couldn't put my finger on what was different and attractive. This guy was in the middle of rock 'n' roll, and he wasn't getting drunk or doing drugs or chasing women every night. But he was having fun, being creative and enjoying music.

"I had no idea that my wife and I were beginning to have marital problems. When Nancy and I separated for seven months, I hit the bottom. That's when I finally prayed with Al, and that's when I found God's plan for me. I had wanted to be a star, but stars burn out."

After injuring his hand while chopping wood near his Colorado home, Furay was forced to suspend his playing until his convalescence was complete. Nearly a year later, he re-emerged

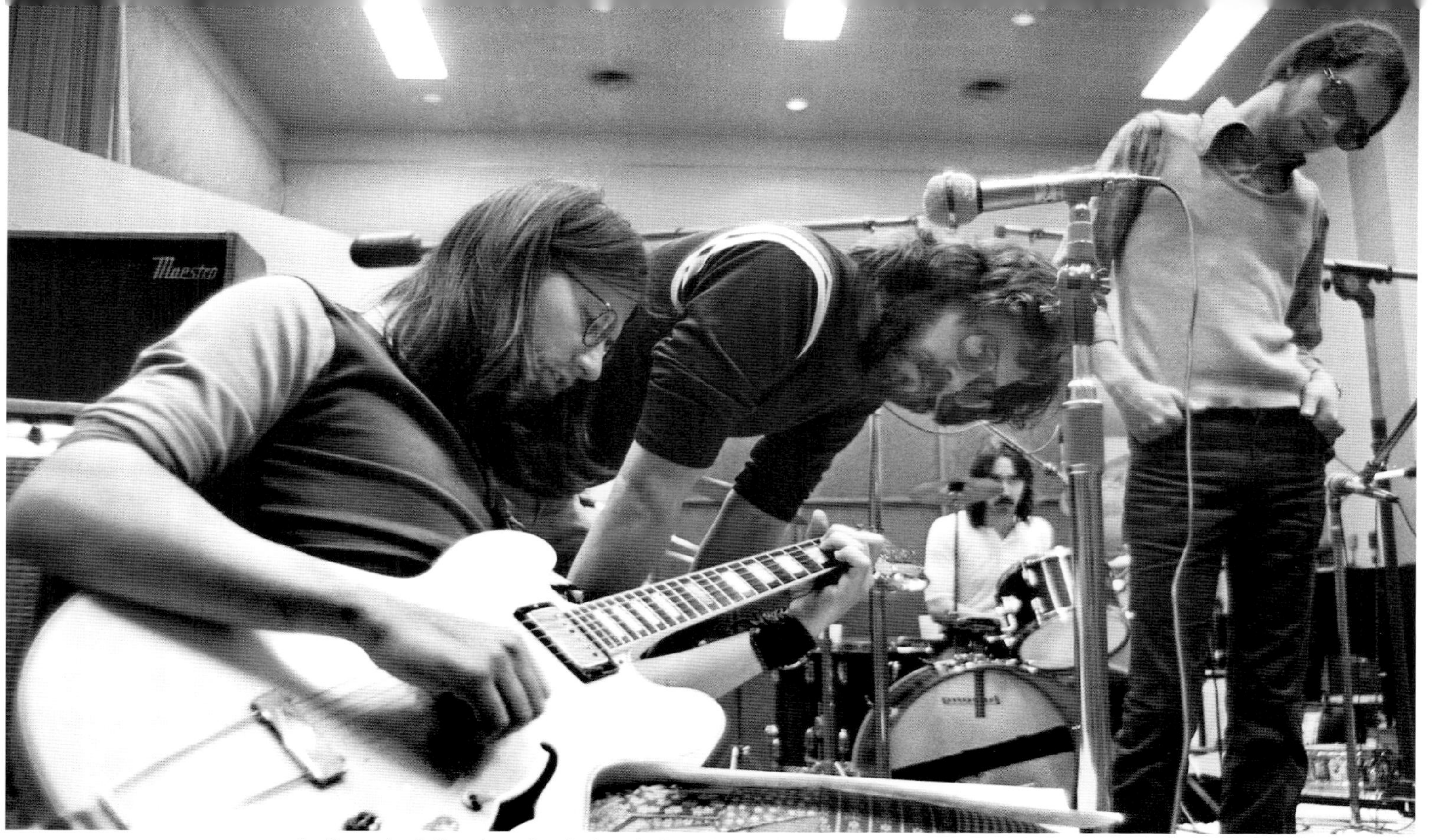

Poco (Furay, producer Jim Mason, drummer George Grantham and pedal steel guitarist Rusty Young) recording *A Good Feeling to Know*, c. 1973

and pursued a solo career, one of the first rock stars to make Christian music for the general market. Three late 1970s solo albums failed to find wide acceptance, but "I Still Have Dreams" debuted on *Billboard*'s pop singles chart in October 1979 and peaked at #39.

"I was on another mission. I had it in my mind and in my heart that I was going to put together the rock 'n' roll band for Christ. People knew what my life was about," Furay said.

But Furay severed his ties with a major label following a controversy over a song that had some spiritual content.

"They wanted me to compromise the lyric, which I couldn't do. It came down to the wire after five years. I said, 'I've tried, and it hasn't worked. What do you want, Lord?'"

In 1982, Furay abandoned music and devoted himself to pastoring for Boulder's 150-member Rocky Mountain Christian Fellowship (now Calvary Chapel, in Broomfield).

"I never went to divinity school. I've never been to a seminary," Furay allowed. "We started a home Bible study group, and that turned into a church!"

When Rusty Young orchestrated a Poco reunion in 1989, he urged Furay to give the rock world one more try. Poco's *Legacy*, Furay's first secular musical project in a decade, earned a gold record. The one stumbling block was the choice of songs dealing with sex. Having given his life to the Lord, Furay made no secret of his disdain for the rock-star life that clashed with his religious beliefs. He didn't participate in the second leg of Poco's tour.

Furay continued to record and perform as a solo artist and with the Richie Furay Band.

"Early on, I wasn't secure enough in who I was in the Lord, and I let people influence me," he said. "I know now that it's Him who I have to answer to. He's given me a gift, a talent.

"Nobody has been as blessed as I have. I've got the wife I married in 1967, four daughters, grandkids. I left Ohio as a boy to become a folksinger and I've lived my dreams—my name is written in the Rock and Roll Hall of Fame with Buffalo Springfield. A lot of people can't say they've experienced all of the things I have in life and still say they're fulfilled spiritually. That's the bottom line." ●

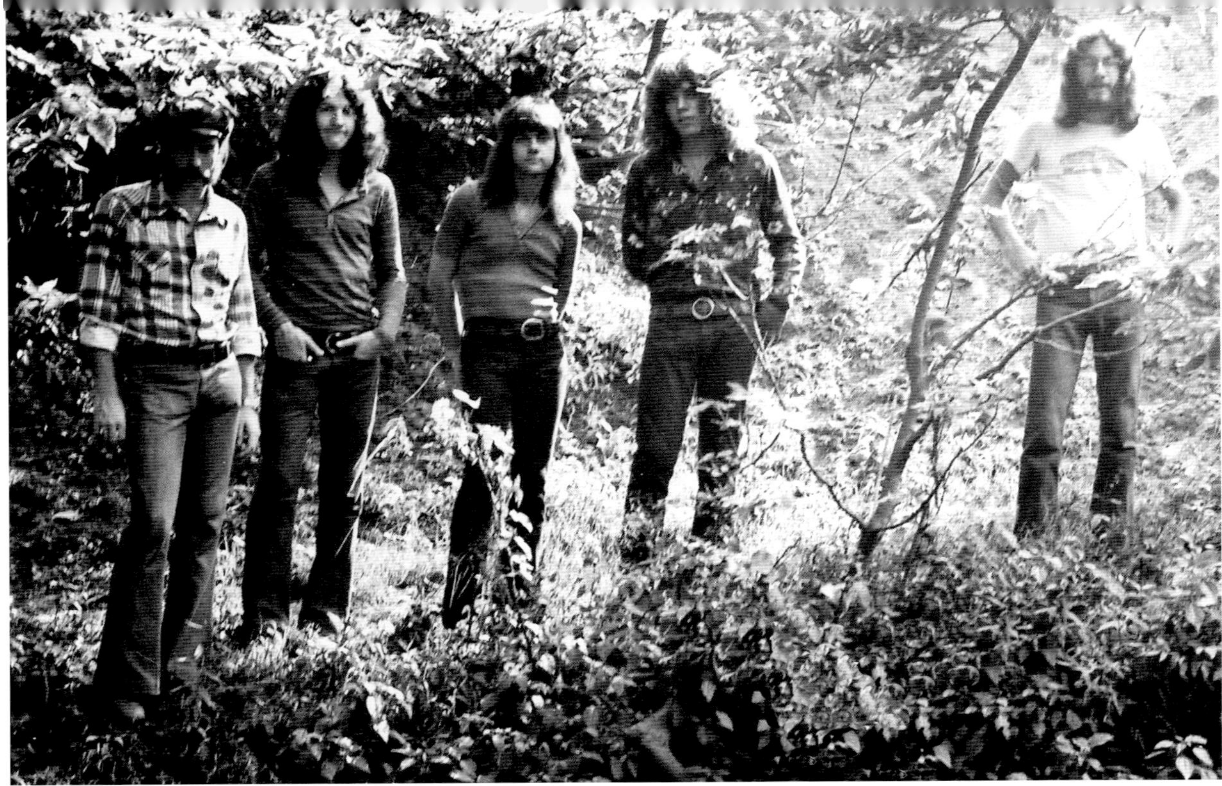
c. 1973

REO SPEEDWAGON }

LIKE OTHER Midwest bands in the 1970s, REO Speedwagon was constantly on the road, eventually becoming a regional star attraction. Lead singer Kevin Cronin and guitarist Gary Richrath wrote the classic rock staple "Ridin' the Storm Out" in 1973 when REO played Tulagi in Boulder, Colorado.

"We were kids—20 going on 15. We had a record deal, and we were goo-goo eyed," Richrath recalled.

"In combination with that, we were romantics from Illinois where there are no hills—we hadn't been far enough west to see mountains. And we freaked. We were driving across the plains saying, 'Shit, look at that stuff!' We were dying when we got to Boulder.

"Kevin and I were like two brothers. We did everything together at the time. We got a few provisions to go up to the Flatirons to hike around. Our tour manager said, 'You're not going up there'—a big blizzard was coming in. We ditched him and went anyway."

"We ended up getting lost," Cronin continued. "It started snowing, and we thought for a moment that we were goners."

"It was confusing for a couple of kids from the Midwest," Richrath said. "We got nervous and scared and walked around in circles for an hour. Then we saw a flagpole in a park and ran to it. Our road manager had brains enough to sit and wait for us.

"It was an inspiring moment, walking in the woods and hoping to get our asses out of there. The next morning I woke up and said to Kevin, 'I've got some lyrics. Let's work on them.'

"Kevin always says he knows a new hit when he writes one. I didn't quite see 'Ridin' the Storm Out' becoming the stalwart REO song of the '70s, but now you've got to give the song the respect it deserves."

REO Speedwagon's first million-seller was a 1977 live album titled *You Get What You Pay For*, and the "Ridin' the Storm Out" single reached #94 on the *Billboard* charts.

REO became America's No. 1 rock band in 1980, reaching a zenith with a carefully crafted blend of hard rock and high-energy ballads such as "Keep On Lovin' You" and "Can't Fight This Feeling."

"We weathered neglect from New York and Los Angeles music circles, critical drubbings, personnel changes and years of opening-act status," Cronin said. "'Ridin' the Storm Out' was the one thing that held the band together for all those years. It closed our shows for over a decade." ●

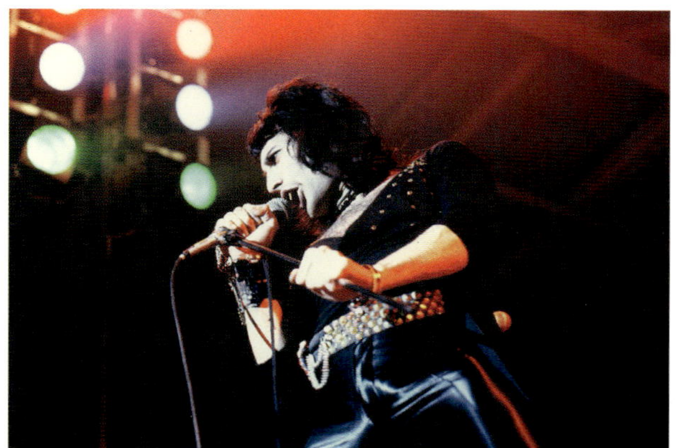

Freddie Mercury at Regis College, April 12, 1974

QUEEN }

A PIONEERING band in many ways, Queen assembled a brash, theatrical stage act well before glitter bands emerged as a potent pop vehicle.

In 1974, with an attention-getting U.K. tour behind them, Queen was looking forward to bigger gigs in the U.S. as the *Queen II* album was released. On April 12, the band began its first American tour, supporting Mott The Hoople at Regis College in Denver. The English newcomers were received rather quietly at first. Folks in the audience had obviously heard of Mott, but they weren't too sure of Queen frontman Freddie Mercury wearing satin and nail polish.

By the end of the set, however, they were won over. Mercury's outrageous onstage theatrics set a new standard for rock showmanship.

"It was wonderful, mind-blowing," guitarist Brian May said. "After the gig, the most incredible bunch of people turned up and we had a party in the (hotel) room. I'd never been in a situation like that. In England, we had made very little ground. Suddenly, we were in a place where there was a rock culture, and we were perceived as generating a new one, unwittingly close to the center of it. I had so many incredible conversations, and I remember the record company people being surprised—'This doesn't feel like Denver tonight.' From there on in, it was a constant high."

The U.S. tour was abandoned when May contracted hepatitis, but the untimely reversal worked to Queen's benefit. The members returned to England, and what emerged from their enforced hiatus was a fresh group effort, *Sheer Heart Attack*, and the hit single, "Killer Queen." Queen went on to international stardom, and the songs "Bohemian Rhapsody," "We Will Rock You," "We Are the Champions," "Another One Bites the Dust," "Crazy Little Thing Called Love" and many others became mega-hits.

Intensely private about his personal life, Mercury never revealed how or when he contracted AIDS. He died in November 1991, only one day after publicly announcing that he was HIV-positive, a fact he had concealed from nearly everyone. ●

BOB SEGER }

IN 1976, AFTER a decade of being rock's "Beautiful Loser," Bob Seger began his overdue breakthrough to stardom when his *Live Bullet* album went gold. *Live Bullet*, recorded at two sold-out shows at Cobo Hall in his hometown of Detroit, featured versions of such early Seger classics as "Ramblin' Gamblin' Man," "Katmandu," "Turn the Page" and "Get Out of Denver." The 1974 single "Get Out of Denver" had peaked at #80 on the *Billboard* chart.

Was the tune based on a real life experience? In his first-ever Denver gig, at Ebbets Field in July 1974, Seger introduced the song as "...a little story that took place real near here, up near Loveland Pass."

"Sorry," Seger grinned later. "At that stage of my career, I tried to write a rocker for every album that would be fun to do live. 'Katmandu' was also done that way.

"I wanted to write a Chuck Berry song, and I liked the cadence of Denver in the lyrics—Albuquerque wouldn't fit.

"But I made it all up. I never got run out of Denver."

The song became a classic, covered in the next decade by Dave Edmunds, Eddie & the Hot Rods and Dr. Feelgood. ●

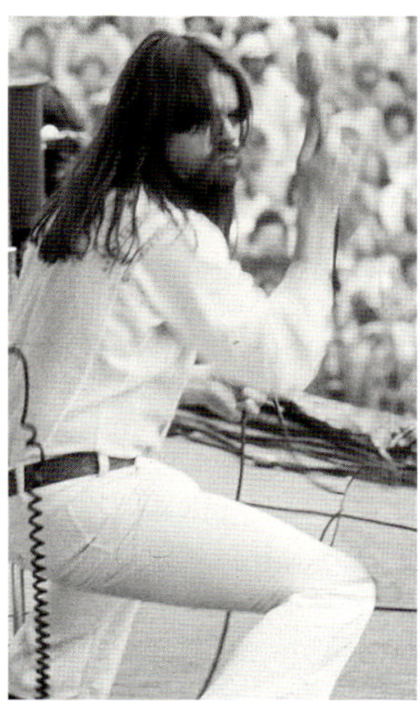

Seger at Folsom Field, May 1, 1977

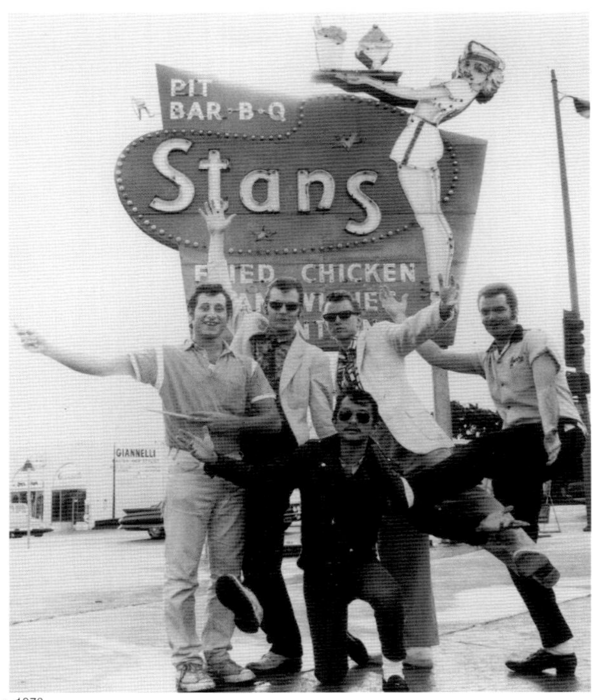

c. 1970

FLASH CADILLAC & THE CONTINENTAL KIDS }

WHAT BAND would audition its sax player with a four-part questionnaire: "Are you single? Do you drink beer? Do you play basketball? Can you play 'Yakety-Yak'?"

Only Flash Cadillac, the best-loved 1950s oldies band in America.

"Sha Na Na started up about the same time in New York. They were on the East Coast and got all the notoriety, but we may have predated them," original drummer Harold Fielden recalled.

Flash Cadillac & the Continental Kids were formed in 1968 at the University of Colorado as a means to pass the time, an oldies rock alternative to the then-popular hippie sound. Mick Manresa eventually signed on as the lead singer. As the original "Flash," he hid his Asian features behind wraparound shades and slicked-down hair.

Two of the first people recruited for Flash Cadillac were future stars Tommy Bolin and Jock Bartley. "They had long hair—Tommy's was red, green and purple—and the last thing they wanted to do was get a greaser haircut and wear tight pants and pointed shoes and do dance steps," Fielden explained. "So neither of them joined."

Word quickly spread about the neo-greasers' rabid live performances.

"It's hard for us to distinguish our actual first job because the first practice was a party—every practice was a party," keyboardist Kris "Angelo" Moe explained. "And the first job was a party. So how do you distinguish a practice party from a job party?"

The first paying job came on February 9, 1969, but things got serious quickly. The lewd and rude Flash Cadillac shows at Tulagi became the biggest events in Boulder.

"The pressure was really on," Moe said. "Six months before, we were just another group of guys waiting for our book assignment. Suddenly, the whole town of Boulder was mobilizing every Tuesday night for some spectacular happening that we had no idea about—we were still trying to figure out the week before. We didn't feel in control. Everybody in town just decided, 'Well, Flash is playing, let's go do it there.' All of the loonies would show up. And let's not kid anybody—people took off their clothes all the time."

The "skin to win" rules for the twist contest, the "wild elephant" for guys (unzipping pants and pulling the front pockets inside-out) and other group participation bits were hatched by Fielden.

"You just can't match the old Tulagi days for sickness," Fielden said of Boulder's thriving late-1960s club scene. "*Playboy* named all the best party schools in the country, and they didn't include CU because they said they didn't want to lump the professionals in with the amateurs."

"We had the entire crowd choreographed and programmed in Boulder, and Harold wanted to see as much lewdness as possible," Moe said. "We didn't want to play a lot, and everyone thought we were trying to raise our prices, so they offered us more money! We would turn down everything unless it was for mondo bucks, so we were doing four times better than other local bands. So we figured we'd go to Los Angeles."

Exactly one year after their formation, the members of Flash Cadillac drove to L.A. to play a "hoot-night" at the legendary Troubadour. That day they called agents from a pay phone across the street.

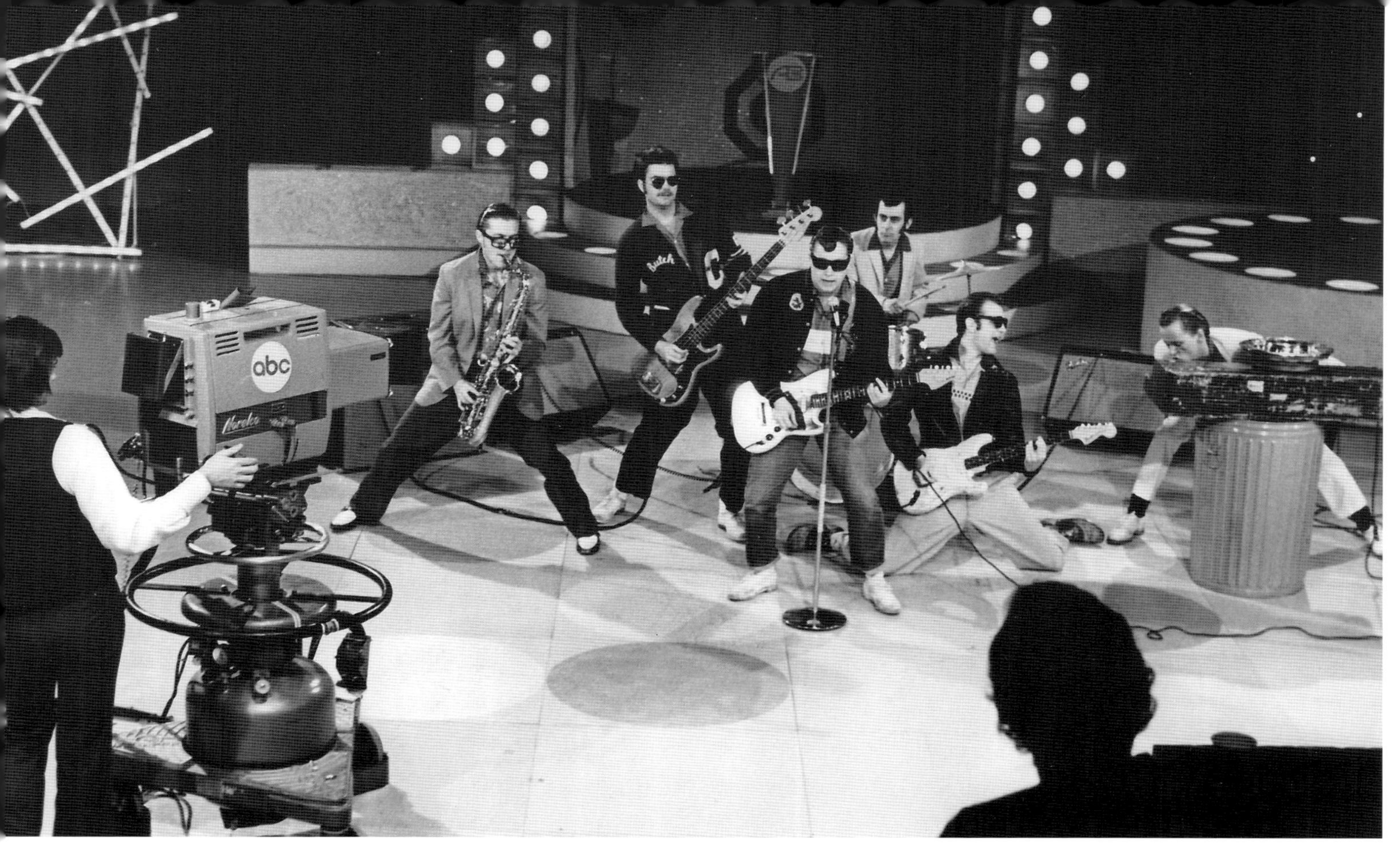

Appearing on *American Bandstand*, c. 1972

That night they came on last to a half-empty club and soon had the place packed with patrons dancing on the tables.

"It was nice because it proved we weren't just good in Boulder, we were good anywhere," Moe said. "All these guys in suits crowded into the dressing room after the show handing us business cards and saying they wanted to sign us.

"And we were saying, 'Well, we've got class tomorrow—we have to leave.'"

So the group quit school and hit the road. Within a year, Fielden and Manresa decided it wasn't fun anymore and returned to Boulder. Fielden became an attorney in the area and Manresa an engineer, but they remained in pursuit of the ultimate gross-out, performing oldies sets with the 4-Nikators and backing up oldies acts like Bo Diddley and the Crystals when they came to town.

Having lost their singer and talker, the other members of Flash Cadillac made the big decision to make a go of it as a real working band in 1971. The first step was to find a new Flash. Sam McFadin, a Colorado Springs fan of the band, was the only person considered for the job.

"When I knew they were going to audition me, I went down in my basement and drank beer to see if I could still play Chuck Berry riffs behind my back," he explained. "It was the only intensive training I got before I was out on the road."

Fronted by McFadin, Flash Cadillac gained instant popularity within the music industry. The band became the first act to perform on *American Bandstand* without having a record. Flash Cadillac earned acclaim in the movies, appearing as the sock-hop band Herby & the Heartbeats in George Lucas' *American Graffiti* in 1973, and also a scene with San Francisco rock promoter Bill Graham in Francis Ford Coppola's 1979 Vietnam epic *Apocalypse Now*.

And Flash Cadillac's work on television's *Happy Days* in March 1975—the episode "Fish and the Fins" was written especially for the band—won the highest weekly rating.

Flash Cadillac also began recording albums of oldies and catchy 1950's-styled pop originals for Epic Records, and the nightmares with record labels began. With the live show, the group never had a problem communicating its patented fraternity-style humor. It was on record that it didn't come across as well.

The band's second album, *There's No Face Like Chrome*, was recorded using three different producers. In 1974, "Youngblood" was the No. 1 song in more than 20 markets, and "Dancin' (on a Saturday Night)" cracked the *Billboard* pop singles charts at #93.

"But they didn't know how to market what we were, and they never let us take any chances," Moe said. "We recorded the greatest belch in the history of the world, and they said, 'There are ten other records with that.' Well, somebody likes it!"

Flash Cadillac gave the big time one more shot on Private Stock Records, recording minor hits in "Did You Boogie (With Your Baby)" (with spoken interludes by Wolfman Jack) and "Good Times, Rock and Roll." But a great version of "See My Baby Jive" (a hit for Roy Wood in England) was left hanging in January 1977 when the company's promotion staff quit over a salary dispute.

By that time, Flash Cadillac was looking for land in the Rocky Mountain area. The members—McFadin, Moe, Linn "Spike" Phillips III (guitar), Warren "Butch" Knight (bass), Dwight "Spider" Bement (sax) and the latest in a long line of drummers—purchased a little ranch located near Woodland Park, outside Colorado Springs. All of a sudden, after years on the road, they found they had real lives to lead. Several of them got married, and they began to scale back their careers.

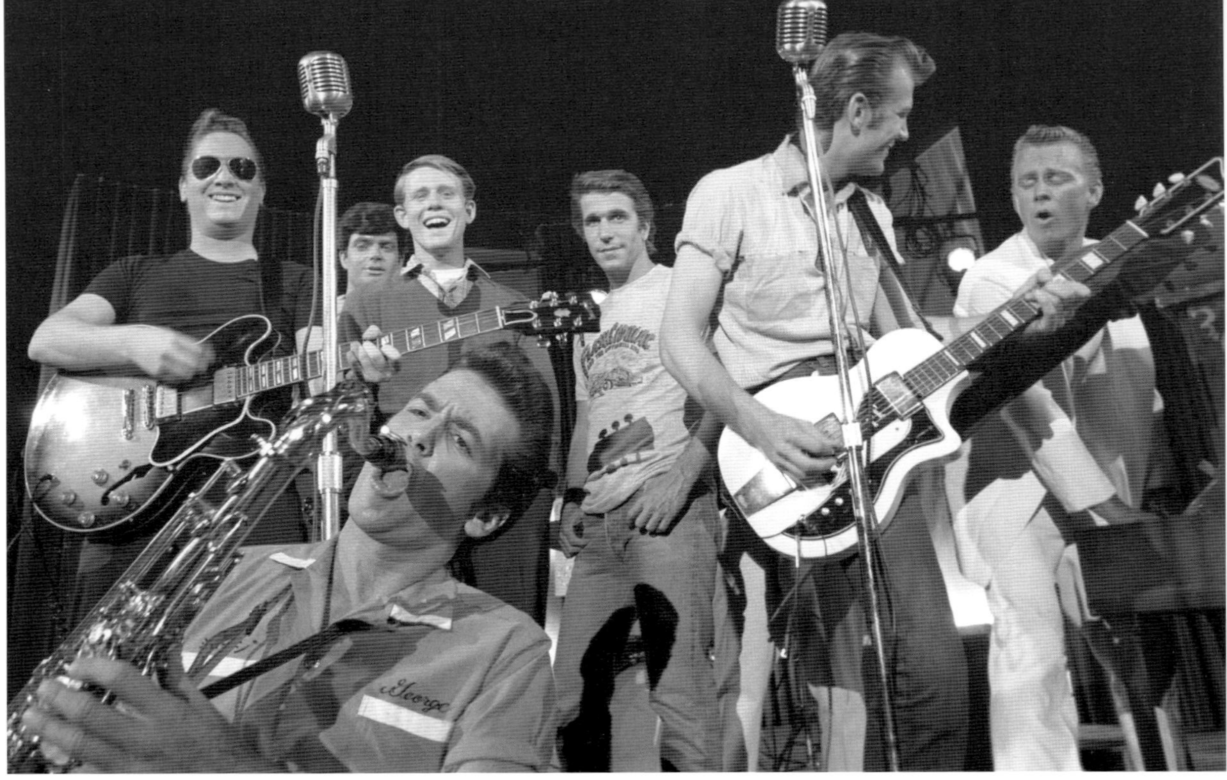

Between scenes on *Happy Days*, c. 1975

The ranch served initially as a rehearsal hall, but after several years the band built up the facility into a 24-track studio. Several businesses were running at once—Flash Cadillac on the road, in the studio and doing commercial work. In the 1980s, the nationally broadcast *Super Gold* weekly radio program featured Flash Cadillac as the house band.

In 1992, the band was reborn performing with symphony orchestras across the country, one of the hottest pops concerts going, and easily the most fun. The symphony musicians got with it, getting old poodle skirts and letter jackets out of mothballs.

"There's a type of music Flash Cadillac plays—good time, high energy—that has existed throughout rock 'n' roll history," McFadin said. "Rather than being nostalgic about it, saying it's all coming around again, we just consider it to be all that we know how to do. There are people who keep this kind of music alive."

Flash Cadillac lost cylinders over the years. In March 1993, Phillips, who was known for his crazy on-stage antics, suffered a heart attack backstage after a show and died. He wasn't replaced in the band, and the use of nicknames was dropped. The heart and soul was taken out of the group when McFadin died of a heart attack in September 2001. Moe, who had retired to the studio due to increasing weakness from ALS (Lou Gehrig's disease), died after a long struggle with the debilitating muscular disease in July 2005. Knight and Bement continued to lead a rockin' Flash Cadillac band, with Dave "Thumper" Henry on drums and "new kids" Timothy P. Irvin, Rocky Mitchell and Pete Santilli. ●

EMMYLOU HARRIS }

DURING HER five-decade journey as an interpreter and distinctive stylist, Emmylou Harris took her mentor Gram Parsons' distinct vision of country music to a new, larger audience. She didn't really start writing her own material until she hit her fifties, with one exception being her heartbroken paean to Parsons, 1975's "Boulder to Birmingham."

"It's not like I set out to write a song about Gram, but it was inspired by some of the feelings I had after his death," Harris said.

In the late 1960s, when the blues and British pop were all the rage on the rock scene, Parsons crusaded for country music's merits. Concocting his notion of "country soul" or "cosmic American music," the Georgia-bred singer-songwriter developed the genre that would later be termed country-rock.

Parsons' journey began when he was a member of the Byrds (he appeared on the countrified *Sweetheart of the Rodeo* album), and he later founded the Flying Burrito Brothers before releasing a pair of solo albums. Harris first came to prominence in the early 1970s, adding heart-tugging harmonies to Parsons' solo efforts. Her clear soprano perfectly complemented his lived-in lead vocals.

In the winter and spring of 1973, Harris toured briefly with Parsons in support of his last album, as the centerpiece of his touring outfit, the Fallen Angels. The performances established her as a decorous honky-tonk angel.

"Our first gig was in Boulder," Harris said of a show at the Edison Electric Company. "We actually got fired from that club—we forgot to work up beginnings, middles and ends of songs!

"Then we went up to the mountains and played in Nederland. It was like seeing *McCabe and Mrs. Miller*—two women were fighting in the parking lot. I thought, 'Yeah, this is for me.'"

Parsons' tragic overdose in September 1973 cut his life short and fixed him as a legend. It also marked the end of Harris' apprenticeship, and the profound experience gave her a sense of purpose and mission. Her debut album, *Pieces of the Sky*, yielded the achingly beautiful original "Boulder to Birmingham," co-written with Bill Danoff, who'd had major success as the co-composer of John Denver's "Take Me Home, Country Roads."

"The song just fell out of the sky," Harris said. "I didn't labor over it—it was kind of there.

"Gram really bequeathed me an extraordinary life." ●

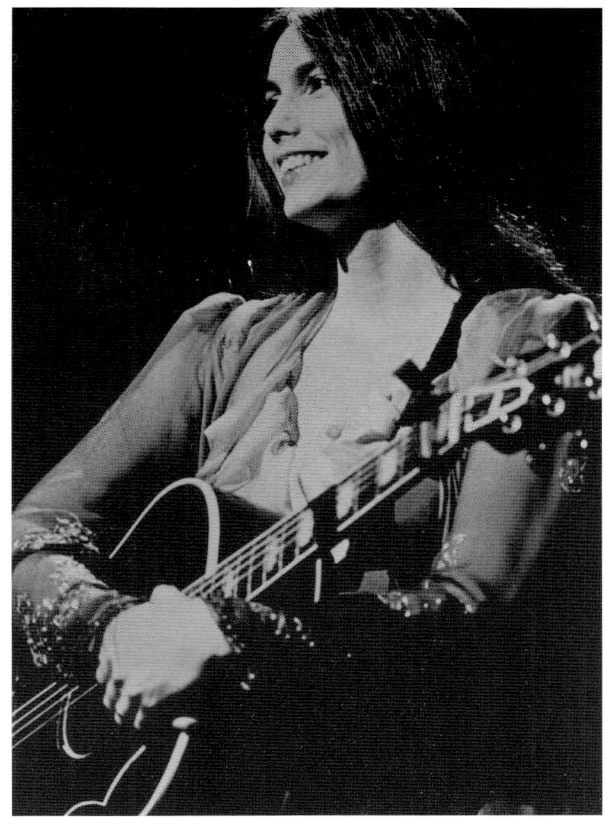

c. 1975

ELTON JOHN }

IN THE mid-1970s, before the recording industry faced the early 1980s economic recession, the rage among top recording stars was to hole up at "destination studios." Wouldn't it be inspirational and less distracting, they reasoned, to record outside of the usual Los Angeles or New York circles?

So they packed up their bags and headed for Caribou Ranch, the legendary recording complex near the Boulder County foothills hamlet of Nederland, Colorado.

Caribou, in its idyllic setting nearly 9,000 feet up in the Rocky Mountains, had been the largest privately owned Arabian stud farm in the country. The 3,000-plus-acre site also served as a dude ranch and a motion picture set.

Owner Jim Guercio, who was best known as Chicago's producer, bought Caribou for a reported $1 million in 1971 and installed the studio in 1973. Then he transformed the place into an opulent retreat for pop music's aristocracy while developing an exclusive image for himself.

"We didn't run the place like a Holiday Inn," Guercio noted. The life-in-the-fast-lane ambience that usually accompanied a recording session disappeared at Caribou. During the ranch's glory days, an entourage got full use of the facilities for a basic rate of $1,500 a day.

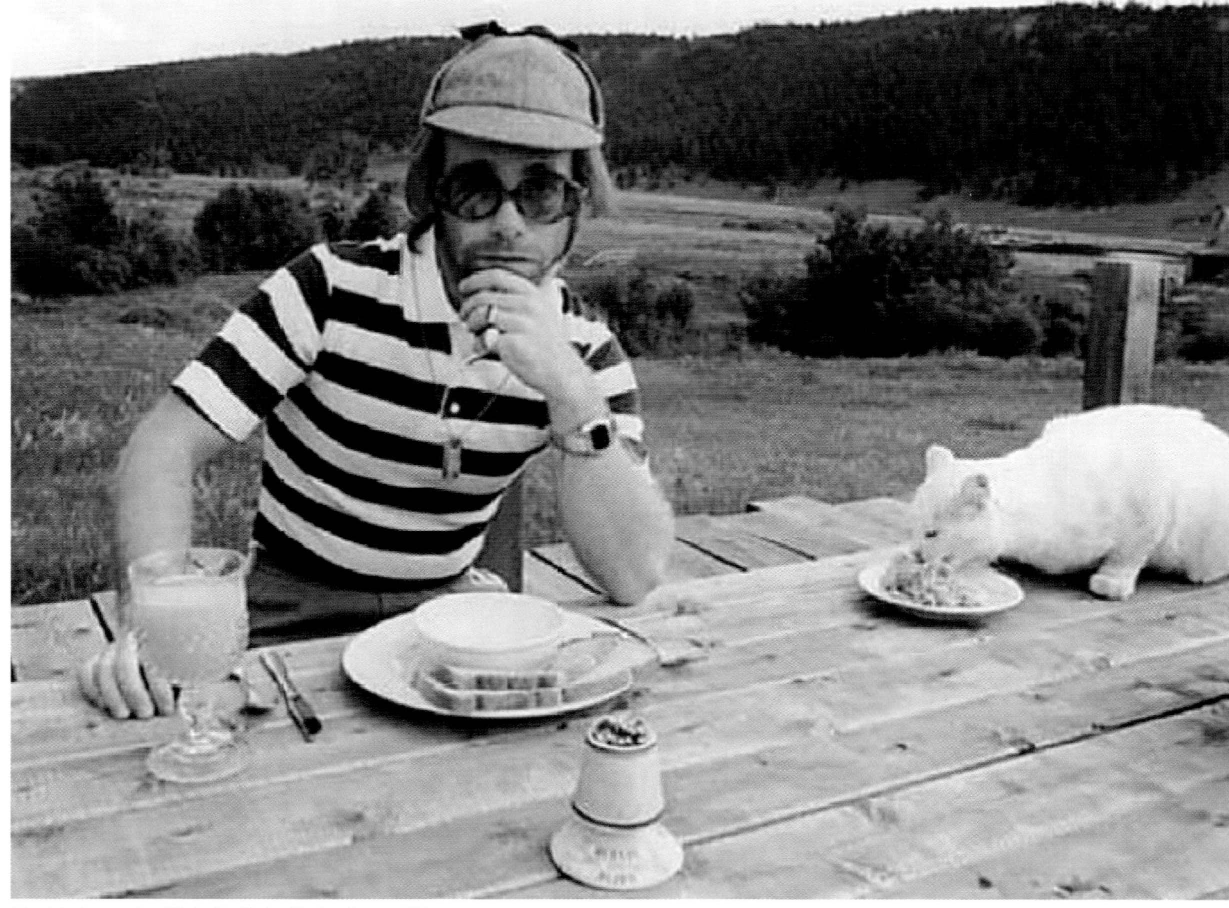

John during the recording of *Rock of the Westies* at Caribou Ranch, c. 1974

The studio was the main lure, but the lodging was equally seductive. The cabins, which slept up to 36 people, featured brass beds, lace curtains, leather-upholstered furniture, huge rock fireplaces, hardwood floors, dark cedar walls and massive stereo systems. Steinway baby grand pianos lurked in the corners of several cabins.

To while away the off-hours, there was a comprehensive library of movies and games, an antique pool table, horseback riding or skimobiling. A staff of friendly cooks remained on call 24 hours a day to prepare any snack or meal that came to mind. And every evening, there was a sit-down dinner with candlelight and wine.

What appealed most to Caribou clientele was the insulation from the usual rock 'n' roll circus. There wasn't a nightclub down the street, and artists didn't have to send for food or commute back and forth from a hotel or even worry about the laundry.

Record companies were only too willing to shell out the money during their boom years. Caribou gained additional prominence when Elton John recorded the gratefully titled *Caribou*

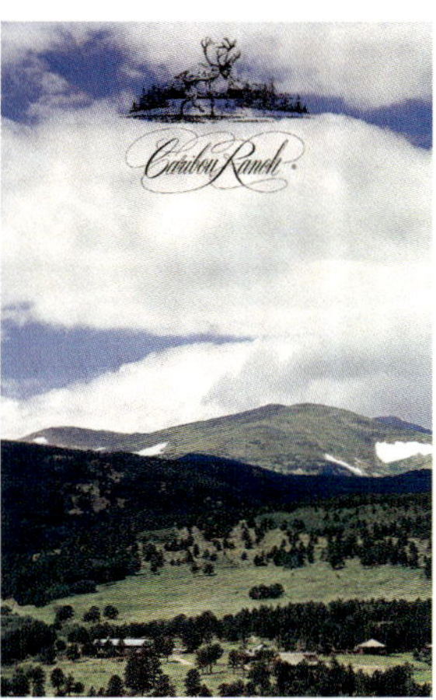

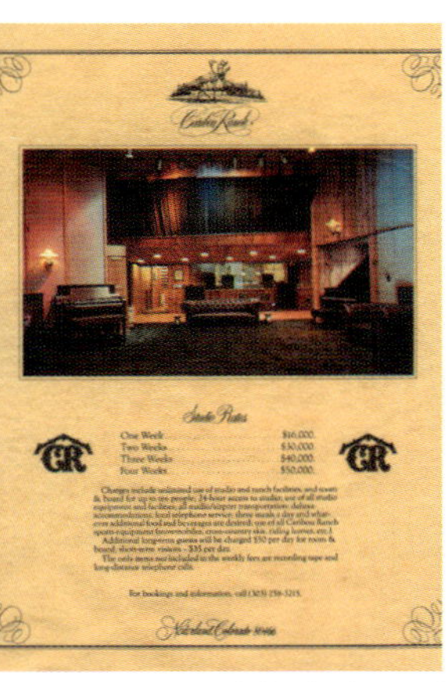

Caribou Ranch rate card

in the spring of 1974.

"It really is luxurious," John raved. "The only thing you have to get used to is that it's so high up, you keep gasping for breath all the time."

Each of John's first eight studio albums had been made in Europe. The flamboyant star, always on the go, was in the middle of another of his traumatic periods because of the rigors of his commitments. Although many of his early albums were recorded quickly, the making of *Caribou* was particularly stressful, squeezed into the smallest time frame yet.

"We were under unbelievable pressure to finish the album in just over a week because we had to go right into a tour of Japan and Australia," he said. "We wrote and recorded *Caribou* in eight days—14 tracks in all."

Caribou topped the album chart on both sides of the Atlantic, remaining in the *Billboard* Top 200 albums chart for over a year. It spawned John's fourth million-selling single in eight months, "Don't Let the Sun Go Down on Me." The emotional ballad became a classic, yet it was the most troublesome track.

"I thought it was the worst vocal of all time," John said. "I said, 'I hate it, so don't you dare put this on the album.'"

John recorded several other classic albums at Caribou Ranch, including *Captain Fantastic and the Brown Dirt Cowboy* and *Rock of the Westies*, which reached the No. 1 spot on the charts its first week out.

Lyricist Bernie Taupin, the celebrated collaborator who put the words in John's mouth for three decades, said, "Some of my favorite work that we ever created was done at Caribou. *Captain Fantastic* is one of our finest records, and probably the most underestimated of our career.

"Oddly enough, it wasn't a particularly good point in my life. We were pretty wacked out in those days. I don't know where there was more 'snow,' in the mountains or in the cabins!

"But there were some great moments, like having Stevie Wonder drive me in a Jeep from the cabin to the studio. I think he set me up—he probably practiced it with somebody else. The funny thing was, I didn't pay any attention to it—a blind man driving didn't faze me at all!

"And spending time with John Lennon doing 'Lucy in the Sky with Diamonds'..."

John had suggested Lennon stop in Colorado on his way back from a trip to California. The session took place at Caribou Ranch in July 1974, with Lennon's contribution billed as "the reggae guitars of Dr. Winston O'Boogie."

John's smash "Philadelphia Freedom" was inspired by one of his bouts of fan worship. The World Tennis League was started in 1974, and he was an ardent supporter of Billie Jean King's team, the Philadelphia Freedoms.

"We had the playoffs in Denver," the tennis great said. "Elton came because he'd been recording up at Caribou. He was all excited, saying, 'You've got to listen to this tape. This is it, the song I wrote for you.' So he played me a rough mix of 'Philadelphia Freedom,' and it was great. And when he got to the chorus he said, 'Listen to this part. Hear the beat? That's when you get mad on the court.'"

"Philadelphia Freedom" took just five weeks to become John's fourth No. 1 single.

In August of 1975, Elton John joined the Rolling Stones onstage in Fort Collins, dressed in a cowboy hat and a Los Angeles Dodgers windbreaker. He wanted to give a barbeque for the Stones at Caribou, but after the show, the Stones turned down his offer.

A veritable who's who of rock music's elite passed through Caribou Ranch's gates—America, Jeff Beck, Rick Derringer, Earth, Wind & Fire, Dan Fogelberg, Michael Murphey, Chicago, the Souther-Hillman-Furay Band, Rod Stewart, Stephen Stills, War, Frank Zappa, the Nitty Gritty Dirt Band, Joe Walsh, Eddie Rabbitt, Sheena Easton and more. Supertramp's crew dragged a grand piano up to Caribou on a snowy mountain top to photograph the *Even in the Quietest Moments...* album cover.

Ultimately, other studios cropped up around the world that offered similarly exotic atmospheres—refurbished medieval castles in Europe, complexes in the middle of the Caribbean—and the "in" place to record among top bands shifted. Caribou stayed busy, but when boom turned to bust, labels scaled back recording budgets and expensive destination studios fell out of favor.

Caribou finally shut down after a March 1985 fire destroyed the control room, causing about $3 million worth of damage. Guercio donated the remaining equipment to the University of Colorado-Denver in 1986 and shifted his interests away from music. ●

IN MAY 1975, under producer Jim Guercio's direction, Chicago teamed up with the Beach Boys in one of the most successful tours in rock history—a 12-city odyssey that grossed $7.5 million and played to a total of more than 700,000, despite a general recession that had hit the rest of the music business hard.

Guercio had gotten his start producing a string of hits for the Buckinghams circa 1967, including "Kind of a Drag," "Don't You Care" and "Mercy, Mercy, Mercy." He became a staff producer for Columbia Records and began working with Blood, Sweat & Tears and Chicago.

Through five albums with Chicago, Guercio gathered up enough money to own Caribou Ranch near Nederland, Colorado.

"We were still recording in New York," keyboardist Robert Lamm said. "Guercio said, 'I think it would be a smart idea for us to find a place where we could go and make music, and we wouldn't have to deal with hotels and taxis and studio time. We could work any time we want for as long as we want.'

"We looked at footage of properties; he had people looking for him. We made the move to Caribou. It was a big financial commitment on Jim's part."

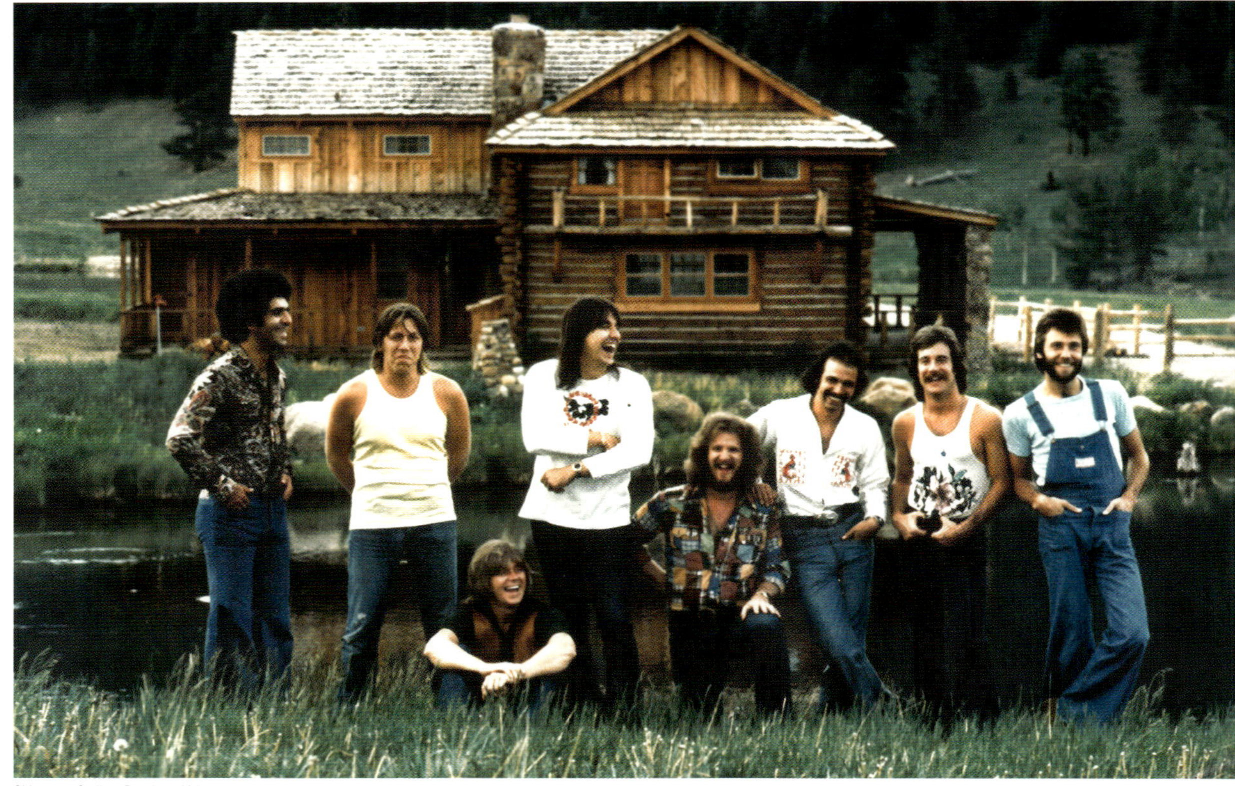

Chicago at Caribou Ranch, c. 1975

"It was a climate where you could get away from any influence or distraction that would take away from creativity. It would result in new fits of inspiration and make for better art, supposedly," Chicago trumpeter Lee Loughnane recalled. "And it worked for quite a while."

In 1973, the year Caribou Ranch opened, Chicago filmed a network television special there, *Chicago: High in the Rockies*. A second TV special, *Meanwhile, Back at the Ranch*, aired in 1974. That same year, Chicago met the Beach Boys at Denver's Stapleton Airport.

"They had come into town to do a show. We started talking at the luggage carousel and we wound up inviting them to the studio," Lamm said. "Peter Cetera was putting down a track for 'Wishing You Were Here,' and he had always envisioned having the Beach Boys' vocals on that record. Bang, there they were at the ranch. Three of them sang on that hit.

"I looked at Carl (Wilson) and said it would be nice to do something with the two bands in concert. It was like Mickey Rooney and Judy Garland saying, 'Let's put on a show! My dad's got a barn!' The light bulbs went off over everybody's heads. In that era, as today, everybody wanted to be a headliner. There weren't many times when a couple of superbands would get together to do something."

The Beach Boys had battled over their live show in the early 1970s, with Carl Wilson insisting that a constant updating was necessary, and Mike Love fighting to give the people what they seemed to desire desperately—an in-concert jukebox. The conflict became academic. In June 1974, Capitol Records released *Endless Summer*, a two-record set of early hits, and *Spirit of America* followed the next year. The collections sold in the millions.

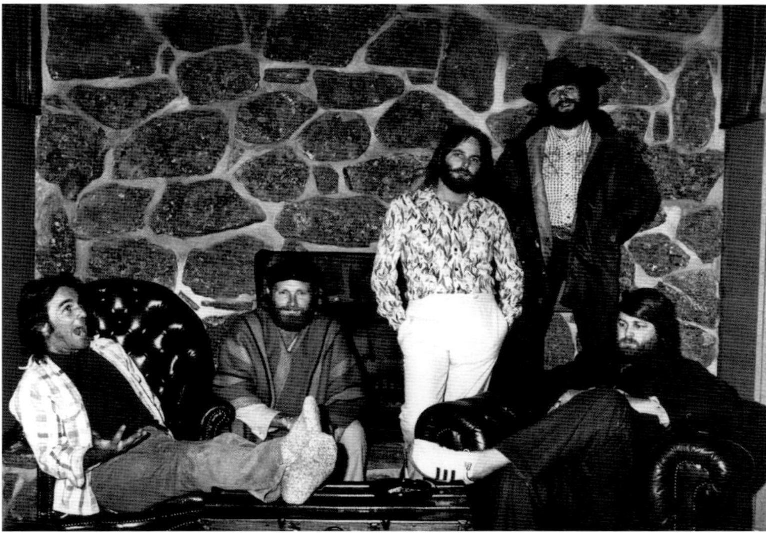

The Beach Boys at Caribou Ranch, c. 1975

The Beach Boys were forced to admit that their only future was in their past, and Guercio played an important role as they made that transition. He quickly moved up the ranks into a full managerial position. His company, Caribou, was officially named as the Beach Boys' management arm, and Caribou Records the band's label. He did double-duty, playing bass with them on the tour and whipping the road band into shape.

"That tour was our comeback," Wilson said.

The two bands appeared in a sold-out show at Fort Collins' Hughes Stadium.

"We flew up to Colorado State University in our private plane," Loughnane said. "I was getting ready in the dressing room, and all of a sudden I heard this 'tea bag' voice saying, 'I say, chaps, how are you?'"

And there was Elton John.

"He'd been at Caribou; he'd heard about the gig," Lamm said. "I told him to hop on stage during the encore. The show was one of those that worked from the get-go. Then Elton jumped up, played a little piano, banged a lot of tambourine, did a lot of singing and smiling. It was one of those magical moments. Everybody who was there got their money's worth."

It seemed almost miraculous that within a year the Beach Boys were back on top, grossing as much money without any newly recorded product as they had in their heyday. But Guercio and Caribou Management didn't stay with them for long. The following spring, he was released from his business responsibilities with the Beach Boys.

Chicago's situation with Guercio also had been deteriorating, and the band members eventually eliminated their dealings with him in 1977.

"We had five years of incredible success. Along with that success came problems of adjusting to a crazy rock star lifestyle. I don't know that we did a very good job of it on a personal level," Lamm said. "We were not ready to look inward to see what else was in there, as the Caribou situation should have encouraged—being out there thinking about what was important and having that come through the music. A number of us weren't ready for that—we wanted to party. We were in our mid- to late 20s. We were interested in coming down to Boulder to chase girls."

"Caribou Ranch was the beginning of the end," Loughnane said. "Jimmy presented it to us as a band investment, and we said, 'Okay, we'll take a pass at it.' But I think he had it in mind that he'd buy it and control it. We had some successful albums out of the studio. There was nothing wrong until we wanted to square up with Jim.

"Well, there was one other thing. We discovered if you stayed too long at Caribou, you got a little buggy. You'd find yourself hiding out in the woods with an elk shirt on." ●

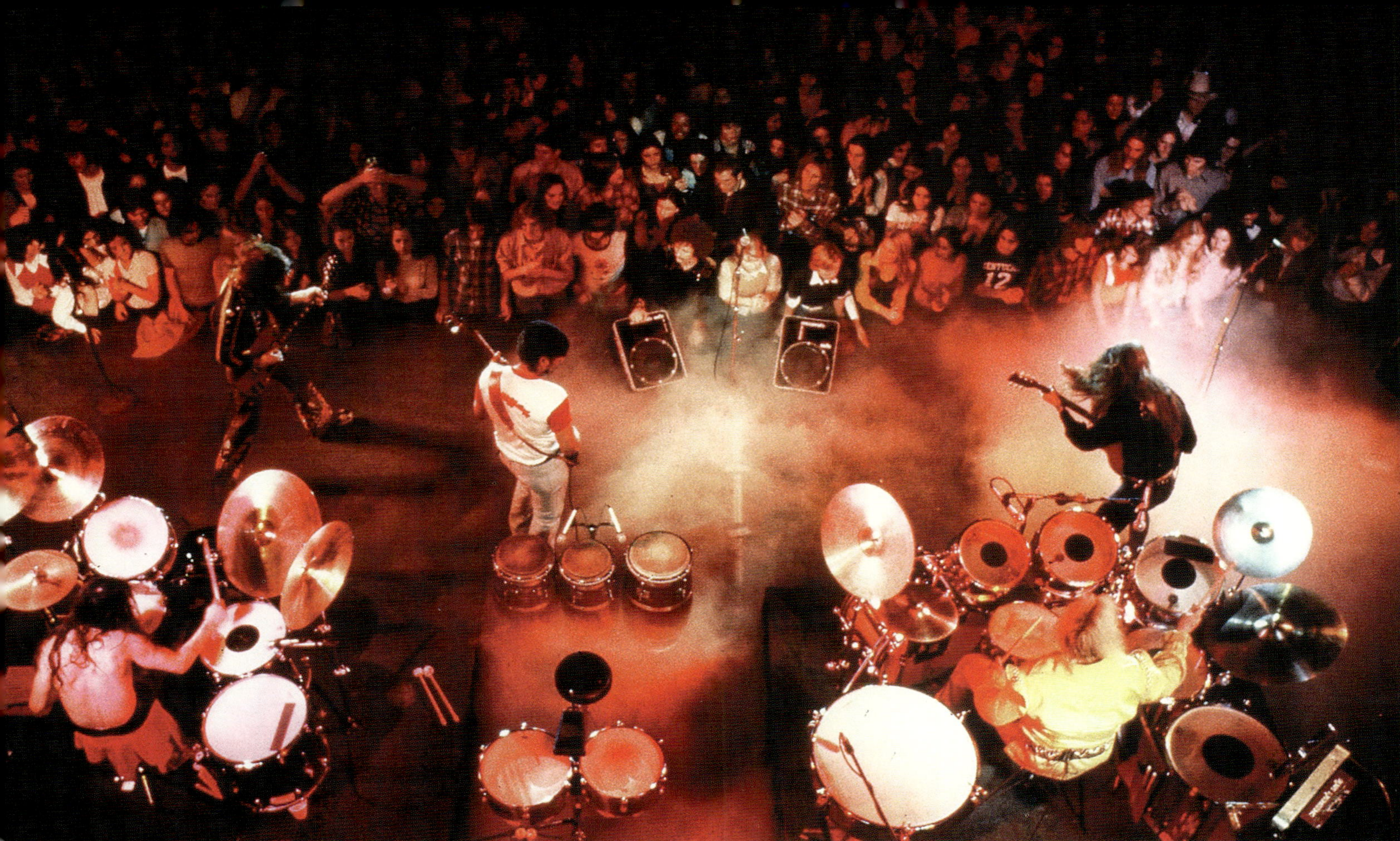

Cover photo by Dan Fong for *What Were Once Vices Are Now Habits*

THE DOOBIE BROTHERS }

THE DOOBIE Brothers' numerous hits collectively formed one of the most impressive repertoires of any American band. Their legendary 1970s shows were marked by the percussive thrust of dual drummers, a full arsenal of guitar chops and the patented Doobies harmonies. The band cited a number of ties to Colorado, the only state where they headlined stadium shows twice—at Folsom Field in Boulder in 1975 and 1979.

Marty Wolff, the group's longtime lighting director, was a Denver/Boulder concert promoter in the early 1970s. Through Wolff's Star Lighting, many Colorado denizens were part of the Doobies' heyday, including Chas Barbour (the graphic designer behind the *What Were Once Vices Are Now Habits* album), Dan Fong (the official photographer/media coordinator) and former concert promoter Doug Brunkow.

And percussionist Bobby LaKind once lived in Boulder and managed the Tulagi nightclub (where the Doobies performed in 1971). LaKind, who originally signed on as a member of the Doobies' lighting crew, became a full-time member after the release of the *One Step Closer* album. His congas and percussion graced every Doobie release and tour from 1976 until the band broke up in 1982.

"He was bouncing around the local scene in Colorado and became one of the crew," drummer and founding member John Hartman said. "We had pyrotechnics when we were out on the road. He had a mishap setting up before a show, and fireworks blew up in his face. We felt sorry for him, so we paid attention to the little guy and he edged in. He could play congas and sing a little bit, so we added another guy to the percussion team."

LaKind died of inoperable colon cancer on Christmas Eve 1992 at age 47. ●

TED NUGENT }

WORKING THE arena circuit in the 1970s, Ted Nugent's act couldn't be ignored. The self-styled "wild man of rock" was a carnivorous, hysterical showman—a noble savage sporting a loincloth, shaking torrents of dirty-blonde hair and wielding a massive hollow-body Gibson like it was a shotgun.

His demeanor was inspired not by drugs, he said, but by blood lust. His skills with rifle and bow and arrow became legendary. His first two solo albums, *Call of the Wild* and *Tooth, Fang and Claw*, were indicative of his highly-publicized passion.

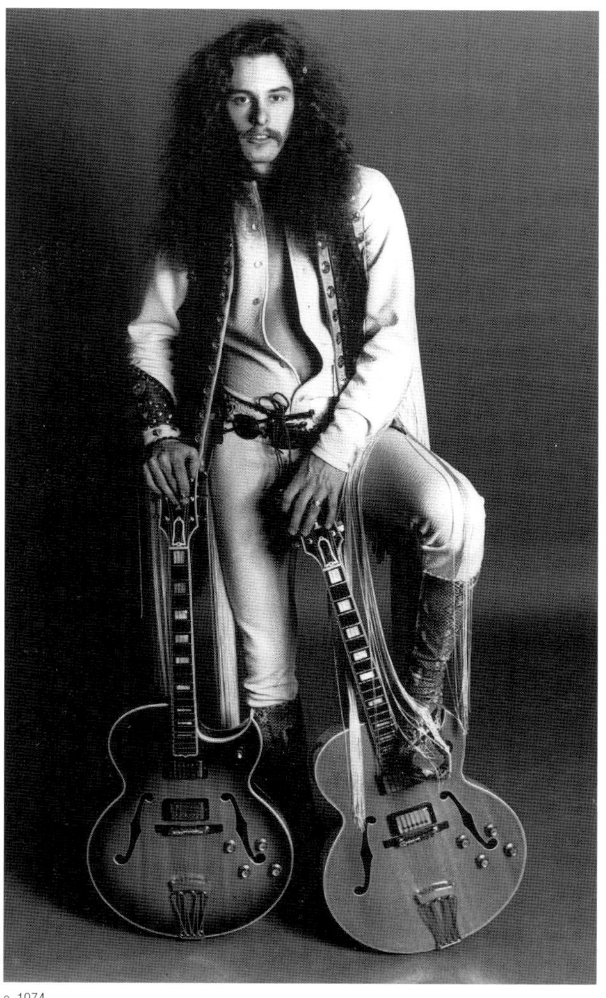

c. 1974

"There's no question that it was my experience in the Rocky Mountains that brought about those album titles and songs like 'Great White Buffalo.' They come from camps on Colorado's western slope, the Grand Mesa and Uncompaghre," he recalled.

In 1975, Nugent bagged his first whitetail buck with the bow and arrow outside of Grand Junction.

"I'll never forget it. I was long overdue. So far as I could tell, my success rate was one deer per 1,000 hours of hunting. Something had to change.

"October 10. The conditions were my favorite—misty, wet, dark and stalky, with a steady east wind. Deer-hunting weather!

"In the fog I could see shapes in the field approaching. A larger deer brought up the rear. Now I could see antler.

"My arrow was nocked, and I was cocked, locked, and ready to rock, Doc, as he moved perfectly broadside. Instinctively, I anchored and released. The aluminum arrow arched the 40 yards—smack-o, whack-o, right behind the shoulder. He went 100 yards and over he goes. Bingo! Still! Don't ask me why, but I immediately sat down and stared at him lying over there in a heap. Goofy. Then I picked up the blood trail and peeked at him, then the blood, then him, then the blood! I guess my psyche just wasn't accepting the scene yet. Halfway to him I figured, 'What the hell am I doing? He's dead, Nuge—go get him!'

"I charged over, knowing only that I saw headgear when I shot. I grabbed his rack and counted 12 points and thought I was going to die. A 12-pointer! Holy guacamole! Eight points with four-inch kickers. A buck! Dead! Mine! Oh, the glory of it all. I be-bopped all the way home in nothing flat. I called my dad, uncle, brothers, buddies and neighbors. They all thought I was nuts. It was wonderful. It's always wonderful. I strapped that beautiful animal to the top of my truck and showed him off to everybody.

"That was hundreds of deer ago, and that Colorado connection is still powerful today. I come back in the fall for hunting season and go just as nuts. I can hunt in the swamps of my native Michigan, but there's no comparison to mountain time. It's always a thrill." ●

KATY MOFFATT }

FOR MOST of the 1970s, Katy Moffatt was a fixture in the Denver folk music scene, playing clubs and small rock venues and spending countless hours at musicians' haunts like the Denver Folklore Center.

"I consider myself to have grown up in Colorado," the Fort Worth, Texas, native said. "I went through so many major life-changing experiences there."

Moffatt's skills as a songwriter and performer initially brought her to Austin, where cowboy hippies first began to turn redneck heads around with their progressive outlaw brand of country music.

After her act with another female singer split up, Moffatt headed for the Colorado mountains, hoping to find fame in Boulder. Late at night, she took a wrong turn and ended up in Denver, alone and broke.

"I was literally living on the streets, trying to get gigs. And there was no interest from anybody. But I was bound and determined to take care of myself, so I did odd jobs. I was a window washer in the dead of winter, a waitress, a factory worker—just about everything.

"The only reason that people latch on to my brief period in the Austin scene as a formative musical time is that Denver wasn't as heralded or widely known. But to my way of thinking, what was going on in the streets of Denver at that time, concurrent with Austin, was easily as fertile. It just wasn't as easily grasped because of its eclecticism. Peter McCabe, Randy Handley, Mary Flower, the bluegrass band Monroe Doctrine—it went on and on, so many great singers, songwriters, players and arrangers who were all young and just coming up. We all knew each other and played together. It was a genuine scene."

After a year and a half of "scrounging in bars," Moffatt eventually met Chuck Morris, who co-owned and managed the Ebbets Field nightclub in downtown Denver. Morris secured a meeting with CBS Records A&R vice-president Billy Sherrill, who had produced over a hundred gold records.

Sherrill signed Moffatt to a multi-record deal in 1975, saying, "Katy Moffatt has got the best pipes since Tammy Wynette." It was Sherrill who discovered Wynette, and he co-wrote and produced the country classic "Stand By Your Man" with her.

Sherrill brought Moffatt to Nashville to personally supervise the recording of her first album, entitled *Katy*. Her first single, the self-penned ballad "I Can Almost See Houston from Here," climbed the country charts and sold well in the western states. But the album was a commercial flop, and Moffatt was pushed into turning out product. She completed three albums for Columbia, yet only two were released. The commercially slanted albums won rave notices, but the ever-eclectic Moffatt found herself found herself caught in the crossfire between the country and pop divisions of a large record company.

Labels, female stereotypes, marketing problems and studio pressures, coupled with Moffatt's confusion in finding her musical direction, all contributed to stunting her career.

"Boy, did I learn some lessons in a hurry," Moffatt said. "The timing was great—labels were signing everybody with a guitar, and underground FM stations were breaking new talent every day. It should have been a perfect situation, but something went terribly wrong with the business."

After living in Los Angeles and having endured the music business grind, Moffatt eventually won a loyal fan base with her acoustic folk-country style and her pure, sparkling voice. She never stayed within a recognizable style long enough to become a star, but she made a living and enjoyed a career marked by consistent critical acclaim, industry appreciation, movie appearances and songs being covered.

"My career has been sort of backwards," Moffatt admitted. "Early on, I had the big label throwing money around and the heavily greased agents and lawyers. But it all had to break down so I could learn what I had to do to survive as an artist." ●

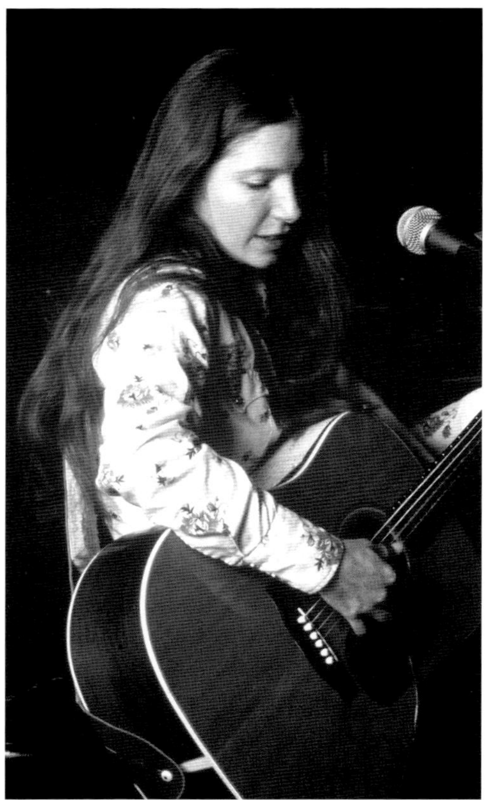

c. 1976

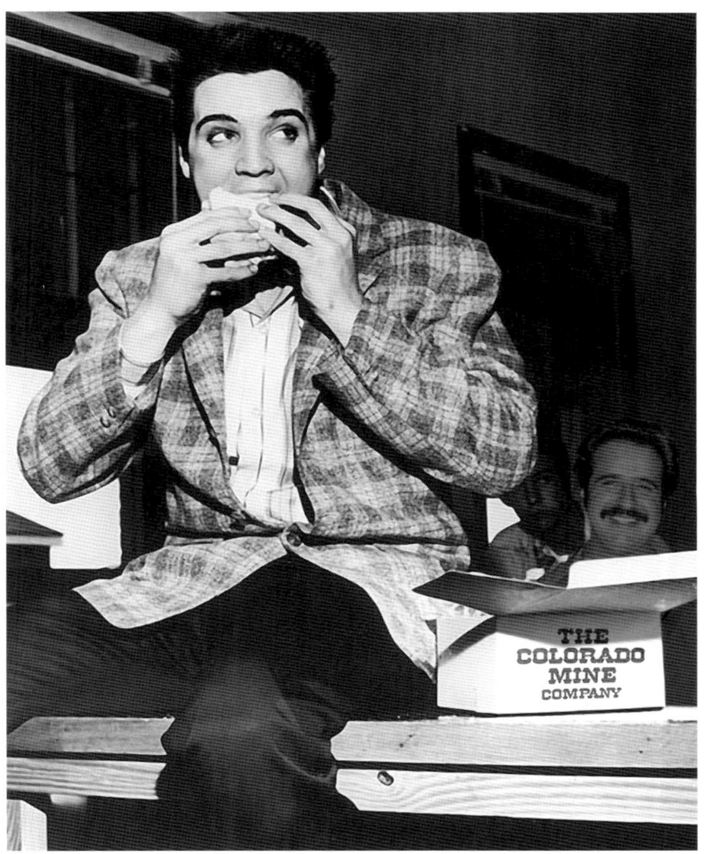

Presley and the Fool's Gold Loaf, 1976

ELVIS PRESLEY }

THE DIETARY needs of Elvis Presley made his other pursuits appear tame. "The King" once flew from Memphis to Denver to fetch a concoction from the now-defunct Colorado Mine Company restaurant in the suburb of Glendale. It was a house specialty he had sampled only once after a concert and apparently couldn't find anywhere else—the Fool's Gold Loaf, a particularly sumptuous feast.

The main ingredients? One loaf of sourdough bread, smeared with butter and tossed into an oven at 350 degrees, and one pound of lean bacon, fried until crisp and drained on paper towels. After 15 minutes, the loaf was removed from the oven and sliced lengthwise. The interior of each half was hollowed out, the insides were filled with one large jar of smooth peanut butter and one large jar of blueberry preserves. The bacon slices were added, and the loaf was closed. The cost was $37.95 per sandwich—hence the name.

In December 1975, Presley decided to leave the lonely confines of Graceland, his mansion in Memphis, for the holidays and his 41st birthday (January 8, 1976). He took Linda Thomson, his girlfriend, and several of his "boys" to Vail, Colorado, to celebrate.

"He flew in on his jet, and we rented a Trailways bus," Captain Jerry Kennedy, head of the Denver vice squad, said. "We sang Christmas carols on the way up. We took off work for ten days; we got him lodging and ski outfits."

Kennedy obtained permission to use the ski slopes at night, and Elvis and his entourage rented snowmobiles for noisy 3 a.m. rides through the woods.

Shortly after the holiday revelry, Presley went on a legendary car-buying binge. Wearing a white woolen ski mask and bulky snowsuit, he visited Kumpf Motors, a luxury automobile showroom in Denver, arriving three hours after closing time with a large party. He told three in the group—Kennedy; Detective Ron Pietrofeso, who had been Elvis' police guard during concerts in Denver months before; and Dr. Gerald Starky, a police physician—to pick out the cars they wanted.

Presley purchased a top-of-the-line Lincoln Mark IV for Kennedy and Cadillacs for Pietrofeso and Starky. The $13,000 cars were his way of saying thank you.

Kennedy had known the King since 1969. "I was the off-duty work coordinator, and he had a concert at the Denver Coliseum," Kennedy said. "He stayed at the Radisson Hotel and had the whole 10th floor. We had to keep the girls out.

"Elvis came out of his room, and he was very friendly. He liked policemen. Elvis and I struck up something of a friendship. He felt like he was part of the Denver Police."

And the force treated Elvis accordingly. He owned an officer's uniform that he wore on visits to the Mile High City and was given an honorary Denver police captain's credential.

Watching the morning news the day after the car-purchasing spree, Elvis saw local anchorman Don Kinney quip that he wouldn't mind getting a car, too. The King had a new Cadillac delivered to the station the following day and then went home to Graceland.

"He was generous to a fault," Kennedy said. "He ended up purchasing a dozen vehicles in Denver. If he gave something to one person, he had to give it to somebody else, too." ●

1976-1987

IN THE late 1970s, the music biz was flush with cash and excess. Guitarist Tommy Bolin, a prodigy of the burgeoning music scene in Denver and Boulder, was another casualty of the rock 'n' roll lifestyle. People danced to disco music in nightclubs that played records instead of using live music, but Denver's Rainbow Music Hall, a 1,300-seat venue, became a prime concert destination for a slew of iconic acts after opening in 1979. The "newgrass" genre was being created by a generation of young musicians—Sam Bush and New Grass Revival, John Hartford, Peter Rowan, Tim O'Brien—who loved both traditional bluegrass and the rock music of their peers; they came together in the beauty of the Colorado mountains for the party and legendary musical ferment that endured as the Telluride Bluegrass Festival.

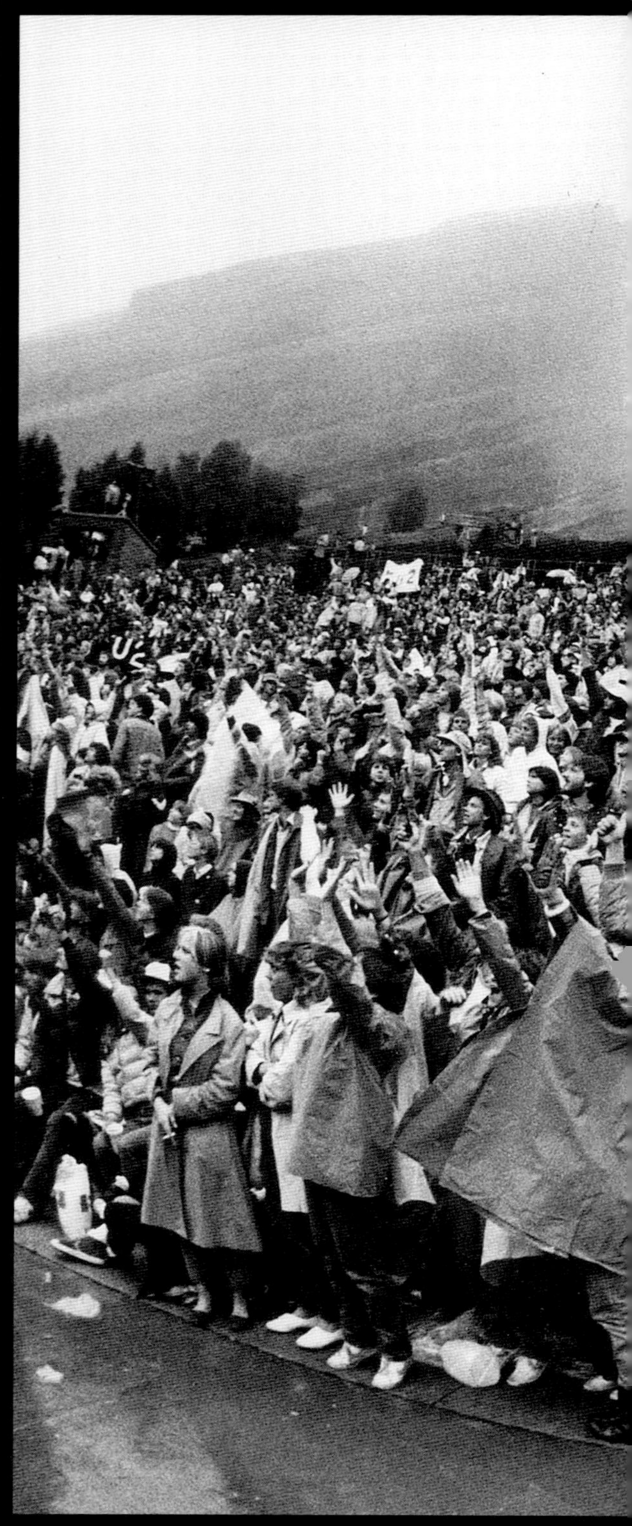

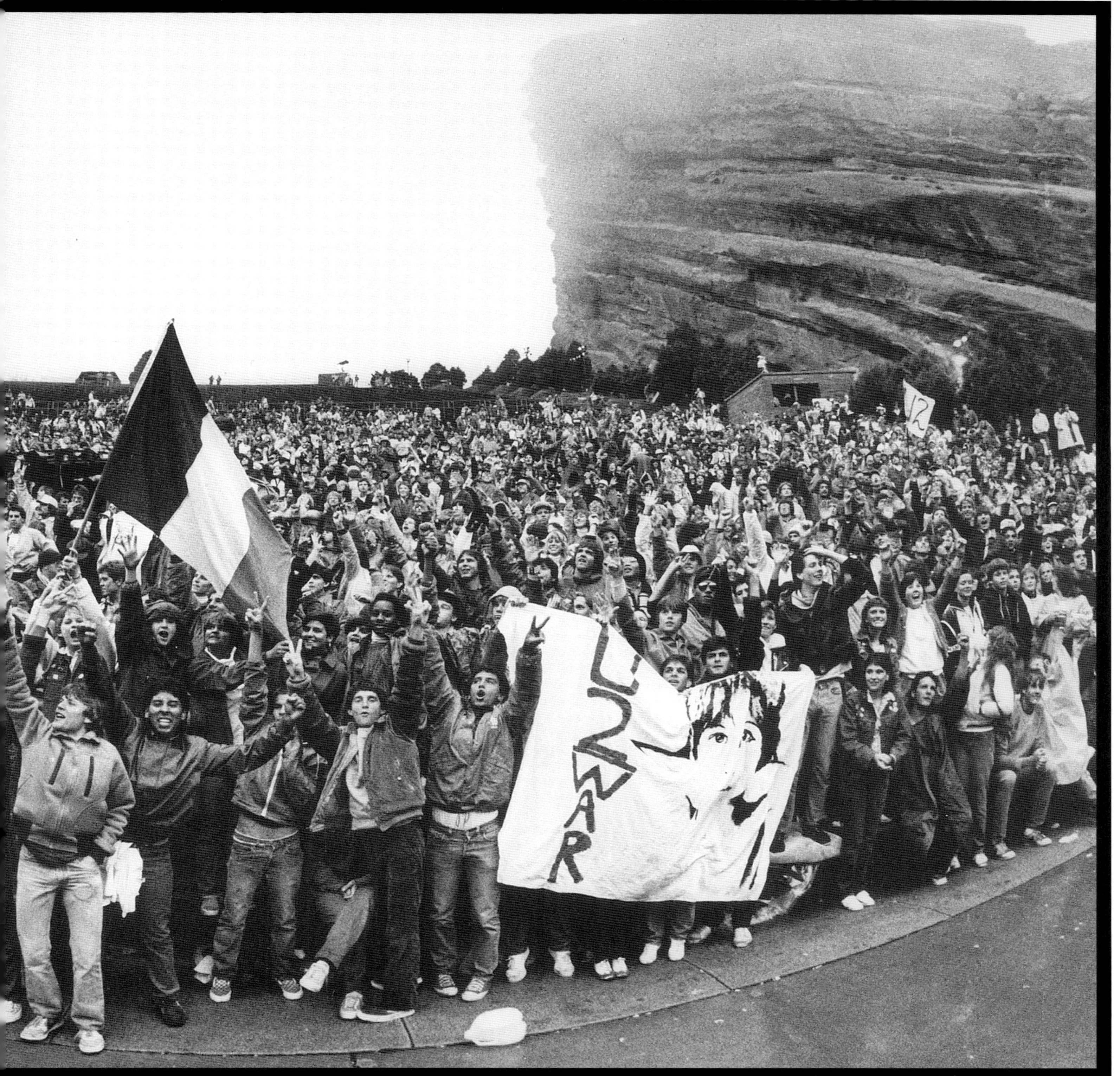

Rain-soaked fans at U2's legendary *Under a Blood Red Sky* concert at Red Rocks Amphitheatre, 1983

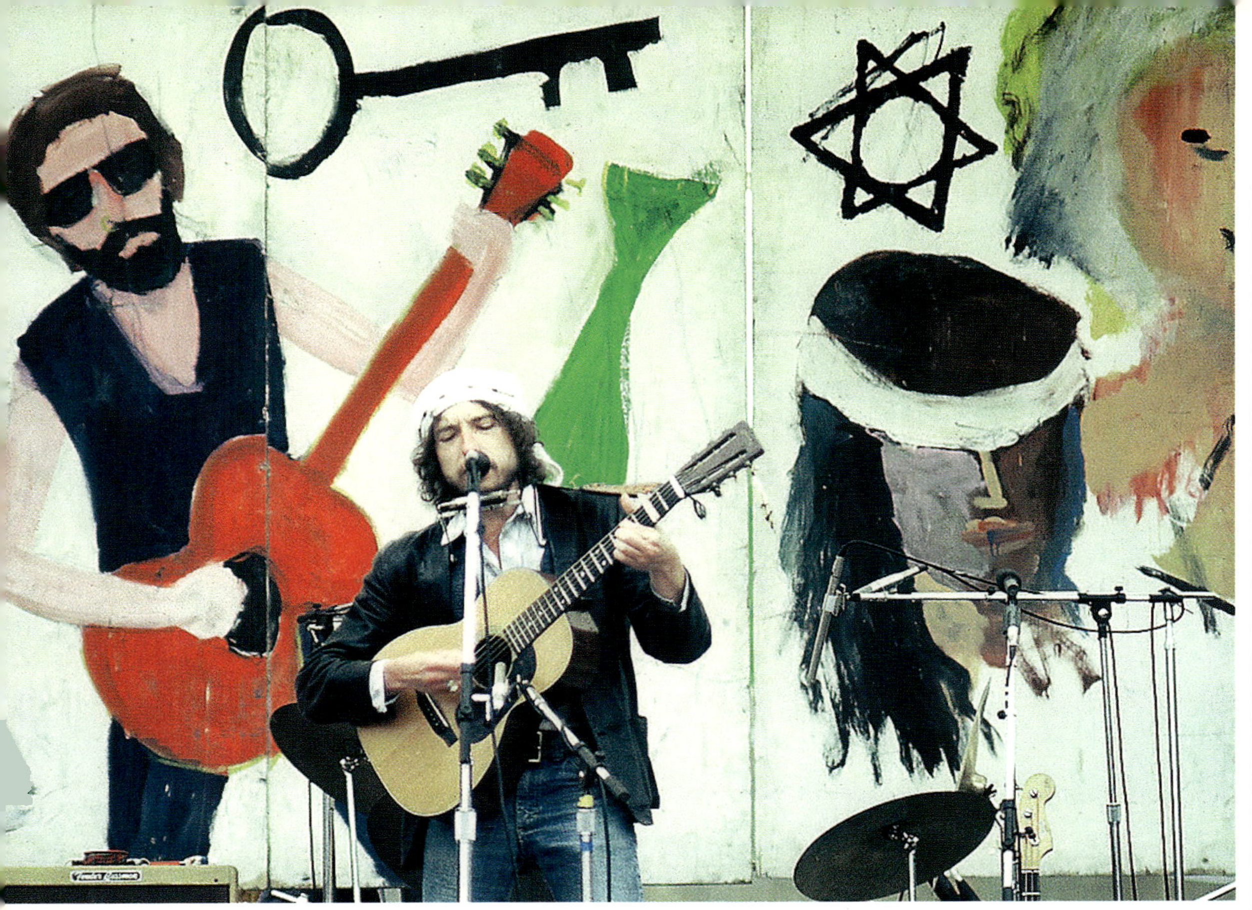

Dylan in Fort Collins, May 23, 1976

BOB DYLAN }

AT 18 YEARS of age, still lacking any real direction and learning his craft, Bob Dylan was essentially a scrawny kid trying to be a folk singer. He arrived in Denver in the summer of 1960 and wandered over to the Satire Lounge on Colfax Avenue to play some Woody Guthrie music. Then he was offered his first job as a professional entertainer at the Gilded Garter, a honky-tonk palace in Central City, a restored frontier town that had become a Colorado tourist attraction, complete with saloons and bad-guy actors with Western outfits and blanks in their six-shooters. His experience lasted for a week and a half.

15 years later, Dylan was once again an ascending star after spending the late 1960s and early 1970s refusing to behave like the counterculture hero that the previous decade had made him. The next logical step was to hit the road, but little about the ensuing tour followed any logic.

The Rolling Thunder Revue embarked in October 1975 with the idea of a communal tour. Rather than playing formal concerts at large rooms and coliseums, Dylan assembled a loosely knit group of merry old friends. The large, shifting entourage—including Joan Baez and such Greenwich Village regulars as Ramblin' Jack Elliott and Bobby Neuwirth and guests Allen Ginsberg, Joni Mitchell, Mick Ronson, Roger McGuinn and Arlo Guthrie—toured until spring 1976.

The Rolling Thunder Revue started out with surprise concerts at small halls and worked up to outdoor stadiums. Dylan and his production taped a show in Clearwater, Florida, and the program was auctioned off to NBC-TV after being offered to all three networks. A few weeks later, Dylan then rejected the tape. Instead, he gave his nod to a group of documentary makers who filmed the May 23 concert under cloudy skies at Colorado State University in Fort Collins. 25,000 fans were drenched by rain.

The footage of the Colorado concert, appropriately titled *Hard Rain*, was broadcast on NBC in September. Most mainstream TV critics panned the show. That month also saw the release of the live *Hard Rain* album, which consisted of nine songs, four of which came from Dylan's TV special; it was certified gold.

While Dylanologists considered other concerts superior, Dylan remained unrepentant. "I don't really talk about what I do," Dylan said to *TV Guide*. "I just try to be poetically and musically straight. I think of myself as more than a musician, more than a poet. The real self is something other than that. Writing and performing is what I do in this life and in this country. But I could be happy being a blacksmith. I would still write and sing. I can't imagine not doing that. You do what you're geared for." ●

BILLY JOEL }

WITH "PIANO Man," Billy Joel notched his first chart hit in 1974. But, as he later explained, "My career was neither here nor there at that time."

For 1976's *Turnstiles*, his third album, the piano man from Hicksville, Long Island, put together top-notch material, the major consequence of returning home to New York City from California (as reflected in the song "Say Goodbye to Hollywood").

Yet it took a long time getting the project off the ground. Jim Guercio, the producer for brass-rock bands such as Chicago, the Buckinghams and Blood, Sweat & Tears, began working with Joel. He wanted to use drummer Nigel Olsson and bassist Dee Murray, both part of Elton John's band.

"Guercio, who I later became a good friend with, had an idea—'Aha, Billy Joel, piano player!' Joel remembered. "I didn't think it was a good idea. I said, 'No, no, I'm not Elton John. I'm Billy Joel.'"

Still, Joel tried that lineup for two months, without satisfactory results.

"I was not a big entity at Columbia Records. I'd had a modest hit with 'Piano Man,' but that was it. So I said, 'I'll give it a shot,' and I cut a couple of tracks. It was awful."

Joel introduced the seemingly novel idea of recording his regular band. Ultimately, he headed to Long Island with his own guys and produced *Turnstiles* himself.

"I had played the Village, a few clubs here and there," he explained. "With the *Turnstiles* album, I put my own band together. They knew the music cold."

The basic tracks were done in New York, but most of the vocals, the overdubs, the mixing and the production were done at Guercio's Caribou Ranch in Colorado.

"I flew in the face of the commercially successful machine, because I ended up leaving Guercio and Caribou Management and producing my own album," Joel said. "Which in a way sealed my fate corporately. I can't tell you that I produced it any better than it could have been produced, but it was the first time I got to work with my own road musicians."

The first ten days of April 1976, Joel played his first gigs with the band, at the Good Earth, a Boulder nightclub on the third floor of a building on what became the Pearl Street Mall.

"While we were at Caribou Ranch, it was time to start playing live," Joel said. "What I remember about Boulder is a lot of Earth shoes and hippie hair.

"It was the first incarnation of the touring band that

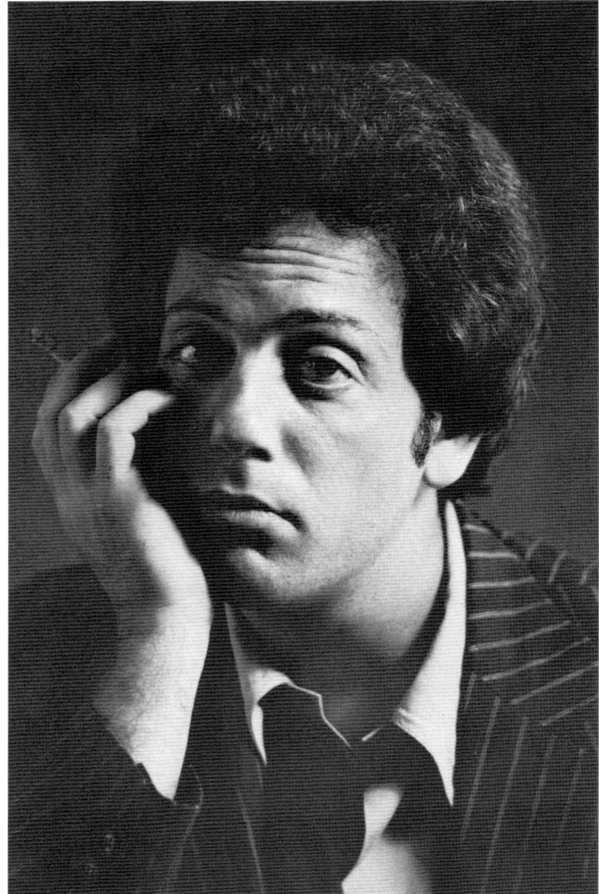

c. 1976

I would keep in place for 17 years. That was the jelling of that particular group of musicians. I'd had Liberty (DeVitto, drums) in place for some time. Doug (Stegmeyer, bass) was fairly new. Richie Cannata on sax, Russell Javors on guitar...it came together at the Good Earth. We started making our bones there."

Turnstiles was released in June 1976, and the success of "Say Goodbye to Hollywood" proved Joel's decision to self-produce to be right. Suddenly everyone was paying attention. *Turnstiles* peaked at #122 on the *Billboard* album charts.

"Guercio, being the gentleman that he is, came to me and said, 'You were right, I was wrong—good for you for sticking to your guns.'"

Then came a breakthrough with *The Stranger*, and a string of multi-platinum hits followed. Joel found himself at the summit of the pop heap.

"And you can trace our success as a touring and performing band back to the training ground of the Good Earth in Colorado." ●

CHRIS HILLMAN }

STAYING WITH the Byrds for four years and six seminal albums, Chris Hillman then departed with Gram Parsons to develop acoustic country sounds in a new band dubbed the Flying Burrito Brothers. He remained with the band until its demise in 1971. At that time, he was the only remaining original member.

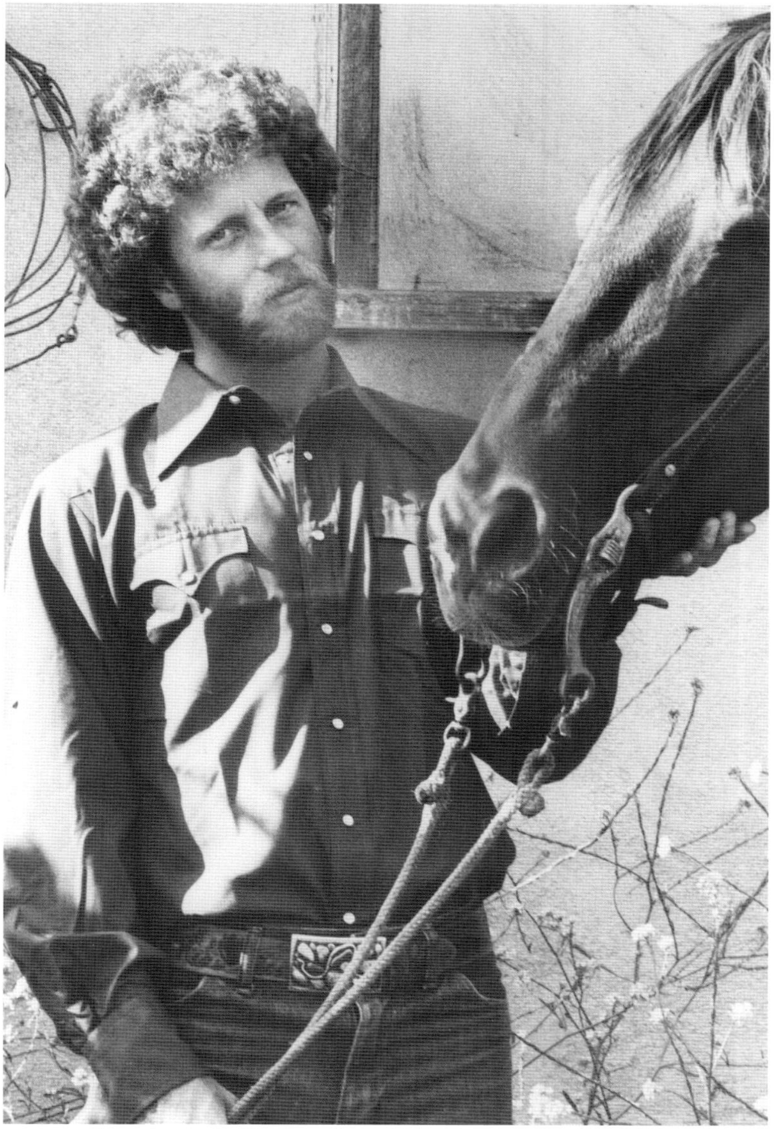

c. 1976

In 1972, Stephen Stills offered Hillman a partnership in the formation of Manassas, and he moved to Colorado. It seemed a comfortable solution to post-Burrito depression.

"Stills had showed up when the Burritos played at Tulagi in Boulder," Hillman said. "After the show, we went up to his real nice cabin in Gold Hill and hung out."

In Manassas, Hillman emerged as Stills' musical foil, collaborating in the writing and contributing vocals as well as instrumental versatility. When Manassas disbanded after two years of road work and two albums (which he co-produced), Hillman produced Rick Roberts' second solo album, *She Is a Song*. He then joined forces with J.D. Souther and Richie Furay in the Souther-Hillman-Furay Band. The group recorded two albums, the first earning a gold record, and toured nationally before splitting up in the summer of 1975.

Back in Colorado, Hillman prepared his first solo album, *Slippin' Away*, a summation of his rock, bluegrass and country roots, aided by old Burrito, Manassas and S-H-F pals. It peaked at #152 on the *Billboard* album chart in June 1976.

Amidst the recording of *Slippin' Away*, Hillman began to utilize his talents behind the board in the studio, producing the demo tapes which led to Firefall's contract and Dan McCorison's self-titled solo album.

"There were some good times in Boulder," Hillman said. "On the plus side, there was a lot of interesting music coming up. There were a couple of clubs that were fun to play, and I had a lot of fun working with people.

"Unfortunately, there was a very heavy negative lifestyle prevalent. Drugs all over the place—a lot of cocaine. I think there was a dealer on every corner. It affected me. It affected everybody. And some people died. It was very excessive. I think the '70s were a very strange time in the history of this country, but, boy, there was some bad stuff going on in Boulder then." ●

FIREFALL }

THE BOULDER scene's biggest success story, Firefall defined the "Colorado sound" of the 1970s. The group's soft-rock blend of country and pop landed six singles on the Top 40 from 1976 through 1981, including the Top 10 "You Are the Woman."

Firefall was founded by singer-songwriter Rick Roberts and former Zephyr guitarist Jock Bartley in the summer of 1974. Roberts was the itinerant young Florida folksinger-songwriter who'd served as the de facto spark of the "second edition" of the Flying Burrito Brothers from 1970 to 1972 (after Gram Parsons left the band) before undertaking his own career as a solo artist. He'd recorded a pair of albums under his own name.

For Bartley, the beginnings of Firefall marked another turning point in his career. He'd started as a student of jazz guitar great Johnny Smith, who had settled in Colorado Springs.

"From eight years old, I was taking lessons from a master," Bartley said of Smith, who wrote the instrumental classic "Walk Don't Run." "I wanted a little Sears red guitar, but Johnny said no. My first guitar was a 3/4-size Gibson. By the time I was 13, I was already pretty good. I was always the youngest guy in bands until I went to college in Boulder in 1968."

With a few band stints around the Denver/Boulder area under his belt, Bartley moved into Zephyr, taking over the lead guitar post of Tommy Bolin. In 1972, he switched over to Gram Parsons' band, the Fallen Angels (which also featured Emmylou Harris).

"After Zephyr broke up, I played with every drummer and bass player in town trying to get something going. I was paying rent by painting apartments," Bartley remembered.

"I got a call to come down to the Edison Electric Company—Boulder was the first date of Gram's tour. The guitar player wasn't any good. He was nervous and he got really drunk and the managers were backstage saying they might have to cancel the tour. And then I showed up. They invited me up to the Pioneer Inn in Nederland to sit in, the second night they played. They put me right next to the guy on the hot seat. At the end of the night, they took a vote. They said they needed three things—a good rhythm player, a rock soloist for songs like 'Six Days on the Road' and a good country picker. They looked at me, this

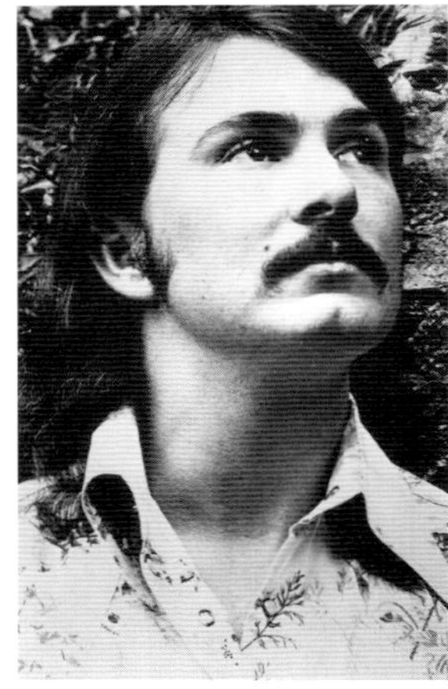

Rick Roberts, c. 1973

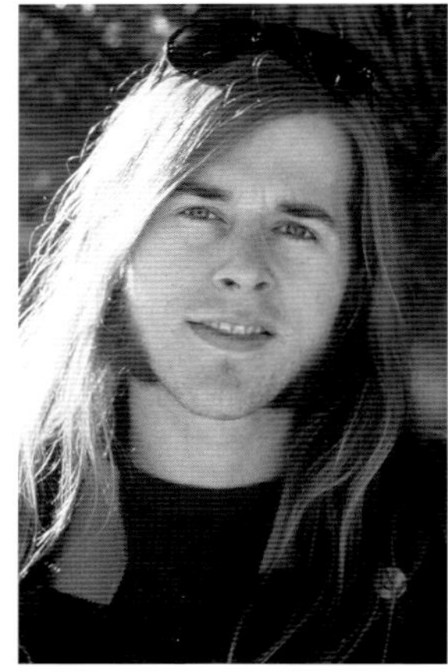

Jock Bartley, c. 1972

long-haired hippie guy, and said, 'Well, you can tell he's not a country player, but two out of three beats the guy we have—he's zero for three.' I got hired. I learned all the songs on the bus to Texas."

That year, Bartley first met Roberts, whose touring schedule with the Burritos often overlapped that of Parsons.

The third charter member of Firefall was another Colorado latecomer, Mark Andes. After four years as a founding member of Spirit, one of the most influential Los Angeles combos of the late 1960s, he and Spirit's lead vocalist Jay Ferguson formed Jo Jo Gunne. When that hard-driving rock troop's first album was released in early 1972, the touring grind began, and Andes realized how far he'd strayed from his roots. By year's end he'd moved to Nederland, and it wasn't long before he'd joined with Roberts and Bartley.

Roberts began an informal series of jam sessions at his home in Boulder. As the jams became more productive, Roberts thought of a fourth participant, a singer-songwriter he'd met in Washington, D.C., named Larry Burnett, who was a taxi driver at the time. With his addition, the alliance made its initial appearances around the Boulder area in September 1974.

At Chris Hillman's suggestion, the band added drummer Michael Clarke, an original member of the Byrds (1964-1968) and later the Flying Burrito Brothers (with Roberts, through 1972). The five-man lineup took the stage of the Good Earth club shortly after Christmas, and Firefall was born.

"We had all these pedigrees," Bartley said. "With the core of the band, we had 30 original songs on the first

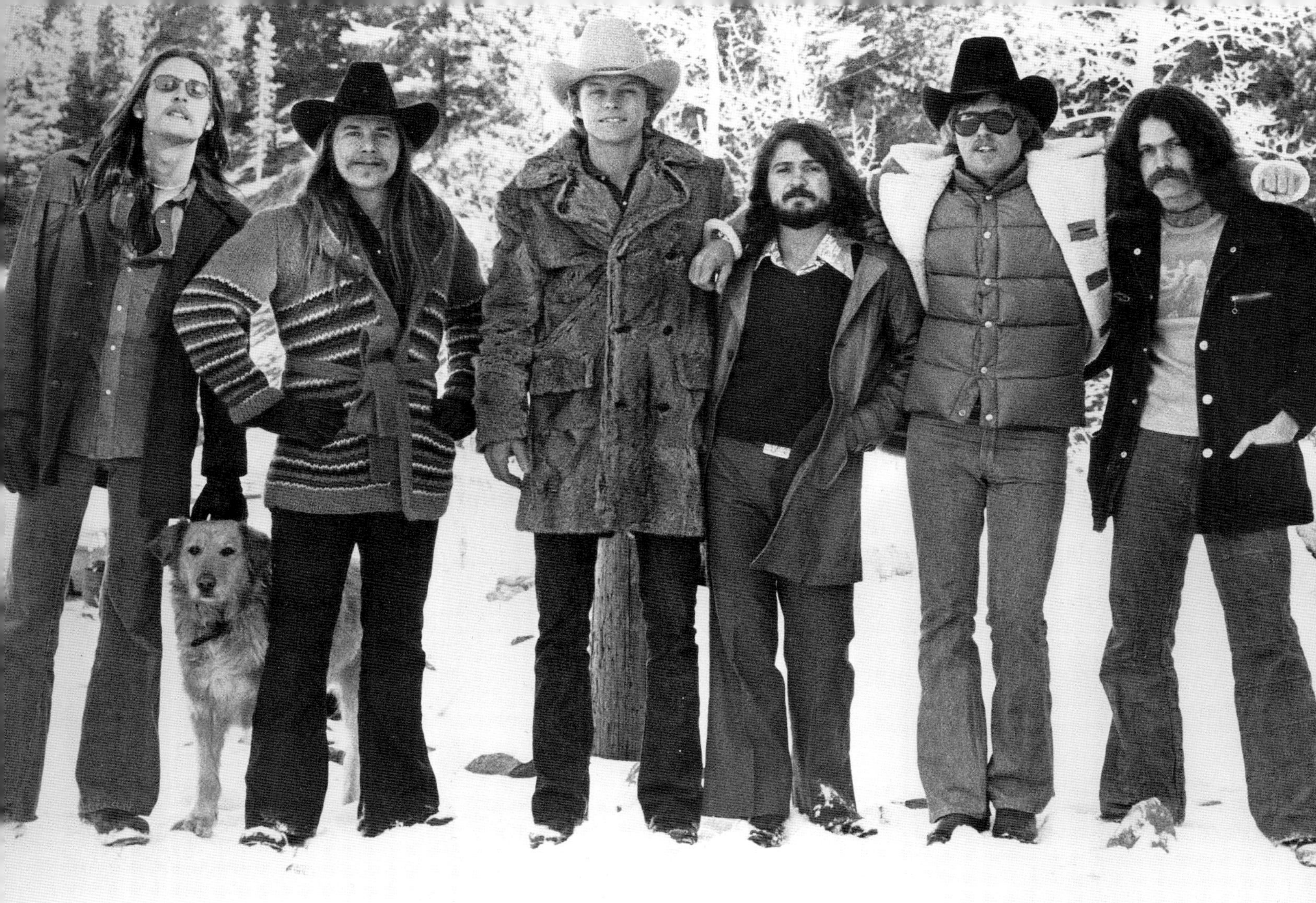

c. 1976

day of practice."

The local gigs increased with frequency and then, in June 1975, came the break. Roberts, Bartley and Andes had been woodshedding on tour as Hillman's backup band when Hillman fell ill in New York during a date at The Other End. The club owner accepted a proposal to bring Burnett and Clarke into town, and Firefall finished out the engagement in Hillman's stead. The first night they played, an Atlantic Records A&R chief was sold on what he heard and saw.

By January 1976, the group had fully completed recording the debut Firefall album with producer Jim Mason (of Poco renown). At the same time, Firefall confirmed the addition of a sixth member who was brought into the ranks during the sessions—David Muse, whose work on keyboards, synthesizers, flute, tenor sax and harmonica gave Firefall a depth that set them apart from other bands in their genre.

Firefall cemented a legend that had been brewing in the Rockies. Three singles—"You Are the Woman," "Livin' Ain't Livin" and "Cinderella"— together sold in excess of one million copies, and the album turned the magic platinum mark.

"With the players we had and the vocals on top, we sounded magical," Bartley said. "Rick and Larry wrote. Rick was this formula guy—'You Are the Woman' was a three-minute love song to get women between the ages of 18 and 35 to call the radio stations. Larry was the junkie from the streets, purging his soul when he wrote a song like 'Cinderella.' Those different

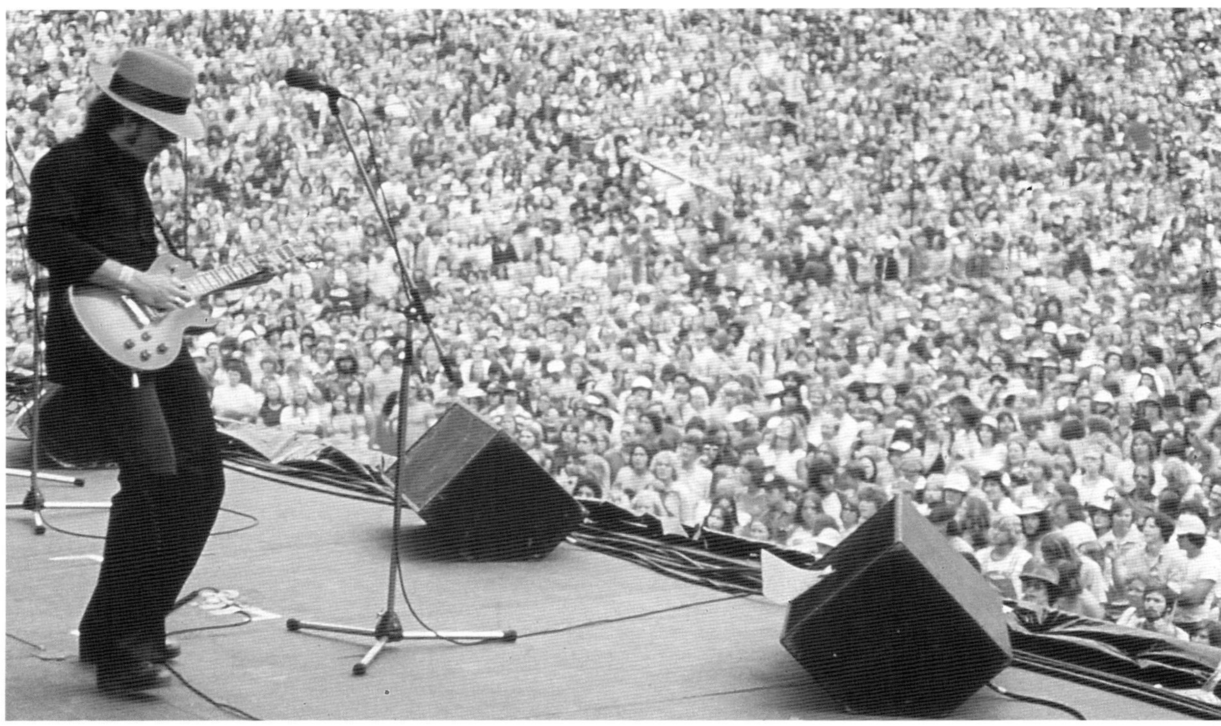

Firefall at Boulder's Folsom Field, May 1, 1977

songwriting halves became the basis for Firefall."

Firefall notched more hits—"Just Remember I Love You" and "Strange Way"—and two more best-selling albums in the late 1970s, *Luna Sea* and *Elan*. The band's heady time culminated in an opening slot for Fleetwood Mac's "Rumours" tour in 1977, which included a hometown Folsom Stadium gig before 61,500 Coloradans. There was broad populist acceptance for a rock 'n' roll band that avoided the trappings of glitter or heavy metal flash in favor of acoustic guitars, mellow pop melodies and vocal harmonies. Firefall's success with softer ballads also stereotyped the group.

"Someone along the chain of consumption—be it in merchandising, radio or the actual listening audience—preferred that we be a ballad band," Roberts said.

"In the short run, the 'Colorado sound' was a good marketing tool. In the long run, musical styles and fads come and go. When the Colorado sound became passé, it was an albatross. It wasn't really accurate. I thought of us being in the same category as the Eagles, in terms of our sound being rock with a lyrical and melodic content."

Many lineup changes and internal tensions followed.

"For a couple of years, we were on top of the world," Bartley said. "Unfortunately, we also had drug and alcohol problems and some huge egos. Everybody was brought into the band for their musicianship, but we ended up having five or six diametrically opposed personalities. We had three guys who couldn't stand each other from the get-go. After a while, the cracks started showing. We caused our own demise."

The band ran out of commercial momentum by 1980, and members began to leave. Bartley continued to tour with the Firefall name. "Once the dust settled, I ended up owning the name by default," he said. "I kept the band going. The reason I didn't quit is that the songs were so great."

The song "You Are the Woman" has been played on American radio more than six million times. ●

GARY GLITTER }

IN THE pantheon of sports anthems drawn from rock songs, Gary Glitter's "Rock and Roll Part 2" (nicknamed "The Hey Song") joined the strains of Steam's "Na Na Hey Hey Kiss Him Goodbye" and Queen's "We Will Rock You."

It got its start in 1974, when 22-year-old Kevin O'Brien was the public relations and marketing director for the Kalamazoo Wings, Michigan's entry in the International Hockey League.

"Back then, organ music was nearly synonymous with hockey games. But there was a movement to introduce some canned music during the games," O'Brien explained. "So I started rummaging through my old collection of vinyl 45s."

Tucked in a box in his basement was Glitter's "Rock and Roll Part 2." "I tossed it on the stereo and immediately thought, 'This is the song we have to use to bring the team out onto the ice.'"

In 1976, O'Brien took a job as marketing director for the Colorado Rockies of the National Hockey League. His copy of "Rock and Roll Part 2" went with him. He persuaded franchise officials to play it as a rousing celebration after Rockies goals. It didn't blare through McNichols Arena that often because the team stunk, but soon local radio stations were playing the three-minute tune, referring to it as the "Rocky Hockey Theme Song."

It was solely identified with the Rockies until 1982, when the hockey team moved east to become the New Jersey Devils. Denver's other pro teams felt free to adopt the song. The Denver Broncos were the first to introduce "Rock and Roll Part 2" to the National Football League, admitting they took the song from the Rockies, while the Denver Nuggets did the same in the National Basketball Association.

"Rock and Roll Part 2" was then played incessantly on the public address systems and by bands in every high school, college and professional arena and stadium in America. Fans got on their feet, clapping, some punching the air as they belted out the song's trademark "Hey!"

"I can't believe that happened to my song," Glitter said.

Glitter began life in England as Paul Gadd, and he tried almost everything seeking to get off the chicken-in-a-basket circuit before aspiring Svengali Mike Leander suggested a radical "image overview." Gadd adopted the name Gary Glitter and created an outlandish, outrageous persona. Somehow, his endearingly silly

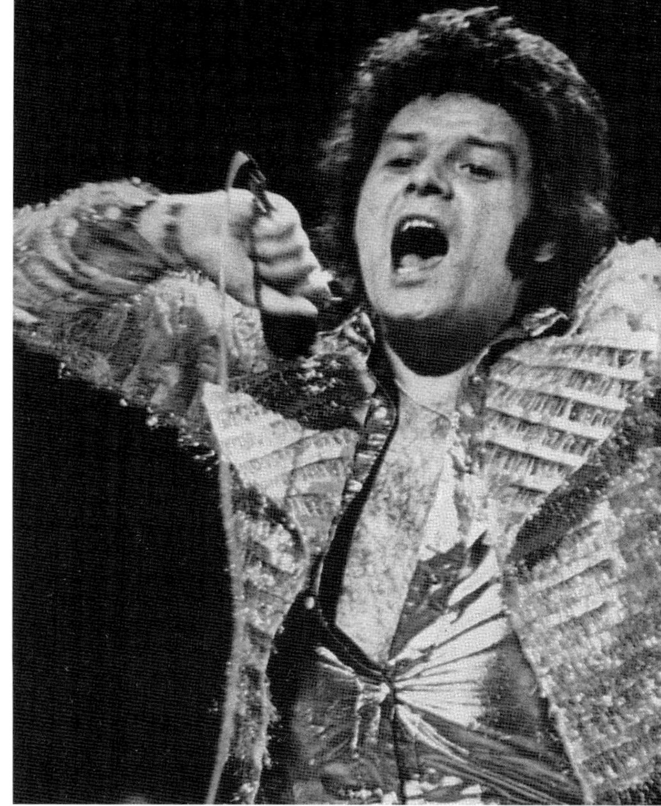

c. 1973

glam-rock struck a chord with the British public. Glitter and his Glitter Band sold millions with troglodytic variations on repetitious but engaging tunes. In 1972, "Rock and Roll Part 2" bulldozed its way onto the U.K. charts. The inspiration for it came from movies Glitter saw as a kid.

"When I went to cinema on Saturday mornings, I loved cowboys and Indians, and remember how the Indians used to run around the fire before the battle chanting, 'Hey, hey, hey, hey!'? Years later, I was trying to create a '50s kind of sound with a song. I wanted something totally different with a great beat, and I remembered the Indians chanting. I wanted it to sound like 50,000 chaps at Wembley Stadium."

All the eventual stadium and arena airplay didn't make Glitter rich. Venues buy a blanket license for the rights to use music, but the fees simply augment the royalties pool, regardless of which music is played most frequently in those places.

In 1999, several National Hockey League arenas stopped playing "Rock and Roll Part 2" in light of Glitter's arrest on child pornography charges. After he was convicted on child sexual abuse charges in Vietnam, the National Football League teams and some professional and college sports teams discontinued using the song. ●

TOMMY BOLIN }

THE BLINDING speed and precision of Tommy Bolin's guitar work was extraordinary. He was just as adept at silky acoustic stylings and jazz improvisation as he was at hard-rock riffing. Going in to the last half of the 1970s, when Bolin was fast on his way to becoming a rock music legend, some Coloradans felt he could be the next Jimi Hendrix.

Before proving it, the highly talented player died at the age of 25.

After being booted out of high school in Sioux City, Iowa, in 1967 for refusing to cut his hair, Bolin drifted west to Denver. His earliest gig, with singer Jeff Cook in a group called American Standard, was forgettable, but Cook went on to become Bolin's frequent songwriting collaborator.

Bolin then established a reputation with Zephyr. Colorado's premier boogie band brought Bolin his first album-making experience (he recorded on two of the group's three albums) and regularly attracted large audiences to its gigs. There was a huge buzz surrounding Bolin. The era of the guitar hero was dawning, and locals who saw him perform knew he not only played the fastest but he was all over the fretboard.

Bolin blew off Zephyr for a largely unprofitable stint with Energy from 1971 to 1973. Players were Kenny Passarelli, who soon joined up with Joe Walsh; Stanley Sheldon, who went on with Peter Frampton; Max Gronenthal, who established himself with Jack Mack & the Heart Attack and 38 Special; and jazz-rock flutist Jeremy Steig. Other members of Energy included Cook, Tom Stephenson on keyboards, Bobby Berge on drums and vocalist Gary Wilson.

Around 1973, Walsh recommended Bolin for a spot in the James Gang. Bolin penned most of the songs on the group's *Bang* and *Miami* albums, and "Must Be Love" was nearly a smash, peaking at #54 on *Billboard*'s pop singles charts and reaching the Top 20 in some markets.

During that time, Bolin's prominence had risen to the point where he also played most of the churning guitar on master drummer Billy Cobham's *Spectrum*. The orientation of the jazz-fusion album, particularly a cut called "Quadrant 4," was monumental—Jeff Beck often credited it as a major influence in sparking his jazz pursuits.

At age 24, Bolin had vaulted into the ranks of electric guitar masters. Everybody

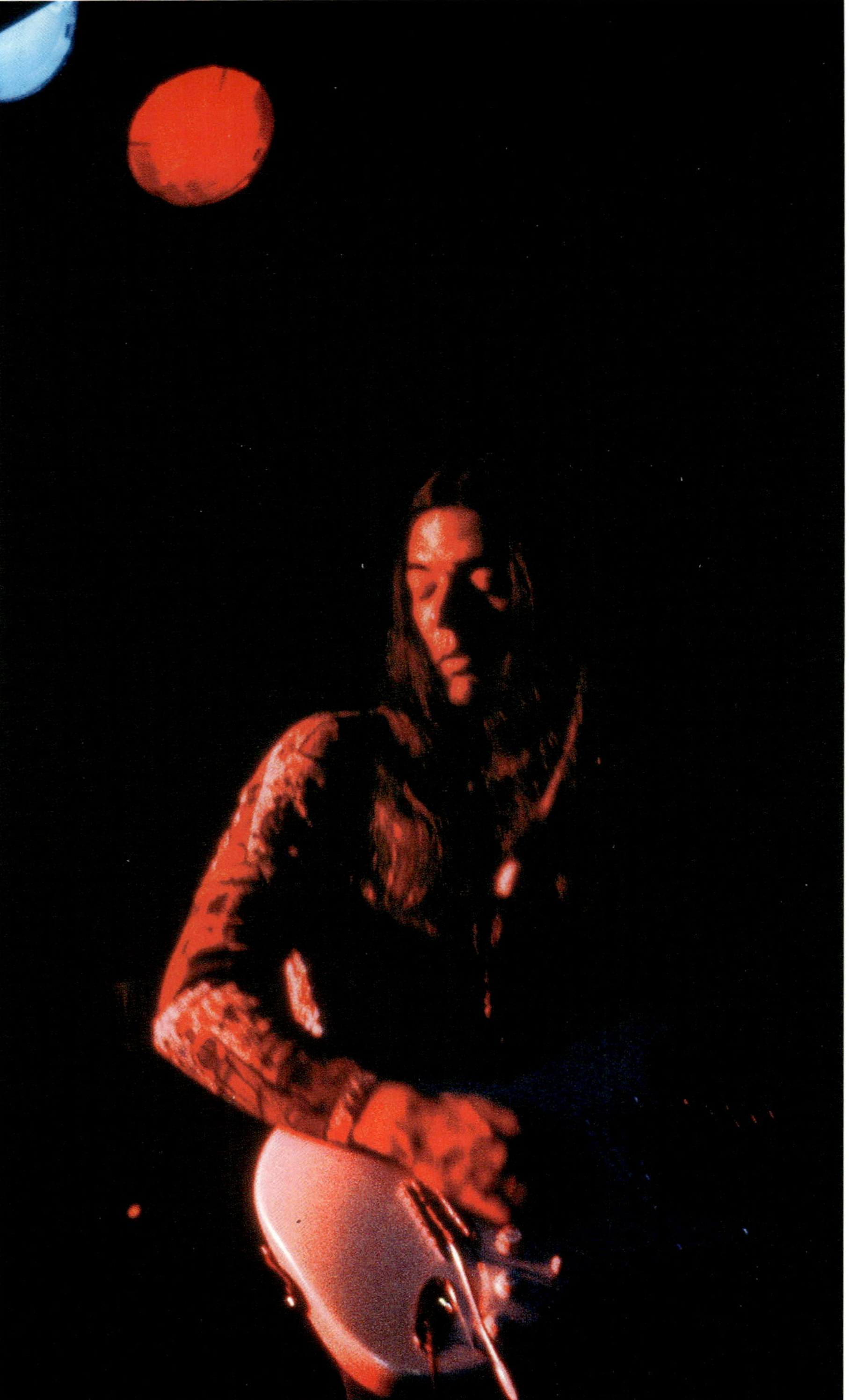

c. 1973

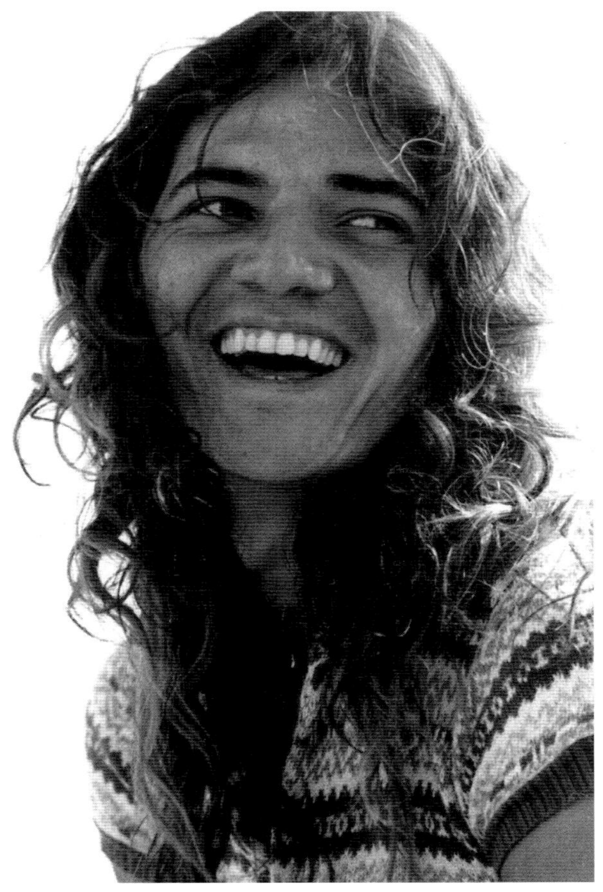

c. 1975

believed in him, and he was always able to get what he wanted from people. He left the James Gang in August 1974 "when it was no longer a learning process" and lived off royalties until he signed a contract with hard-rock band Deep Purple, confronting devotees of the departing Ritchie Blackmore head-on.

"To be honest," Bolin said, "I'd never heard anything but 'Smoke on the Water.'"

He co-wrote seven of the tunes on Deep Purple's *Come Taste the Band* album (#43 in *Billboard*). Live, he mesmerized fans with the soft, melodic parts of "Owed To 'G,'" his solo spot.

During that year, Bolin recorded *Teaser*, his masterpiece. The solo album featured him ripping it up in the company of such diverse talents as saxophonist David Sanborn, drummer Michael Walden and keyboardist Jan Hammer. *Teaser* explored Latin rhythms ("Savannah Woman") and reggae along with grinding rock, and it became a full-blown hit—one of the most requested records on the FM airwaves.

Bolin's period in Deep Purple was a hectic one. On a world tour stop in Indonesia, his roadie was killed in a hotel elevator shaft fall. Returning from the tour, he found himself named a co-respondent in Blackmore's divorce suit (15 others were also named).

In the spring of 1976, Bolin returned triumphantly to Denver, raising the roof at Ebbets Field. Happy and outgoing, he talked about being a rock 'n' roll outlaw, and he spun tales about his appetite for revelry.

"I have the best of both worlds," he said. "I can make money with Purple and be as artsy as I want on my own."

After Deep Purple disbanded that summer, Bolin returned to his solo career and launched a fall tour to support his second album, *Private Eyes*.

Shortly after his band played support at a Jeff Beck concert, Bolin collapsed and died in the bathroom of a Miami Beach hotel on Dec. 4. His body was ravaged by alcohol, barbiturates, cocaine and heroin. According to friends, Bolin had been having periodic problems with drugs and drinking for some time. The pressures that came from being constantly broke and his breakup with longtime girlfriend Karen Ulibarri appeared to have added up to a severe depression.

Bolin was buried in the family plot in Sioux City. Ulibarri put a ring on his finger that Jimi Hendrix had been wearing the day he had died, a gift to Bolin from Deep Purple's manager that she had been saving for Bolin because he kept losing it. ●

BABYFACE }

BOBBY BARTH'S first musical interest was the drums, but he learned guitar basics from his stepfather and, after finishing his formal education at Fountain-Fort Carson High School in Colorado, left home in 1968 to become a full-time musician. He joined the group Wakefield as lead guitarist and singer; the Colorado band performed in clubs across the country until parting company around 1973.

Barth then launched Babyface, and the band gigged around Colorado before signing with the now-defunct ASI Records and recording *Babyface*, its first and only album.

The group—Barth, Colorado drummer Bobby Miles, bassist Mike Turpin and keyboardist Edgar Riley—felt betrayed by producer Dan Holmes, who changed the direction of the record without the members' knowledge.

"ASI was his company, and his thing was to get some recognition no matter what he had to do," Barth said. "'Never in My Life' was this little guitar ditty I had written years earlier, like the Beatles' 'Blackbird.' After we left the studio, he took the guitars off the record and wrote schmaltzy string arrangements for everything. The problem came when 'Never in My Life' went on the charts."

"Never in My Life" quickly reached #30 on the *Billboard* adult contemporary charts in December 1976.

"The reason it was a hit isn't that it was a great song. It's that it was only one minute and 56 seconds long—it fit in perfectly before a radio station's news at the top of the hour," Barth recalled. "It got airplay all over the country because of that, an easy-listening hit among 40-year-olds. They'd show up for our shows in dinner attire, suits and gowns, expecting to see the Carpenters. We were more like Pink Floyd. They'd wait until we played that song, then everyone would leave."

"Make Way Miami" peaked at #50 on the a/c charts in March 1977. "That year the Super Bowl was going to be in Miami. Someone had sent Dan that song and he asked if we would do it. We said absolutely not—the band never played it—but somehow he talked me into just singing it. And it became some kind of hit, too. We were distraught over the whole thing. We couldn't go on that way."

Barth, Turpin and Riley evolved into the hard rock act Axe. Barth then worked with Blackfoot, Angry Anderson and the Denver-based

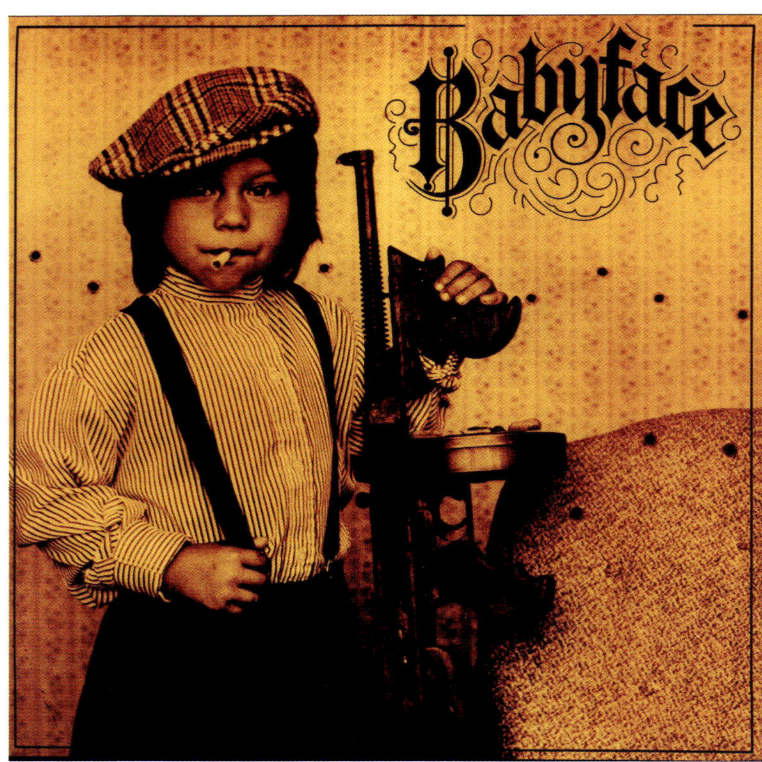

Babyface LP, 1977

Caught in the Act (C.I.T.A.) and started N.E.H. Records in Denver. Although a working musician all his life, Barth claimed his greatest accomplishment was receiving the Colorado Master of the Year Award in 1998 while serving as the Worshipful Master of Denver Lodge #5, Colorado's oldest Masonic Lodge.

"You lead such a selfish life when you're a musician," he said. "You're always focused on yourself, learning how to play and improve. I woke up one day and realized that I hadn't been concerned with anyone but myself. I read a book by Manly P. Hall and the

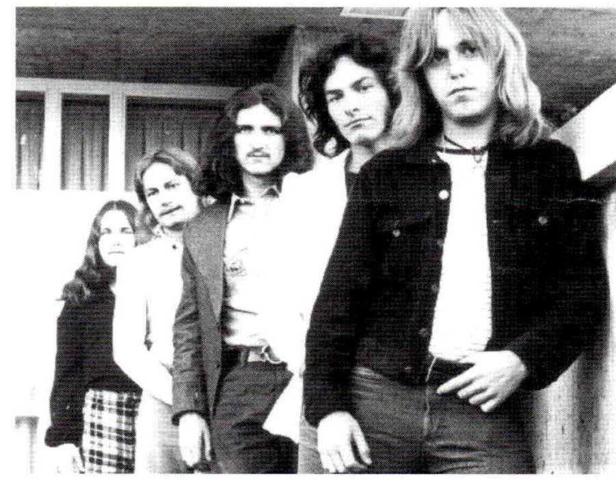
Wakefield, c. 1971

books he recommended, and all of the things that touched me turned out to be Masonic in origin. I found a Masonic Lodge in the phone book, became a member and wound up working my way through the chairs in Denver." ●

STALLION }

POLISHING ELEMENTS of Western music with an upbeat city-bred approach, Stallion moved into Denver from the streets of Chicago.

"I joined the group late, in '75," lead singer Buddy Stephens said. "They flew me out because they wanted a singer. In those days you needed to add a high baritone so you could get the vocal harmonies."

Working with producer Dik Darnell of Pyramid Productions, the Denver-based quintet—Stephens, Danny O'Neil (guitarist), Jorge Gonzales (bass), Wally Damrick (keyboards) and Larry Thompson (drums)—signed with Casablanca Records. In March 1977, the band had a Top 40 record, "Old Fashioned Boy (You're the One)." Four months later "Magic of the Music" bubbled under the Hot 100, reaching #108.

"Casablanca pushed us to fashion a little more of a rock sound," Stephens said. "Casablanca was an image-conscious label—they had Kiss and popular disco acts such as Donna Summer and the Village People. We weren't the tall, skinny rock stars that everybody loved. We dressed out as dudes, a bunch of city guys gone out West. Three of us in the band were balding, so they made us wear hats. I wore a $900 suit, boots and a multi-colored vest. I looked like Bat Masterson."

Stallion was the group's identity and its symbol. "Our logo was the Mile High Stadium horse," Stephens said.

While most of the band members were relative newcomers to Colorado, Stallion took an interest in a humanitarian issue, choosing to adopt the cause of the Wild Horse Organized Assistance program (WHOA), designed to preserve the endangered wild mustangs in the western states. The group took on KIMN disc jockeys in a charity softball game at Mile High Stadium.

"We were trying to be worthwhile," Stephens said. "We were like the group Chicago was when they first started out, a brotherhood thing."

Stallion toured with Elvin Bishop and Styx, but the record company and management didn't quite see eye to eye. The band broke up in 1979.

"We got a lot of advertising, got a lot of airplay," Stephens noted. "I can honestly say we came about as close to 'making it' as anybody could, without doing so." ●

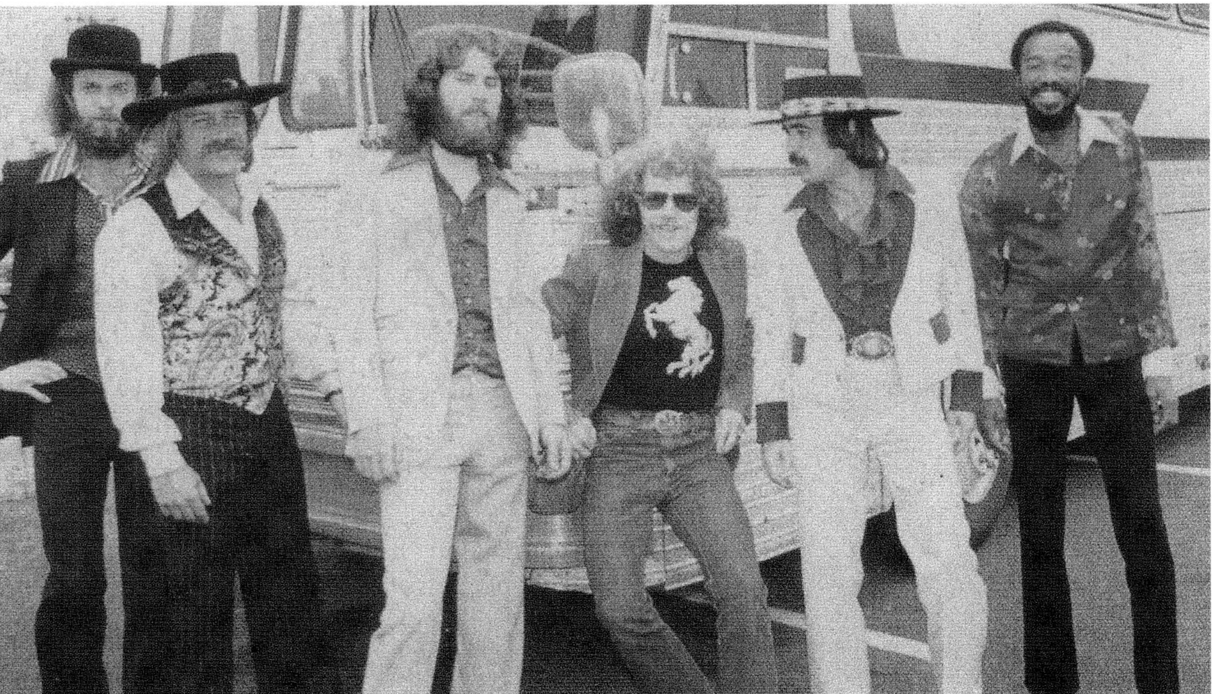

c. 1976

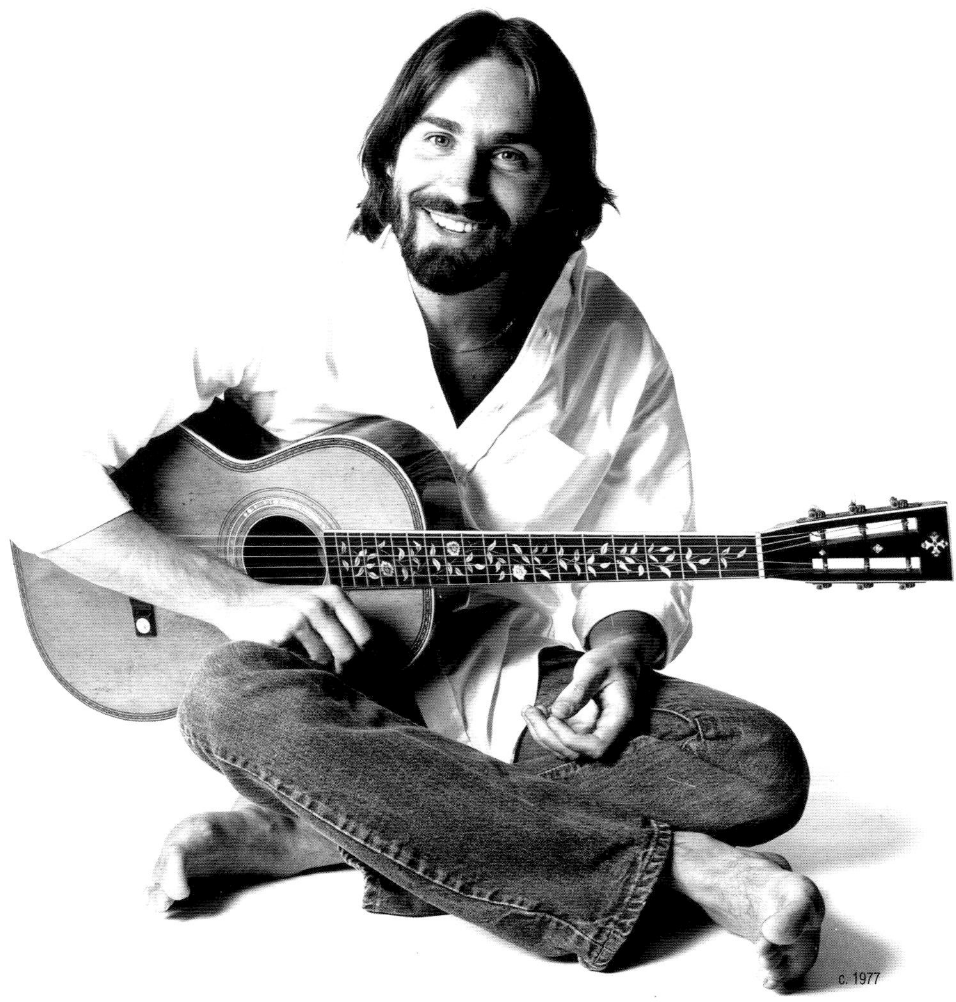

c. 1977

DAN FOGELBERG }

HE WENT from being a folksinger from the Midwest to an international star. But Dan Fogelberg ended up in Colorado, an appropriate destination for "a quiet man of music," to adapt one of his best-known lyrics.

Under the aegis of Eagles manager Irving Azoff, Illinois native Fogelberg rose to prominence amidst Southern California's burgeoning scene of the 1970s. Fogelberg was good friends with the Eagles, and in 1974 he and band members Glenn Frey and Don Henley went to Aspen with J.D. Souther.

"The Eagles were putting their show together, rehearsing at the Gallery, a club under the Little Nell hotel," Fogelberg recalled. "A lot of L.A. bands went up to Aspen and broke in their show before they went on the road. There was nothing there but waitresses and ski bums and bartenders. It was my first real taste of Colorado, the first time I had hung for any length of time, and I really liked it.

"But Aspen wasn't my place. Even then, the lifestyle was a little fast-paced for the likes of me. I was good for about two or three days, and I'd crawl out with my tongue dragging down to my legs. I

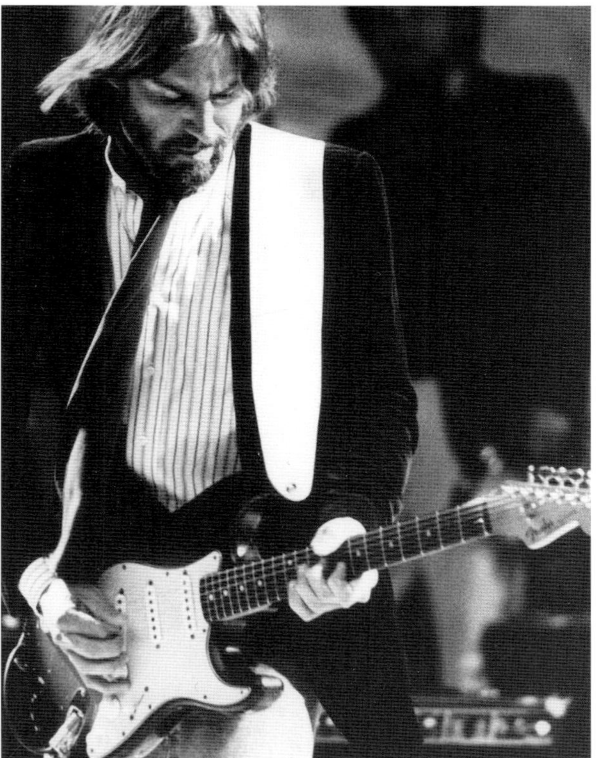

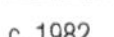
c. 1982

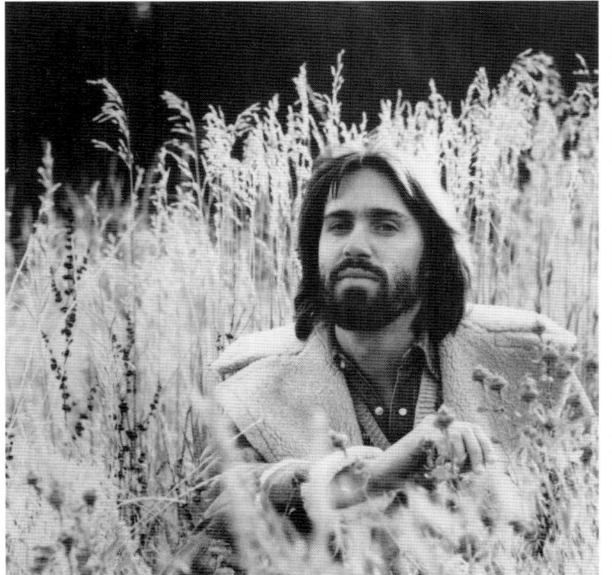

c. 1979

didn't have the liver those guys had.

"When I was touring with my band Fool's Gold, we played a couple of nights at Ebbets Field, an industry showcase for the Denver area. My road manager at the time, Patrick Cullie, mentioned that Chris Hillman had his house up for sale. I went and looked at it, fell in love with the mountains and impulsively bought the house. When the tour was done in 1975, I moved to Nederland."

From his 9,000-foot perch in the Rocky Mountains, the songs began to spill out. Vivid, emotional, personal and ambitious, the *Nether Lands* album found him singing about "living on the edge" and emerging from his Colorado hideaway, an exchange of naïveté for the temptation of new experience.

"I grew up with that album," Fogelberg said. "We called my road the Ho Chi Minh trail, because it was literally impassable most of the year. The title cut was inspired by living a fairly solitary life high up in the mountains. There's a spirituality in those mountains that I love. The first year it hit me the hardest, and the grandeur came out in the symphonic arrangement of 'Nether Lands.' I was trying to create a sonic atmosphere of the Rockies as well as singing about it.

"When I made *Nether Lands*, I didn't feel like I was imitating anyone, paying tribute to my influences like the Beatles and Buffalo Springfield. Suddenly it felt like, 'This is my music. This is what I'm about.' When you discover your own voice, it's so incredibly exciting that you never want to let go. Once that fire is set in you, I don't know that you can ever extinguish it."

Nether Lands peaked at #13 on the *Billboard* pop album charts in 1977 and was a platinum seller.

"Colorado was a very different place, very unpopulated. It was a hip "new age" hideout in Boulder and Nederland. California's charm had been exhausted, and a lot of the people that had started quests there ended up gravitating to the mountains—myself included," Fogelberg said.

"It was never a huge music scene as much as an inside family. For years, my nearest neighbor was Mark Andes. The Navarro boys were below me living in a communal setting. Richie Furay was over on Sugarloaf Mountain. Stephen Stills and Manassas were there with Chris Hillman. Everybody gravitated to Caribou Ranch—it was our boys club."

Fogelberg's signature sound—a combination of light harmonized folk-rock, highly dramatic orchestration and introspective lyrics laden with sensitivity—endured beyond all critical predictions.

In 1980, Fogelberg found and bought land near Pagosa Springs on the western slope of Colorado. He built a house and barns and led a quiet life in the San Juan Mountains.

"I cherish my privacy. As an artist, to create, I've got to keep some anonymity," Fogelberg said.

During the many hours spent in his truck driving back and forth between Boulder and Pagosa Springs, Fogelberg listened to a lot of bluegrass tapes, feeding the desire to play some roots music. After sitting in with Hillman's acoustic band at the 1984 Telluride Bluegrass Festival, he decided to make a record with his favorite acoustic pickers. The resulting album, *High Country Snows*, became one of the best-selling bluegrass albums of all time.

But shuttling between his Colorado redoubt and the recording studios of Los Angeles was taking a toll. Fogelberg found his records took longer to make. So in the late 1980s, the singer-songwriter built his own studio at his Mountain Bird Ranch.

1990's *The Wild Places* was self-produced and mostly tracked at his spread. The album, about the sweetness of his seclusion in Colorado, included a tender, soulful cover of the Cascades' 1963 hit, "Rhythm of the Rain." The tune, with a touch of the Beatles' "Rain" added to the coda, was a Top 10 adult contemporary hit.

"That song was a result of having my own studio in Colorado, the freedom to experiment," Fogelberg said. "I could ski during the day and work at night.

"It's a pretty calm existence here. I'm not a very social person. I'm an avid skier during the winter, and I prowl around the state. Summertime, there's so much to do—I enjoy the solitude of hiking and mountain biking.

"The mountains have always been a very healing place for me. You go through a lot of changes in life, but these mountains will always be here."

Fogelberg's long career was interrupted by a health crisis in 2004, when he was diagnosed with advanced prostate cancer. After battling for three years, he succumbed to the disease in December 2007. ●

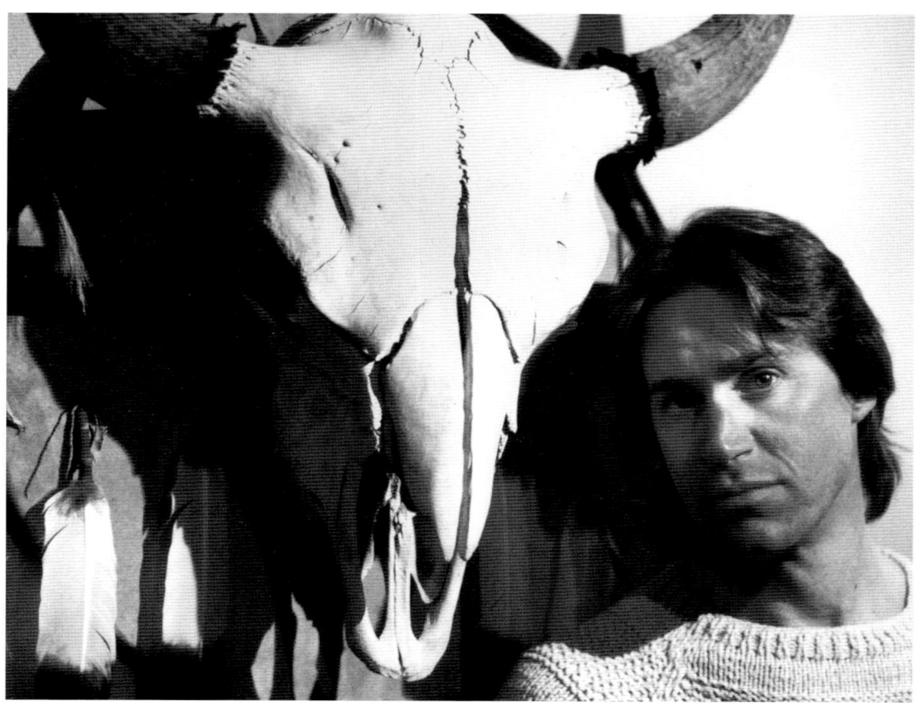

Fogelberg with stage prop "Kevin," c. 2002

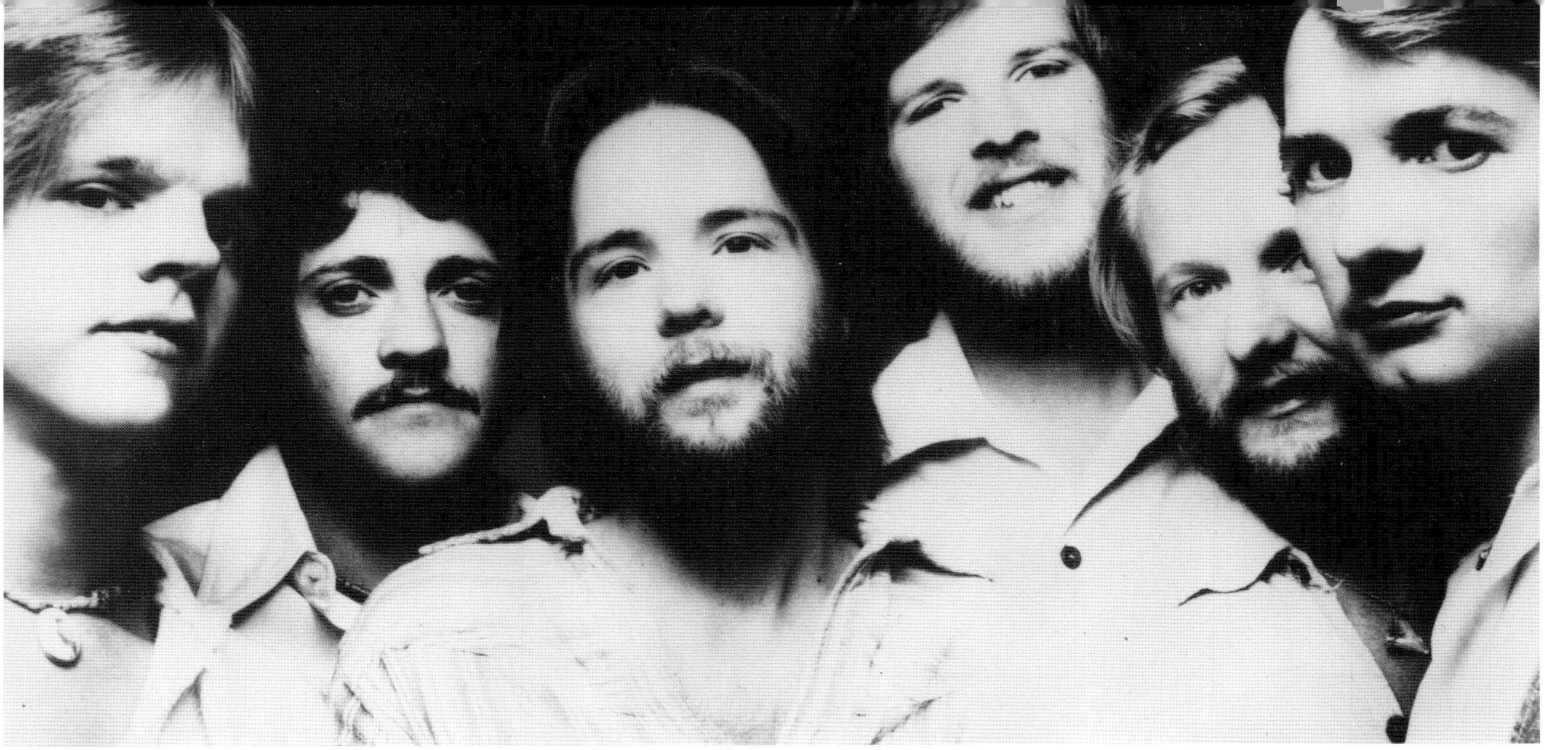

c. 1977

CAROLE KING & NAVARRO }

RECORDING AT Caribou Ranch in 1977, Carole King was on the lookout for a backup band. Dan Fogelberg, who lived in neighboring Nederland, suggested Boulder's Navarro.

King saw Navarro perform in the tier of the Stage Stop, a barn near Boulder in Rollinsville, and went on to sign the act to her own label. King enlisted Navarro as the "side-by-side" band for her *Simple Things* album, which reached #17 on the *Billboard* pop album charts and went gold. Navarro's own debut collection of mellow rock music, *Listen*, was released simultaneously with *Simple Things*, and the group also recorded *Straight for the Heart* for Capitol Records in 1978.

What was a reclusive legend (in 1971, King's *Tapestry* had become one of the most popular albums in music history) doing with a "positive energy" band from Boulder?

"I have never been happier with a band," King said simply. She and the six young members of Navarro all clasped hands and meditated together in "the circle," as they called it, before every session and show. In concert, King opened solo, slowly introducing musicians until she had left the audience in Navarro's hands.

"She loved the band,"

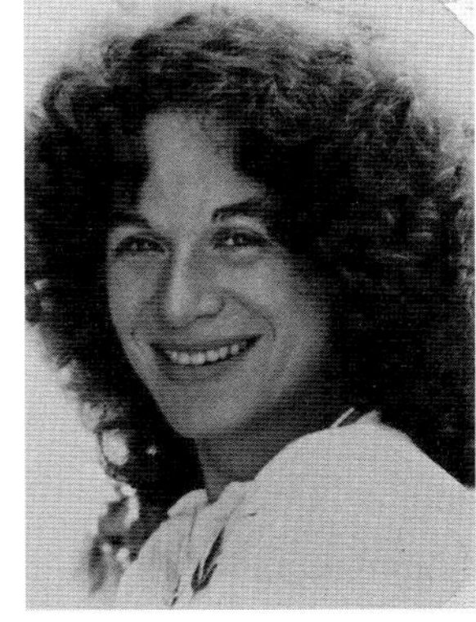

c. 1977

lead guitarist Robert McEntee said. "We were treated to a wonderful and generous education with her."

Right before King latched onto Navarro, the band had, in fact, broken up. "We'd split up and reformed so many times that it was a big joke around town," McEntee said. "But this time was for good...or so we thought."

Local promoters jokingly called Navarro "granola rockers," and the image stuck nationally, too. A 1977 *Rolling Stone* story about the band was headlined "Carole King and Navarro Mellow Out," and was accompanied by a picture captioned "Good Vibes in Boulder."

After parting ways with King, Navarro moved to Austin, Texas for a time before drifting back to Colorado. McEntee and guitarist-songwriter-singer Mark Hallman played in Fogelberg's touring band. ●

MARY MACGREGOR }

IN THE summer of 1972, Mary MacGregor, a pop singer from Minnesota, moved to Steamboat Springs, Colorado, a small ski town in the Rockies populated by many small clubs featuring live music. For the next four years she and her husband lived in a secluded ranch house with no running water and an outhouse, and she sang folk and soft rock music in the area's nightclubs.

While still living in Steamboat circa 1974, she began commuting to Minneapolis, Chicago and Nashville, where she sang for commercial agencies. During that time, she was invited by Peter Yarrow of Peter, Paul & Mary fame to join his tour as a vocalist.

"My career didn't take up that much of my time. I was on the road with Peter for a couple of months out of the year. And maybe every other month, I would fly to do a couple commercials and be gone for a week," MacGregor said.

In the spring of 1976, Yarrow took MacGregor into the studio to record, and the first song produced was "Torn Between Two Lovers," co-written by Phil Jarrell and Yarrow. Yarrow brought the record to the new Ariola America label, with MacGregor as part of the package. The record's success was so unexpected that she didn't even have a deal with Ariola when it was released.

"Torn Between Two Lovers" became the only 1977 single to top the pop, country and easy listening charts simultaneously, resulting in her capturing the Top New Female Artist award in *Billboard*, *Record World* and *Cashbox*. But MacGregor hated her No. 1 single.

"I think it's a real implausible situation—a lady who wants to have her cake and eat it too," she explained. "At the time I recorded the song, I was married and people thought I'd written it and wanted to know if I was 'torn.' It was real aggravating for me, although the success that it had was definitely not."

The song had a traumatic effect. MacGregor had been happily married for five years and had no intention of ever being unfaithful to her husband. Yet the record's appeal soon put a devastating crimp in their relationship.

"When 'Torn Between Two Lovers' happened, it was like getting on an already fast moving train. My life changed drastically—I was gone a lot—and my husband just couldn't deal with it. It was just hard on both of us, and we separated for a couple of years. I moved to Los Angeles during that time, and we eventually divorced." ●

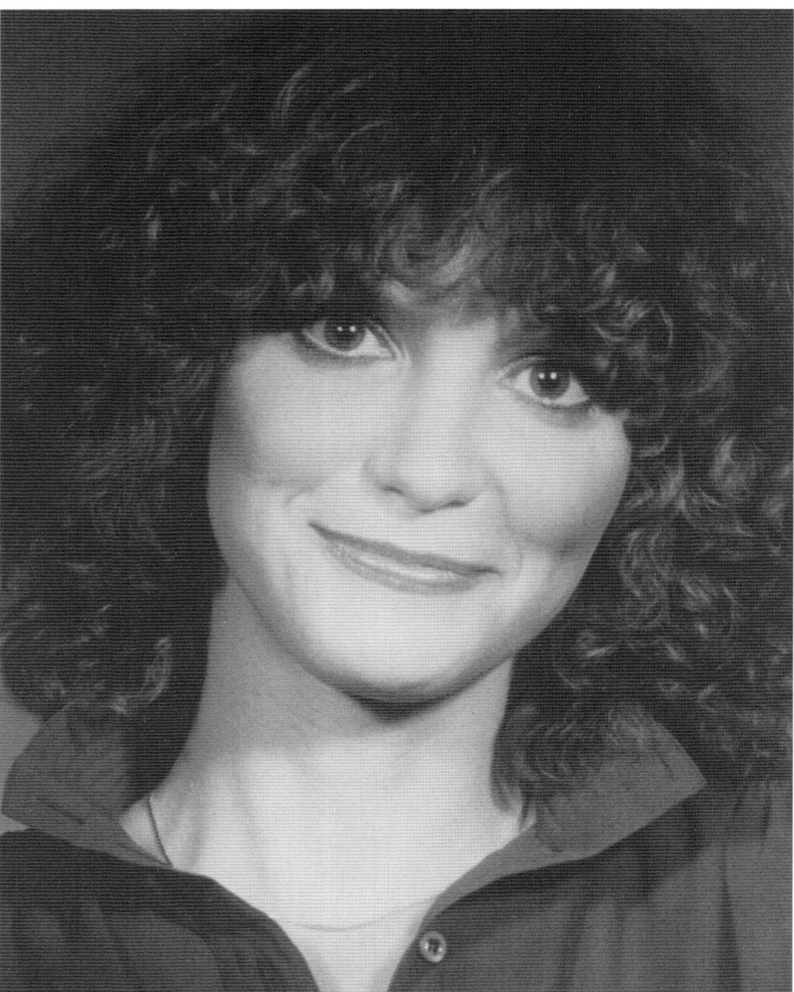

c. 1977

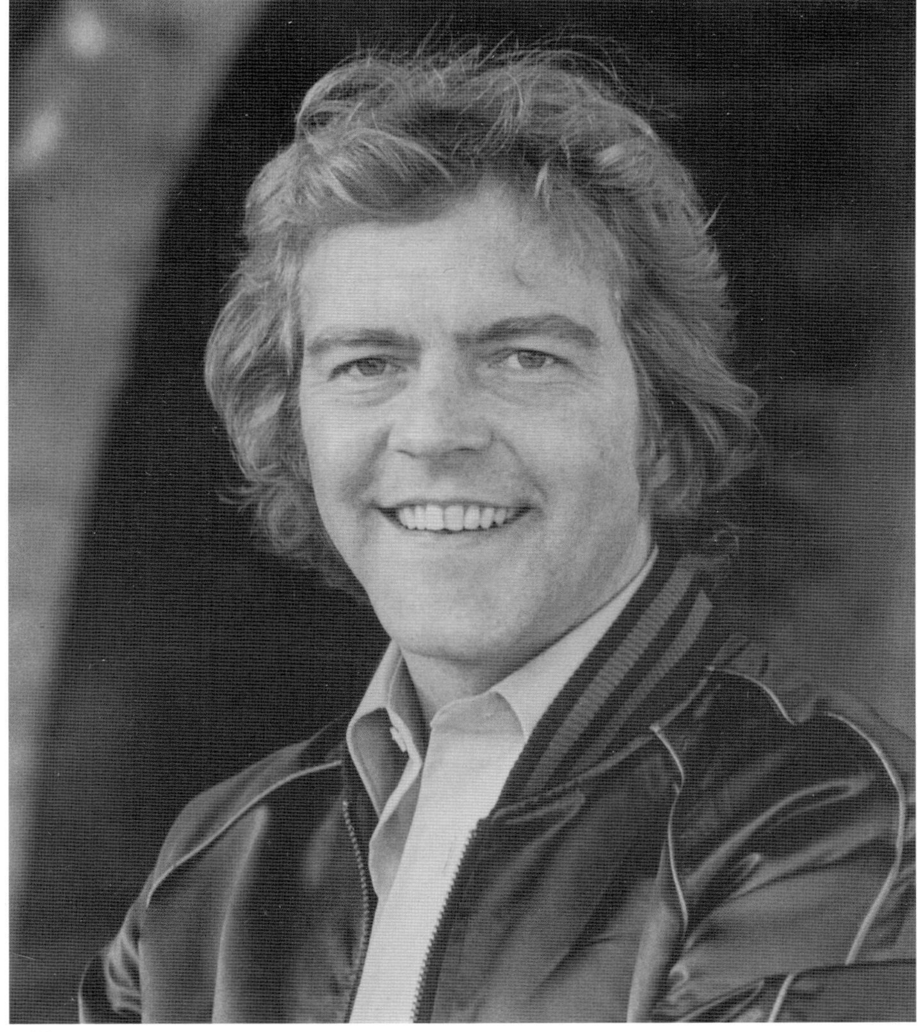

c. 1978

MICHAEL JOHNSON }

POP SINGER and guitarist Michael Johnson's wide-ranging experience started with his natural attraction to music as a 13-year-old in his native Denver. In 1958, he and his older brother Paul (then 20) began teaching each other the basics of playing guitar. Their first professional gig was at the local VFW hall that year.

"We played for five bucks a night and all the screwdrivers we could drink," Johnson recalled. "I played in high school dances in Denver as soon as I was able to. I played bars and clubs—the Exodus, another called the Green Spider. They're probably selling plumbing fixtures out of there now."

Johnson grew up in a Catholic family of six. He attended Denver's North High School and Holy Family High School, but got kicked out of the latter, a Catholic school. "I mooned a nun," he explained.

In 1963, Johnson went off to Colorado State University to study music education, but his college career was truncated. He left for Spain, studying at the Conservatory of Liceo in Barcelona, then returned to the States and signed on with Randy Sparks in the Back Porch Majority (a sort of feeder team for the New Christy Minstrels). He was a member of the Chad Mitchell Trio for two years, spending some of that time co-writing with another member, John Denver.

Johnson returned to creating and performing his music, his popularity increasing with each new recording and his continued touring. It was time to pursue national recognition. From 1978 to 1980, he scored big pop and adult contemporary hits—"Bluer Than Blue" (#12 on the *Billboard* singles charts), "Almost Like Being in Love" (#32), "This Night Won't Last Forever" (#19) and "You Can Call Me Blue" (#86).

"I never lived anywhere longer than a year," Johnson said. "I lived out of a suitcase." In the mid-1980s, Johnson moved into country music, conquering the charts with "Give Me Wings" and "The Moon Is Still over Her Shoulder."

By then, he had circled the world with his music.

"Denver's not where most of my clothes are anymore, but it's my home, where my heart is. Every time I come back, I wonder why I don't live in Colorado." ●

STEVE MARTIN }

GROWING UP in Southern California, Steve Martin first picked up the banjo when he was around 17 years of age. He learned his way around the instrument with help from high school friend John McEuen, who later joined the Nitty Gritty Dirt Band. McEuen's brother William later managed Martin as well as managing and producing several early Nitty Gritty Dirt Band albums.

Martin exploded onto the comedy scene in the mid 1970s, and the banjo was a staple of his stand-up career. The young comic performed at Tulagi in Boulder and Ebbets Field in Denver, most memorably at a 1974 New Year's Eve concert during a blizzard; after the show, he led the entire audience across the street and ordered 300 doughnuts, then changed his order to one cup of coffee.

In 1974, Martin discovered the charms of Aspen and found a solar-heated home in the mountains to be closer to his friends the McEuens and members of the Nitty Gritty Dirt Band. By 1978, the Colorado resident was the most successful concert draw in the history of stand-up, earning the level of commercial success usually reserved for rock stars. The second side of his comedy album *A Wild and Crazy Guy* was recorded at Red Rocks Amphitheatre in front of a roaring audience; they got treated to a rare onstage appearance of Yortuk, one of the Czech Festrunk Brothers (the "two wild and crazy guys" he'd popularized with Dan Aykroyd on *Saturday Night Live*). *A Wild and Crazy Guy* reached #2 on *Billboard*'s Pop Albums Chart. It was eventually certified double platinum and won the Grammy Award in 1979 for Best Comedy Album.

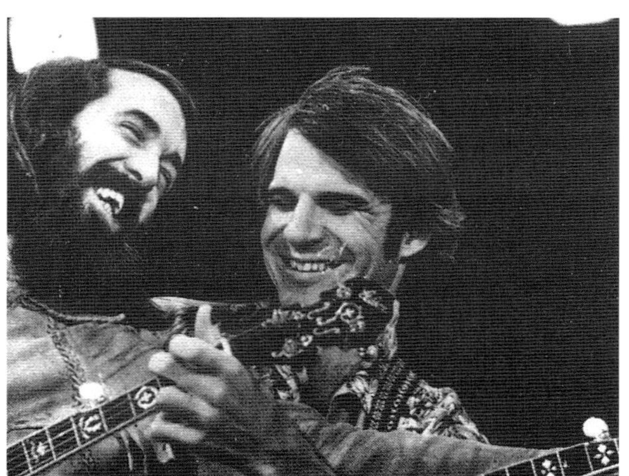

Martin with John McEuen, c. 1974

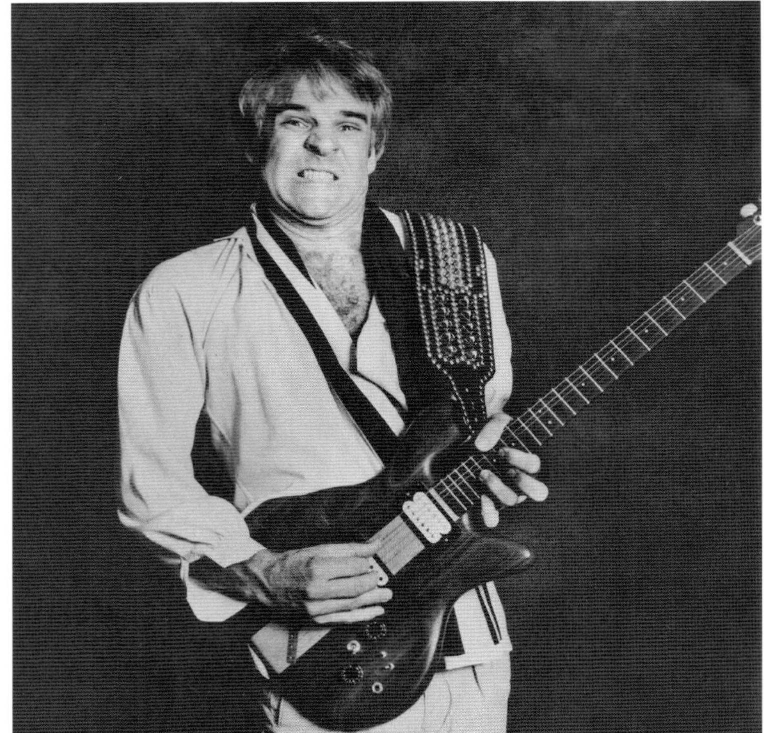

c. 1978

"My recollection of the general period is precise, but my memory of specific shows is faint," Martin said. "Every place was the same—I stood onstage, blinded by lights, looking into blackness. I don't really remember much about Red Rocks except watching Doug Kershaw and the Nitty Gritty Dirt Band as a fan. Beautiful place, though."

A Wild and Crazy Guy contained the hit novelty single "King Tut," performed by Martin and the Toot Uncommons (actually members of the Nitty Gritty Dirt Band). Produced by William McEuen at his Aspen Recording Society studio, it paid homage to the boy king who "gave his life for tourism," Egyptian pharaoh Tutankhamun; the "Treasures of Tutankhamun" traveling exhibit toured seven United States cities from 1976 to 1979 and attracted approximately eight million visitors. "King Tut" sold over a million copies and reached #17 on the *Billboard* Hot 100 chart in 1978. Martin also performed it on *Saturday Night Live*. ●

BRUCE SPRINGSTEEN }

DURING HIS first visits to the Rocky Mountain region, Bruce Springsteen learned that rock 'n' roll is an indoor sport.

On June 20, 1978, Springsteen and his E Street Band made their Colorado debut at Red Rocks Amphitheatre in support of *Darkness on the Edge of Town*, his first release in nearly three years. The interim had been spent battling his ex-manager and letting the hype from the *Born to Run* album settle down.

He had agreed to do his first-ever outdoor show only after weeks of cajoling by his manager and booking agents. A gig in the wide-open spaces? He was dubious about the havoc that it might wreak among his sound crew and cautious of problems with audience communication and a lack of intimacy.

But on that Tuesday night, Springsteen put on a legendary performance, one that he later claimed was the best of the entire tour. Springsteen and the band had the charm of kids who had just hopped out of their folks' station wagon and seen the mountains for the first time. Springsteen managed to keep his Jersey sensibilities intact—"Nice place you got here...a bunch of big rocks," he said with a laugh.

Only 6,200 persons had the foresight to catch Springsteen's maiden area performance, but his loyalty to his new western friends was incredible. The kid from Asbury Park played for three hours, racing around the stage and exhorting the crowd.

"The idea is to deliver what money can't buy," Springsteen said backstage after the gig.

However, playing at Colorado's famed outdoor venue set a precedent. Springsteen returned to Red Rocks on August 16 and 17, 1981, his first outdoor dates since he had played there in 1978. On the first night, a torrential summer rainstorm drenched the audience, and Springsteen opened the show with a cover of Creedence Clearwater Revival's "Who'll Stop the Rain." A few songs into the set, Springsteen tried to talk the crowd out of continuing. He thought it would be better to start all over on a night with better weather. The proposal was shouted down in a spirited voice vote, and the show went on in an intermittent downpour.

In 1985, Springsteen played stadiums across the U.S. during his *Born in the U.S.A.* tour, ending his prevailing holdout against playing outdoors. But two shows at Denver's Mile High Stadium were scheduled late in the summer concert season—September 22 and 23—and Springsteen lost the gamble. An icy rain fell on the morning of the first show, a Sunday, and the temperature fell into the low 30s with 25-mile-per-hour winds. It was decided to delay the performance until Tuesday.

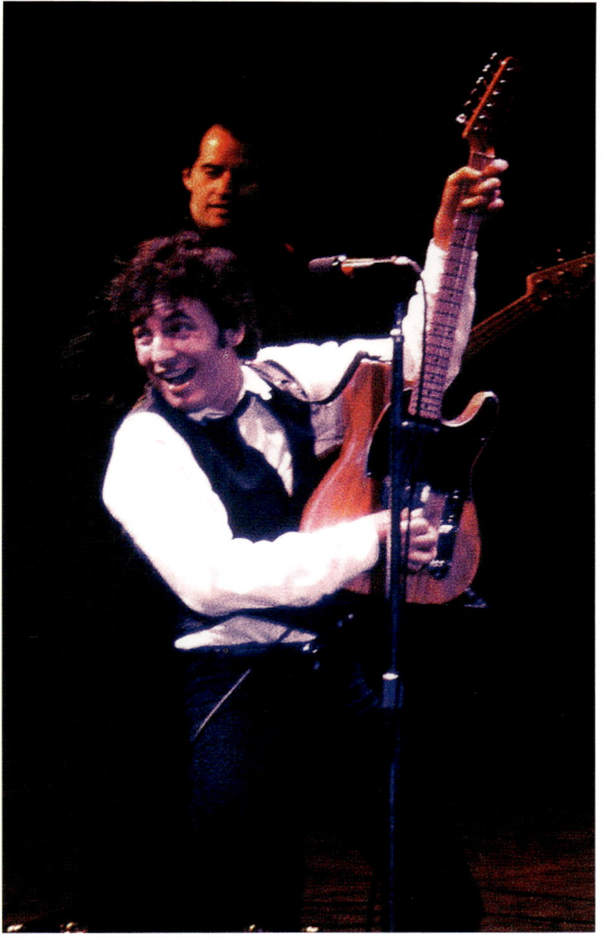

Springsteen at Red Rocks, June 20, 1978

On stage both Monday and Tuesday, Springsteen was profuse in his apologies for Sunday's postponement—but the weather during those shows wasn't much better. By the time Monday's show ended, temperatures were back in the 30s—a heck of a way for Springsteen to spend his 36th birthday. On Tuesday, the E Streeters played in a cold, drenching downpour that made everything slippery. At one point, Springsteen had to quit playing his acoustic guitar because he couldn't pick it up. ●

PHILIP BAILEY | EARTH, WIND & FIRE }

IN THE annals of pop R&B, Earth, Wind & Fire's place is assured as a multi-platinum, multi-Grammy-winning supergroup. The band's hits ranked as some of the most joyous moments of the 1970s.

Earth, Wind & Fire featured the vocal acrobatics of Philip Bailey, who was born and raised in Denver and had graduated from East High School. With schoolmates Larry Dunn (on keyboard) and Andrew Woolfolk (on sax), he played with a local group, Friends & Love.

"Denver wasn't a heavy black urban area, so we did all kinds of music—Blood, Sweat & Tears, Three Dog Night, Sly & the Family Stone, Carole King," Bailey said.

Bailey had heard Earth, Wind & Fire's first album. "Friends & Love opened the show when the group came to town in '71 to play a promotional gig at the Hilton. Then I hooked up with them in Los Angeles and joined. I brought a certain pop sensibility to the band."

Earth, Wind & Fire had originally recorded as a brassy, jazz-like band. But founder Maurice White reworked the concept, and Bailey recommended Dunn and then Woolfolk, who had been busy in New York studying sax with jazz maestro Joe Henderson and was on the verge of taking up a career in banking when Bailey called. The group began presenting exuberant dance music that had life-affirming, often metaphysical lyrics wrapped around exciting rhythms.

Bailey's distinctive falsetto, pure and sweet, became as legendary as Barry White's basso. Earth, Wind & Fire had six Top 10 singles, including the Beatles' "Got to Get You into My Life" (#9 in September 1978), which it performed in the ill-fated *Sgt. Pepper's Lonely Hearts Club Band* movie.

"We recorded the *That's the Way of the World* album and more at Caribou, but 'Got to Get You into My Life' was recorded at Northstar Studios, a little studio in Boulder," Bailey said. "We were on a deadline—we were writing the arrangement while we were on the road, and we rehearsed it in another city on the way to Denver, then had a concert the next night. Then we went to Boulder and did the track. We brought out George Massenberg, who was an innovator of engineering. He brought his outboard gear and hot-rodded the soundboard.

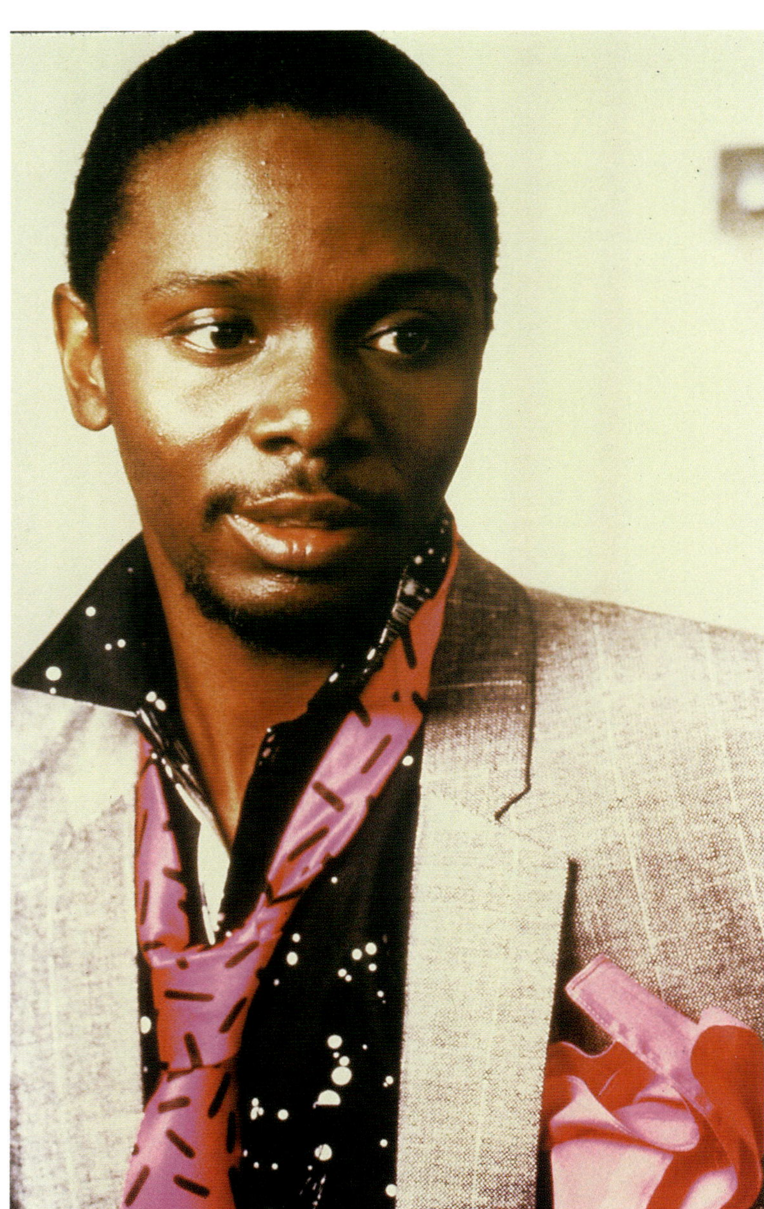

c. 1982

"At the time when we started reworking the original, I was wondering if the whole treatment that we had was going to be too different from what the Beatles song sounded like. But it was the single off the *Sgt. Pepper* record and it went pop for us. It ended up being a major smash."

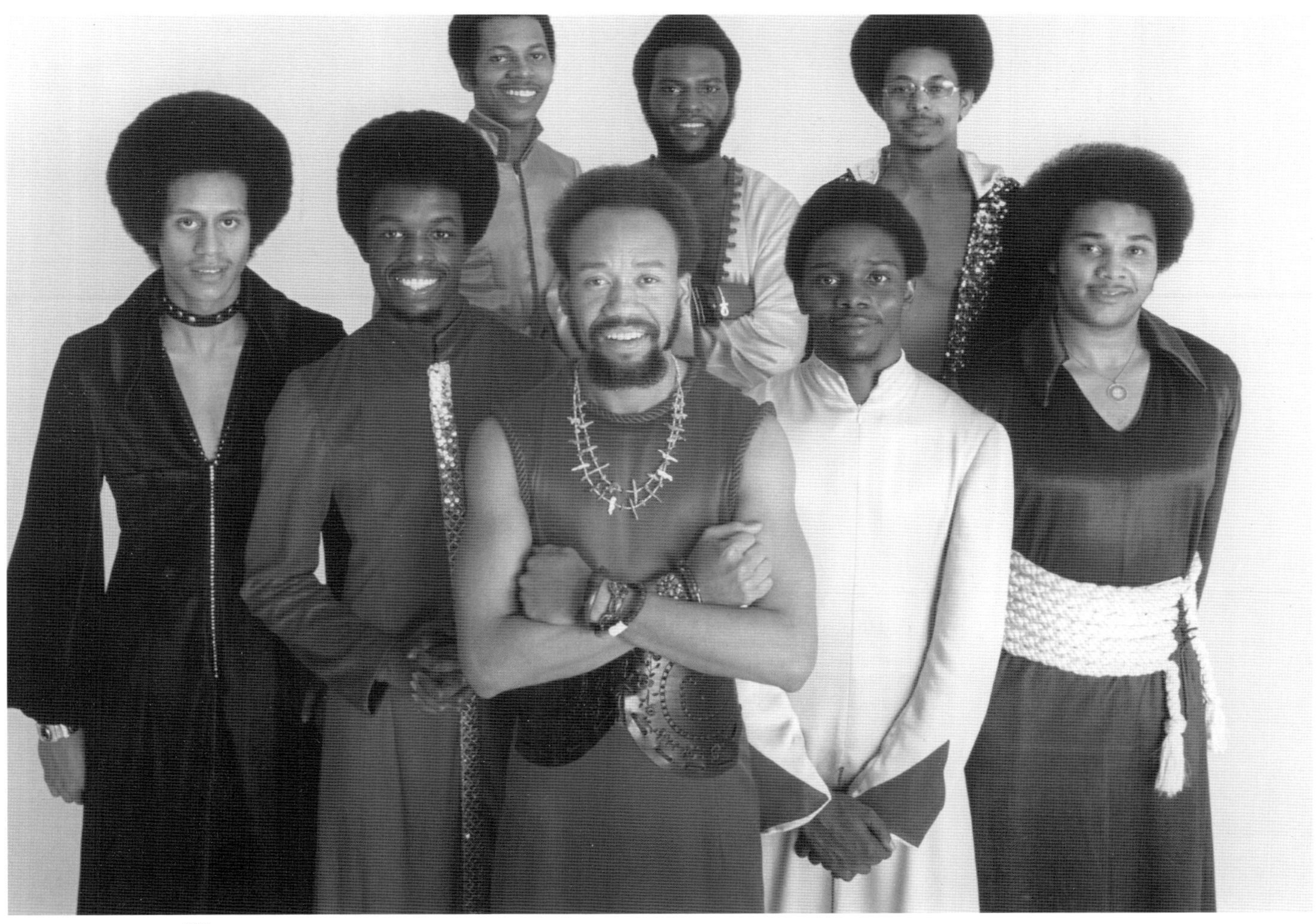

c. 1978

Bailey had his own solo career—in 1982, he hit #2 with "Easy Lover," a duet with Phil Collins. And he had a dual identity as a singer—he also recorded Christian music.

"The time spent away from one another was necessary for everybody in the band. I came in at age 20, straight from a year of college and getting married. I literally grew up in EWF, so it was more than a band. It was a family, and a lot of multi-faceted relationships were established as a result."

Earth, Wind & Fire added fresh chapters in the 1980s and 1990s, and the long-lived band was inducted into the Rock and Roll Hall of Fame in 2000.

"Over the years, I've been exposed to things I could never dream of as a kid in Denver," Bailey said. "At the end of the day, I've been able to support my family and work for myself. I get paid for being the best me I can possibly be. How many of us get the chance to say that?" ●

POCO }

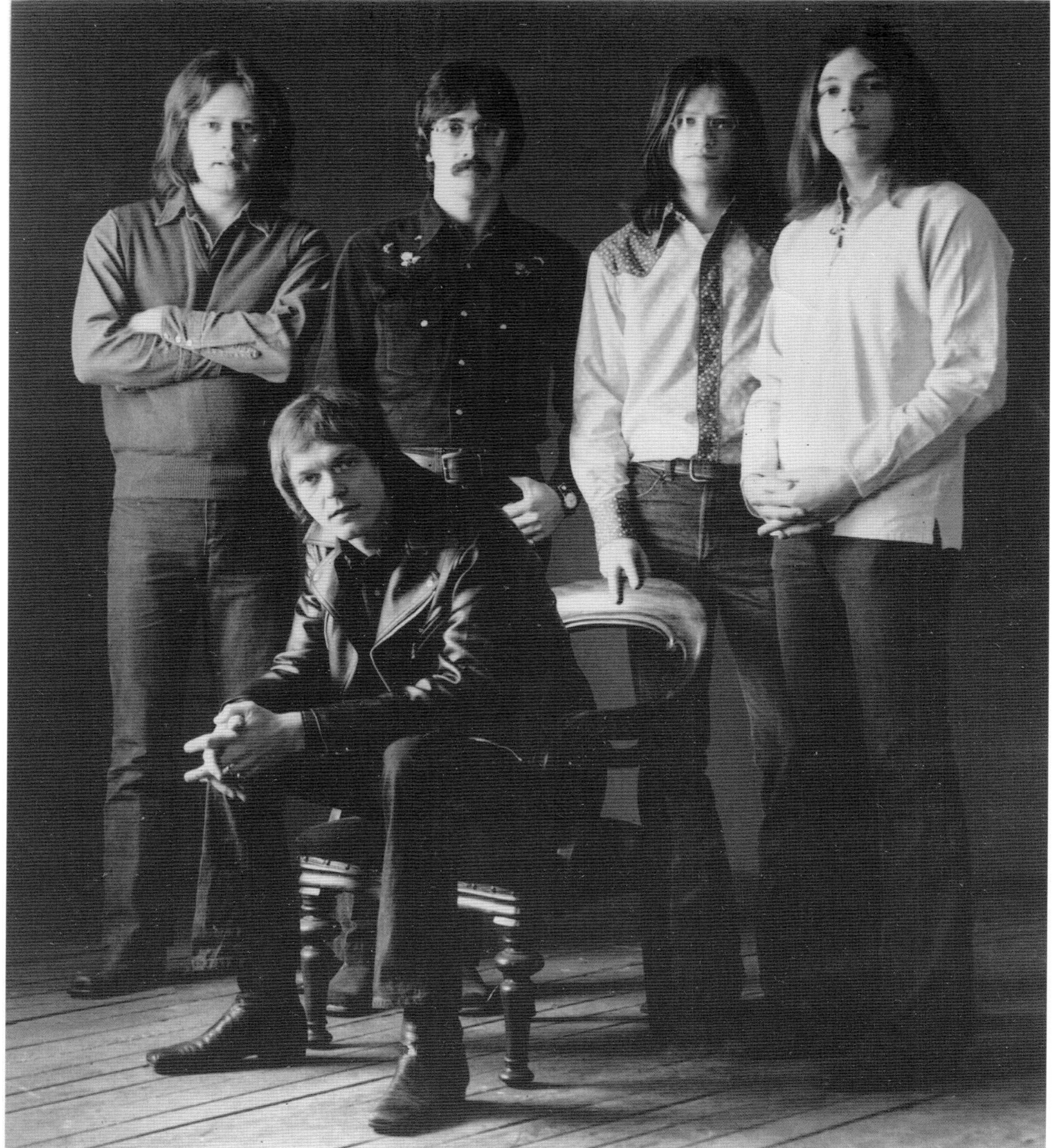

c. 1973

RUSTY YOUNG got his musical start in Böenzee Cryque, a Denver-based band whose odd moniker was inspired, perhaps apocryphally, by the local business sign on an appliance store. Getting local airplay, a single got placed with Uni Records, and "Still in Love with You Baby"/ "Sky Gone Gray" went to No. 1 on the hit list of KIMN, the dominant Top 40 station in Denver, in April 1967.

Böenzee Cryque went to Los Angeles, where the group promptly broke up, and Young found himself playing pedal steel guitar on sessions for Buffalo Springfield's "Kind Woman." In 1968, with Springfield in disarray, two members, Richie Furay and Jim Messina, quickly set about assembling a band of their own. They recruited Young, who called in two buddies from Colorado—George Grantham, also from Böenzee Cryque, and Randy Meisner, who came from a rival band, the Poor, to play drums and bass, respectively.

The new band originally called itself Pogo, but Walt Kelly, the creator of the *Pogo* comic strip, sued.

Poco started out with great commercial promise. Then Meisner left to co-found the Eagles, and guitarist Messina slipped into the Poco bass slot until Timothy B. Schmit signed on in February 1969. In November of that year, Messina split to form a prosperous duo with Kenny Loggins, and guitarist Paul Cotton stepped in to sing and play guitar. In 1973, Furay departed to form the Souther-Hillman-Furay Band. It was a near-mortal jolt to the group.

Poco plugged on for the next three years, recording such classics as Schmit's "Keep on Tryin'," Young's "Rose of Cimarron" and Cotton's "Indian Summer." They watched the Eagles adopt the group's sound and emerge as the triumphant synthesis of L.A. country-rock. "We had such a tremendous influence," Young allowed.

When Meisner left the Eagles and retired to his native Nebraska, Schmit quit Poco

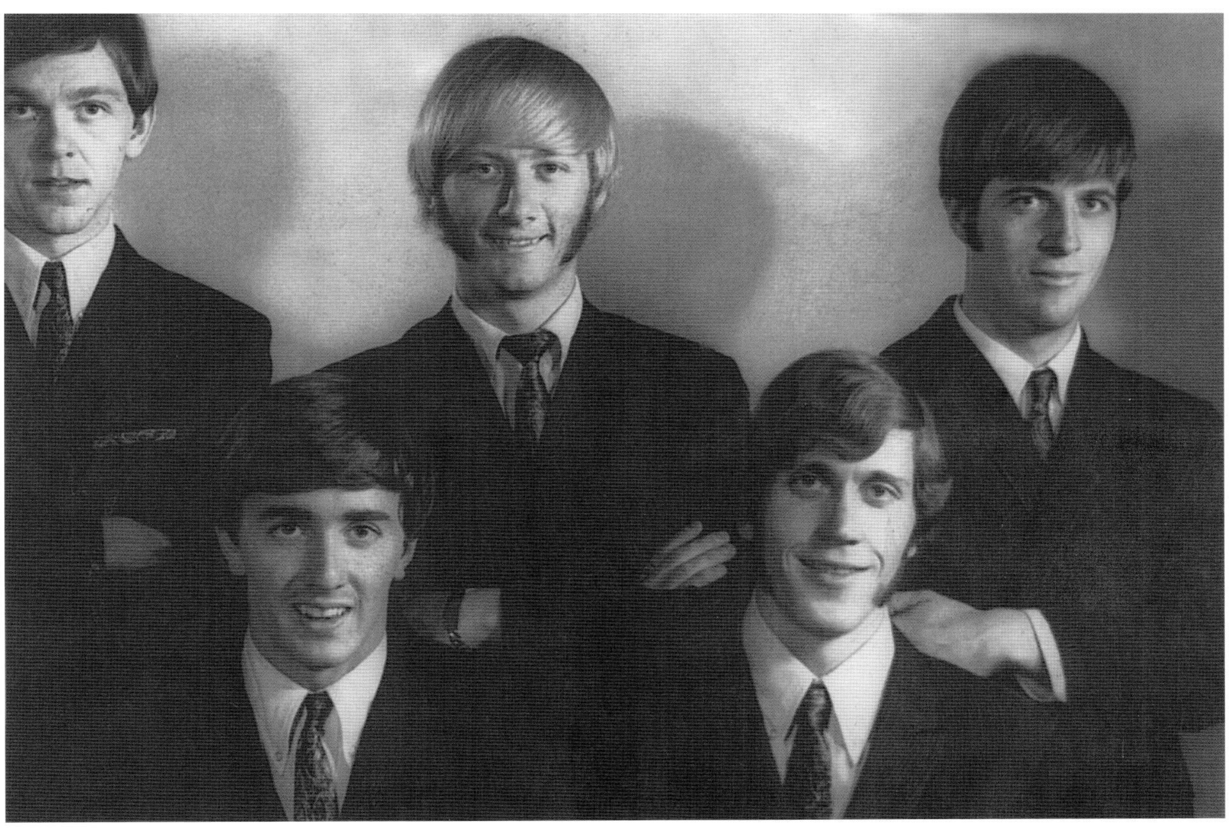

Poco predecessor Böenzee Cryque, c. 1967

to take his place. Young alone remained of the original lineup. He, with Cotton, had had it with Poco—they were going to start the Cotton-Young Band and were writing songs for and auditioning female singers, "like a Fleetwood Mac situation."

But the band recruited keyboardist Kim Bullard and an English rhythm section, Steve Chapman on drums and Charlie Harrison on bass, to take on the road for a final tour, releasing one more record as Poco in 1979. With *Legend*, its 14th album, Poco finally cracked the top of the charts—the breakthrough, at last.

Legend resurrected the Poco spirits. Young, fittingly, wrote and sang on the gold album's surprise hit single, "Crazy Love." Cotton's "Heart of the Night" was a second Top 20 hit—not bad for a band that some had written off as a dusty anachronism of the country-rock era.

"A lot of people helped and did us favors and went out on a limb for us over the years," Young said. "We couldn't let them down. We owed them something. We believed in the value of the future, not the past."

Poco disbanded five years later. Young moved to Nashville in 1985, hoping to follow such country-rockers-gone-country as the Nitty Gritty Dirt Band and Michael Murphey onto the charts—"a Colorado boy battling the bugs and humidity, staying out of the ballpark for a while, waiting to see what's going to happen in country and rock music."

Young orchestrated a Poco reunion of the five original members in 1989, and the band's *Legacy* was certified gold.

"I thought it would be interesting to put it back together, and I missed my original partners. Things were never as exciting as that first period coming out of Colorado."

The team of Young and Cotton carried as Poco until 2010. ●

CHUCK E. WEISS }

FOR HIS offbeat blend of Americana, Chuck E. Weiss was regarded as one of the coolest cats on the Los Angeles creative scene. What he described as "twisted jungle music"—inspirations that ranged from New Orleans dirge jazz to demented electric country-blues, brazenly mixed with boozy attitude and jive poetry—bristled with both cultural and historical value.

The synthesis represented the breadth of experience he gained growing up in northeast Denver in the 1950s and 1960s, where his aura (his idea of awesome was gold pointed-toe shoes and black cut-off t-shirts) gave him a reputation for being a little offbeat—but right on the beat.

"I was the only Jew for a hundred miles. I felt like a Ubangi dropped in Times Square on New Year's Eve," Weiss recalled with a laugh.

"Denver was more cosmopolitan then. When our parents were kids, it was a hub for the railroads. Hence you had that huge skid row downtown that's now been yuppified as LoDo. The con was born there. All the grifters came in the early part of the century and they'd get their training and then they'd go to Chicago and other cities. That gave rise to all the bohemians coming to Denver.

"When (Jack) Kerouac discovered the place, it was already wide open. As a kid, I caught the tail end of that. People were different. The place had a lot of soul. There was a jazz station. There were so many little coffeehouses and clubs down in the Capitol Hill area—the Sign of the Tarot, the Exodus.

"We used to take the bus down to Larimer Street to go find stuff in pawnshops. You could hear a million great Mexican rock 'n' roll bands. There was one I liked called Mando & the Chili Peppers. Of course, they never went national, but there were always little things like that happening.

"I don't think anyone was ever there to document it. I don't think anybody ever took it seriously. Naturally, it molded me, so I took it seriously."

Weiss learned to drum, and circa 1970, Chuck Morris, a local manager and promoter, asked him to sit in during an appearance by Lightnin' Hopkins at Tulagi, a Boulder nightclub. The gig went well, and Weiss persuaded Hopkins, one of the last great exponents of Texas blues, to take him on tour.

Weiss hit it off with singer-songwriter Tom Waits at Ebbets Field, the now-defunct Denver club where

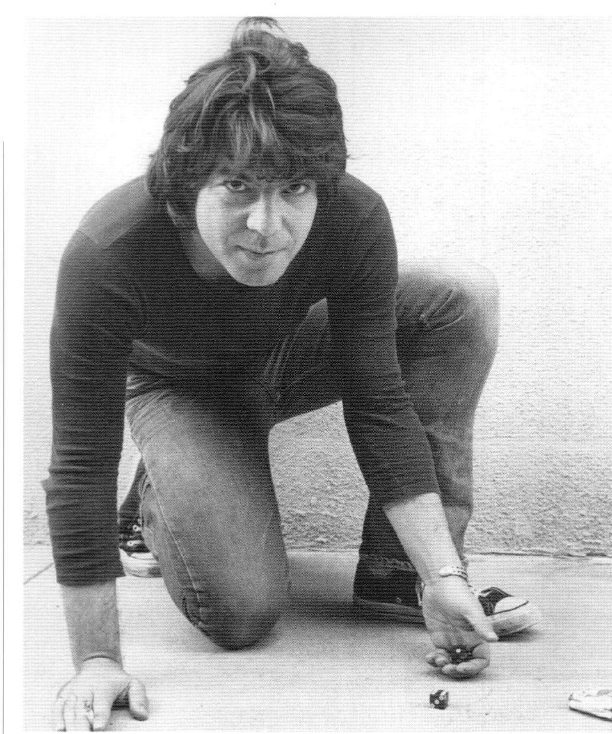

c. 1981

Waits was performing. The pair cultivated a lasting friendship.

Weiss subsequently moved to California, and in the late 1970s he joined Waits and an up-and-coming female artist named Rickie Lee Jones at the vanguard of an "alternative singer-songwriter" trend based out of West Hollywood's famed Tropicana Motel.

Jones later immortalized Weiss in her Top 5 hit "Chuck E.'s in Love" and won the 1979 Best New Artist Grammy. Waits sprinkled Weiss' likeness around a lot of his music.

Perhaps that encouraged the perception of Weiss as some sort of hipster novelty artist, but his music retained a life-learned authenticity. He played with his band at the Central, a Los Angeles nightclub, and later partnered with friend Johnny Depp to convert the space into the trendy Viper Room.

"I always wanted to sing like a black man and do business like a Jew. Instead, I sing like a Jew and do business like a black man," Weiss said.

In time, L.A.'s club-crawling night owl settled down. "The only bohemian thing that happens is the music, when I'm rehearsing and gigging with hepcat musicians. Other than that, I lead a pretty normal middle-class life. I go to the barbershop, I got my cats at home, I watch sports on TV... I got a routine." ●

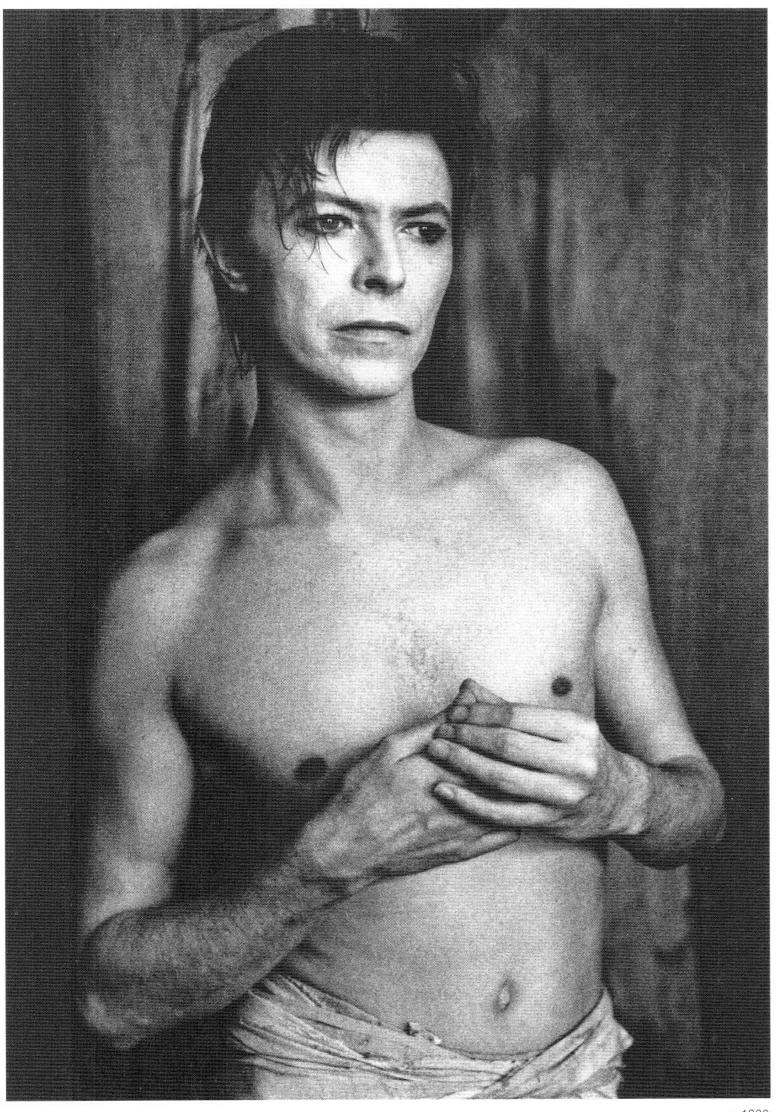

c. 1980

DAVID BOWIE }

ROCK'S ULTIMATE chameleon in the 1970s was David Bowie. From the glam-rock of his Ziggy Stardust character to the R&B of his Thin White Duke persona, he went through musical styles faster than he went through clothes, always moving on to another role, or even films.

On July 19, 1980, Bowie showed he had another surprise up his sleeve. He made his theatrical debut playing the title role in Bernard Pomerance's play, *The Elephant Man*. The Tony Award-winning hit opened its run in Denver, as the producers wanted to work out the kinks in a smaller market.

"The first moment on that Denver stage was probably the most scary moment of my life," Bowie recalled.

"Around music, with something I've written or a piece that I've designed, I've got a fair amount of faith in what I'm doing. But I didn't really know what was going to happen that first night. It was great just to be allowed to continue the performance."

A few years prior, Bowie had lived in Berlin as "a frame of reference," avoiding the United States unless he was working. But an appearance on the popular *Saturday Night Live* television show brought him to New York City during Christmas of 1979. There he saw *The Elephant Man* and met its director, the voluble Jack Hoffiss.

"It was nuts. It made no sense at all," Bowie admitted. "I'd never been offered a play before, and because of that, I accepted! Jack really convinced me that if I was going to fall on my face, he'd fall with me.

"I thought it was a wonderful performance piece, strange enough to keep my interest. So I jumped at the chance. I'd run out of good books to read."

Bowie always had more than a passing fancy in wedding theatrics and rock. He'd worked with Lindsay Kemp's mime troupe circa 1966 as David Jones, and his past experience helped him to prepare for *The Elephant Man*. In the drama, set in early 19th century England, Bowie played John Merrick, a young man horribly deformed from birth who was gradually transformed from a sideshow freak into a darling of aristocratic British society.

Bowie performed sans makeup or padding, letting his body illustrate the contortion—his twisted torso slumped to one side, his head arched at an uncomfortable angle, his right leg dragged.

"I get headaches. I take aspirin," Bowie allowed after opening night.

"It's the idea of putting over various points of view which intrigues me. It's creating environments that aren't there, seeming illusions. Rock productions and the theater stage are both very similar. You have to employ the same methods of vision to create a microcosm or a macrocosm. It's your yin and yang, ain't it?"

Bowie shortly took over the lead role in the New York production of *The Elephant Man* and won rave notices. ●

VAN HALEN }

WHEN ITS members were just a bar band, Van Halen looked up to groups that defined the rock 'n' roll party lifestyle. Perhaps intoxicated with their recent rise to predicted stardom in 1980, they were ready to do their own impersonation of hopelessly spoiled rock stars.

Van Halen's concert rider—the part of a performing contract that lists a act's requirements—stated that meals always included servings of M&M candies, with the brown ones removed. This was real power in the band's eyes, as the promoter was confronted with the task of hand-removing the offending candies.

At the start of the tour in support of the *Van Halen II* album, at a college show at the University of Southern Colorado in Pueblo, the band decided that the proviso was not being met. They trashed the facilities—and did $10,000 worth of damage.

"We were taking a ginormous production out on the road," singer David Lee Roth explained in his usual overdrive hyper-jive way. "Nobody was used to the kind of manpower and logistics it took to wrench that around.

"Every backstage looks identical—you have a bowl of Pringles and soda pop. So an idea was tossed around—'How do we prevent technical errors in this monster production? We'll write something about M&Ms in the middle of the contract rider!'

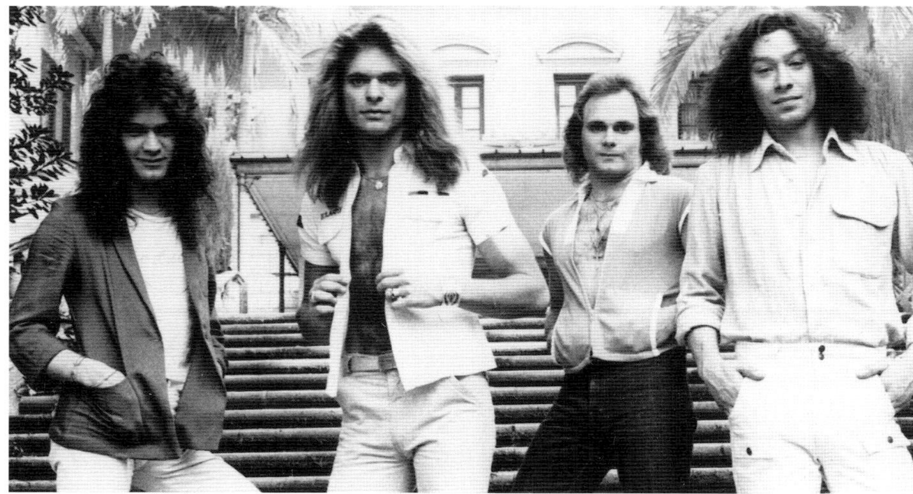

c. 1980

"If there were no brown M&Ms, it meant that the promoter read the contract and things were going to run smoothly. If you saw a brown M&M, guaranteed if you ran a line check you'd find technical error after error—all of which would happen during the show. And when you have moving pieces...c'mon, those tickets ain't cheap."

Ten thousand dollars was a lot of money even for Van Halen, but the result was national publicity for the tour—even *Time* magazine ran a piece on the band. It helped catapult Van Halen into superstar status. ●

HEART }

DELIVERING ACOUSTIC serenades and tomboy rock 'n' roll with equal aplomb, Heart found immediate success in the 1970s and racked up a string of hits—"Crazy on You," "Magic Man," "Barracuda," "Straight On" and others.

The two-record *Greatest Hits/Live* pulled together the obvious highpoints, fleshed out with six spirited live tracks—including a warmly elegant cover of "Unchained Melody" recorded at McNichols Arena in Denver.

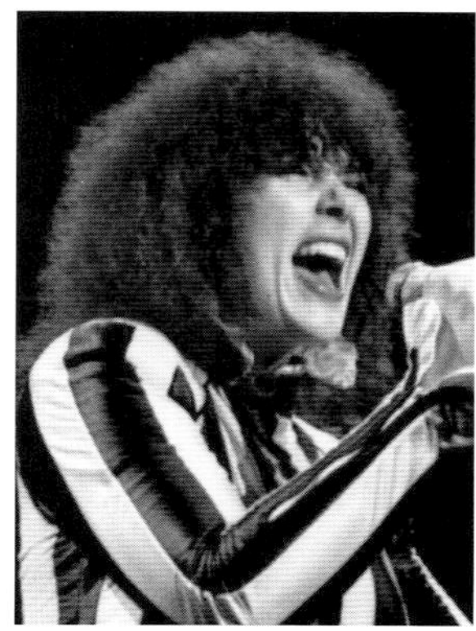

Ann Wilson at McNichols Arena, 1980

"It's one of those songs they used to write a long time ago—beautiful, no effects," singer Ann Wilson said.

Wilson had incurred oxygen debt singing it in the Mile High City in September 1980.

"When you sing rock 'n' roll or do something athletic, you use up more oxygen. We went up to the mountains to check out Caribou Studios, and they had oxygen bottles on the wall like a cigarette machine. We did a casual track and my voice sounded thin.So I kept a tank of oxygen stage left when Heart played Denver."

"Unchained Melody" was left off the CD reissue of Heart's *Greatest Hits/Live*, but the version was included on 2002's *The Essential Heart*. ●

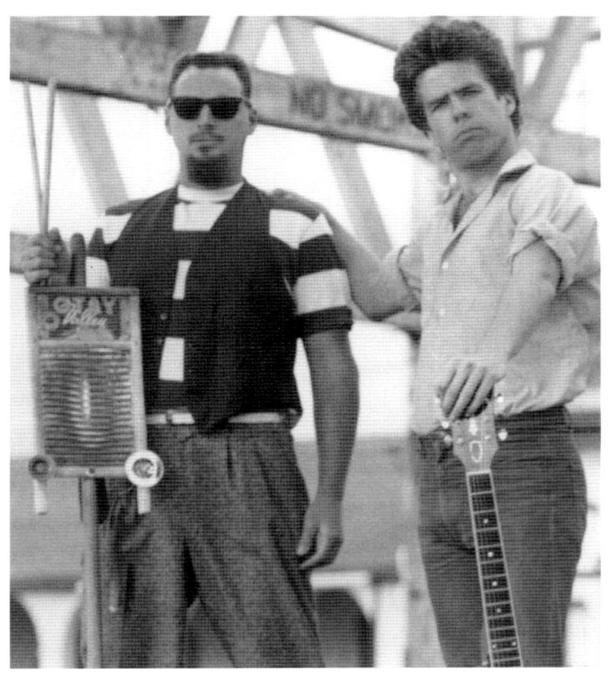
With Skid Roper, c. 1985

MOJO NIXON }

ROCK ECCENTRIC Mojo Nixon parlayed an irrepressible personality, a roguish sense of humor and a fondness for lusty rockabilly into swaggering punk originals like "Elvis Is Everywhere," "Debbie Gibson Is Pregnant with My Two-Headed Love Child," "Don Henley Must Die" and "Stuffin' Martha's Muffin," achieving a measure of national fame throughout the late 1980s.

Nixon had always been gonzo. The singer lived in Denver circa 1980-1981, when he was still appearing under his birth name Kirby McMillan. He and his punk band Zebra 123 were questioned by the U.S. Secret Service for their part in the Assassination Ball at the notorious Malfunction Junction in the Capitol Hill area.

"It took place on Nov. 22, 1980, which happened to be the anniversary of John F. Kennedy being caught in the triangulation at the grassy knoll. Zebra 123 had been banned from everywhere. We weren't 'skinny-tie, new wave' cute, we were pissed off—three chords and a cloud of dust.

"We got together with two other bands and decided to put on our own show. This girlfriend of mine took a picture of Jimmy Carter and Ronald Reagan—the presidential election was going on then—and made it look as if they'd been shot from below and their heads were exploding, not unlike JFK's.

"That got the Secret Service on us. They came and gave us a big lecture, and they didn't like our show. So there's a file on me somewhere."

McMillan moved to San Diego and came up with his stage name (a combination of "voodoo and bad politics"). The newly christened Mojo Nixon began performing with a partner, washboard-harmonica player Skid Roper, and quickly expanded his cult audience. ●

TIM GOODMAN }

CIRCA 1980, Denver rock promoter Barry Fey got the go-ahead from CBS Records to assemble talent for his own custom label. Under the arrangement, his Feyline Presents handled all of the basic record company functions but got to use the corporate muscle of CBS for distribution.

Feyline Records got off to a slow start. Fey recorded a band called the Flyers, but CBS heard the final tapes and raised a corporate eyebrow, saying the band sounded like a watered-down Firefall.

The next signing was Tim Goodman, another artist with a Colorado past whose *Footsteps* was a more suitable debut release for Feyline Records.

Goodman had spent years honing his craft in locales across the entire country, including the mountains of Colorado. The singer-songwriter-guitarist was managed by Marty Wolff, who, ironically, was Fey's rival as they both promoted shows in the Denver area in the mid-1970s.

Footsteps was produced by Doobie Brothers lead guitarist John McFee. In September 1981, "New Romeo" bubbled under the *Billboard* Hot 100 at #107.

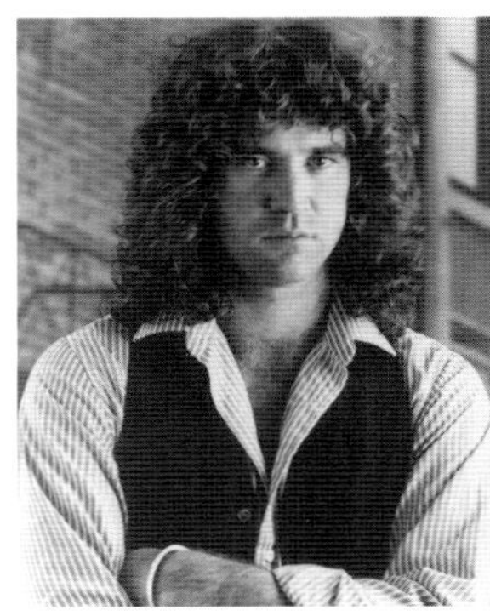
c. 1981

"A guy named Alex Call wrote it," Goodman said. "He was an original member of Clover with McFee. He sent me a cassette and, on the flip side, there were some titles scratched out. The first tune was 'New Romeo.' I called Alex and asked him about this tune. He said, 'Oh, I'm holding on to that for myself.' I worked on him for a year before he let me cut the song."

But that was the extent of Feyline Records' legacy. The imprint went under, not with a bang but a whimper. In 1983, Goodman cut his hair and pursued a country rock sound as Southern Pacific's vocalist. ●

CARL WILSON }

DURING THE 1960s, the Beach Boys' ability to surf the waves of commercial success and artistic development made them America's preeminent pop group. By the late 1970s, the venerable band was threatening to splinter. Carl Wilson, guitarist of the Beach Boys and the man who many people credited with keeping the group together all those years, ventured out on his own to release his self-titled solo debut for Caribou Records in 1981.

"I never pushed to do a solo record because my first responsibility had always been to the Beach Boys," he explained. "But they had mostly just done concerts for the last couple of years. The group can't really provide me with an outlet for the other music I love to play—good, straight-ahead rock 'n' roll. I just wanted to get some of that off my chest."

That funkier, rocking side of Wilson dominated *Carl Wilson*. Myrna Smith, formerly of the Sweet Inspirations, co-wrote all of the songs with Wilson and supplied vocals.

When it came time to choose a producer, Wilson gravitated to Jim Guercio, the Chicago mentor who ended a three-year absence from the studio to undertake the project at his home base, Colorado's Caribou Ranch.

"I moved to Colorado and lived in the mountains very near Caribou," Wilson said. "It's beautiful. I love it."

Guercio also played bass and percussion on several tracks. "Heaven" was the song that manifested the magic and passion of a Beach Boys work.

Carl Wilson charted for two weeks on the *Billboard* Top 200 in May 1981. In support of his album, Wilson embarked on the first solo tour by a Beach Boy.

"I feel like a lucky dog—we always have been," Wilson said. "Gosh, it's been a wonderful run."

Wilson died in February 1998 from complications of lung cancer at the age of 51. ●

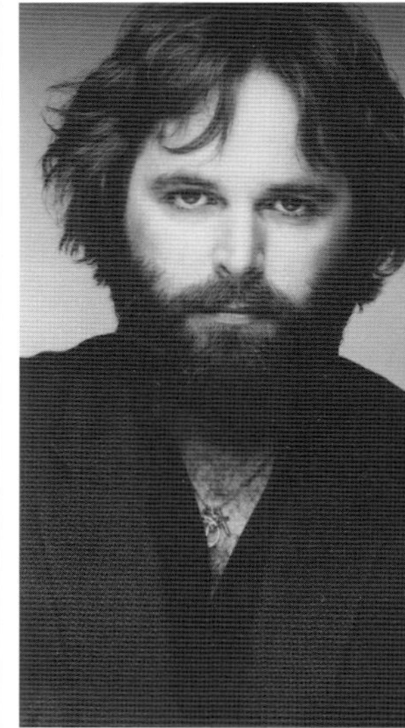

c. 1981

DAVID CROSBY }

THE ESTABLISHMENT of the 1950s told drug horror stories—notably, that marijuana leads to harder stuff. David Crosby didn't believe them, but in his case they were right.

The musician, a pivotal member of two seminal groups, the Byrds and Crosby, Stills, Nash & Young, first smoked pot in Boulder, Colorado.

"The year was nineteen-hundred-and-frozen-to-death," the singer reminisced. "I spent a winter playing in a basement coffeehouse on the Hill called the Attic. A fellow musician gave me my first joint and I loved it. I was driving a car at the time—thought I was going 85, but the speedometer read 40."

In the 1960s and 1970s, Crosby managed to out-drug Stills, Nash and Young combined. But the 1980s were rough on him. His well-documented substance-abuse problem and the resultant paranoia left him a shell of a performer. He got busted so often he should have installed a drive-through window. The arrests piled up: cocaine, heroin, guns, assault and battery. By 1985, he was rock's most tragic figure, lucky to be alive.

A five-year jail sentence stemming from drug and possession charges in Texas caught up with Crosby before death did. When he finally surrendered to authorities, by his own admission, he and girlfriend Jan Dance were consuming approximately seven grams of cocaine a day as well as a half a gram of heroin.

But Crosby beat his addiction. He finally went cold turkey, serving nine months of hard time before leaving prison on parole.

"For two or three years before I went in the can, I didn't write a song. And that's what scared me to death in prison. Not the guys saying, 'Hey, rock star, c'mere—where's all yer money?' It was the fact that God put me on earth to write songs, and I'd gotten to the point where I couldn't do it anymore.

"But after six months, I woke up one day and it came to me. And now I know the reality of it all—it's not hip to be fucked up anymore, not if you want to do creative work. I got very loaded for a long time. I enjoyed it at first, started with a few joints. But when I got strung out, it was very hard for me. I'm not going to preach about drugs—that's up to everyone to decide for themselves. But if you watched my life, you can figure it out."

Crosby bounced back musically, remaining as colorful and newsworthy a character as before. "I still can't believe I was that stupid—but I'm proof that it's never too late to wise up." ●

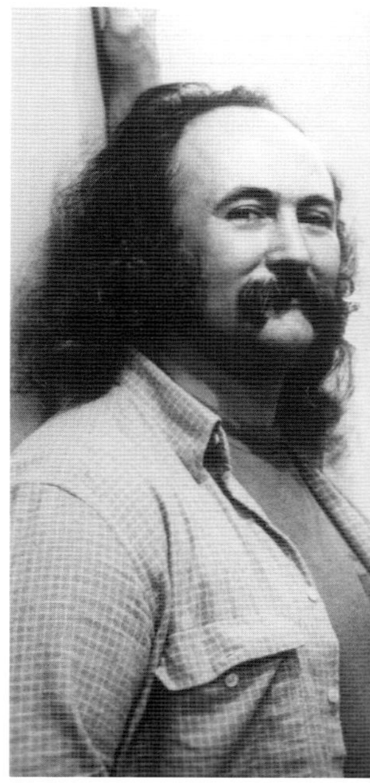

c. 1981

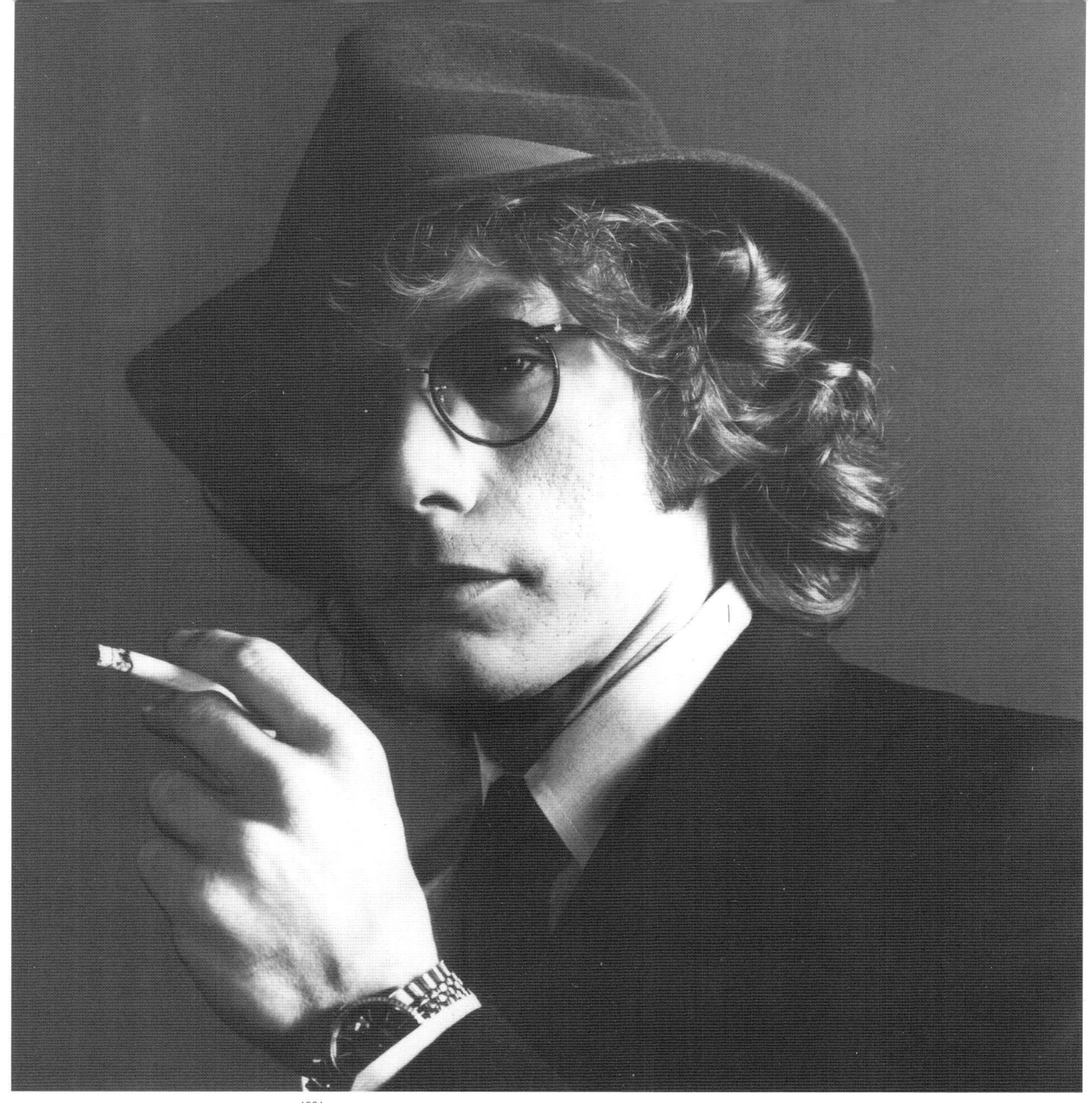

c. 1981

WARREN ZEVON }

AS THE Everly Brothers' pianist-bandleader in the early 1970s, Warren Zevon spent a couple of years touring. After the duo's breakup, he worked alternately with Phil and Don Everly—and sojourned to Aspen long enough to be appointed honorary coroner of Pitkin County, Colorado.

"My ex-wife grew up in Aspen, which is a sort of rarity, I presume," Zevon explained. "So we ended up there. A friend of mine was running for councilman, and late one night in the Hotel Jerome bar, I said that if he won, I wanted to be appointed coroner. He said, 'Well, it is an appointment.' He won, and I was. I think of it like a perpetuity."

Singer-songwriter Zevon's ironic tales of physical and psychological mayhem had earned him a cult following, and he was dubbed "the Sam Peckinpah of rock" after the director who opened the door for graphic violence in movies. In 1978, he'd had a Top 10 single with "Werewolves of London." But his career was temporarily set back by alcoholism.

After a year in the studio and "in training," Zevon's 1980 release, *Bad Luck Streak in Dancing School*, represented something of a comeback for him, and he was eager to tour. First, he enlisted the aid of East Coast guitar ace David Landau. Then he met the group called Boulder.

Boulder was seven players, most of them writers and five of them singers. The nucleus formed in Florida in 1972, and the other members, all veterans of bar bands throughout the U.S., joined in installments. The act was complete by 1976, when the members relocated to Colorado and acquired their name.

Boulder did college and club dates, but the members were wary of becoming a copy band and burning out on the road. They finally built their own rehearsal studio in a two-car garage in the vicinity of Denver.

"One of our roadies was a carpenter, and we went all out with hammers and nails and plasterboard," drummer

Marty Stinger recalled.

Boulder began recording material in Florida in January 1978 and did additional work at Caribou Ranch in Colorado. The band signed with Elektra/Asylum Records in November and moved to Los Angeles. The debut album, *Boulder*, included a harrowing and intelligent version of Zevon's "Join Me in L.A."

"We liked the theme of the song, and we were moving to L.A., where we'd never been before," lead singer Bob Harris explained.

So Zevon took to the road, not with the L.A. session guys from his albums, but with the little-known Colorado group. The so-called audition consisted of a spirited version of "Johnny B. Goode." Zevon's somewhat sudden decision to record his new touring band in concert spoke volumes about the guy's essential rock 'n' roll attitude.

"The idea always appeals to me to find a self-contained band, or at least find musicians who are accustomed to playing with each other," he said.

The difference was apparent on the live recording, *Stand in the Fire*, cut at the Roxy in Los Angeles. One of Zevon's best albums, *Rolling Stone* called it "a portrait of the artist defiantly walking the line between emotional exorcism and mass entertainment."

Throughout, Boulder anchored the star's feisty roar with a tight, tenacious beat. Zevon struck up the band for the title track, a vigorous celebration of the rock 'n' roll spirit driven by guitarist Zeke Zimgieble: "Our lead guitar player's scalding hot/And Zeke's going at it, giving it every thing he's got," he shouted proudly in a lusty, Elvis Presley-like baritone.

Zevon often performed shirtless on the summer tour, which was titled "The Dog Ate the Part We Didn't Like," a line borrowed from his friend, novelist Thomas McGuane.

"That was the culmination of a two-year physical fitness period in my life. I think I was celebrating the Chuck Norris-like physique of that era," Zevon said.

"It was a real turning point for Warren because he had just gotten out of rehab and kicked the bottle," Harris said. "He had this incredible amount of energy. All of a sudden he knew where to put it, and he could turn it into being good.

"He went to some tailor in Beverly Hills and bought these $1,200 suits and was going to play in them—he'd been doing dancing and karate and was going to come across really classy. And about two weeks into the tour, he'd ripped the pants and the coats just leaping around on stage. So after that, he went out in blue jeans and t-shirt.

"Seeing him onstage every night, he was probably the most consistent performer I've ever seen. On the bus one night, he said, 'Man, I had to realize that these people out here are my friends.' It went from being good to phenomenal."

But the success wasn't enough to keep Boulder going.

"The producer from Elektra scammed the whole deal and screwed the band—which is not an uncommon situation, but we had our turn at it," Harris said.

Meanwhile, Zevon continued his solo career. *Time* magazine's reviewers gave "Song Title of the Year" to his rollicking "Things to Do in Denver When You're Dead" from *Mr. Bad Example*, his 11th album. *People* magazine called it "a hoot."

"Um, it had to be a two-syllable town—Indianapolis wouldn't work," Zevon explained. "It had to start with a 'D.' It had to have a Rattlesnake Cafe. Those were kind of the parameters. Everyone seemed to enjoy it the last time I played Colorado."

In 2003, Zevon died of mesothelioma, a form of lung cancer, at age 56. ●

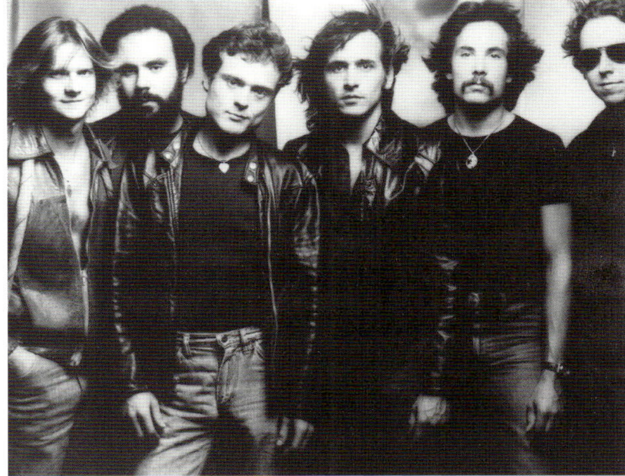

Boulder, c. 1979

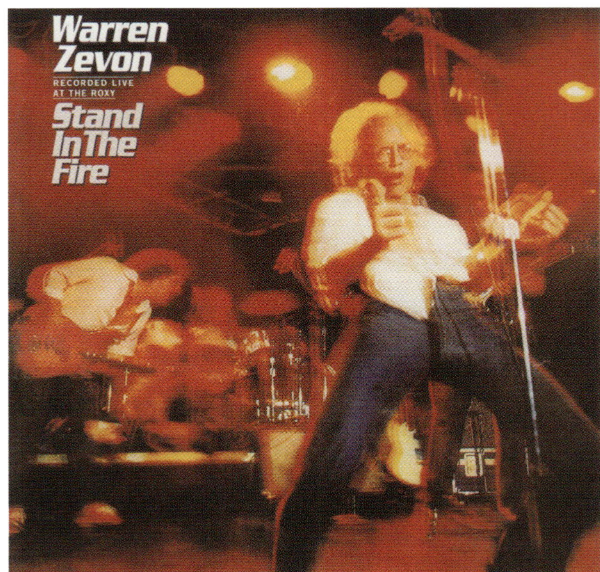

Stand in the Fire LP, 1980

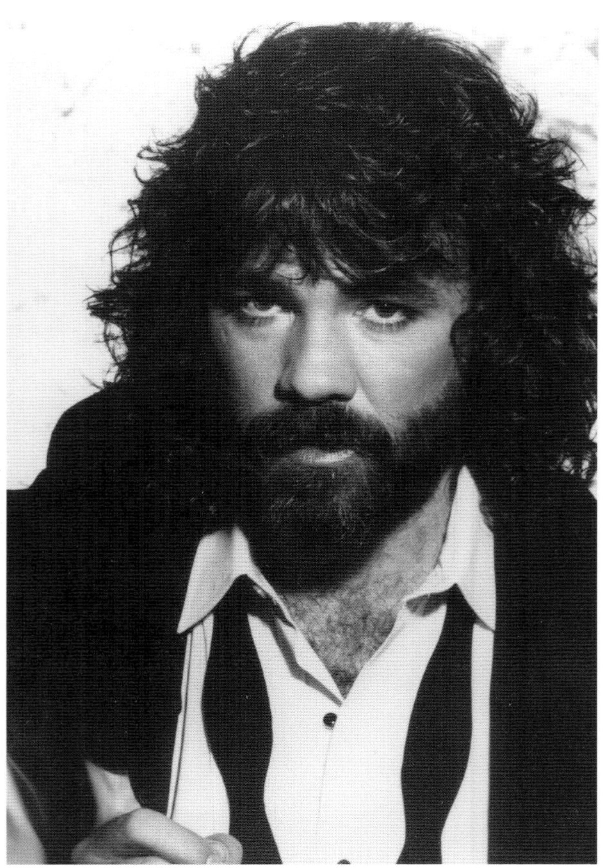

c. 1983

GARY MORRIS }

SUSTAINING A string of smash country records in the 1980s, Gary Morris credited Colorado as the place where he gained his most valuable experience.

The Texas native had intended to enroll in college and play football, but the summer after finishing high school he and two buddies went to Colorado.

"That was the beginning of my singing career," Morris said. "We stopped at a bar in Colorado Springs called the Golden Bee. We asked the bartender if we could do a few songs. We stood up on some tables and did 'Gentle on My Mind,' 'Early Morning Rain' and 'Visions of Sugar Plums.' The audience just went crazy. We collected $35 in tips and quickly translated that figure into what we could make singing 20 songs. We thought, 'This is it!'"

The trio traveled on to Boulder, where Morris rented an apartment and got a job as a construction worker. They also sang at a bar called the Three Kings "for beer and cheeseburgers." As summer's end drew near, Morris opted to forego college and turn his attention to singing and performing. For several years, he fronted a trio that entertained regularly at Taylor's Supper Club in Denver. He also gained valuable studio experience under the direction of Maryruth Weyand of Carousel Productions, singing and writing jingles for accounts such as Coors Beer and Frontier Airlines.

From 1976 to 1979, Denver was a full-time address for Morris when he fronted Breakaway, a seven-piece country rock band, with his writing and vocals as the driving force.

"The band was conceived to support my singing," Morris recalled. "In time, though, it became a 'personality' band with everyone involved using a nickname and so on. As I became more serious musically, I saw the need to make some drastic personnel changes. We were vying to get signed as a pre-Alabama, pre-Charlie Daniels Band type of group, but it wasn't in the cards at that time."

Morris eventually made the decision to go solo, even though Breakaway "was as good a band as you'll ever hear." He made the trek to Nashville to take a shot at the real music business. "Headed for a Heartache" and "The Love She Found in Me" were the records that established him as a Music City brand name.

Morris had 16 singles reach the Top 10 on the country charts, including five No. 1 hits. He is probably best known for his original recording of "The Wind Beneath My Wings," which won "Song of the Year" awards from both the Country Music Association and the Academy of Country Music. *Why Lady Why* peaked at #174 on *Billboard*'s pop album charts in 1983 and earned a gold certification.

Morris took a break from touring and pursued a successful theatrical career. He also hosted and produced The Nashville Network's *The North American Sportsman*, which related his love of the outdoors. He then resided in southern Colorado at his own hunting and fly-fishing executive resort, Mountain Spirit Lodge.

"I once missed an elk hunt in the Bob Marshall Wilderness Area because of a commitment to perform in the Broadway adaptation of Puccini's 'La Boheme' with Linda Ronstadt. I swore, 'Never again!' I'm forced to spend at least half of the year in Nashville because of my touring and producing schedule, but every spare moment I get, I'm back in Colorado."●

DAVE GRUSIN }

PIANIST, CONDUCTOR, arranger, composer, producer—Dave Grusin covered a lot of ground in the music business. But he saw no rationale in keeping score.

"I'm not keen on the idea of competition in my area," Grusin mused. "If they want competition, they should have eight guys sit down and write the same thing and see who does it the fastest. It's not really important to pit different types of work against each other. So I've tried to take a low profile. I'd rather just do the work."

Born in June 1934 and raised in Littleton, Colorado, Grusin was exposed to music right away. His father, Henri, a watchmaker and accomplished violinist, had performed chamber music in hotels throughout the East Coast for 30 years. It rubbed off on Grusin, who started playing piano at the age of four. He credited his father with instilling in him and his brother, Don, an understanding of classical music and "the literature of great orchestration."

As a teenager, Grusin was taken to jazz concerts, where he heard Lester Young, Ella Fitzgerald, Ray Brown and Oscar Peterson, and he began enjoying artists like Art Tatum and Count Basie.

"I started to go wrong sometime around 13 or 14 years old," Grusin quipped. "I could relate to Art Tatum from a technical standpoint primarily. I liked early Brubeck, too, when he was doing the contrapuntal arrangements of standards."

Enrolled in the University of Colorado at Boulder's music school, Grusin played with some jazz groups, working the usual frat parties and clubs.

"We thought we were creative, but we didn't know what we were doing," he recalled. "It took me a while to realize that bass players were supposed to hit specific notes for certain chords."

Grusin wanted to play jazz more than dance music, however, and that attitude got him fired. While still a piano major in Boulder, he found time to play with visiting artists like Art Pepper, Terry Gibbs and singer Anita O'Day. But film composers became his real heroes.

In 1959, Grusin moved to New York, planning for an academic career. He eventually became the music director of *The Andy Williams Show*, a job that brought him to Hollywood. During that time, he also did his first recording dates.

Grusin left Williams after three years to score television sitcoms, hoping they would pave the way for movie assignments.

In 1967, he broke into film with *Divorce American Style* and then *The Graduate*. More commissions quickly followed. Records created the next challenge. Sergio Mendez with Brazil '66 called upon him to arrange such hits as "Fool on the Hill" and "The Look of Love." Quincy Jones recruited him as a player and arranger on many of his sessions as well as the Brothers Johnson albums.

In the 1980s, the Colorado native brought his talents into focus.

As a producer and businessman, Grusin ran GRP Records, a classy mainstream jazz label with popular artists like the Rippingtons, Spyro Gyra, David Benoit, Lee Ritenour and Tom Scott.

As an artist, the jazz pianist recorded his own records. Four cracked the *Billboard* album charts. 1981's *Mountain Dance* was the most successful, peaking at #74.

And as a film composer and producer, Grusin worked on the soundtracks for such notable pictures as *Heaven Can Wait*, *The Champ* and *On Golden Pond*. His many awards include a 1988 Oscar for best original score for *The Milagro Beanfield War*. "It Might Be You" from *Tootsie* received a Best Original Song nomination. He scored *The Fabulous Baker Boys* and was a 1989 Grammy Award winner. For television, he composed "Theme from St. Elsewhere," which hit #15 on *Billboard*'s easy listening charts.

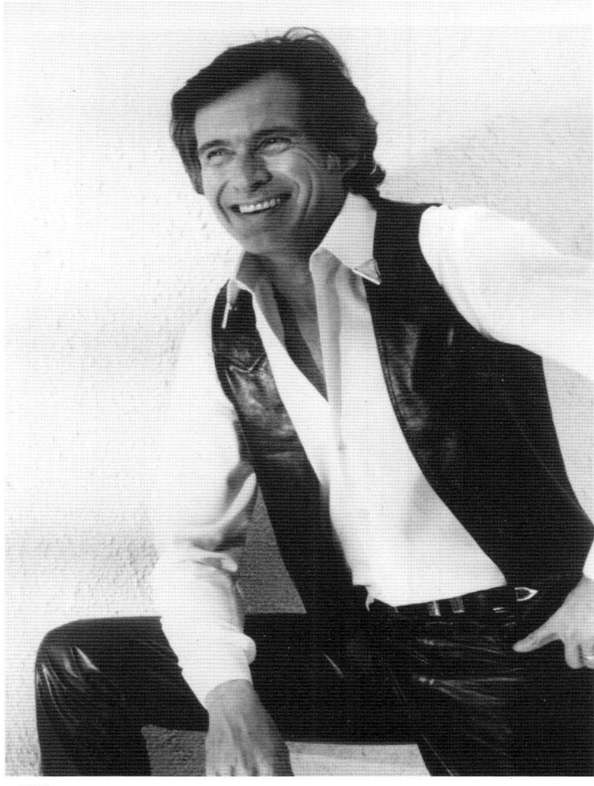

c. 1982

Grusin, with a filmography of about 100 titles, received an honorary doctorate from the University of Colorado in 1989. He continued doing numerous projects through the 1990s, from fusion and pop recordings to working with symphony orchestras. In 2002, he added a further Grammy to his collection for arranging on the James Taylor album *October Road*. ●

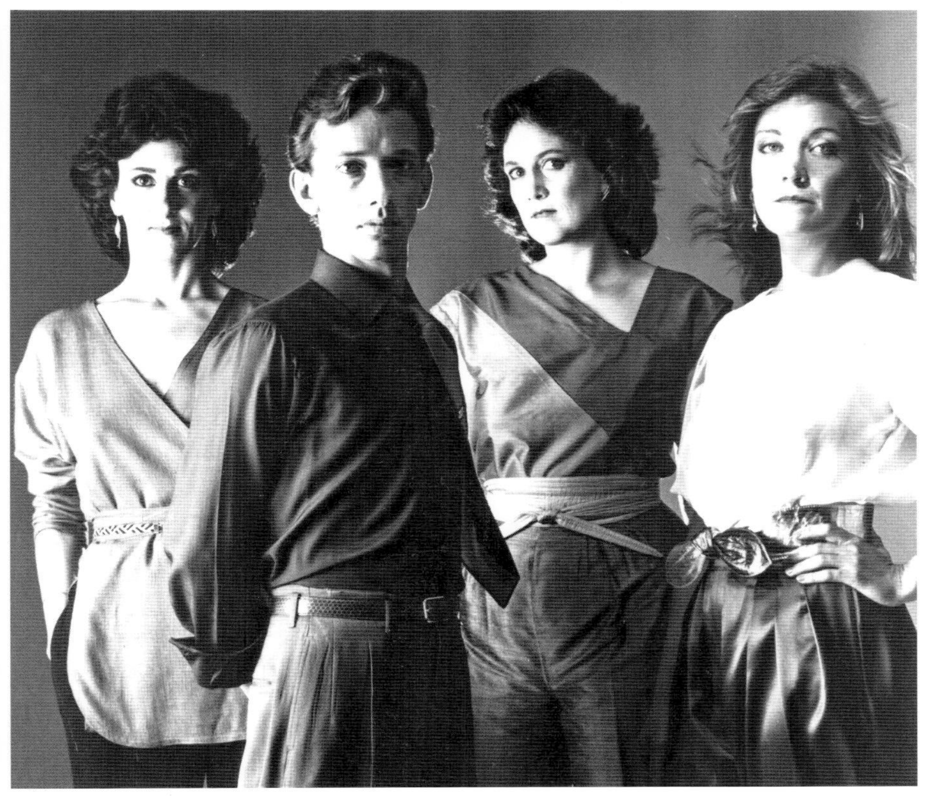

c. 1983

RARE SILK }

BASED IN Boulder, Rare Silk emerged as a Grammy-nominated vocal group, climbing the jazz charts with a contemporary harmonic sound and marvelous, imaginative arrangements.

Originally a female trio consisting of sisters Gaile and Marylynn Gillaspie and Marguerite Juenemann, Rare Silk started out revisiting tunes from the swing era of the late 1930s and early 1940s. At the 1978 inception of KGNU, a community radio station for Boulder, they created a regular public access show.

"We would go in and record three songs every week," Marylynn Gillaspie said. "And that's how we built our repertoire, drawing on the vocal styles of the Boswell Sisters and the Andrews Sisters. We wore vintage dresses and built a small following in area clubs."

The three got their break in 1980 when they met Benny Goodman, "the King of Swing," opening for him at Macky Auditorium in Boulder. Goodman fell in love with the girls' tight, precisely harmonized material and asked them to go on his tour. They made their debut with the clarinetist at the Boston Globe Jazz Festival, which was live broadcast on PBS, and performed at Carnegie Hall, the Playboy Jazz Festival at the Hollywood Bowl and the Aurex Jazz Festival in Japan.

Goodman wanted the trio to sing standards, but Rare Silk was restless. Joined by male vocalist Todd Buffa, the innovative ensemble began modernizing its approach. The echoes of the past were gone; programs now came from stylistic versions of Keith Jarrett and Chick Corea songs.

"We didn't sound like any other four-part harmony group," Marylynn Gillaspie said. "Manhattan Transfer, the other leading vocal jazz group at the time, had the standard two men, two women lineup, and they stacked their voices in typical intervals. But we didn't come from tradition; Todd had his own way of putting harmonies together. He and Marguerite were trained, and Gaile and I had a street sense. That was the magic."

Rare Silk's sound was soon heard by a PolyGram A&R exec. The group recorded a debut album with illustrious session players such as Michael and Randy Brecker backing up their vocal performances. *New Weave* made its way to #2 on *Billboard*'s Jazz Albums chart, where it stayed for many weeks. It contained a notable version of "Red Clay," and Buffa was nominated for the Arrangement–Two or More Voices category at the 1984 Grammy Awards; *New Weave* was nominated for Best Jazz Vocal–Duo or Group category.

Juenemann wanted to pursue more traditional jazz styles; she was replaced by Barbara Reeves, then Jamie Broumas. Rare Silk recorded *American Eyes* on the Palo Alto label in 1985 and toured perpetually, traveling by van and trailer with its backup musicians. At clubs and musical festivals, the group won over audiences with perfected harmonies, choreographed sequences and a diverse mixture of material.

"We didn't isolate ourselves in the jazz world," Marylynn Gillaspie said. "Driving across the country, we all had our Walkmans and headphones, listening to whatever was going on that was good. In the scat singing and improvisational parts of our live shows, we'd incorporate Talking Heads and David Bowie stuff, even go into Culture Club's 'I'll Tumble 4 Ya.'

"We had a good run for ten years, but it got to the point where it was more of a struggle than fun."

Rare Silk made the decision to disband by 1988. ●

THE NAILS }

LED BY PATTI Smith lookalike Marc Campbell, the Nails began their musical life as the Ravers, Colorado's punk rock forefathers.

In 1976, Campbell arrived in Boulder from San Francisco, where he'd been turning out 16mm films and performing "sexually explicit" songs in small clubs with another guitarist-poet in a duo they called the Pits of Passion. One day Campbell was reading the University of Colorado bulletin board and noticed a card posted by David Kaufman, who sought to form a reggae band. "My interests were moving in that direction anyhow, so I called him," Campbell said.

The Ravers' nucleus was formed, and the five-piece band soon developed a cult following. The combination of reggae, ska, mid-1960s rock and high-volume tone poems set the Rocky Mountain music scene on its edge. This was at the very beginning of the New York/London punk explosion—and in Colorado, Firefall and the like still ruled the area's numerous country bars.

The Ravers recorded "Cops Are Punks" at Boulder's Mountain Ears Studio, and the single received national attention from the magazine *Trouser Press*. One fateful day, the police raided the band's basement rehearsal hall, mistakenly thinking it was a bomb factory. Shortly thereafter, Campbell and Kaufman elected to search out wider vistas, and they moved the entire group to New York City. Years of steady gigging in the Manhattan clubs followed.

"We had a friend in real estate who let us use an empty five-story house on the Upper East Side. The bad news was that it had no furniture, so we all slept on the floor," Campbell said.

Once transplanted, the group slowly began its transition to the Nails, mining the rich "American poetic tradition" also worked by Lou Reed, the Doors and Bruce Springsteen.

Campbell explained that the Nails' music emanated from "a mystical and sexual area. I write in a cinematic way, trying to create through language and sound, texture and atmosphere, a specific mood. Each of the songs—little fictions, I call them—tells a story to explore those moods."

Originally recorded for the 1981 EP *Hotel For Women*, "88 Lines About 44 Women" was re-recorded and distributed nationally on RCA Records in 1984. The sardonic song made people everywhere sit up and take notice. Certainly many members of the male species knew at least a few of the archetypal females in the lyrics, and a lot of women recognized themselves in the tightly compacted two-line life stories. The Nails had constructed a tune that took an unflinching look at real life in the New York tradition of Lou Reed's "Walk on the Wild Side," the New York Dolls' "Personality Crisis" and Jim Carroll's "People Who Died."

Los Angeles progressive radio giant KROQ-FM put "88 Lines About 44 Women" in heavy rotation and the song zoomed up the dance floor charts. The Nails subsequently played their first U.S. tour, concentrating on southern California and Colorado.

Over the years, "88 Lines About 44 Women" continued to appear on new wave compilations. In the late 1990s, a television commercial for the Mazda Protégé showed a group of hip twentysomethings driving a vehicle through a surrealistic city accompanied by a vocal set to the Nails' "88 Lines About 44 Women," bemoaning the trials and tribulations of their workday lives. ●

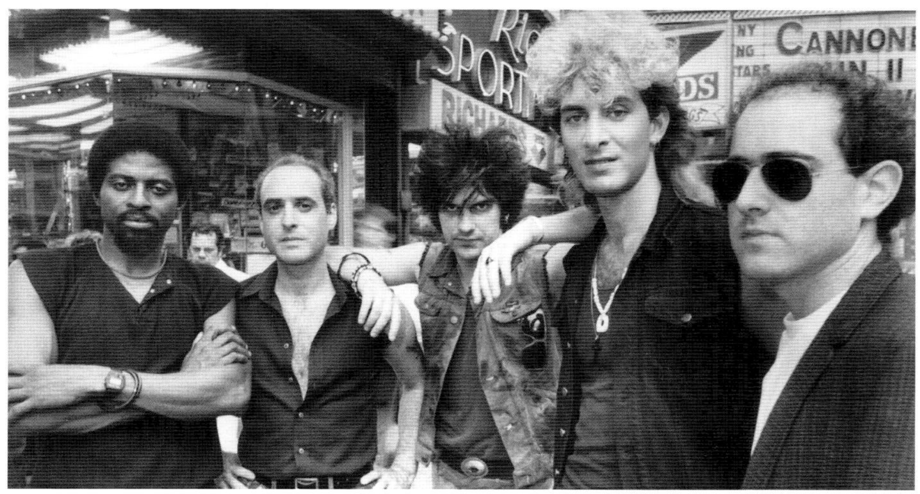

c. 1983

Red Rocks Amphitheatre, June 5, 1983

U2 }

NESTLED IN the foothills of Morrison, Colorado, 20 minutes from downtown Denver, Red Rocks Amphitheatre is a geologic phenomenon—an acoustically perfect outdoor venue not duplicated anywhere in the world, a visual marvel of natural rock formations. Today, it ranks as one of the planet's most awesome and important concert locales.

The natural wonder of the Red Rocks setting wasn't cemented in the imaginations of rockers everywhere until U2 staged a now-famous concert video, *Under a Blood Red Sky*. However, a lot of things had to go wrong in order for the show to come off so right.

In 1980, U2 came through Denver on its first American tour, playing at the Rainbow Music Hall. Promoter Chuck Morris knew the young Irish band was destined for greater things and wanted to show off Red Rocks to the members. They immediately fell in love, and manager Paul McGuinness vowed that one day they would film a performance there.

Three years later, U2 carried out the commitment when Red Rocks was booked for June 5, 1983. By that time, the college-radio underdogs had made a mark on the rock scene by dint of honest, emotional performances.

"It was the first U.S. trip where a record (*War*) was doing quite well, a (writer and a) few people in radio got behind us—we might have made some money," lead singer Bono said. "We were going to invest that money into documenting our victorious tour."

From day one, the logistics proved to be formidable. No one had ever attempted such a project before, and it was a costly proposition. For the full effect of the mountain scenery to be caught on camera, the huge rocks had to be lit up at a cost of $40,000, according to McGuinness.

However, the band proceeded with the lofty plans. Gavin Taylor, the director of *The Tube* (an avant-garde English video program), was flown over to oversee the filming. Steve Lillywhite, the producer of U2's albums, was also transported from Europe to properly record the live audio on location. Special effects including backdrops and two bonfires on the rocks were generated.

But on the day of the show, miserable weather moved in and threatened to ruin the entire scenario. Temperatures dropped to 40 degrees at showtime, and a day's worth of drizzle evolved into a deluge. It was no place to be holding a concert, but with all the investment in one show, canceling or moving it was out of the question economically.

"The Red Rocks area was in a cloud, a rainstorm," Bono said. "We'd paid all the camera people's wages, we'd paid their flights over. We had to go on with the concert.

"We heard that (promoter) Barry Fey was coming back into town, very cross that this concert was still taking place at Red Rocks. We had to explain to him there was no way we could afford for it not to take place. We had all our savings invested in it. We had to do it."

U2 decided to play without a warm-up act for all who braved the weather. They then planned to do a proper show with Divinyls and the Alarm at an indoor venue on the University of Colorado campus the following night. Bono went on the radio—he called local stations KBPI, KPPL, KPKE, KTCL and KAZY.

"I said, 'We're going to do the show tonight at Red Rocks. If you want to come, then come, and if you don't, then we'll do the show over again tomorrow at CU.'"

Out of the 6,000 advance sales, 4,400 ticketholders showed up to deal with the nightmarish elements. U2 took the stage despite all of the operational torments.

"If only eight people turned up, we were still going to play like our lives depended on it," Bono said.

The 19-song show has gone down as one of U2's defining moments. The event ceased being a concert after the second song. From that point on, it was more akin to a church service, a tangible exchange between a band fulfilling its promise as a premier musical outfit and its soaked, shivering fans.

Later, the drama made its way to the wonderful *U2 at Red Rocks* (a rock documentary aired on the Showtime national cable television service) and *Under a Blood Red Sky* (a video and live album). The pelting rain and swirling mists that rolled in over the mountains gave the setting a dramatic, eerie quality, something akin to a Scottish moor. The segments in which the band was delivered to the site via helicopter appeared to be from the epic war movie *Apocalypse Now*. And the concert pieces were exceptionally striking—in the video of "Sunday Bloody Sunday," Bono immortalized his holy gladiator profile, unfurling and waving a huge white flag in the crowd against the hellish glow of the large, flaming torches high on the cliffs surrounding the stage.

It's doubtful that any other band could have turned the adversity at Red Rocks into its favor so convincingly. The subtle peace-and-brotherhood appeal was attributed to the Christian beliefs that three of the four members shared.

"We're not just 'sentimental Irish lads'—I think there's more depth to us than that," Bono insisted after the show. "We just want to share a message. John Lennon, Bob Dylan—those people were artists who wrote about what was happening in their lives.

"But I detest the way religion is turned into an industry in America. I want to kick in the television in disgust when I see people begging for funds—we'll never do that."

The mystic, against-all-odds performance was a spiritual and commercial break-

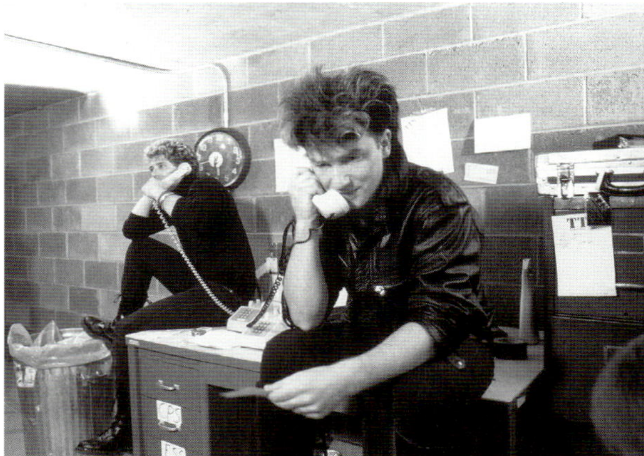

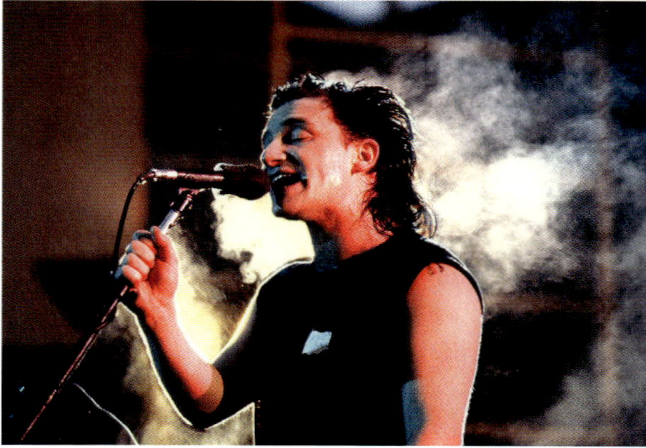

Bono backstage (top) and onstage, June 5, 1983

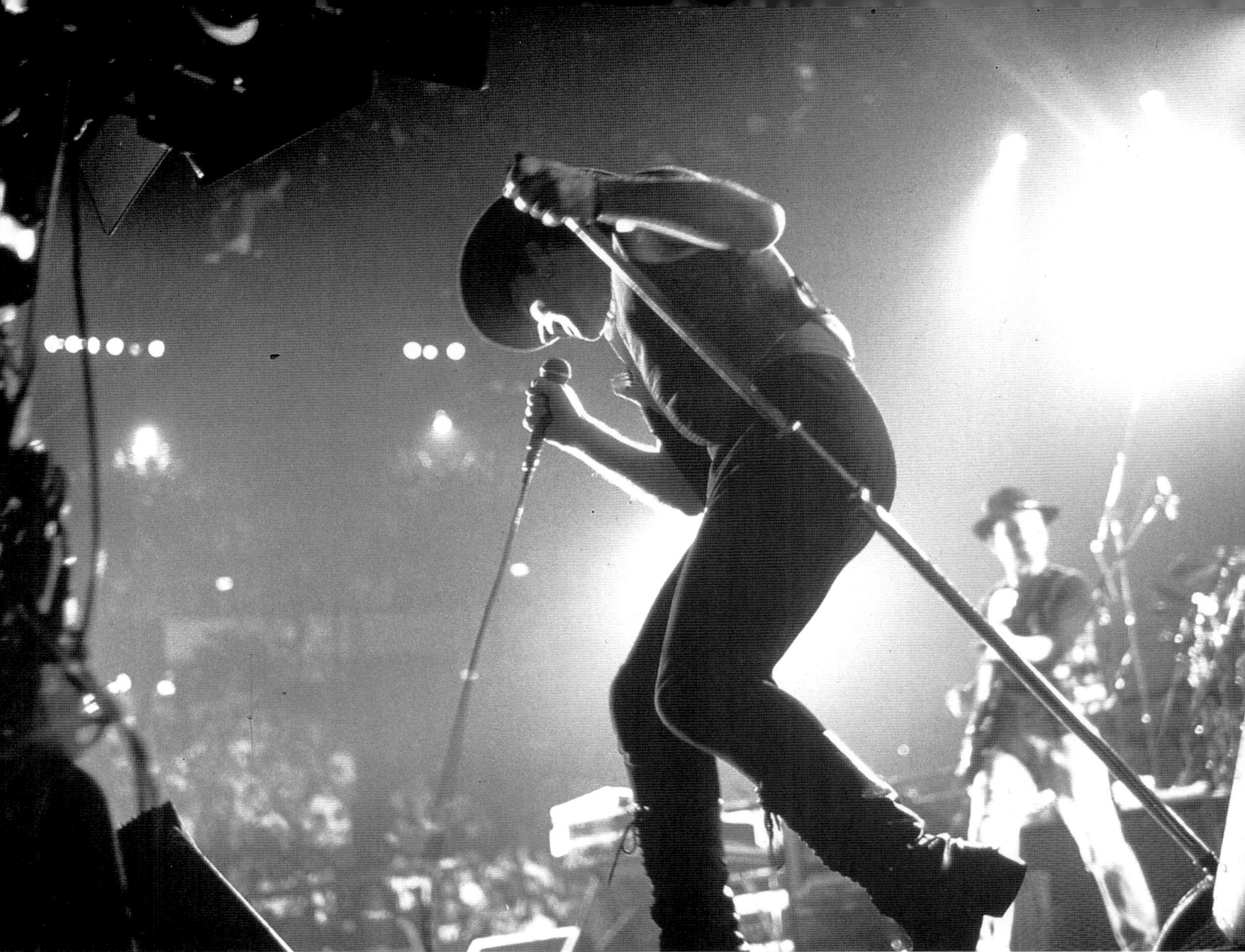

U2 at McNichols Arena, November 7, 1987

through, and it turned U2 into A-list rock heroes.

"That was the turning point for us," guitarist the Edge said. "In Europe, nobody knew who we were. They saw this visually spectacular video and said, 'Who are these guys?'"

"I'd like to thank the man who invented the wide-angle lens," Bono added. "He made the 4,000 people there look like millions!"

U2's motion picture *Rattle and Hum*, a documentary of the Irish superband's 1987 world tour, featured live recordings from concerts at Denver's McNichols Arena on November 7 and 8. During the first show, the band battled the distracting presence of cameramen on stage—Bono eventually dropped his microphone in disgust and muttered, "I feel like a book that shouldn't have been made into a movie." But three songs from the second night made the *Rattle and Hum* soundtrack—"Pride (In the Name of Love)," "Silver and Gold" and a cover of the Beatles' "Helter Skelter." ●

JELLO BIAFRA }

LEADER OF the punk band Dead Kennedys and the target of one of rock 'n' roll's most spectacular censorship trials, Jello Biafra was born Eric Boucher in 1958 and grew up in hippie-happy Boulder.

Like a lot of disillusioned punk rockers, he left town after high school.

"In some ways it was a great place to grow up, but then it turned miserable," he explained. "The hippies discovered Colorado and came in droves. That's when they were considered very dangerous: 'Don't go down on the Hill, Eric, you might run into some hippies!' Of course, that was where I went.

"By the time I was coming of age in junior high and high school, when I could really start to immerse myself in this culture, the culture was gone. It wasn't the '60s anymore, and people were just beginning to realize how stupid and boring it was to be 18 in 1975.

"The music was much more salable, respectable and slowed down. They had figured out how to take the rebellion out of everybody from Bob Dylan to Steppenwolf—yes, Steppenwolf scared people at one time—and water it down into Bad Company, Lynyrd Skynyrd and, worst of all, country-rock and disco.

"Country-rock ruled in Boulder. That and jazz fusion was pushed to the gills by media and record stores. Some L.A. country-rock mafia had moved to Colorado and lived around Boulder, so you'd also have these pre-yuppie monied hippies swaggering into town: 'Hi, I'm Rick Roberts of Firefall—give me a free meal!' 'Hi, I'm Stephen Stills—get the fuck away from that pool table!'

"But one thing saved me. Starting in the ninth grade, I got so fed up with radio that I began buying records just on the basis of which covers looked the most interesting. I discovered the used record stores. At Trade-A-Tape, I scoured the 25-cent bins and especially the free box, where they'd throw in anything they didn't think they could sell. Looking back, this was the advantage of living in a country rock town—Stooges for a dime, MC5 for a quarter, 13th Floor Elevators, Nazz and Les Baxter for free...

"I went to see the Ramones live at the Rainbow Music Hall in Denver, and my whole life changed. They were so powerful, yet so simple—'Yeah, I could do that, too. Why not? I think I will!' And the rest, as they say, is sordid history. Myself, Wax Trax Records, Ministry, the Nails—we all grew out of that show."

Boucher chose his stage name by combining the brand name for gelatin desserts and the name of the country where hundreds of thousands starved to death at the peak of Nigeria's civil war. A self-described "cultural terrorist" and born provocateur, Jello Biafra went to San Francisco and decided to form a band. He made bad as lead singer for the Dead Kennedys, upholding an aggressive anti-capitalist style that featured smart but harsh political lyrics with furious music. The Dead Kennedys always refused to sign with a major label—the band could have, but Biafra wouldn't change the name (which came from his friend Radio Pete, a participant in the Colorado musical underground who would go on to become a successful publicist and consultant under his real name, Mark Bliesener).

Biafra constantly challenged the status quo. In the fall of 1979, he even ran for mayor of San Francisco on a dare. He cut his hair, circulated petitions and made the talk-show rounds, and with zero political clout he still managed to finish fourth in the race.

Then California authorities charged Biafra based on a parent's complaint about the inclusion of artwork by Swiss surrealist H.R. Giger titled "Penis Landscape" (a poster depicting sexual organs) in the Dead Kennedys' *Frankenchrist* album, released in 1985. Biafra was held on the grounds of distribution of harmful material to minors. Though he was eventually acquitted and the prolonged legal confrontation left a powerful anti-censorship legacy, the ordeal strained morale, and the Dead Kennedys broke up soon after. The obscenity trial left Biafra in debt up to his ears, without a group and unable to record for years.

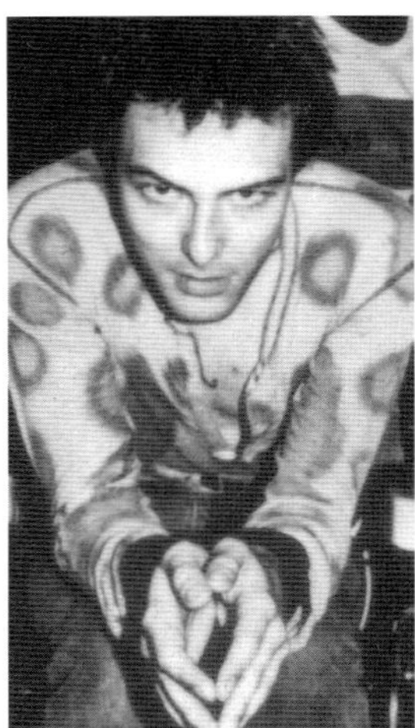

c. 1984

But his controversial spirit raged on. By and by he harnessed his sharp observations about American politics and culture, doing spoken-word tours and releasing spoken-word albums on Alternative Tentacles, the record label he created in 1981 for the Kennedys. ●

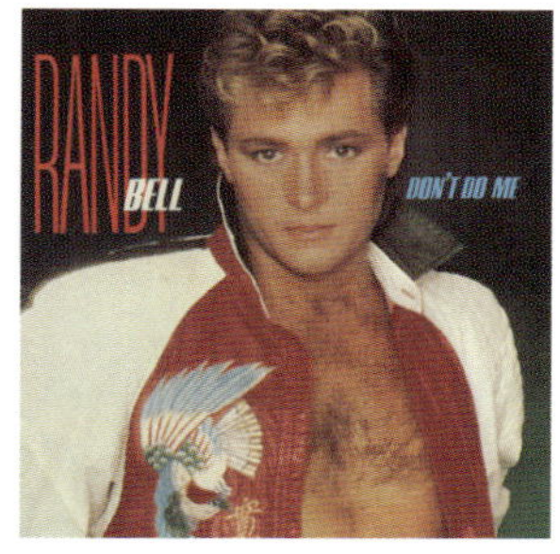

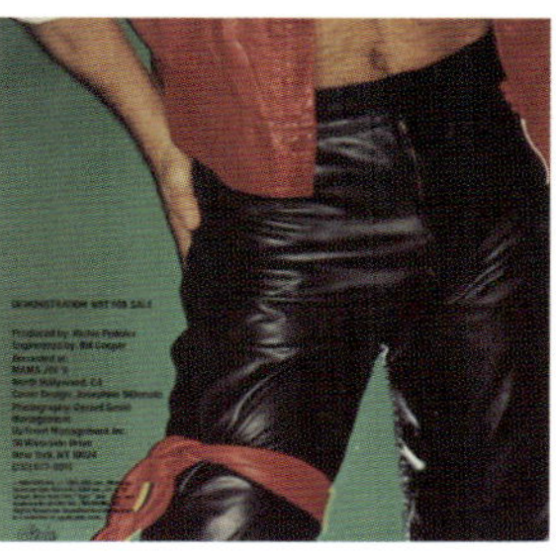

"Don't Do Me" picture sleeve

RANDY BELL }

A 24-YEAR-OLD resident of Thornton, Colorado, Randy Bell hadn't played many concerts when he struck a deal with a major label. Epic Records released the single "Don't Do Me" in July 1984, and the power-pop ode made a brief appearance on the *Billboard* singles chart, peaking at #93.

"I never played the bars," Bell said of his nascent career. "I put my money into good-quality home-recording equipment—I started doing that when I was 18 or so. I'd go down to the basement and listen to what was popular on the radio, then write my own material based on that and try to record it."

One of Bell's first homemade efforts, an original tune called "More Than Alive," was voted No. 1 by the listeners of Denver's KTLK in the radio station's *Colorado Music* album contest. Bell entered it under the name "Randy Rock," but ditched the moniker soon after. The local showing led him to the finals of Miller High Life's "Rock to Riches" talent search. At the finals, held in New York's Palladium in April 1982, he wound up with second place.

"Don't Do Me" was the first product to come out of Bell's "long term, multi-album" contract with Epic. He quit his day job at Rocky Flats, a nuclear plant near Denver, in his continuing search for a smash. But Epic styled him as a teenybopper act—his bare-chested visage appeared in such fan magazines as *Teen Beat*. The one-dimensional marketing plan didn't work, and it put an end to Bell's musical path. ●

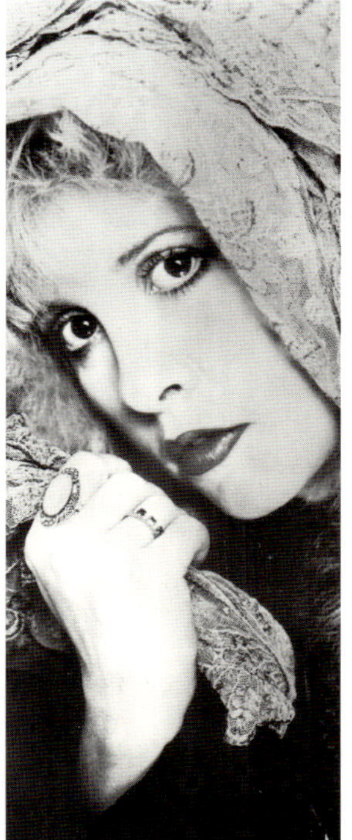

c. 1985

STEVIE NICKS }

HOW DOES Stevie Nicks love Colorado? Let her count the ways.

"My ancestors immigrated there from Cologne, Germany. My late great-aunt lived up in Cripple Creek—she ran a brothel. I have a lot of relatives in Colorado Springs. And I have real bad asthma, and Denver has the best doctors in the world. "I feel like Colorado is mine."

In 1974, Nicks and guitarist Lindsey Buckingham were not getting along; their *Buckingham Nicks* album had been a commercial failure. Nicks wrote "Landslide" and "Rhiannon" when she was staying in Aspen.

"Lindsey was on the road with Don Everly. I wasn't making it big in the music business. It had gotten to a point where I was unhappy, tired, lonely and confused. I was in Colorado and surrounded by these incredible mountains, the only time in my life that I've lived in the snow, and you realize everything could tumble around you. That's where the line 'If you see my reflection in the snow-covered hills' in 'Landslide' comes from. I was trying to figure out what I was going to do, make a decision. I went, 'Okay, I'm sure we can do it.' Three months later, Mick Fleetwood called and asked us to join Fleetwood Mac."

Both "Landslide" and "Rhiannon" became two of the most popular tracks from the 1975 *Fleetwood Mac* album.

Nicks embarked on a solo career in 1981. On August 20, 1986, Nicks filmed the final concert on her "Give a Little" tour at Red Rocks Amphitheatre—just eight weeks after she had played two sold-out shows at the legendary outdoor venue.

"They told me, 'You can't go back so soon and film there—nobody's going to come.' I said, 'I can. You don't understand—this is a sacred thing to me and everybody who will be there.'

"And it sold out. I knew in my heart where I should do my movie, where my feet are planted. "

The results were broadcast on the Showtime cable network and made commercially available on the hour-long *Stevie: Live at Red Rocks* concert video, which featured her Top 10 hits ("Dreams," "Stand Back" and a 15-minute version of "Edge of Seventeen") and guest performers Peter Frampton and Mick Fleetwood.

Nicks' Red Rocks show ended when 25 doves were released into the crowd. One of them refused to leave her hand—and 15 minutes later she was still clutching the bird backstage and demanding that a separate cage be found. "I want to find a good home for him," she explained. "I want to visit him when I come back next time." But Nicks kept him—only it was a her, named Rhiannon, of course.

"She wouldn't leave. I couldn't get her away, so I said, 'I guess this is my dove.' " ●

CHUCK PYLE }

AN IOWA native, Chuck Pyle made his way to Colorado's Front Range in 1965, "when Boulder was mostly gravel streets." His path as an accomplished songwriter was set in 1975 when Jerry Jeff Walker scored a modest hit with a rendition of "Jaded Lover." Through the 1980s and 1990s, John Denver, the Nitty Gritty Dirt Band and a number of popular artists recorded Pyle's songs. Suzy Bogguss covered "The Other Side of the Hill" in 1980; Chris LeDoux renamed the song "Cadillac Cowboy" and took it to the top of the country charts in 1991.

Pyle emerged as a celebrated artist in his own right. The title track to his 1985 album *Drifter's Wind*, about a hitchhiker he once picked up, peaked at #60 on *Billboard*'s Hot Country singles chart. A reviewer labeled Pyle the "Zen cowboy," and he took the nickname to heart—"Ride the horse in the direction it's going," he said—shaving his head and mixing Eastern truisms with Old West horse sense.

"Zen is very cowboy-like," Pyle explained. "There are lots of spaces in a cowboy's life, which promotes a meditative lifestyle."

In concert, Pyle became known for a delightful amalgam of western themes, folk and rock music, a touch of "cowboy logic" poetry and an enlightened sense of humor about his self-help outlook. He also developed a unique finger picking style he called "Rocky Mountain slam picking," which married rhythm guitar strumming and lead guitar lines.

"At some point, I became more of an entertainer," Pyle said. "I was always nervous about performing until one night I made an audience laugh, and it relaxed me so much that I wanted to do more."

Pyle continued to live in Colorado and play across the country. "Colorado" became the theme song for a PBS series called *Spirit of Colorado*; he was invited to sing it for the opening session of the 2005 Colorado State Legislature. ●

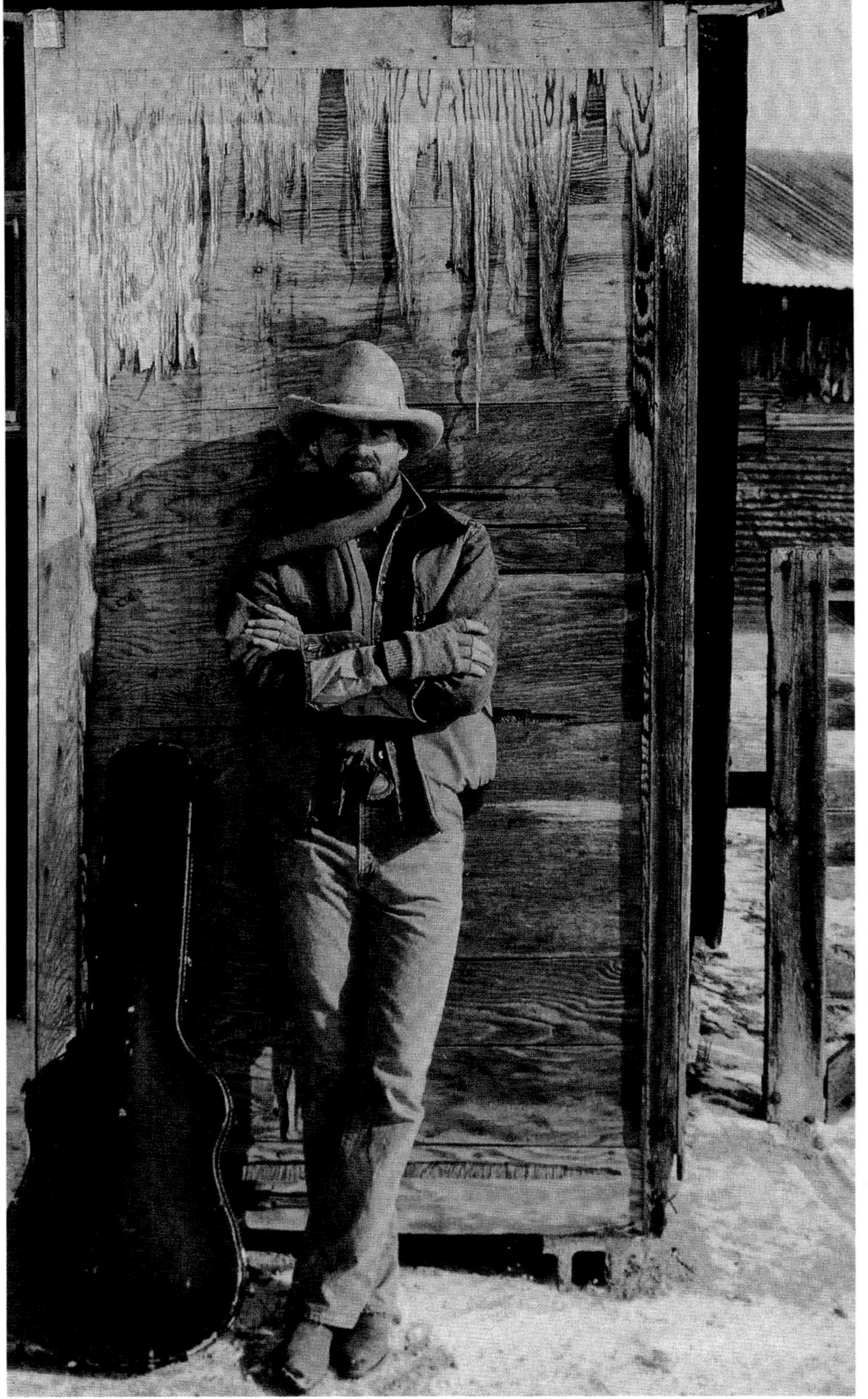

c. 1985

ROB MULLINS }

WITH A string of releases in the contemporary jazz field, Rob Mullins rose to international acclaim as a composer and performer.

Born in Oklahoma, Mullins was raised in California before moving to Denver at age 14; he was already playing drums with big bands professionally. Leaving for school one morning, a car jumped the curb and struck him, fracturing his leg and forcing an important career decision.

"You can't play drums in a cast," he said. "So I took up piano."

Mullins' parents loved jazz, so he was well versed in the genre. "While my sisters were listening to the Beatles and the Monkees and the Doors, I was listening to Buddy Rich, Count Basie, Glenn Miller and Thad Jones and Mel Lewis," he said. "I kind of skipped rock 'n' roll early on."

Mullins mastered other instruments and, at 16, formed a jazz quintet. His high school music program included field trips to clinics where he received guidance from bandleaders such as Oliver Nelson, Clark Terry and Urbie Green.

"The school system back in Denver had a wonderful thing going on," he noted. "If it hadn't been for that, I think I would have gone into accounting or something."

Mullins attended the School of Music at University of Northern Colorado before accepting an invitation to study with the audacious composer-pianist George Russell in New York circa 1977. "There were only four of us; I was 19," he recalled. "The first class was held in the kitchen of the Village Vanguard."

Back in Denver by the mid-1980s, Mullins was hugely popular. He anchored the jazz club Regas' Cafe on a beautiful white grand piano the owner bought to make him happy. "Regas Cristou was the first guy to give me the opportunity to play five nights a week," he said. "I could try out new material, perfect it over weeks and take it into the recording studio." Mullins started his own RMC Records, and *Soulscape* peaked at #12 on *Billboard*'s Top Jazz Albums chart in 1986; the single "Making Love" was nominated for a Grammy.

In due course, projects brought the versatile keyboardist to California, where he became an in-demand arranger, producer and session musician. Mullins played and recorded with a who's who of the jazz and pop scene, spreading his musical reputation in venues throughout the world. He wrote more than 400 songs and recorded more than a dozen CDs.

And he was a dedicated music teacher since age 14, back when he taught music theory to older musicians in Denver at the Happy Logan Music Company. He went on to hold teaching programs in his Los Angeles studio and did workshops in other cities. ●

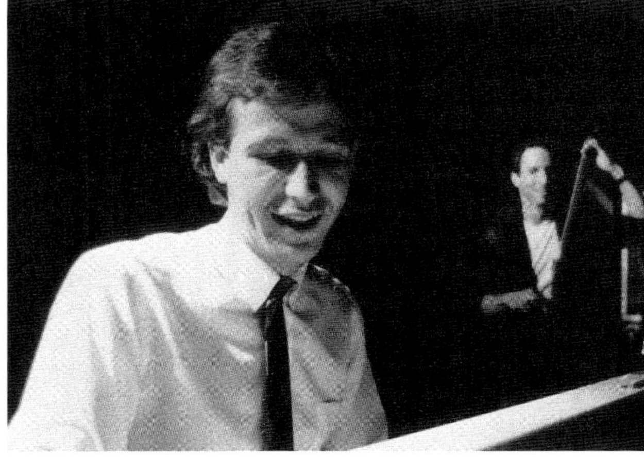

c. 1986

HOT RIZE }

A TALENTED, innovative quartet, Hot Rize not only inspired artists within the progressive bluegrass genre, but also fueled the rise of the jam band scene in Colorado.

Named after the secret ingredient of Martha White Self-Rising Flour (an early sponsor of the legendary bluegrass act Flatt & Scruggs), Hot Rize formed in 1978. Four stellar musicians made up the band—Tim O'Brien on lead and harmony vocals, mandolin and fiddle; "Dr. Banjo" Pete Wernick on banjo and harmony vocals; Charles Sawtelle on bass guitar, guitar, harmonies and lead vocals; and bass player, guitarist and vocalist Nick Forster, who also became their emcee.

"The Denver Folklore Center was the full realization of '60s ideals in a commercial venture," Forster explained. "It was wild—seven consecutive storefronts. On one end was a concert hall, then there was the instrument repair shop where I worked, then there was a music store in two storefronts where Charles was the manager. Then there was the bead shop for all your beading needs, then the next store front over was a record shop where you could by all the records you couldn't find at the chains. And then the next door over was a music school where some of us guys taught. It was an amazing environment—30 people all working for minimum wage, hanging out and playing music all day long.

"There was a band based at the Folklore Center called the Rambling Drifters. Sometimes it was called the Drifting Ramblers, or the Rebuilt Ramblers or the Tumbling Rafters. Every week they had a different name, but it was basically a bluegrass pickup band. Charles and Pete were at the core, and they had a revolving cast of guests. Tim and I were two of those guys. We were about ten years younger than Pete and Charles. They had the wisdom and experience that really helped us. We set attainable goals—whatever we dreamed of, we got to do it very quickly."

Hot Rize was capable of playing straight bluegrass as well a quirky mix of folk, jazz and rock elements.

"We tried to be traditional bluegrass, did the best we could," O'Brien said. "We wanted to dress like the old bands and sing around one microphone, but our hair was too big. We were different from other bands. Colorado is friendly to all kinds of music, a great place to learn our craft. We were looking to make records, and it seemed like a good idea to write songs. Lester Flatt's advice was, 'If you sing something no one else sings, then they have to hire you to do it.'"

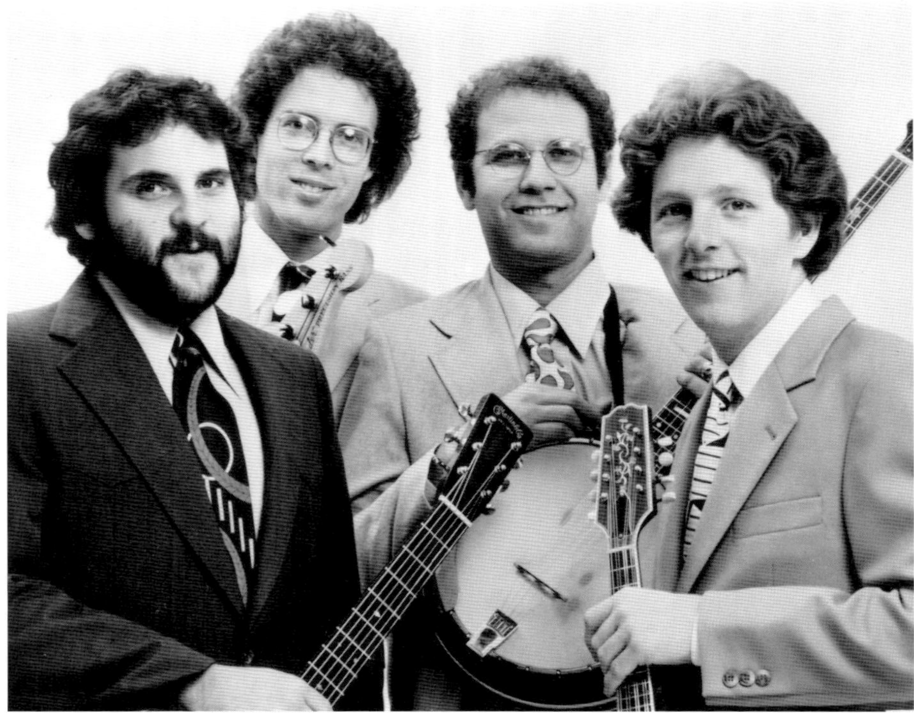

c. 1981

At the beginning of their career, the musicians traveled in a black and silver '69 Cadillac, their equipment behind them in an old U-Haul trailer that matched. Tapes recorded by Sawtelle for the band's road trips provided an education in what Forster calls "the soul of music."

"These mix tapes were enormously diverse—they had traditional bluegrass, then Freddie King and Blind Willie Johnson, then a Jimi Hendrix cut. We listened to a lot of country blues. We agreed on certain qualities that songs either had or didn't have."

Hot Rize took those special song traits and infused them into a unique and exciting style, reaching the upper echelons of the bluegrass world.

"I was one of the first troublemakers in the world of bluegrass during the '70s," Forster said. "We'd play the long-established festivals, and I'd walk out on stage with my electric bass and get boos and catcalls from the audience.

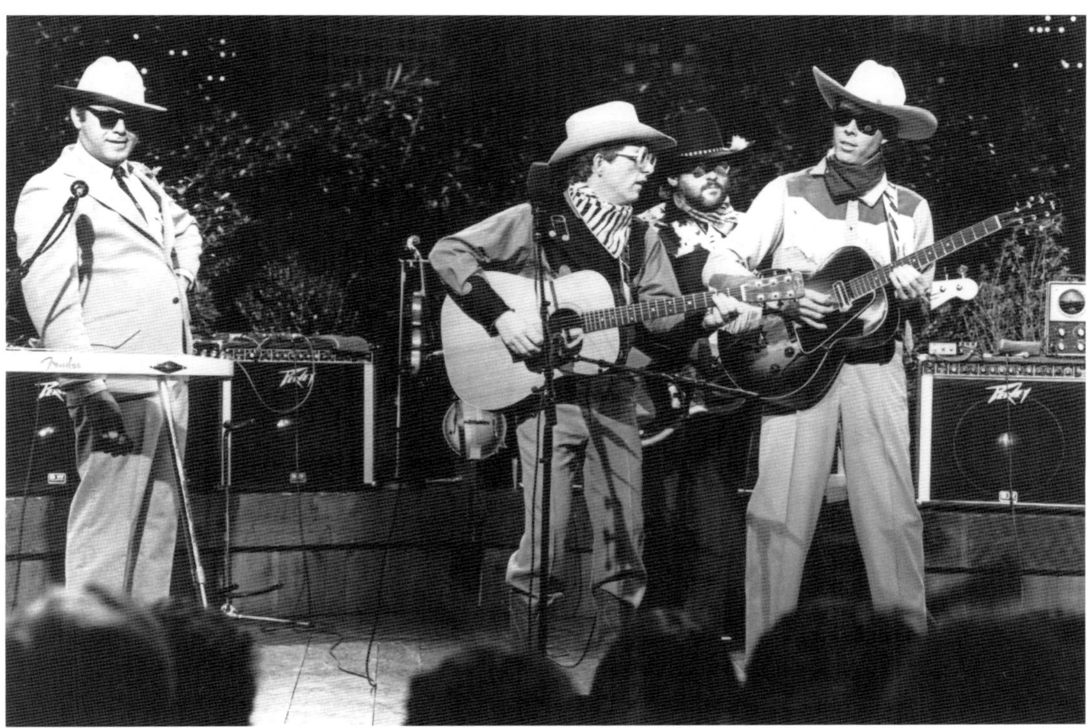

Hot Rize's wacky alter-ego, Red Knuckles & the Trailblazers, c. 1988

"But we weren't Mister Bluegrass kind of guys. I went to Swiss boarding school. Pete has a doctorate in sociology from Columbia. Tim had gone to military academy and private college up in Maine. That's not exactly the same background that Earl Scruggs had."

The band recorded numerous albums for Flying Fish Records, the independent Sugar Hill label and Rounder, including the Grammy-nominated *Take It Home* in 1990. The group performed at the top festivals, touring Europe, Japan, Australia and the U.S., and also appeared on *Austin City Limits*, The Nashville Network and at the Grand Ole Opry.

As part of their act in concert, the four members of Hot Rize left the stage and were gradually replaced by the four members of Red Knuckles & the Trail Blazers who, wearing the tackiest Western wear imaginable, parodied hardcore 1950s country music.

"We had this schizophrenic show," Forster explained. "The part where we were playing bluegrass in suits and ties was serious. But through our evolution as musicians, we also knew that there were other interesting things to explore, like playing plugged-in electric music. So the Trailblazers gave us an outlet for staying true to a different traditional form, but also having a wacky time with it."

"We liked to disparage each other when we were onstage," O'Brien added. "Hot Rize would complain about how Red Knuckles was unwashed and not very sophisticated. And then the Trailblazers would come on and talk about the terrible sounding banjo and this twangy, whiny music. The Trailblazers were never at the concession stand—they were always working on the bus when the money got shown. So Hot Rize would be at the merchandise table, and people would come up and say, 'You shouldn't treat those guys so poorly. They really are pretty good.' And we'd say, 'Oh, I wouldn't know. I hate that kind of stuff.' It was fun. Halloween every night. We didn't take ourselves seriously, but we played the music well."

Hot Rize parted ways amiably in 1990 to pursue other musical ventures. The group's members performed together occasionally until Sawtelle died of leukemia in 1999. Forster remained a Boulder mainstay who, together with his wife Helen, hosted the national weekly radio program *eTown*. Wernick still performed, and O'Brien, based in Nashville, was a Grammy Award-winning singer, songwriter and multi-instrumentalist.

Hot Rize regrouped for a few gigs in 2002, adding Bryan Sutton on guitar. The band released a new studio album (*When I'm Free* hit No. 1 on *Billboard*'s Bluegrass Chart in its debut week) and embarked on a full tour in 2014. ●

1988-1995

IN THE 1980s, with the advent of MTV, music was all about image, and a song's success totally depended on its video. A flock of glitzy new wave and glam metal bands performed at Red Rocks, while the Telluride Bluegrass Festival had become an annual musical and cultural phenomenon. But Colorado artists mostly fell short of triumphing nationally. Talent scouts from major record labels stopped sniffing around the state until the Subdudes inked a deal in 1988 with Atlantic Records at the Governor's Mansion. Yet the local metal, funk, R&B, jazz-fusion and hip-hop scenes thrived, thanks to stores like Denver's Wax Trax Records, which had become the fountainhead of Colorado's underground musical culture in the late 1970s. Local Anesthetic, an independent label run by Wax Trax co-owners Duane Davis and Dave Stidman, ignored mainstream conventions and showcased the area's post-punk and hardcore bands.

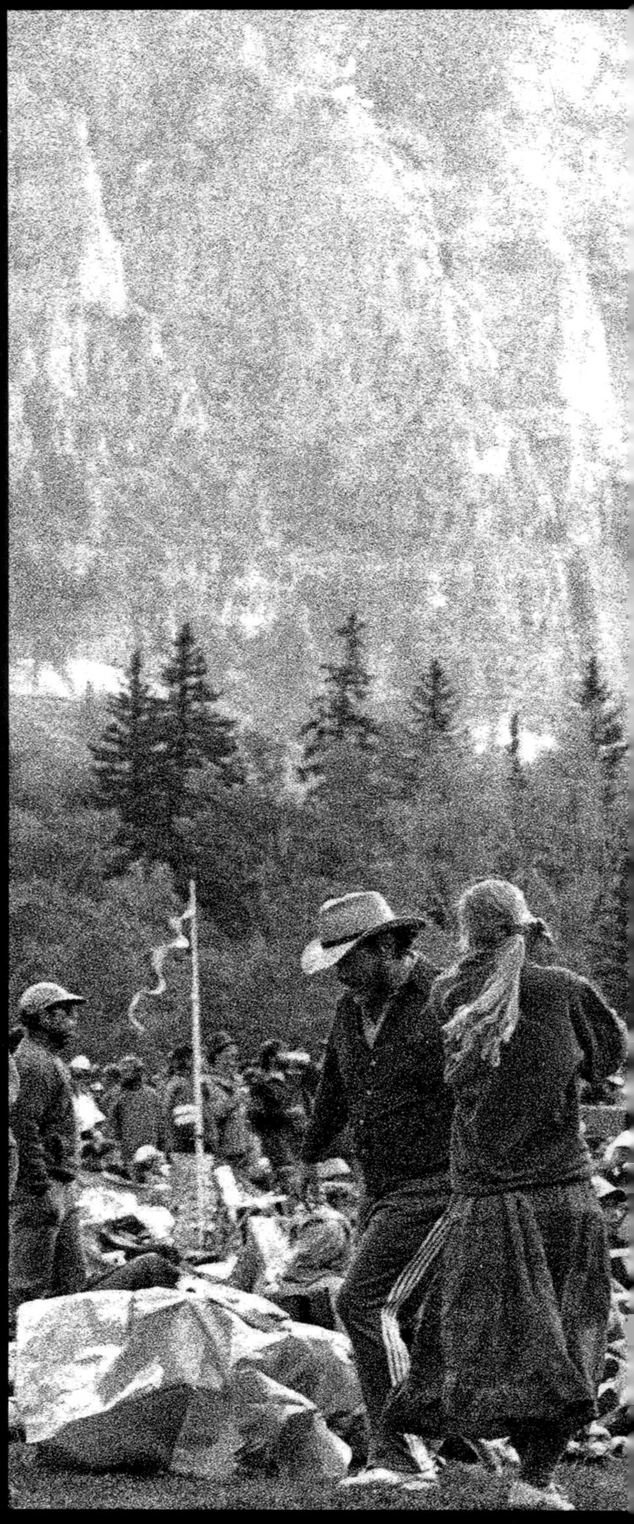

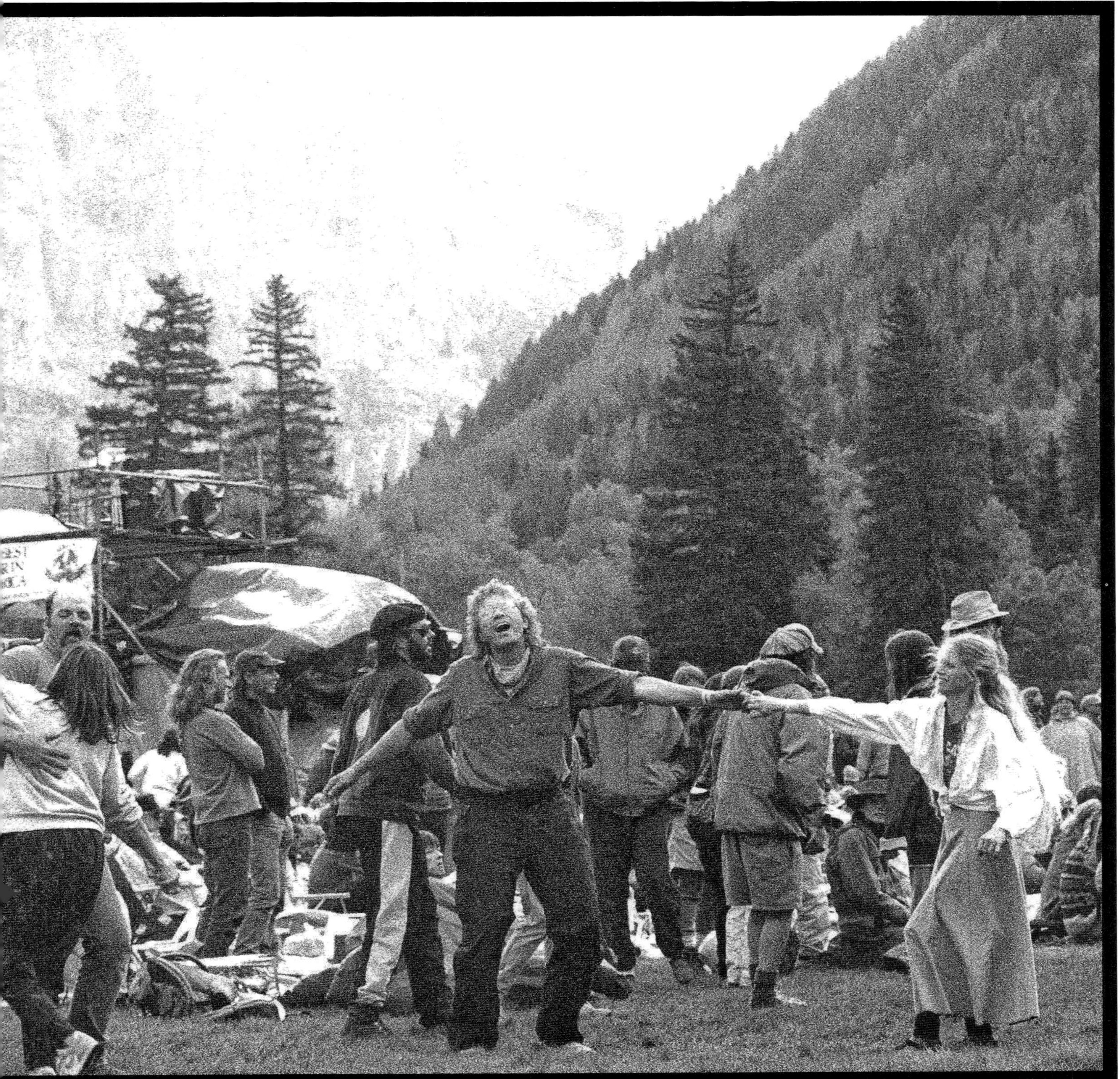

Dancing fans at the Telluride Bluegrass Festival, 1991

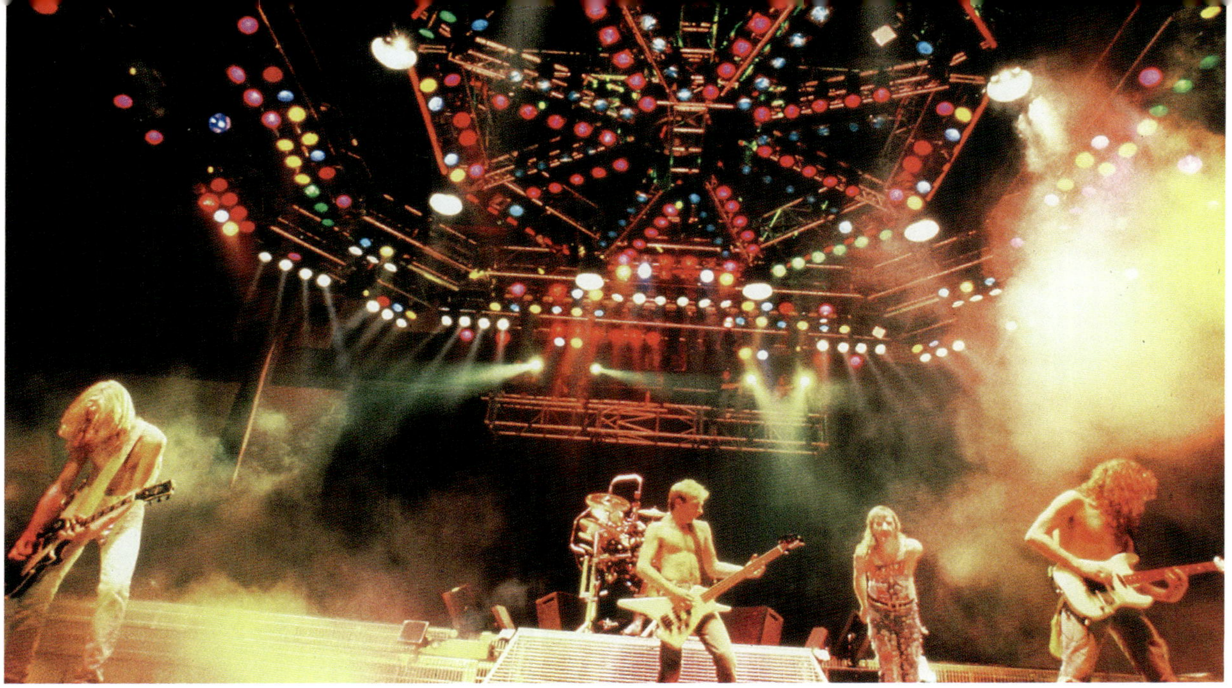

At McNichols Arena, February 12, 1988

DEF LEPPARD }

TO COMMEMORATE the 227-date "Hysteria" world tour, Def Leppard filmed a concert video at Denver's McNichols Arena on February 12 and 13, 1988, titled *In the Round–In Your Face*.

Initially, the superstar British quintet had planned to film a performance video for the hit single "Pour Some Sugar on Me."

"But then we said to hang on a minute—we'd be daft to shoot just one song," singer Joe Elliott recalled. "So we decided to do the whole show and see what we got.

"We wanted to do it in the best possible place. On that leg of the tour, the *Hysteria* album hadn't really taken off nationwide. Denver was the first place we were doing two nights, and they were both sold out. It was obvious—we were kings in Denver.

"And we wound up with a hell of a lot of good footage. The audience was beyond belief."

The band members financed the filming themselves—"We couldn't get the record company to pay for that one," Elliott said—and the project served as a memorial to their massive high-tech circular stage construction.

"We wanted to make an event, so we put the stage in the middle. I described it as a 60-by-40-foot boxing ring without the ropes. It was a lot of fun—the director (Wayne Isham) auditioning girls that you wanted to shove against the fence down at the front, all the usual rock 'n' roll trappings.

"For us Englishmen, the only drawback with doing it in Denver was the altitude. When you listen to the tape, you can hear me getting out of breath big-time. It's a good thing we were in our mid-20s, because we would have been in cardiac arrest after five songs."

The 90-minute *In the Round–In Your Face* video contained 30 seconds of additional footage from a trio of shows in Atlanta "because the director decided he needed more audience shots," according to Elliott.

The "Pour Some Sugar on Me" clip became a finalist for both Best Stage Performance and Best Heavy Metal Video in the MTV Music Awards. *In the Round–In Your Face* showcased 13 more pop-metal hits, including "Foolin'," "Rock of Ages," "Photograph," "Animal," "Armageddon It," "Bringin' On the Heartbreak," "Rock! Rock! (Till You Drop)," "Women," "Too Late for Love" and "Hysteria."

The most riveting aspect of *In the Round–In Your Face* was the effort put forth by drummer Rick Allen. In a much-publicized incident, he lost his left arm in an automobile accident during the recording of the *Hysteria* album. But Allen was determined to continue playing with one arm, and onstage, he unveiled his new drumming style for everyone to see. He fostered a technique where his left foot substituted for his missing limb to go along with a specifically designed Simmons electronic drum kit. ●

WINGER }

IN 1988, WINGER'S self-titled debut album was certified platinum for one million sales, part of the wave of stylish pop-metal that also sent Bon Jovi and Def Leppard to the top of the charts.

Ten years earlier, Denver native Kip Winger was holding court—underage—at the Godfather and other Denver-area 3.2 beer emporiums for teens.

"It was Christmas 1968 when I got my first bass—I was seven, and I wanted to be Paul McCartney. I had fiddled around with piano lessons the year before, but my other two brothers and I wanted to do a band, so our parents got me a Panoramic and my brothers a guitar and drum set."

The brothers' first gig was at Walnut Hills Elementary School in 1970. Prior to his sophomore year at Golden High School, Winger, then 16, took the GED and went on the road.

"The band was still me and my brothers at the time. We were getting a lot of gigs, and school was getting in the way," he recalled. "We linked up with producer Beau Hill, who was working out of Denver's Applewood Studios. He drove up in his Porsche, and we rode up on our ten-speed bikes."

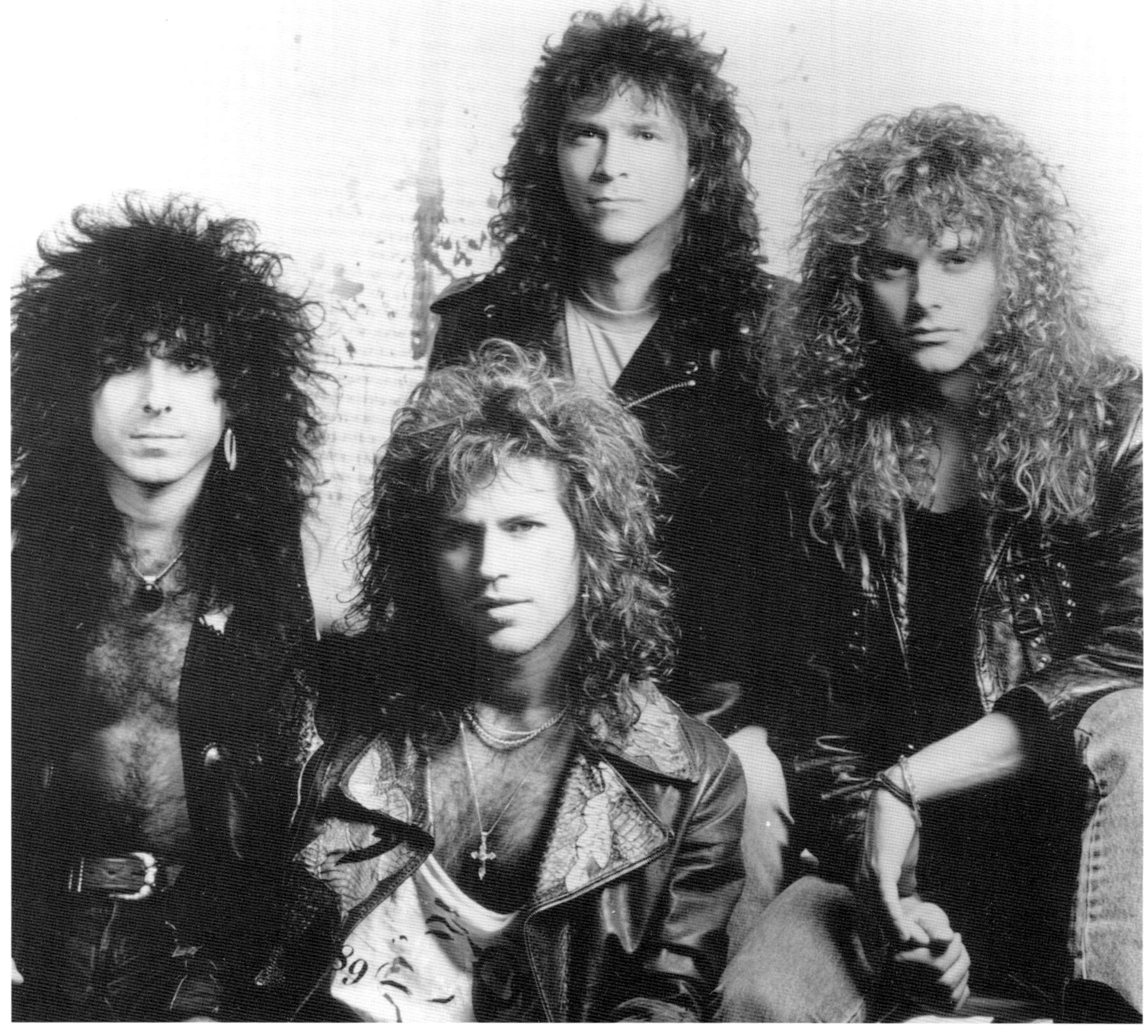

c. 1988

Winger spent 1980 in New York opening in bars for the likes of Zebra and Twisted Sister. When the city's scene lost its momentum, he returned to Colorado to study acting, music and voice at the University of Denver. But he was always sending tapes to Hill, who stayed in New York. Winger eventually rejoined him, sleeping on the floor of Hill's apartment.

"I had never done anything but play music, and I had an ego. I had always made money at it. But when I got to New York, there were a thousand of me, waiting tables and getting treated disrespectfully. It was overwhelming and intimidating, but it was the best thing that ever happened to my songwriting."

Hill finally cracked the big time by producing Ratt's breakthrough hit, "Round and Round," and he allowed Winger to play bass on some sessions. Winger got some equipment together and his hopes up—prematurely—for a record deal.

"When you grow up in the Rockies or Midwest, you don't have any connections. You think if you had some, you'd be happening. But they don't mean shit. You've got to have the goods as a songwriter or you don't make it."

Winger's demos were repeatedly turned down by record companies. He finally made some money writing horn and background vocal parts as Hill's production assistant for the *Hearts on Fire* soundtrack, featuring Bob Dylan. Alice Cooper then asked him to play on two albums and a tour.

"I remember the 1987 concert at McNichols Arena in Denver. When I was a kid, I used to ride my bike down to McNichols and stare at it and say, 'I'm going to play there someday.' And when I finally did, I couldn't move—I dislocated my knee the week before. I had to be carried on and off the stage."

The Cooper gig was good-paying, guaranteed work, but Winger decided to pursue his goal of leading his own band. He went into Boulder's Mountain Ears studio and didn't emerge until his contacts and experience landed him a recording contract.

Winger was a surprisingly accomplished debut, and Kip Winger's chiseled good looks were seen on MTV, where videos for "Seventeen" and "Headed for a Heartbreak" received heavy exposure. The band's second album, 1990's *In the Heart of the Young*, was equally successful, selling over a million copies and featuring the hit power ballad "Miles Away."

"It's weird," Winger said. "I was accustomed to hanging out wherever I wanted, but then people were waiting at the hotel for autographs and pictures," he said. "But I dug it. I waited for years for that to happen, and then it was all of a sudden."

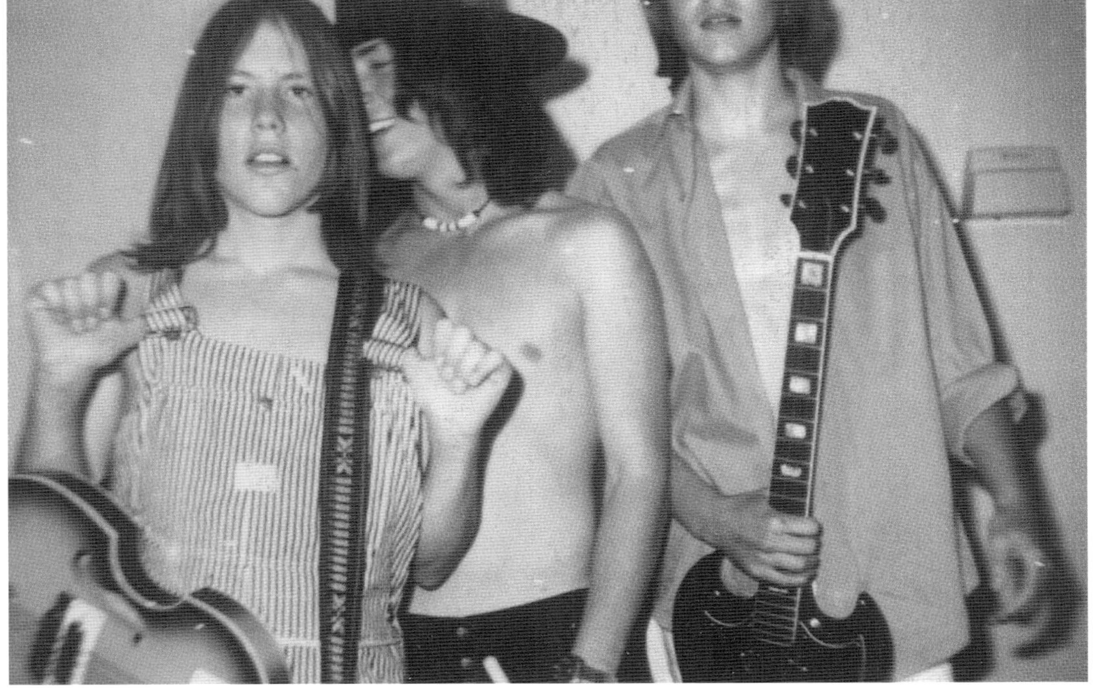

Kip Winger with brothers, c. 1970

Although he based himself in New York, Winger maintained, "Denver is the best place to be. It gave me a perspective on life.

"In Denver, you get a chance to nurture yourself and grow spiritually. It doesn't cost a million dollars to rent space and the players are in close proximity, so you get a vibe, a sound, a longevity. That's much more preferable."

The musicianship in the ensemble bearing his last name was stronger than that of any other "hair metal" band. In addition to lead singer and bassist Winger, the lineup featured guitarist Reb Beach, rhythm guitarist/keyboardist Paul Taylor and drummer Rod Morganstein, formerly of the Dixie Dregs. But with the rise of grunge and alternative rock, a backlash overtook the group. On *Beavis & Butthead*, MTV's top-rated animated series of the mid-1990s, the heavy metal-loving adolescents used to torture the neighborhood kid Stewart for wearing a Winger t-shirt.

"It was over," Winger said. "I could have released *Sgt. Pepper's* and it wouldn't have mattered."

After dissolving the band in 1994, Kip Winger went on to a solo career, releasing three albums. He then reunited members of Winger for several tours and recordings. ●

CHRIS DANIELS }

FOR OVER 30 years, Chris Daniels & the Kings entertained Colorado music fans with a souped-up mix of jump blues, blue-eyed soul and horn-infused rock. The Kings also earned something of a worldwide fan base—in the Netherlands, they even coaxed the nation's queen to shake her royal booty.

"You're not supposed to make a living playing guitar for a quarter-century plus," Daniels said. "Who would have thunk?"

Originally from Minnesota, Daniels moved to Martha's Vineyard and then New York City as a teenager, where he worked as a backing musician for David Johansen, later a founder of the glam-rock band the New York Dolls. He relocated to Colorado in 1971 and served a stint in Magic Music.

"We did the hippie thing—Leftover Salmon before there was a Leftover Salmon," Daniels said. "They had all been living in school buses and a donut truck in Eldorado Canyon. We had two acoustic guitars, a flute, bass and percussion, usually tablas. The songs had a lot of elves, druids and fairies in them. We had all kinds of brushes with fame."

Magic Music performed at the second and third Telluride Bluegrass Festivals in 1975 and 1976. It also held its own in local clubs and was often booked at Boulder's the Good Earth, with the funky Freddi-Henchi Band.

"The hippies would get all blissed-out and mellow with Magic Music," Daniels remembered, "then Freddi-Henchi would take the stage and everyone would get the soul shakes.

"In the early '70s, there was a whole series of communes and 'families' living in little mountain towns above Boulder, stretching from Nederland, Gold Hill, Ward, Allenspark, Estes Park and even down to Horsetooth Reservoir.

"Some were pretty insulated, like Stephen Stills and the whole Caribou crew—unless you were part of a chosen few, you did not enter. Others, like Magic Music, were porous and seemed to attract both camp followers and satellites. Magic Music set up headquarters in Allenspark, and the Hummingbird Cafe was the focal point. Bands like Rosewood Canyon and performers like Michael Covington (of Joni Mitchell's 'Michael from Mountains' fame) either lived nearby or played the cafe with Magic Music."

Daniels left the area to earn a B.A. in music and journalism at Macalester College and Berklee College of Music

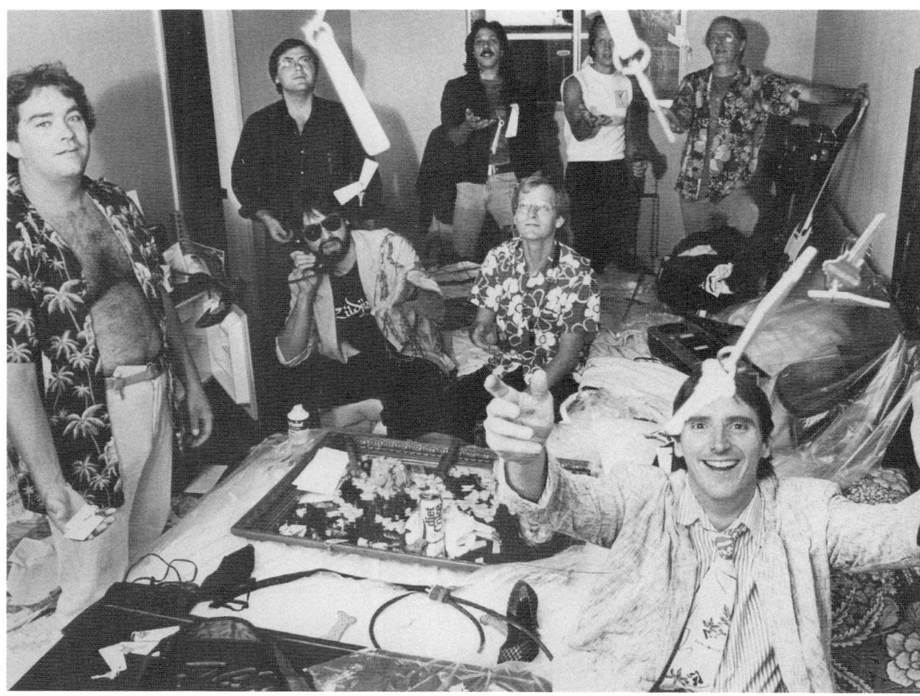

Chris Daniels & the Kings, c. 1989

in Boston. He then returned to found Spoons, an influential Boulder country-rock band. In the early 1980s, he toured with former Amazing Rhythm Aces frontman Russell Smith, whose manager lived in Boulder.

In May 1984, Daniels formed a rhythm & blues horn band as a "one-night party" at the old Blue Note in Boulder. Three decades later, Chris Daniels & the Kings had produced twelve albums, toured Europe 18 times and remained a top local concert draw.

"We wanted to do anything with horns," said Daniels of the Kings' post-new wave genesis. "Everybody thought it was real cool, and they'd say, 'What's that stuff?' But it's really a love affair with what happens with horns. One of the things we did was push the hard rock 'n' roll sound with horns, which no one had ever done before.

"In the days of the fabled 'downtown Boulder music scene,' there were six or seven clubs in a five-block radius. Sonny Landreth would be at JJ McCabe's, the Kings at the Walrus, Steve Conn at the Boulderado, Woody & the Too High Band at the Blue Note, and everybody going back and forth on the breaks, even timing our breaks so we could sit in with each other's bands. It was like New York's

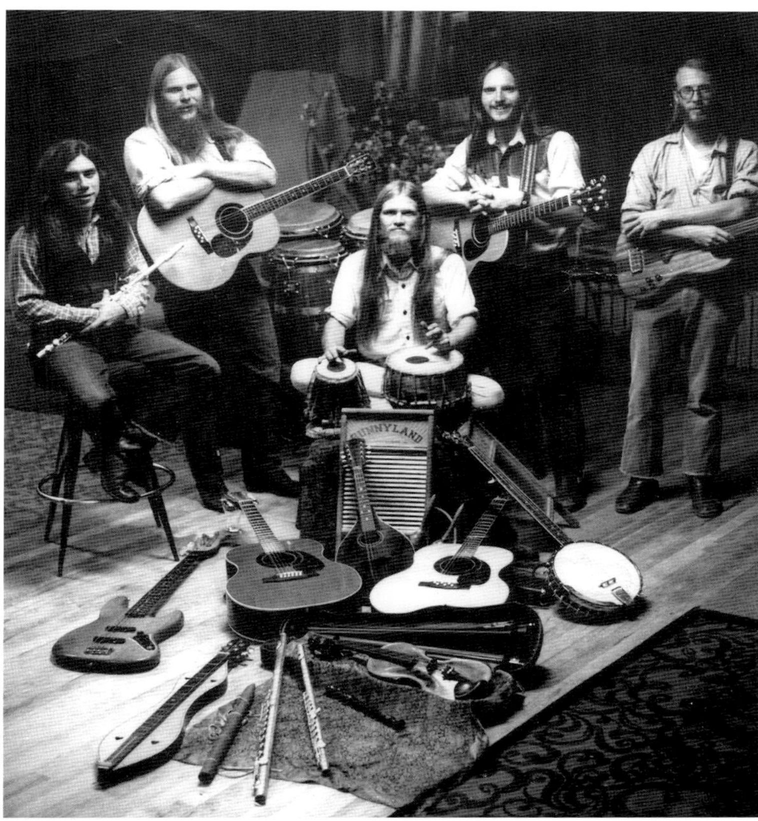

Magic Music, c. 1975

52nd Street in the '40s."

After building a following on the local circuit, the Kings hit the road and built loyal regional audiences in such places as Nashville, Minneapolis and New York, even parts of Europe.

The band made a dent on the new "adult-album" format in larger markets. In 1987, the title track from their debut, *When You're Cool*, hit No. 1 in Minneapolis, Denver/Boulder and Detroit, and broke the Top 20 in San Francisco, Washington, D.C. and Montana. The video for the track "Gloria, Come Back to the Record Store" gained a significant amount of play on VH1 and took third place in the International TV and Film Festival in New York. *That's What I Like About the South* was produced in 1989 by Al Kooper (famed for playing with Bob Dylan, starting Blood, Sweat & Tears and producing Lynyrd Skynyrd and the Tubes). "Depot Street" made the Top 40 in *Radio & Records*, and "I Like Your Shoes" became a KBCO favorite. *That's What I Like About the South* was released in Holland, where a cover of Chuck Berry's "Roll Over Beethoven" went to No. 1.

"It's real roots music, which is why we've had such success over there," Daniels said. "The basis of this music is blues, R&B, funk, swing—all very American stuff. When we come over we're not bringing them what they get when they hire a Stevie Ray Vaughan clone. With us it's something much, much more, and it flips them out."

Landreth and Hazel Miller, a Denver blues-soul singer, recorded with the Kings on *Is My Love Enough* in 1993.

"Hazel Miller and I sang together for the first time at the first Boulder Blues Festival—I saw Hazel in the wings and pulled her on stage. She blew the doors off the place. She's probably my best buddy as far as 'band leaders' go. We talk about the trials and tribulations of keeping it going. We've sung the national anthem together at sports events and done a zillion shows together."

Louie Louie (1998), the Kings' collection of jump blues and swing, was done in tribute to Louis Jordan and Louis Armstrong. On 2003's *The Spark*, Daniels traded his trademark Stratocaster for an acoustic guitar, horn-based music for intelligent singer-songwriter material with hints of blues, bluegrass and funk. In 2005, *10* marked a return to roots music, and 2008's *Stealin' the Covers* featured the band's favorite cover tunes. Released in 2009, *We'll Meet Again!* was a live recording in collaboration with BMaster, a Dutch band. Daniels' 2012 album, *Better Days*, marked a return to his folk roots and cracked the national Americana charts.

In addition to making great music, Daniels played a hefty role in shaping the Front Range music scene. The Mile High mainstay spent five years as executive director of the Swallow Hill Music Association, which promotes folk and acoustic music in Denver. He taught courses at Arapahoe Community College and became an assistant professor at the University of Colorado's Denver campus teaching music business.

"I studied the various people throughout history who were not trapped by their circumstances, who kept going farther. You can also see it in music, but one of the most painful stories is people who got into doing one thing and it reached some pinnacle of success, and from that point on they had to keep recreating it. It's tough for all the bands out there with one original member selling memories.

"So I looked at those examples and tried to diversify. It's always been an adventure. There's an old saying—when you hit a wall, turn left!" ●

THE SUBDUDES }

A MAGICAL, marvelous musical treasure, the Subdudes' enjoyed favored status during their long stint in Colorado. The critically acclaimed band's rich, soulful harmonies, insightful lyrics and rootsy grooves kicked off the Americana genre before the term became clichéd, winning over listeners across the country.

Frontman Tommy Malone, bassist Johnny Ray Allen and percussionist Steve Amadee grew up together in Edgard, Louisiana. They formed their first band in high school, inspired by Malone's older brother, guitarist Dave Malone of the legendary Radiators.

Keyboardist John Magnie, a Denver native, was then introduced to the trio in 1984. "I thought he was from Louisiana," Allen admitted. "He played that Professor Longhair style of piano that you have to be from New Orleans to understand."

"I grew up in East Denver and graduated from Cathedral High School," Magnie said. "I got into a band—Meatball, or the Righteous Meatball Boogity Band. The name came from a Zap Comix character by R. Crumb where this meatball got released into the world and would hit people on the head and they'd become enlightened. We moved up close to Steamboat Springs and played for a couple of years. We had an actual hippie commune up there—12 of us, 20 dogs, raising pigs and goats. That band broke up, but it got me going on music. I fell in love with New Orleans piano, that polyrhythmic roll that they got from the Caribbean. I had to go down there for my schooling. I got there in 1974. I ended up staying for 13 years."

The four friends performed in various combinations with other local musicians for several years. They had a lot of strange names and played a lot of strange dives. But as players came and went, frustration grew.

"New Orleans is a place where the music is pouring out of every crack, with lots of bands in different styles," Magnie explained. "But there is very little business opportunity. Bands will get a repertoire together and get hot, and nobody will help them get to the next step and they fade away.

"Tommy and I were in one of those bands around town, the Continental Drifters. We had some good songs, but they didn't seem to be in the right format. A lot of electric bands just get louder and louder. My wife complained one night about how damn loud we were, so Tommy and I said, 'Let's do a night where we play in a subdued way.'"

One spontaneous evening in April 1987, the Subdudes were born. Magnie was playing piano at Tipitina's bar in the Crescent City, and the three other musicians came down and started jamming. Amadee, a drummer who liked to travel light, used a tambourine—"It was ripped off from my landlady"—and the scaled-down acoustic sound worked. They wound up playing every Monday night.

Later that year, the Subdudes, unable to make a living at music in New Orleans, decided to relocate with their families, en masse, to Fort Collins, Colorado, where it was quiet and inexpensive.

"Most of the bands struggling down in New Orleans that go to New York or L.A. try to be like other bands," Magnie said. "It was September 1, 1987 that we came up from New Orleans with the idea of trying to make a new start. I'd had a little time in Fort Collins going to college and I just loved the town. I thought that we'd be able to work there doing our original material. We got to Colorado, and dang if it didn't go just as good as it could, because we were the only band around with that sound."

Magnie scouted out some gigs, and the members quit their day jobs. The chance paid off. The Subdudes' reputation spread throughout the state almost immediately, as they were being booked three and four nights a week. They became a fixture at Herman's Hideaway on South Broadway in Denver, where a loyal following continuously packed the place.

Anyone who ever saw the quartet live likely will always remember them, mostly for the way Amadee worked the tambourine as if it were a full drum kit. His percussion and Magnie's wheezing accordion began imbuing Malone and Allen's concise three- and four-minute songs with the ethnic R&B associated with the varied styles of the New Orleans region. Their funky, danceable performances garnered rave reviews from the local media.

The band soon attracted the attention of entertainment attorney Ed Pierson and manager Patrick Cullie, and a demo of the song "On His Mind" won *Musician* magazine's Best Unsigned Band contest. It sounded like a timeless classic, something Ben E. King might have considered recording in his heyday. By the fall of 1988, the Subdudes had acquired a recording deal with Atlantic Records. The label signed the foursome in an official ceremony in Governor Roy Romer's office.

The Subdudes didn't light

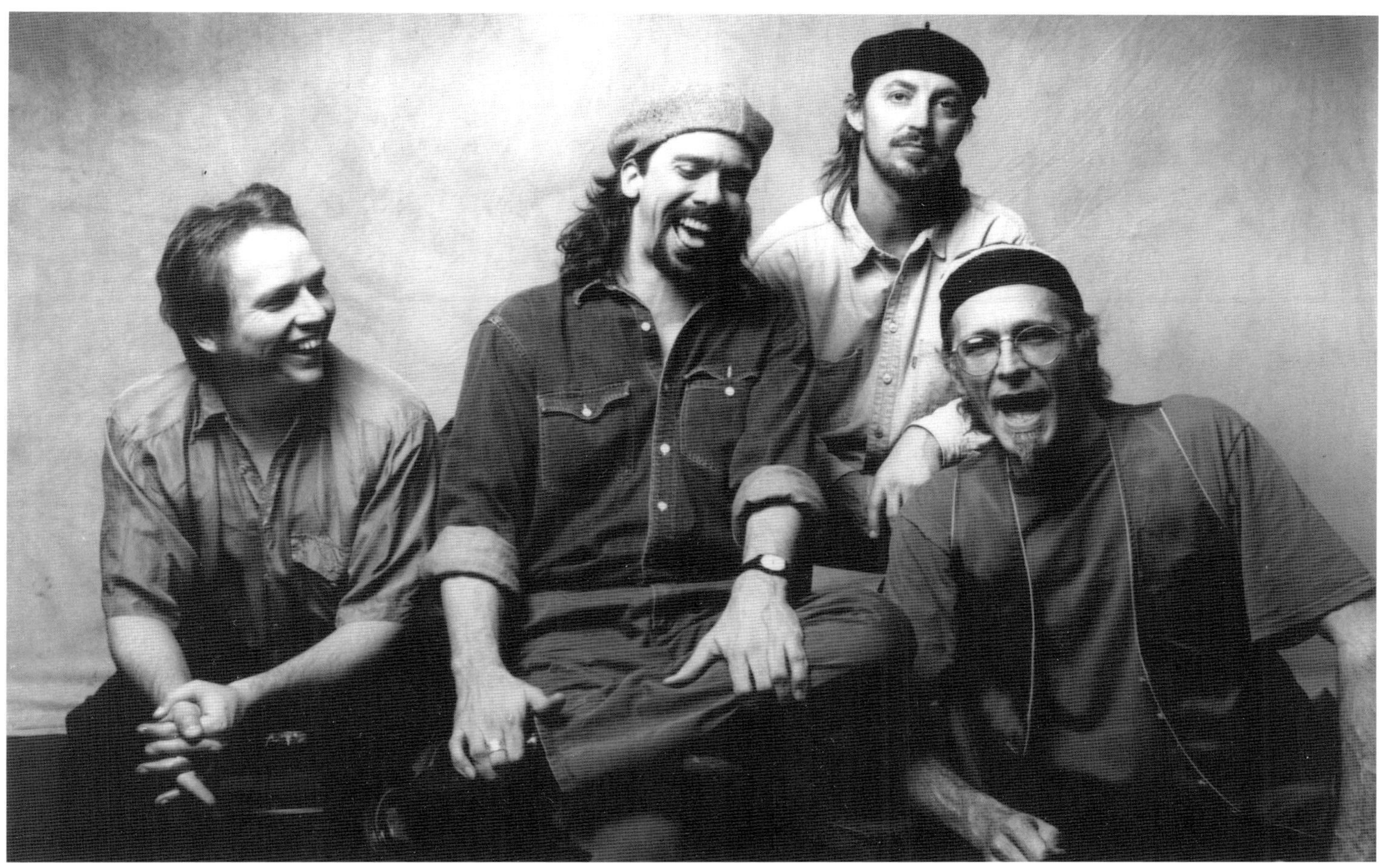

c. 1994

up the charts—it sold nearly 30,000 copies—but the national music community loved the band's mastery of American music styles. They had good word-of-mouth from peers. Bonnie Raitt, Linda Ronstadt, Huey Lewis, John Hiatt and especially Bruce Hornsby were zealous fans. The band also built a reputation for session work, accompanying Shawn Colvin, Roseanne Cash, Joni Mitchell and others, and toured frequently.

"We learned a lot," Magnie said. "Before we moved to Colorado from New Orleans, we weren't in road bands—we gigged in and around town because we weren't well-known enough to travel."

On record, the Subdudes always delivered both charm and first-rate chops, masterfully mixing elements of New Orleans R&B, roots rock, gospel and country. 1991's *Lucky* featured a cover of Al Green's "Tired of Being Alone."

But by 1997, the rigors of the road and the burden of being a unique band had taken a toll. The members decided to call it quits.

"The Subdudes had a real intricate balance that involved songwriting, especially," Magnie said. "We just ran out of gas, used up what we had there—the process fell apart."

Spinoff projects ensued—Tiny Town, 3 Twins, the Dudes. Sans Allen, the Subdudes reformed in 2003, adding Tim Cook (vocals, bass percussion) and Jimmy Messa (bass, guitar) to the mix. The band secured a recording contract and released *Miracle Mule* in April 2004. Keb' Mo' produced the 2006 effort, *Behind the Levee*. *Street Symphony* (2007) and *Flower Petals* (2009) followed.

The four original members reunited for several concerts in 2014. Allen's sudden passing shocked the reanimated band.

"I'm proudest of us getting back together," Magnie said. "We had a lot of animosity towards each other, and we all felt like we'd never play with those other blankety-blanks again! It took us over six years away from each other to realize that we do better when we unite our forces, that we're going to be playing music anyway. It was a second chance." ●

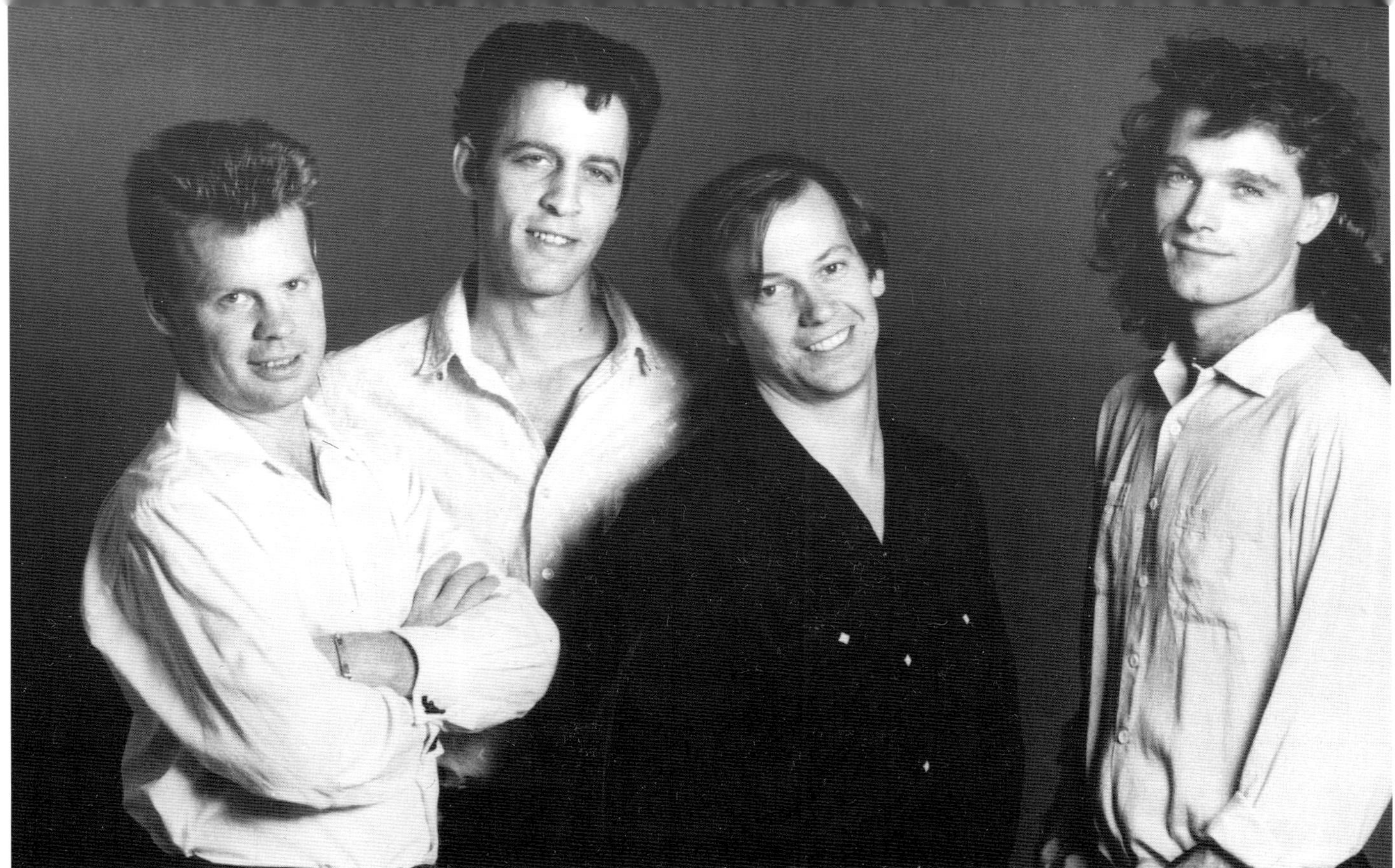

c. 1988

TREAT HER RIGHT }

UP TO the time Treat Her Right recorded "I Think She Likes Me," one of the best oops-she's-married songs since Lynyrd Skynyrd's "Gimme Three Steps," the punk-blues quartet was considered Boston's best-kept secret. The song made waves on the U.S. college charts and in the U.K., and RCA Records picked it up in 1988.

The inspiration? Guitarist Mark Sandman wrote it after an incident in Fairplay, Colorado.

"I will remain mute about the specifics, but I maintain it's true," Sandman said.

After graduating from the University of Massachusetts, Sandman worked a variety of blue-collar jobs. He noted he would often earn considerable overtime pay, which allowed him to take leave of work and travel outside of New England to places such as rural Colorado, the setting for a number of his songs, including "I Think She Likes Me." Sandman sang about the confusion of walking into a bar and being approached by a woman whose husband later makes an unwelcome appearance:

She'd told me things about her life
She'd never told me she was someone's wife
The man with the gun says, "Why'd you buy her a drink?"
I said, "I think she likes me that's what I think"

Sandman played only the bass strings of his guitar. "We're not revivalists or purists," he said. "But we do have an aesthetic—keep it simple at all costs. Resist the temptation to add. If you're going to do something to a song, subtract."

After the demise of Treat Her Right, Sandman formed Morphine, an unlikely rock 'n' roll trio. The instrumentation was guitarless, "low-rock" played on baritone sax, drums and Sandman's homemade two-string slide bass. The song "Thursday" became a college-rock success in 1994, with Sandman delivering particulars about weekly infidelity and jealousy.

"And I'm not kidding, I imagined 'Thursday' taking place outside of Fairplay," he reported. "It's like the continuing adventures of the character, getting involved with the wrong woman."

In July 1999, Sandman suffered a heart attack on stage at a festival outside of Rome and died on the way to the hospital. ●

STEVE TAYLOR }

IN THE 1980s, Steve Taylor emerged as perhaps the most intriguing artist in the contemporary Christian genre.

Taylor, a Northglenn High School graduate (class of 1976), recorded his demos during his last year at the University of Colorado in Boulder. In the summer of 1982, he got a slot at the annual Christian Music Conference in Estes Park, Colorado. It was his first live set. The crowd's reaction impressed the head of Sparrow Records, and a deal quickly followed.

Songs like his quirky debut "I Want to Be a Clone," "I Blew Up the Clinic Real Good" (about violence at abortion clinics) and "This Disco (Used to Be a Nice Cathedral)" (a No. 1 hit on Christian radio) outlined Taylor's perspective without sounding preachy or self-righteous. *Meltdown* (1984) was one of the all-time biggest-selling rock albums in contemporary Christian music history. *Newsweek* called him "evangelical rock's court jester."

But Taylor's tendency toward satire, black humor and witty metaphors didn't endear him to gospel-weaned members of the church. He couldn't conform, so he formed a secular alternative rock band called Chagall Guevara. The song "Murder in the Big House" could have been a hit, but the band worked for MCA Records (the industry joke was that it stood for Music Cemetery of America).

So Taylor returned to the contemporary Christian fold in 1994.

"It's a little different now, having had the chance to do the other side," he said. "The blinders came off.

"In gospel music, I felt constrained by expectations, people assuming things about me that weren't true. But the same thing happens in pop music on another level. There are just as many regulations you're not supposed to cross. I traded in one set of rules for another."

Taylor produced two gold-certified albums for Newsboys and the platinum-certified self-titled album for Sixpence None the Richer. All three earned Grammy nominations. His work as a director earned him two *Billboard* Music Video Awards. In late 1997, he launched Squint Entertainment, a record label and film production company. While still running Sprint, he began working full-time as a filmmaker. ●

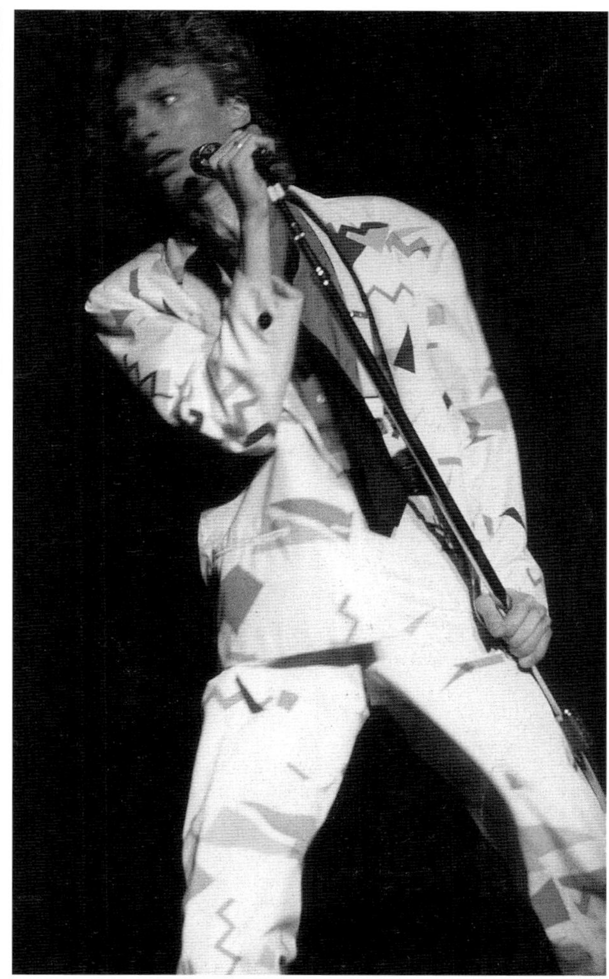

c. 1984

WIND MACHINE }

STEVE MESPLE was proud to live in Louisville, Colorado, even if he found the "local musician" stigma uninspiring. "Heck, even I wouldn't go to see a band from Louisville," the guitarist said.

Yet Mesple's music with his band Wind Machine got attention from the entire country.

Wind Machine never met a style it didn't like, playing guitar-based, mostly instrumental music described as "mass fusion." Its members dabbled in sounds that ranged from blues to bluegrass to jazz to new age. They utilized a vast arsenal of instruments, ranging from the guitar to the mandolin to the dobro; from the trombone to the electric fretless bass to their own invention, the "guitjo," a six-, seven- or eight-string guitar with the bass strings restrung with higher pitched treble strings.

"We were never bored in this band," Mesple said. "We played at jazz festivals and folk festivals, bluegrass festivals and blues festivals. I had friends who said, 'Don't spread yourself too thin—you need to specialize in one style.' I tried to, but I was unhappy."

The sincerity and honesty of Wind Machine's music could be sensed in the atmosphere of family and friendship that surrounded the band since its 1986 inception, with Mesple on guitars, mandolin, harmonica, banjo and vocals; Joe Scott on guitars, guitjo and banjo; and Blake Eberhard on fretted and fretless bass and trombones.

The band started as the house band at the Bratskellar in Larimer Square.

"We knew there was something different happening," Mesple said. "Joe and I would play four-minute songs of rapid-fire 16th notes, and our timing was right together."

The predominantly electric first album, *Wind Machine Featuring Steve Mesple*, and the second, *Unplugged*, were released independently. But after *Unplugged*, Mesple was in a car accident during a blizzard near Berthoud.

"I was lucky I wasn't killed. I was smashed by a delivery truck going 60 miles an hour, climbed out the window of my car and got hit by another car. My hands were messed up, and for quite a while I couldn't hold a pick. My finger would swell up like a pickle.

"But interestingly, I could fingerpick—that didn't bother my hand. So for four months of rehabilitation, all I did was sit around and write acoustic stuff. And that's where the *Rain Maiden* album came from."

Released in 1989, *Rain Maiden* put Wind Machine's signature acoustic style in the national spotlight, with Boulder's Silver Wave Records offering the band distribution and promotion.

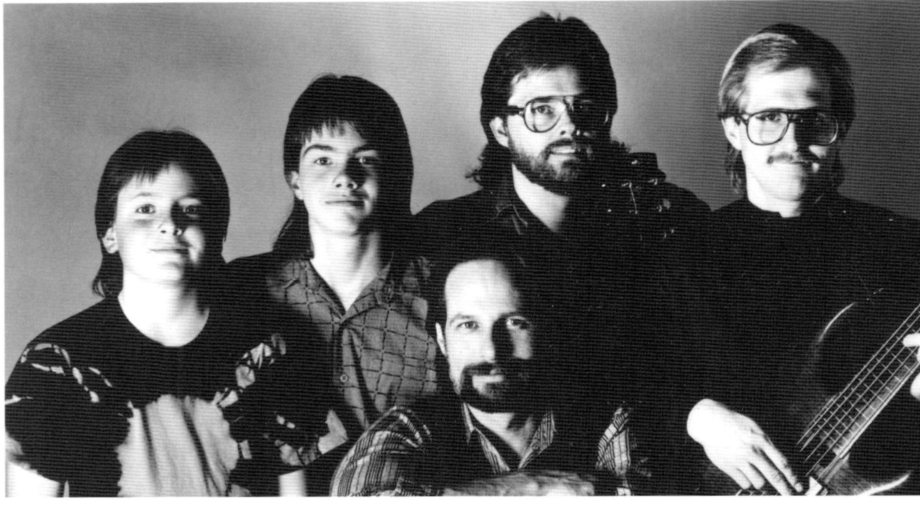

c. 1990

For *Road to Freedom*, the personnel then included the teenaged sons of Mesple, Taylor (keyboards) and Ethan (percussion). Mesple harbored reservations about his boys joining the band, but they shared their bandmates' dedication.

"They are two of the finest musicians I've ever met," Mesple stated. "They are adult musicians temporarily trapped in the bodies of 13- and 15-year-old boys. It's a fascinating story, but I wanted the music perceived on its merit, not as a gimmick. Wind Machine was getting national attention, and I didn't want to be 'Louisville's Partridge Family.'"

Road to Freedom reached the Top 5 in the major NAC (new adult contemporary) and related radio airplay charts. The title track reached the No. 1 spot in *Radio & Records*' Hottest Tracks chart. More than 250 stations played cuts from the record.

Wind Machine rehearsed obsessively. "If you want to be a world-class act, you have to make a world-class effort," Mesple said. But Wind Machine was also a fun group. Concerts often ended with "Eat Your Heart Out, Stanley Jordan," a tune where everybody played one guitar at the same time.

Wind Machine released 13 critically acclaimed albums. The group ended its run in the spring of 1998. At that point Mesple focused on running Wildwood Guitars, his shop in downtown Louisville renowned for its custom pieces. ●

DOTSERO }

THE ROOTS of Dotsero's part in the smooth jazz genre's uptick could be traced back to a garage band in Denver. Performing together was nothing more than a whim to Stephen Watts (tenor and soprano saxophones, wind synthesizers) and his brother David (guitar) while they were students at the University of Colorado. They moved to gigs in local clubs, taking the name Dotsero from the Ute Indians. It means "something unique," but it was also, as explained by the Watts brothers, the site of one of their favorite fishing spots—Dotsero, a little Western Slope burg on the banks of the Colorado River.

"The town of Dotsero is named for all the 'out of the ordinary' geothermal activity up there," Stephen Watts noted. "But anybody there will tell you that it was 'dot zero' on the first topographical mining map in Denver. And about eight miles up a narrow gauge railway that's not running anymore is a town called Orestod, which is Dotsero spelled backwards!

"I wanted desperately to be part of the music business. You can play gigs and express yourself and get instant gratification from your audience if you're good. But I grew up watching the Grammy Awards, and I wanted to be part of the recording industry."

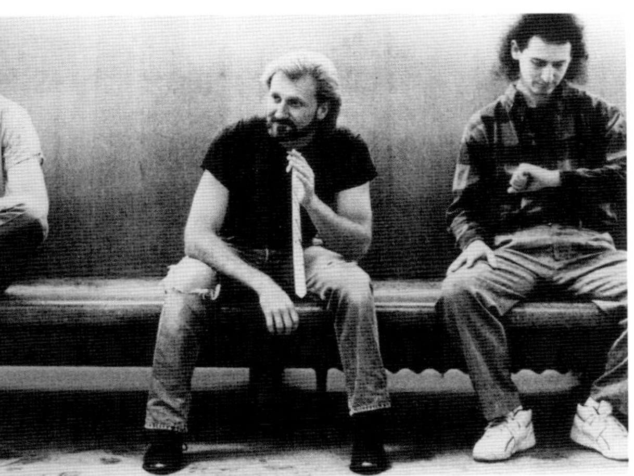

c. 1991

Dotsero broke onto the national music scene with its 1990 release, *Off the Beaten Path*, a blend of jazz, pop, R&B and rock. The band followed up with *Jubilee* in 1991 and became one of contemporary jazz's hottest ensembles. The album spent five weeks at No. 1 on the *Radio & Records* charts, hit No. 1 on the *Gavin Report*'s Adult Alternative chart and spent 10 weeks on the *Billboard* Contemporary Jazz chart. In 1994, Dotsero released *Out of Hand*, which cracked the charts again.

"It was a time when the radio stations all picked their own music," David Watts said. "You could hear anything from Pat Metheny to Kenny G to David Sanborn to Yellowjackets any given day, depending on which disc jockey was playing which music.

"Five tunes from *Jubilee* charted—stations from 'The Wave' in Los Angeles, WNUA in Chicago, KKSF in San Francisco, 'The Oasis' in Dallas, all had their own favorite. If they liked you and your tunes, they were very accessible. You could call them up and say, 'Thanks for playing our record,' and they'd record an interview and say, 'How can we get you out here?' We found ourselves on five different charts—adult alternative, adult contemporary, contemporary jazz, new adult contemporary and new age. We didn't know how to classify ourselves. We just went with it."

Dotsero continued to record, mainly at Colorado Sound Studios with producer Kevin Clock. Core members over the years included Michael Friedman on bass, longtime cohorts Tom Capek (on keyboards) and Kip Kuepper, and Larry Thompson and Mike Marlier on drums.

"I understand purists who want to keep their straight-ahead jazz—that's our American art form," Stephen Watts said. "But that art form is like a tree trunk that grows branches. Our influences weren't limited to John Coltrane and Charlie Parker. We were also influenced by the Beatles and Steely Dan. It's healthy and understandable growth to take the jazz we love and meld it into a music that has all those aspects. Also, the recording process evolves as well, with electronic instruments and keyboards that are unbelievable."

"We consider ourselves more contemporary jazz, which means it's a little harder," David Watts added. "A lot of pure jazz players think they're above the audience—'Most people just can't begin to comprehend how great we are.' We wanted to do the opposite. We decided we were going to be the Van Halen of jazz. We've always tried to be engaging visually as well as with our sound."

Dotsero played big festivals and small clubs. In 1998, the act designed the Denver venue Jazz@Jack's to be a home base. The club, operated and co-owned by the Watts brothers and located in the heart of downtown Denver, proved to be a mainstay in the city's nightlife.

In 2001 the University of Colorado named David and Stephen Watts, along with jazz greats Glenn Miller and Dave Grusin, among its top five Arts graduates of the last 125 years. ●

WILLIE NELSON }

ONCE A Nashville renegade, later a favorite son of Texas, Willie Nelson boasted a popularity that elevated him to a stature approaching that of a contemporary national folk hero.

In the 1980s, the venerable country singer maintained residences in Texas, Malibu Beach—and a mountain home in Evergreen, Colorado, described as a two-story, 4,700-square foot Swiss chalet on a 116-acre estate. It included a large teepee.

Nelson also found the Little Bear, a nearby bar that gave him a place for his music.

"I had lived down in Texas for a long time," he explained. "I wanted to get away for a little while just to check out the rest of the world. My nephew, Freddy Fletcher, had a little band, and they were traveling around. He was coming up to Colorado a lot. So one day I took my daughter Suzie and we drove from Austin up to Evergreen, where Freddy had a little cabin. I thought, 'Well, this is a spot to come to.' The first place I had was up on Turtle Creek; then we bought a place over in Evergreen, on upper Bear Creek.

"But I only had a few days to spend at either Colorado or Texas because I was touring so much. I had a place in Austin with a recording studio and a lot of other different things—a golf course, for one—that were calling me back there. I had a run of bad luck with the weather in Colorado—every time I'd fly back home, it would be snowing! So I got to thinking, 'Wait a minute, it's snowing here, there's a golf course over there—what do I really want to do?'

"So mid-'80s, I decided to head back and spend most of my time off down in Texas."

Nelson owned the house in the Colorado mountains until November 1990, when it was seized by IRS agents who nabbed him for $16.7 million in "unpaid back taxes" for the years 1975 through 1982.

"I wrote a lot of songs while I was living in Colorado, had a lot of fun, did a lot of nice things that you can only do there," Nelson said. "It affected me a lot of ways. I sure hated to leave, I know that." ●

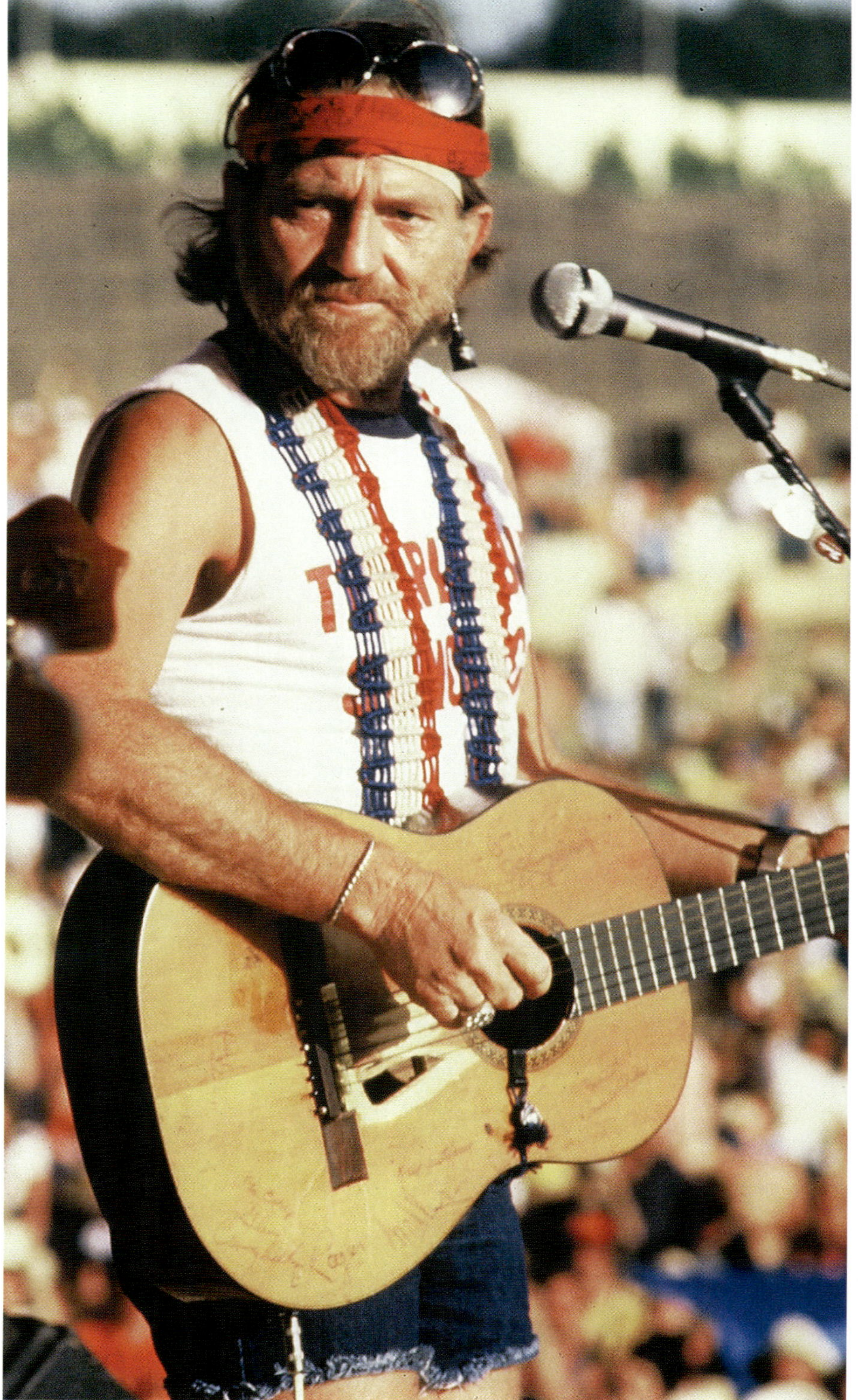

Fourth of July picnic, 1984

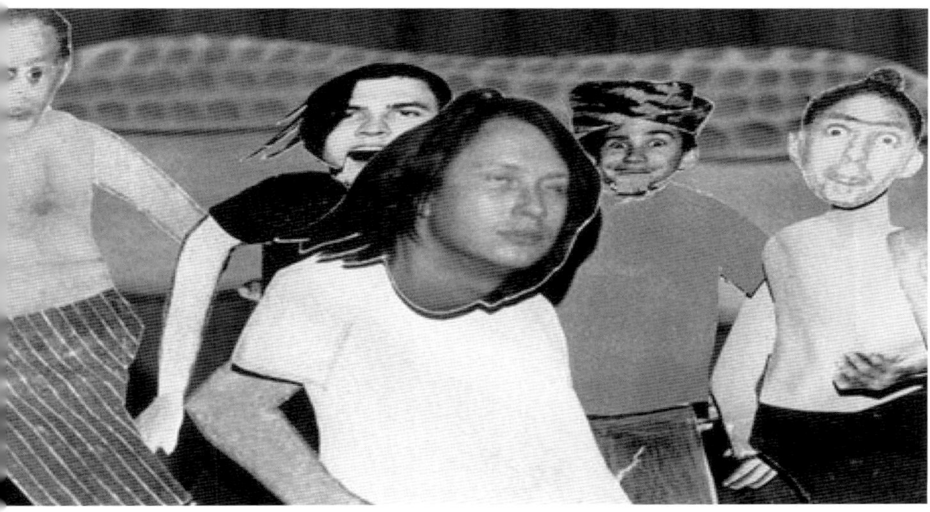

c. 1989

WARLOCK PINCHERS }

BY PUTTING out false information and pernicious publicity stunts, the Warlock Pinchers created a legacy of creative mischief in the annals of underground shows in Denver and Boulder.

"We are the band who cried wolf," admitted KC K-Sum, a.k.a. percussionist Andrew Novick.

The noisy, bratty and crude quintet started in 1987, lampooning the effect of mass marketing on the suburban middle-class in the name of having fun and entertaining themselves.

In 1989, the Warlock Pinchers trashed teen pop star Tiffany's No. 1 hit version of "I Think We're Alone Now," recording it with cut-up interviews and samples as "I Think We're Tiffany."

"And in our concerts, we'd let the drum machine keep going for ten minutes after we stopped playing the song," Novick said. "We wondered if we could get sued and sell thousands of records because of the publicity. But we couldn't find out—nobody would pay attention to us."

So the band members scammed. They wrote a letter from Tiffany's management to themselves on fake letterhead, "received" it and then issued a press release saying they were going to be prosecuted. The media was referred to the band's manager, Wil Wheaton. "That's the name of the guy who played 'Wesley' on *Star Trek*," Novick laughed.

Local writers took the bait until Tiffany's manager admitted the hoax, and the Warlock Pinchers had zero credibility. "We had trouble getting our concerts listed in the papers," Novick said. But then the musical pranksters recorded a hard-core punk-rap song, "Morrissey Rides a Cockhorse," and garnered more notoriety.

Morrissey, the former lead singer of the Smiths, was turning shameless self-absorption and hand-wringing angst into mega-stardom in his native England. "Morrissey Rides a Cockhorse" satirized his flightiness and outrageous neurotic fantasies—the record featured a photograph of him on the jacket and a cartoon on the label depicting him chanting "Ouija Board Ouija Board" as he simulated sex with a skeleton over the grave of James Dean. The sneering lyrics ("Crybaby son of a bitch, no talent motherfucker") were an unabashed attack. The record also featured two samples of Morrissey himself in an interview. "As much as the song was a string of obscenities about Morrissey, it was way more than that," Novick said. "If you listen to the lyrics, it's obvious we know a lot about him."

The British had a tremendous love-hate thing with Morrissey, and "Morrissey Rides a Cockhorse"—released two years later in Morrissey's homeland—made them laugh out loud. It was named "Single of the Week" in the country's leading music weeklies, *Melody Maker* and *New Musical Express*. The former erroneously identified the Pinchers as "a Boston-based" band and ran a picture of another group, but both reviews were raves: "A hilarious iceberg that gets bigger and better with each subsequent listen...Their level of sustained invective is staggering...One meticulously planned vindictive assault...Snide, cynical, parasitic and hilarious." The song briefly hit the U.K. indie charts in June 1991.

A spokesman for Morrissey said, "Who are (the Pinchers) anyway? They seem to be intent on making a name for themselves on the back of other artists' reputations." He denied that legal action would be taken against the Warlock Pinchers or their record label over the lyrics and artwork. But he confirmed that Morrissey was aware of the record's existence.

Novick attempted to present Morrissey with his very own copy of "Morrissey Rides a Cockhorse" when the high priest of blatant solipsism performed at Denver's Paramount Theater.

"His gofer took everyone's gifts—mostly flowers," Novick reported. "He gave our record and T-shirt a weird look, but we assured him, 'Take it, Morrissey'll love it.'" ●

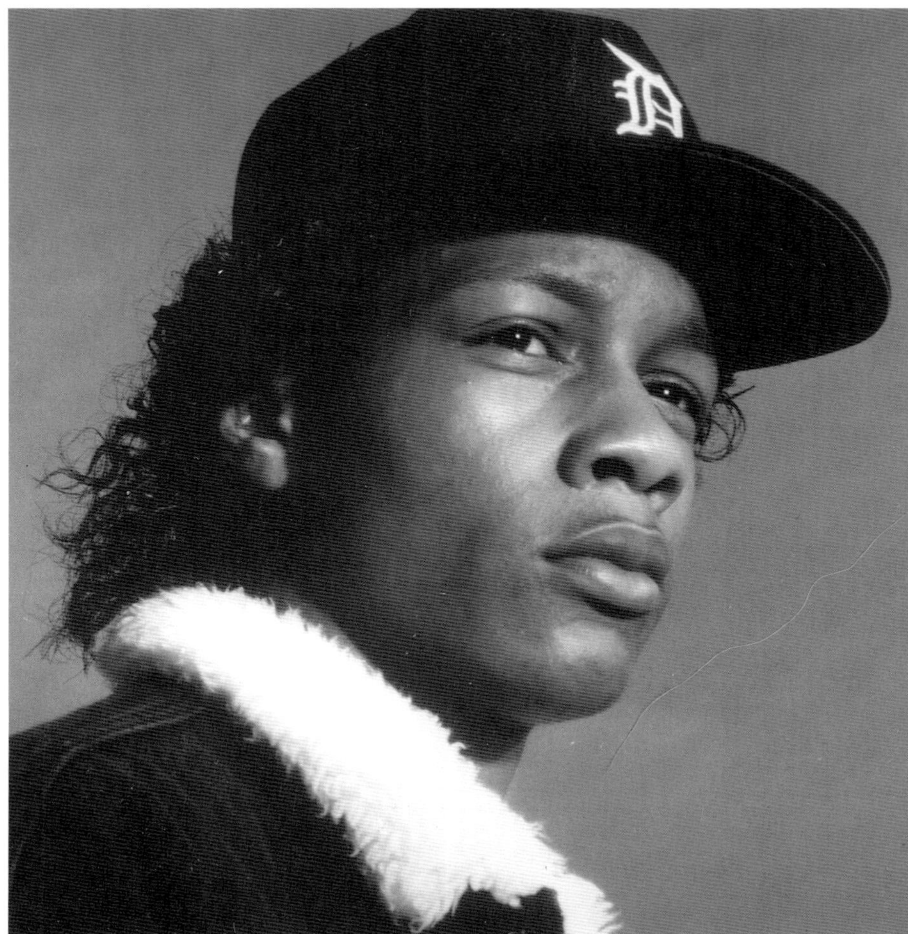

c. 1991

DJ QUIK }

IN THE fall of 1991, Los Angeles rapper DJ Quik was arrested for allegedly throwing a bottle into the crowd during a concert at Denver's Mammoth Events Center. A fan was struck in the cheek, though one witness said another band member had thrown the bottle.

Quik, born David Blake, was booked for investigation of second-degree assault and released on $5,000 bond. He then proved his mettle with the song "Jus Lyke Compton," a definitive bit of regional touting which reflected his thoughts after being exposed to life outside of South Central L.A.

The rhymes took on a resigned, almost dispassionate tone as Quik recounted the gangsta hood resistance he had experienced on tour—how the self-destructive violent lifestyle had become endemic to urban life, how the scene in each city reminded him of home:

"How could a bunch of suckers in a town like this/ Have such a big influence on brothers so far away?"

The "Jus Lyke Compton" video was shot on the locations of the cities in the song—Oakland, St. Louis, San Antonio and Denver—and briefly re-enacted each telling outbreak of violence. In St. Louis, it was a Blood/ Crips gunfight.

"In Denver, it was a simple case of a bunch of hard heads trying to prove a point," Quik said. "A long time ago, I made an underground tape and it contained some Blood shit in it. I wasn't gangbanging. I made it for some friends—I knew they would buy it. I didn't know motherfuckers everywhere were liking the raps. It's a word-of-mouth thing. It all is. And one thing led to another."

Concertgoers saw Quik flashing gang signs and inciting fans in the Denver crowd.

"So I was the aggressor then? I got more to lose. I'm out here trying to do something for myself. I didn't jump up there in Denver and start provoking those motherfuckers. They started throwing stuff on stage, throwing gang signs. So I flipped them off and threw rival gang signs. They hit somebody in the head—nobody knew who threw the bottle, but they put me in jail.

"I go through this shit everywhere. In the song, I didn't mention Houston, Memphis or Phoenix—those were serious scenarios, too. I'm not singled out as a Blood. I'm singled out as a successful little motherfucker."

The single's intensity and wit made Quik a household name in hip-hop circles and helped him earn a gold album—*Way 2 Fonky* later reached the 24th spot on comedian Chris Rock's list of "The Top 25 Hip-Hop Albums of All Time" for *Rolling Stone*. ●

JINX JONES | EN VOGUE }

GROWING UP in Colorado, Jinx Jones spent his teen years playing guitar and singing at Christian youth dances around Denver. He moved on to perform at long-departed 3.2 beer clubs such as My Sweet Lass, Dirty John's and Sam's. It was the 1970s, and his bands had names like MacBeth, Waves and Emerald City.

By the early 1980s, an original music scene began to brew, and for the rest of the decade, Jones was ubiquitous. If he wasn't fronting one of a half-dozen bands—from Jinx Jones & Friends to the Tel Rays to the Blue Jets—he was backing Chuck Berry at a local gig or tending to his own retail establishment, Cadillac Guitars.

c. 1992

Jones was partial to a pink Stratocaster and a retro wardrobe pulled from the racks at Value Village, and he had a handful of varying musical allegiances. After bouncing from rockabilly to funk to everything in between, Jones had done all one musician could in Colorado. As the 1980s came to an end, he packed up his guitars and moved to San Francisco.

"One day, I just impulsively decided to pull up stakes and move out of town," he said. "My intention was to get into a different musical environment, get into the record industry in a bigger way."

Jones fulfilled a lifelong dream when producers Denny Foster and Thomas McElroy recruited him to tackle both guitar and bass duties on En Vogue's 1992 breakthrough album, *Funky Divas*. One day in the studio, Foster and McElroy had Jones piece together a heavy funk track inspired by Funkadelic's "Free Your Mind and Your Ass Will Follow." Jones played everything but

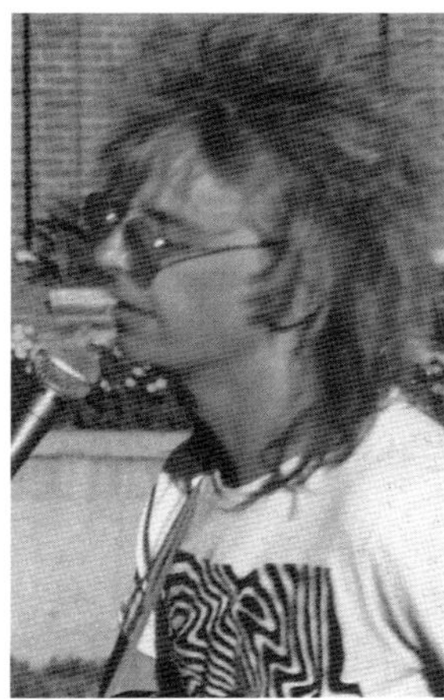

c. 1992

the drum machine on the song, but the label worried that the song was too aggressive and balked at putting it on the album.

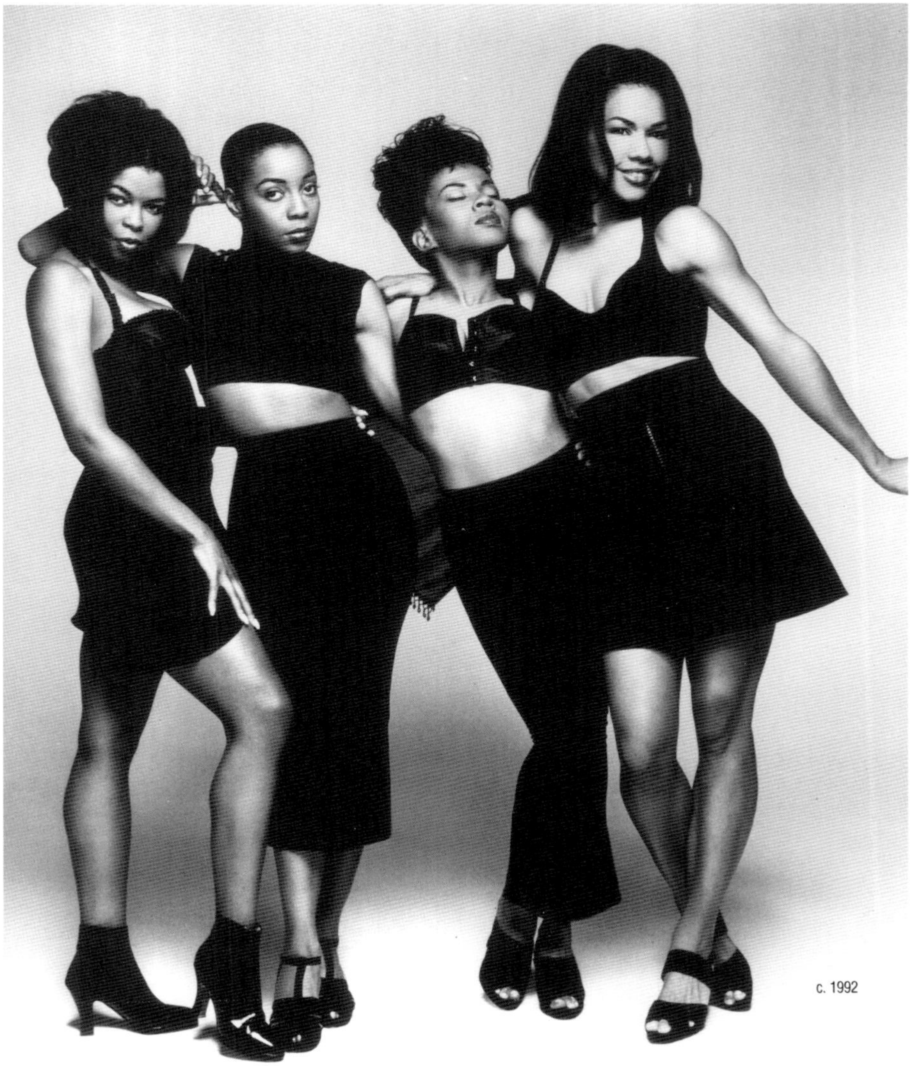

The execs relented, and the tune—"Free Your Mind"—became one of En Vogue's biggest smashes, making #8 on *Billboard*'s Hot 100.

"Then they were getting ready to take it out on the road. My wife was pregnant, and she basically told me that if I went out with those four good-looking black women, she was going to leave me," Jones said with a laugh.

"Spending years and years playing music is a wonderful journey. You get to sample a lot of different great experiences. One thing I really wanted to do was participate in a recording that would be on everyone's radio. And I was very lucky to do that." ●

SPINAL TAP }

THE FUNNIEST movie ever made about rock 'n' roll was 1984's *This is Spinal Tap*, a fictional and admirably accurate spoof of heavy metal stereotypes and the music business (penned by director Rob Reiner and actors Christopher Guest, Michael McKean and Harry Shearer).

The "rockumentary" introduced a gracelessly aging British band. The music was passable fare with bright, imaginative lyrics ("My baby fits me like a flesh tuxedo/I want to sink her with my pink torpedo" from "Big Bottom"), so many of metal's youthful adherents didn't get it. But *This is Spinal Tap* became an inside joke for anyone who had spent a few minutes backstage at a rock concert. The people laughing hardest were the very folks the band lampooned—musicians like Ozzy Osbourne and Aerosmith's Steven Tyler claimed to be the inspiration for the film.

In 1992, Spinal Tap reemerged. The new conceit? The band members turned their collective backs on rock stardom after the disastrous "Smell the Glove" tour documented in *This is Spinal Tap* (the group had a history of constant personality clashes and musical differences). But Spinal Tap had decided to reunite, claiming that the movie was "a gross distortion."

"It was a double-edged gun—it made us infamous, but it made us look pathetic," guitarist Nigel Tufnel said. "The director, Martin Di Bergi, chose to show us not finding the stage. But you saw us performing. We must have found the stage on those occasions."

A tour celebrated Spinal Tap's 25-year reunion, and it opened at the Air Force Academy's Arnold Hall in Colorado Springs. (In *This is Spinal Tap*, the band was mistakenly booked at an Air Force base—Tufnel stormed off during the gig when his radio-miked guitar picked up air-traffic control messages.) Spinal Tap amplified the absurd pomp of metal music, and the devastating parody earned sustained laughter, not just scattered giggles.

Prior to the concert, Tufnel explained his latest invention.

"Guitarists are always saying, 'Could you make the tone a bit warmer?' I've designed something. It's made of wool and goes over the knobs of the guitar—it's a 'tone cozy.'"

Spinal Tap assaulted the media, and the poker-faced band cropped up giving comical interviews to every magazine and talk show in sight. People commented that the single "Bitch School" was sexist. "It's about dog obedience," Tufnel said. "The three of us love dogs. Read the lyrics—'You're so fetching when you're on all fours.' How can you misconstrue that?" ●

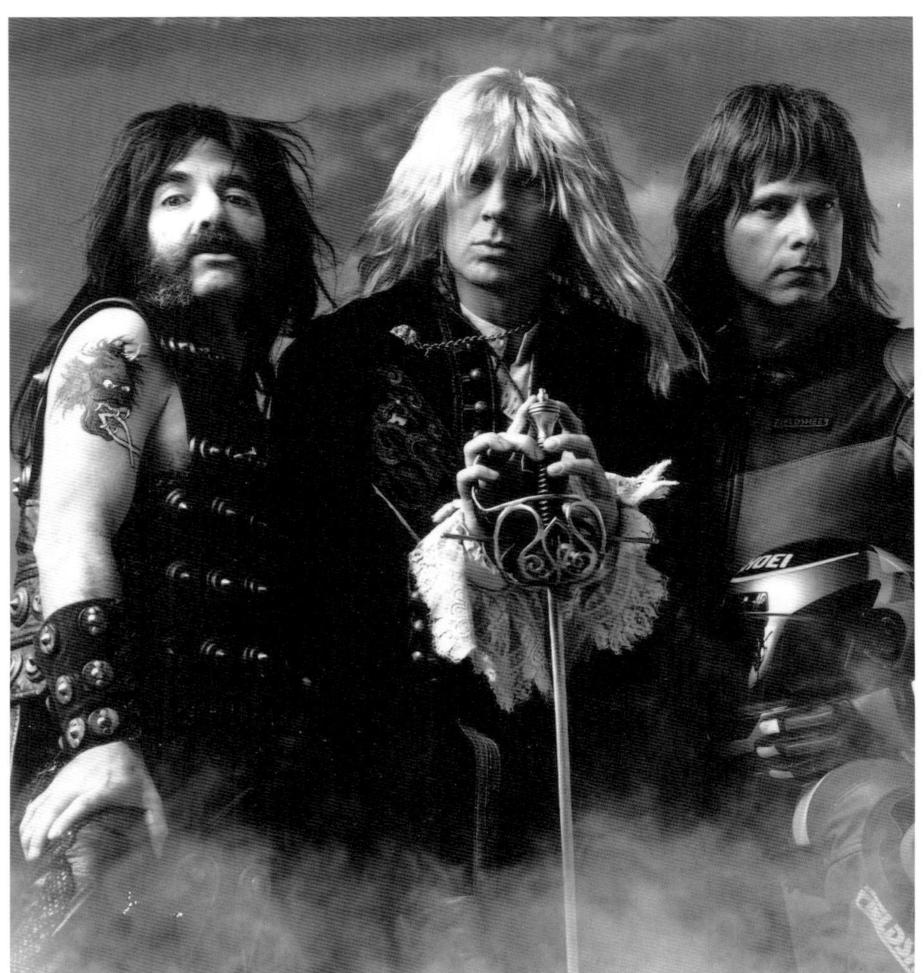

c. 1992

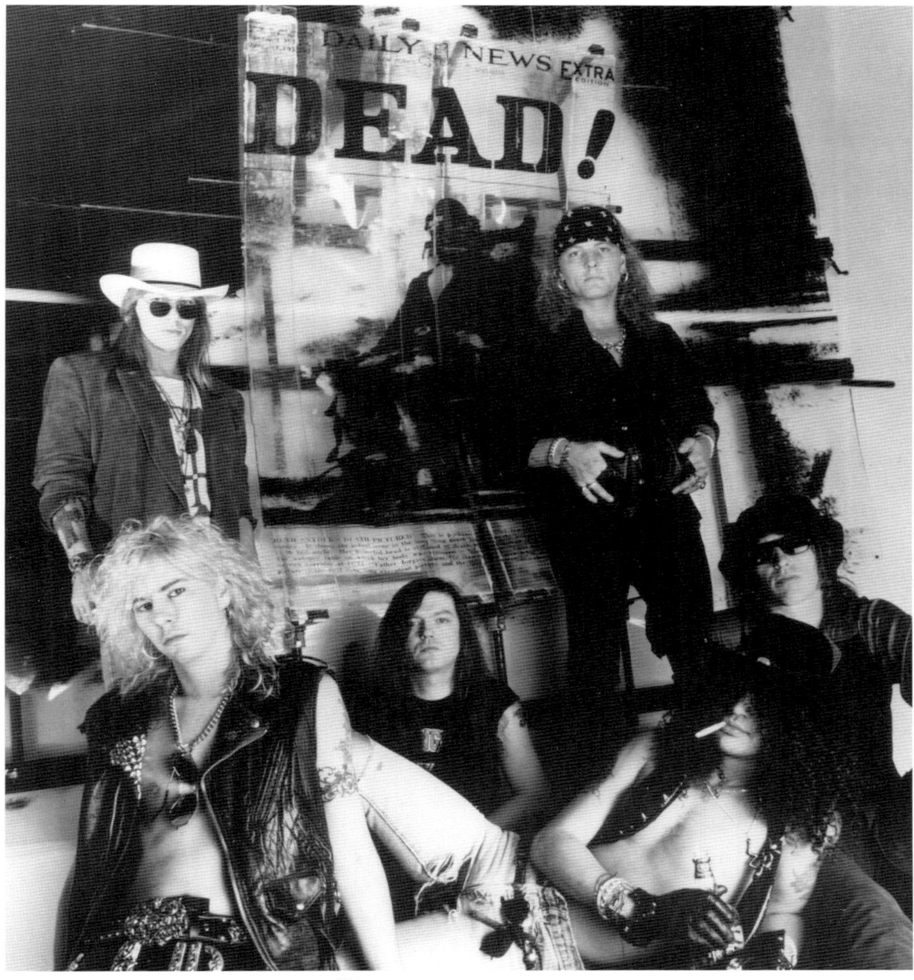

c. 1991

DIZZY REED | GUNS N' ROSES }

MANY LOCALS knew Dizzy Reed from his performances in Colorado with bands like Bootleg and Gauntlet. Then the keyboardist achieved more success than most regional musicians ever dream of—Guns N' Roses recruited him in 1990 to give some additional color to their sound. Reed provided support on the two *Use Your Illusion* albums and toured with the controversial band.

"I was born in Chicago, but my family moved to Colorado when I was six years old. I grew up in Boulder and

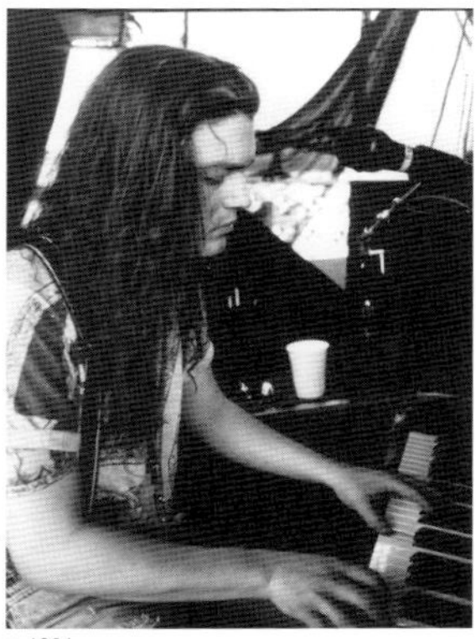

c. 1991

graduated from Fairview High School," Reed said.

"Pat Gill (of the Feds) and I started our first band together in the sixth grade. We were called the Hairy Bananas. We went through a few names and finally settled on Bootleg. We played together for ten years, until we were 20, and finally went our separate ways."

Reed journeyed to Los Angeles in 1983—"I goofed off and ran out of money"—and came back to Colorado, hooking up with a band called Gauntlet.

"Every time I would meet a girl at a club, she would say, 'Do you know the guys in Gauntlet?' They opened for Ratt at the Rainbow Music Hall. I walked in and saw the girls screaming and the guys sitting down and booing because their girlfriends were into it. Immediately I knew, 'I have to join this band.'"

After recording a demo at Colorado Sound Studios, Gauntlet split to Hollywood and changed its name to the Wild, living in a studio apartment behind Sunset Boulevard for two years. Guns N' Roses moved in next door on the way to becoming the biggest band in Hollywood, and Reed got to know frontman Axl Rose. "I slept on floors with the guys," he said. Eight years later, Reed ended up with Guns N' Roses.

"I didn't really audition, because I was a friend from their early club days. They called up when it was time to get a keyboard player, and I said, 'Let me think about it...okay!' If you audition a bunch of people, you don't get someone who fits in. There's more to it than music."

Reed became an accepted part of the group, known for his keyboard, piano and backing vocal work on albums and during live performances and music videos. He continued to record and play live with the Guns N' Roses lineup, the only band member, besides Rose, to remain from the *Use Your Illusion* era. ●

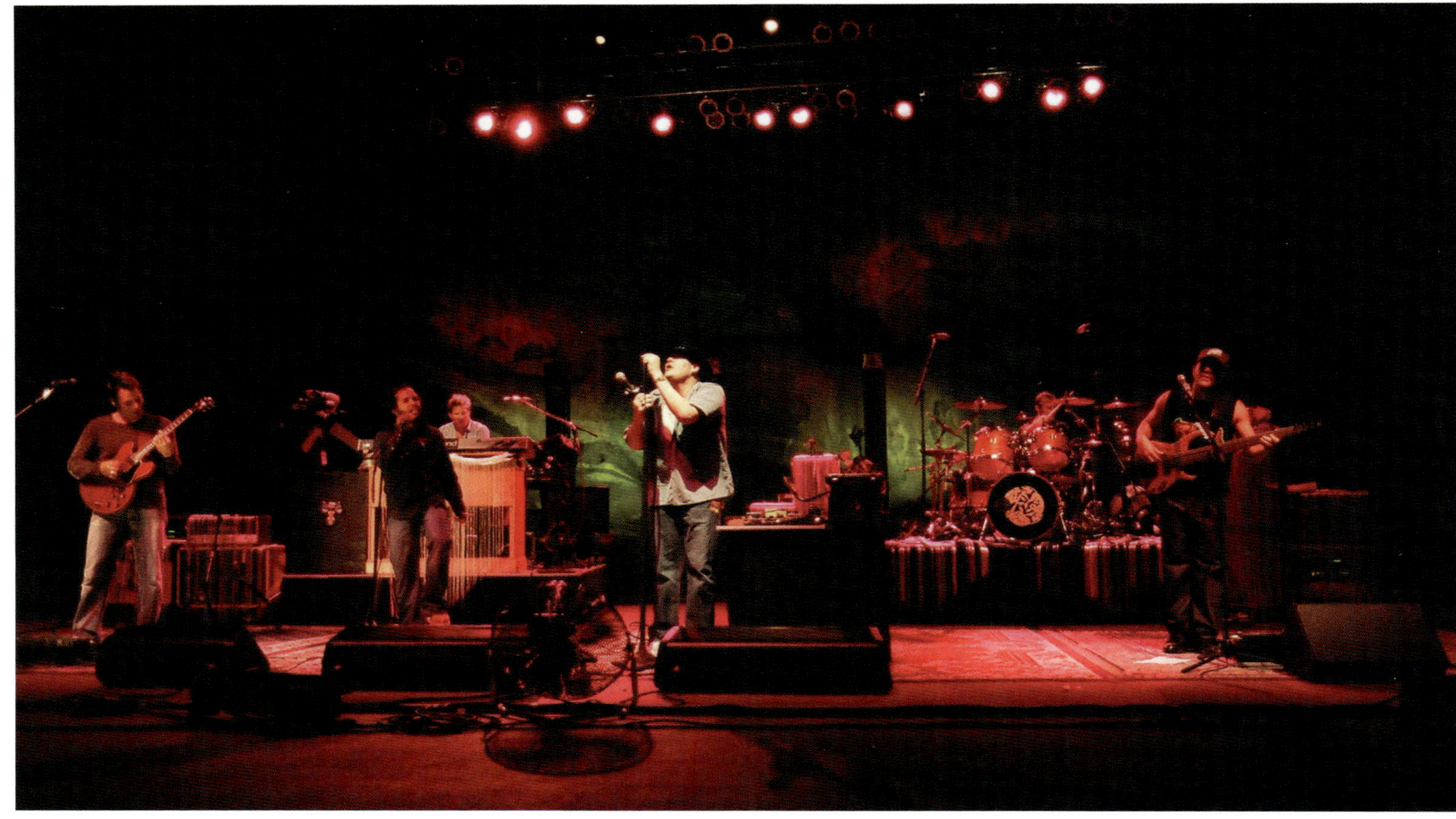

July 4th concert, Red Rocks Amphitheatre, 2009

BLUES TRAVELER }

IN THE 1990s, Blues Traveler gained a reputation in the revival of the extended jam-friendly style of 1960s and 1970s groups. Devotees celebrated with a level of zeal and enthusiasm once reserved for the Grateful Dead, following the New York-based blues-rock quartet to Colorado—since 1992, Blues Traveler was a Fourth of July fixture at Red Rocks Amphitheatre.

Opening for the Allman Brothers Band on July 3 and 4, 1992, marked the beginning of Blues Traveler's run.

"Past New York City, Colorado had been the first place that really opened up for Blues Traveler," guitarist Chan Kinchla said. "From the very beginning of the band, we had great support in there, way before we had any following at all in the rest of the country.

"Red Rocks was just sitting there for us. The fans are just as incredible as the venue—it's such a high-energy, open, rocking crowd of mixed, diverse people. That mentality is what's great about Colorado. It just happened—the next thing we knew, we'd done Red Rocks seven times."

Blues Traveler grew its following with extensive touring, sometimes with over 300 dates a year. The band, fronted by heavyset singer and harmonica player John Popper, crossed over into mainstream success in 1994 with its fourth album, the multi-platinum *Four*, which spawned the Top 10 hits "Hook" and "Run-Around."

Blues Traveler's tradition of Independence Day shows at Red Rocks was interrupted only in 1999 when Popper—who'd been experiencing chest pains for months—was hospitalized and forced to undergo an angioplasty. Weeks later, trage-

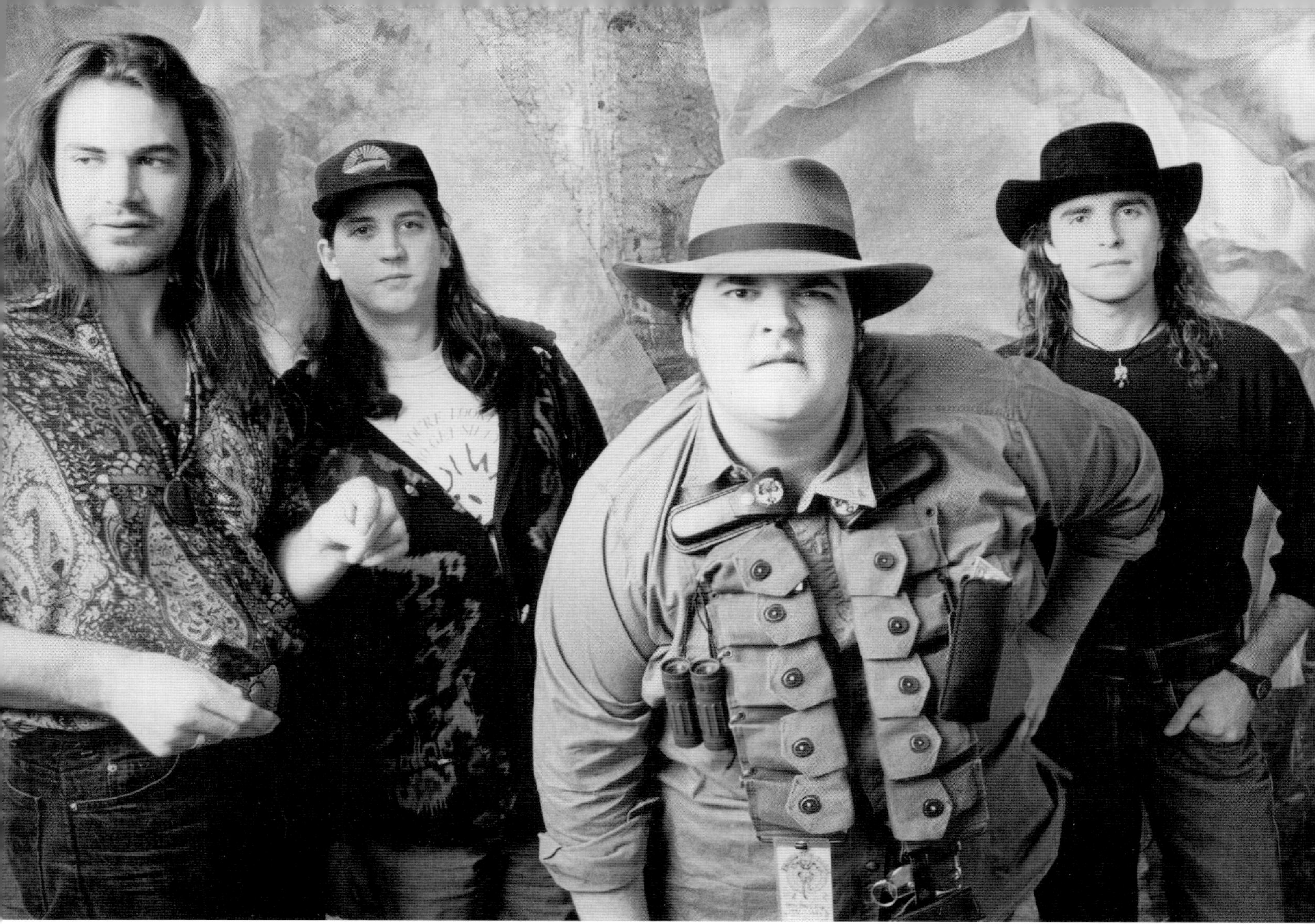

c. 1992

dy struck when bassist Bobby Sheehan was found dead in his New Orleans home.

Sheehan's death and Popper's struggle with obesity put a damper on the group's success. However, the new millennium saw a renewed vigor, with Blues Traveler starting in new musical directions and releasing work on smaller independent labels. *Live on the Rocks*, recorded at Red Rocks on July 4, 2003, was one of the band's strongest live albums, featuring plenty of solid improvisation and funky blues jamming.

"Through all the changes in the entire history of the band, Red Rocks on the Fourth of July is the only constant thing we've done," Kinchla said. "The opportunity to play there almost 20 years in a row is just insane to me, something I'm thankful for.

"When we opened for the Allman Brothers in 1992, someone said, 'When the fireworks come, we've got to go to the top.' So a bunch of us climbed all the way up and watched the Allman Brothers with the fireworks crackling in the background. And since then, Blues Traveler has been the headliner—every year I've been down on the stage playing. When the fireworks start going off, the crowd goes nuts, and it always brings me back to the first time I was there—'God, this must look amazing to them right now. I'm a little jealous. I wish I was up there!' But I have those memories. I know what they're screaming about." ●

THE MOODY BLUES }

DURING THEIR initial heyday from 1967 to 1972, the Moody Blues had some sensationally successful recordings in their "cosmic" symphonic rock style.

In the mid- and late 1990s, the Moodies enjoyed another period of great success. The band ranked as one of the decade's top concert draws, playing around the world augmented with symphony orchestras.

The concept started with a show in Colorado on September 9, 1992, when the band recorded a live album and television special, *A Night at Red Rocks with the Colorado Symphony Orchestra*.

"We wanted to celebrate the 25th anniversary of our *Days of Future Passed* album," singer-guitarist Justin Hayward revealed. "In the absence of a record company revitalizing it, we figured we'd do it ourselves.

"We thought we'd perform with an orchestra before a live audience—we'd never done it. And Red Rocks had been a favorite venue of ours. It's a stunning, beautiful setting."

Released in 1967, *Days of Future Passed* was one of the earliest collaborations between a rock band and an orchestra. The Moody Blues were a trifle ahead of their time. "Everyone thought we were crazy," Hayward laughed.

Uniting the group with the London Symphony Orchestra, *Days of Future Passed* was a landmark in rock recording, establishing a wave of progressive concept albums characterized by classical overtones. The album spawned the massive hits "Nights in White Satin" and "Tuesday Afternoon," and the Moody Blues' following increased to messianic proportions.

On that special summer night at Red Rocks a quarter-century later, the Moody Blues were able to recreate their majestic studio sound as originally envisioned.

After years of struggling financially, the Denver Symphony had disbanded, only to rise again as the Colorado Symphony Orchestra. The 84-member-strong CSO backed the Moody Blues with arrangements supplied by Denver-based travelling conductor Larry Baird, a rock and classical buff who studied theory and composition in college. Nobody had saved the orchestral scores on the classic *Days of Future Passed* for the musicians, so Baird had to listen to the record and recreate the parts. Other songs were also newly scored for the august occasion.

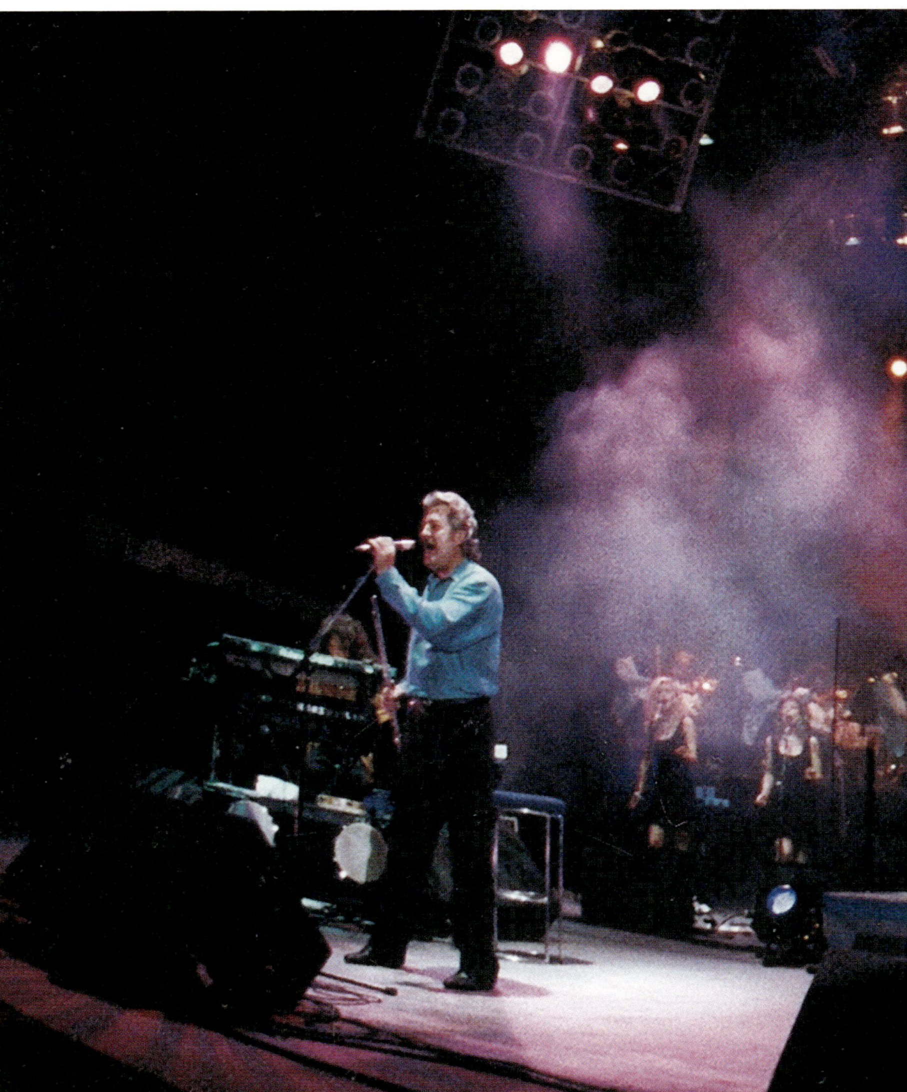

Performing with the Colorado Symphony Orchestra at Red Rocks, September 9, 1992

The symphonic sumptuousness of the Moodies' early hits was discovered by a new generation of young fans.

"We did that one night at Red Rocks for a PBS special," Hayward said. "It was really the brainchild of our late manager, Tom Hulett—he had a desire to see us with an orchestra, and he went about putting it together. We thought it would be a one-off thing.

"And the response came from all over, from orchestra

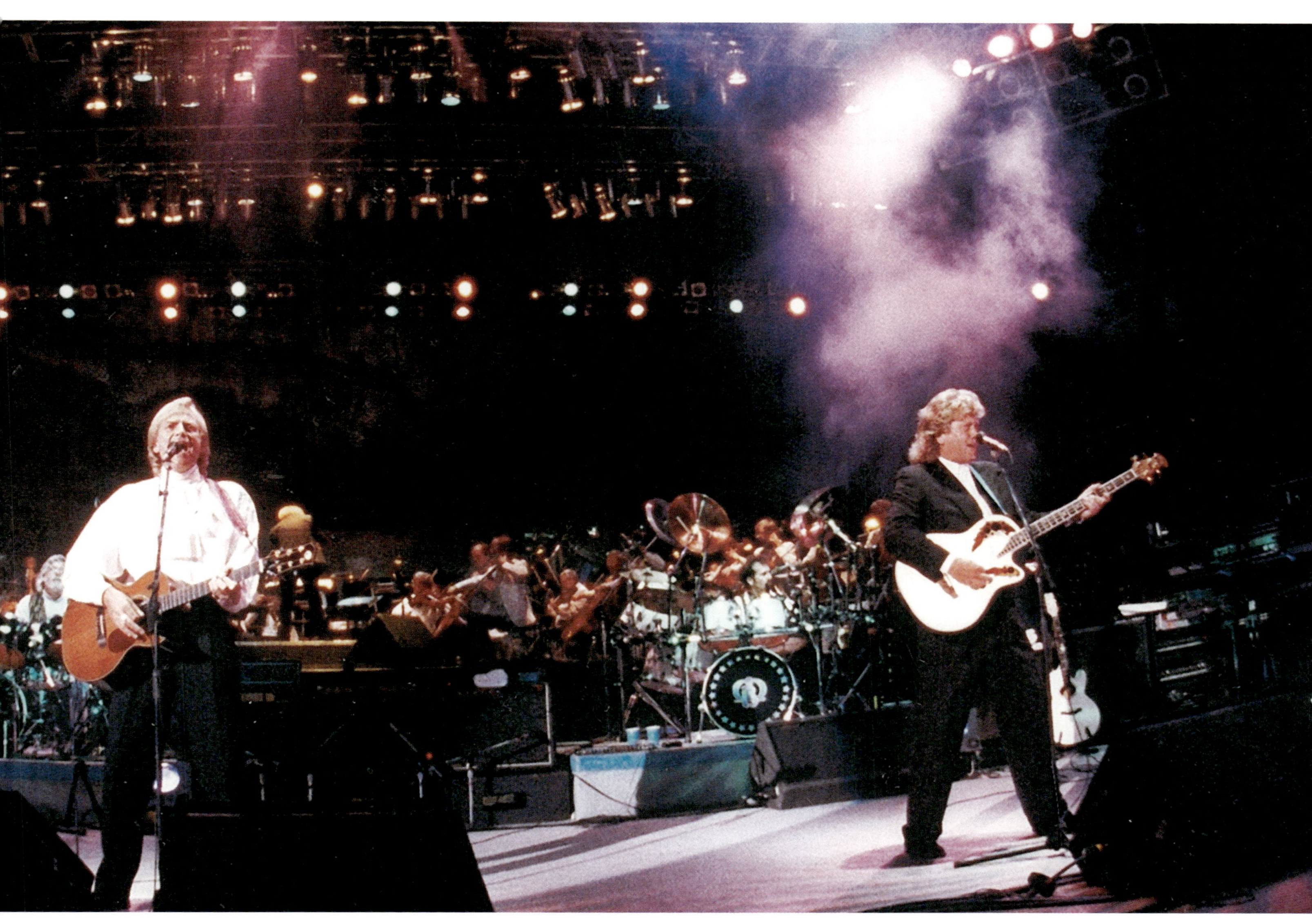

directors and even mayors of towns—'Can you come and do this show with our orchestra?' That's when we realized that most decent-sized cities and towns in America have their own professional-quality orchestra. That doesn't exist in Europe, so we didn't know about it. I thought the logistics would be impossible.

"But of course they're not. Tom had toured with Elvis Presley—'Hey, Elvis used to pick up 47 musicians every night and it sounded great.' So we thought we'd try it. The stage is ours, the seats are ours, the microphones are ours—the only thing that changes is the players. I'm not sure a lot of people know they've got an orchestra in their town until they come and see the Moodies."

A deluxe edition two-CD set of the Moody Blues' *A Night at Red Rocks with the Colorado Symphony Orchestra*, released in 2002, presented the entire two-hour concert for the first time. ●

OZZY OSBOURNE }

AN IN-CONCERT home video and double live disc—both titled *Live & Loud*—documented Ozzy Osbourne's "Theatre of Madness" and "No More Tours" treks in 1991-1992.

Both releases were jump-started when "Changes," a version of the Black Sabbath song from the 1972 *Vol. 4* album, was issued. A live performance clip culled from the *Live & Loud* video hit MTV. Osbourne had performed the ballad at Red Rocks Amphitheatre in Colorado, backed by Zakk Wylde on piano.

"I'm going through a different change," Osbourne explained. "I had a hard time on this farewell tour." The 1993 releases marked the final performances of Osbourne with the lineup of guitarist Wylde, bassist Michael Inez and drummer Randy Castillo.

Castillo, a Denver native, was a familiar face around town back in the 1970s. The muscular drummer played with the Wumblies before forming the Offenders, a band on the edge of the local punk scene (they used to spray-paint their hair instead of springing for dye). Castillo had joined Mötley Crüe when he lost his battle with cancer in March 2002. ●

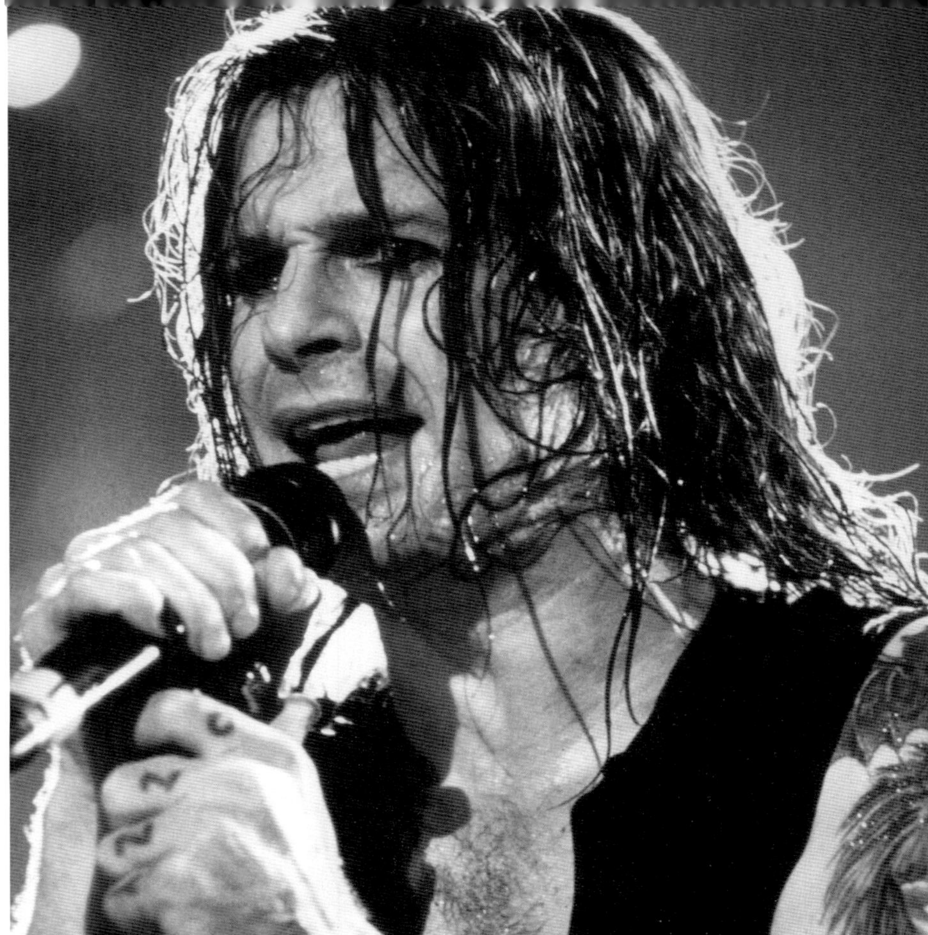

c. 1993

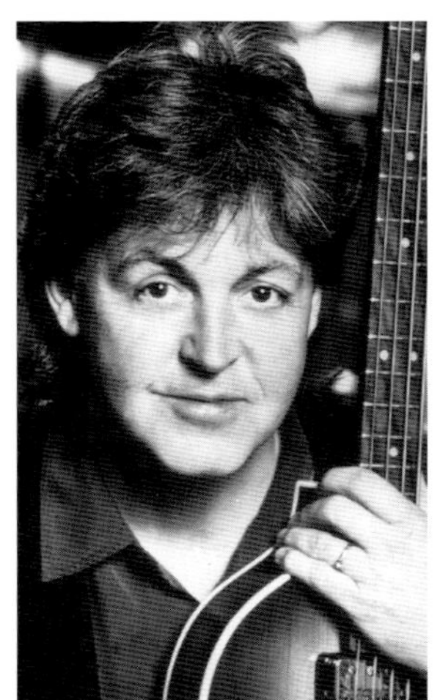

c. 1993

PAUL McCARTNEY }

IN 1993, PAUL McCartney's U.S. "New World Tour" served up Fab-tinged family fun for nearly two million fans at 78 concerts, including a performance at Folsom Field in Boulder on May 26. He put eight songs from that show on his 24-track album, *Paul is Live*, including "Live and Let Die" and "Let Me Roll It."

McCartney, 50, was happy to be playing. "I always thought you had to finish in rock 'n' roll at 24 or so. But it just keeps on going. When you're 30, then you think you'd better finish at 40. When you're 40, you think you'd definitely finish at 50. At 50—I don't know, I suppose you just stop thinking about it. I'm still enjoying it, and as long as audiences keep coming, and I keep seeing smiling faces out there, I'll keep showing up."

The *Paul is Live* video was intended to complement the live album, but there were differences between the two. In the video, there was an obvious lack of continuity within each sequence to underline the breadth of the tour. For example, the color footage of "Let Me Roll It" was shot in Boulder, the black-and-white in Paris, and the audience bits were Milanese. ●

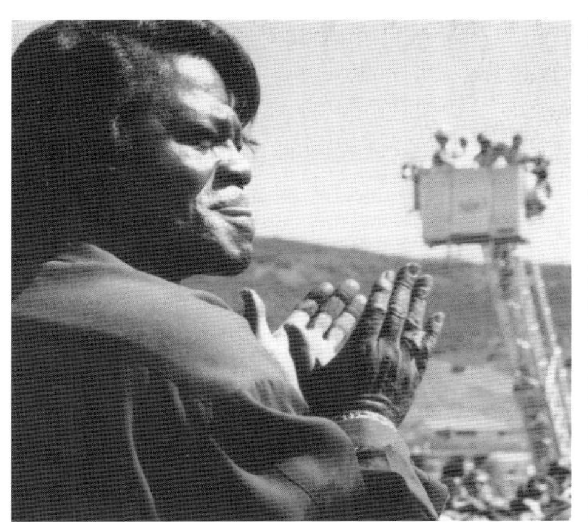

In Steamboat Springs, 1993

JAMES BROWN }

THE COLORADO mountain resort of Steamboat Springs had a contest to name an otherwise unnoticeable highway bridge north of town in 1993. Locals were sharply split. After much public debate and two elections that pitted factions such as long-time area ranchers against ski-bum newcomers, the residents voted and overwhelmingly selected "The James Brown Soul Center of the Universe Bridge" in honor of the Godfather of Soul over one of the region's historic names.

Brown himself showed up in a stretch limousine for the official dedication, leading the crowd in an a cappella version of "I Got You (I Feel Good)." The span had already been defaced by racist graffiti, but Brown said he wasn't bothered by the vandalism: "I hope they use the writing to teach the kids how to spell."

Town officials wouldn't put up a dedication plaque, saying it would only wind up on someone's college dorm room wall. ●

TAG TEAM }

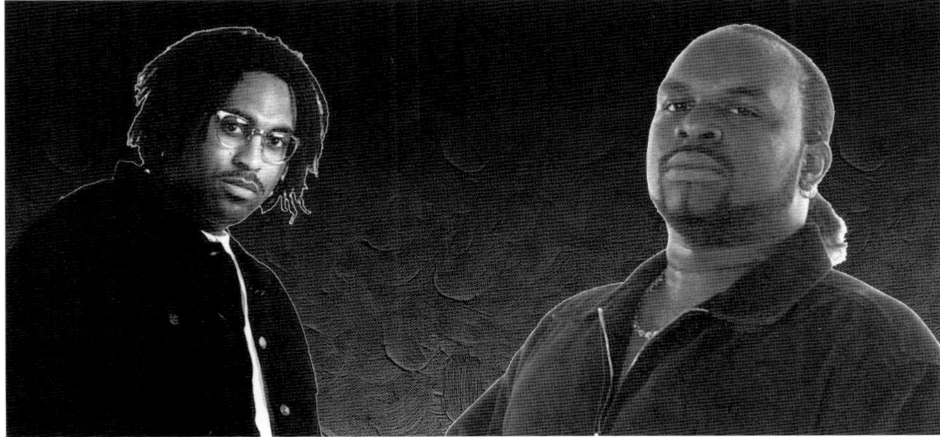

c. 1993

IN THE summer of 1993, Tag Team's "Whoomp! (There It Is)" was every B-boy and B-girl's jeep-ready anthem. The slammin' slang caught fire nationwide after Chicago Bulls fans shouted it during the NBA playoffs.

Partners Cecil "DC" Glenn and Steve "Roll'n" Gibson—two "old fools from the old school that are so cool"—were Denver natives. They met while attending Manual High School during the early 1980s. The local hip-hop scene was in its infancy at the time, so they relocated to Atlanta.

Glenn claimed to have coined the phrase while spinning records at Atlanta's Magic City club—"America's number one adult entertainment complex," he intoned.

"People had been saying 'There it is' forever. Everybody in Arsenio Hall's television audience used to do the 'Wooof' chant. We put that together with the 'There it is' dance floor chant we were hearing at the club."

Gibson recalled that "DC said, 'Oh, man, we need to do a song called, "Whoomp, there it is."' All I said was, 'How do you spell it?'"

Chanted on street corners, in clubs and at concerts, the exuberant double-edged street phrase spawned not one but two hit singles, Tag Team's "Whoomp! (There It Is)" and 95 South's funkier "Whoot, There It Is." Hall pitted the two groups in a competition on his *Arsenio* show. Viewers prefered "Whoot," but record buyers judged "Whoomp!" the best—it lasted 45 consecutive weeks on the *Billboard* Hot 100. A #2 pop hit and a No. 1 R&B hit, it became a pop culture phenomenon.

But Tag Team didn't come close to matching that initial level of commercial success, and the duo was considered a one-hit wonder. ●

THE FLUID | SPELL }

DENVER'S EARLY 1980s hardcore punk scene gave the Fluid its roots. Rick Kulwicki (guitar, vocals) and Matt Bischoff (bass, vocals) were in the Frantix and gained a measure of national notoriety with "My Dad's a Fuckin' Alcoholic," a single that radio deejays wouldn't even consider playing, let alone say the title over the air. James Clower (guitar, vocals), Garrett Shavlik (drums, vocals) and Bischoff were in White Trash. In 1985, rookie vocalist John Robinson joined up, and the Fluid debuted.

"They had a gig and were auditioning singers," Robinson recalled. "In my own head, I thought I was sculpting myself to be a singer, but the Fluid was my first band. That had been my boyhood dream."

The Fluid earned good reviews on a self-produced first album. A package was put together and mailed to clubs in the Midwest, where enough owners liked it to book the group.

"They weren't willing to give us more than $100 or a pizza as payment, but that's definitely what made us a national band and not so much a Denver band," Robinson noted.

"We got out there continually and basically starved. That's just what it takes. It's not that you have to suffer for your art, but you have to be willing to sacrifice. There's one underlying element that's consistent—we enjoy playing live. It's less of a work ethic and more of a passion."

The Fluid started raising hell in the indie-rock world. The group was the first non-Northwest signing for Sub Pop Records, the tiny record label that launched Nirvana and other Seattle acts. The Fluid acquired a substantial following and significant success on college radio, with records charting high in the trade magazines *Rockpool* and *CMJ* and in the British weeklies. In addition to releasing three of the band's albums, Sub Pop also put out a split 7-inch single featuring the Fluid and Nirvana. But the Fluid's appeal was more punk than grunge.

"Grunge is just a lot of screeching going on, with no competence in harmony and melody. Those pop things are what separates us," Robinson said.

"We've always had a hard time describing what our music is, even though it's not that complicated," Clower added. "We got lumped in with the whole grunge thing, but it's always been pretty much straight-up rock."

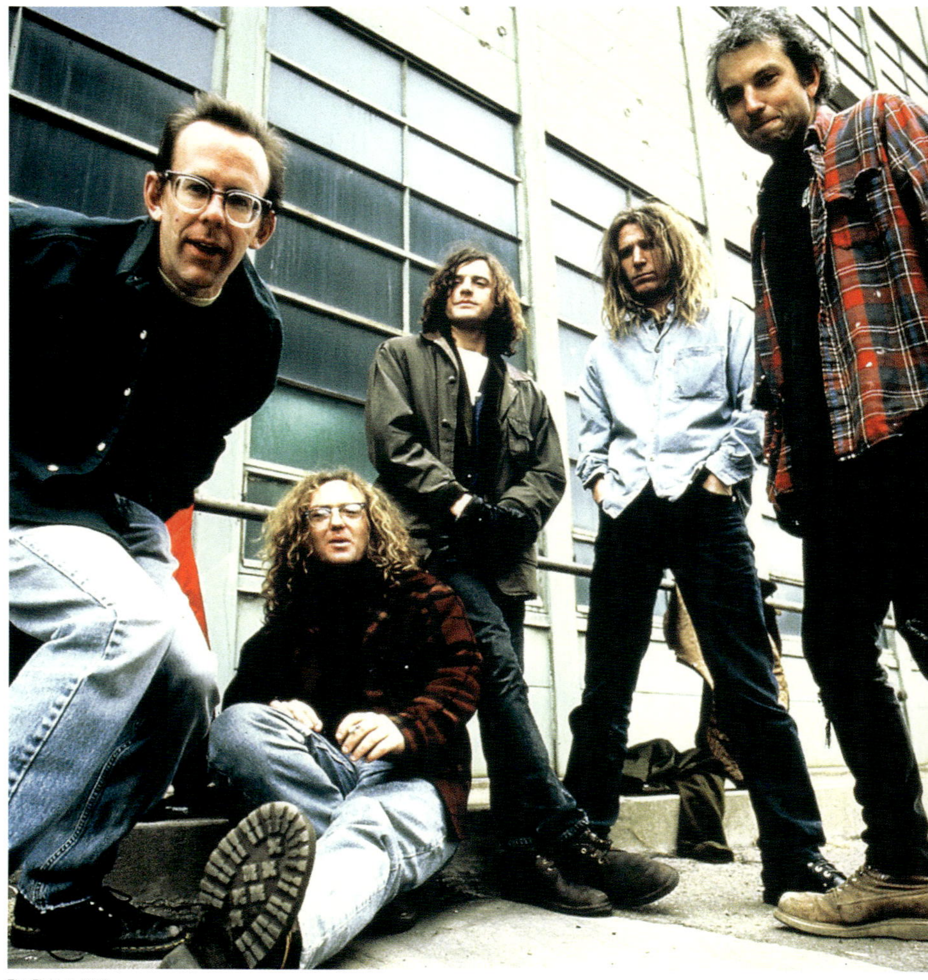

The Fluid, c. 1993

The sound was captured on *Purplemetalflakemusic* (1993), a wonderful, ugly roar of a debut on Hollywood Records, a Disney-backed label. The pumped-up track "Mr. Blameshifter" and the heavier "7/14" featured big, threatening guitars and Shavlik's careening, driving beats.

But the Fluid's career on a major label was brief. Weak sales and a tour from hell killed the band.

"Signing to a major was the worst thing we could do. Once we got signed, we got lost in the shuffle," Clower said.

"The majority of the team we were working with got fired, and we were left to deal with complete strangers who didn't know what we were doing and vice versa," Kulwicki noted. "We got sent out on the road and had zero communication, as this was before the days before cellphones and laptops. It was a difficult last tour for us. We never took a break from each other, and we should have. That's what led to the demise of the band."

Shavlik was the first to quit. "I didn't have my heart in it anymore," he explained. "I would have rather had a page-turner than a roadie—I could have read Tolstoy while I was on stage. I still played my ass off, but I was bored. And I think everybody else in the band felt that way, too. We weren't progressing.

"What we did was amazing, and I'm really proud to have been a part of that. But I was so lucky and fortunate to have the link with Spell."

Spell took shape when Shavlik, who had penned much of the music and lyrics on early Fluid albums, lost his creative responsibility as Robinson started contributing songs. Out of boredom, Shavlik (who went to Boulder High) wrote some songs with Tim Beckman (of Rope, who went to Westminster High School) and Chanin Floyd (Beckman's wife, who was in 57 Lesbian and went to Littleton High).

The trio formed Spell and it became Shavlik's new project. The band's tape circulated among friends in the music underground, and it landed the trio on the cover of *CMJ* as Best Unsigned Artist of the day. The phone started ringing.

The decision was hard on Shavlik, who had put in years with the Fluid. But he realized that Spell offered him the opportunity to test some new ideas with Beckman and Floyd. Spell signed to Island Records (home of U2 and Melissa Etheridge) and released *Mississippi*.

"Basically, the record was our demos from four different sessions over three years in Denver with a local producer—we just released the whole recording process. The hardest thing to get was the continuity."

The official bio called Spell's sound "sexually charged noise pop energy." Beckman called it "three chords and the truth."

"Superstar" was one of the first songs written by the fast and loud trio. The boisterous, cynical take on fitting in led off with a hard power-pop guitar riff and a vocal sound similar to X and Sonic Youth. The song was added in eight markets, including Detroit and Boston, when it was sent to alternative radio stations. KTCL-FM played it in the Denver area.

"It's was very polarized. In some circles, we were the little darling bastards of Denver," Shavlik said. "It was special for the people who were there from the beginning—to them, we were a cool noise band with hooks. But the day the news broke that we signed on the dotted line, all of a sudden we were arrogant sellout rock stars."

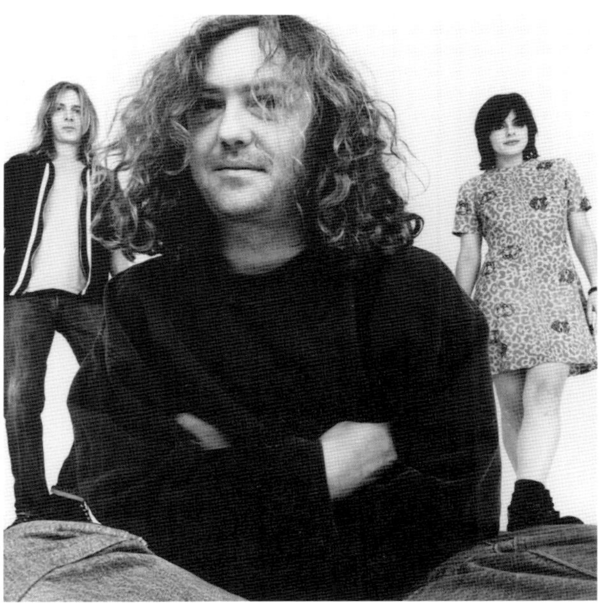

Spell, c. 1994

"Superstar" didn't find a big audience. "I wish they could have made a better video—it was lame, just a performance shoot," Beckman said. "MTV liked the song—they played it as a theme for their sport shows—but they wouldn't show the clip.

"That's okay. Everybody makes mistakes."

In 2008, all five of the Fluid's original members reunited to perform at Sub Pop Records' 20th Anniversary Festival in Seattle and at selected dates in Denver.

"Once everyone talked to each other, it's amazing that all it took was someone to ask us to do it," Kulwicki enthused. "It's still ridiculously fun." ●

PEARL JAM }

IN THE 1990s, Pearl Jam had its turn as rock's hottest new band. The Seattle quintet's debut album *Ten* sold more than five million copies in the United States. In late 1993, the *Vs.* album debuted at No. 1 on *Billboard*'s chart and sold nearly a million copies in the first week of release.

The burden of Pearl Jam's popularity fell hardest on singer Eddie Vedder. "These shows are a difficult situation," the reluctant messiah said. "I want fans to be able to see the show like it should be. But instead of making 2,000 people happy, you end up upsetting 20,000 people who can't get in. The letters I get—'They don't care about their fans or they'd play bigger places.' It's the opposite. I'm really surprised how all this happened. You just become this huge band."

In late November, controversy struck in the form of an abruptly cancelled gig at the University of Colorado in Boulder. Pearl Jam had been booked for a three-night stand, and the first show, on a Friday night, went on without a hitch. A crowd-control plan that had worked well in Europe was implemented. Fans in front were packed into where their surging energy could only be released upward. "Surfing"—passing people overhead—was directed toward the stage barricade, where security personnel fished out the bodies and funneled them to the outskirts.

When Pearl Jam took the stage on Saturday, though, the band members were angered to see teams of headset-wearing policemen wandering through the crowd of about 4,000 people. For seemingly no reason, the campus had augmented the venue's normal peer group security force with dozens of stern-looking uniformed officers. The disagreement focused on a university concern brought by "moshing"—in which participants in the crowd slammed into each other.

At the end of Saturday night's show, Pearl Jam, which was "pro-mosh," started criticizing the stage security, complaining that the fans were being treated too roughly. Vedder took the opportunity to vent his displeasure over the unnecessary police presence during the last few minutes of the show, confronting a few of the cops present and reportedly grabbing one officer's headset.

On the morning of the Sunday show, during a meeting with campus officials and the promoter, the band insisted that the venue ease its security. When the school wouldn't budge, alleging that Vedder's actions the previous night had "created some tension," Pearl Jam canceled the gig, promising to return in the spring at a different locale to honor the tickets held by disappointed fans.

The third Pearl Jam performance was rescheduled for March at the Paramount Theatre in Denver. The Paramount's reserved seating didn't allow moshing.

Midway through the set, after a false start on a song, Vedder alluded to the Boulder dispute.

"It's an interesting situation...This is a nice theater, really, and we don't want to damage it...There were problems at the last show—I won't say anything until the lawsuit's over...But it seems like you're bored, and we've been so excited to come here..."

After the frenzy, Vedder milled about backstage.

"My lawyer has advised me not to talk about it," he said. "But I won't just pay the fine and be done with it. I didn't do anything. I don't want a charge of obstructing government operations on my record."

Six months later, a judge in Boulder threw out the charge against Vedder of interfering with police. ●

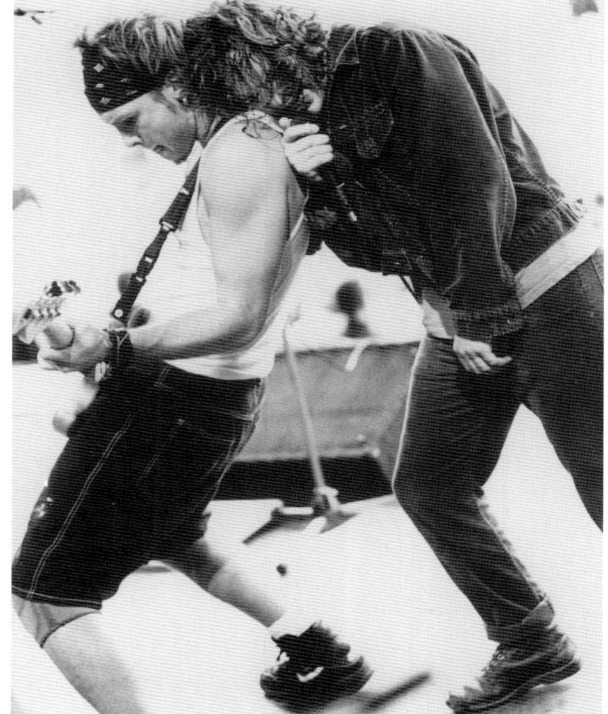

c. 1993

MICHAEL JACKSON }

IN FEBRUARY 1995, Denver songwriter Crystal Cartier thought she had a rock-solid case against the planet's most famous music man. The local crooner had filed a lawsuit in federal court in Denver, claiming that she wrote "Dangerous" in 1985, and that she produced and recorded it five years later for her album *Love Story: Act One*—a long time before Michael Jackson released his *Dangerous* album in 1991. The lawsuit sought $40 million, claiming a violation of copyright and trademark laws.

The trial's crescendo came on the seventh and final day of testimony. After Cartier—the "Queen Size Lover," as she once billed herself—had been booted out of the courtroom by the judge for wearing fishnet stockings and a skin-tight black leather miniskirt, Jackson, the "King of Pop," captured the attention of courtroom spectators and possibly boosted his defense by breaking into song.

A string of questions gave Jackson all the prompting he needed to deliver abbreviated a cappella renditions of his hits, ostensibly to explain how the vocal melodies were conceived on the spur of the moment "like a gift that's put in my head." During his 49 minutes on the witness stand, Jackson sang portions of "Billie Jean" and "Dangerous" into the court microphone. Eyes closed, head bobbing, fingers snapping, he immersed himself in brief segments of bass line and melody.

The pop superstar adamantly denied Cartier's claim. "I wrote the words to 'Dangerous,'" Jackson testified between samples of his songs. "No one at all" assisted with the writing, he said.

"The first time I sang the lyrics, it was kind of a funny day (in September 1990). Well, not really a funny day. I usually sing in the dark because I don't like people looking at me unless I'm on stage...

"Then (while singing 'Dangerous' for the first time) this huge wall, maybe seven feet tall, fell on me."

Jackson wore black pants and a black shirt with red and yellow epaulettes and collar tabs. He pulled his hair back in a ponytail, one strand trailing down the right side of his face. He said he didn't read music because "you don't have to." He also said he had never heard of Cartier before she filed her lawsuit against him.

It took the four-man, four-woman jury less than four hours to rule that Jackson hadn't swiped Cartier's tune. Cartier retreated to her Capitol Hill apartment, refusing to leave except for special occasions, notably a TV appearance on *Geraldo*. A cappella passages of Jackson singing "Billie Jean" and "Dangerous" on the witness stand became available via mail order through U.S. District Court at $15 a copy. ●

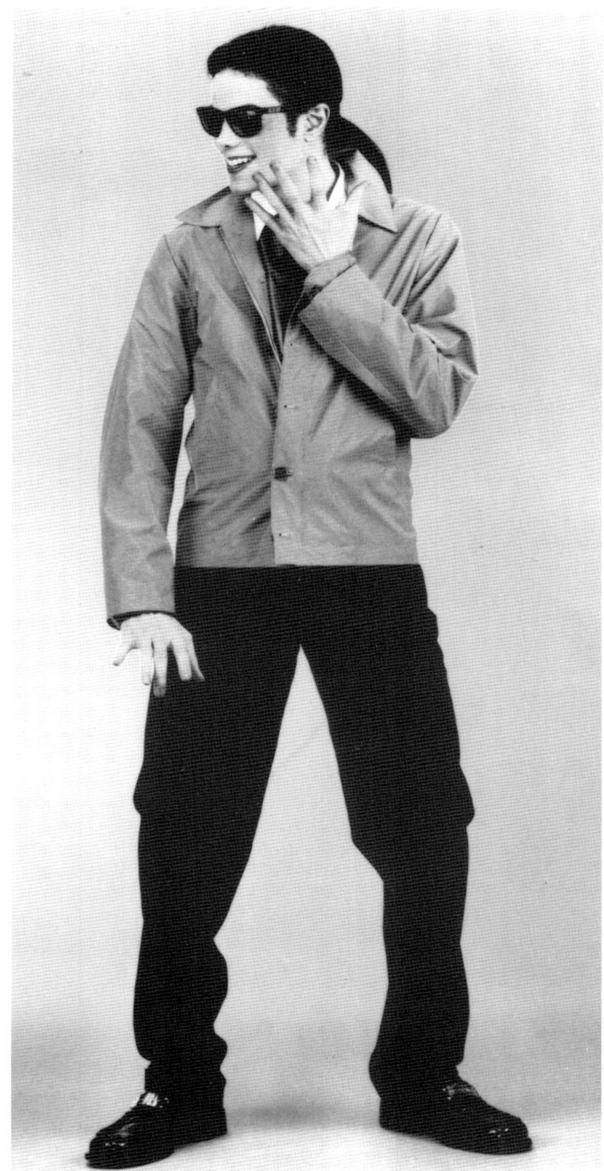

c. 1995

THE SAMPLES }

EMERGING OUT of the burgeoning Colorado music scene, the Samples grew to become one of the most popular touring bands of the early 1990s. It was no fluke.

In 1987, Sean Kelly (vocals and lead guitar) and Charles Hambleton (acoustic guitar, mandolin and banjo) played their first gig at a frat party in Vermont.

"We knew we wanted to play music, but it was so cold there, and jobs were hard to find—I'd had it," Kelly recalled. "Charles' brother was attending the University of Colorado, and he told us the weather was good that winter. We packed up our guitars and amps and moved to Boulder within a week."

They found bassist Andy Sheldon, who had played with Kelly since high school. They put a drummer-wanted ad on a campus bulletin board, which was answered by student Jeep MacNichol, and met keyboardist Al Laughlin (a Boston transplant) at a party. The members took their name for their survival technique of making meals from free food samples at local supermarkets.

The Samples played their first show in front of a handful of people at Tulagi nightclub on Easter Sunday 1987. The band soon became a sensation in local clubs, taking over rooms like JJ McCabe's and the Boulder Theater. The group then went on a North American tour and built a solid grassroots following.

"When bands from New York or Los Angeles or San Francisco try to tour outside of those cities, they rely on national promotion machines. We happened by ourselves," Kelly said.

"In Boulder, our fans were supportive students. They would buy our tapes, and during summer vacation they'd spread out across the country to go home. We recognized people from Boulder in every strange little bar in every university town we played. We got letters from Texas and California, and we heard stories of Samples tapes playing in a hotel on an island off of Greece and in a bar in Nepal.

"And we created a big base. We knew that there was an audience that liked the music, that we were on to something fresh."

The Samples played atmospheric pop, mixing rock melodies and reggae rhythms. Most of the band's songs were written by Kelly, who frequently referenced rain, oceans and other environmental aspects.

Already popular in concert, the band chose to release 5,000 copies of *The Samples* on its own. With the initial shipment sold out, the quintet signed a major label deal with Arista Records under its own terms.

The situation should have meant wide distribution, promotion and possible financial stability. It never developed. *The Samples* sold over 50,000 copies nationally, but when asked specifically to write "hits" to push to radio and MTV, the band discerned the label's meddling and opted to be dropped. Hambleton left the band.

One of the Samples' goals was to let other bands know they didn't have to "feed the machine."

"Major labels are like drift nets," Kelly said. "They go out to sea and fish for big tunas like Mariah Carey and Whitney Houston, but they kill everything else that gets tangled in the nets, the beautiful dolphins. We were lucky enough to slip through the netting and survive."

In four years, the Samples had risen from a freethinking Boulder band to a group with national impact, opening for UB40, the Wailers and Johnny Clegg & Savuka. They found new ways to distribute product to their audience, and a 7,000-person fan club gave them the means to spread the word.

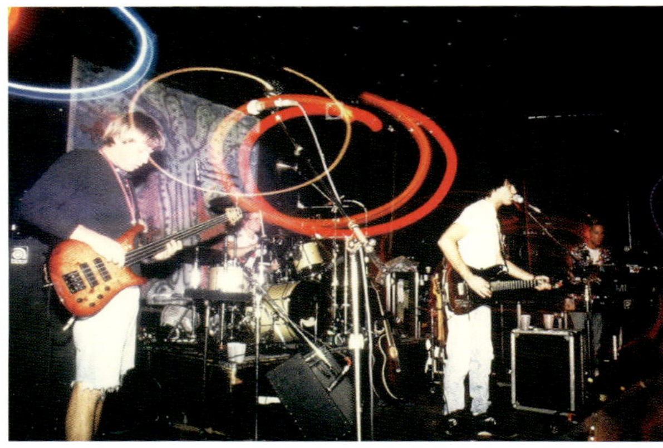
c.1989

To take control of their career, the Samples were the charter act signed to W.A.R.? Records, a tiny Boulder-based operation founded by disenchanted refugees from the corporate atmosphere. W.A.R.? distributed directly through stores that fell through the cracks of a major label's network.

Through constant roadwork and such beguiling tunes as "Underwater People," "Did You Ever Look

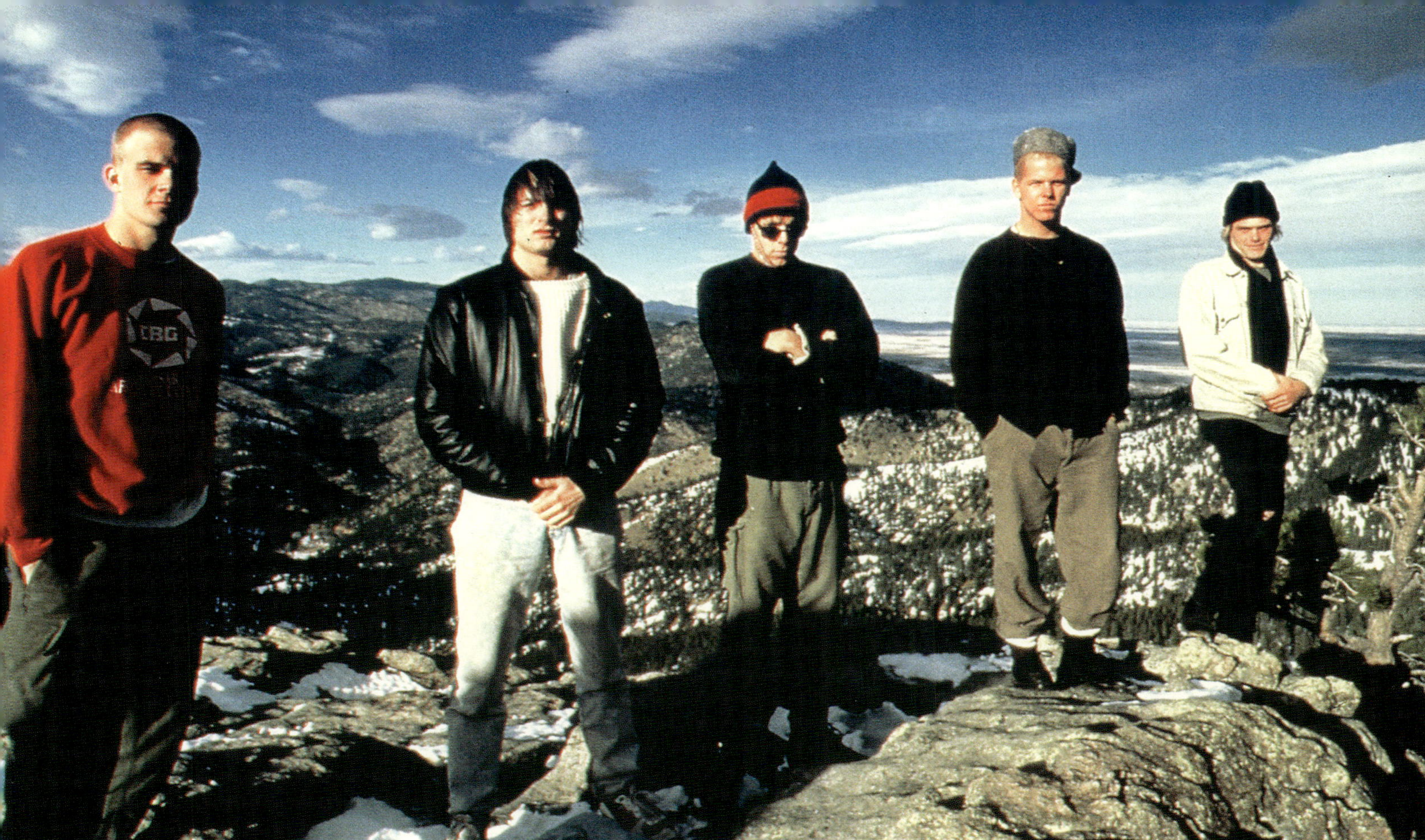

c. 1989

So Nice" and "We All Move On," the Samples made the leap to appearing on the H.O.R.D.E. tour and *The Tonight Show*. Kelly wanted the band to be a part of a nationally recognized Denver/Boulder music scene.

"We travel so much, we know better than anybody—there's no better place to be making music than right here," he insisted. "I really support the Wine Bottles, the Reejers, local bands that have potential. I tell them not to focus on getting signed—don't get caught up in that stuff. Play music, tour and build an audience. It will give you better leverage when the day comes."

The Colorado quartet's fourth CD, *Autopilot*, debuted at No. 1 on *Billboard*'s national Heatseekers chart, listing the best-selling titles by new and developing artists. The Samples had managed great success without the backing of a big-time record company.

Yet when the Samples' contract with W.A.R.? expired, they looked to sign with a major label for the second time in their career. The band had a brief stint at MCA Records, but the *Outpost* CD did poorly (a changing of the executive guard at the label didn't help matters).

MCA paid off the Samples contract. Laughlin battled a substance-abuse problem, and he and MacNichol departed the band. Kelly introduced a brand new Samples featuring Rob Somers, the acoustic guitarist who had accompanied his solo projects. In 1997, the Samples rejoined W.A.R.? and released three more albums, then began to issue recordings on their own. There were numerous personnel changes with the exception of Kelly, the only remaining founding member. The rebirth as an independent band rejuvenated the group's career in the 2000s.

"You have to be a very committed individual for a career in music, because you have to put up with a lot of heartache," Kelly admitted. "The joys are unbelievable, like the very heartfelt letters we get from people. But you have to be really tough." ●

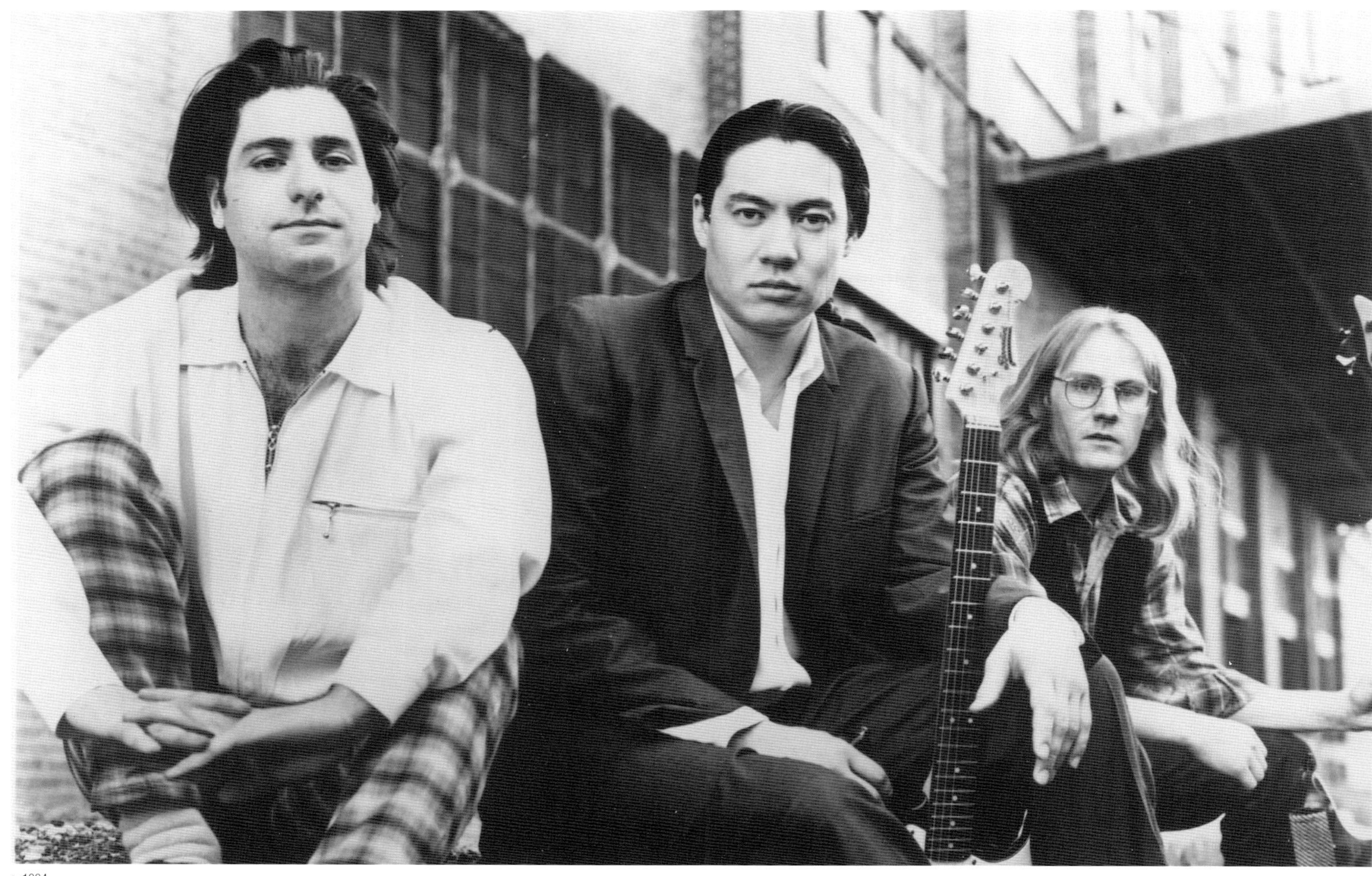

c. 1994

BIG HEAD TODD & THE MONSTERS }

COLORADO NEVER had rock heroes like Big Head Todd & the Monsters. The trio, graduates of Columbine High School, took the local buzz to a national level through hard work, representing a truly organic success story.

"There's no gravy train to stardom from Colorado, I'm afraid," guitarist and lead vocalist Todd Park Mohr said. "There's not a lot of music industry around, so we had to learn how to do things ourselves. It became habitual for us to run our own business after that."

Mohr, bassist Rob Squires and drummer Brian Nevin formed Big Head Todd & the Monsters in 1987. The young band's slightly jazzy, neo-1970s rock 'n' blues sound, fronted by Mohr's strong writing, powerful vocals and charisma, started gaining steam.

The not-so-big-headed guys demonstrated the ability to tour relentlessly and get people to shows. They filled area clubs and grabbed attention in other towns such as San Francisco, Los Angeles, Chicago, Austin, Minneapolis and Boston, where they would sell out venues with capacities of 1,000 or more—they had a built-in crowd of University of Colorado alumni or people who'd seen them in Boulder.

And Big Head Todd & the Monsters got people into record stores. *Another Mayberry* and *Midnight Radio*—

two albums recorded and released on the band's own Big Records label—moved about 40,000 copies without a major distribution deal and garnered response from publications such as *Rolling Stone* and the *Washington Post*.

By 1990, Big Head Todd & the Monsters were clearly ready for the national limelight. In January 1991, the band finally signed with Denver management company Morris, Bliesener & Associates. A month later, the band caught the attention of music mogul Irving Azoff's Giant Records, a label distributed internationally by the mega WEA Corp.

The trio recorded its Giant debut at Paisley Park studios in Minneapolis. *Sister Sweetly* was the killer album that served to define the band. Listeners across the nation caught on to what Colorado already knew, and "Broken Hearted Savior" was a Top 10 track on the album-rock charts. Subsequent hits like "Circle" and "Bittersweet" made *Sister Sweetly* the eighth most played album on rock radio in 1993, according to the trade journal *Radio & Records*.

There were performances on *The Today Show* and *Late Night with David Letterman*, and a tour supporting Robert Plant, former lead singer of Led Zeppelin. The album's steady development, on the back of word-of-mouth and constant gigs, took it to platinum status (one million in sales) three years after its release.

"But success always comes quickly, and nobody can be prepared for what happens to your humanity when you become a celebrity," Mohr said. "It was honestly one of the worst times of my whole life—it was that troublesome for me. It wasn't that I felt like I didn't deserve the acclaim, but it took a lot of adjustment for me to feel comfortable playing in front of people and talking to audiences.

"There was a lot of commercial pressure, and I have to take responsibility for bowing to it. I wanted our music to reach as many people as possible, and we knew that the opportunity had certain contingencies attached to it. You just have to be a man and do the best you can with it. I'm very proud of *Sister Sweetly*. The problem is, if you're successful, then the only way to continue that success is to repeat what you did, to make the same thing over again. I can't ever do that. That's my problem."

Big Head Todd & the Monsters recorded the follow-up, 1994's *Strategem*, by themselves, setting up shop at home and at the Boulder Theater with two inexpensive eight-track digital tape machines. The band joined Blues Traveler's H.O.R.D.E. tour and embarked on a maiden trek across Europe. The group worked with producer Jerry Harrison on 1997's *Beautiful World*, an energetic, honest batch of songs that blended gritty blues, easy funk and acoustic charm. A dream came true for the members when blues legend John Lee Hooker agreed to perform his boogie classic "Boom Boom" with them (he happened to be working in the same San Francisco Bay Area studio down the hall).

But *Strategem* and *Beautiful World* didn't expand the band's audience like the consistent, satisfying *Sister Sweetly*. There was rarely a mention on MTV or in music magazines. Big Head Todd & the Monsters were content to continue their touring schedule, gratifying a fiercely loyal fan base. The group chartered several Caribbean and Hawaiian cruises, filled with devotees.

"There's nothing that prevents us from communicating our music to peo-

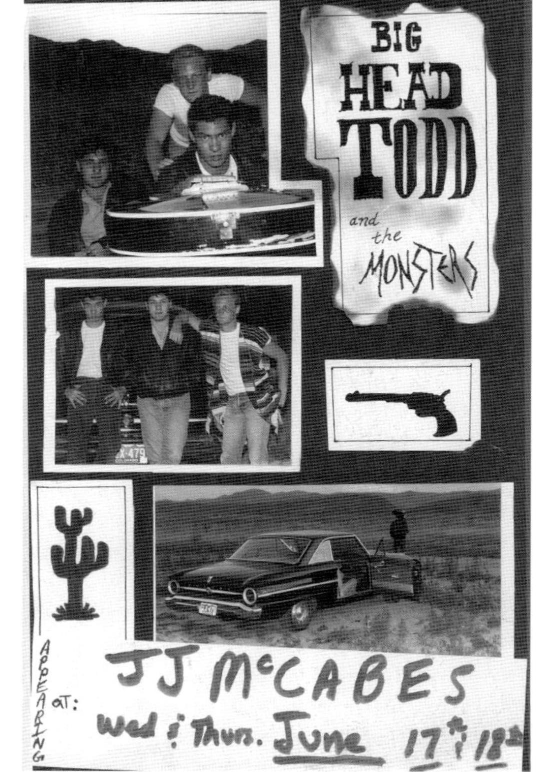

Early poster

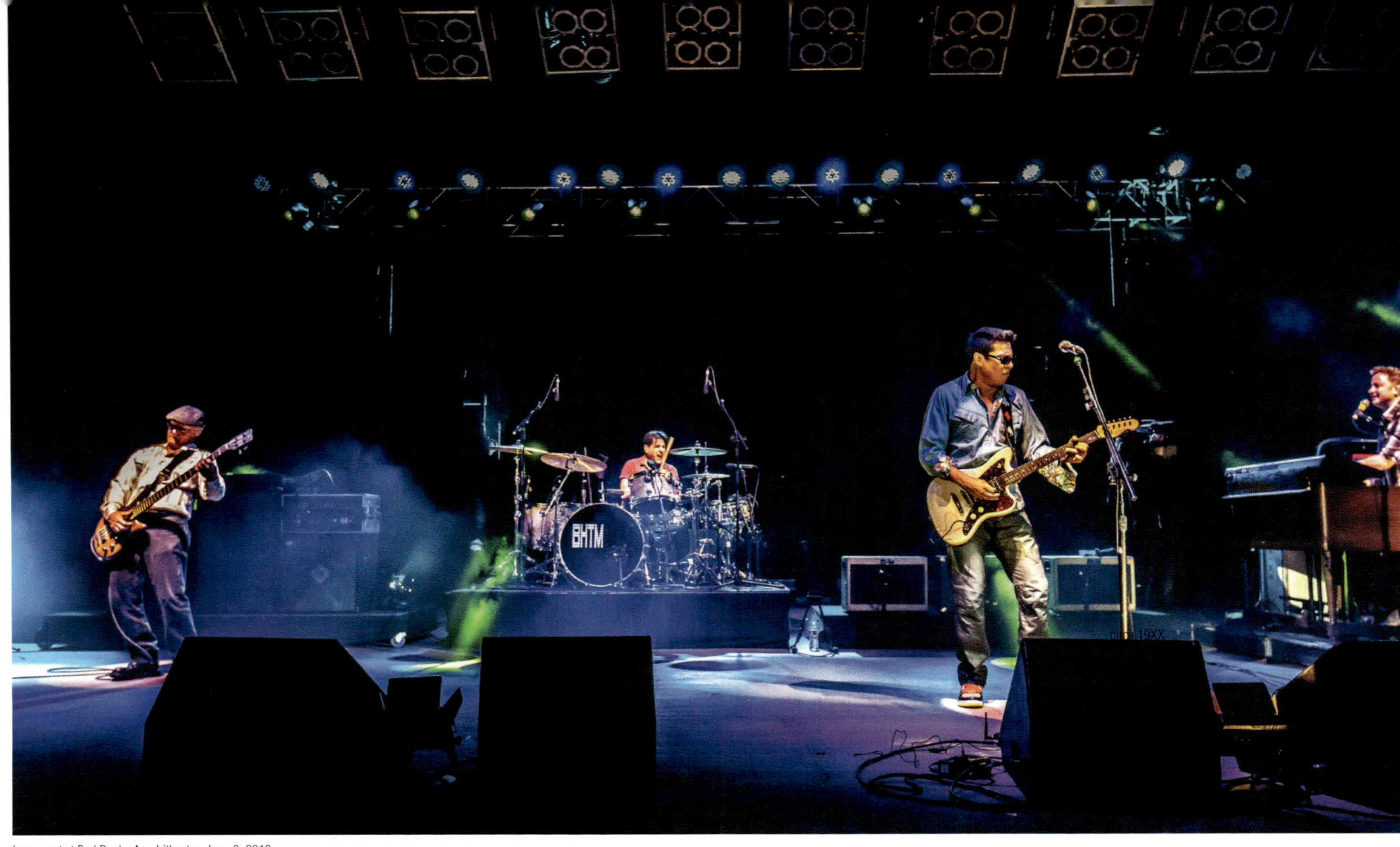

In concert at Red Rocks Amphitheatre, June 8, 2013

ple," Mohr said. "In our minds, our live show has become central to who we are as a band.

"The touring business is really difficult, but it's one of the last bastions of value for music fans. CDs and radio seem less and less valuable every day, whereas touring is something that you can't just download away. A lot of people are still interested in seeing performers live. That's pretty special."

After three records on a big label, the trio was back to rebuilding its career with the same do-it-yourself spirit it had at the beginning. In 2000, the trio headed to Mohr's solar-powered recording studio in the Colorado mountains and recorded *Riviera*, released on the band's own Big Records. 2004's *Crimes of Passion* was licensed to Sanctuary Records, which issued the album on the Big/Sanctuary imprint.

"It was a great time in my life," Mohr said. "I began to feel like there wasn't a middleman between my being musical and the audience. For a while, I felt like I had to write to please executives. Now I just had to write to please people. It brought a freedom that I've enjoyed ever since."

Keyboardist Jeremy Lawton joined, and the group affiliated with internet-based music distribution in 2005 by releasing music for free via podcasting. The single "Blue Sky" was written as a tribute to the men and women of the American space program. *All the Love You Need* arrived in 2007.

As evidenced by their shared maturity and experience, the three original members' friendship endured, a feat that precious few acts ever match.

"You wouldn't toss a good marriage away if it works and great things are coming out of it," Mohr said. "I've always searched for what makes it exciting to be in a band—looking back on our career, remembering when we were first beginning. It's cool to be committed to the idea of a band. I like that three people argue and conflict and have an equal platform for ideas. That democracy is what a band is about. It has an energy and human quality you can't get any other way." ●

DAVE MATTHEWS BAND }

HAILED AS one of rock's few emerging superstar acts of the late 1990s, Dave Matthews Band came out of Charlottesville, Virginia, in 1991, its success fired by a tenacious do-it-yourself approach. By playing nearly 200 gigs a year and releasing its own CDs, DMB built a zealous following based largely on word-of-mouth publicity. It wasn't long before the members ventured farther afield, first to resorts in Colorado, an area of the country that had a history of supporting acts from outside the mainstream.

"All of Colorado was huge," Matthews said. "I was surprised that we could go so far away and be received with such open arms. Our not-quite-suffering audience is made up of a lot of middle-class and upper-middle-class, because we initially were aiming at the university audience on the East Coast. They spend a lot of time in Colorado during ski season."

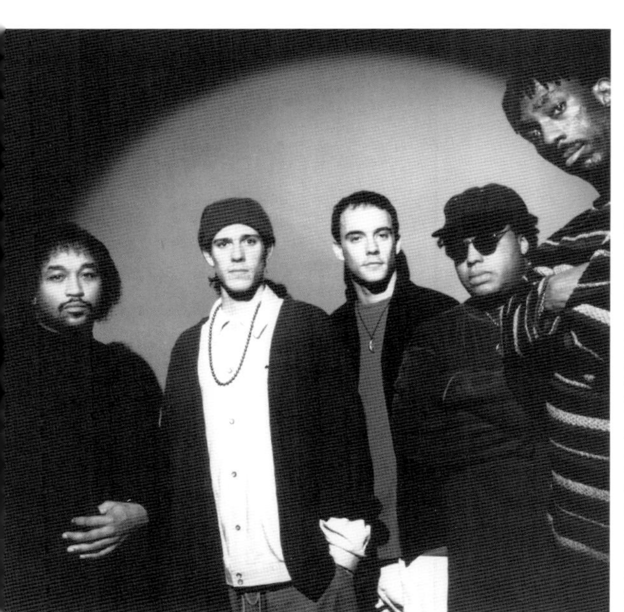

c. 1994

In 1994, Dave Matthews Band chose to film the video for "What Would You Say," the group's first smash, at three sold-out shows at the Fox Theatre in Boulder. The marketing was intentionally low-key—the band didn't shoot the clip until three months after the release of its major-label debut album, *Under the Table and Dreaming*.

"It was a way of saying thanks. Everything fell together there—the synchronicity, the fact that we'd always had a vibe there," Matthews said. "It was one of the most ambiguous songs on the album, so we put the video together slapdash with no story—no disgruntled babes walking out of the house, slamming the car door and driving away."

"What Would You Say" became a Top 20 MTV video, sales of *Under the Table and Dreaming* took off and Matthews became a star.

Because Dave Matthews Band's sound—jazz-rock fusion grooves and improvisations, melodies carried by violin, saxophone and acoustic guitar and Matthews' earnestly delivered, world-weary, impressionistic lyrics—was so mutable, and no two gigs were ever alike, the band, like other rootsy jam acts such as Phish and Blues Traveler, encouraged its army of fans to record shows and trade bootlegs among themselves.

Live at Red Rocks 8.15.95, released in the fall of 1997, was the first in a series of live albums the band issued to give fans an alternative to the many bootlegs on the market. It landed in the Top 10 and sold a million copies with barely a flicker of marketing and promotion.

"We just felt it was a good way to give something back to the people who care about the live shows, including the improvisational elements," Matthews said. "It's not that we have a problem with bootlegs, because nothing could be further from the truth. We have no intention of stopping people from bootlegging our shows. The trouble comes with the idea of some guy who doesn't really give a crap about the band or the music, just simply trying to cash in on an easy buck."

The double live album was an unedited soundboard recording. Perhaps as a nod to the fact that the band was performing in Colorado, snippets of John Denver's "Sunshine on My Shoulders" cropped up in both "Proudest Monkey" and "Recently."

Another live album, *Live at Folsom Field*, was a two-CD set of the band's rain-soaked performance recorded and filmed July 2001 at the University of Colorado in Boulder.

In 2005, Dave Matthews Band already had three sold-out concerts booked for Red Rocks Amphitheatre. Immediately after Hurricane Katrina struck, the band added a fourth show featuring New Orleans' own Neville Brothers on the bill to benefit the victims of the natural disaster. Everyone from the concessionaires to the City of Denver pitched in, and every cent related to the show—proceeds from food, drink, t-shirts, tickets and parking—went to relief charities in the Gulf Coast, over $1 million total. The Red Rocks concerts were released as a two-CD/single-DVD compilation titled *Weekend on the Rocks*. ●

GRETCHEN PETERS }

ACCLAIMED AS one of country music's top songwriters, Gretchen Peters wrote hits for Faith Hill, Martina McBride, George Strait and many others. She spent her formative years in Boulder, honing her singer-songwriter chops before heading to Nashville in 1988 and growing into one of the most successful creative minds in that competitive town.

Peters was eight when her parents divorced. Her mother eventually moved to Colorado.

"Boulder was a hippie town, a whole other universe," Peters said. "But it reinforced the notion that you could escape the stifling suburbs of John Updike novels—you didn't have to have a house, a husband and the four kids."

Peters developed an appreciation for the music of Jackson Browne, James Taylor, John David Souther and Gram Parsons. "I was born in the era when everything was either a novelty song or a love song," she said. "Then these writers came around. It opened my mind to the possibility that writing a song was as limitless as writing a novel or poem or anything else."

Peters played anywhere she could in the town's thriving live music scene. "The whole nexus of the hippie country-rock breed happened in Boulder. We always thought we were on the cusp of becoming Austin," she said. "The music that was coming out of the West had a spiritual, hopeful quality that really affected me. At its worst, it could be perceived as sort of California flaky, but the wonderful thing was that it was a very open place, spiritually and physically. I felt lucky to be a part of that.

"I did everything wrong—playing five and six nights a week, living in shacks, playing whatever I liked. It was two electric guitars and a rock 'n' roll drummer. We had a ball. We didn't do 'Orange Blossom Special.' Instead, it was Bonnie Raitt songs, Emmylou Harris. By midnight, all the drugstore cowboys and honky-tonkers would be liquored up enough that we could play a Dire Straits song and they'd love it. That's the thing about music. It all basically comes from the same place, so if you give it a chance, it'll lift you up."

Staring down 30 years of age, Peters decided to pull up stakes and move to Nashville.

"My friend Michael Woody had moved from Boulder to Nashville the year before. He had a hit with the Desert Rose Band—he wrote 'He's Back and I'm Blue.' I thought, 'If he can do it, I can do it.'"

c. 1996

Peters got a publishing deal, and her closely observed story-songs hit a sweet spot with some of mainstream country's finest voices. "Independence Day" with Martina McBride, an anthem in the fight against spousal abuse, won 1995 honors as the Country Music Association's Song of the Year. Patty Loveless topped the charts with Peters' second Grammy-nominated song, "You Don't Even Know Who I Am."

Non-country artists such as Bonnie Raitt, Bryan Adams and Etta James also recorded Peters' compositions. In the mid-1990s, she got a record deal and the chance to make her own studio albums every few years. The title track of her debut album, *The Secret of Life*, was later made into a Top 5 country hit by Faith Hill in 1999.

"It was a bit of a shock when I got to Nashville, where there was the idea that you could break people up into little pieces between writers and artists and be part of a machine," Peters allowed. "I was used to this very sweet, innocent homegrown approach that my formative years in Boulder had in spades. People wrote and sang and recorded—they did it all. Music was just music—I saw the same band doing a bluegrass song and then an R&B song. That state of mind I grew up with stuck with me. I still carry it around like a badge." ●

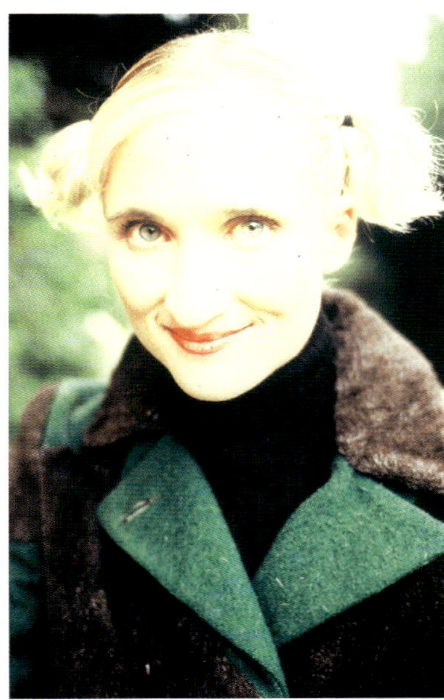

c. 1995

JILL SOBULE }

THANKS TO "I Kissed a Girl," Jill Sobule's self-titled album of 1995 garnered a lot of publicity.

In the Denver native's innocent yet seditious ode to sexual experimentation, two women compared notes about what jerks their boyfriends are and end up dabbling in the love that dares not speak its name. The singer described the act as "just like kissing me, only better." Thanks to a wacky yet provocative video (featuring supermodel Fabio playing a sometime sweetheart described as "dumb as a box of hammers") that got heavy airplay on MTV and VH-1, "I Kissed a Girl" took on a novelty-song stigma.

Sobule, a clever songwriter with anecdotal approach to lyrics, didn't understand why her ditty caused such an uproar—WYHY, a radio station in Nashville, broadcast parental advisories before playing it—but she refused to fuel the fire by confirming whether it was as autobiographical as it appeared.

"It's a pretty innocent comedy song," Sobule said. "I mean, it reminds me of a bad '90s version of *Love, American Style*. It certainly isn't a Melissa Etheridge 'Yes I Am' thing, you know?"

The alternative folk singer grew up in Denver in the 1960s—"I'm a home girl, a third-generation native on one side of my family." Despite her Jewish upbringing, she was enrolled in St. Mary's Catholic school for the strict discipline. She played and quit the electric guitar as a child; then, studying at the University of Colorado, she started singing and playing acoustic. But she never had the nerve to play her songs for other people.

As a junior, Sobule spent a year abroad and played her first public gigs in Seville, Spain. She was persuaded by a friend to gain experience playing in the streets like the Spanish musicians.

"I thought, 'What do I have to lose? No one will ever see me in another country,'" she said.

Sobule headed back to the United States and started shyly playing in front of Denver audiences, doing her own material and singing with several local groups.

"What was great about Denver was the venues," she recalled. "I had the chance to grow, because I don't think I was very good at first. I went through so many different kinds of bands and sounds, but you could get paid to play original music, and I actually made a meager living. I would never have been able to do that in New York. The only reason people pick up a guitar there is to get a record deal. That takes a lot away from the creative process. Playing in Denver, I did what I wanted to do."

Sobule migrated between Denver, New York City and Nashville before a showcase gig led to her discovery and a recording contract. Her 1990 debut, produced by Todd Rundgren, was all but unheard in the States. She opened Joe Jackson's tour and completed a follow-up album with him, but her record company turned it down and released her from her contract.

"Then my management dropped the ball, and I couldn't get arrested. It was a complete disaster, really bleak," Sobule said. "And then it just happened out of nowhere, as a fluke."

By way of a lawyer acquaintance, she came to the attention of Atlantic Records. *Jill Sobule* was permeated with her melodic instincts and wry whimsy. With "I Kissed a Girl," she breezed past social taboos to ponder the notion of attraction to a member of the same sex. The satirical "Supermodel" was featured prominently in Amy Heckerling's 1995 hit teen comedy film *Clueless*.

The album *Happy Town* followed in 1997, solidifying Sobule's critical reputation with a new level of depth and maturity. But when sales were stagnant, it hit her hard. After taking some time off from her recording career to regroup, Sobule landed a new recording contract and reinvigorated her muse. In the following years, she dabbled in off-Broadway musicals, made an appearance on NBC's *The West Wing*, composed songs for the popular Nickelodeon network series *Unfabulous* and played one of five leads in the indie film *Mind the Gap*.

In 2009, Sobule was in the news when Katy Perry's pop smash "I Kissed a Girl" shared little but a title with her "lesbian chic" landmark, and she spent much of the year fielding questions about the song. ●

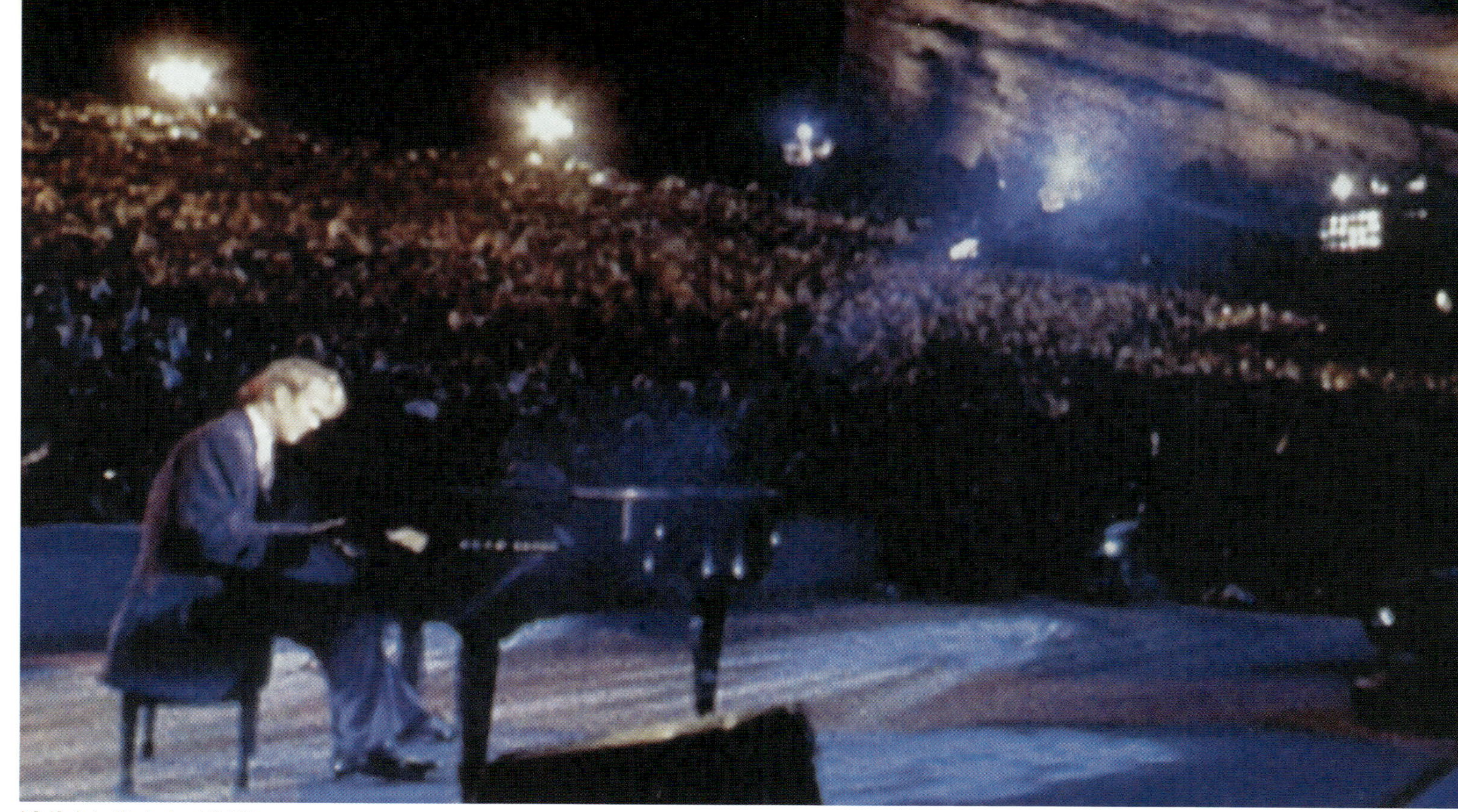

At Red Rocks Amphitheatre, August 18, 1994

JOHN TESH }

AS THE co-host of television's *Entertainment Tonight* for ten years, John Tesh became a household name. But the role sidetracked him from his true love—music.

His breakthrough came when he first appeared on PBS with *Live at Red Rocks*. Broadcast in 1995, it was hugely successful, repeated endlessly by stations nationwide during pledge drives. The attendant album went gold and the video reached double platinum sales.

The next year, Tesh daringly left the security of *E.T.* and its seven-figure salary to concentrate on writing and recording music. Most pop music critics would run screaming from his over-the-top pop instrumentals, but new age music fans feted Tesh as an icon, a star whose mix of styles sold more than five million albums.

"Denver is, in my mind, the reason I was able to do that," Tesh said. "Certain people are defined by certain things. Steve Martin is defined by, 'Ex-cu-u-u-se me!' I'm defined by, 'Hey, Red Rocks!' I love that. I really didn't want to be known as a talking head my whole life."

Ironically, the man associated with Red Rocks didn't want to do the show there.

"I knew the Moody Blues had already done something," Tesh said. "I didn't think we could afford to light the place. The budget increased to $1.5 million. I financed it myself—took loans from three banks."

Pianist Tesh had won Emmys for televised sports contests, and in the *Live at Red Rocks* special, he paid tribute to the spirit of competition—Olympic champions Nadia Comeneci and Bart Conner performed choreographed gymnastics routines to his music.

Tesh and his eight-piece ensemble battled inclement weather. His wife, actress Connie Sellecca, came to town, got altitude sickness and ended up in the hospital.

"It was magical, and I made my money back," Tesh said following the concert. "But it would be difficult for me to play Red Rocks again, let's put it that way."

Tesh revisited the venue with the 2004 release of *Worship at Red Rocks*, a family-friendly live set of contemporary Christian music.

"Nine years ago, in a driving rainstorm, my life changed forever at Red Rocks Amphitheatre," he explained. "It was inspiring to be back with a new concert." ●

KITARO }

ALREADY WIDELY recognized throughout Asia and other parts of the world, Kitaro unified his work for worldwide distribution circa 1986. Suddenly, the American market burst open for the Japanese composer and synthesizer player. He never used "new age" to describe himself or his music, but he helped pioneer the genre, combining a thoughtful compositional style with a refined execution.

When his tour visited Boulder, Kitaro was smitten. He acquired mountaintop living quarters, a 180-acre spread in Ward, nearly 10,000 feet above sea level. He played his huge ceremonial log drums so passionately that he was heard from two miles away in Nederland.

"There is an old Japanese legend about a man who travels from his home to do something positive in another land. In turn, he will return to his home larger than life," Kitaro said. "Japan is quiet—you never see standing ovations. But in the U.S. and Europe, the reaction is more hot. I like to feel that."

Because Kitaro wished to "instill harmony and a peaceful co-existence, building a balance between nature and humanity," his devotees deemed him a spiritual leader. A visitor might have expected "Camp Kitaro" to be crammed with candles, wind chimes, crystals and jewelry. But Kitaro had what locals called "Ward zen." There was a Humvee parked next to a snowmobile in the driveway, and a few golf balls littered a makeshift driving range. "It's a party house," he explained.

There was no denying the serene beauty of the wildlife and pond and wind-damaged trees. In his Mochi House studio, big enough to hold a 70-piece orchestra, Kitaro recorded his projects and rehearsed with his touring band.

"Living in the mountains is nice for thinking about music," he said. "I like to be quiet and peaceful and feel the energy from nature. I spend many hours outside, walking, and then I go back to the studio and create."

Kitaro's innovative soundscapes crossed over classical, jazz and pop charts and sold in the millions. His music for Oliver Stone's Vietnam War film *Heaven & Earth* achieved the 1993 Golden Globe for Best Original Score, and 2000's *Thinking of You* won the Grammy for Best New Age album in 2001.

Colorado wasn't Kitaro's last stop. In 2007, he moved to Sebastopol, a small city in northern California. His studio in Ward still existed and could be rented. ●

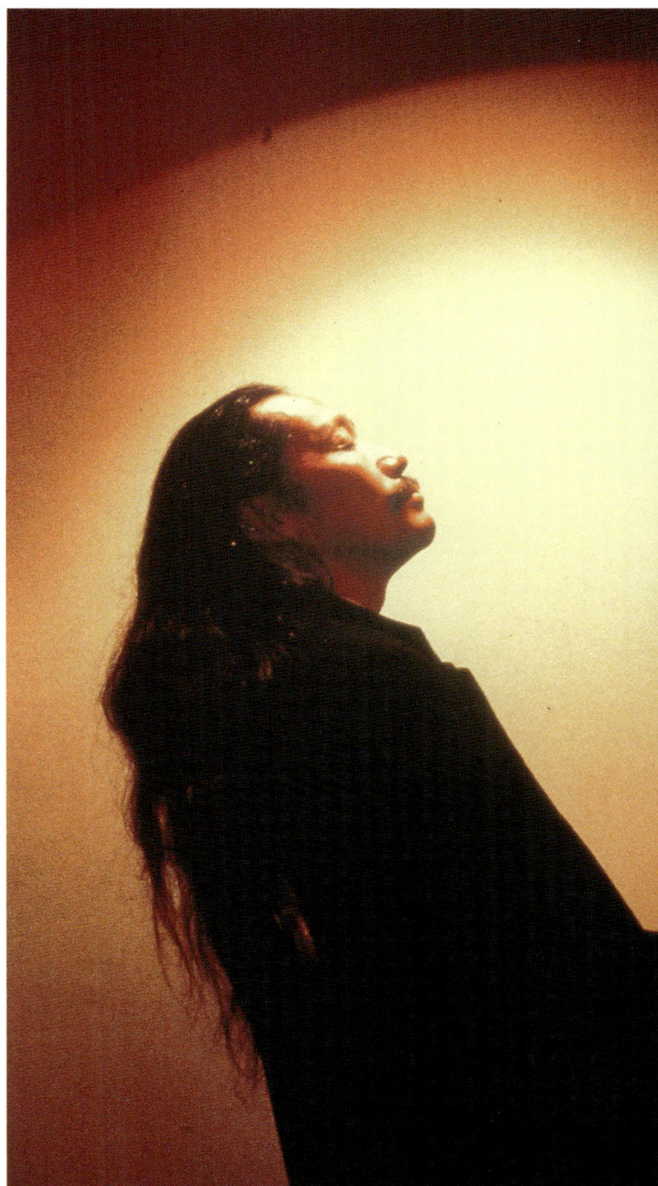

c. 1994

1996-2003

THE FLASHY excesses of the 1980s spawned a reaction embodied by jam bands that focused on creating unique concert performances for every show. The Fox Theatre in Boulder opened its doors in 1991 to great fanfare, as the old-movie-theater-turned-concert-hall welcomed both the neo-hippie subculture and the giants whose music reshaped the world. After U2's success at Red Rocks during the previous decade, the amphitheater had become a mecca for artists wanting something different for recording and filming—from Neil Young's acclaimed "Music in Head" tour to the Stray Cats' Brian Setzer Budweiser commercial with the "guitar granny." ZZ Top played the last rock 'n' concert at McNichols Arena before the bulldozers made room for a new stadium.

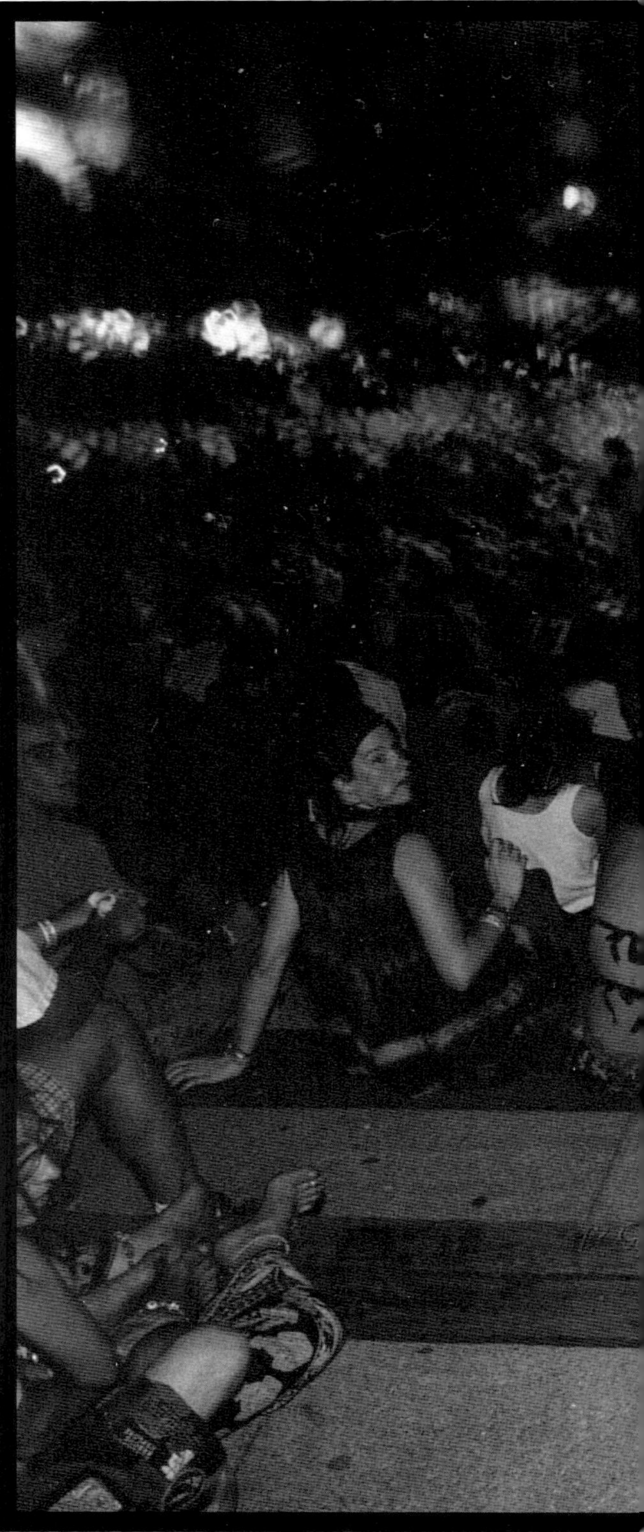

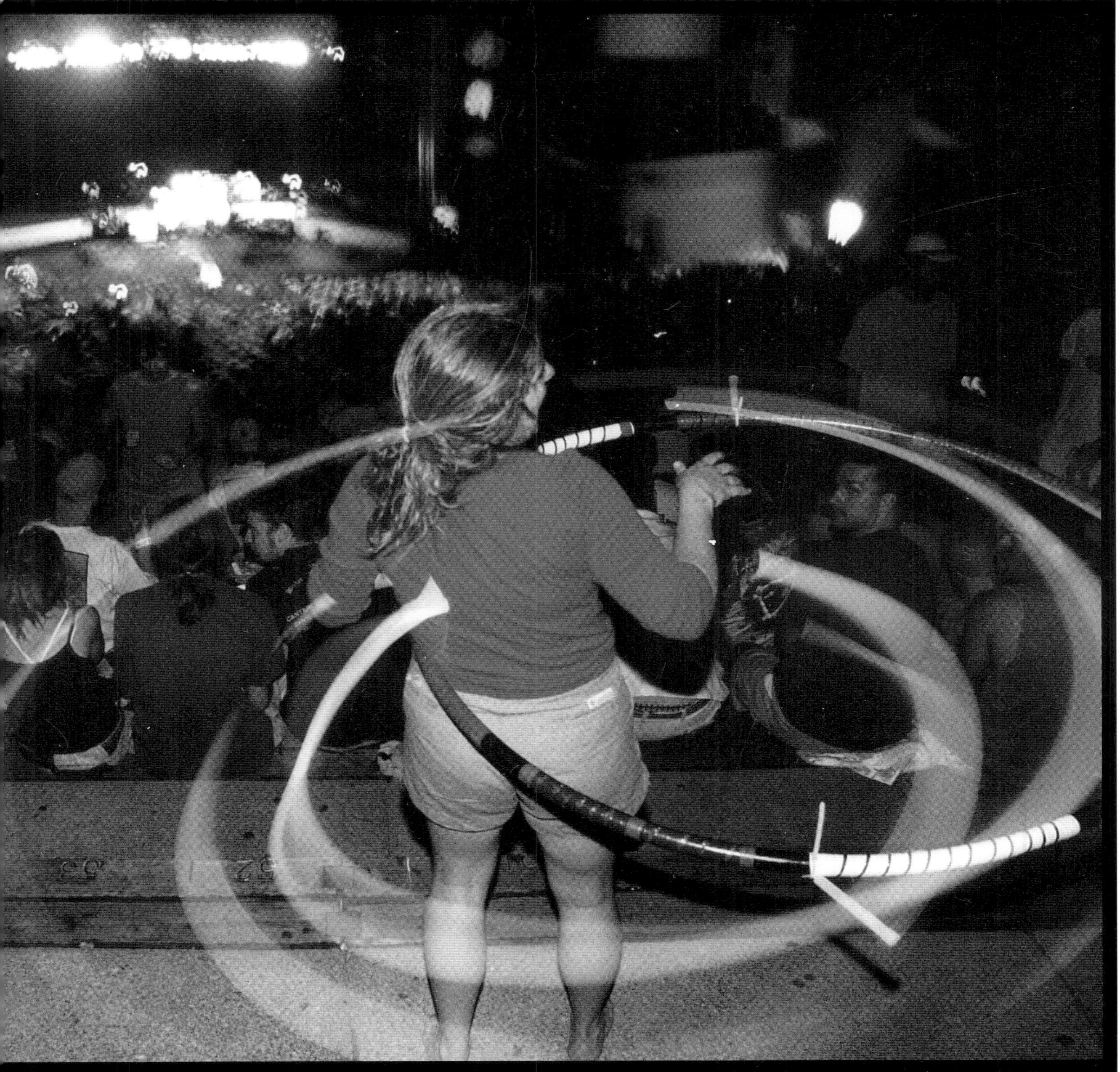

Hooping devotees of String Cheese Incident at Red Rocks Amphitheatre, 2000

PHISH }

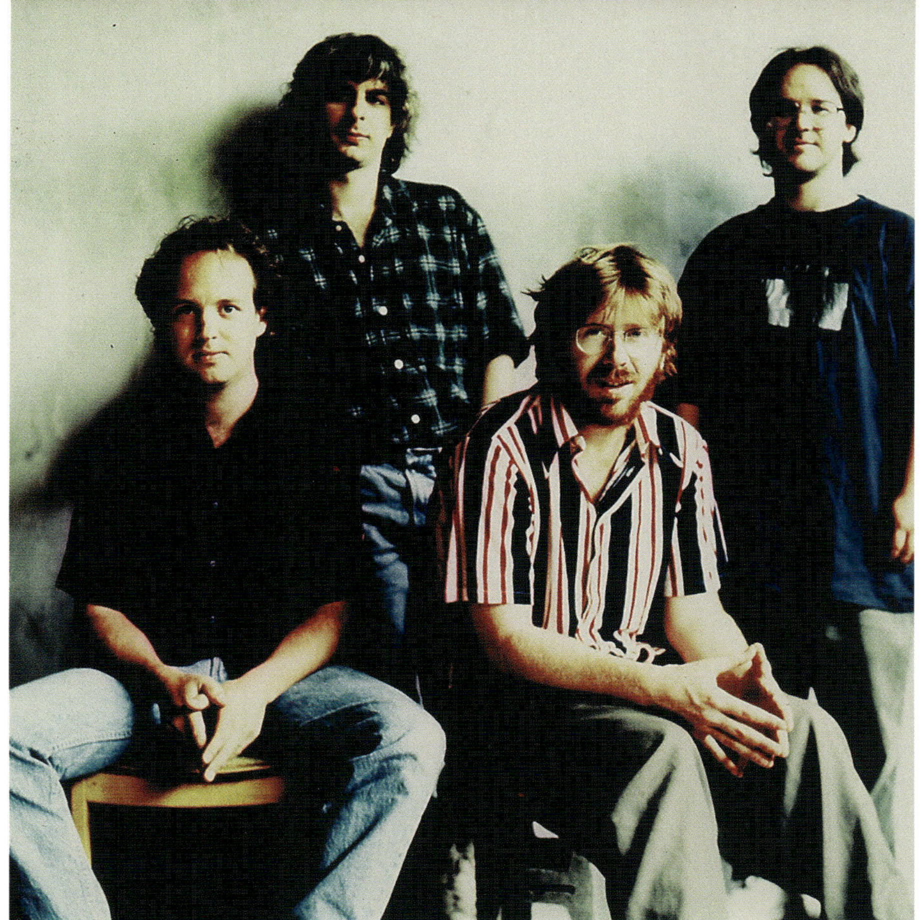

c. 1996

THE LEFT-FIELD success story of the 1990s, Phish was one of the biggest concert draws in America. The determinedly eccentric Vermont quartet—guitarist Trey Anastasio, keyboardist Page McConnell, bass player Mike Gordon and drummer Jon Fishman—was beloved by an army of noodle-dancing, sandal-wearing, tie-dyed nomads. Since the demise of the Grateful Dead, no band had created that kind of musical and social environment.

But there were growing pains. When Phish played the first of four sold-out gigs at Red Rocks Amphitheatre in August 1996, hundreds of itinerant fans from across the nation flooded the town of Morrison, looking for a "miracle"—a free ticket to the show of their dreams. Few had more than a car or campground to stay in, and the overflow packed the streets.

Despite months of planning—Phish had its own security expert—things deteriorated when a truck accidentally hit and injured a 21-year-old Phishhead. A mob formed, dancing to the beat of bongo drums and chanting at heavily armed police, who temporarily shut down the main road into town as they tried to move the gathering, estimated at more than 400, out of downtown. Bottles were thrown and a melee broke out. Several people were injured. Authorities reported 10 arrests.

McConnell looked back at the Red Rocks affair with displeasure, sorrow and acceptance.

"We didn't hear about it until well after we got off offstage," he explained.

"From our perspective, we understand that the nature of our crowd creates certain idiosyncrasies that most concert promoters and local authorities don't have to deal with. We do everything we can to prepare for the numbers of people who might show up for a show with no tickets.

"In preparing for Red Rocks, we knew there was a potential situation there, and we met with all these people to make sure we were doing everything we could to make everything as smooth as possible, where our fans would be as low-impact as possible on the community. We pledged money and support to make it go as well as we could. And nobody bothered to accept it, I guess. Unfortunately, none of the preparation that we put into it was followed through.

"We can't prevent everything all the time. And when a situation does happen, it's a shame that it gets blown out of proportion—I saw it on CNN—because, more often than not, our fans are really peaceful, nice people and not troublemakers."

In 2003, Phish led the trend of offering online access to live shows via the Live Phish Downloads. In addition, the band made several shows from its archives available for purchase, including *10/31/90 Armstrong Hall, Colorado Springs*, an early Halloween gig. ●

SIXTEEN HORSEPOWER }

AT THE time that Sixteen Horsepower formed in Denver circa 1992, fans labeled the gripping, atmospheric music "prairie-goth," "roots-gloom" and "spooky campfire." Whatever the band was doing, it wasn't a take on post-grunge alternative music. The haunting, lingering sound was a mix of rustic blues wailings, old-time country tunes and modern-rock dramaticism.

The vibe reflected David Eugene Edwards' love of traditional music. The Colorado native grew up in Englewood and Littleton and attended Arapahoe High School.

"I played electric guitar in punk rock bands in high school, but I've always played the acoustic guitar," Edwards said. "I started getting into other types of music—not necessarily quiet, folky music, just 'rootsy' music from all over, Russia, Hungary, Czechoslovakia. That's my family's heritage."

For a good portion of his youth, Edwards was raised by his grandparents. His earliest memories were of traveling from town to town in Colorado listening to fire-and-brimstone sermons by his grandfather, a Nazarene preacher.

"It's a real old, Southern-style sect," Edwards said. "I always like the music around church. That's my main influence."

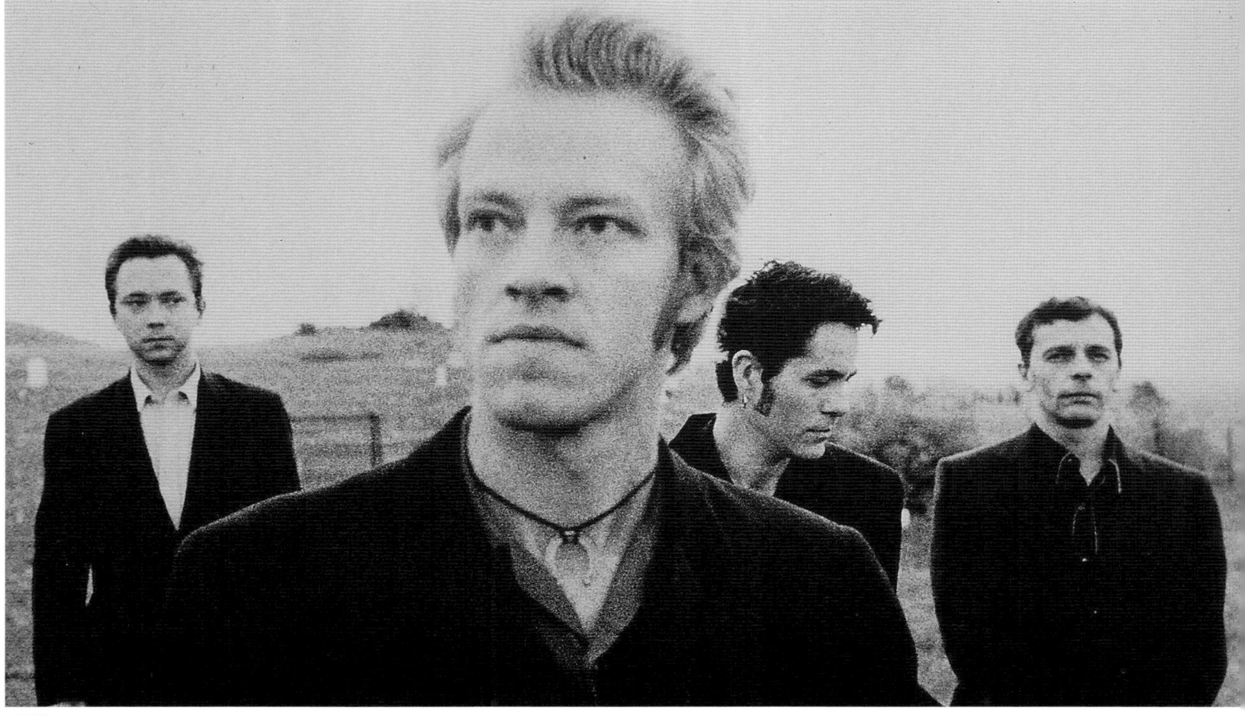

c. 1997

Married at 17, Edwards left his grandfather's church (with the old preacher promising eternal damnation) to seek a more individualistic Christian path. He became the foundation of Sixteen Horsepower. Other members included bassist Keven Soll and drummer Jean-Yves Tola, then Pascal Humbert on bass and Jeffrey Paul Norlander (a co-founder of Edwards' original band, the Denver Gentlemen) on strings and guitar.

"I sing about the things that are important to me, plain and simple," Edwards said. "Things that are lasting and worthwhile don't change. There are a million bands out there to listen to, but there's a certain amount of responsibility that comes along with making music. I refuse to take the attitude of 'I'm an artist, so I can do what I want.' Your work affects people, and you have to be conscious of it.

"There are different aspects of what we do. Some people latch on to the Americana thing. Some people latch on to the European traditional music part. Some people latch on to the spiritual aspect. It's difficult to please all of them all the time."

Edwards' mournful voice and the edgy emotional content of his lyrics were driven by vintage acoustic instruments—bandoneón (a turn-of-the-century button accordion), violin, cello, hurdy-gurdy and banjo.

"At the beginning it was a matter of money—I couldn't afford anything new or of any certain quality, so I would go to pawnshops and used instrument stores," Edwards said. "The guitars that I played weren't very popular—they were considered cheap and no one really wanted them, so I basically got them for nothing.

"A friend of mine knew I love hillbilly music, so he found a banjo in the trash and gave it to me, and I started playing it. I saw the used bandoneón in the window of a Boulder music store and got it for $130—it was a $2,000 instrument, 150 years old, but they had no clue what it was. They just wanted to get rid of it. I played it for years to the point where it fell apart.

"I just love older instruments. They have a different character and quality that you can't get out of newer ones. I try to get as old as I can possibly use to be roadworthy and function every night."

Sixteen Horsepower's attitude was determinedly antique, and Edwards unleashed his doubts about sin and redemption with a religious fervor that echoed kindred spirits Nick Cave and the Gun Club. Two fine major-label albums, 1995's *Sackcloth 'n' Ashes* and 1998's *Low Estate*, built up the band's following in Europe. In the annual best-of list in *OOR*, the Dutch equivalent of *Rolling Stone* magazine, as voted for by Dutch critics, *Sackcloth 'n' Ashes* reached #4. *Low Estate* reached #9 in the *OOR* list.

The irony? Internationally, the Denver-based band's rugged American music was embraced and understood on a more mainstream level than on its home turf.

"We went to Europe constantly since '95, and each time the interest expanded to new countries and cities, and the crowds were bigger," Edwards said. "And then to come back here and people in Colorado don't really care, or don't believe it in a way—it's odd.

"On an overall level, traditional music is so much more accessible and everyone is more interested in Europe. Even teenagers aren't as distant from their folk music as Americans are. They're a little more conscious of keeping their own creativity, discovering something new for themselves instead of being told what to listen to.

"To me, it seems like they listen to this music because they're not associated with it in the way that we are. The reasons most Americans don't take it to heart like they do other types of music is because it makes them think of an earlier time that is depressing to them, of slaughtering Indians and slavery—a time of cruelty. America is trying to go into the future as fast as possible to escape that. But you can't."

Sixteen Horsepower released two more studio albums and toured extensively, taking a break in late 2001, as the group Woven Hand became the dominant outlet for Edwards' music and lyrics. Sixteen Horsepower finally called it quits in April 2005 after years of sitting on the fence, citing "mostly political and spiritual" differences. Edwards remained active in Woven Hand. ●

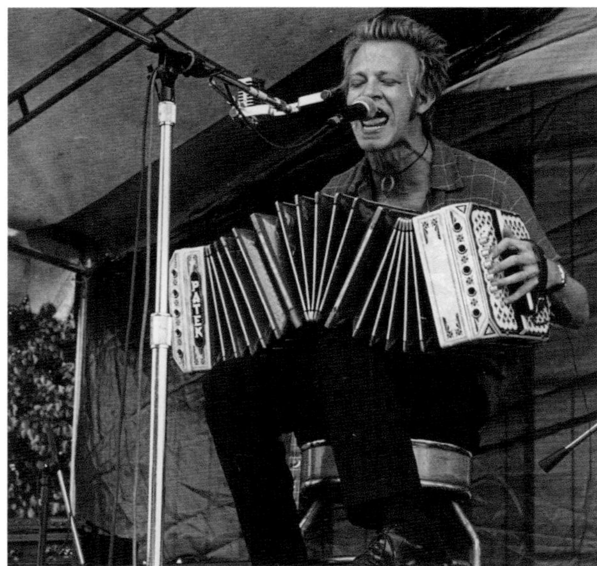

David Eugene Edwards, c. 1998

311 }

WITH SINGLES like "All Mixed Up," "Don't Stay Home" and the smash hit "Down," 311 won 1996's alternative-rock lottery.

The funk-rap-rock group had been on a steady climb toward success since 1992, conquering the Omaha, Nebraska rock scene and moving its base of operations to Los Angeles. Rather than rely on airplay, the guys of 311 built on the early buzz that surrounded their frenetic, charged live performances.

Thanks to radio station KBPI's support, 311 headlined a 1996 sold-out show at Red Rocks.

"We played two shows that day," drummer Chad Sexton said. "We played in California during the day, and then we hopped on a private jet, flew to Denver and played our Red Rocks show. That was cool."

The band then released a long-form home video, *Enlarged to Show Detail*, that was certified platinum. It captured a moment at the Red Rocks concert.

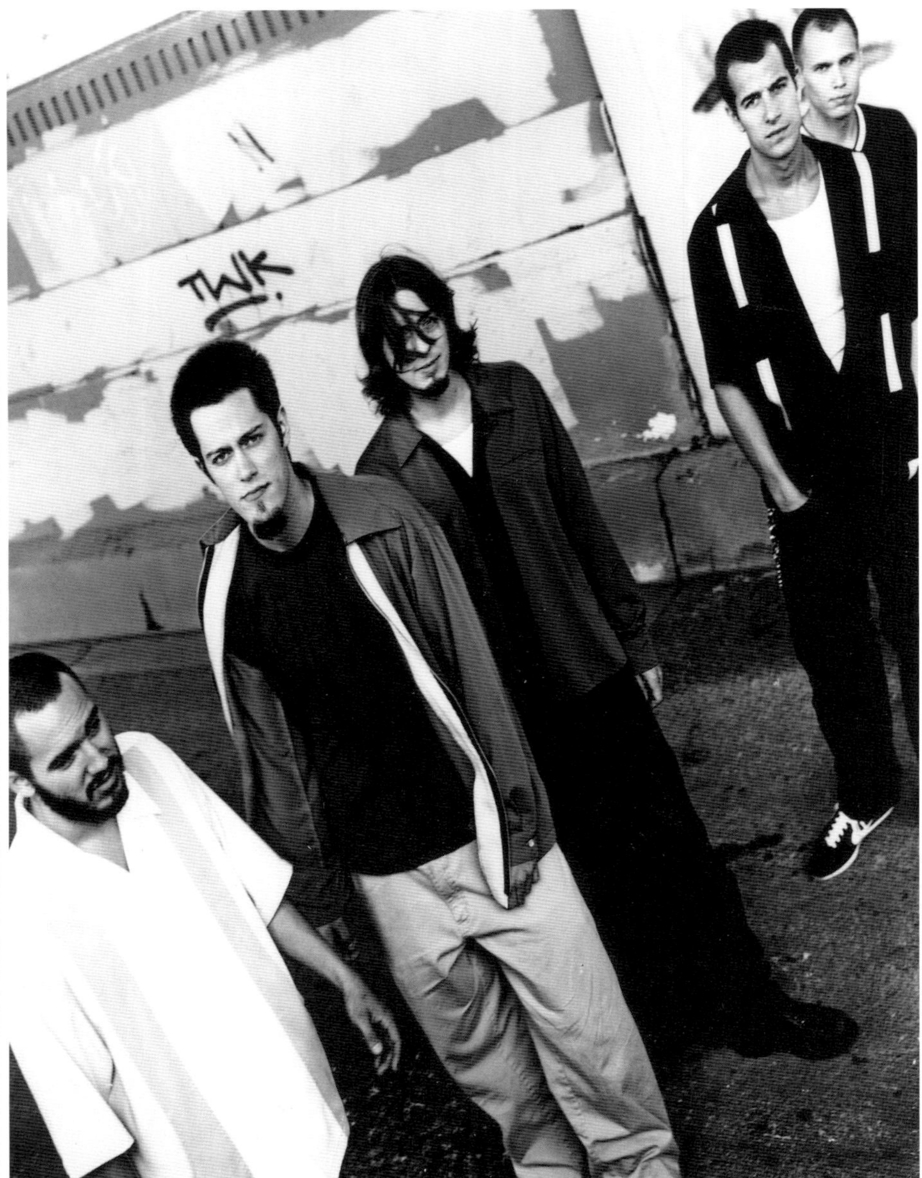

c. 1996

"Denver always supported us. It's one of the biggest markets where people were excited to see us," vocalist-guitarist Nick Hexum said. "We tell a story in the video. Before we were signed, when we were moving to L.A., we had some friends in Denver. We stopped there and hung out for a day. We made it up to Red Rocks when the place was empty, stood on the stage and said, 'Yep, someday we're going to rock this place.'

"You get really ecstatic when your dreams are coming true. Recalling that moment to a full audience at Red Rocks was very emotional for me." ●

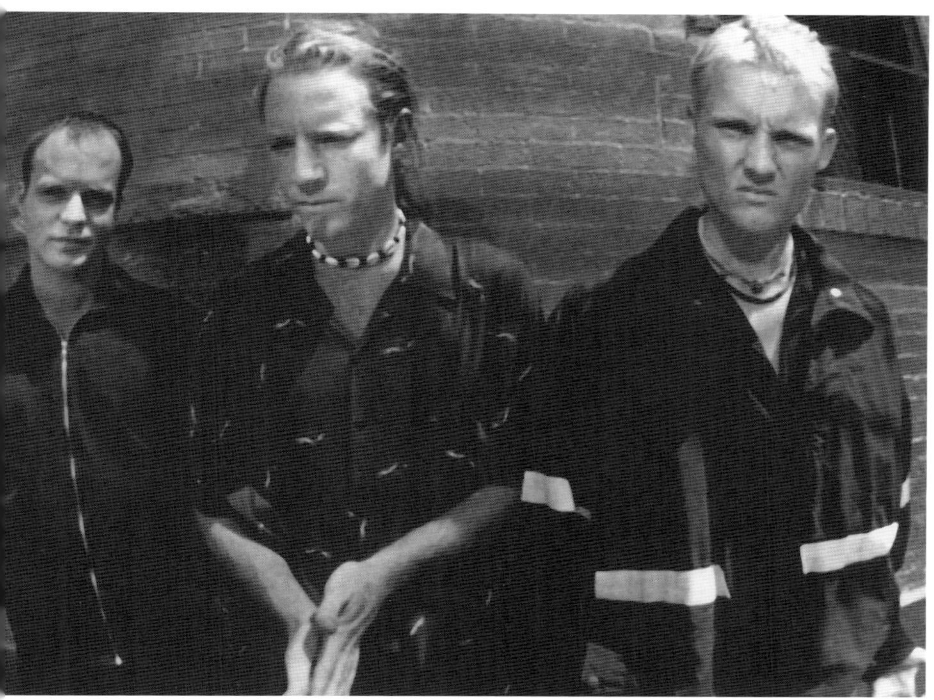

c. 1997

MEDESKI MARTIN & WOOD }

ONE OF America's hottest instrumental groove bands and a surprising pop music phenomenon, Medeski Martin & Wood was an organ-bass-and-drums trio with neither a guitar nor a vocalist. Chris Wood, the youngest kid in the band, remained humble, perhaps the lingering affects of a Rocky Mountain high.

When he was six years old, Wood's family moved to Boulder, Colorado, where he studied composition and classical bass. During his teen years, he signed on with a musicians service that would mix and match random professional players (many of them much older and more seasoned) with a huge songbook that included country, pop, ethnic and jazz standards. He would play at bar mitzvahs, weddings and corporate events in Denver, gaining fantastic practical experience. Wood was voted "Most Musical" by his senior class of Boulder High School. After graduating in 1988, he left for the East Coast.

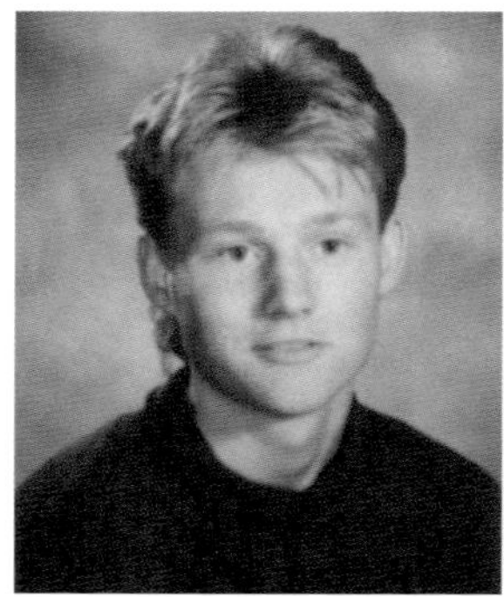

Chris Wood, c. 1988

"I expected to spend years as an obscure sideman for some famous jazz musician," Wood said. He envisioned toiling most nights in New York nightclubs or on tour in Europe and Japan, where there was more money and greater appreciation for the genre.

Instead, he met organist John Medeski and drummer Billy Martin in 1990 while gigging around New York's innovative and energetic downtown scene. Playing loose, groove-based jazz with a touch of hip-hop and a flair for long, 1970s-style jams, the threesome found a following in the New York clubs.

Then Medeski Martin & Wood did the unthinkable. "We attacked our career more like a rock band than a jazz group," Wood said. They loaded up the van and took to the road, crisscrossing the country on a mission of groove. The three-piece instrumental outfit began building a considerable cult fan base nationwide, much the same way Dave Matthews Band, Phish and Blues Traveler had. They played to a storm of interest among college-age crowds.

It exploded with the help of Phish, which played Medeski Martin & Wood tapes before its concerts. MMW's fourth album, *Shack-Man*, debuted at #7 on *Billboard*'s jazz chart and #34 on the Heatseekers chart. It was #19 on *Billboard*'s Top 25 contemporary jazz albums of 1997.

Medeski Martin & Wood were signed to leading jazz label Blue Note Records. The band's albums delved deeper into dense, electronic funk, although the three core members continued to experiment with free jazz and improvisation.

In addition, MMW contributed to numerous other projects, both as sidemen and leaders. Circa 2005, Wood formed the Wood Brothers with his sibling, guitarist Oliver Wood, who also grew up in Boulder but had moved to Atlanta and soaked up the origins of blues. They continued to tour and record together, channeling the influence of American roots music. ●

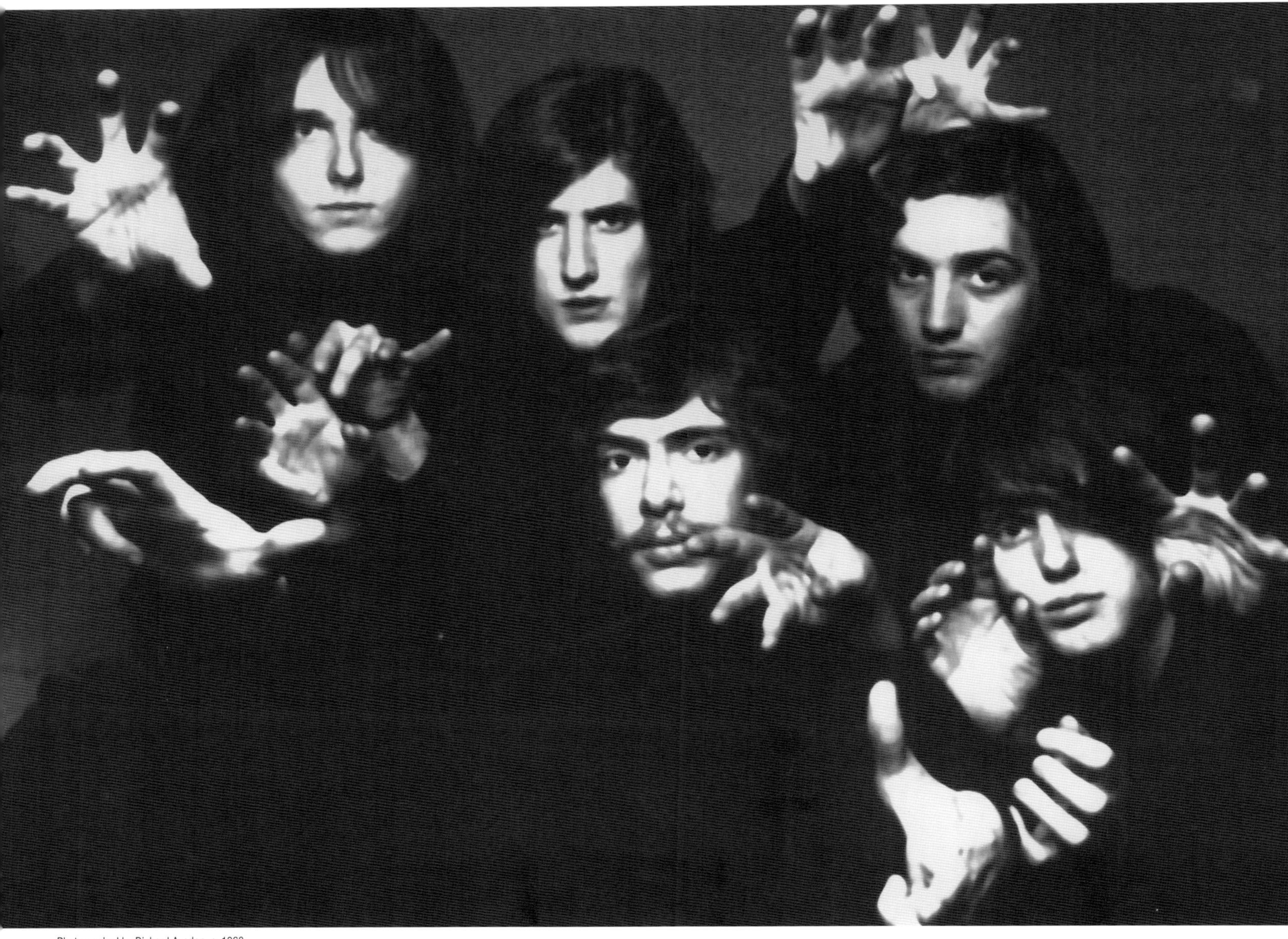

Photographed by Richard Avedon, c. 1968

LOTHAR & THE HAND PEOPLE }

IN 1997, BRITAIN'S Chemical Brothers reigned as the kings of electronica—pulsing dance music with frenetic beats, lots of computer or synthesizer treated sound effects, minimal vocals and a generally ecstatic ambience. Unlike many of their brethren, "Chemical Brothers" Ed Simons and the bespectacled Tom Rowlands understood the potentially psychedelic nature of electronic music. On *Dig Your Own Hole*, (a U.K. No. 1 album), the track "It Doesn't Matter" was a high-tech adaptation of a 30-year-old Lothar & the Hand People song, "It Comes On Anyhow."

Lothar & the Hand People were the first rockers to tour and record using synthesizers, thereby remaining a touchstone for many contemporary electro-warriors. The musicians came together in Denver in 1965. Singer John Emelin, a native of New York State, had already embraced the burgeoning East Coast folk scene before heading west to study at the University of Denver, where he decided to form a group.

"We played our first professional gig on New Year's Eve in Aspen," Emelin said. "We all called our parents on New Year's Day of 1966 and told them we were dropping out of school."

Lothar was not a person but a theremin, an electronic wand that uses an oscillator to translate nearby physical movement into woozy, high-pitched sounds. The electronic space-age sounds heard in so many vintage horror movies were produced by a theremin, and it also formed the basis for the eerie whistling in the Beach Boys' classic "Good VIbrations."

"We were just looking for a freaky name, and it got hung on our theremin, the first electronic performance instrument, invented in the '20s," Emelin said. "It's a wood box with a metal aerial protruding from one end. As you move your hand to the aerial, the frequency goes up. Move father away from the aerial and the frequency goes down. You could control the circumference of this field, and if you got real good at it you could make it sound like a violin or a human voice.

"We had the idea that it would be possible at some point to have whole bands with synthetic sound rather than instruments. In 1966, that was a relatively weird idea."

For the next six months, Lothar & the Hand People played exclusively in and around Denver—their stomping ground was the Exodus club—but they eventually found themselves rather restricted. For what proved to be their last gig in Colorado, they were the support act to the Lovin' Spoonful at the Denver Coliseum. They made a strong impression on the headliners, who suggested a move to New York. The band won a respectable following there in the fall of 1966, becoming part of a fascinating subculture.

But their hopes were sadly slow in being realized. The band did two albums of atonal and staccato material for Capitol Records—1968's *Presenting Lothar & the Hand People* and 1969's *Space Hymn*. In Denver, KMYR played "Machines" and "Sex and Violence" from the first album, but there was no other chart action. Singles failed to sell outside New York.

"They gave us every chance in the world, I must say," Emelin said. "Those were the days when record companies would sign people with the idea that it would take them two or three albums to get used to the process, and they'd see what happened. It was a time when anyone who had an idea, no matter how wild, could probably get the backing to do it."

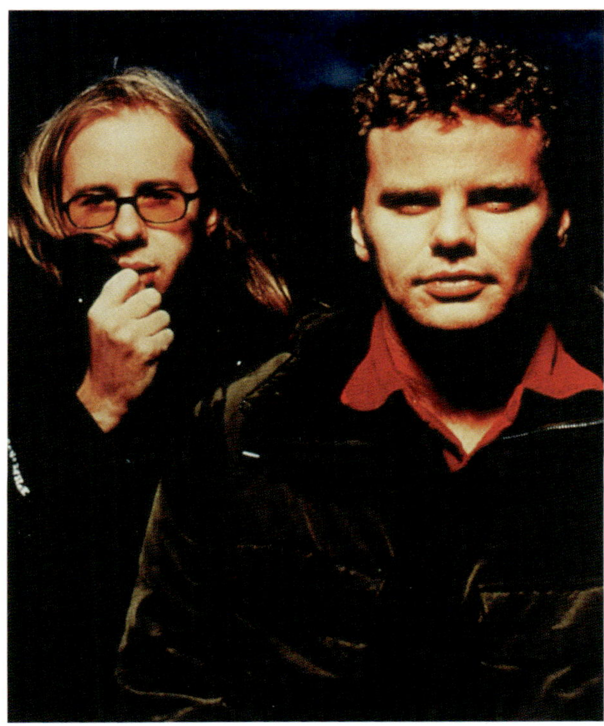

Chemical Brothers, c. 1997

Someone at Capitol must have carried a soft spot for the band, as *Presenting...* was repackaged as a budget album in the mid-1970s. By then, it was too late for Lothar & the Hand People, who had gone their separate ways circa 1971.

For "It Doesn't Matter," the Chemical Brothers "sampled" a passage from "It Comes On Anyhow," Lothar & the Hand People's early and strange experiment with electronics—a sound-effect-laden tape loop on which Emelin repeatedly chanted, "It doesn't matter"—and added a whopping, thumping dance track to it. As a result, the English spin-jockey duo shared the songwriting credit with two Lothar members, Emelin and Paul Conly, who were pleased with the recognition.

"That was our most advanced and free-form piece," Emelin opined. "We're really happy that, 30 years later, someone used our music on a record. That's a long span.

"We were a little too far ahead of our time." ●

ALL }

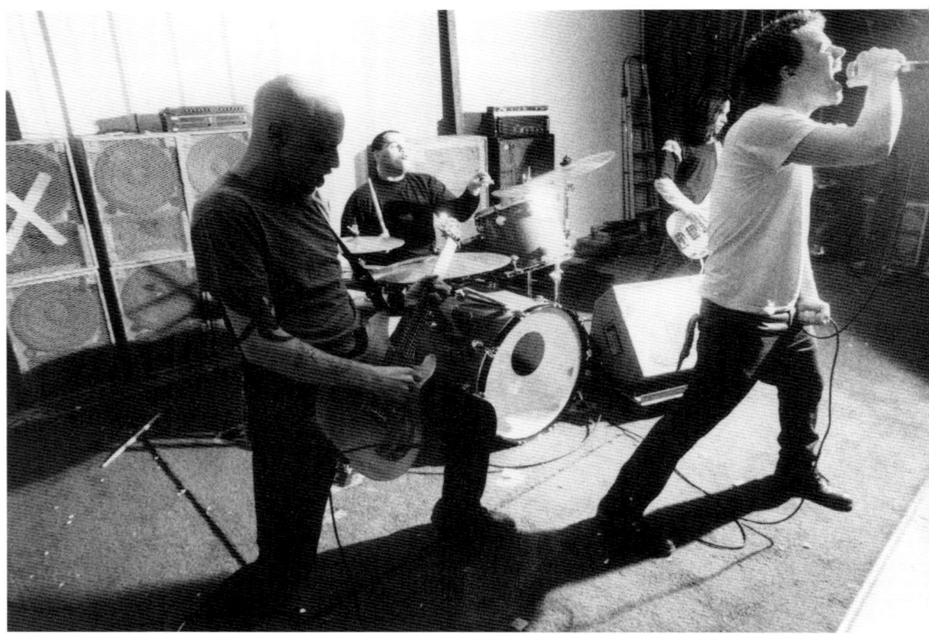

c. 1995

LOS ANGELES and New York had been the traditional headquarters of the music industry, but the business had become decentralized by the late 1990s. In local scenes—Minneapolis, Seattle and Athens, Georgia—it wasn't uncommon to find labels not affiliated with major companies.

While most folks in Colorado were still waiting for the Denver area to turn into that kind of musical mecca, several indie labels kept busy in Fort Collins.

Hapi Skratch, an independent music production company founded by Morris Beegle, worked with some of the region's top artists. Bruce Brodeen ran his Not Lame Recordings, a label and distribution company devoted exclusively to "power pop."

And Bill Stevenson—the drummer and songwriter of All, a spinoff of the Descendents, a near-legendary punk rock group—became co-owner of Owned & Operated Recordings. His own recording studio was appropriately dubbed the Blasting Room.

It smacked of Stevenson's days with the Southern California-based SST label, which helped develop and popularize the American punk of Hüsker Dü, the Minutemen, the Meat Puppets and many others. Owned & Operated was a parallel opportunity to pull some good bands together, groups that were having a hard time finding a label to treat them right. O&O could offer experience and the studio—a chance to record without big cash advances.

Stevenson got his start drumming for Black Flag, the original purveyors of the D.I.Y. rock ethic. While still in high school, Stevenson co-founded the Descendents, which released eight albums before singer Milo Aukerman left in 1987 to pursue a doctoral degree in biochemistry. Stevenson then formed All with remaining Descendents Karl Alvarez and Stephen Egerton and recruited Chad Price for vocals, and they stayed the punk-pop course.

"But we left Los Angeles in '89 for all the obvious reasons—cost of living, pollution, crime, racial tensions, traffic," Stevenson said.

All landed in Missouri for four years. "But we were in the middle of nowhere. So Fort Collins was randomly chosen as a middle ground. We could just as well have landed in Austin, but the guys wanted to be in the mountains. Bands make decisions in weird ways."

They built the Blasting Room "one step at a time—'Oh, let's buy a truck, a mixing board, a bigger one...'" When All was signed to Interscope Records, a major label, Stevenson was astute enough to negotiate for two albums. Most bands are signed for one, then dropped when they don't perform, and they wind up owing an arm and a leg. But Interscope had to pay All to leave.

The money was used to purchase a 48-track board, and Owned & Operated stepped into the marketplace in earnest at the turn of the millennium, releasing punk rock CDs, several of them by Fort Collins-based bands—Wretch Like Me, Someday I, Tanger and Bill the Welder. By 2008, Rise Against was recording at the Blasting Room, and the Chicago-based band's *Appeal to Reason* peaked at #3 on the *Billboard* 200 albums chart. NOFX's *Coaster* was also recorded there.

"It seemed like the progression of the earthworm—we inched our way in, and somehow threw together a half-assed career," Stevenson said.

"If you had told me when I was 15, 'So, Bill, when you're in your forties, you're going to co-own a studio and have a record label and your punk band is still going to be playing,' I would have just laughed and said, 'Well, first of all, I won't even be alive because I'm going to kill myself when I hit 30. And there's no way I'm still going to be a punker.' So all this took me by surprise." ●

RICK JAMES }

KNOWN FOR his 1981 hit "Super Freak," Rick James also gained notoriety for his wild lifestyle. Later in life, his drug abuse led to widely publicized legal problems. After serving a two-year prison term for assault, James was on tour to promote his comeback album *Urban Rapsody* in November 1998.

At Denver's Mammoth Gardens, right before his first encore, the self-described king of "punk funk" became ill backstage, barely able to move. He regained his strength to perform "Super Freak" but he had ruptured a blood vessel in his neck, causing a blood clot. After the concert, James returned to his hotel and collapsed.

"I was kicking it with my security guys when I felt a funny sensation in my neck and elbow, a tightening on the left side. Rubbing it didn't help. Then my whole right side, from my head down to my toes, went to sleep. Whatever it was, I knew it was no joke," he said.

Doctors in Denver examined James and advised him to return to Los Angeles, where he lived, for further evaluation. The doctors performed a battery of tests and diagnosed a stroke.

"When I was onstage, I noticed it was really hot. Maybe being a mile above sea level had something to do with it. I can't really say. I played Denver before, in the '80s and I was doing cocaine up the ying-yang and shaking it up.

"But I don't do those things now—I'm older."

Doctors called James' stroke the result of "rock 'n' roll neck," caused by the head's "repeated rhythmic whiplash movement."

"It's just me moving my head too fast, while I'm playing bass," James said. "Like any athlete, you shouldn't go out there cold—you should warm up backstage. I don't."

Clean and sober at 50 and thinking times were promising, James was sidetracked. And the irony wasn't lost on him.

"It's God's way of saying, 'Well, me and you got to chat. It doesn't seem like you know how to talk to me, moving around like this, and I've got some things you really got to know. So let me just sit you down for a minute—*bam*! I'm going to give you this stroke. I'm not going to make it real heavy, but you'll feel it."

A recuperation period at Cedars-Sinai Medical Center was necessary before James could walk again, and the stroke effectively ended his musical career. He died of a heart attack at his Los Angeles home in August 2004. ●

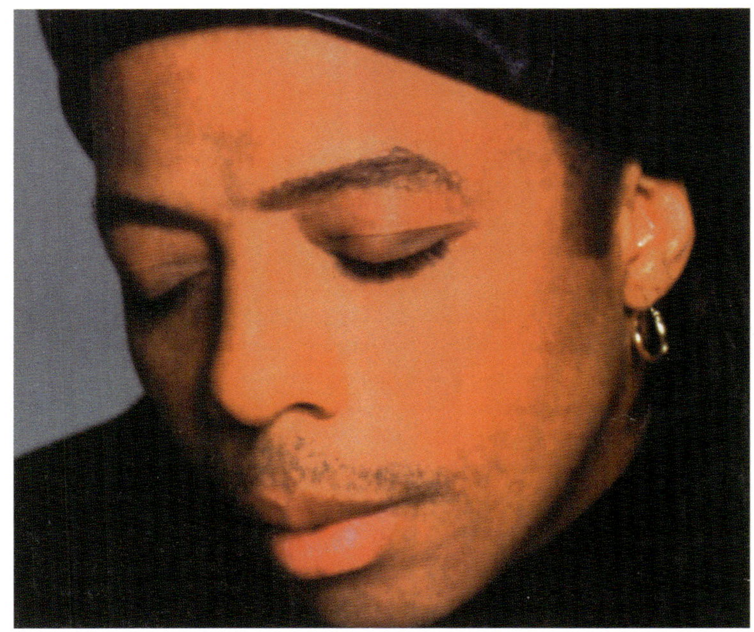

c. 1998

JOE COCKER }

AFTER HE reinvented the Beatles' "With a Little Help from My Friends" and Traffic's "Feelin' Alright" in the late 1960s, Joe Cocker descended into a haze of alcohol and drugs, often seeming like one of rock's saddest casualties. But the gruff-voiced singer got his career back on track in the 1980s, staging a heart-warming comeback that saw him sing at the Oscars and win a Grammy for "Up Where We Belong." Immensely popular in Europe, he had survived in the music business, seemingly more focused and confident than in any period in his life.

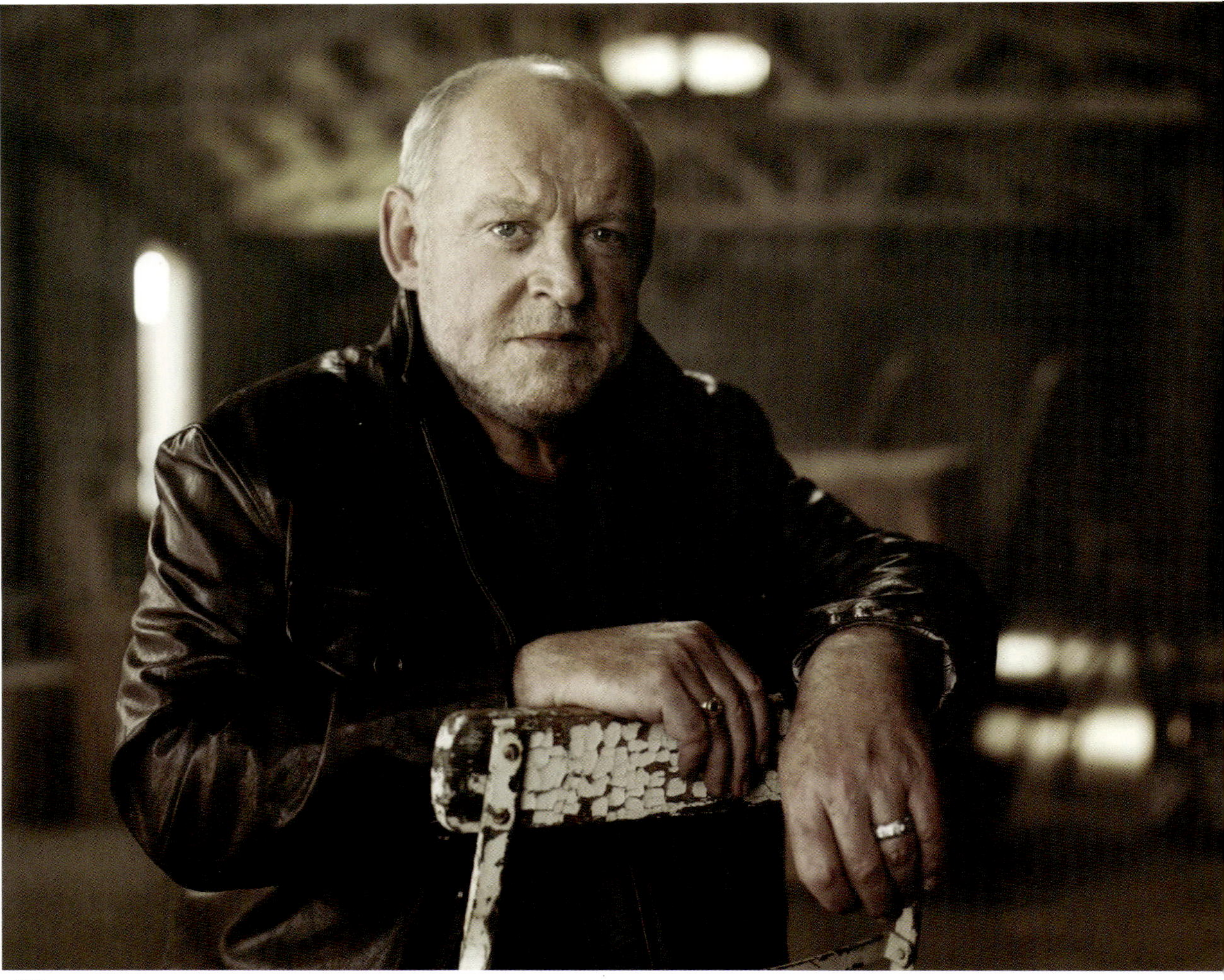

c. 2012

Since 1991, the clean-living Cocker lived in Colorado.

"My wife, Pam, and I had been living in Santa Barbara for going on ten years. I did a gig in Telluride, and we met a lot of old friends who had strangely enough all ended up in the North Fork Valley. We thought we'd buy a bit of land and go up there in the summertime. But once we got a feel for the place..."

The Cockers hurried back to Santa Barbara and put their home on the market, then packed their belongings and moved to tiny Crawford, a self-described cowtown of 250. They built a 243-acre ranch and opened and ran the Mad Dog Ranch Fountain Cafe and Trading Post for a few years.

In 2007, Queen Elizabeth II honored the singer as an Officer of the British Empire (akin to knighthood), but around Crawford, Cocker was always just an average Joe.

"I go in total reverse when I'm home," he said. "I love to walk with the dogs and be out in the open. I relish those days when I rarely see a soul. It sounds a bit strange, but it's such an opposite to the rock 'n' roll way of life of being in hotels and living at nighttime."

At Christmastime, 150,000 lights turned Cocker's adopted hometown into a holiday extravaganza that drew visitors from around the state. His spouse donated the decorations to all the businesses in Crawford.

In December 2014, Cocker died in his Colorado home after battling lung cancer. He was 70. ●

GINGER BAKER }

IN JUNE 1966, Ginger Baker recruited guitarist Eric Clapton and bassist Jack Bruce to form Cream. The group's success catapulted them to stardom—in the second half of the decade, Cream set the pattern for the power-trio format, and Baker virtually created a new lexicon of rock drumming, elevating his instrument to co-lead status.

After leaving Cream, Baker never attained as high a profile. He resurfaced with Clapton in 1969 as half of another short-lived supergroup, Blind Faith. He developed Ginger Baker's Air Force and, later, the Baker-Gurvitz Army before retreating from the scene to found a studio in Nigeria. He re-emerged with a solo career, moving to Los Angeles from Italy in 1988. In 1992, he joined the metal group Masters of Reality, and in 1993, Cream reformed for a performance at the trio's induction into the Rock and Roll Hall of Fame.

That same year, Baker moved to Colorado. He hadn't been encountering any problems getting his visa, but he had three counts against him that were never going to go away—two drug busts (in 1970 and 1971) and fraudulently obtaining a visa (when he toured in 1972 and failed to mention the busts on his visa permit). Under no circumstances was he ever going to get a green card.

"I could live here permanently as long as I behaved myself or didn't leave the country," Baker said. "But I couldn't not leave the country."

Baker did a lot of work on his ranch in Elbert Country, near Parker, building two barns, a guesthouse and a home. His son Kofi, a drummer, played clubs in Denver.

Baker had secured a spot on the jazz scene by releasing two acclaimed albums with Charlie Haden and Bill Frisell. Then he hooked up with his own group, the DJQ2O—the Denver Jazz Quintet To Octet, a unit of local musicians known to perform following games Baker had organized at the Denver Polo Club. *Coward of the County*, with special guest James Carter, featured Ron Miles on trumpet and Artie Moore on acoustic bass, plus Fred Hess (tenor sax), Eric Gunnison (piano) and Shamie Royston (organ).

Then, in 1997, the Department of Justice showed up.

"Somebody made a phone call after a polo game," Baker said. "My groom was English, and we were still working on getting her green card. She'd been with me for two and a half years. I trusted her with my horses."

The groom was handcuffed, jailed and eventually deported. Two weeks later, the Department of Justice showed up again to deliver a subpoena stating that Baker's status in the country was under investigation. Baker spent nine months waiting for the other shoe to drop.

His lawyers said Baker was only going to be fined, but then he appeared on radio station KRFX and dissed the INS on the air. The Justice Department reopened the investigation, saying Baker didn't live in America, he lived in the United Kingdom.

At the same time, the Internal Revenue Service considered Baker a U.S. resident for tax purposes. Baker, in turn, refused to pay taxes for two years—and he used the money to move to South Africa in 1999.

"They'll never let me back in? Big deal, so I'm heartbroken," Baker said sarcastically. "America is not the world, although they seem to think so." ●

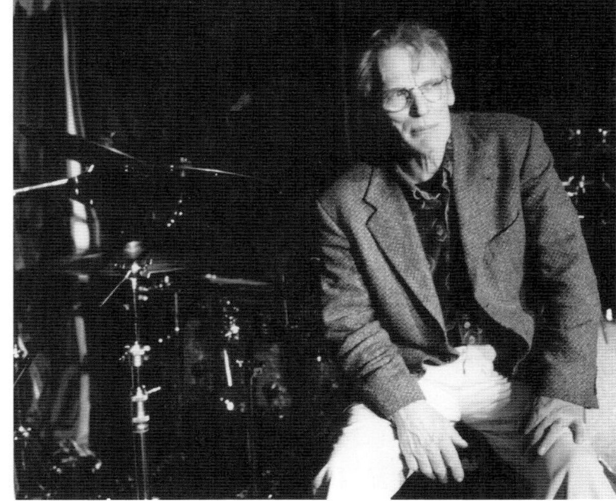

c. 1999

JIMMY EAT WORLD }

ROCK CRITICS in charge of names for musical trends reckoned Jimmy Eat World had an "emo," or emotion-based, style, and the Arizona-based four-piece emerged as trailblazers in the genre. The outfit's influence widened considerably with the single "Lucky Denver Mint," which used droning and ambient guitar tones and drum loops under the band's alt-pop-rock sound.

"Lucky Denver Mint" was first released as the lead song on Jimmy Eat World's self-titled EP. The track was added to the rotation early on KROQ, a quintessential modern rock radio station in Los Angeles. Then Capitol Records released the band's album *Clarity*. The hard-edged sensitivity of "Lucky Denver Mint" was played on modern rock stations in Chicago, Phoenix, Boston and Cleveland.

But the Denver market responded slowly. KTCL ignored "Lucky Denver Mint" for weeks, and KBCO played the song only occasionally. Granted, the deeply personal lyric didn't really play up a connection—the city was only mentioned in the first verse: "This time it's on my own/Minutes from somewhere else/Somewhere I made a wish with Lucky Denver Mint..."

"It's about getting drunk in Las Vegas," guitarist-vocalist Jim Adkins explained.

"Um, we've always had really good shows in Denver," guitarist-vocalist Tom Linton added.

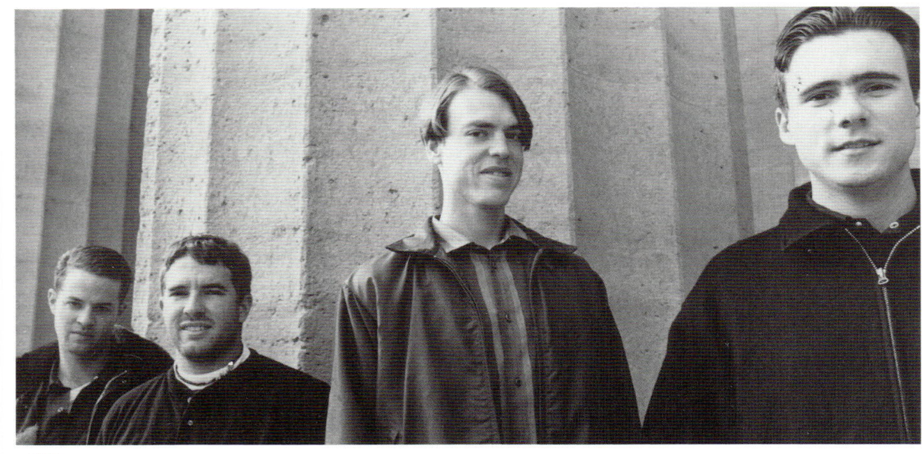

c. 1999

"And there was a band from there called Christie Front Drive—we did a split 7-inch single with them."

"Lucky Denver Mint" was featured in the movie *Never Been Kissed*, starring Drew Barrymore, and a companion video for the single interspersed footage from the film.

"The soundtrack was released and promoted worldwide at a time when our albums were not," Adkins said. "Thanks to Ms. Barrymore, we got at least one of our songs across the water."

Jimmy Eat World's follow-up album, *Bleed American*, crowned them as major figures in commercial rock, and "Lucky Denver Mint" then become an emo standard.

"I used to cringe when someone asked us how it feels to play music in the emo movement," Adkins said. "I still cringe. But people need labels." ●

NEIL DIAMOND }

GIVEN THE ephemeral nature of pop culture, Neil Diamond's enduring popularity was astounding. For more than three decades, the entertainer was one of the biggest draws in America, consistently setting attendance records at major venues across the country.

Diamond decided to culminate his 1999 world tour with a New Year's Eve concert at Denver's Pepsi Center. As the media prepared for big Y2K/Millenium coverage, ABC planned a marathon broadcast that girdled the globe and carried dozens of musical performances, including Diamond from Colorado.

But Diamond's original intention was to spend the night quietly at his streamside cabin in the Rocky Mountains—he'd lived in the Roaring Fork Valley for over 20 years.

"Colorado became my home when I wasn't touring and I didn't have specific recording obligations," Diamond said. "I even have pictures of my little log cabin in my dressing room kit."

Diamond was born in Brooklyn, New York, and he spent his childhood in the working-class neighborhoods of the borough. But for a couple of years in the mid-1940s, his family lived in Cheyenne, Wyoming, where his father was stationed in the Army.

"I was five, but that experience in the West had a big influence on me," Diamond recalled. "That's where I got to idolize cowboys—they had some kind of attraction. I always thought I was one when I went back to Brooklyn. I loved the singing-cowboy movies—a guy on a horse with a cowboy hat and a guitar." ●

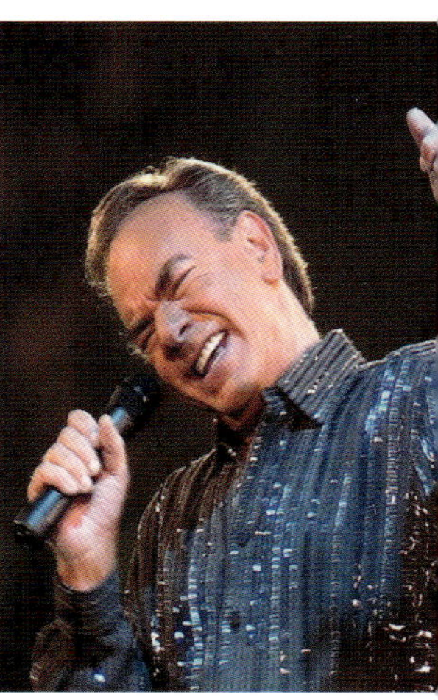

At Pepsi Center, December 31, 1999

THE APPLES IN STEREO }

SINCE MAKING their recorded debut in 1993 with a self-titled EP, the Apples in Stereo forged a career in summery, sweetened pop music. Founder Robert Schneider, his wife and drummer Hilarie Sidney, rhythm guitarist John Hill and bassist Eric Allen were zealous students of the tradition's standard elements—brisk tempos, brief run times, fuzzed-out guitars and trebly vocals.

"When we started, everything was so heavy and dark with all the grunge stuff," Hill observed. "Although we liked that at the beginning, we were trying to do something going against that. We knew that pop songs could get across, and maybe even a lot of people would like it. We didn't set out to do anything specific other than be the best fucking band in the world."

Schneider helped start a musical collective called Elephant 6, which included like-minded groups that made jangly music reminiscent of 1960s pop acts, especially as produced by the Beatles and Beach Boys. The innovative Schneider spent much of his time at the band's recording studio—named Pet Sounds, after the Beach Boys album—tucked away in the alleys of Denver's Golden Triangle, and forged a sophisticated sound using low-tech equipment.

The connection between Schneider's big ideas and his financial constraints was his peculiar gift for producing and engineering. He supervised albums for some of the bands in the collective, including Neutral Milk Hotel, the Olivia Tremor Control, the Minders, Beulah and Elf Power.

"Our obsession was always the best audio and production quality possible, and we attacked it from the beginning, on our own and together," Schneider said. "We just didn't have any resources at all. We were working along at crappy little jobs. Even if we had a good bit of money, we would have done it the same way. We wanted complete control.

"We started out on a four-track cassette deck because that's what we knew how to do. We never tried to be a part of the 'lo-fi' scene—we just had hardly any equipment at our fingertips."

The Apples used their D.I.Y. beginnings as a launching pad. Sound expanded from recordings made in Schneider's bedroom to 100-track sonic experiments. The Apples invented their own scene because they were outsiders in Denver's music community,

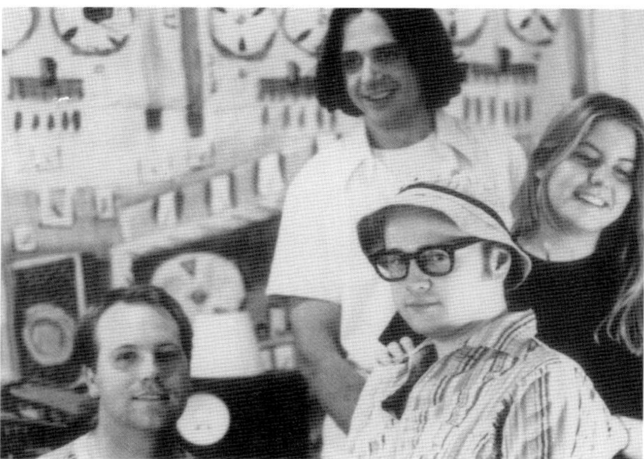

c. 1997

becoming well known across the U.S. with write-ups in *Rolling Stone*, *Spin*, *Details* and other national publications and in Great Britain and Japan as an indie-rock institution. They regularly played for packed houses almost everywhere except their hometown. Live, the band's noisy, grinding distorted guitar chords against trash-can drums created a catchy, loose power-pop romp.

The Apples in Stereo's cute, winsome outlook transformed them into a children's band when "Signal in the Sky (Let's Go)" was included on the Powerpuff Girls' souvenir album and the video aired on Cartoon Network.

In the summer of 2001, Schneider and Sidney moved to Kentucky in pursuit of affordable housing. Allen and Hill, both associated with other local acts (Hill also played guitar for Dressy Bessy), continued to tour with Schneider and Sidney as the Apples, but they remained in Denver. The members went on hiatus and focused on other projects. When they reconvened, their lineup suffered a blow with the departure of Sidney (since divorced from Schneider) in late 2006; new players Bill Doss (keyboards), John Dufilho (drums) and John Ferguson (keyboards) joined the group.

The Apples in Stereo got a boost in December 2006 by the appearance of Schneider on the infamous "Green Screen Challenge" episode of *The Colbert Report*, singing a typically tuneful ode to Stephen Colbert's attractiveness and his "number one TV show." In April 2009, the song "Energy" from *New Magnetic Wonder*, the band's sixth studio album, was performed by the contestants on the television show *American Idol*. ●

LEFTOVER SALMON }

SERVING UP self-described "polyethnic Cajun slamgrass"—a unique brand of bluegrass-based boogie that drew from miscellaneous influences—Leftover Salmon won an astounding national following on the jam-band circuit.

The group formed in 1990 with the merging of two Boulder outfits—the Left Hand String Band, known for progressive bluegrass, and the Salmon Heads, who did crazy Cajun music.

"I had moved to Colorado after I attended the University of West Virginia," frontman Vince Herman explained. "In Appalachia, there are a bunch of old-timey music festivals. But the Colorado scene was different. Progressive bluegrass was happening with Hot Rize and the Telluride Bluegrass Festival. It was the meeting place between California and the East Coast scene.

"Leftover Salmon came together as an accident. I had started the Salmon Heads in 1989. A couple of guys in the band didn't want to leave Boulder to do a New Year's gig in Crested Butte, so I got Drew (Emmitt, mandolin and guitar) and Mark (Vann, banjo) from the Left Hand guys to go with us. It was strictly 'Let's have some fun and play some rock 'n' roll folk music,' because that's what we knew. On the way to the gig, we were joking—'How are we going to put the Salmon Heads and the Left Hand String Band together?' We did all the mathematical permutations, and Leftover Salmon was the worst!"

The lineup eventually settled with Herman, Emmitt and Vann, Michael Wooten (drums) and Tye North (bass).

"We had a ton of gigs because the scene was real tight in 1990," Herman said. "All the promoters and bar owners knew each other, and there was a lot of work in the ski areas. We didn't leave the state for over two years.

"We were a bluegrass band with drums, and respectable people didn't play traditional bluegrass that way, so we knew we couldn't make much of a living on that circuit. We decided to play in bars, and that took a different approach. We became more of a slamgrass band, because that's what ski bums wanted. Even after skiing all day, they had plenty of energy left, and they loved slamming into each other. The rowdier we got, the more that circle kept going."

Joyous freeform sets at traditional events (the Telluride Bluegrass Festival and the Merle Watson Festival in North Carolina) and raucous rock jaunts (a two-week stint on the H.O.R.D.E. tour) resulted in the band's 1993 self-released debut album, *Bridges to Bert*. The band crisscrossed the country in an old yellow school bus, a grueling schedule that continued for years.

"We named the bus Bridget, and we put 800,000 miles on her," Herman said.

"We created this thing in our minds, and we were lucky it happened," Emmitt added. "The big dream was to bridge the gap between the rock 'n' roll world and the bluegrass world. We were one of the first bands that got to play with our bluegrass heroes at festivals like Telluride, and we got to tour like a rock band with Widespread Panic and play huge stadium shows as well."

Ask the Fish was a 1995 live effort recorded at the Fox Theatre in Boulder, but hundreds of concert recordings existed—the band encouraged fans to tape its shows. In the studio, Leftover Salmon searched for ways to incorporate the variety of musical styles heard at its concerts. *Euphoria*, 1997's major-label debut on Disney's Hollywood Records, peaked at #3 on *Billboard*'s Mountain Regional roundup.

But the band did better serving up bluegrass hippie hardcore in charismatic live performances for loyal followers, or "salmon heads."

"We're a strong touring band, and 'rehearsal' is one of those French-sounding words that we don't quite understand," Herman said of the band's devotion to the road. "That 'L.A. process'—'Let's make a record and then try to get somebody to listen to it'—is one part of the music industry that I've never understood.

"It's a very 'high-touch' kind of music. We don't need bodyguards to get in and out of our shows. We're just geeks like everybody else, interested in the same things and wearing the same clothes. We have that sharing of the culture in common."

By the end of the 1990s, Leftover Salmon had the opportunity to record *The Nashville Sessions*, which teamed the band with an A-list of Music City's most notable session players.

2002 started out on a sad note for Leftover Salmon with the melanoma-related death of Vann at age 38. The group experienced some internal restructuring and continued to hit the open road relentlessly, taking part in a tour with bluegrass giants the Del McCoury Band and releasing an album with the band Cracker. But the last

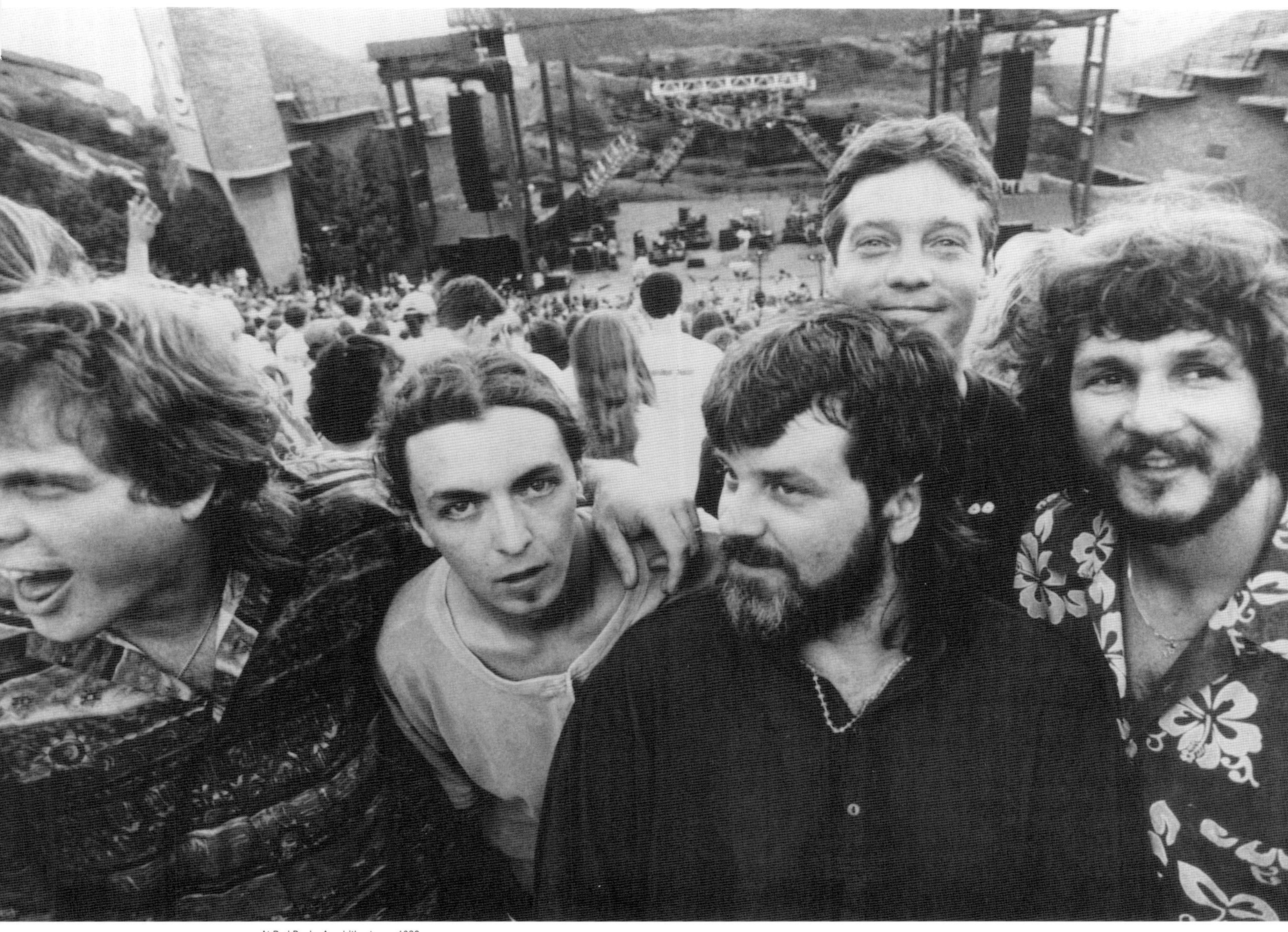

At Red Rocks Amphitheatre, c. 1999

months of 2004 brought an end to Leftover Salmon.

"Leftover Salmon was like a family, with a great amount of mutual admiration going on. There was an undeniable chemistry between Vince and Mark and me, the heart and soul of the band," Emmitt said. "It was like three legs of a stool. When Mark went and that leg was gone, the stool wasn't standing up on its own too well anymore."

In 2007, Leftover Salmon brought banjo player Andy Thorn into the group and returned for a handful of reunion shows; Bill Payne of Little Feat became a full-time member in 2014. The band's bluegrass roots remained.

"Over the years, we've certainly done one or two live shows that have centered around the Led Zeppelin musical universe more than Doc Watson's," Herman said. "But the bluegrass scene in Boulder is the reason I moved from West Virginia to Colorado. I held Hot Rize as a model of successful musicians. They weren't selling a ton of albums, but they were playing what they wanted to fun, interesting crowds and having a good time and making a living at it—which I thought beat the hell out of flipping eggs at Nancy's Restaurant." ●

FIVE IRON FRENZY }

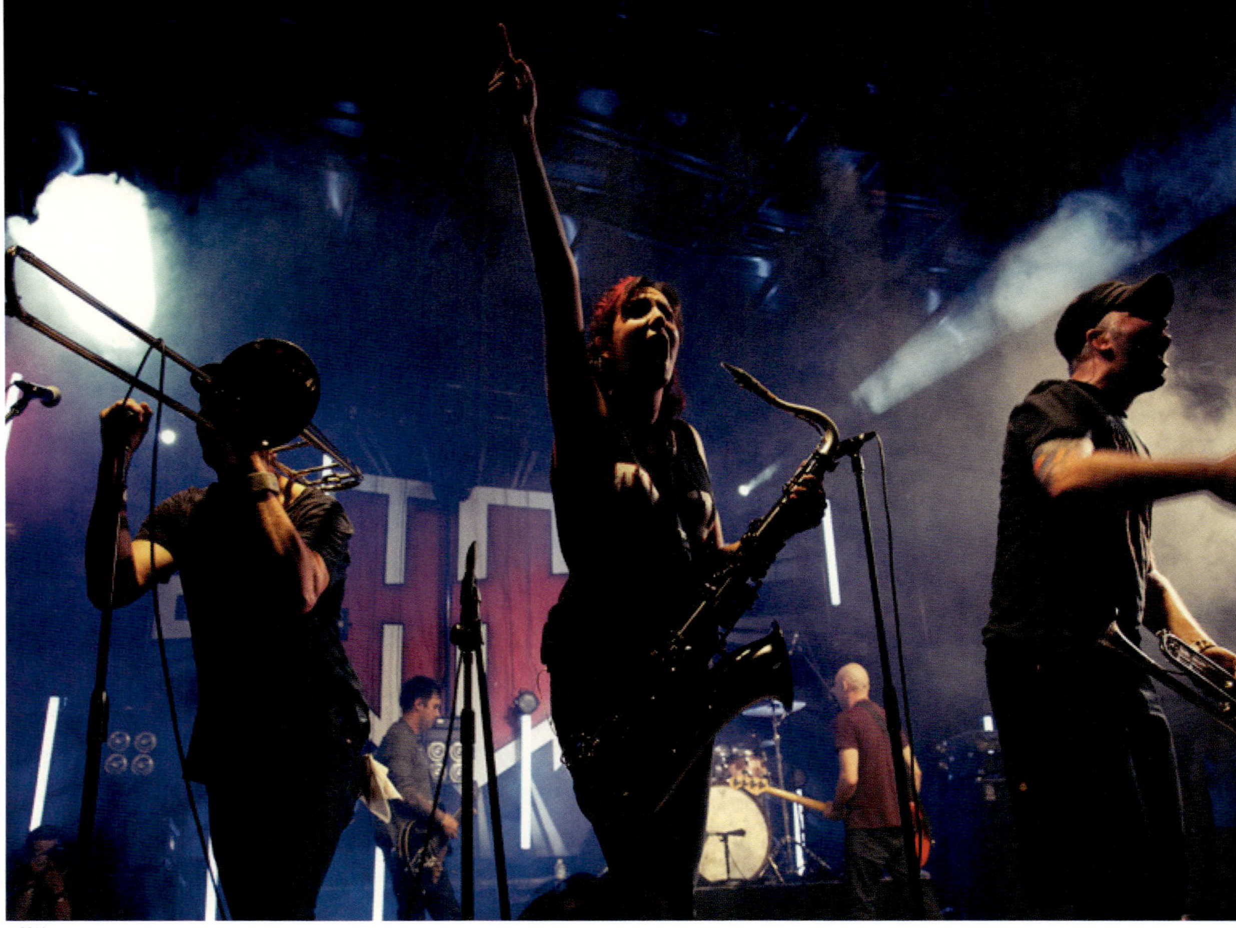

c. 2012

DURING THE late 1990s and early 2000s, several ska-punk bands broke through to mainstream popularity. Along with No Doubt, Goldfinger and Skankin' Pickle, the Denver band Five Iron Frenzy helped contribute to the scene, combining the tangy sound of ska with a horn section and catchy alternative pop-rock songs—and the positive message unified by the band's shared Christian faith.

"We were outcasts, riding the fence between a secular fad and a Christian phenomenon," singer Reese Roper said. "We never quite belonged in either place."

Formed in 1995, the core members—Roper, Keith Hoerig (bass), Micah Ortega (guitar) and guitarist-lead songwriter Scott Kerr—had been a staple in the Denver area's Christian-rock scene with their first project, an industrial-strength thrash outfit called Exhumator.

"Five Iron wasn't supposed to be a full-time gig," Hoerig said. "We were getting into some poppier punk and thought it would be fun to try something like that. We found horn players naturally—Micah's cousin played sax, and Scott was like, 'I've got a friend who plays trumpet.' It wasn't a big decision. We never had any idea we would be able to make a living at it."

They soon added Andrew Verdecchio (drums), Dennis Culp (trombone), Nathanael "Brad" Dunham (trumpet) and Leanor "Jeff the Girl" Ortega (sax). After a few months of constant gigging, the band attracted a strong regional following and their 1996 debut album *Upbeats and Beatdowns* became a local hit.

"Initially, we didn't have any goals, except to have some fun and play music," Hoerig said. "What helped us was that local promoters were bringing a lot of national poppy ska-core bands to Denver, and they wanted local bands to open. We were able to get in front of an audience."

Five Iron Frenzy punctuated its horn-drenched, fast-and-loose live shows with salsa-style shouting and elaborate trombone solos. Before social media took hold and sites like MySpace, Facebook and Twitter turned the music industry on its head, the hard-working band built a rabid fan base by incessant touring.

"Our living expenses were extremely low; a lot of us rented a house that we shared together," Hoerig said. "So when we went on tour, we didn't have to make a lot of money."

Early on, the members used tours to raise awareness for social causes—on the "Rock Your Socks Off" tour, fans were encouraged to bring clean socks for donation to local homeless shelters. Songs also tackled somber themes, such as the homophobia of Christian subculture, the plight of the Native American people and corporate hegemony. Notwithstanding, the group often incorporated its signature goofy humor into lyrics and Roper's many onstage costumes (e,g,, a cape, crash helmet and metallic leisure suit). On the "SkaMania" tour in 1998, the entire band wore Star Trek uniforms.

The manner in which the ska-punk band displayed its faith sometimes was too much for traditional Christian marketing channels.

"Five Iron was always locked in some struggle for legitimacy that we could never quite obtain in the Christian marketplace," Roper allowed.

"Our record company never understood that we had cut our teeth playing club shows, and so they kept putting us on to play the better-paying church shows. They were usually bigger and almost always edifying, but the bigger question was, was it ministry? More importantly, was it where we belonged?"

The band did as many secular shows and tours as appearances at Christian tours and festivals. On the 1997 "Ska Against Racism" tour, featuring Less Than Jake and the Toasters, Five Iron Frenzy was the only openly Christian act.

Album releases broke into *Billboard*'s Top 200—*Our Newest Album Ever!* (peaking at #176 in November 1997), the live *Proof That the Youth Are Revolting* (#190 in November 1999) and *All the Hype That Money Can Buy*, the band's most eclectic collection of tunes (#146 in May 2000). The octet toured internationally, playing in South Africa and Europe. Kerr left the band in 1998, replaced by guitarist Sonnie Johnston.

In 2003, Five Iron Frenzy announced its impending breakup and parted ways with a sold-out final show at Denver's Fillmore Auditorium. The show was released as the double-disc set *The End Is Here*.

Claiming "We can't even quit good," members of the band reunited in November 2011 (Hoerig chose not to participate) and returned to the stage. Two years later, Five Iron Frenzy released its first new studio album in a decade, financed by a Kickstarter campaign; *Engine of a Million Plots* peaked at #118 on the *Billboard* albums chart. ●

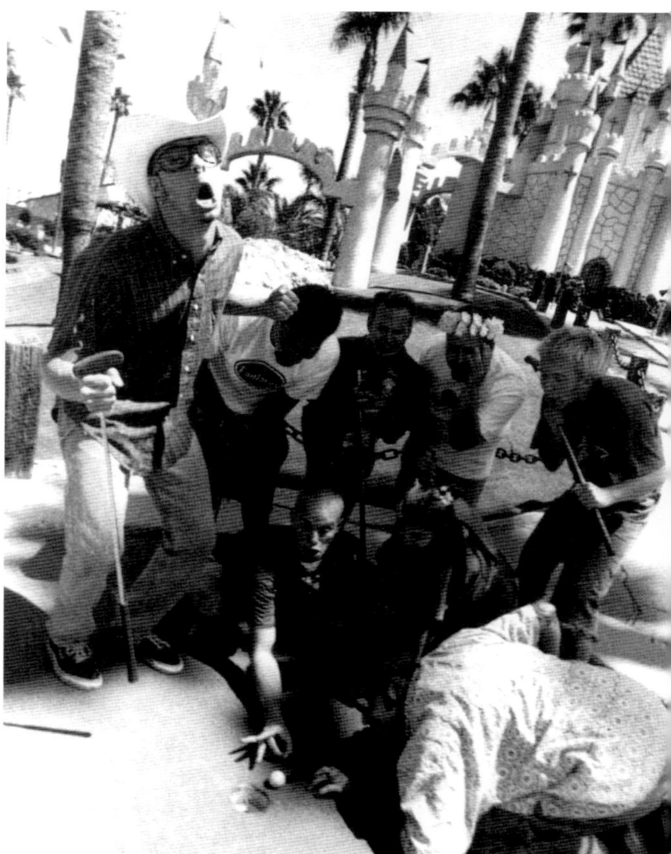

c. 1998

MATT STONE & TREY PARKER }

CREATED BY Trey Parker and Matt Stone, *South Park*, the Comedy Central television network's controversial and wildly successful animated sitcom, became infamous for lampooning a wide range of topics with crude, absurd, satirical and dark humor. Music always contributed mightily in the show's success; several characters often played or sang catchy songs in order to advance the storylines.

Parker forged his love of musical theater, a hallmark of the franchise, as a teenager with the Evergreen Players, a venerable mountain community theater 30 miles west of Denver. He was a 14-year-old chorus boy in *The Best Little Whorehouse in Texas* and helped build the set for *Little Shop of Horrors*. "When I was a kid, to me, the Evergreen Players were the big time," Parker said. There, he hung out with other theater geeks on the fringe of the in-crowd. He played piano, was president of the choir counsel and played Danny Zuko in Evergreen High School's *Grease*. Stone went to Heritage High in Littleton.

After meeting at the University of Colorado in 1992, Stone and Parker were outsiders in what was then a largely avant-garde film school. "We were kind of looked down on in Boulder," Parker said, "because everyone was doing these crazy exploratory kinds of things, and Matt and I just basically wanted to do Monty Python."

Stone and Parker made an animated short entitled "The Spirit of Christmas," created by animating pieces of cut-out construction paper with stop motion. In 1995, after seeing the film, a Fox executive hired the pair to make a personal video Christmas card; the duo developed "Jesus vs. Santa." Out of that came *South Park*, created for Comedy Central, which debuted in August 1997. Consistently earning the highest ratings of any basic cable program, the ongoing narrative revolved around four children—Stan, Kyle, Cartman and Kenny—and their bizarre adventures in and around the titular Colorado setting, also home to an assortment of frequent characters such as students, families, elementary school staff and other various residents.

Isaac Hayes voiced the character of Chef, a black, amorous soul-singing elementary-school cafeteria worker. One of the few adults the boys consistently trusted, Chef made conversational points in the form of original songs written by Parker and performed by Hayes in the same sexually suggestive R&B style he had utilized during his own career. The band DVDA, which consisted of Parker and Stone, along with show staff members Bruce Howell and D.A. Young, would perform the music for these compositions, listed as "Chef's band" in the closing credits.

"When we first approached Isaac to do the show, I don't think he was in the best financial shape," Stone said. "I think he did the voice for the first time for the cash, to tell you the truth. But he got into it after a while."

The song "Chocolate Salty Balls (P.S. I Love You)" was released as a single in the U.K. in 1998 to support *Chef Aid: The South Park Album* (a compilation of original songs from the show, characters performing cover songs and tracks performed by guest artists) and became a No. 1 hit. It also reached No. 1 on the Irish singles chart and peaked in Australia at #14 in February 1999.

The song's first and second verses featured Chef listing the ingredients of the titular confection, and urged people to "suck on them" during

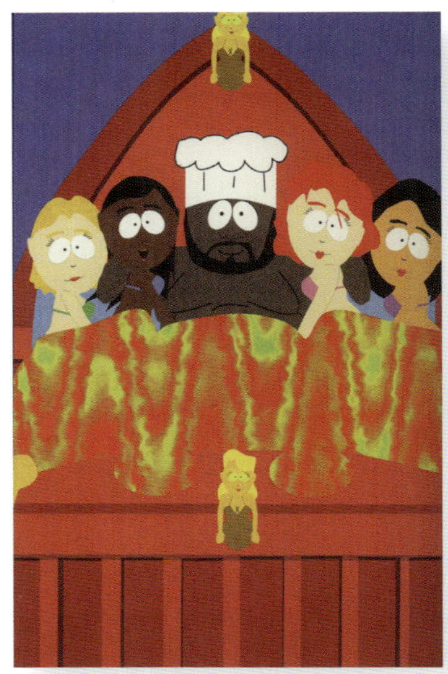

Chef in *South Park*

the chorus. During the final verse, Chef, concerned that his chocolate salty balls had become burned, insisted his lover blow on them. The radio version featured an additional verse, in which Chef begs his lover to retire with him to his bedroom before her husband comes home.

"When I did 'Chocolate Salty Balls,' I asked them, 'Are you sure you want to do this stuff, man?'" Hayes remembered. "But then I looked into the studio and saw the whole crew in there cracking up. I said, 'Shit, they might have something.' So I went on and did it, and I'm glad I did, because it was such a huge hit."

Hayes left the show in early 2006, and the character of Chef was killed off in

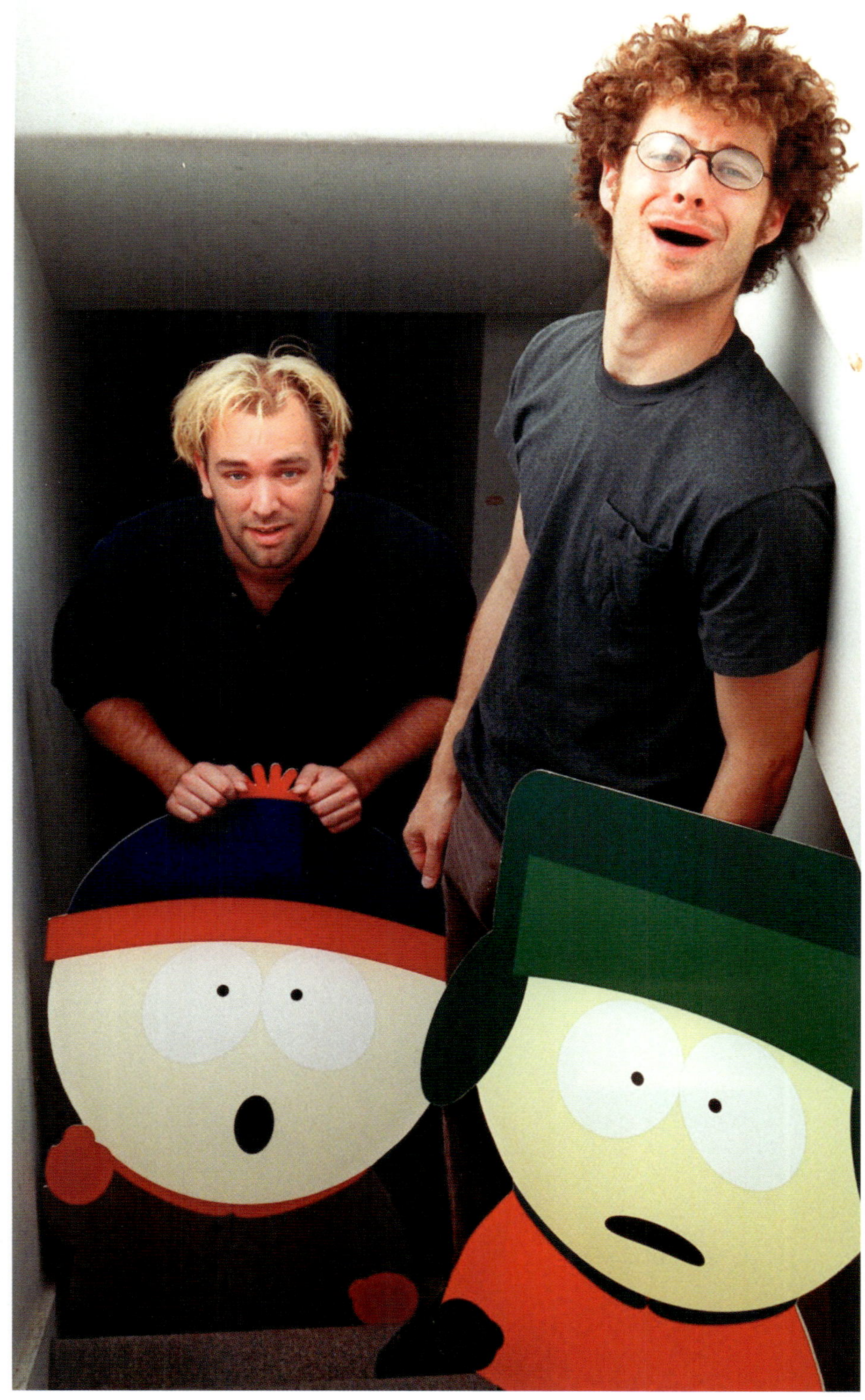

c. 1997

the season 10 premiere, "The Return of Chef."

"He was never offended by anything we did in the slightest until we did the thing about Scientology," Stone said, referring to an episode lampooning Tom Cruise and other disciples of L. Ron Hubbard. (Hayes was a Scientologist.)

Following the early success of the series, the feature length musical film *South Park: Bigger, Longer & Uncut* had a widespread theatrical release in June 1999. The songs were written by Parker and composed by Marc Shaiman. In "Blame Canada," which satirized scapegoating, the fictional parents of South Park decided to blame Canada for the trouble their children had been getting into since watching the Canadian-made fictional movie *Terrance and Phillip: Asses of Fire* and imitating what they saw and heard in the movie. "Blame Canada" was nominated for the Academy Award for Best Song. That created controversy, because all nominated songs are traditionally performed during the Oscar broadcast, but the song contained the word "fuck," which the FCC prohibits using in prime time broadcasts. Comedian Robin Williams performed the song with a chorus that gasped when the word was to be sung (Williams turned around at the crucial moment, and did not actually sing it). The Academy Award was instead awarded to Phil Collins' song "You'll Be in My Heart," which was parodied on an episode of *South Park* in 2000 as "You'll Be in Me."

When Stone and Parker premiered their religious satire musical *The Book of Mormon* on Broadway in spring 2011, it became an instant hit, grossing more than $200 million. When it was announced the show would go off-Broadway in 2012, tickets became nearly impossible to obtain. *The Book of Mormon* garnered nine Tony Awards, one of which was for Best Musical, and the Grammy Award for Best Musical Theater album. An original Broadway cast recording was released in May 2011 and became the highest-charting Broadway cast album in more than four decades, reaching #3 on the *Billboard* charts. ●

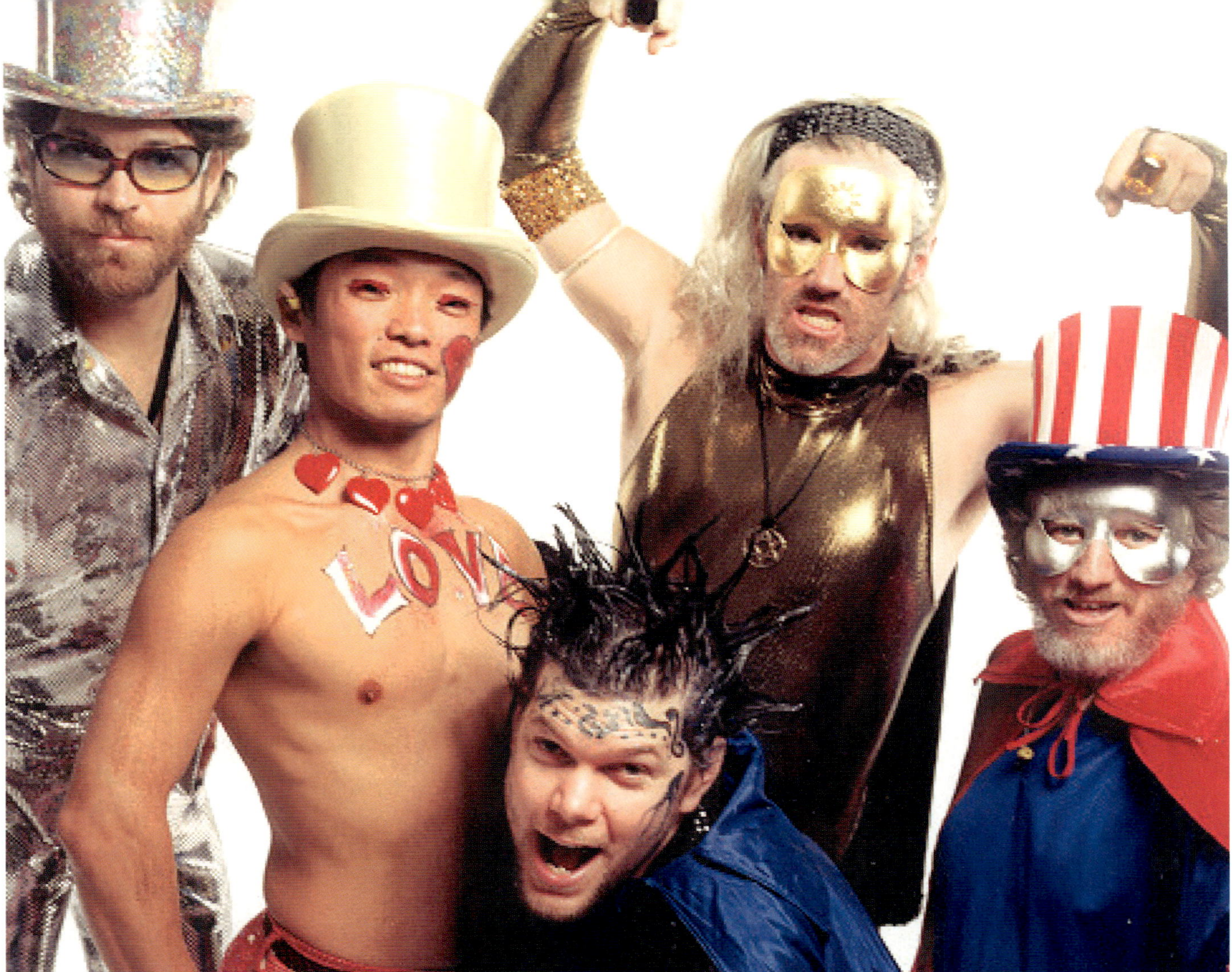

c. 2001

STRING CHEESE INCIDENT }

A HEADY approach to a musical career established Colorado-based String Cheese Incident as one of the most popular neo-hippie jam bands from west of the Mississippi. The members didn't concentrate on selling records. They devoted themselves to live improvisation, cultivating a dedicated fan base that followed them from show to show and a carnival-like atmosphere when they threw their festivals.

"It was always a very interactive scene, ever since we played the first gig at a variety show in Crested Butte," acoustic guitarist Billy Nershi said. "People are just as much a part of the show as we are. It takes everybody listening and involved to have a really good 'incident.'"

In 1993, String Cheese Incident was playing après-ski bars in Crested Butte and Telluride. Soon after, the five unassuming ski bums—Nershi, Michael Kang on violins, Keith Moseley on bass, Kyle Hollingsworth on keyboards and Michael Travis on drums and percussion—moved to Boulder to pursue seriously a career in music, a self-described "sacrilegious mix" of bluegrass, funk and jazz with breezy Latin and African influences.

Stretching the noodly extremes of folk music, the energy and enthusiasm exuded from the stage established String Cheese Incident. Taking a page from the Grateful Dead and Phish, the band carried the positive communal vibe and idealism of the hippie era into the 21st century, building a fan base so loyal and involved that it became somewhat of a phenomenon itself.

Whether it was following the group for national and international shows or collecting merchandise or trading live-show tapes, set lists and concert reviews via the internet, devotees made the group a way of life. Silver-haired Deadheads, well-to-do college kids, suntanned ski bums and middle-aged professionals—all shared in the carefree happiness. A craze was spawned when the band started throwing hula hoops into the audience, encouraging their followers to "hoop" and dance.

Early poster

String Cheese Incident grossed several million dollars in revenues every year, yet the band had no major-label contract, hardly got any radio airplay and did not have a video on MTV. As the group continued to elevate both the sound and the shows, it attracted the support of a zealous business team.

The enterprise included String Cheese Incident's own management and booking company. It launched its own record label, SCI Fidelity, and an in-house merchandising department. There was also an SCI-run ticketing service and in-house travel agency, set up to help fans arrange transportation plans to "incidents." The band also employed a tape archivist who maintained recordings from each SCI show.

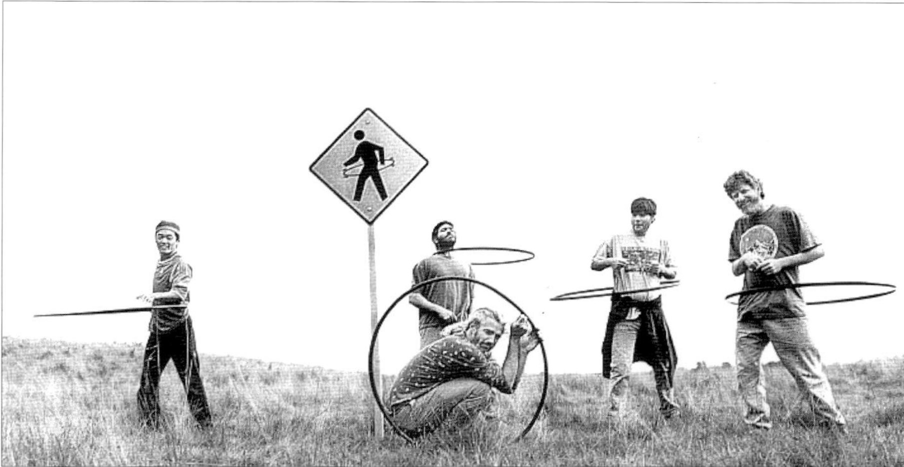

The band with its emblematic hula hoops, c. 2003

All told, the String Cheese empire had two dozen casually clad staffers—and a few dogs—running around a Boulder office building.

"It began as a dream, something we set out to do from the beginning—'Let's tour like maniacs and build a grassroots following, and let's start our own record company because everyone we talk to has nothing but horror stories,'" Moseley said.

"Then, by enlisting people to run the company, we saw it grow. There was a sense of responsibility that weighed on my shoulders. I not only played in the band, but I was a part of all these different wings of the organization."

To make their tiring tour schedules more pleasant, the band members often played multiple dates in the same city so they and their dreadlocked, patchouli-soaked disciples could settle into a festive atmosphere. For hot summer gigs, String Cheese Incident played exotic beachside locations in Jamaica, Mexico and Costa Rica. For the band's annual Winter Carnival shows, venues near the best ski resorts were favored.

"We're doing the same thing onstage, whether we're playing to 500 or conceivably 50,000—that is, communicating as a musical unit, trying to blend five instruments into a single voice, and have some feedback from the audience...get them involved, feel their emotion," Moseley said.

In May 2001, String Cheese Incident's *Outside Inside*, a studio release recorded with producer Steve Berlin (Los Lobos), debuted at #147 on the *Billboard* Top 200 and #5 on the Independent Band Chart. The title track climbed the AAA charts. The group also documented its live concerts, releasing nearly every show through its massive *On the Road* CD series. The darker *Untying the Not* arrived in 2003, followed in 2005 with the roots-based *One Step Closer*.

During summer 2007, members announced to their fans that the String Cheese Incident would take a break from touring. They rode out into the sunset with a last blowout at Red Rocks Amphitheatre that August. The band reunited in summer 2009 to tour with small runs throughout the country. In 2014, *Song in My Head*, the fifth studio offering by the group, reached #123 on the *Billboard* 200. ●

WIDESPREAD PANIC }

THE ROAD-FRIENDLY group never had an album crack the Top 40 or a music video on MTV. But Widespread Panic, formed in the early 1980s in the college town of Athens, Georgia, dominated the Colorado market in a way few bands have ever accomplished.

From their early days in small bars, the neo-hippie jam band staked its reputation on a freewheeling, amorphous mix of country-blues with touches of jazz-fusion and Southern rock. Without traditional music industry support, the sextet used extensive touring and the Internet to cultivate a vast, dedicated following. It changed its set list every night, allowed fans to tape shows and generate hundreds of Web sites dedicated to the music and mission. Standout performances at Blues Traveler's H.O.R.D.E. festival and other locales increased Panic's grassroots appeal.

In the late 1990s, Panic targeted Colorado, and fans were quick to get on board. Photos of Red Rocks Amphitheatre appeared prominently on 1998's two-CD live release, *Light Fuse Get Away*, and Panic's 2000 summer tour kicked off at the famed outdoor venue, with the three shows (some 27,000 seats total) selling out in 44 minutes. For several summers, the band headlined three consecutive nights at Red Rocks. It officially holds the record for sellout performances at the amphitheatre.

"It might not be the path that everybody treads down, but it seems to be working with us," lead singer and guitarist John Bell said. "You just do what you feel is right at the time. We're well-practiced at that kind of loose formula."

That formula, Bell explained, dates to the 1980s. "Back in '87, America was experiencing a recession. A lot of the 'hair bands' had big light shows, very flashy and effect-laden presentations. That stuff carried such a high dollar that it wasn't really affordable.

"We were still in our little world, just getting our sea legs as far as touring went. We endured for a couple of years, and then there was the recognition that there was some value to what we were doing. We didn't have to be gimmicky. We could just be ourselves, and there was a market out there that would help sustain us as a band, to where we could eat once a day and play music.

"A few years later, we met Blues Traveler, Phish and Col. Bruce Hampton & the Aquarium Rescue Unit. From Colorado, we met Leftover Salmon and Big Head Todd & the Monsters. Here were bands that had also acquired established niches. We were very different, but we all seemed to attack the music and crave what was going on—'Hey, there's a common experience in different parts of the country.'

"That was a good feeling right there. Nobody was into hyping themselves as a band—the egos were at a minimum. You could just get on with playing music. You were satisfied with pushing yourself, and you were excited to see what other people were doing. Instead of competition, there was inspiration."

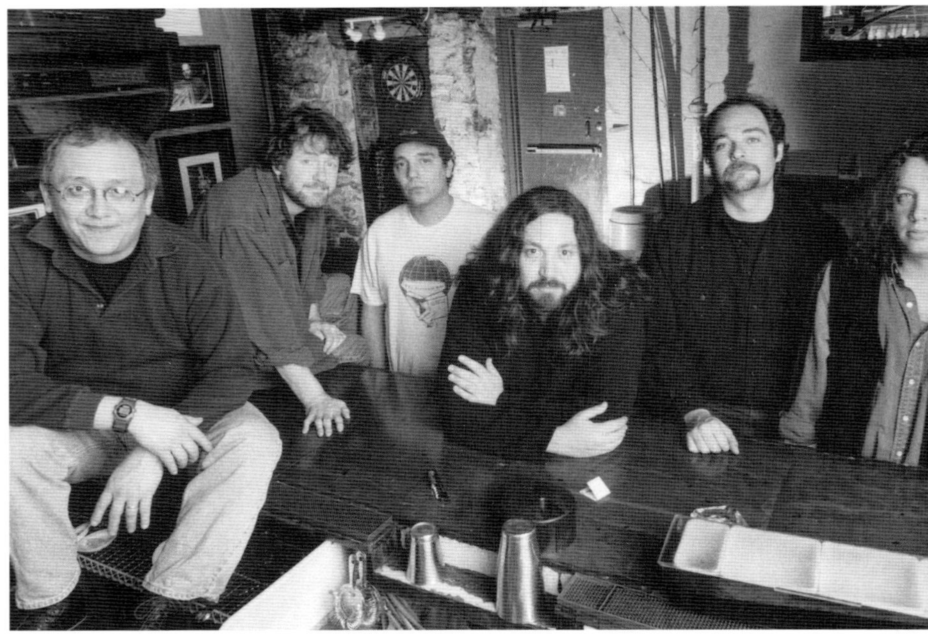

c. 1998

The band did big business on the road—according to trade publications, Panic was a Top 30 concert draw in 1998. In the South, the group's influence was legendary. A record 63,000 people came to its New Orleans Jazz & Heritage Festival show in 1999, and 100,000 to a record release party in the streets of Athens.

In Colorado, the band continued to inspire unprecedented devotion. June 27, 2008 marked Widespread Panic's 32nd sold-out show at Red Rocks Amphitheatre, more than any other band in the venue's history. Mayor John Hickenlooper proclaimed it "Widespread Panic Day" in Denver. ●

YONDER MOUNTAIN STRING BAND }

IN THE late 1990s, the phrase "jamgrass" emerged. As groups across the country blended bluegrass, folk, country and improvisation into a new creation, Yonder Mountain String Band experienced a meteoric rise.

Mandolin player Jeff Austin and banjoist Dave Johnston had moved from Illinois to Nederland, Colorado, where they met bassist Ben Kaufman and guitarist Adam Aijala.

"The reason I moved to Nederland was the music scene," Austin said. "I knew what I wanted to do with music and I had an idea of what kind of folks I wanted to meet. Luckily, we all had the same mindset of what we wanted to do with bluegrass, the common language that we all knew.

"The musical climate was huge. At that time you could go to open 'picks' and bluegrass jams five or six times a week. Leftover Salmon was playing like crazy, and String Cheese Incident was getting going, and Runaway Truck Ramp and the Tony Furtado Band were there. There was just a lot of bluegrass-influenced music going on, rock bands that had bluegrass instruments and played bluegrass songs. But one thing was missing—there was no traditional bluegrass lineup that was stretching the limits."

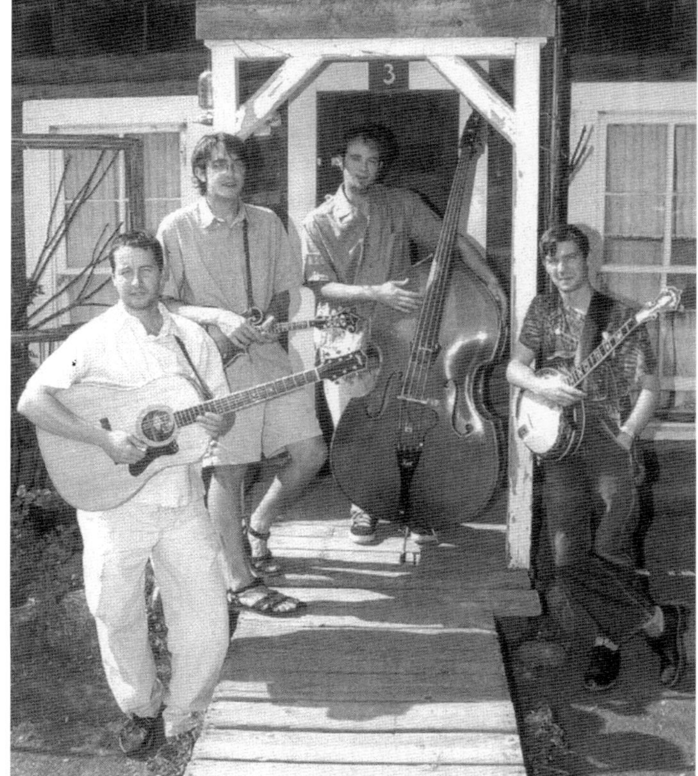

c. 2001

"People were very respectful and open and welcoming," Aijala added. "It made me and a lot of other people feel comfortable, because I didn't know hardly any of the songs."

Yonder Mountain String Band, which formed to play an opening set at the Fox Theatre in Boulder, developed a loyal following among bluegrass and jam band fans, playing fests in New York, North Carolina, Kansas, Oregon and California, and big summer sheds like Alpine Valley and Deer Creek. The band was known to stretch its tunes out to great lengths, and to insert surprises like Ozzy Osbourne tunes and Michael Jackson songs.

"Our roots all come from a rock background," Aijala said. "If you'd have asked me back in 1986 when I was listening to Black Flag and Dead Kennedys if I'd end up in a bluegrass band... well, first of all, I'd have said, 'What's bluegrass?'

"Obviously, we try to play as good as we can each night, but we're not about perfection. We go for the energy, and it works. Not having that pressure makes us happier."

In 2002, Ryko Distribution began distributing Yonder Mountain String Band's four albums, which had sold a combined 100,000 records. The group then released two studio albums with rock producer Tom Rothrock (Beck, Elliott Smith, Foo Fighters) and several live recordings. YMSB was a regular at bluegrass festivals like the Telluride Bluegrass Festival and the band's own Northwest String Summit as well as massive multi-stage events like Austin City Limits Festival, Bonnaroo and Rothbury.

In 2008, Yonder Mountain String Band performed at the Democratic National Convention in Denver at Invesco Field at Mile High, opening for Barack Obama, who accepted the nomination for President in a speech before a record-setting crowd of 84,000 people in attendance. Austin parted ways with the band in 2014. ●

DIANNE REEVES }

BY THE beginning of the millennium, the divas of the jazz world had passed, leaving a new generation of singers to carry on. One of the most significant jazz vocalists to fill the void was Dianne Reeves, whose performances could recall the era of Carmen McRae, Ella Fitzgerald and Sarah Vaughan while imparting her own technically adept yet emotive style.

Reeves had known that music was the path she would take since she was a 13-year-old student.

"My family moved to Denver from Detroit while I was still a toddler," she said. "When I was a kid, I went to Hamilton Junior High, and we were one of the first busing programs in the Denver public school system, to attempt racial integration and balance. There were a lot of neighborhoods that we didn't even know existed, and there was a lot of tension in the school. But I had this wonderful music teacher, Bennie Williams, who felt the best way to bring all of these students together would be through music."

Williams heard Reeves singing in the hallway one day and invited her to join the school's choir. Williams organized a concert to help unite kids of different cultural and racial backgrounds, and Reeves ended up singing a solo. For the first time, Reeves got on stage and discovered the power of her voice.

"When I first heard myself with a microphone and saw how my voice affected people, I knew what I wanted to do. I walked past the music room and said, 'I'm putting all my eggs in this one basket.' I found something that was mine, that was stronger than any kind of peer pressure. I needed that at that time. My father had passed away when I was very young, and I felt lost. But when I found that, it was special.

"In the late '60s and early '70s, the songs were very conscious politically—'You've Got a Friend,' 'Bridge over Troubled Water,' 'Let It Be' and 'He Ain't Heavy, He's My Brother' were meant to unite people. At the same time, black radio had just come into Denver, so we had access to my favorites, Marvin Gaye and Stevie Wonder. From that point on, I was hooked."

Reeves' uncle, Charles Burrell, an acclaimed jazz bassist as well as a bass player with the Denver Symphony Orchestra, introduced her to the music of jazz singers, from Billie Holiday to Fitzgerald and Vaughan. At the age of 16, Reeves was singing in a jazz ensemble, the choir and a madrigal group at George Washington High School in Denver. Winning a citywide competition in 1973, Reeves' high school jazz band traveled to Chicago to perform at the National Association of Jazz Educators conference. It was there that she met noted jazz trumpeter Clark Terry, who became her mentor. Terry was so impressed with Reeves that he asked her to sing with him at Dick Gibson's Colorado Jazz Party at the Broadmoor Hotel in Colorado Springs later that year.

Reeves began studying music at the University of Colorado and was also kept busy performing on the club circuit before she moved in 1976 to Los Angeles. Her interest in Latin-American music grew, and she toured with Eduardo del Barrio's group Caldera, worked with pianist Billy Childs' avant-garde outfit Night Flight and accompanied Sergio Mendes on a world tour. In the early 1980s, Reeves moved to New York and toured with Harry Belafonte as a lead singer.

Reeves launched her solo career and was the first vocalist signed to the revived Blue Note label in 1987. She rose to the top echelon of jazz singers, performing on some of the most prestigious stages of the world. She was the recipient of four Grammy Awards for Best Jazz

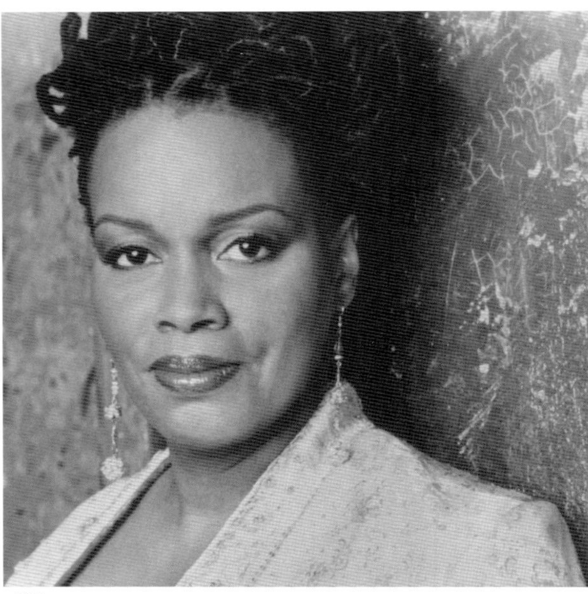

c. 2000

Vocal Performance: for her 2000 release *In the Moment: Live in Concert*; for 2001's *The Calling: Celebrating Sarah Vaughan*; in 2003 for *A Little Moonlight*, a lush set of ballads; and in 2006 for the soundtrack to the film *Good Night, and Good Luck*.

Reeves could have sought a higher profile career elsewhere, but she preferred to keep her base of operations in Colorado. She moved back to Denver in 1992 after years away from home.

"Denver is sort of in the middle of the country, and it's easy to get to both coasts," said the long-time Park Hill resident. "This is home, the place where I'm the most comfortable—it's beautiful and peaceful, and my family is close by. No one could ever pay me to leave Denver." ●

INDIA.ARIE }

WITH HER 2001 album *Acoustic Soul*, R&B singer India.Arie made one of the most notable debuts in music history, traveling down the trail blazed by like-minded soul sisters Lauryn Hill, Erykah Badu and Jill Scott. The song "Video" from the CD became an anthem for many listeners with its positive message about loving yourself. It made India.Arie a household name.

"It's not a stage name—Î was born India Arie Simpson at Rose Medical Center in 1975," the Denver native laughed. "My first name was chosen in honor of Mahatma Gandhi, because I share his birthday. My mom came up with my middle name. I later found out it means 'lion' in Hebrew."

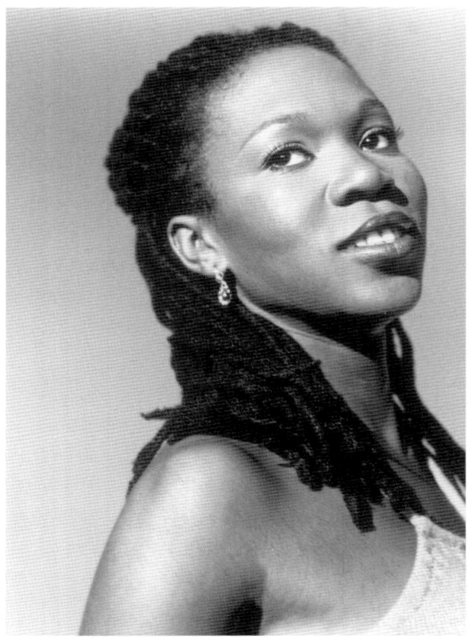

c. 2001

Arie's father, Ralph Simpson, was a standout high school basketball player in Detroit and spent a year at Michigan State University before getting a hardship exemption to enter the draft of the American Basketball Association as a 19-year-old. Drafted by the Denver Rockets (later the Denver Nuggets), he became one of the now-defunct league's top scorers (he also played with three National Basketball Association teams before ending his athletic career in 1980). Arie's mother, Joyce Simpson, also grew up in Detroit, where she pursued a career as a singer during her teenage years.

"Growing up in Denver, I always liked music—my family sang at church, at home, at Christmas," Arie said. "But my parents never pushed me in that direction. They told me that I could accomplish anything."

The Simpsons were divorced in the mid-1980s, and at age 13 Arie moved from Denver to Atlanta with her mother and her two younger siblings. But she found Atlanta schools to be less tolerant, and after a few years of being ridiculed for her physical appearance and attitudes, she decided to move back to Colorado with her father to finish her secondary education at Rangeview High School in Aurora.

"Growing up, I looked different, I dressed different, I liked different music. I was made to feel that I wasn't as good because of that," Arie said. "But it never occurred to me to change."

Arie had taken up a succession of musical instruments throughout her schooling in Denver. After graduation, she studied at the Savannah College of Art and Design in Georgia. It was there that she got a nylon-stringed acoustic guitar from her first boyfriend and began writing songs.

"When I went to college, I decided it was time to accept myself," Arie said. "It was a direct result of writing songs. When I started tapping into my own sensitivity, I started to understand people better."

Arie signed with Motown Records in 2000 and started the 18-month process of writing and making *Acoustic Soul*. Her acoustic guitar playing had spare folk stylings, but with soul and funk in the vocals and arrangements, a cross of Stevie Wonder and James Taylor, two of her idols. "Video," her debut single, was India.Arie's declaration of independence, outlining her intentions and personality with unfashionably affirmative lines: "I'm not the average girl from your video and I ain't built like a supermodel/But, I learned to love myself unconditionally/Because I am a queen...My worth is not determined by the price of my clothes..."

Arie received seven Grammy Award nominations for 2002, including Best New Artist, Album of the Year for *Acoustic Soul* and Record of the Year and Song of the Year for "Video." Although she did not walk away with any of the awards, the publicity catapulted her into the front ranks of contemporary female R&B performers. Arie followed the success of her debut with the release of *Voyage to India*, which debuted at No. 1 on the *Billboard* R&B chart and won her two Grammy Awards. Her third studio recording, *Testimony: Vol. 1, Life & Relationship*, was released in 2006, gaining her first No. 1 spot on the *Billboard* 200 album chart. *Testimony: Vol. 2, Love & Politics* and *Songversation*, issued in 2009 and 2013, respectively, debuted in the Top 10.

"When I come back to Denver and drive through the same streets I grew up on, it's an awakening," Arie said. "It makes me realize how life can take you to so many places." ●

OTIS TAYLOR }

CURIOUSLY, THE 2002 winner of the prestigious W.C. Handy award (the blues equivalent of the Grammys) for Best New Artist was a 53-year-old man who began playing as a teenager in the 1960s. But there are no overnight success stories, and writers and performers of Otis Taylor's caliber hardly come out of nowhere.

Born in Chicago, the son of a railroad man, Taylor grew up in Denver after his family relocated, motivated by an uncle's murder. An adolescent Taylor began not only listening to music but aching to create it. He spent afternoons and weekends at the Denver Folklore Center, where he bought his first musical instrument, a used ukulele. Next up was a banjo.

"All the instructors taught me how to play music during their breaks—I never had to pay for a guitar lesson," Taylor said. "I already had an attitude about being different. I was making sandals back in '64 way beyond when that hippie stuff started up—that all came out of the folk scene that I was hanging out with.

"At home, we were what some people might call a little eccentric. I'm 'first-generation hip'—I was raised in an environment that was too hip, sometimes. My father was a big jazz buff, and he loved that be-bop lifestyle—start partying Thursday night and go on until sometime Sunday."

Taylor began playing folk blues after meeting such masters as Son House and Fred McDowell. By the time he drifted to Boulder, he had already led a couple of groups. He managed to save enough money to travel to London in 1969, where a brush with Blue Horizon Records lasted only a few weeks.

"They didn't get what I was doing over there," Taylor said. "I ran out of money. They wouldn't give me any. So I came back home. I was homesick anyway."

Back in Boulder, he hooked up with Tommy Bolin, who was on the rebound from the personnel changes and business chaos that surrounded Zephyr. However, Taylor retreated from the music business in 1977. During a sabbatical that lasted almost two decades, he did not perform in public, preferring to refine his gruff vocals and technique on guitar, harmonica and banjo. He became a successful antiques dealer and then organized one of the first all-black bicycling teams.

In 1995, a friend and longtime investor in Taylor's bicycle racing team opened Buchanan's, a coffeehouse on the Hill in Boulder, and decided he wanted to do live music in the basement. "He asked if I could put a band together for the opening," Taylor said. "All of a sudden, I was back in again."

Taylor and his accompanists, longtime friend Kenny Passarelli (whose resume included stints in the 1970s with Elton John, Dan Fogelberg, Stephen Stills and Joe Walsh) on bass and Eddie Turner on venomous and ethereal lead guitar, played together and found their sound—a drumless yet driving groove, reminiscent of John Lee Hooker's one-chord boogie—was too "cool" and uneasy to disregard. Some called it "trance blues."

Taylor's scary, stinging style relied little on the standard 12-bar blues structure and "woke up this morning" lyric clichés. Besides thoughtful, vivid first-person storytelling, Taylor applied fables and allegories from distant times and places. In a breathy style, he talked/moaned his dark vignettes. Some of them touched on the pain and misery of romantic infidelity, but most were peppered with vitriolic social commentary about the African-American experience.

Taylor self-released *Blue-Eyed Monster*, a mini CD. It caught just enough critical acclaim to convince him to record a full-length CD, *When Negroes Walked the Earth*. He sang about the lynching of his grandfather on his 2001 follow-up, *White African*, and the buzz eventually landed him some national exposure, leading to his four 2002 Handy nominations. He released a steady cavalcade of intriguing, critically acclaimed albums—*Respect the Dead*, *Truth Is Not Fiction*, *Double V*, *Below the Fold* and *Definition of a Circle*. Augmenting his band on several songs were Ben Sollee's evocative cello lines and the background vocals of his daughter, Cassie.

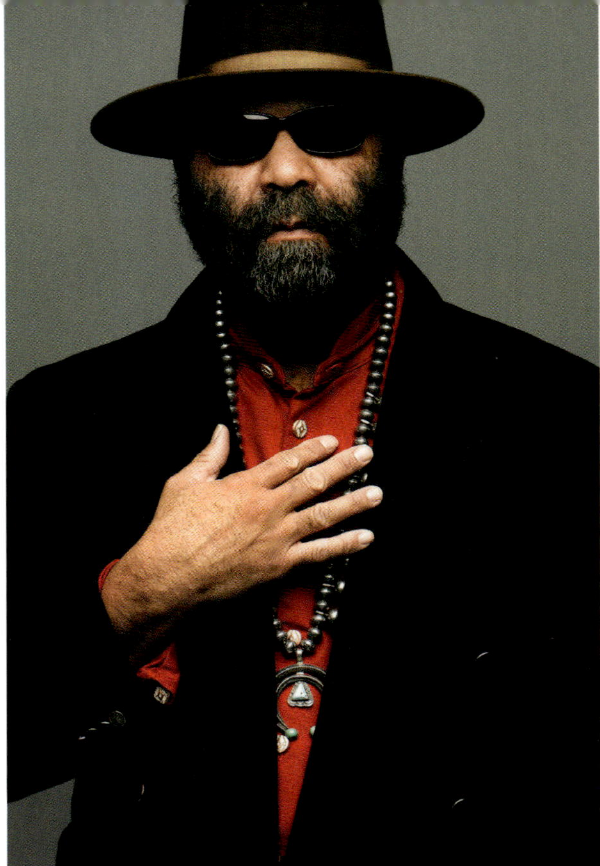

c. 2011

The Boulder resident saw the blues as a forum for more than just good-time boogie. Through his "Writing the

Blues" program, he shared the genre's history and heritage. "I've done it for elementary schools, and I've done it for universities. If I don't get the young kids involved, I won't have an audience. You have to do it on an emotional level, not just an intellectual level. I have them write the blues on paper and sing or speak it. Once they understand that everybody has the blues, they can relate to it."

The revelatory *Recapturing the Banjo* appeared in 2008, a mission statement to present the banjo in a clearer historical light; the banjo was originally an African instrument, arriving in the New World via the slave trade and turned almost exclusively into a white bluegrass instrument. *Pentatonic Wars and Love Songs*, released in 2009, was a dark and jazzy examination of desire.

Taylor toured in clubs and at festivals, achieving arguably more prosperity in Europe than in the States, in some respects mirroring the traditional blues success overseas.

"I still don't have much of a reputation for playing in Colorado. You talk to a musician, they're always saying how they get no credit in their hometown. The soul of humanity is the arts, and people turn their back on their own community. It's backward—it should be the community that rallies behind you. When somebody says you can't be a prophet in your own land, well, that's somebody not paying attention to their own land."

Taylor continued to bring a spellbinding intensity to his music. Taking the easy route never appealed to him.

"I rode a unicycle to school when I was 16, and there were not a lot of black rugby players, either," he said. "No matter what I do, I'm just a born outlier." ●

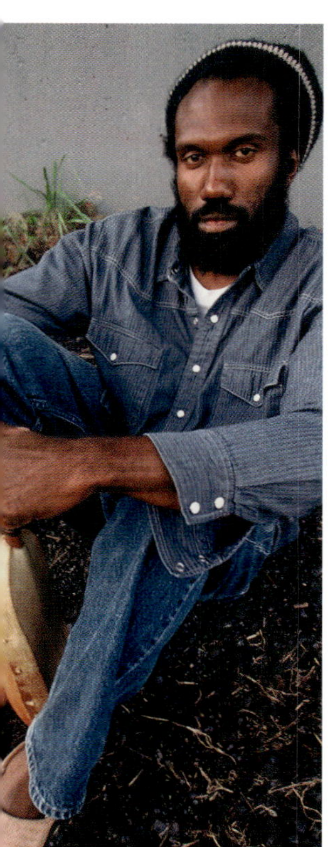
c. 2003

COREY HARRIS }

TRADITIONAL ACOUSTIC Delta blues attracted a host of young performers in the 1990s and early 2000s, but Denver native Corey Harris was credited with revitalizing the breadth of black musical traditions.

"People are surprised that I come from Denver, but it doesn't make sense to me," Harris said. "The people I grew up around were all from the South. They moved to Denver for jobs, and wherever people move, they're inclined to carry what they liked with them. My parents loved music, and I heard the blues at house parties and family celebrations from the time I was small. There's an old saying that the roots of a tree cast no shadow. Everyone has roots, and they come out in their creations."

Harris's mother had wide-ranging musical tastes, and she encouraged him to listen to her collection of records. He gravitated toward the songs of bluesman Lightnin' Hopkins. But his first instrument was the trumpet, which he played in the marching band at Isaac Newton Junior High.

"But I didn't think the trumpet was as cool as the guitar," Harris said. "So I switched."

At Littleton's Arapahoe High School, Harris played in a rock band, wrote songs and poetry and strummed guitar on the sidewalks of downtown Denver and Boulder.

"Littleton wasn't known as a melting-pot," Harris said. "I never felt like I belonged there, and a lot of the time I was made to feel that I didn't belong there. But that's often the truth of race relations in this country. And I had my family, thankfully."

After graduating in 1987, a scholarship took Harris to Bates College in Maine, which led him to postgrad work in Africa, which brought him back to America—and the blues.

Harris' second release, *Fish Ain't Bitin'*, won the W.C. Handy Award in 1997 for Best Acoustic Blues Album. His critically acclaimed releases then explored new sounds that incorporated reggae, ska, hip-hop, Latin and country styles. Comfortable in the pop-rock community, he toured nationally with Dave Matthews Band and Natalie Merchant. In 1998, he was invited to participate in the Billy Bragg/Wilco collaboration *Mermaid Avenue*, which set a selection of unfinished Woody Guthrie songs to music.

In 2003, Harris served as the guide in the first episode of Martin Scorsese's PBS series *The Blues*.

"But I think it would be a misrepresentation to say I am a bluesman," Harris said. "That's just a label that people put on me. I don't really call myself anything but a musician." ●

BUBBA SPARXXX }

DENVER BRONCOS players traded their mouthpieces for microphones over the course of the team's history. Leading up to the 1977 National Football League playoffs, fullback Jon Keyworth cut a record called "Make Those Miracles Happen"—appropriately enough for

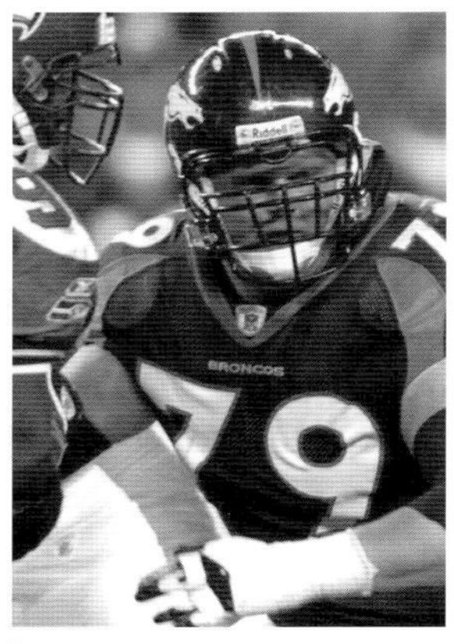

Steve Herndon, c. 2001

the upstart Broncos, who marched to Super Bowl XII. In 1989, Broncos running back Melvin Bratton, who was raised in the same Miami neighborhood as 2 Live Crew leader Luther Campbell and sang on the group's early releases, had a personal interest when the raunchy rap group appeared in court to fight obscenity charges. In 1998, defensive lineman Trevor Pryce launched Outlook Music Company, an indie label that boasted several bands and issued his own instrumental project, and defensive back Ray Crockett rapped the lyrics on a song titled "Salute to This" on a 1999 CD that celebrated the defending NFL champions' season.

Offensive guard Steve Herndon became something of a rap star after signing with the Broncos in 2000. Herndon grew up with Georgia rapper Bubba Sparxxx, maintaining a close association with him.

"Steve's my best friend—we've known each other since we were 11 years old," Sparxxx said. "We were inseparable, from middle school on up. We played football in high school, and Steve left to go to the University of Georgia with a full football scholarship. About a year later, I ended up moving on up there and did some time in community college. I stayed about seven years, working with rappers in Atlanta and Athens.

"Then we shot my first video, 'Ugly,' in Athens."

Herndon was front and center in the raucous music video for Sparxxx's hick-hop anthem, which received heavy rotation on MTV in 2001. "Ugly" was unabashed in its stereotypical Southern imagery—Sparxxx and Herndon were seen covered in pig slop on the farm, while pickup trucks rolled by like Escalades in the 'hood.

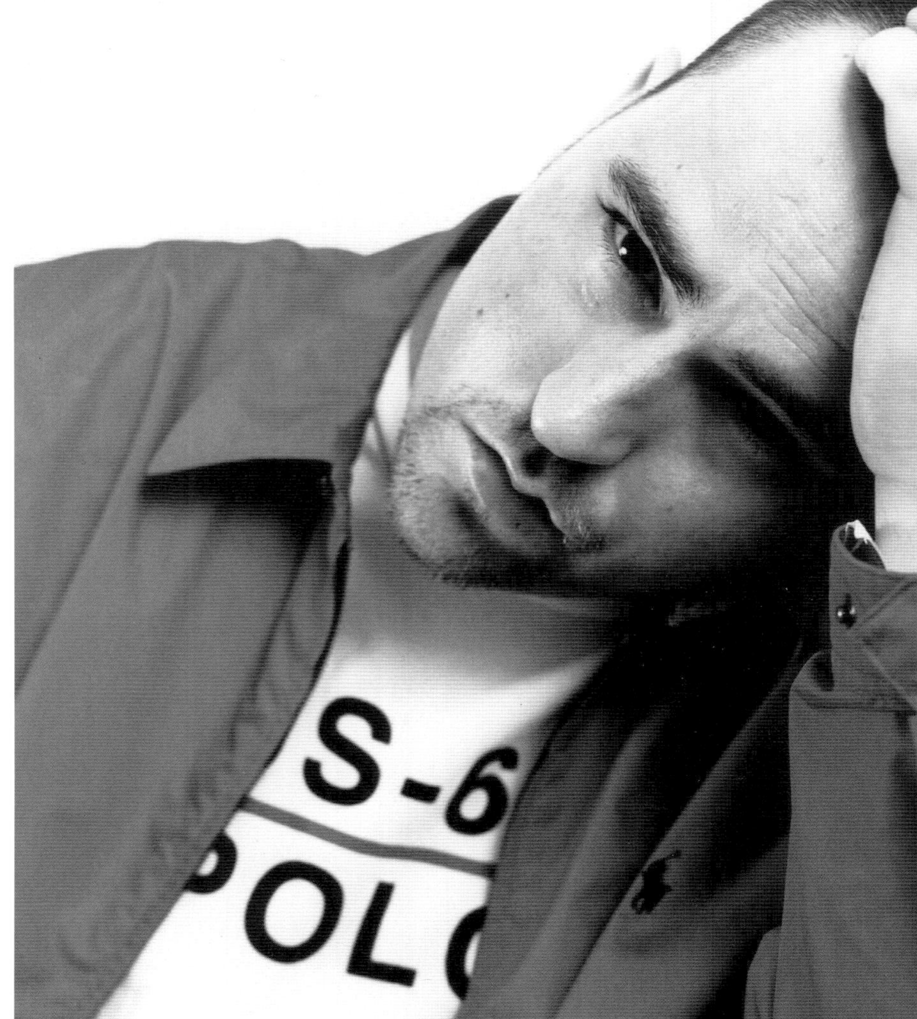

c. 2001

Heardon was a recurring video character—in July 2003, before Broncos training camp, the two pals did a video shoot for "Deliverance," the title track to Sparxxx's followup CD.

"If I wasn't playing football, I'd have probably been the road manager," Herndon said. "I'd run the show and then be on the stage doing my little dance.

"We both had an opportunity to fulfill our dreams at the same time. We were two white kids who grew up in a small town in Georgia saying, 'I want to play in the NFL,' and 'I want to be a rap star.' Just to be able to stay in touch and talk about everything he's experiencing and I'm experiencing is terrific."

Herndon played six seasons for the Broncos and the Atlanta Falcons. ●

STACIE ORRICO }

IN 2003, STACIE Orrico's major label debut introduced her to the world of pop stardom. The 17-year-old songstress got her start at an early age when her family moved to Colorado.

One of five children, Orrico sang at church and in school as a child. At home she listened for hours to pop divas and R&B artists while singing along in front of the mirror.

"I listened to Whitney Houston, Mariah Carey and Celine Dion," Orrico said. "Lauryn Hill was my favorite musical influence, ever since I saw her in *Sister Act II* when I was in second grade."

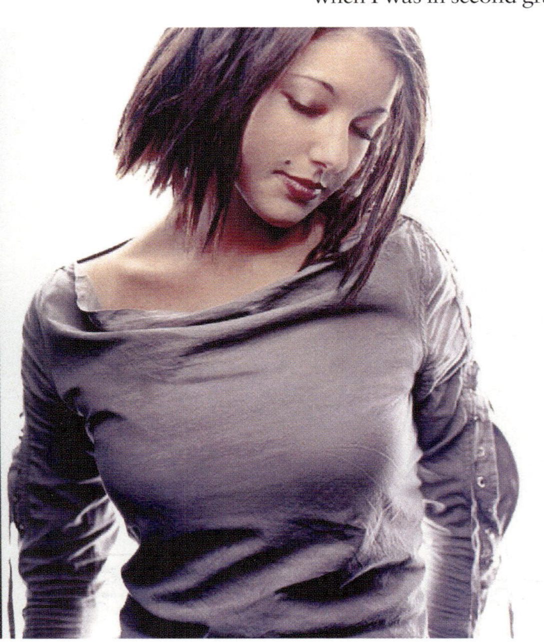

c. 2003

Orrico's parents were Christian missionaries who loved travel, requiring the family to move frequently. In 1998, they lived in Louisville, Colorado, a small town just outside of Boulder. They decided to attend "Praise in the Rockies," a Christian-music seminar held in Estes Park, a popular summer resort and the headquarters for Rocky Mountain National Park. With a friend's encouragement, Orrico, who was only 12 at the time, entered what she thought was just a little competition for the fun of it. It turned out to be a much bigger event than she or her family realized, and much to her astonishment, she won.

An executive at ForeFront Records heard her limber and mature vocal style and approached her family about signing her to a development deal. Orrico's family moved to Nashville for her career.

She had a big-selling debut release, *Genuine*, which held the No. 1 spot on *Billboard*'s national Heatseekers chart (listing titles by new and developing artists), and was a Dove Awards nominee for New Artist of the Year. Destiny's Child took notice and invited her to be the opening act for a string of dates on the pop-R&B combo's 2001 tour.

Orrico received comparisons to fellow teenage Christian artist Rachael Lampa, who debuted the same year. Lampa also grew up in Louisville and signed a deal with Word Records when she was 14. She won a Dove Award with the album *Live for You* and became a regular performer of the national anthem at Colorado Rockies baseball games.

"Then I had my second album ready to go to the Christian market," Orrico said. "Two months before they were going to release it, Virgin Records came into the picture. They added a couple of songs."

The secular label paired Orrico with some of the top producers in the business, including Dallas Austin (TLC, Pink) and Virgin CEO Matt Serletic (Santana, Matchbox Twenty, Aerosmith).

"Stuck" was the first single from *Stacie Orrico*. The sassy, catchy tune had a slick urban flair—especially the hook, "I hate you, but I love you, I can't stop thinking of you"—and it was the No. 1 most-added song at Top 40 radio in its first week, according to *Radio & Records*, a trade journal. Not bad for a single released to mainstream radio from a Christian artist.

"Stuck" climbed the *Billboard* Top 40 and was in the Top 10 on MTV's *Total Request Live*. It became a bigger international hit, reaching the Top 5 on the majority of the world's charts. "(There's Gotta Be) More To Life", the second single, debuted at #30 on the *Billboard* Hot 100. Orrico was sent off on a whirlwind of touring, promoting and recording. Still a teenager, she was driven out of the music business for a few years by the demands of a successful career. After a break from the public eye, she started recording again.

"Life has definitely changed a lot since I was living in Colorado," Orrico said with a giggle. "I don't know that I would sit down with every parent of a talented child and say you should try to get them record deals when they're twelve. It has the potential to be a very dangerous industry, and my whole life was so abnormal starting at such a young age. I never went to high school, didn't go to proms, didn't play sports. At the same time, I feel very fortunate to have experienced more places than a lot of people get to in an entire lifetime." ●

2004-2015

AS NEW technology provided new tools, the mainstream media and record labels no longer held a monopoly on musical tastemaking. Performers could now grow their profiles and fund their art using social media, becoming big hits without ever being mentioned in newspapers or magazines, or even getting radio play. Terrestrial radio, which had ruled the airwaves for almost a century, declined in popularity, as listeners invested in internet radio or digital streams and downloads. Songs commercially placed in films, on TV, in advertisements and video games became a chief means of exposure and big business in a new music economy paradoxically defined by grass-roots "viral" marketing and ubiquitous corporate sponsorships of live music.

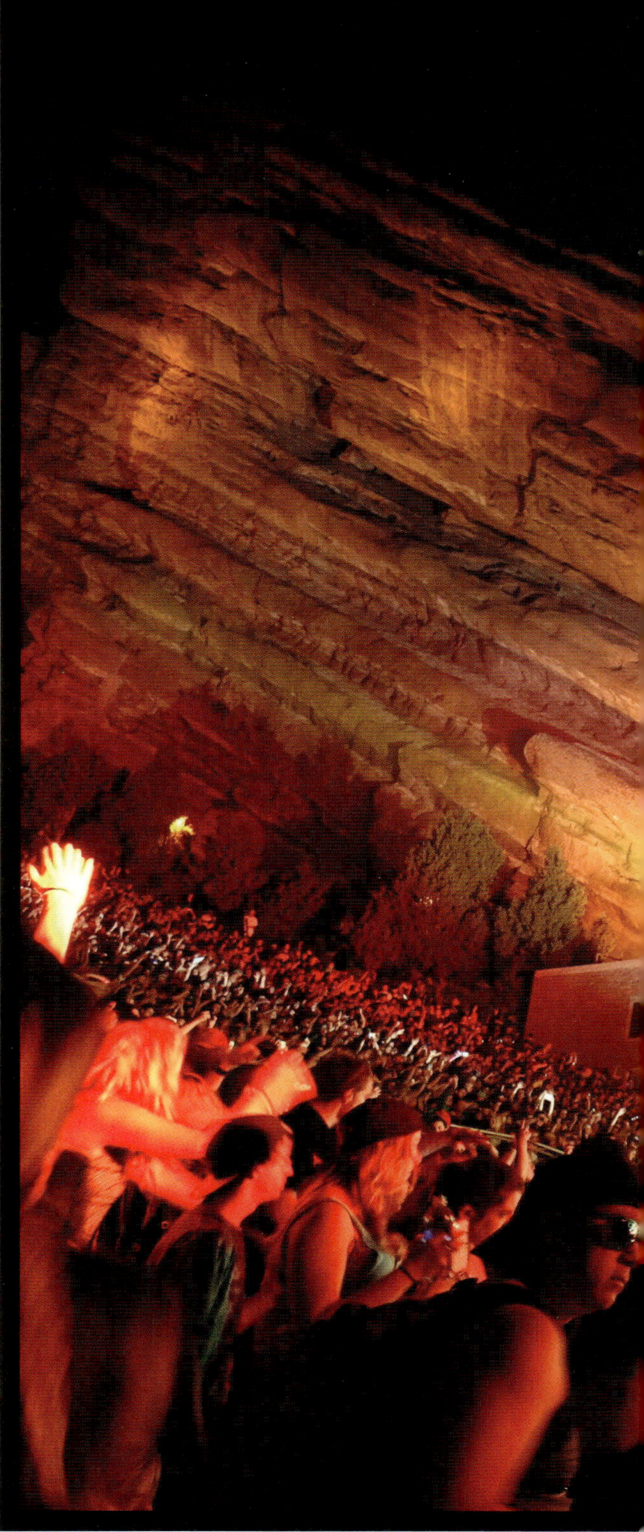

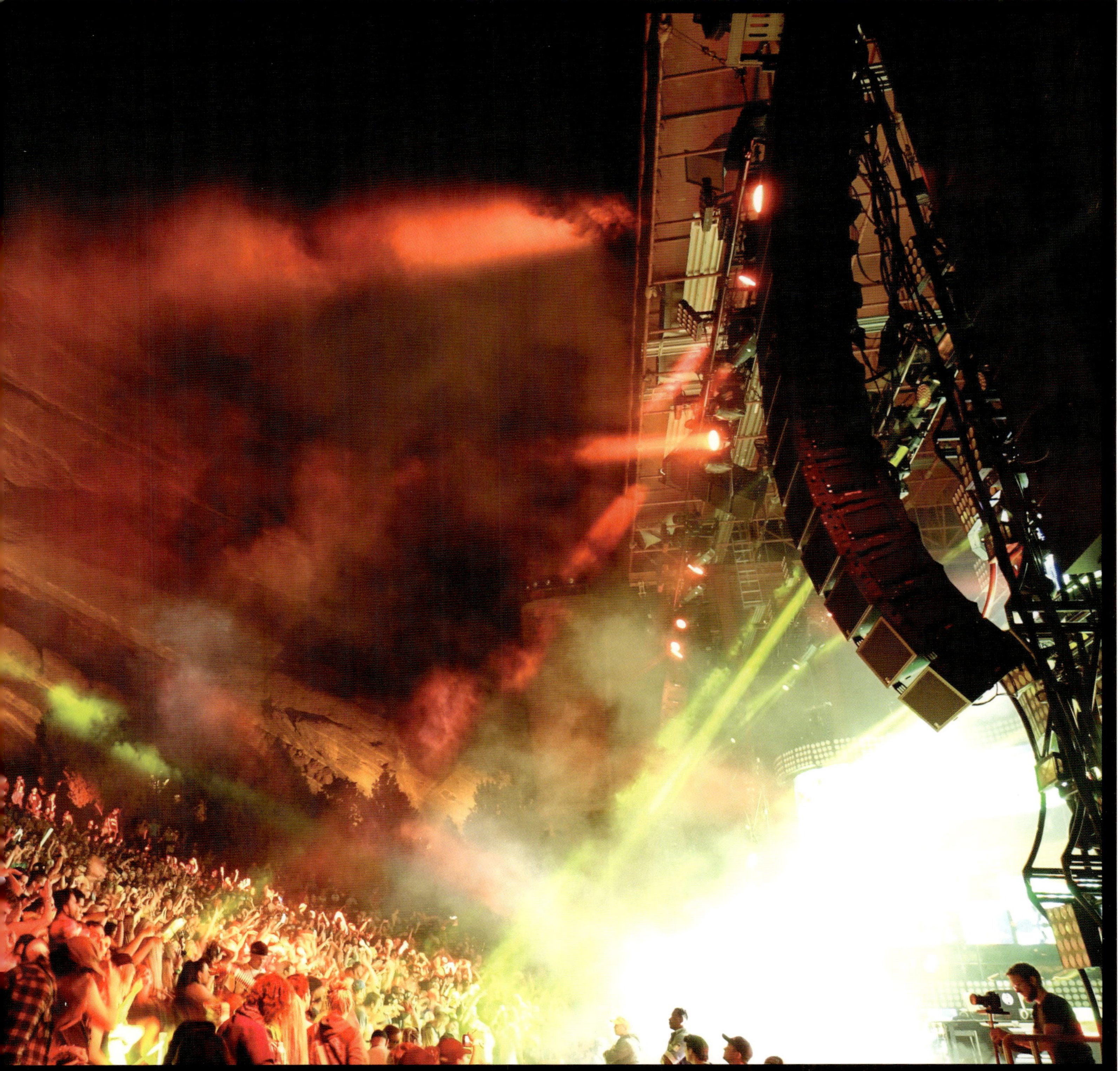

Bassnectar fans at Red Rocks Amphitheatre, 2014

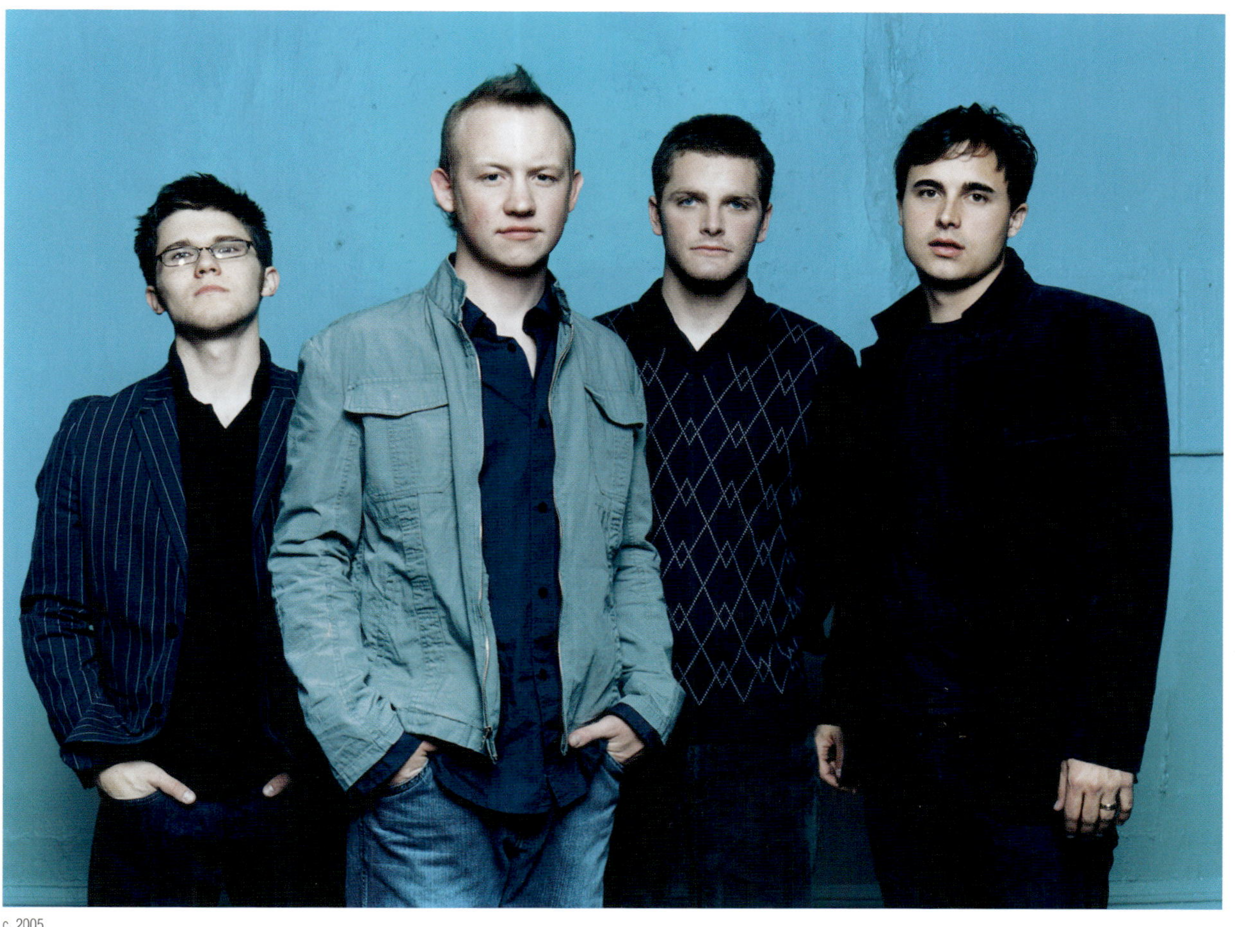

c. 2005

THE FRAY }

NO COLORADO band has had a more astounding trajectory into rock's galaxy of stars than the Fray. In two years, the affable group of churchmates went from playing gigs for mostly friends and family to commanding international attention, becoming one of the most successful and visible acts Colorado had ever produced.

In the early 2000s, singer Isaac Slade was a student at the University of Colorado-Denver, working as a barista at Starbucks.

"When I was ready to jump into college, my parents were trying to convince me that I should not follow my dad's footsteps and go into engineering, that I should really do music because they saw it made me come alive," Slade said. "And I was telling them, 'I don't know if it's a smart idea, I need a backup plan...'

"I saw that CU-Denver offered music business courses. I got a combination degree of business, studio and performance."

Although he couldn't have known it at the time, the seeds for what would become the Fray had been planted before college. He and guitarist Joe King had both attended Faith Christian Academy in Arvada, Colorado, where they rarely spoke to each other.

"I was the math nerd, and he was the soccer player," Slade explained. "For some reason we both sang in choir. After high school, we lived in the same neighborhood and didn't even know it."

During a chance encounter at a local music store, they realized they were kindred spirits. Each had been playing predominantly Christian music, and both wanted to write songs that were less pious and touched more on interpersonal issues. Slade set about peppering his lyrics with secular themes of redemption and hope.

"I had played one show outside of a Christian circle, at my Starbucks," Slade recalled. "The customers were complaining to the manager because all my songs were heavy spiritual songs. She came up to me and said, 'Could you make these less…God-ish?' I went home and threw away all my songs and tried to write about my life."

Slade took his new songs to a music conference at Estes Park called Praise in the Rockies. "My buddy got me into an open mic. I said, 'This song is called "Vienna."' The chorus is, 'There's really no way to reach me/'Cause I'm already gone'—it's about a tragic relationship with a girl I had broken up with. Everybody clapped, and then the three panelists looked at me and sighed, and one of them said, 'Y'know, Isaac, it's a good song, but it's just not true. There really is a way to reach you, and that's Jesus.' I thought he was going to start laughing, and he didn't, and everybody else in the crowd nodded along like that was a good point.

"And in a flash, I felt like a jerk in the confines of the Christian market. There are plenty of good people in it, but the framework was just not working for me. I had to get out as fast as I could and join the regular music scene and stay there for the rest of my life."

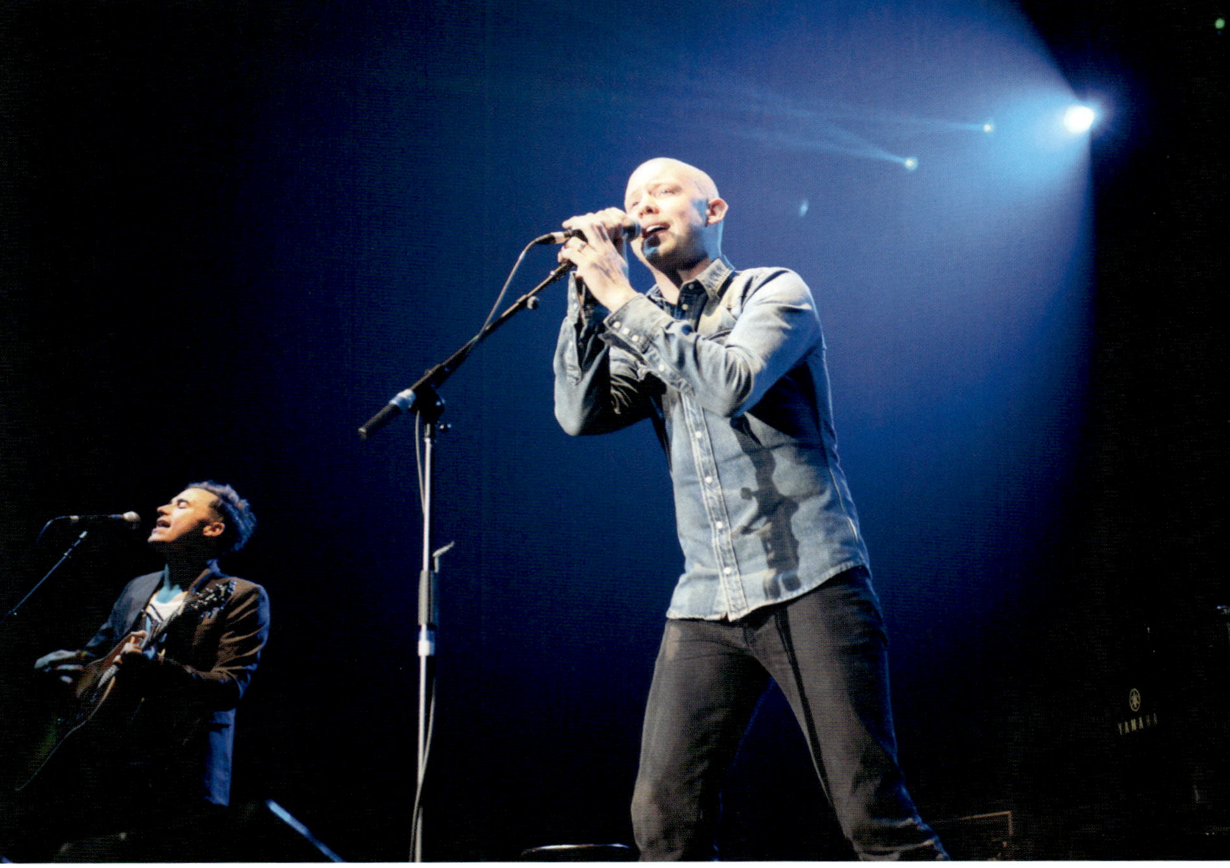

At 1stBank Center, October 27, 2013

Slade and King eventually picked up drummer Ben Wysocki and guitarist Dave Welsh. "Ironically, they were both in my high school band Ember at certain points," Slade noted. "We broke up because we sucked—we prayed way more than we practiced."

Playing sparsely attended gigs along the Front Range, the Fray started earning buzz in a hurry. The crew at Boulder's Fox Theatre booked the group as a headliner, and the quartet earned Best New Band honors from Denver's *Westword* alternative newsweekly in 2004. Area FM station KTCL jumped on the demo of a song called "Cable Car." In a short time, Epic Records came calling, and the quartet signed a major label deal on stage at the Fox.

"We were either getting the chance of a lifetime or dooming our career with a five-record deal—it was scary," Slade allowed. "The music business model was in transition, but it was still a country club, and you had to get membership. We figured that if we kept writing and kept playing and kept recording, somebody was going to hear it and call us. That was the dream."

"Over My Head (Cable Car)" broke nationally in 2005 and pushed the Fray beyond its Colorado fan base; the piano-driven hook and lofty vocal melody drew comparisons to Coldplay. The single was certified double platinum, selling more than two million digital downloads. Slade wrote the

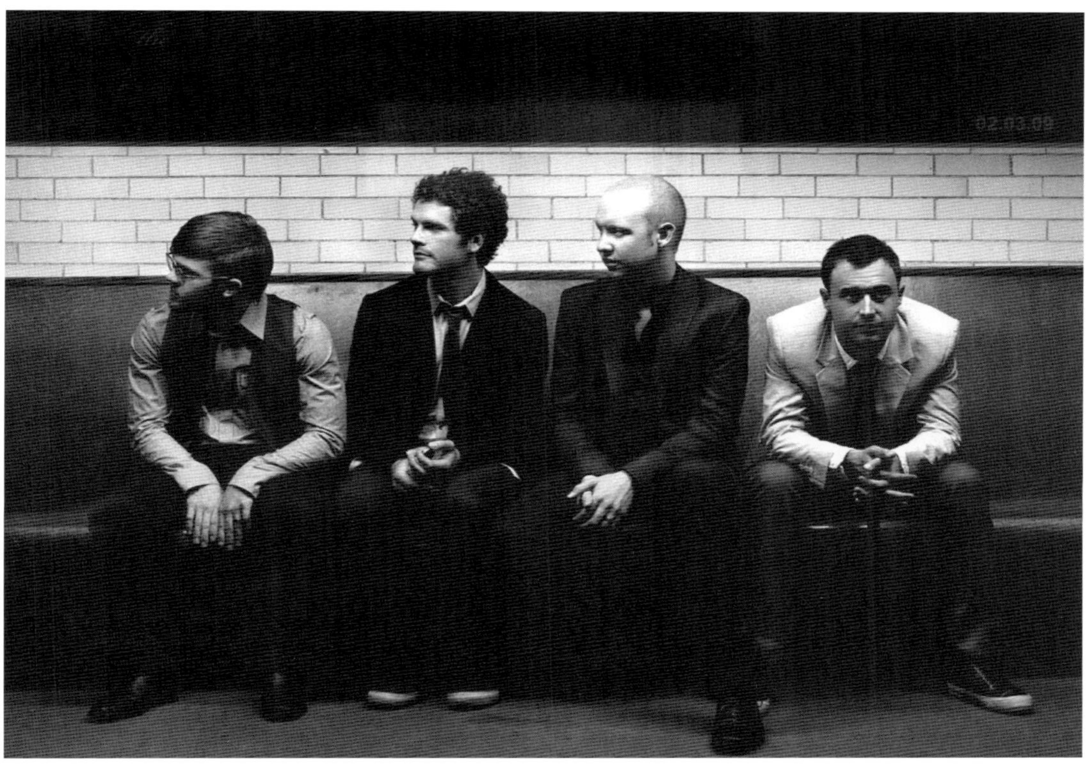

c. 2009

song about a disagreement he had with his brother.

"It's not what we were fighting about, but that we weren't talking about it," Slade explained. "Ideally, hit songs are about things you've figured out five years ago—everything's resolved, the dust has settled, and you can stand up in front of people and look like you have it all together. For us, all the songs that were hitting big were the most vulnerable, least comfortable lyrics that really cut to the bone. But it's okay to be honest in front of people. It's what they connect with the most."

The debut CD, *How to Save a Life*, peaked at #14 on the *Billboard* 200 and went on to sell more than two million copies. The melancholy title track tied for the sixth longest-charting single on *Billboard*'s Hot 100, became a VH1 staple and was used to promote the ABC-TV medical drama *Grey's Anatomy*. On the road almost constantly, the Fray was a double Grammy nominee in 2006. Television appearances included *The Tonight Show with Jay Leno*, *The Late Show with David Letterman*, *Late Night with Conan O'Brien* and *Late Late Show with Craig Ferguson*.

"It never felt like we were one in a million," Slade said. "We were just trying to navigate the road in front of our car."

Debuting with so much success caused high expectations for future releases. In 2009, *The Fray* sold more than 500,000 copies, with the hit "You Found Me" becoming the band's third single to top two million digital downloads; the band was an opener for a leg of U2's 360° tour. *Scars & Stories*, the band's third studio album, was a departure from its contemplative style, recorded with Grammy-winning producer Brendan O'Brien (known for his rock-oriented work with Bruce Springsteen, Pearl Jam and Rage Against the Machine). 2014's *Helios* marked the band's first time working with fellow Colorado musician Ryan Tedder of OneRepublic, who wrote and produced "Love Don't Die," which peaked at #60 on *Billboard*'s Hot 100 chart.

The Fray weathered a number of storms to create artistically true but commercially viable work.

"I tend to live in the future in my mind," Slade said. "I hope we have what it takes to be the next stadium band from our generation, but I don't know if we do, honestly. I wonder if we're missing something in the pandering to the commercial side, where we're a little afraid to say no—we as a generation are a little afraid not to play the game. It's all about focusing on quality and letting that define your success. So whether we're playing to 300 people or 30,000 people, if the four of us aren't proud of these songs, it's going to feel just as soulless as doing karaoke tracks." ●

DRESSY BESSY }

NAMED AFTER the popular learn-to-dress kiddie doll, Dressy Bessy built a sizable cult following in the U.S. and internationally with a sugary 1960s retro-pop style—fuzzed-out twin guitars, delicious melodies and jangling tambourines. Tammy Ealom had the perfect voice for the Denver group's cartoonish charm, and her playful sense of fashion and love of bold-colored vintage outfits (high-mod miniskirts, Day-Glo tights, go-go boots) saturated the act's art.

Ealon lived in various places while her father was in the military before he retired to Colorado Springs in 1984. She moved to Denver in the mid-1990s and began singing backup with the band 40th Day before boyfriend John Hill bought her a guitar. Hill was learning his chops playing in the Apples in Stereo, the Denver area's premier pop act.

"John taught me some chords and showed me how to use his four-track cassette recorder. I began writing songs and trying to find musicians who would let me boss them around a little bit," Ealom said with a chuckle.

She recruited drummer Darren Albert and his friend, bassist Rob Greene. Hill joined around the time they started recording, moonlighting in Dressy Bessy while handling guitar duties for the Apples in Stereo. The band was singed to the Kindercore indie label and had two songs used in the feature film *But I'm a Cheerleader*.

For 2003's *Dressy Bessy*, the members got out of their Denver basement and traveled to a New York recording studio, retaining the hooks and simple approach but adding a harder sound.

"It's hard to go hi-fi when you're recording your own records, and I'm into cute, colorful things visually, so we got lumped into that late-'90s bubblegum-pop genre," Ealom said. "But we've always said we're a rock band first and foremost. Before, we had always recorded ourselves—we'd overdub everything and constantly be second-guessing each other and adding things. But this time, we were able to go in rehearsed and go at things live."

The record got a great response from critics, with reviews in *Rolling Stone* and *Entertainment Weekly*, and it was in the Top 10 for weeks at college radio. The band also performed on *Last Call with Carson Daly*. In 2005, the players issued *Electrified*, which caught people's attention when the album received high praise from National Public Radio rock critic Ken Tucker, who proclaimed it a "far more efficient pleasure machine" than Coldplay's massively advertised *X&Y*. The unexpected boost led to a high-profile performance on *Late Night with Conan O'Brien*. 2008's *Holler and Stomp* followed, but it was through extensive tours beyond the Mile High City's borders that Dressy Bessy gained wider exposure and new fans.

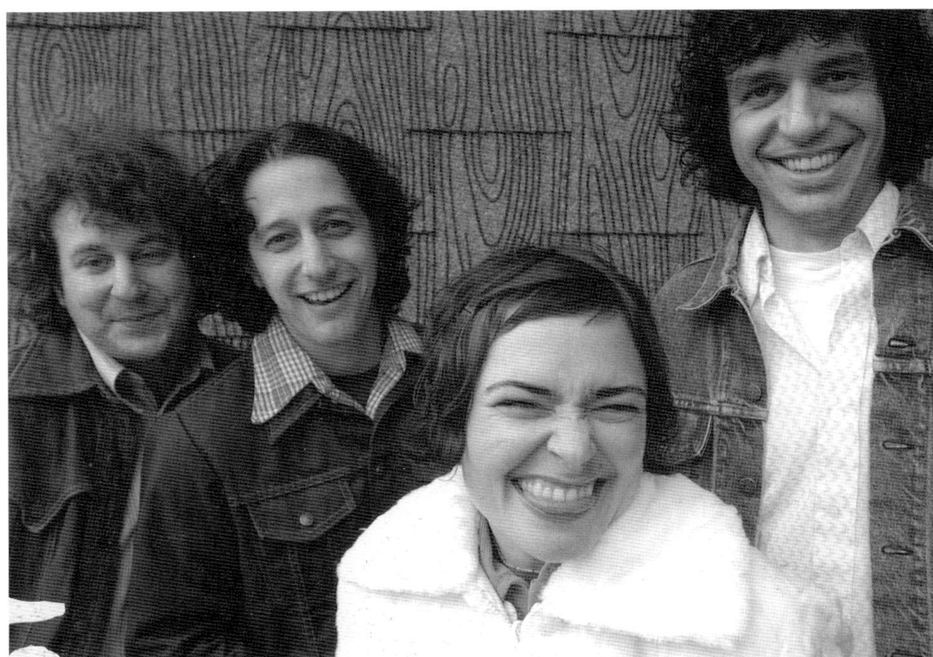

c. 2003

"I've always hated the term 'local band' because you're treated differently by club owners," Ealom said. "Not so much that they look down on you, but it's hard to get attention over touring bands because they think you're always available.

"It's not so much like that for us anymore. We're just a band that happens to love living in Denver. The music scene isn't the reason—not to take anything away from other bands, but I don't know that Denver is the next Seattle. It's not anything in the water or the altitude. It's just a nice place to lie low and live cheaply." ●

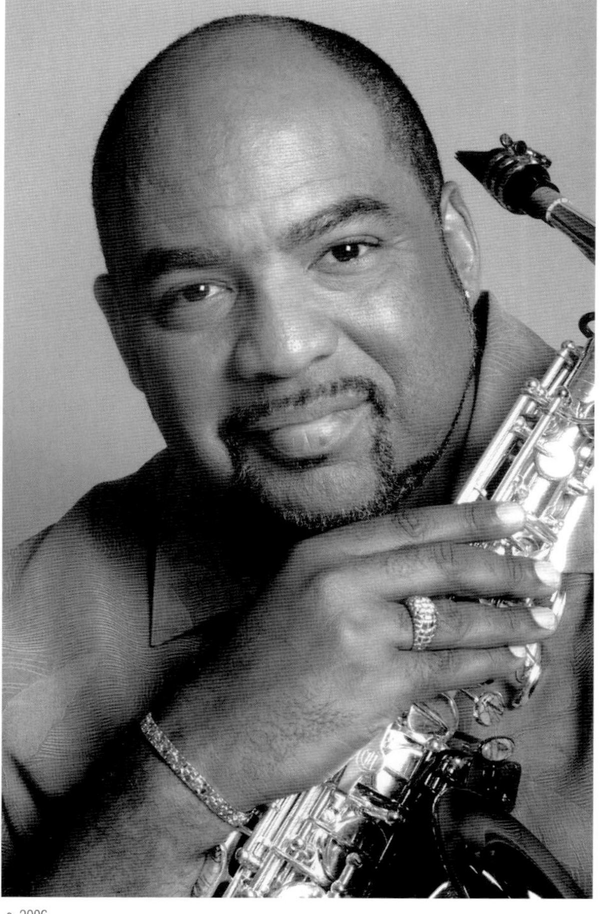

c. 2006

GERALD ALBRIGHT }

LOS ANGELES native Gerald Albright ranked among the most revered performers in jazz and R&B instrumental music. The saxophone master became a highly requested studio musician during the 1980s, assisting noted artists ranging from Anita Baker to Whitney Houston, and he toured with Phil Collins and Quincy Jones. When he wasn't maintaining a busy schedule as a session player, he recorded numerous successful solo albums; his versatility resulted in a stellar reputation for improvisational skills and soulful creativity.

Since 2005, Albright lived in Castle Pines, Colorado. "It was a step out in faith," Albright said. "Up until the move I'd always lived in California—born in Hollywood, raised in South Central L.A.—but a lot of negatives were developing. In our travels my wife and I finally came to Colorado. I was performing a benefit fundraiser, and one of the perks was staying a couple of extra days. A realtor took us around; we saw 25 homes and some golf courses in two days. Before we flew back to L.A., we saw the house we're in now. We walked in and it felt so good, we moved 45 days later."

Inspired by his relocation, Albright's *New Beginnings* reached the Top 5 on *Billboard*'s Jazz Albums chart, topped *Billboard*'s Heatseekers Albums chart and received a Grammy Award nomination. Photographer Carl Studna captured the mountains of Colorado on the CD cover artwork.

"I'm one of those transparent guys—I try to make the music mirror where I am in my life at that given point in time, and *New Beginnings* was reflective directly of my move to Colorado," Albright said. "It's hard to put a finger on it, but I do know I had a different feeling living here, and when I started to create the music, it came out with a different flavor, a different overtone to it, than the CDs I recorded and released in California. Even though I'm known to be a high-energy player, even the funkier stuff came out with a more relaxed, smoother overtone to it."

Albright continued to self-produce tracks in his home studio, and his solo recordings *Sax for Stax*, *Pushing the Envelope* and *Slam Dunk* also received Grammy Award nominations.

"Living in Colorado is conducive to songwriting," Albright said. "The pace is a little slower, the air's a little cleaner. Everybody's happy to be here, closer to nature, and you never get tired of the scenery. You wake up in the morning and you look out the window and you go, 'Wow, man—God really knows how to put it together!'" ●

DEVOTCHKA }

TAKE UNORTHODOX instrumentation—sousaphone, trumpet, violin, accordion, clarinet, guitars and percussion. Liberally season with varied influences—traditional Eastern European dance, Argentine tango, Spaghetti Western instrumentals, Mexican folk, American roots music and angular post-punk. Top off with a crooning tenor—equal parts flamboyant lounge singer and sensual balladeer.

For Devotchka, this unique recipe made for an indie-rock strain not normally associated with Colorado's musical climate.

"People are taken aback when we say we're from Denver," singer and guitarist Nick Urata said. "But I don't think geographical stereotypes hold true anymore."

After Urata's Chicago-based alt-country band failed to gain a following, he set out for the Denver/Boulder area in 1997 and formed Devotchka (from the Nadsat vocabulary of *A Clockwork Orange*, meaning "young woman").

"Boulder is one of those places you end up because you have friends there," Urata said. "In my mind, I had laid out the fantasy of what I wanted Devotchka to be. I had a bunch of songs written, and I had an open door policy—anyone who wanted to work on them with me was welcome. I would con friends from the music school into coming over and playing. That became Devotchka's first album.

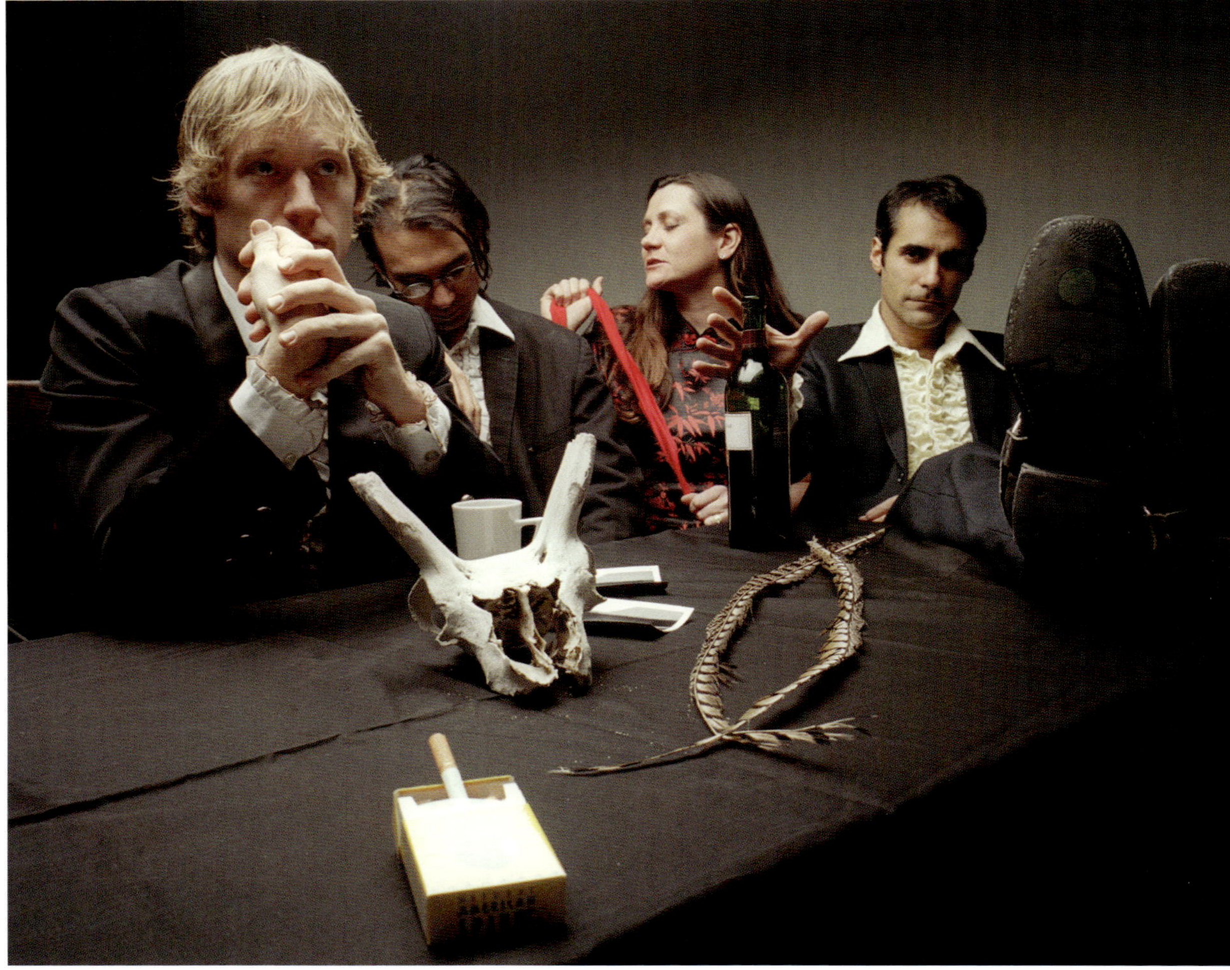

c. 2006

"I had a lot of people move on and not stay in the camp. With persistence, I found three other like-minded individuals who wanted to make a life out of it."

Devotchka—Urata, who sang and played theremin, guitar, bouzouki, piano and trumpet; Tom Hagerman, who played violin, accordion and piano; Jeanie Schroder, who sang and played sousaphone and double bass; and Shawn King, who played percussion and trumpet—released its own records and toured on its own dime.

The band promoted its *Una Volta* album in 2004 by accompanying burlesque queen Dita Von Teese.

"At the time, the art of the tongue-in-cheek striptease was being revived," Urata said. "We were developing our sound, and we were drafted as the pit orchestra for these variety shows. It was a big break for us, and very inspiring—it made us devour some vintage sounds, and we had to play more instruments."

The members were continually flirting with poverty, as record labels deemed their circus of styles unmarketable.

"It's almost a form of insanity," Urata admitted. "You get knocked down, and you just pick yourself up and keep going. Everybody has that one path that they're supposed to go on. I couldn't stop. I had no choice in the matter."

Urata braided the band's sensibilities into a sound that was haunting, sweeping, ecstatic and romantic. "How It Ends," the title track of an album released in 2004, introduced the band to a wider audience when it was used in the trailer for the motion picture *Everything Is Illuminated*.

"As a songwriter, I've sat down at my little desk a thousand times and come up with crap, but that one wrote itself for me," Urata said. "In that way, 'How It Ends' is very special. That's why I shy away from taking any personal credit for this work. I think it's borrowed from the universe and the collective consciousness."

"How It Ends" left its impression. Devotchka was asked to compose and perform the majority of the music for *Little Miss Sunshine*, a 2006 indie film that became the surprise hit of the year, garnering four Academy Award nominations. Devotchka was nominated for a 2006 Grammy Award for Best Compilation Soundtrack Album.

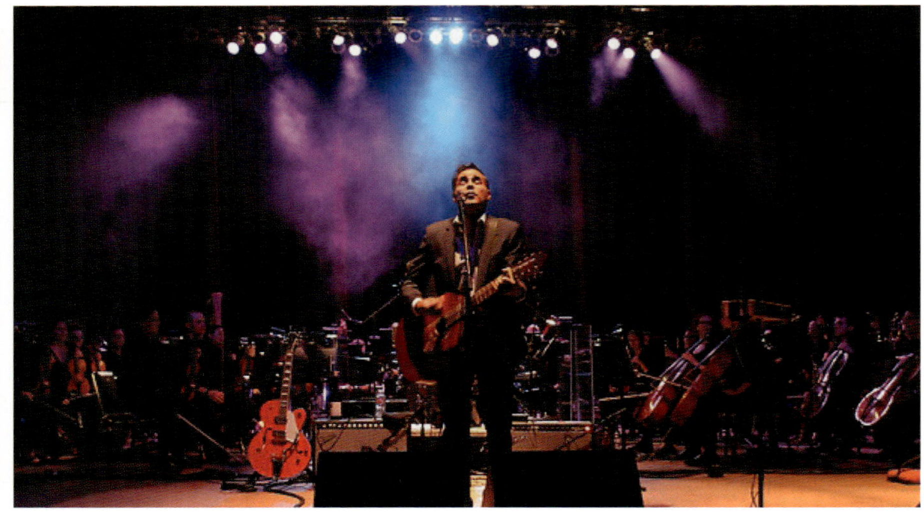

With the Colorado Symphony Orchestra, Red Rocks Amphitheatre, June 14, 2013

"It wasn't a backdoor management deal, it was a pure stroke of fate for this band," Urata said. "The husband-and-wife team of Jonathan Dayton and Valerie Faris directed some cool music videos of the 1990s—we grew up watching their videos for the Smashing Pumpkins and Red Hot Chili Peppers. They were music-conscious, and when they were ready to make their feature film debut, they had the idea to have a band do the score. When they were lying around one Saturday morning, the Los Angeles radio station KCRW played our song 'You Love Me'—which is a miracle in itself, because we didn't get much radio airplay. They called up, asked who it was and got in touch with us, and we hit it off."

With the movie's success and the attention surrounding the soundtrack, Devotchka's sound was suddenly in vogue. The band was later signed to Anti- Records, an imprint known for releasing music from such diverse artists as Tom Waits, Nick Cave and Billy Bragg. In 2008, Devotchka's album *A Mad & Faithful Telling* reached #9 on the *Billboard* Heatseekers chart and #29 on the Top Independent Albums chart. 2011's *100 Lovers* peaked at #74 on the *Billboard* 200.

Devotchka had also built a reputation for manic, extravagant live shows, often featuring belly dancers and trapeze artists, and the band's notoriety was buoyed by acclaimed appearances at Coachella, Bonnaroo and various festivals across the country. Sharing the spotlight with sixty musicians, the members turned a February 2012 performance into a live album, *Devotchka Live with the Colorado Symphony Orchestra*.

Urata flew solo to compose the soundtrack for the Jim Carrey movie *I Love You, Phillip Morris*, and his phone rang with other offers. He juggled his time between Devotchka's career and writing music for several films, including *Crazy, Stupid, Love* and *Ruby Sparks*. He scored the 2014 films *Paddington* and *The Cobbler*, and the 2015 crime romance *Focus*.

"I've always been in love with film music—early on, it opened up my heart and my mind," Urata said. "In the back of my mind, I've aspired to this. I take it very seriously. I thought I would be in a room with a grand piano watching a film and composing whatever I wanted. But that's not the case! It's a moving target, and it's subject to committee, but in the end I can't get enough of it." ●

ROSE HILL DRIVE }

THE BOYS in Rose Hill Drive grew up fostering a style of hard-driving classic rock influences—and wound up opening for the Who and Van Halen.

Brothers Daniel Sproul (guitar and backup vocals) and Jacob Sproul (bass guitar, vocals) and childhood friend Nate Barnes (drums) spent hours practicing in the basement of the Sprouls' house on Rose Hill Drive in Boulder's University Hill neighborhood. Set in the laid-back college town, it made their heavy power-trio riffage all the more surprising.

"Jake and I were making music together since elementary school," Daniel Sproul said. "My dad was always passionate about music, and we got into it just being around electric guitars and a stereo."

"During high school, we would play every day after classes, and I'd sleep over every weekend so we could jam," Barnes added.

The young players were blessed with virtuosity beyond their years, and Jake Sproul's soaring tenor and Daniel Sproul's searing solos were hailed as a throwback to the heyday of Cream and Led Zeppelin. They found day jobs around town and played as many shows as they could, then headed out on the road, where Rose Hill Drive ascended relatively quickly, performing with the Black Crowes, Wilco, Queens of the Stone Age and Aerosmith, among others, and also at the Bonnaroo, Wakarusa and Austin City Limits music festivals and on the Warped Tour.

"The record industry was slowly crashing, and we rode that wave perfectly—it kept us jamming on the road," Jake Sproul said.

Despite interest from several major labels, there had been no full-length album release. Brendan O'Brien, the producer and creative consultant who had worked with a long list of heavyweights (Pearl Jam, Red Hot Chili Peppers, Bruce Springsteen), signed on to do Rose Hill Drive's first album after the band played a private showcase. But the members did the unexpected—they shelved the project. With engineer Nick DiDia, Rose Hill Drive went back into the studio and recorded its self-titled debut album, released in 2006 on Megaforce Records. *Rose Hill Drive* debuted at No. 1 on *Billboard*'s regional Heatseekers (Mountain) chart for up-and-coming artists.

While on tour in support of the album, the group played the same stage as the Who at the Hyde Park Calling Festival in London and attracted the attention of legendary guitarist Pete Townshend. Rose Hill Drive supported the Who on select U.S. and European dates, and Townshend invited the band onto his weekly internet talk show called "In the Attic." The group was named one of the "10 New Artists to Watch" in 2007 in *Rolling Stone* magazine.

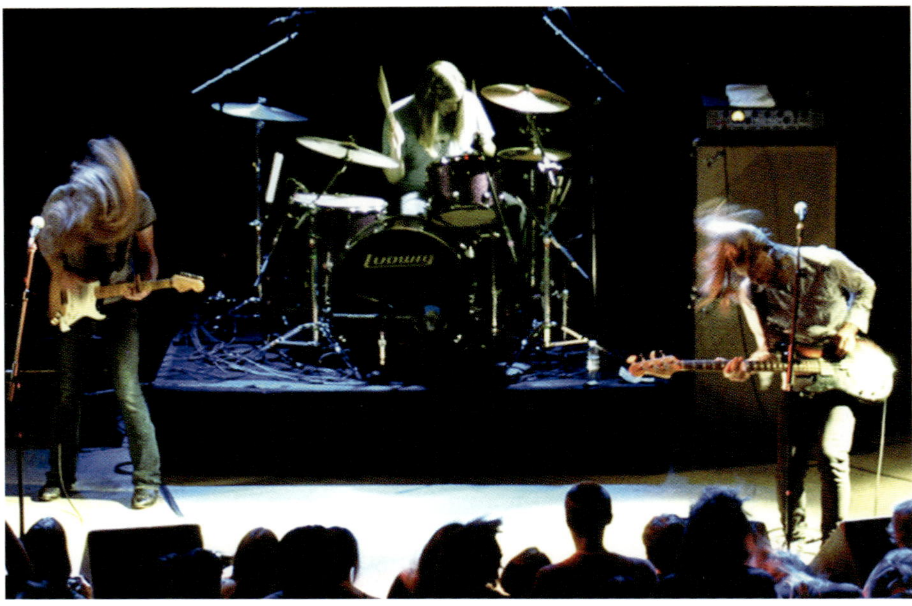

c. 2007

Rose Hill Drive returned to Boulder to write and record a second album, *Moon Is the New Earth*. It positioned the band as an innovator in the revival of traditional blues-rock and psychedelic metal, and the song "Sneak Out" appeared in the popular music video game "Guitar Hero 5." But the tight-knit trio took a hiatus and almost broke up.

"We'd been in close quarters for ten years together," Barnes said. "We had a desire to try something new and different. We got to a point where we all needed to go do our own thing for a while."

The band then added bass player Jimmy Stofer and became a two-guitar quartet, recording a third album in Boulder. *Americana* fizzled. "It was more keyboard and vocal oriented," Barnes said. "We'd have changed the name of the band if it wasn't already established."

After a fast start, Rose Hill Drive couldn't hold on.

"I thought that we were going to be the biggest thing ever and people had to recognize it—and it's just not like that," Daniel Sproul said. "I don't think that realization would have been easy when I was eighteen." ●

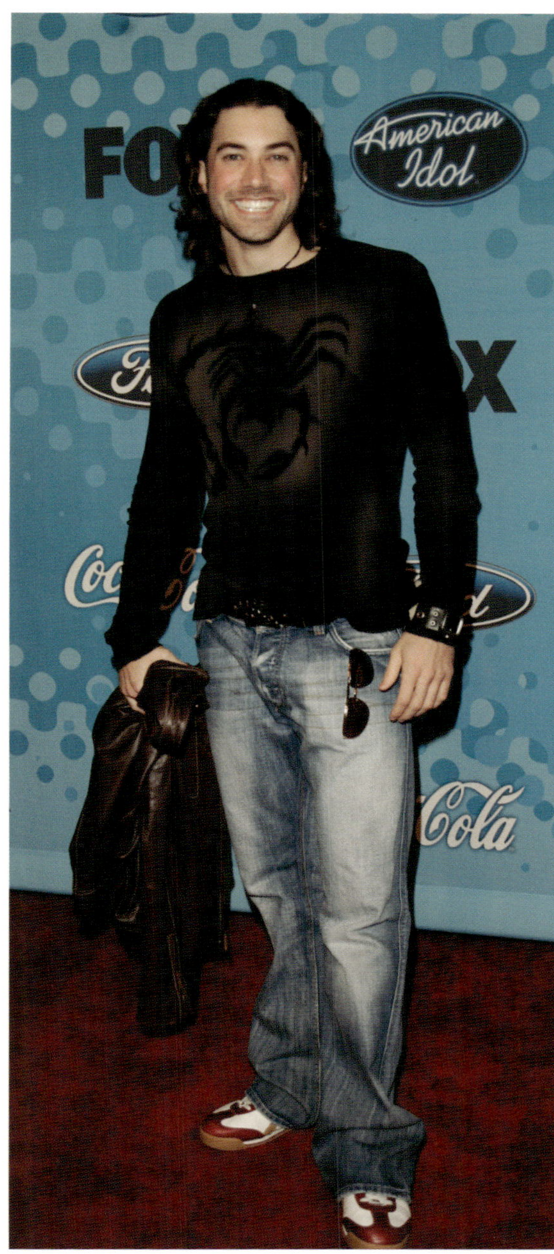

Young on *American Idol*, c. 2006

ACE YOUNG }

IN THE mid-2000s, reality television shows—from dating competitions to survival contests—changed the landscape of broadcast television and dominated prime time. "Reality TV" was not to be confused with reality—the patter was scripted, the action carefully choreographed—but on the talent show *American Idol*, ultimately contestants did have to perform. And America went crazy for it. *American Idol* became a ratings behemoth, and the program's unique ability to market its contestants to millions of viewers weekly created a new business model for the music industry.

Ace Young, who grew up in Boulder, Colorado, came to national recognition during the fifth season of *American Idol*. He attended voice lessons and performed at local shopping malls and recreation centers during his youth. After his high school graduation, he moved to Los Angeles; he eventually met Brian McKnight and got a chance to make his mark as McKnight's opening act.

American Idol was auditioning for contestants, but the Los Angeles area auditions were finished. The final audition was in Denver, so Young jumped on a plane. More than 14,000 contestants showed up at Invesco Field at Mile High to try out. Young sang a rendition of Westlife's "Swear It Again" and was unanimously passed on to the next round. The long-locked Boulder boy had the virtues of a serious *Idol* contender, a sensitive heartthrob who could hit high notes. A Top 10 contestant, he won over swooning fans, but in April 2006, the sixth week of the finals, Young was eliminated from the competition, finishing in seventh place.

"They loved that I was from Colorado," Young said. "But they didn't want to say on the show that I'd been in L.A. for a few years at that point, that I'd done anything musically. They asked me all the questions, they had all the footage—they just never showed it. I learned they can make the story whatever they want."

During his *Idol* experience, Young had befriended fellow finalist Chris Daughtry, whom he met at the Denver audition; the two lived in the same apartment complex during the show's runtime. Young helped write the chorus to Daughtry's debut single, the international smash "It's Not Over," which was among the top ten digital selling songs of 2007. For his songwriting credit, Young was nominated for Best Rock Song for the Grammy Awards.

Young teamed up with veteran songwriter and producer Desmond Child and co-wrote seven of the eleven tracks on his self-titled debut album. *Ace Young* was released in July 2008 and peaked at #160 on the *Billboard* 200. His single "Addicted" landed at #77 in the *Billboard* Hot 100.

But Young's post-*American Idol* career was largely theater-focused. He made his Broadway debut as Kenickie in the revival of *Grease*, and he played the impish Berger in the recast production of *Hair* alongside fellow *Idol* alumnus Diana DeGarmo; they were married in 2013. Young then starred as Joseph in the national tour of *Joseph and the Amazing Technicolor Dreamcoat* with DeGarmo as the Narrator.

"When I 'made it' on *Idol*, I still hadn't done what I wanted to do, a career in entertainment," Young said. "Every time I'm in New York, I love the food. Every time I'm in Los Angeles, I love working on music. But when I'm in Colorado, I'm home." ●

SINGLE FILE }

THROUGH HARD work, unswerving dedication and frontman Sloan Anderson's cheeky charm, the likable power-pop punks of Single File drew the attention of a major label before concluding their career.

In the mid-1990s, Anderson (vocals, guitar, bass) and Chris Depew (drums, backing vocals) started playing music together at Mandalay Middle School in Westminster, Colorado. A few years later, while attending Standley Lake High School, Joe Ginsberg (bass, guitar, piano) joined them, forming a jazz trio.

But they took separate paths after graduation in pursuit of higher education and stable career paths, living in different states. In 2003, Anderson and Ginsberg reunited in Los Angeles; they recorded an EP and then coaxed Depew to join them. Playing pop punk, the three members spent a chunk of their twenties tooling around the nation in a cargo van and trailer.

"We didn't know dick about what we were doing, other than the desire to get out and play for people," Anderson said. "We knew it was a long uphill battle trying to learn the ropes without having a mentor or outside figure. Once we finally discovered marketing on MySpace, we'd have fans bring us non-perishable canned goods and Top Ramen—that's what we lived off of for the first two years of touring. We'd give them free merchandise, but we spent every penny we had keeping the gas tank full."

Single File self-recorded and distributed two more EPs and scored a spot on MySpace's Top 10 Unsigned Bands chart, which led to a gig on the Vans Warped Tour in summer 2006. The threesome had moved back to the Denver area and recorded an album with producer Ed Rose that was eventually shelved. But one song was made public on the band's MySpace page—"Zombies Ate My Neighbors," inspired by a Super Nintendo video game of the same name Anderson played as a child.

"We had the music written for a long time—Joe came up with this cool guitar part—but I had no idea what I was going to write or sing over it," Anderson said. "The night before we recorded it, the lyrics fell out of the sky. It was one of those divine moments for me—'Thank god we didn't waste all this money in the studio.' It came together and everyone loved it. We knew it was one of our strongest songs and had a fun vibe."

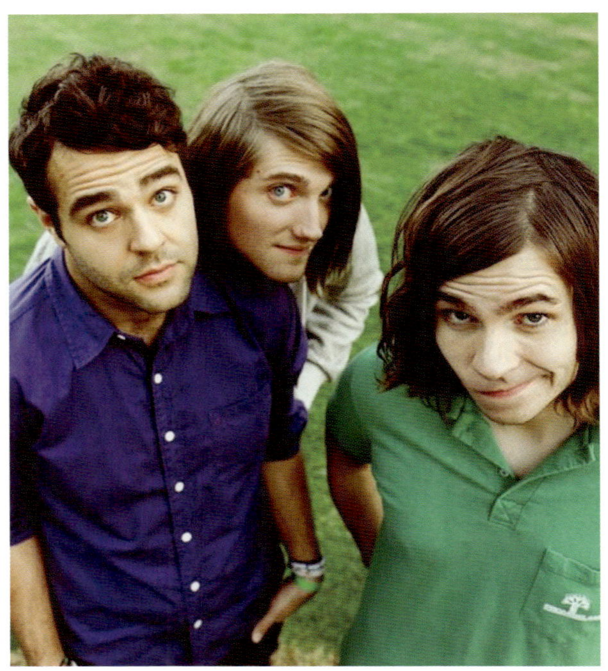

c. 2007

Denver modern rock station KTCL heard "Zombies Ate My Neighbors" and added the pop-punk gem to its rotation. The single became a local smash, and soon Single File was playing packed clubs and theaters across Colorado. Reprise Records got wind of the trio's growing popularity, and the band inked a deal with the label in 2007. *No More Sad Face*, an EP featuring "Zombies Ate My Neighbors," hit #43 on the *Billboard* Top Heatseekers chart.

The band entered the recording studio with famed producer Howard Benson, but capturing the music's potential proved elusive. Finally, Single File's full-length debut, titled *Common Struggles*, was slated for release in April 2009. The lead single, "Girlfriends," was serviced to Denver radio a month early, to show appreciation for the music community's support. The future was bright.

Unfortunately, Reprise then dropped Single File.

"Several songs on that record had been hits in Colorado for months on end, so there was something good going on," Anderson said. "But the label was in serious financial turmoil, and they laid off half their staff and turned their backs on a good majority of their smaller bands. We got kicked to the sidelines—no radio campaign, nothing. It was just heartbreaking to go back to the drawing board." ●

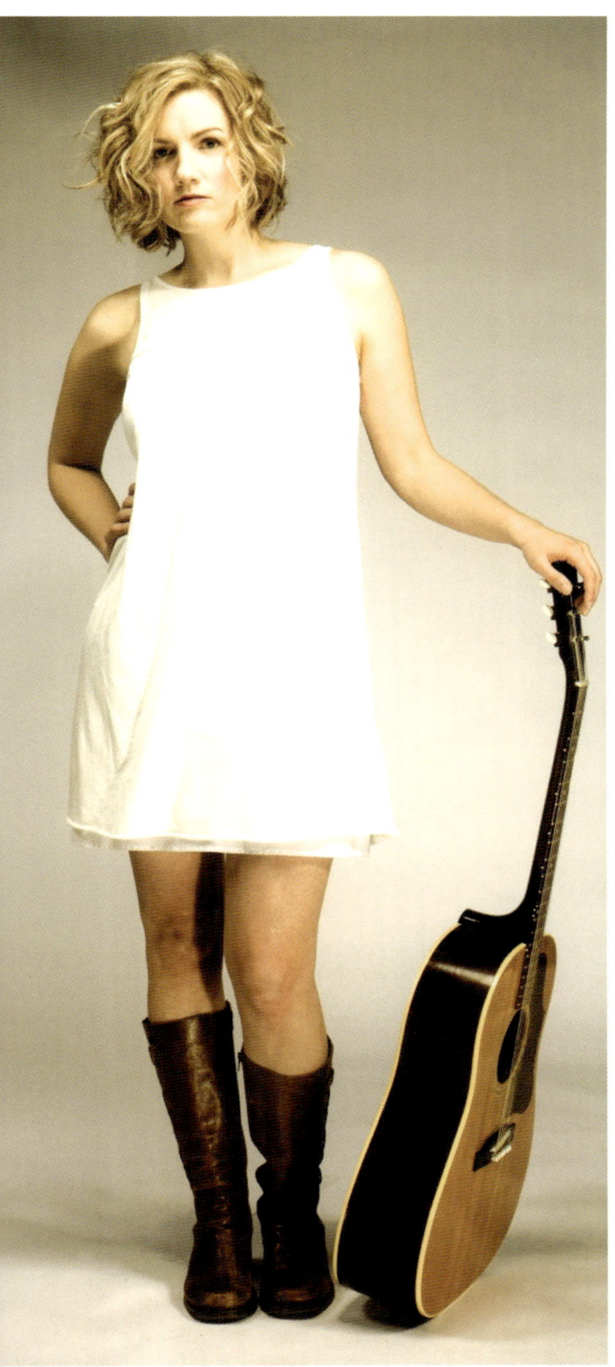

c. 2006

KATIE HERZIG }

AS WELL as her own critically acclaimed albums, Katie Herzig's lovely, confident voice and songs have embellished numerous films and television shows.

Herzig's family hailed from Fort Collins, Colorado, where she attended Rocky Mountain High School. While enrolled at the University of Colorado in Boulder, she formed Newcomers Home with Tim and Laurie Thornton and Andrew Jed in the summer of 1997.

"We were leaders of Young Life, a non-denominational Christian ministry for high schoolers," Herzig said. "We would play in churches and we would also play in bars and coffee shops. For a while, we didn't have to think too hard about it. Then the bigger we got, the more we were socialized to be concerned about being advertised too much as a Christian band, because people wouldn't want to hear us. And it also got harder to play in churches, because we weren't exactly writing worship music. We tried to focus more on being a band that anyone would come to see."

Initially, Herzig suffered from stage fright and confined herself to singing backing vocals and playing percussion. She eventually began to play the guitar and became a lead singer. Over time, Newcomers Home's music became more pop-influenced.

"We were purists in the beginning, wanting to be very acoustic and folky," Herzig said. "We had a large debate on whether or not we should have an electric guitar in our band. Eventually we got more rocked out."

In 2004, Herzig released her first solo album, *Watch Them Fall.*

"At the time, it was a needed outlet for me," Herzig said. "There started to be a lot of extra songs that I wanted to do something with. In the process, I discovered how much fun it was."

Newcomers Home broke up in 2006, leaving Herzig free to pursue her solo career. She released a second album, *Weightless*, which she made using Pro Tools and instruments that she borrowed from friends.

"I recorded over several months in my basement bedroom in Louisville," Herzig explained. "It had to be a solo endeavor—I found that I could do everything on my own."

Herzig collaborated on "Jack and Jill" with veteran singer-songwriter Kim Richey, and two other tracks from the album, "Fool's Gold" and "Sweeter Than This," were featured on the popular television series *Grey's Anatomy*. After the release of *Weightless*, Herzig moved to Nashville and broke into its indie music scene, playing gigs and writing new material. She collaborated with Ruby Amanfu on "Heaven's My Home," which was performed by the Duhks. The song was nominated for a 2007 Grammy award for Best Country Performance.

"It was a rainy day," Herzig recalled. "I had this guitar line in my head, so I kept playing it over and over. Ruby was sick that day and had a stuffed up, groggy voice, so I have some drug companies to thank for the song. There was something about it that felt aged and familiar, like it wasn't written in this decade."

Songs from Herzig's albums *Apple Tree* (2008) and *The Waking Sleep* (2011) were featured in movie trailers and soundtracks, network television programs and commercials; 2014's *Walk Through Walls* peaked at #12 on *Billboard*'s Top Heatseekers chart.

"You have to want it—be persistent and play and play," Herzig said. "If you're doing something that people like, you start to get recognized for it." ●

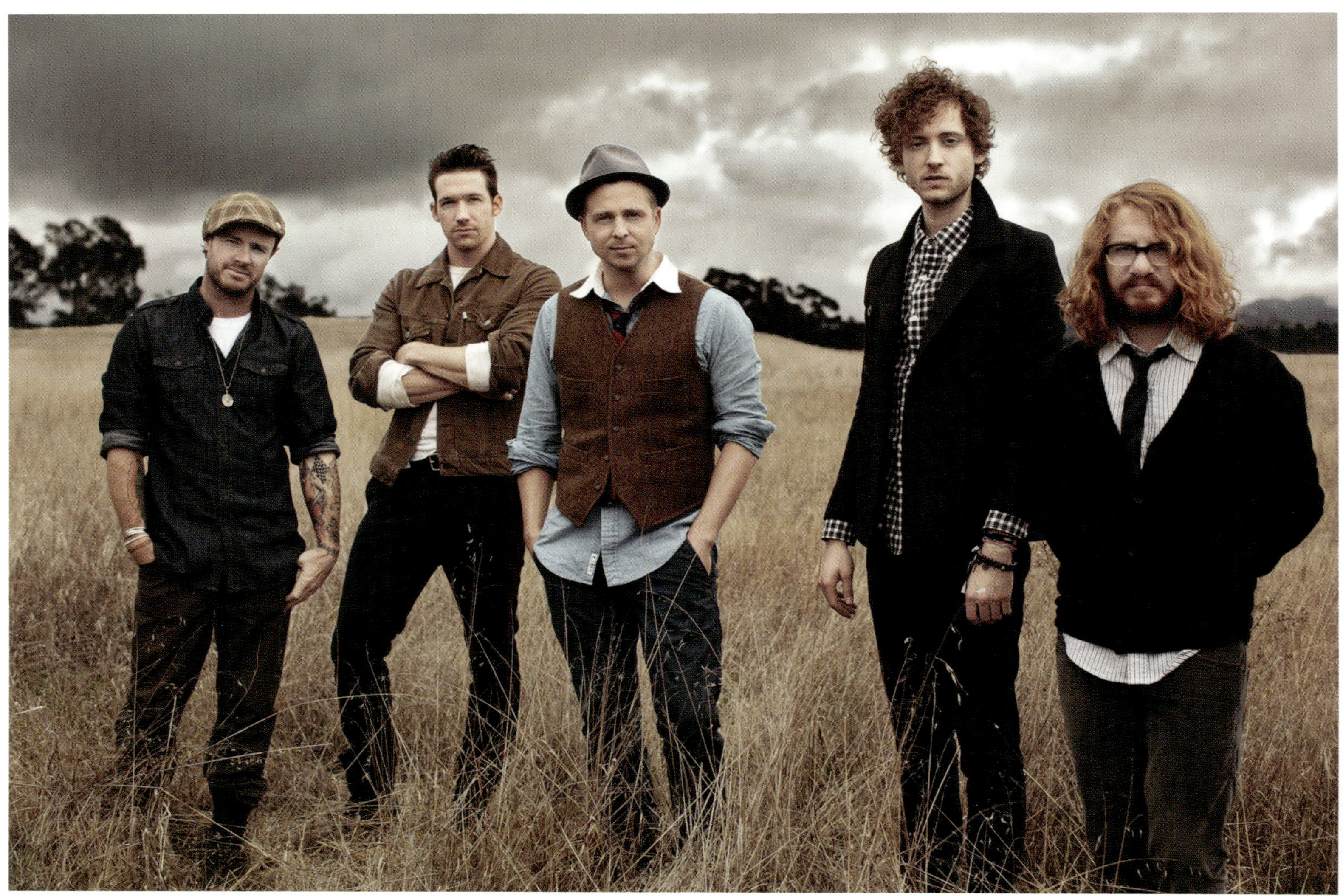

c. 2009

ONEREPUBLIC }

IN THE MUSIC business, the busiest guy of his generation may be Ryan Tedder. The singer-songwriter built a dual career—as frontman for Denver-based OneRepublic, and as a prolific and visible producer of global hits for other pop music superstars.

"My M.O. is not having one style, but taking a 'Swiss Army knife' approach," Tedder said. "No matter what fads come and go, you will always find something to bring to the table."

Growing up in a religious family, Tedder cited his father, Gary, as his earliest musical influence. As a teenager, he had an epiphany that songwriting was the key to a long-term career.

"I was born in Oklahoma, and I bounced between Colorado every summer and holidays because I had over a dozen family members living there," Tedder said. "I thought everybody wrote their own songs—why would anybody sing something they didn't write? Imagine my surprise when I discovered Diane Warren, one of the most prolific songwriters in history. Then I found out Sinatra didn't write his own songs…

"I thought it was an interesting job. I was watching some crappy pop band on TV one day, and I thought, 'Man, I can come up with something this good.' I got my guitar and wrote my first song in two hours."

In his senior year, Tedder

moved to Colorado Springs and became friends with guitarist Zach Filkins at Colorado Springs Christian High School, playing on the soccer team and deciding to start a band. They headed to different colleges; Tedder studied at Oral Roberts University, and Filkins wound up in Illinois.

"I took most of a summer away from college and got an internship at DreamWorks Records in Nashville," Tedder said. "I asked how long it would take to get a record deal or publishing deal—'I've got two and a half months, so if we could squeeze it in that'd be great'—and they just laughed. But I got my feet wet in Nashville. I learned how to write, working with song doctors. It was boot camp, basically. If you want to truly figure out the craft, that's the place to be."

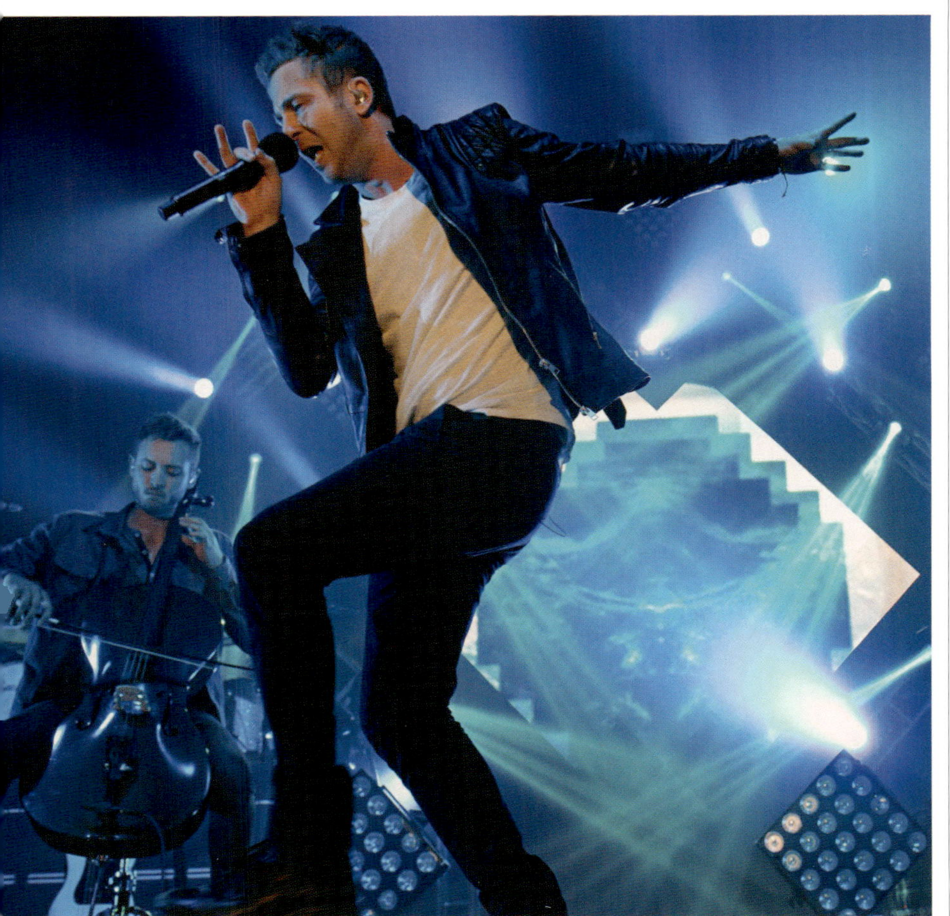

c. 2014

Tedder competed in a singer-songwriter talent search and was selected to perform on MTV. He caught the attention of hip-hop producer Timbaland, who reached out to Tedder a year and a half after the show aired and took him under his wing. Under the alias of Alias, the 21-year-old Tedder started producing tracks.

After two years in studios from New York to Los Angeles to Miami—"like going to college for production"—Tedder's own artistic aspirations took over. He returned to Colorado Springs and reunited with Filkins. They moved to Los Angeles, joined by guitarist Drew Brown (born and raised in Boulder) and drummer Eddie Fisher, eventually adding Brent Kutzle (bass and cello).

The band faced hard times during its five "minor league" years; the members returned from a performance at Coachella to find themselves dropped from their first record deal. Nonetheless, OneRepublic's popularity suddenly started to soar on MySpace, the social networking service.

"In May of 2006, there were only two million people on MySpace, but when I switched our status from signed to unsigned, I saw the immediate reaction of people making comments, and it occurred to me—this is our catalyst," Tedder explained. "I didn't have the next five years to put flyers under people's windshield wipers and hang posters on Sunset Boulevard. That crap doesn't work. We became the No. 1 unsigned band on MySpace. I assigned everybody to take shifts; I was on it eight hours a day, five days a week for a good year and a half, updating and responding. We had every record label coming after us."

When Timbaland launched his Mosley Music Group label with Interscope, he signed OneRepublic as his first rock act. The original version of "Apologize" appeared on *Dreaming Out Loud*, the band's debut album. The remix version, heard on *Timbaland Presents: Shock Value*, was a massive hit internationally, reaching No. 1 in 16 countries; it reigned as the most popular digital download in history. Tedder had written the breakout single in his dad's house in Colorado Springs in 2003.

"For the first time ever, a song I wrote hit me the way those massive songs from growing up did, those all-consuming moments of pop coming off the radio when I was 15," Tedder said. "Every time I listened to the demo, I thought, 'Maybe I'm self-deluded or biased, but if this isn't a hit, then I'll probably never write one, because I don't know how.'"

In 2009, Tedder was honored by ASCAP for writing and producing the two most played singles in Top 40 radio history, Leona Lewis' "Bleeding Love" and OneRepublic's "Apologize." According to Mediabase, which monitors radio stations in North America, "Apologize" racked up 10,331 spins in its biggest week. OneRepublic's second single, "Stop and Stare," also achieved success.

After writing and producing hits for the likes of Beyonce ("Halo"), Kelly Clarkson ("Already Gone") and Jordin Sparks ("Battlefield"), Tedder turned his attention back to OneRepublic. Recorded in Denver, the album *Waking Up* was released in November 2009; the single "All the Right Moves" charted in the Top 10 in several countries and at the #18 spot on the *Billboard* Hot 100.

"I said, 'Guys, if we're going to keep going around the world, we have to camp out in Denver and carve out our own sound,'" Tedder noted. "The first album was Coldplay-like piano-pop. Now you could tell we're a band that loves Brit-pop, that has a thing for movie soundtracks because we have strings riddled through everything, and that uses hip-hop beats."

Tedder did his best to make Denver a go-to destination for pop music production, writing hit songs for his band and other artists from the comfort of his private use studio.

"Los Angeles is a wonderful place, and you go there to be a writer and a performer. But then you get out before it destroys you. I've seen it happen to a lot of people—you completely lose your sense of self. Seeing the Fray guys being able to make their music comfortably from Denver was encouraging for us."

In 2013, *Native*, OneRepublic's third studio album, peaked at #4 on the *Billboard* 200, and "Counting Stars" topped "Apologize" as the band's biggest single, reaching No. 1 in many countries including Canada and the U.K. Tedder continued to work two jobs, as he put it—OneRepublic and dependable producer of major hits. His work on Adele's *21* brought him a Grammy Award for Album of the Year. Tedder had credits on over two dozen charting singles in 2013, from Elie Goulding's "Burn" to Demi Lovato's "Neon Lights." *Billboard* crowned Tedder the songwriter of the year and estimated that he made $2.5 million for his efforts.

Tedder felt the pull between his own multiplatinum band's music and that of his list of flashy music biz clients.

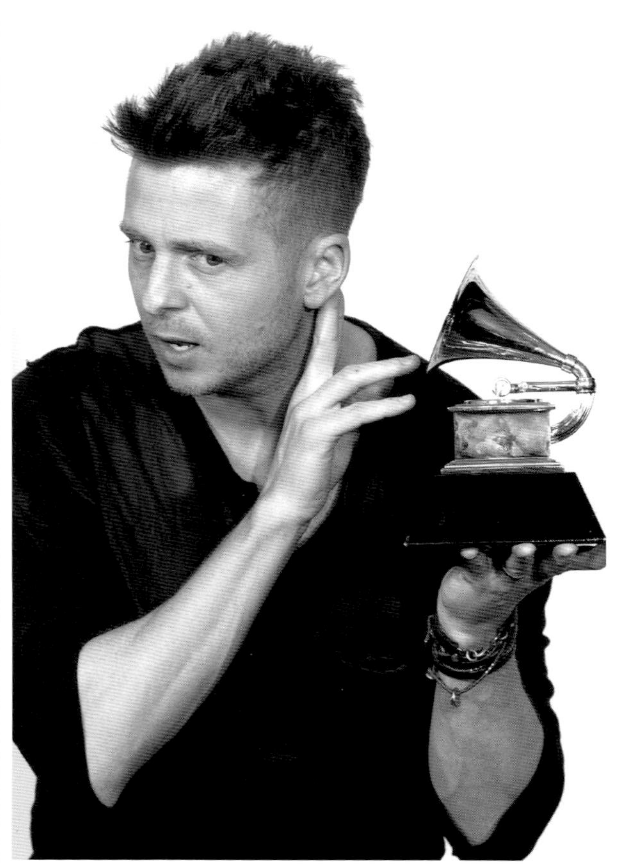

Tedder at the 2012 Grammy Awards

"I could stay in the studio back home in Denver and write songs six days a week, and it would be simpler and more lucrative—and there are days when that sounds appealing," Tedder said. "But that's only part of who I am. I'd be inclined to go that route if I didn't know that OneRepublic has a shot at being one of the biggest bands in the world." ●

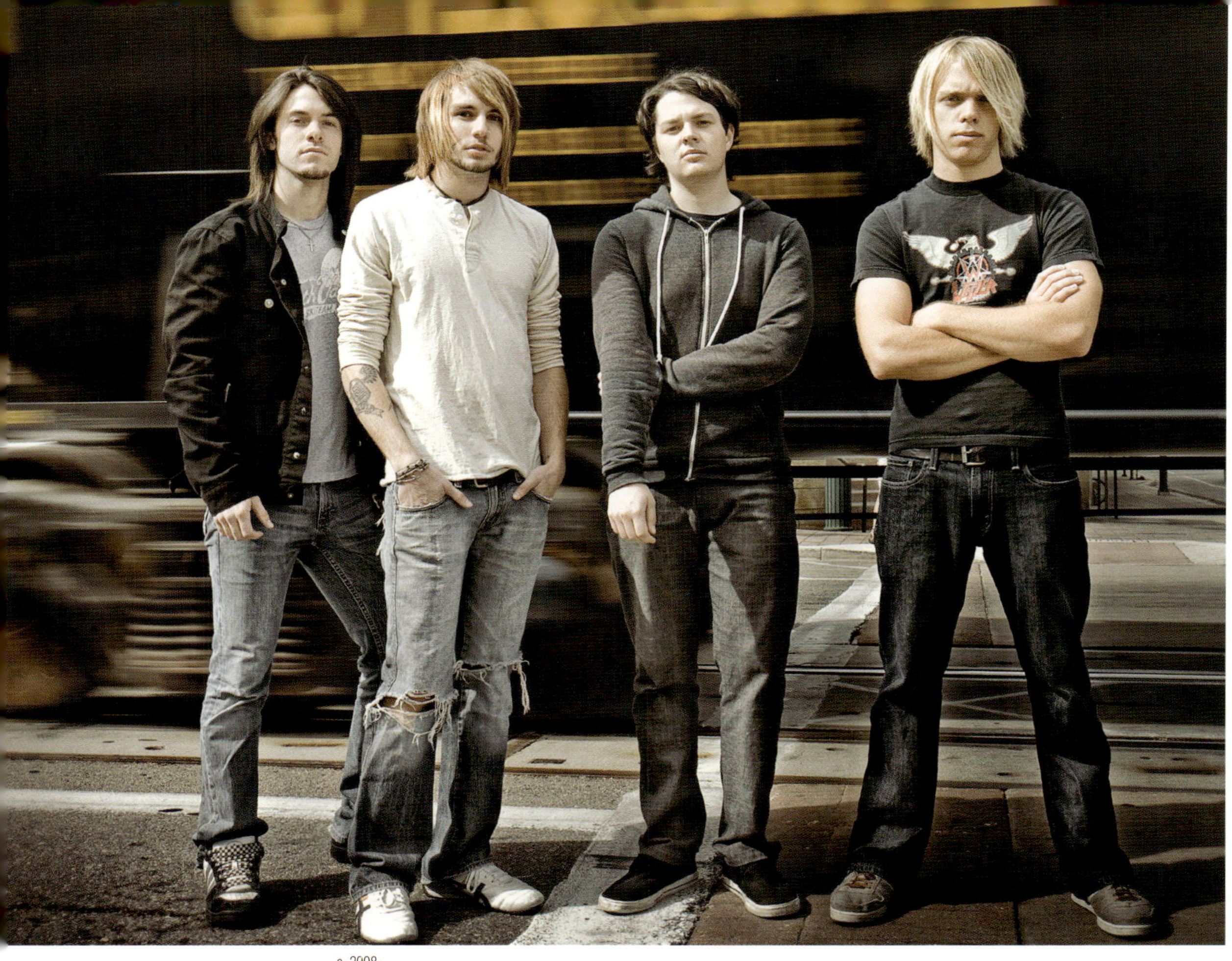

c. 2008

TICKLE ME PINK }

WHEREAS MOST people in their early twenties are told it's the best of times, Tickle Me Pink dealt with the reality of how short life can be.

Formed in Fort Collins in 2005, the pop-punk quartet built a loyal following by playing hundreds of live shows and independently releasing two EPs. Each of the members had considerable musical experience prior to coming together as a group. Singer-guitarist Sean Kennedy had taken lessons for voice and piano as well as training with classical guitarist Dave Beegle. Since the age of 17, bassist Johnny Schou had worked as an assistant engineer at the Blasting Room Studios in Fort Collins.

After making a lot of noise in Colorado, Tickle Me Pink—Kennedy, Schou, drummer Stefan Runstrom and guitarist Steven Beck—broke on Denver alternative rock radio station KTCL with the catchy song "Typical," which drew the attention of the Wind-up Records label. The band recorded *Madeline*, its full-length debut album. Kennedy and Schou wrote the majority of the music, and Kennedy wrote all of the lyrics, which explored mortality, breakups and the trappings of suburbia.

"I was thinking about everything going on in my life," Kennedy said. "I did well in school and got a lot of scholarships, and I chose not to go the college route because we were passionate about our music. I was engaged at 18 and broke that off. My mind was in a darker place. I saw a world around me that I hadn't seen before. Writing lyrics is your voice. If you're not going to state something that doesn't connect with someone, why even do it?"

On the morning of July 1, 2008—the same day of *Madeline*'s release—the 22-year-old Schou was found dead in his bedroom by his bandmates. Kennedy, Runstrom and Beck were left to console one another.

"Johnny and I were best friends," Kennedy said. "We did everything together, and we could have deep, serious conversations about religion and death. When we knew it was going to snow, we'd go to the Blasting Room and get snowed in there—we knew other bands couldn't come in and we wouldn't have to pay for days; we recorded demos and had so much fun.

"He wasn't a junkie. He just slipped up. Everyone loved him. He was a good kid."

Tickle Me Pink had performed just days before at the Vans Warped Tour at Invesco Field and was preparing for a national concert tour and publicity drive for *Madeline*. Joey Barba, a long-time friend, was enlisted to join the band on the road. *Madeline* peaked at #21 on *Billboard*'s Top Heatseekers chart. Tickle Me Pink played its last show in March 2011. ●

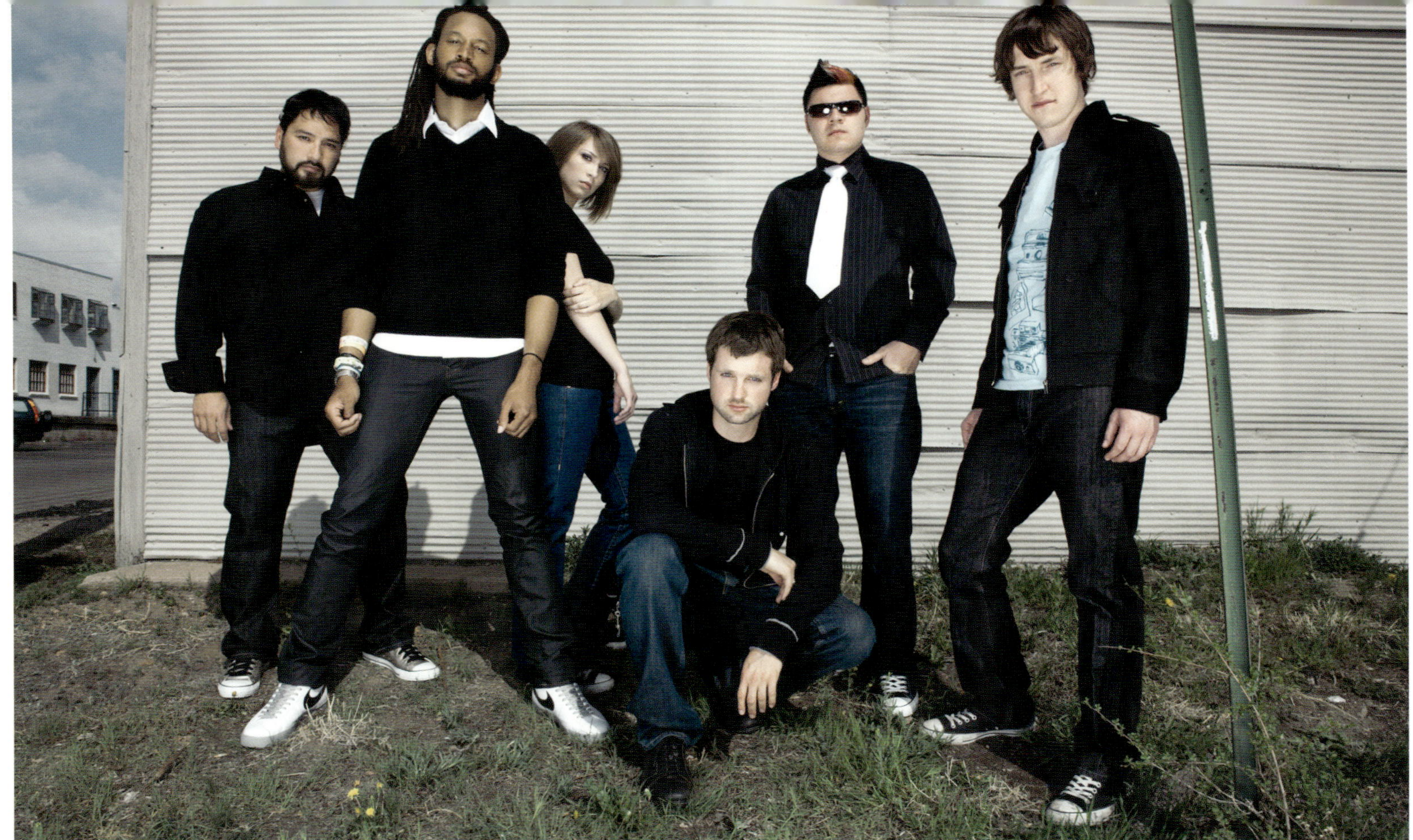

c. 2008

FLOBOTS }

FOUNDED BY Jamie Laurie (a.k.a. Jonny 5), the Denver collective Flobots went from an underground local band to one of the most buzzed-about national acts of 2008.

Laurie formed Flobots with childhood friend Stephen "Brer Rabbit" Brackett; the two emcees began looking for musicians who were politically minded. In 2005, guitarist Andy "Rok" Guerrero and Mackenzie Roberts, a classically trained violist, were recruited. Bassist Jesse Walker and drummer Kenny Ortiz completed the sextet, with an occasional pop from trumpeter Joe Ferrone. Flobots became a full-time project; the band cultivated a strong hometown following by playing live shows and combining the elements of unique instrumentation and rhymes bristling with social commentary.

"We're all products of the Denver Public Schools," Laurie said. "We connected with positive, kind people who were willing to push musical boundaries in the spirit of an inclusive community and curiosity and having fun together."

After a year of writing and producing, Flobots released *Fight with Tools*, its debut album. Laurie rapped about human rights laws, the dark side of globalization, drug prohibition and other sharply contested topics. Flobots never saw the quirky, catchy "Handlebars" becoming a radio success, but after fans bombarded local station KTCL with requests to play it during a contest, the song went into full rotation. Soon the major labels were sniffing around, and after a sold-out show at the Gothic Theatre, the group subsequently signed on with Universal Republic, which re-released *Fight with Tools* unchanged.

The record raced to #15 on the *Billboard* albums chart, fueled by "Handlebars," which became popular on alternative rock radio. The single peaked at #3 on *Billboard*'s Modern Rock Tracks chart in May 2008. The sing-along chorus—"I can ride my bike with no handlebars/No handlebars"—emphasized the value of self-actualization and activism.

"I was in fact riding my bike with no hands on the handlebars, which is something I had just learned to do," Laurie explained. "I was riding home from the sushi restaurant where I worked as a busboy, and I went across this field next to my old middle school. It was a beautiful day, a beautiful feeling—isn't it cool, the things that we human beings can do? And then a devil's-advocate thought reared its head—a lot of brainpower is spent figuring out physical destruction or economic destruction, things that are ultimately negative. So that juxtaposition inspired me. When I got home, I wrote down the chorus and left it on my mom's answering machine. I called Stephen and read it for him. We brought it to the rest of the band, and the rest is history."

"Handlebars" raised Flobots' profile to full-fledged pop phenomenon. The group played shows across the country, appeared at festivals and performed on late-night television. During the 2008 Democratic National Convention in Denver, Flobots led peace-promoting marchers into the streets following a politically charged performance with Rage Against the Machine. A second single, "Rise," was a modest hit.

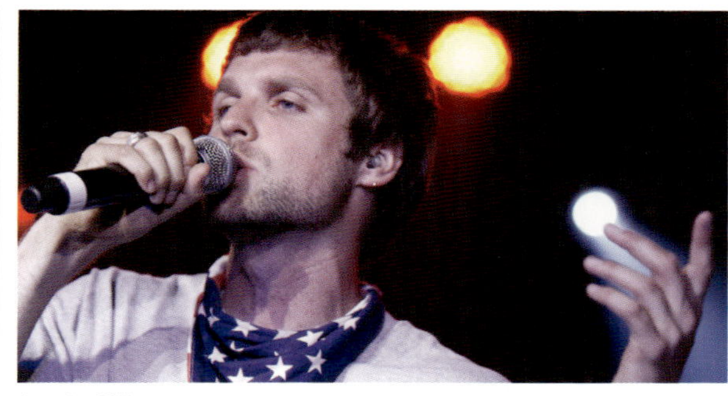
Jonny 5, c. 2008

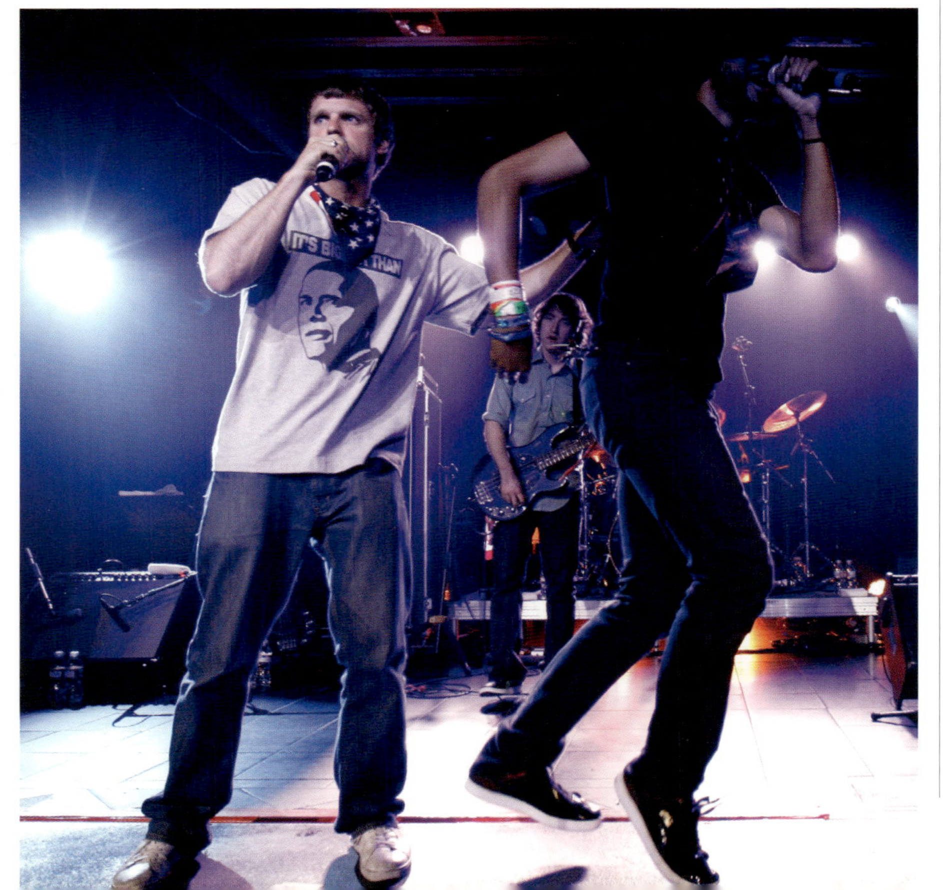
Rock The Conventions concert, August 26, 2008

Flobots continued to facilitate social change. In September 2009, the progressive rap-rock group opened up the Flobots.org Community Center in Denver, headquarters for collaborative work from school arts programs to voter registration (in 2015, the name was changed to Youth on Record).

"We're trying to push the model beyond having an information table in the lobby during concerts—we're committed to building and sustaining a positive organization of people," Laurie said.

With producer/mixer Mario Caldato of Beastie Boys fame, Flobots holed up in the Blasting Room Studios in Fort Collins, Colorado, and recorded *Survival Story*, which reached #9 on *Billboard*'s Modern Rock/Alternative Albums chart. Tim McIlrath from Rise Against joined the band on the chorus of the single "White Flag Warriors"; the anti-war anthem became another modern rock hit.

"A Florida radio station was accusing Rise Against of being against the military, which wasn't the truth, so it was good to collaborate on that song," Laurie said. "There's a huge difference between supporting the troops and supporting the recruitment of young people to fight wars started by politicians."

Released from its major label deal, Flobots returned to the Blasting Room to work on its third album on the same day that Occupy Wall Street protesters camped out in New York. The movement provided a backdrop for *The Circle in the Square*, released in August 2012; it reached #47 on *Billboard*'s Top Independent Albums chart. ●

3OH!3 }

KNOWN FOR over-the-top antics and frat-boy rap sensibilities, 3OH!3 climbed the charts worldwide with some raucous party hits.

Sean Foreman and Nathaniel Motte both grew up in Boulder (with the area code 303) and met in a physics class while attending the University of Colorado. Both were heavily into the underground hip-hop scene.

"Bands just loved touring through Colorado because of the scene—people are supportive, they come out to shows and make them fun," Motte said. "I interned for Radio 1190, the local college radio station, and the 'Basementalism' specialty program featured underground hip-hop, so I got to see a lot of cool shows. I saw Sean at a lot them."

"I was doing MC stuff and writing and doing freestyle," Foreman added. "There was no intention of playing shows. We were both concentrating on school, and music was a fun little hobby—we would hang out and have some beers and put stuff on the computer. After a while we started writing more electronic sounding music, and it just evolved from there."

"We abandoned those hipster notions about music," Motte said. "The most important thing for us was playing live shows and seeing things grow. A lot of it was instinctual and stupid coincidence. I've been to a lot of bland hip-hop shows where you stare at your feet and wait for someone to verbally ejaculate all over everyone with their clever rhymes. Our intention was to have fun."

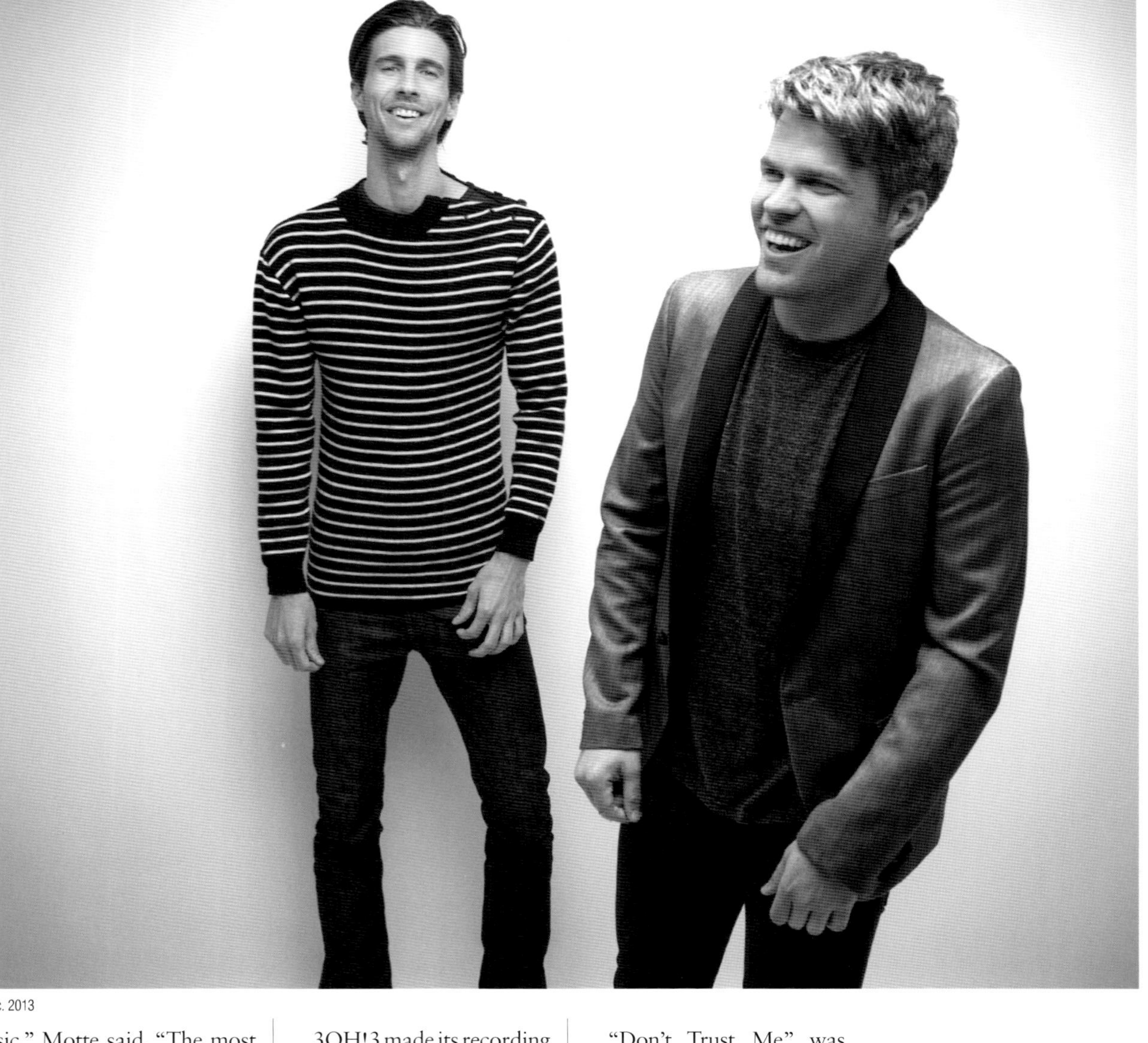

c. 2013

3OH!3 made its recording debut in 2007 with a self-titled, independently released album. It got the attention of Photo Finish Records, and the label released the band's second album, *Want* (2008). "Don't Trust Me" became 3OH!3's breakout hit—the electro-rap single sold over three million digital copies in the U.S. and reached #7 on the *Billboard* Hot 100.

"Don't Trust Me" was controversial, as some argued that the lyrics—"Shush girl, shut your lips/Do the Helen Keller and talk with your hips"—were misogynistic.

"Of course I knew that it was offensive when I was writing it," Foreman said. "But at the same time, the underlying meaning is 'Just dance.' I understand that

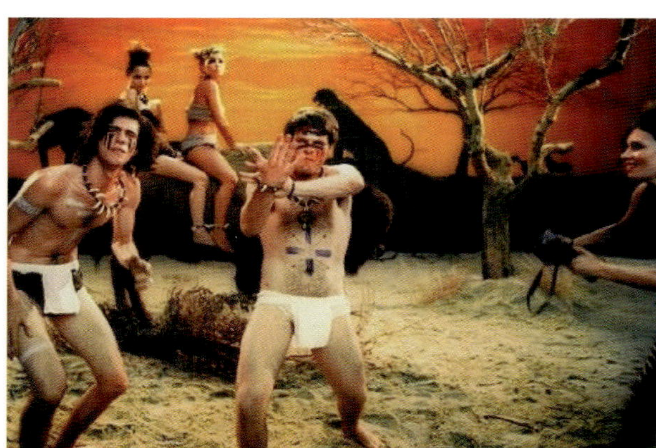

"Don't Trust Me" video

it's trading on the fact that Helen Keller was deaf and blind, but I'm not undermining what she accomplished. I grew up with punch lines in hip-hop that were way worse than that. You just write rhymes that bring it on point, poking fun at relationships."

Both Motte and Foreman had graduated with honors from the University of Colorado. After playing in Denver during the 2008 Warped Tour and whipping the crowd into a frenzy, the wacky Colorado rap duo was signed on for the tour's remaining stops. Their outrageous live performances propelled the joke-hop jesters to national fame.

"Sean majored in math and English, and I was a pre-med student," Motte said. "Once you get accepted to medical school, you have a secure future. You're going to be helping people and make a fair amount of money and have guaranteed work. But we started to do well when we went on our first Warped Tour. I was supposed to go to school in August. It was a tough decision, but I'm glad I deferred. The Warped Tour was the best thing we could have done. It was crazy to see crowds getting bigger and bigger every day. We'd never been anywhere near other major markets with 3OH!3, and it was amazing and flattering to see a few thousand people going nuts and having a good time."

3OH!3's second single, a remix of "Starstrukk" featuring future pop star Katy Perry, was a Top 10 hit in the United Kingdom, Ireland, Finland and Australia. *Want* reached #44 on the *Billboard* 200, but critics received its sophomoric humor either in terms of "It's laugh-out-loud awesome" or "Obscene, obnoxious drug/sex/bro references suck."

"It's tough when people slam you—social media provides anonymous forums for bigotry and hate where people work the kinks out of their lives," Motte said. "Obviously, we want everyone to like our music. As long as the people close to us think what we're doing is cool, we can take the criticism."

3OH!3 provided additional vocals on Ke$ha's raunchy Top 10 hit "Blah Blah Blah." "Follow Me Down" (with Neon Hitch) was written for the compilation album for the film *Alice in Wonderland*. 3OH!3's third studio album, *Streets of Gold*, was out in 2010; the duo issued a video for the song "House Party," and Ke$ha was featured on the song "My First Kiss." The 2013 album *Omens* reached #81 on the *Billboard* 200. Foreman and Motte laid low after its release.

"We're active students of songwriting and production," Motte said. "We've learned a lot over the last few years. There's usually a reason a lot of people like pop music—it's well crafted or interesting in a way. That's intriguing to us." ●

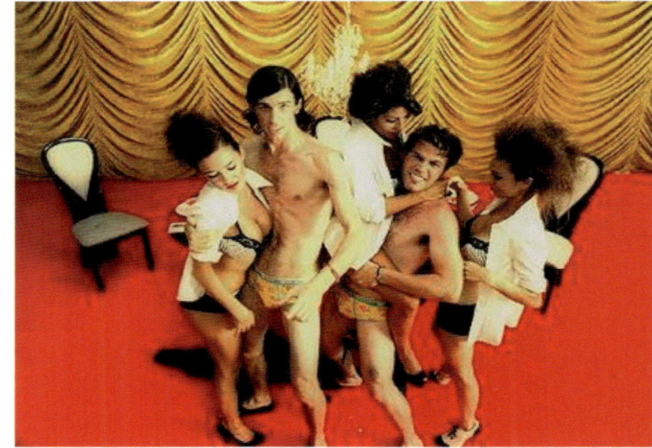

"Don't Trust Me" video

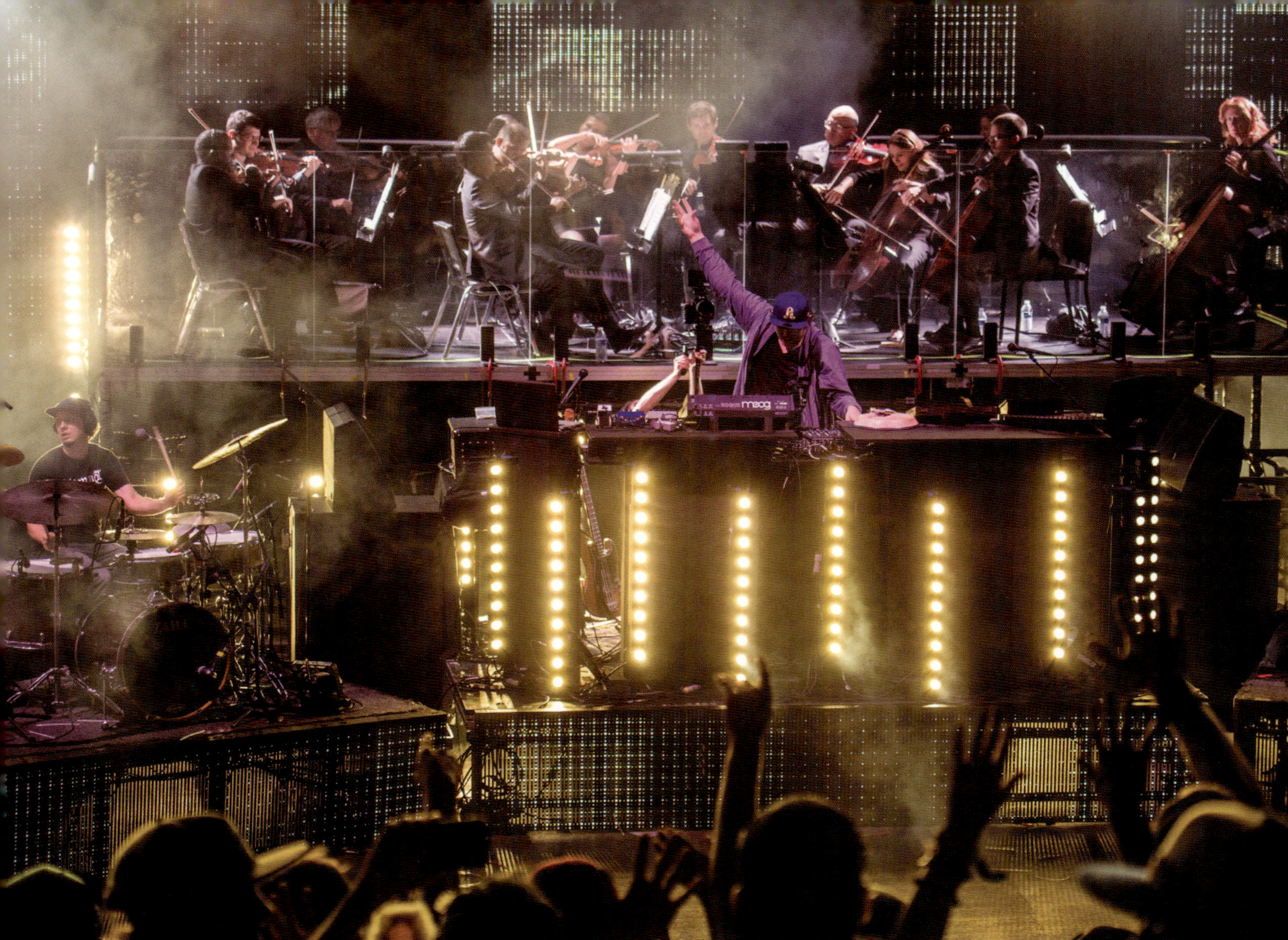

With the Colorado Symphony, Red Rocks Amphitheatre, Aug. 8, 2014

PRETTY LIGHTS }

WHEN THE world of popular music became just a mouse-click away, Colorado's Pretty Lights—the creation of Derek Vincent Smith—built a following by offering his music for free.

Smith spent his high school years in Fort Collins playing bass in rock bands and composing hip-hop tracks. He dropped out of the University of Colorado during his freshman year to focus on his music.

"Growing up in a small city in Northern Colorado, I was exposed to a bunch of styles," Smith said. "The punk scene was pretty big. The underground hip-hop scene blew up—I was able to open for every touring act that came through, and a lot of times they'd come to the after-show party at my house. The rave scene was popping—I got exposed to DJ culture and the subgenres of electronica. That melting pot is why I piece different styles together in my music."

Smith's sound resulted from pulling bits and pieces from many genres, and transforming it into a combination of self-described glitchy hip-hop beats, buzzing synth lines and vintage

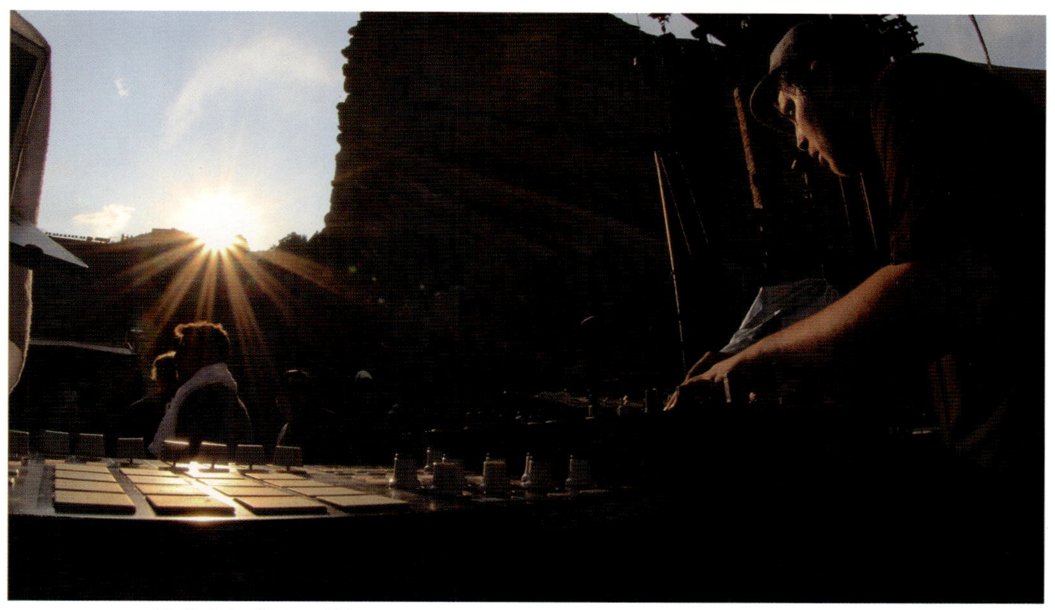

At Red Rocks Amphitheatre, c. 2014

funk and soul samples.

"Some people think artists who sample are thieves who don't have enough creativity to make music on their own," Smith said. "But I always try to use samples in a distinctive way—different records and genres can evoke fresh styles and emotions."

Smith made his recorded debut as Pretty Lights in 2006, making his music available for download without a fee on the official Pretty Lights website. The response was astounding—in a matter of weeks, his site received almost a million hits.

"I want to download music and not pay for it, and so do a lot of people," Smith explained. "So I took a gamble and gave my music away via the internet. Instead of trying to make a minimal amount of money from selling it, I wanted to get it out to as many people as possible. And it turned out to be a good move—the word-of-mouth about it being free picked up momentum. I had no idea it would let me make a living off of touring."

Pretty Lights' busy release schedule was combined with gigs, the beats issued from Smith's laptop accompanied by drummer Cory Eberhard. Spectators were enjoined to party with thumping bass lines and beats weaved with mysterious, gentle sounds and timbres, plus an evocative orgy of active stage lights and lasers.

By 2009, Pretty Lights had sold out five consecutive Front Range shows at the Aggie, Boulder, Fox, Gothic and Ogden Theaters; Smith then played a headlining date at Red Rocks and crisscrossed the country at major music festivals such as Bonnaroo and Rothbury, drawing a wider audience.

The electronic dance music hero released three albums in 2010, posted as free downloads, and took the production of the live show to a full-scale, mind-bending, psychedelic visual experience; stops that year included the Coachella, Ultra, Movement and Electric Zoo festivals, which sold hundreds of thousands of tickets.

"It's had an impact on the way I create music," the EDM mastermind admitted. "I made *Passing By Behind Your Eyes* while I was on tour, during the time between shows in airport gates and airplanes, hotels and green rooms."

Pretty Lights returned in 2013 with *A Color Map of the Sun*, Smith's first new material in over three years. Rather than sampling vintage vinyl records for his elements of folk, blues and jazz, he recorded with musicians—the Harlem Gospel Choir, members of the Preservation Hall Jazz Band and the Treme Brass Band—and pressed the resulting sessions on vinyl. He then reused them to construct the Pretty Lights sound. The first Pretty Lights album to be released digitally and physically on the same date, *A Color Map of the Sun* peaked at #24 in the *Billboard* 200. ●

MEESE }

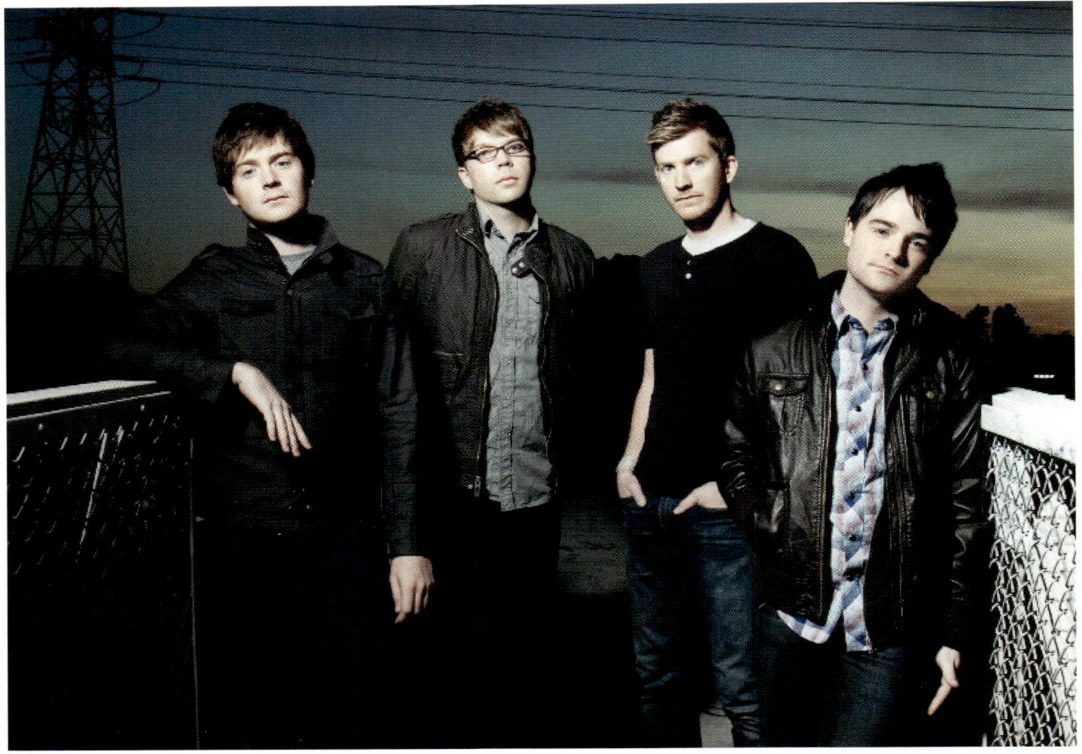

c. 2009

THE BARRIERS to entry in the music business proved insurmountable to Meese's career progression, but the Denver-based quartet's melodic brand of pop-rock was widely admired in the local scene.

In 2002, Ohio native and multi-instrumentalist Patrick Meese moved to Colorado to pursue a career in music; Nathan Meese followed his sibling out west. The brothers, both Colorado Christian University alums, formed Meese in 2005, bringing drummer Benjamin Haley and guitarist Mike Ayars into the fold from another local band, For the Holiday.

Meese crafted and self-released an EP, and the band's music found its way on to local modern rock radio station KTCL, which added "The Start of It." The catchy chorus addressed Colorado audiences directly: "Kids of the frozen Front Range..."

"When I wrote that song, it was a horrible few weeks—record cold temperatures, accumulating snow and no sun, which doesn't happen much in Colorado," Patrick Meese said.

Meese started playing major label showcases and eventually signed with Atlantic Records in the fall of 2007. It didn't hurt that the members were friends of fellow Denver band the Fray, which resulted in national exposure as tourmates. In Denver, Meese opened sold-out shows for the Fray at Red Rocks Amphitheatre and the Paramount Theatre.

Broadcast, Meese's first major studio album, was released in 2009. "Next in Line" was offered as a free single of the week in the iTunes Music Store.

"That started as another darker, weird song with operatic chord changes," Patrick Meese explained. "I wanted to make it more electronic, something that was great to play live and sing along to. The question was, do we make it the first single? You roll the dice on stuff like that. It might not have been the right game plan to steer us towards the alternative radio format in the first place. That's the risk you take with a major label."

After *Broadcast* peaked at #24 on *Billboard*'s Top Heatseekers chart, Atlantic dropped Meese. Writing new songs, the Meese brothers decided it was time to move forward with different projects. With Patrick's wife Tiffany, they founded the Centennial. Patrick toured as the drummer for Gregory Alan Isakov and backed Nathaniel Rateliff; Nathan toured with Churchill.

"That's the great thing about the community of musicians here—we help each other out," Nathan Meese said. "Denver is nine hours away from the next city by car—it's an island with enough culture to have a music scene with so many good and different types of bands. 3OH!3 and the Fray on the same local radio station? You can't have that anywhere else in the country." ●

MATT MORRIS }

WITH A breakout performance in front of millions of TV viewers, Colorado's Matt Morris left his imprint on America's musical landscape.

The son of country music star Gary Morris, who had a string of hit records in the 1980s and starred on Broadway, Morris stayed in Denver with his mother when his parents split up while he was still an infant. Family support led to his stint on TV's *The All-New Mickey Mouse Club* in the early 1990s. His fellow Mouseketeers included future pop icons Justin Timberlake, Christina Aguilera and Britney Spears.

"As a kid, I loved to sing—when I wasn't forced to be talking about something else, you'd hear me singing," Morris said. "I also enjoyed sketch comedy as a kid; I participated in a group called Kidskits at the downtown Comedy Works. That was a chance to act, to be funny. So the idea of performing on a television show that would allow me to sing and act professionally was a dream. I auditioned at age 11. Out of over 20,000 kids in the U.S. and Canada, they whittled it down to ten."

Morris came back to Colorado to attend Kennedy High School. He began working on music, setting his own pace out of the spotlight. It wasn't long before he was co-writing hits such as "Miss Independent" by Kelly Clarkson and "Can't Hold Us Down" by Aguilera. Pop star Timberlake, his close friend since their Disney days, decided Morris should be the debut artist for his label Tennman Records.

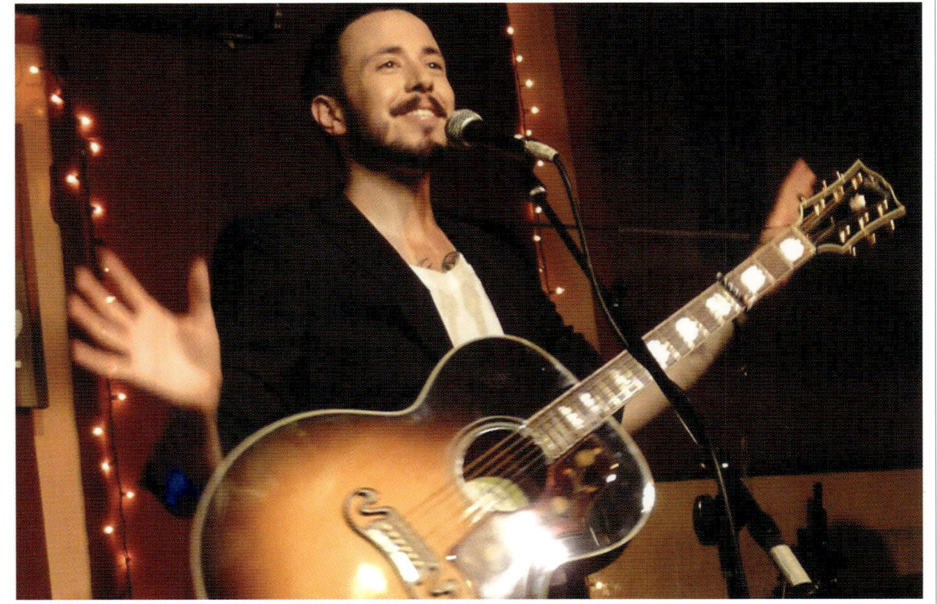

c. 2009

"I had put out an independent record, *UnSpoken*, in 2003," Morris said. "Justin and I had known each other as singers and performers, but those recordings gave him a sense of my diverse artistry in the studio. Working with him was an ideal situation. I knew that, through that partnership, I could maintain creative freedom."

When Everything Breaks Open was co-produced by Timberlake and highly regarded guitarist Charlie Sexton. Morris wrote many of the lyrics with his partner, Sean, whom he married in California when same-sex marriage in the state was legal. The album's strong point was Morris' striking vocal range.

Timberlake invited the tattooed Denver singer-songwriter to perform on the "Hope for Haiti Now" telethon on January 22, 2010, a highlight of the star-studded night. With Timberlake, Morris presented an impassioned rendition of Leonard Cohen's "Hallelujah." According to Nielsen SoundScan, the heartfelt cover notched 64,000 downloads in just two days, leading the pack on digital singles sales from the event's performances; the track went to No. 1 on the iTunes music chart and shot to #13 on the *Billboard* Hot 100.

"Being a part of that was a gift on many levels," Morris said. "I hadn't had a lot of opportunities to perform on stage with Justin and Charlie. And, personally, it was a timely reminder of what music is capable of doing in the world, that it has a greater cause. It's larger and broader than a means to entertain. It's a tool for connecting people in their hearts to one another. If you do that effectively, a positive change can happen in one single moment. I believe we created, with a very reverent intention, that moment for ourselves and for a lot of other people."

Morris' career was taking off, and *When Everything Breaks Open* sparked national interest, reaching #99 on the *Billboard* 200 chart. But the album spawned no hit singles to drive it. Tennman Records let Morris go, and he parted ways with his manager of ten years. He announced he was scaling back and continuing to write songs for other artists. ●

CEPHALIC CARNAGE }

WITH ITS self-styled "Rocky Mountain hydro-grind," Cephalic Carnage managed to pierce the intense global grindcore scene while ensconced in Colorado.

"I was born and raised in Pueblo and moved to Denver when I was 15, and I have no desire to live anywhere else," vocalist Lorenzo Leal said. "The musical spark was seeing Scorpions on the "Blackout" tour—they played with Quiet Riot at the Colorado State Fair in Pueblo. I said that has to be the most amazing job in the world. I tried to find the heavier stuff from there on out."

Cephalic Carnage came together in 1992, founded by Leal and guitarist Zac Joe.

"Around Denver, there were a lot of glam-type bands, so we wanted to be associated with an extreme style," Leal explained. "The goal was to keep up with what was going on in places like California, the East Coast, Canada, Houston. Being from Denver, you have to do the same things as everybody else but a little bit harder to get noticed and stick in people's heads. Our motivation was if we could write songs that would get us into *High Times*, we've made it. We realized we had to tour—'If we make it somewhere else, they'll appreciate us more here.'"

Cephalic Carnage released demo EPs and financed its own tour across the U.S., establishing notoriety for fierce live performances. The Italian label Headfucker Records released the band's debut album *Conforming to Abnormality* in 1998. In 2000, the band signed to the American heavy metal imprint Relapse Records. The members—Leal, guitarists Joe and Steve Goldberg, drummer John Merryman and bassist Nick Schendzielos—evolved into enterprising metal crusaders; later releases sought a more experimental tenor in the doom-death structure.

"I'd rather label our music myself than have somebody label it for me," Leal said. "We're stoners, but we like to play fast, crazy music, so it wouldn't work to be a stoner-rock band. We don't want to be lumped in with the hundreds of brutal death-metal bands doing the exact same thing—we're inspired by a lot of different genres, but if you have a little jazz part, that's where you lose those fans. We had to have a different identity—do it our own way, take it a step further. We came up with 'Rocky Mountain hydro-grind.'"

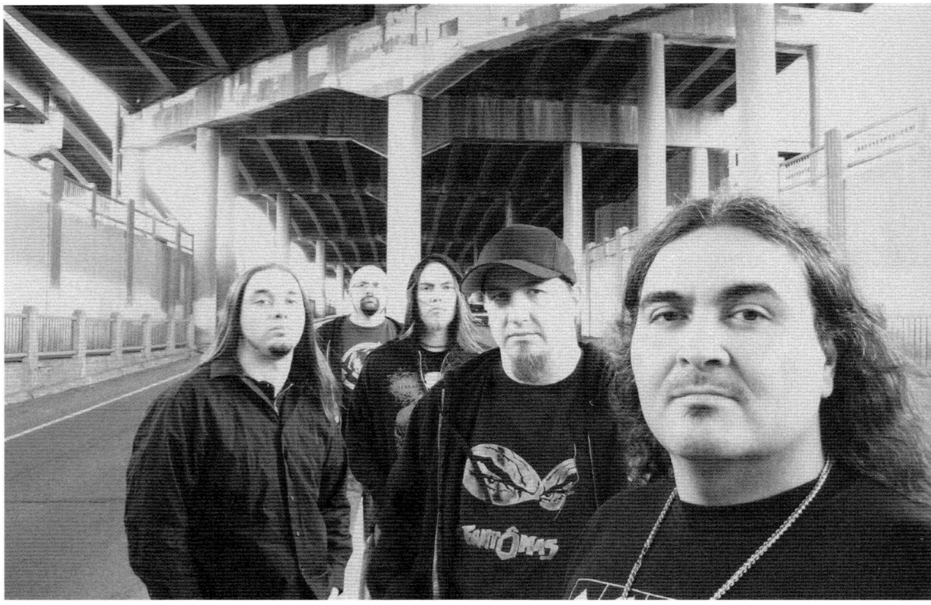

c. 2010

The band's technical proficiency at playing the punishing music was combined with a playful irreverence, evidenced in comedic song titles such as "Dying Will Be the Death of Me."

"Some metalheads have no sense of humor; everything has to be literal," Leal mused. "We're from Colorado—the weather's eclectic, everything's a little quirky, so we try to put that in our music. If we can add a little humor to the darkness, we do."

Cephalic Carnage's endeavors eventually started to yield results. Released in 2007, the band's fifth album, *Xenosapien*, peaked at #13 on the *Billboard* Heatseekers chart. The band's 2010 release, *Misled by Certainty*, was the first album with Brian Hopp as a guitarist, replacing Joe; it debuted in the #24 position on *Billboard*'s Heatseekers chart.

Touring has taken Cephalic Carnage around the world, playing in North America, Europe and Japan and South America.

"But we stay true to our roots," Leal stressed. "Get out there, away from the pack, and stay on the trail. It's a lot of sacrifice if you have a family, but you make it work. Because once you step off the road, things slow up." ●

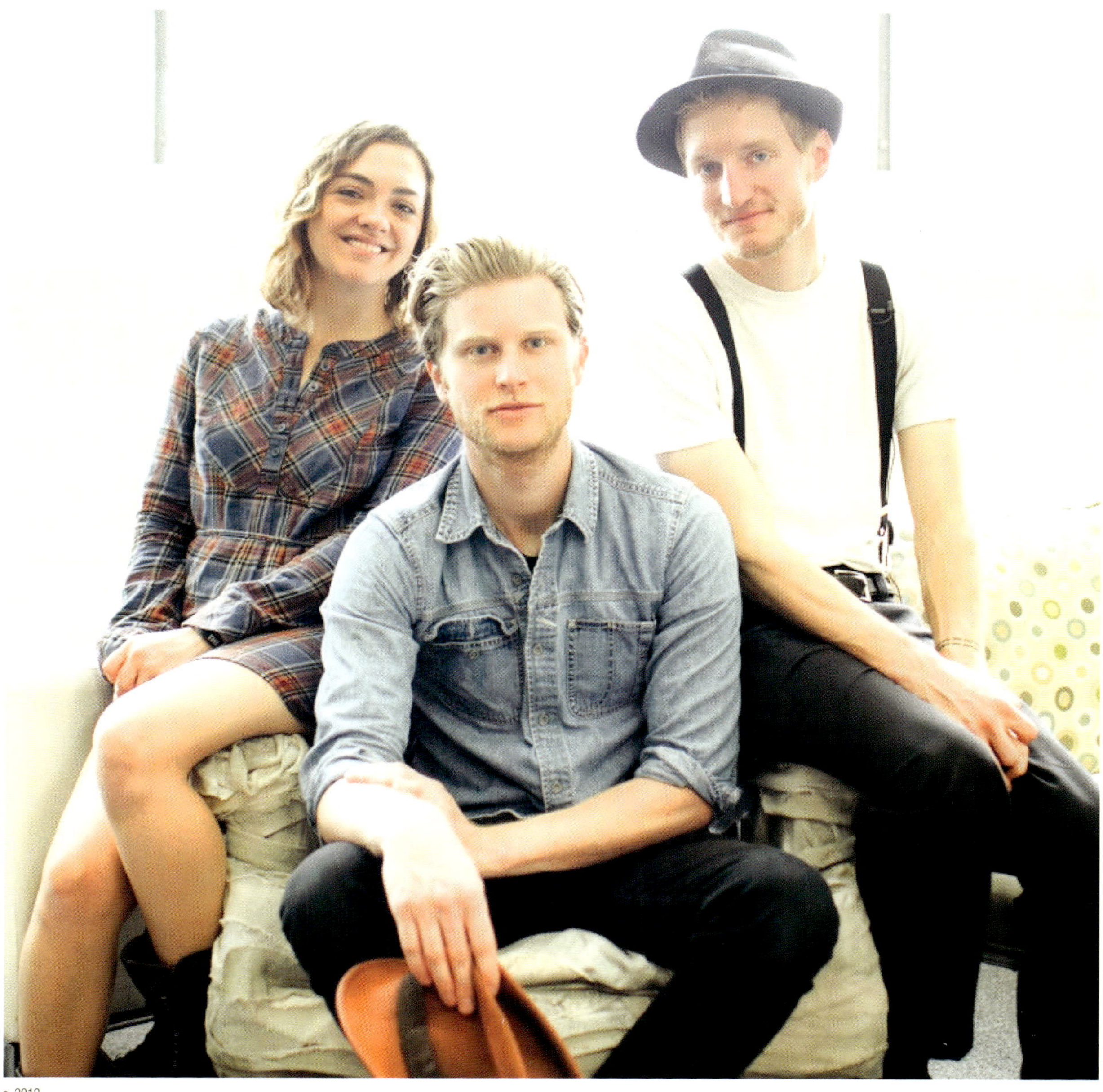

c. 2012

THE LUMINEERS }

WITH THE Top 10 single "Ho Hey," the Lumineers left their indelible mark on pop culture. The push began in Denver, where the band members fostered their talents the old-fashioned way.

Singer and guitarist Wesley Schultz and drummer Jeremiah Fraites grew up in New Jersey; they started playing music together in 2005. In an effort to get noticed, they played open mics in New York City with the ambition of ascending to small clubs.

"We never got close to that," Schultz admitted. "It was so cold and unemotional—people came in, saw their friends play and shuffled out. It was impossible to build something. I was working three jobs to play the rent."

Schultz and Fraites relocated to Denver in October 2009. "In our naiveté, we thought we'd move to the middle of nowhere to find a fresh start and not worry about the cost of living—eliminate distractions and regain our focus playing music. The idea wasn't necessarily to go to Denver. Sometimes you're just drawn to a place. A couple of friends there were moving into a house that was half of what I was paying for an apartment in Brooklyn."

Having come of age during the 1990s, Schultz and Fraites had run through grunge and other styles of music. By the time they took up residence in Colorado, the duo had started developing the kind of Americana songs for sitting comfortably on a front porch.

The Lumineers' initial shows took place at the Meadowlark, an intimate basement club where the local songwriters cultivating Denver's cozy folk-pop scene gathered. Schultz and Fraites performed at open-mic night every Tuesday, depending on word of mouth to fill the 72-capacity space. Their music landed on receptive ears.

"We started meeting unbelievable musicians—Nathaniel Rateliff, Paper Bird," Schultz said. "If you're a part of a community where people work with each other and care about each other and keep raising the bar for each other, that makes for great art. Coming from the ego that exists in the New York scene, where they don't share a lot of information, I didn't expect the Denver scene to be so fertile."

Subsequent to placing an ad on Craigslist for a cellist, the Lumineers recruited Neyla Pekarek, a multi-instrumentalist and harmony singer. They released an EP and began to tour at homegrown places. "Ho Hey," with its call-and-response structure and delusively cheerful chorus—"I belong with you/You belong with me"—emerged as one of the favored folky ditties.

"At house shows and most clubs, we were literally on the same level as the crowd," Schultz said. "So halfway through our sets, we would carry our instruments into the audience and stomp our feet and chant to start 'Ho Hey.' It got people's attention."

The band signed a contract with Dualtone Records. "Our record was an extension of the demos we had done," Schultz said. "But we took months in the studio—we didn't like any of it. We almost left 'Ho Hey' off the album because it was so hard to get the live feel of the song. We re-recorded and remixed and remastered it until it sounded the way we wanted."

After showcases at the South by Southwest festival, the band received favorable mentions in top newspapers (*New York Times*, *Los Angeles Times*, *Chicago Tribune*), and radio airplay picked up steam. After seducing the alternative format, "Ho Hey" made its mark on the pop charts, where its acoustic moves—folksy guitar, tambourine and handclapping—were encircled by electronic beats and synthesized hooks. The hit boosted the Lumineers into ubiquity—"Ho Hey" was heard during a CW's *Hart of Dixie* episode, in a Bing commercial, on a *Saturday Night Live* performance.

"Back in Denver, our friends joked about not being able to get away from us," Schultz said. "Every time they'd watch TV or go on YouTube, they ran into our song."

The Lumineers' self-titled debut album peaked at #2 on the *Billboard* 200 the week before the Grammy Awards; the band got two nominations, for Best New Artist and Best Americana Album. For tours, the members added bassist Ben Wahamaki and keyboardist Stelth Ulvang, and the group found itself leading the worldwide revival toward all things rootsy in popular music.

"For years, we had the benefit of failure—success is a new venture for us," Schultz said. "I take it with a grain of salt, because I know how fickle the industry is. We're lucky—it would be greedy to wish for anything more." ●

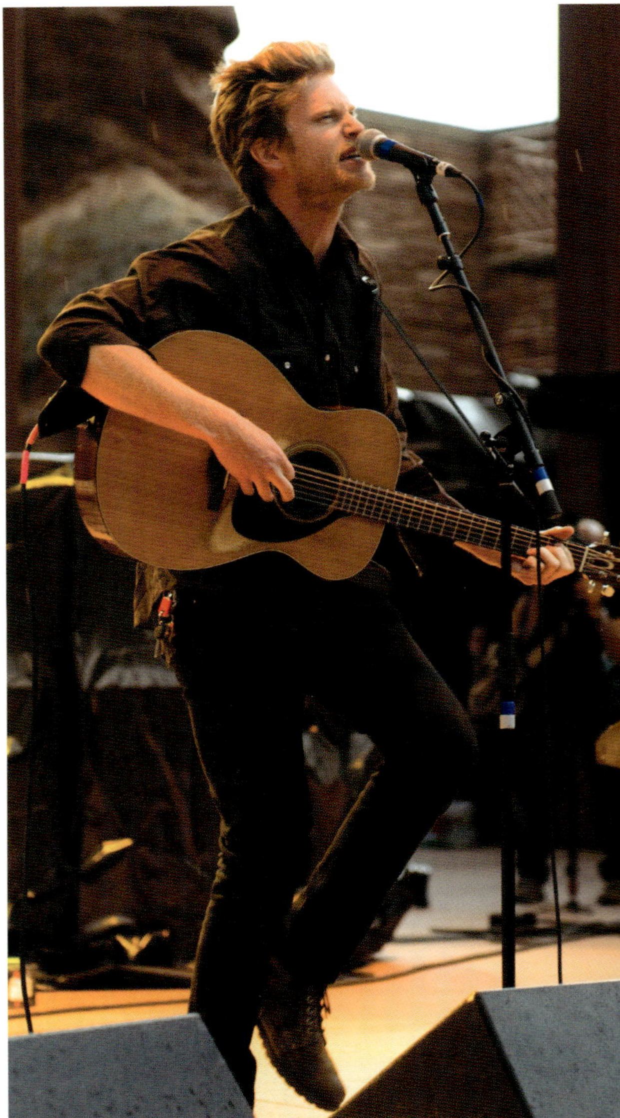

At Red Rocks Amphitheatre, July 28, 2012

TENNIS }

THE ORIGIN of Tennis, from landlocked Denver, resulted from a seafaring venture.

Patrick Riley and Alaina Moore met while studying philosophy at the University of Colorado; they were married in 2009. The couple bid farewell to family and friends and took off on a sailing expedition along the Eastern Atlantic Seaboard, deliberately removing themselves from a world driven by technology—restricting their energy usage, suppressing their food intake and limiting any electronics that weren't necessary for survival.

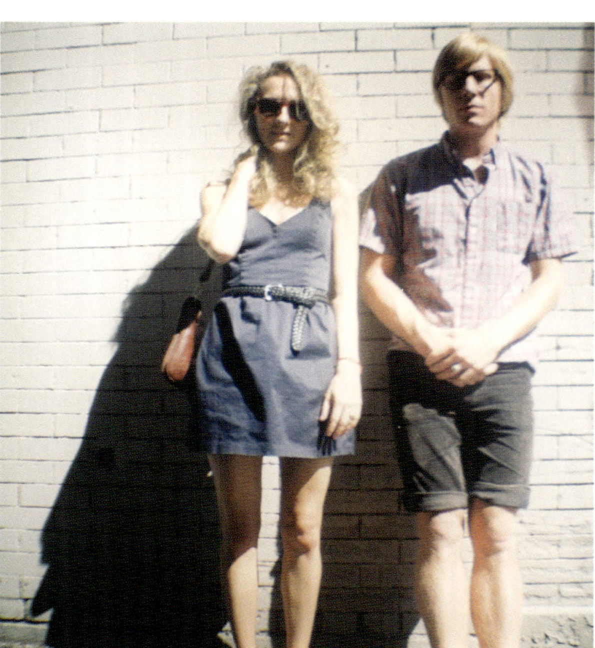

c. 2011

"It was meant to be a huge alteration in our way of life," Moore explained. "We wanted to learn to 'live small' in our own self-contained little world. We were only 22—we thought we'd float around on a 30-foot boat forever, live off fish and fruit would fall off the trees. We made the first step of that dream come true.

"It only lasted eight months. Sailing was like living in the wilderness, exposed to the elements at all times. It's beautiful and amazing, but it's extremely hard work. We returned to society, got jobs. We didn't know how to integrate those memories and lessons into the life we were coming back to in Denver."

Moore and Riley turned to music to express the emprise.

"We realized that writing songs captured the indescribable heart of living on a small sailboat," Moore said. "I gravitated toward sounds that represented that aesthetic—the parallels between the sound of water and reverb, translating those ideas with analog. It set us up to make a certain kind of music."

Tennis' sprightly, unadulterated sound centered on the easy dynamism of Moore's crooning and Riley's guitar. The husband-wife duo posted the song "Baltimore" on a music blog and gained a following through online support. Word about their adventure spread, the sweet take on retro-pop trickled into the ears of lo-fi revivalists, and Tennis got a recording contract.

"We still hardly know how to make sense of that experience," Moore said. "There was this strange, temporary moment where all the blogs would latch on to some obscure new bands, outsiders of the industry, and cover them so extensively that they would take over the internet and be launched into the spotlight. It was scary in a way. Patrick and I had hardly played any live shows, we didn't have an album yet, so all of a sudden there were extraordinarily high expectations. We were doing tons of press, and we had no publicist, no representation, no booking agent, nothing. We didn't know how to take advantage of that organic momentum.

"In hindsight, we're so fortunate because that attention enabled us to have a career. But there was also a lot of skepticism, and I couldn't explain why it was happening. Sure, we didn't deserve it—we'd only written two songs."

Tennis filled its 2011 debut album with songs inspired by the sailing trip. *Cape Dory* entered various charts including the *Billboard* Top 200 and was featured on NPR. During Tennis' first tour, James Barone joined the band on drums.

Riley and Moore then put some distance between their post-college experiment and their next songs. *Young & Old*, the second album from Tennis, was produced by Patrick Carney of the Black Keys and released in 2012; it debuted at No. 1 on *Billboard*'s Heatseekers chart. The couple obtained the help of a trio of producers—Carney, Jim Eno (who worked with Spoon) and Richard Swift (the Shins)—to bring 2014's *Ritual in Repeat* to life.

"We lived in Nashville to make *Ritual in Repeat*, and also worked in Austin and Portland," Moore said. "When we got to Tennessee, the Black Keys career exploded, so we ended up alone with no friends and a lot of time on our hands. When we finally finished the album, Patrick looked at me one evening and said, 'Do you want to move back to Denver?'—which until that point would have felt like quitting—and I immediately said, 'Oh, I'm so happy you said that. Yes, let's move right now.' We were back by the end of the week, exhausted and so happy to be home.

"And that's when I realized where we belonged. The 'Denver sound' might typically be associated with darker folk music, reflective singer-songwriter stuff. We were a little bit different; people would say our music was sunny or surfy. But it's that Colorado context that informs the way that we filter and interpret all of our experiences. We write out of that framework." ●

TYLER WARD }

WITH NO assistance from a record label, Tyler Ward built a rabid fan base throughout the world with a savvy use of the 21st-century tool of social media.

After graduating from high school in Parker, Ward enrolled at the Air Force Academy before seeking a journalism degree at the University of Northern Colorado. He started writing and recording music, posting a mix of originals and his acoustic take on tunes by Taylor Swift, Justin Bieber and others. Spreading songs on Facebook, putting up videos on YouTube and utilizing Twitter, Ward's do-it-yourself approach jumpstarted his career.

"Without that online engagement, I would probably still be making music in my dad's basement, trying to figure out where to go," the singer-songwriter said. "The internet platform expedited the process a thousand-fold."

Ward ranked on *Billboard*'s Social 50 chart and landed a top spot on the iTunes singer-songwriter chart. Making a living as a full-time independent musician, he became a touring act and opened for the Jonas Brothers and the Fray.

Ward then produced most of his music in Tyler Ward Studios in Los Angeles, providing a cadre of colleagues and collaborators the opportunity to record their songs and expose their talent through a featured-artist series on YouTube. ●

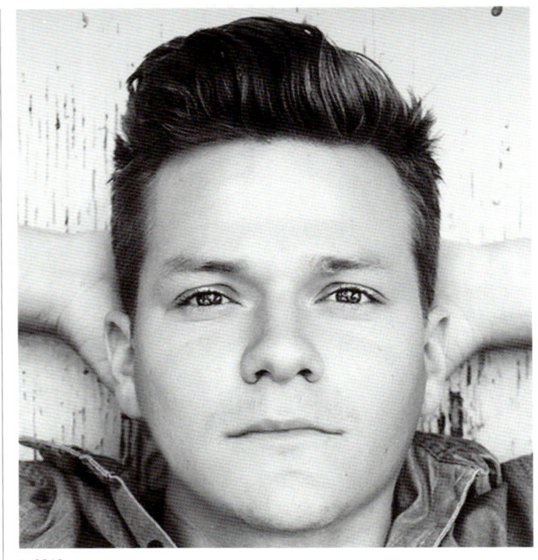

c. 2013

CHURCHILL }

FOUNDED BY frontman Tim Bruns and mandolinist-guitarist Mike Morter in 2008, Churchill expanded to a five-piece band and gained a loyal audience in its hometown of Denver. With a reputation for energetic, charming performances, the members graduated from the club scene to shows at Red Rocks Amphitheatre and 1stBank Center.

"The Denver scene is great for bands trying to help each other," Morter said. "It's like that feeling X-Games skateboarders get cheering each other on during the halfpipe."

The members of Churchill recorded and released the *Change* EP themselves, and the irrepressible title track, sung by Bethany Kelly, started taking off.

"It's the idea that everyone feels that pressure to change at some point, but if you really believe in something, stick to your guns," Bruns said.

Churchill signed with a major label, A&M Octone, and "Change" made its way to #17 on *Billboard*'s Hot Modern Rock Tracks chart. The band planned to release a full-length album in 2013 with premier rock producer Brendan O'Brien, and appeared set to be the next prominent act out of Denver.

Reinforced by the male/female vocal interaction of Bruns and Kelly, Churchill evoked Fleetwood Mac, often drawing tumultuous applause with its mandolin-driven version of the Mac's hit "Go Your Own Way."

"Fleetwood Mac is probably our biggest influence, and *Rumours* is our all-time favorite record," Bruns admitted.

But whereas Fleetwood Mac outlasted the intense inner turmoil brought on by its success, Churchill didn't. In July 2013, the group returned from a European arena tour with Pink and abruptly called it quits, canceling all upcoming shows and scheduled television appearances.

"To protect all of us, we just say that we decided to go different ways," Morter said. "It ended after a great high." ●

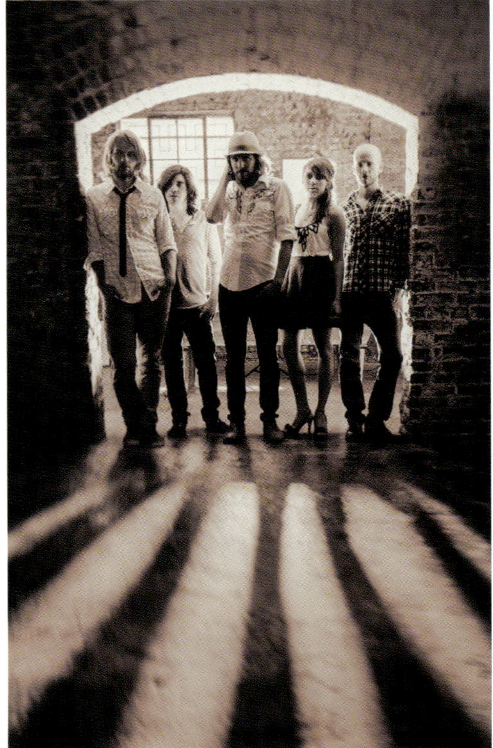

c. 2012

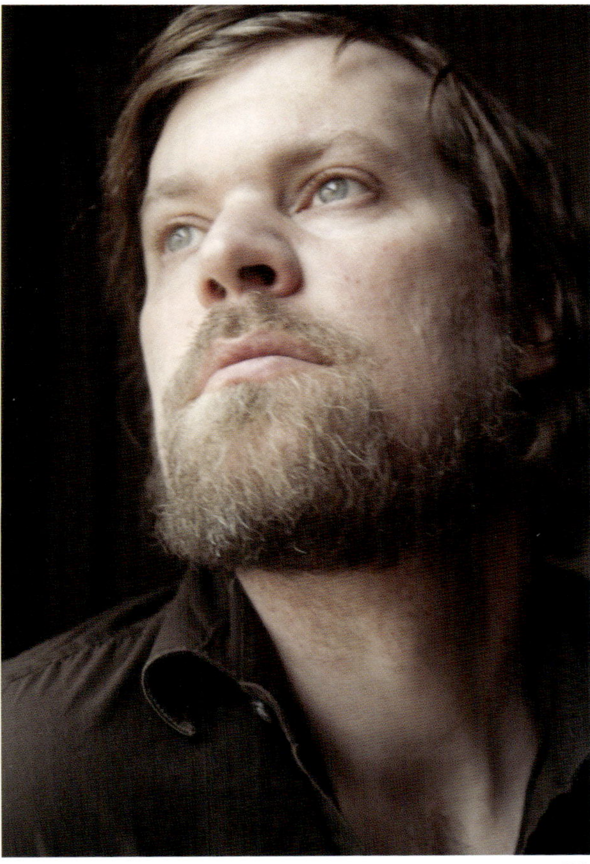

c. 2013

JOHN GRANT }

BEFORE HE finally made a chart showing in America, John Grant had been making records for 20 years. Even then, it was a moderate push, but the emergence of *Pale Green Ghosts* showed that the thoughtful songwriter was inching into the mainstream after a lifetime spent grappling with depression, poverty and addiction.

The album title referred to the luminescent Russian olive trees that lined I-25 in Colorado near his family home in the town of Parker.

"I spent a huge part of my life driving up and down that highway," Grant said. "I always had romantic notions of those trees—the leaves have a silvery quality on one side, so they glow in the moonlight, and I was soothed by the fragrance when they bloomed in late May. The title track of *Pale Green Ghosts* is about wanting to get out in the world and make your mark. It took a couple of decades to crawl out of the hole I fell into."

Grant's family relocated to Colorado from Michigan when he was 12. Oppressed in a religious household, he struggled with his sexual identity; he felt even more discomfort when he endured cruel homophobia for being the only clearly gay boy in high school. At age 20, he moved to Germany to become an interpreter, but he suffered severe panic attacks and agoraphobia, disrupting his education. He returned to Parker to care for his terminally ill mother in 1994.

Grant became reacquainted with a friend, Chris Pearson, and they started a band that evolved into the Czars. Crafting somber country-noir songs, the six-member alternative rock act released five studio albums that were embraced by critics, but the band could only muster a cult following, mostly in Britain. Years of touring took their toll, and Grant's alcoholism, rampant drug use and "dangerous sexual behavior" didn't help matters.

"I hated who I was so much at that time," Grant noted. "I still felt the same as when I was growing up, that I had no future. People interpreted my fear as arrogance, so I started playing the role they'd given me. Everyone just thought I was a prick."

Subsequent to a ten-year career, Grant's bandmates decided to jump ship. Looking for a fresh start, Grant sobered up, moved to New York City to find translation work and abandoned music for six years.

Grant called upon the muse again with the assistance of the Texan folk-rockers Midlake; the band lent him studio time and provided sympathetic musical backing for his new songs. Drawing on his troubled memories and unabashedly influenced by the gentle, melodic soft-rock of the 1970s, *Queen of Denmark*, Grant's debut solo album, was greeted with ecstatic reviews, and *MOJO* magazine crowned it the best album of 2010.

Grant then discovered his HIV positive status. He didn't tell anyone for more than a year; during a performance at London's Meltdown festival in August 2012, he announced his diagnosis in front of the shocked audience.

Grant's career continued on its successful trajectory. The bulk of *Pale Green Ghosts* was recorded in Iceland, where he was living; he added contrasting traces of electronica-influenced sounds to the music. The album peaked at #28 on *Billboard*'s Top Heatseekers chart.

Grant's new profile ensured belated attention for his former band. *The Best of the Czars*, a compilation album, was released in 2014.

"I didn't like myself or the things that were happening to me during that period," Grant explained. "A lot of it is a blur—I've blocked it out because it was painful. But there were a lot of great times. The Czars' music is an important part of my history, so it deserves to be heard." ●

KELLER WILLIAMS }

OWING TO his skill using live phrase looping, Keller Williams made his mark as a "one-man jam band."

A self-taught musician, Williams began performing in the early 1990s. He lived in Steamboat Springs after relocating from Virginia. "I was that dude playing solo in the corners of bars and restaurants, with just a guitar and microphone. No one was coming to see music. The lure was playing music in exchange for a free ski pass. That was the goal, and I successfully completed that goal for two seasons!"

Williams' career got a boost after an encounter with String Cheese Incident in 1996.

"I saw them in the small bars around ski towns in Colorado, probably a half-dozen times before I introduced myself. They played Steamboat, and I invited them to sit in with me the next night. They listened to my first set and by the end of the second they were all on stage with me. A month later I was opening for them. I was jonesing for exposure. My mantra at the time was to get out in front of anybody, anywhere in the country. I didn't require much."

Finding it difficult to attract an audience as a solo acoustic artist, Williams investigated the use of technology, creating samples on the fly in front of the audience. "Looping" allowed him to play a riff once on an instrument, such as a bass guitar, and, operating a pedal with his feet, loop it back to be used as accompaniment as he sang and played guitar. He recreated the sound of a full band, essentially jamming by himself. With nothing pre-recorded, the end result often tended toward a composite of alternative folk and electronica grooves, a genre Williams jokingly designated "funk folk" or "dance acoustic techno."

"The first time I tried to loop was 1997," Williams said. "The looper started out being a tape machine inside a bulky box, essentially a delay unit. I was trying to play within time parameters, and the device was not meant to do that. I had a lot of trial and error in covering my mistakes. But once the correct gear came into existence, something I could control with my feet and tap out tempo, and start and finish a phrase, everything fell into place."

Word about Williams' shows began garnering a buzz in the jam-band world. He signed to String Cheese Incident's label, SCI Fidelity Records; 2003's *Home* ranked #39 on *Billboard*'s Independent Albums listing. Williams won a Jammy Award (for jam bands and other artists associated with live, improvisational music, sponsored by Relix magazine) for his album *Stage* (Live Album of the Year) in 2005, and for his song "Cadillac" with Bob Weir (Song of the Year) in 2008. The album *Dream* ranked #4 on *Billboard*'s Top Heatseekers chart.

While his live gigs were largely solo affairs, Williams invariably used his albums as a forum for collaborations with fellow musicians; the Keller Williams Incident was a joint project with String Cheese Incident. For the 2012 release of *Pick*, which rated as #3 on *Billboard*'s Top Bluegrass Albums chart, he teamed up with the Travelin' McCourys, the royal bluegrass family.

"The Telluride Bluegrass Festival was always the holy grail for me," Williams recalled. "I attended the festival six times before I actually got in for free as a 'tweener,' to play in between sets. The next year, 2001, I actually got on the bill. Seeing Peter Rowan, Béla Fleck, Jerry Douglas, Sam Bush and Edgar Meyer on the main stage put those players on a pedestal in my mind, and the McCourys were right up there.

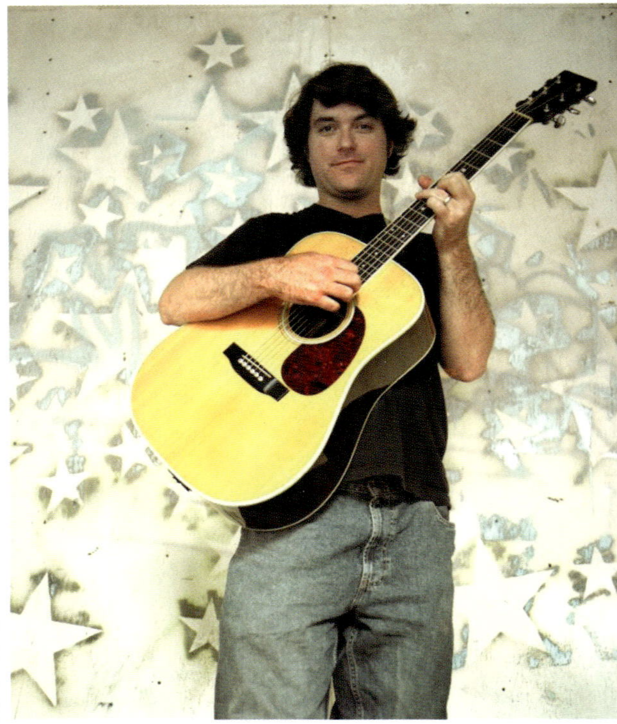

c. 2010

"Telluride was my first stop in Colorado. When you play a ski town, whatever the season, there's a certain energy in the shows—young, open-minded people that migrated there from other places, looking for the Colorado experience. I've always had a connection with that, because I was one of them." ●

HARD WORKING AMERICANS }

THE COLORADO Flood of 2013 impacted communities all across the state, creating significant hardship for hard-working Americans. To get them back on track, Hard Working Americans, a collaboration of all-star musical lifers from the jam-band scene, debuted their project at a benefit performance in Boulder.

Singer-songwriter Todd Snider fronted the group, which featured bassist Dave Schools from Widespread Panic, guitarist Neal Casal of Chris Robinson Brotherhood, Duane Trucks on drums and keyboardist Chad Staehly of Great American Taxi, the Colorado-based band he formed with Vince Herman when Leftover Salmon went on hiatus.

"Taxi had backed Todd in the studio and done a few tours with him," Staehly said. "Todd and I developed a strong connection. I was always the guy in the band who handles the business end of things. He had seen what I was doing for Taxi and wanted that for his own career. I started working on Todd's management team and set him up with Dave Schools to play a gig in California, and that led to the formation of Hard Working Americans."

Snider was a cult hero in Americana circles, known for entertaining crowds with little more than an acoustic guitar, harmonica and his story-telling genius, delivering wry, politically charged sentiments about battered but unbroken outcasts and hippies. He had released more than a dozen albums in the past two decades. Reviewers called 2003's *Near Truths and Hotel Rooms*, his first live album, closer to a comedy act than a concert; the track "Talkin' Seattle Grunge Rock Blues" was recorded at a Boulder Theater show.

Snider had collected lesser-known songs from the folk circuit to cover, bound with notions of class-consciousness and the low economic trajectory that some people face. Hard Working Americans stemmed from the idea of celebrating his selections with a few pals and new bandmates.

"Todd's always been one to root for the underdog; he has his own idea of justice," Staehly noted. "His thing is peace, love and anarchy, and that rings true for me, too. Some people like to hijack the concept of patriotism and manipulate it for their own agenda. Todd had a clear vision of reclaiming it."

"I wanted to poke fun at the flag-waving people who think that the term 'hard-working Americans' applies only to them," Snider added. "It's like Woody Guthrie said, 'Music should comfort the afflicted and afflict the comfortable.'"

Hard Working Americans' very first concert was scheduled at the Boulder Theater, a sold-out benefit concert for Colorado flood relief.

"For ten years, I was the executive director of the Mark Vann Foundation (Vann, banjoist of Leftover Salmon, died of cancer in 2002)," Staehly explained. "An annual show started out small and grew into the Boulder Theater. December is usually a downtime for musicians, so all the great players from Colorado were home, and it was easy to call in favors.

"There were a few years off, and I missed handling the nuts and bolts of that benefit show. Colorado had just gone through that giant flood in September. It was an opportunity to do something for the flood victims and to get the band together for rehearsals and to play its first gig. We didn't know how we'd play or how we'd sound or if we'd be any good. George Boedecker runs the Boedecker Foundation, which does amazing things in Colorado and globally. George said, 'We should film it and call it *The First Waltz*!'"

The resulting documentary by Justin Kreutzmann (filmmaker and son of Grateful Dead drummer Bill Kreutzmann) captured the like-minded souls finding a fertile combination of creative drive and musical muscle. Guitarist Jesse Aycock was added before the band's debut album was recorded; *Hard Working Americans* reached #45 on the *Billboard* 200.

"Todd had a vision of the album narrative being someone's life story, a bit of gypsy wanderer who throws a backpack on his back and hits the highways and byways to get his education, getting to see what this country is all about," Staehly said. "I was that guy, and so are a lot of other people in Colorado." ●

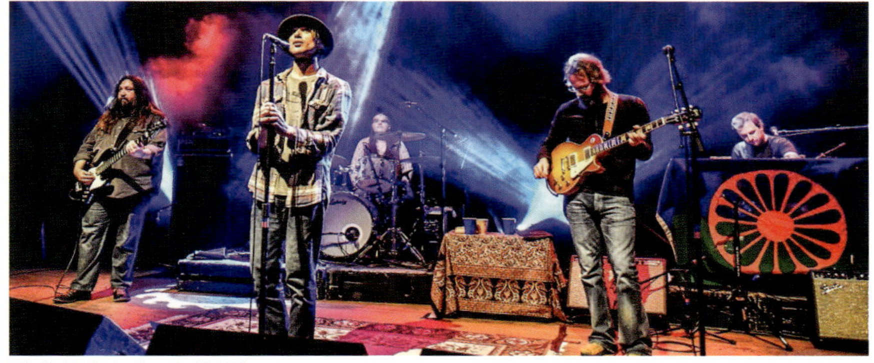
At the Boulder Theater, December 20, 2013

GREGORY ALAN IZAKOV }

AN INDIE-FOLK treasure, Gregory Alan Isakov has patiently cultivated a loyal following in much the same way he has tended his four-acre Colorado garden.

Born in South Africa and raised in Philadelphia, Isakov started touring with a band at the age of 16, moving around the East Coast. He ultimately found a home in the Centennial State.

"I came upon a horticultural program there," Isakov said. "I moved and worked on farms and gardens in Lyons and Boulder County.

"A lot of the music around that scene was bluegrass and old time. Around the campfire, I was an alien in a way—'Okay, Gregory, play another "jam buster" where nothing repeats.' I played with those people a lot."

Isakov began turning heads with his haunting Americana style. Living out of his truck, he roamed the United States, his agreeable combination of shy presence and lyrical storytelling cherished by fans and fellow "road rats." His travels impacted his songwriting; his observations and knowledge of the countryside and lost love provided a constant source of inspiration.

"I've been driven by that curiosity for words," he said.

Isakov benefitted from being a multi-instrumentalist—he could play acoustic guitar, banjo, fiddle and cello.

"I'm not a master of any instrument—I play every instrument kinda," he explained. "The band and I have been tight friends for a long time; we grew up playing together. Now they stylize their playing for me, and I stylize my writing for them. We have a cool schedule. We tour mostly in the winter, and then we're home. It's always busy; we're working all the time. We rehearse in the barn and record our records there."

Isakov's song "Big Black Car" was placed in a McDonald's commercial in Canada in 2011; he donated the proceeds to support non-profit organizations that further sustainable farming practices.

In 2013, Isakov's fifth album, *The Weatherman*, peaked at No. 1 on the *Billboard* Heatseekers album chart for new or developing acts.

"I joke around with friends that it's the slowest career ever," Isakov said.

"I never thought I'd get to do music for a living. I was a landscaper in high school, always a gardener, developing some scenarios for farms and food production. That was the big plan. But making music is a no-brainer part of my life, one of those things that I need to do. That attitude will push you during the tough times. I don't know if the longer you do it, the better you get, especially creating something from nothing. You're always in that moment of noticing and writing, with the purpose of making useful art in some way. I just look at every song like it's the challenge today.

"Gardening, that's different. It's a constant deadline—'I've got to put in potatoes, and now I'm late.'" ●

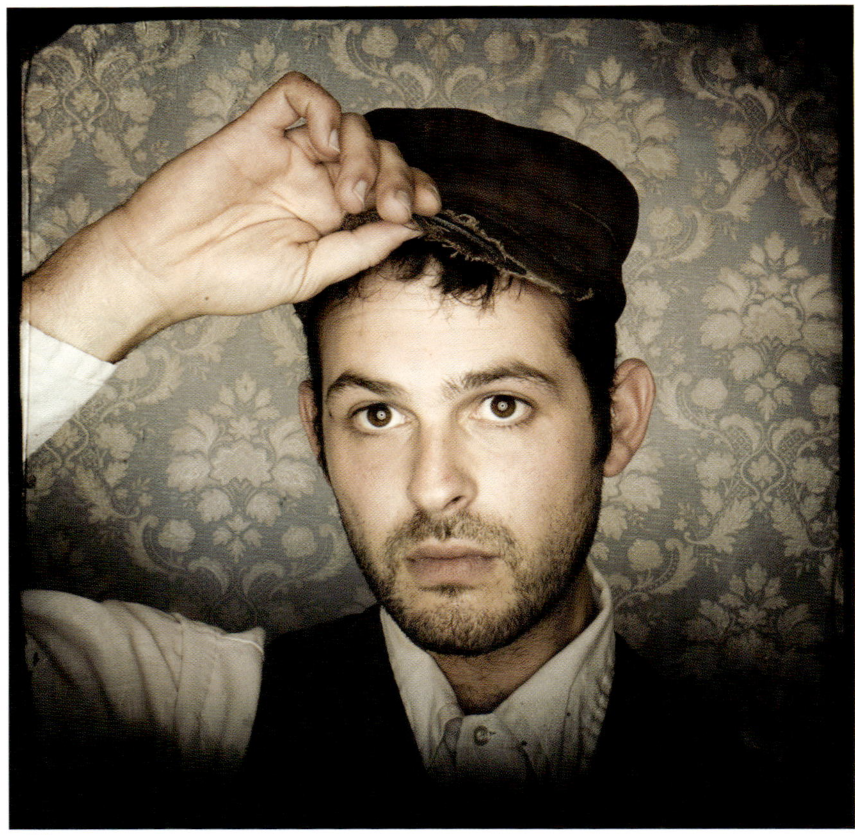

c. 2013

ELEPHANT REVIVAL }

DESCRIBED AS "transcendental folk," Elephant Revival's rustic style centers around bluegrass instrumentation while dabbling in elements of reggae, Celtic fiddle tunes, jazz standards and even an occasional hip-hop beat. The tangled tale of how the five multi-instrumentalists came together and ultimately settled in Colorado is as eclectic as their unique repertoire.

The first linkage came in 2003, when bassist Dango Rose encountered Bridget Law, who had set out fiddling at the Waldorf School in her native Denver.

"I was performing at a bluegrass festival in Keystone, Colorado, and she was doing a fiddle contest," Rose recalled. "We literally met dancing in one of those Colorado summer rainstorms."

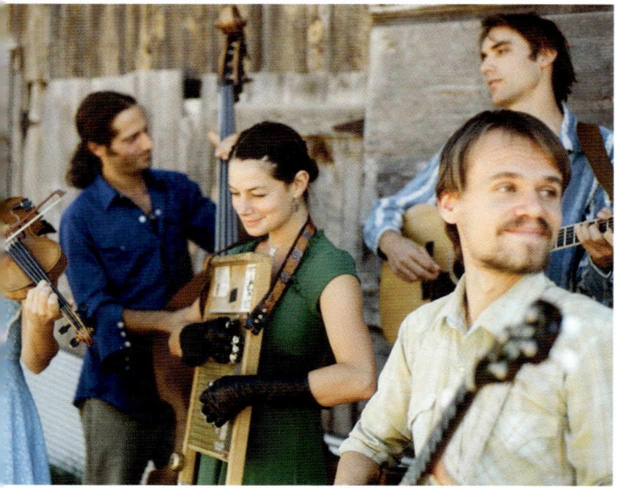

c. 2014

After that came various friendships and musical connections forged in Connecticut, Kentucky and Colorado; a significant gathering point was the Walnut Valley Festival in Winfield, Kansas. For the next few years, the affiliation of musicians—Rose, Law, Bonnie Paine on washboard, stompbox and other percussion; Daniel Rodriguez on guitar and banjo; and Sage Cook on the electric banjo, guitar and mandolin—would play with one another whenever and wherever they could.

"We kept crossing paths for the next few years, different festivals all around the country," Rose said. "We knew we had a very strong connection musically; we heard something in each other.

"In 2005, we started communing in Tahlequah, Oklahoma, which is where Bonnie's from. It's at the end of the Trail of Tears, where the removed Cherokee Nation settled. We spent the summer camped out on Spring Creek, and that's when the songs came together."

The players then relocated back to the thriving music scene of Nederland, Colorado, in the fall of 2006.

"When I was young, I had lived in Nederland for about three years, playing with an old-time string band called High on the Hog," Rose explained. "We were part of the 'picks' that would go on at the Pioneer Inn and the Acoustic Coffeehouse, and I got to know the guys in Yonder Mountain String Band and Vince Herman of Leftover Salmon pretty well.

"Those picks and the support network in Colorado for new innovative acoustic music absolutely played a part in the decision to move back to Nederland to start a band. Vince knew Bonnie and Daniel pretty well through festivals in the Midwest, so he invited them up to live next to him. I started booking shows and invited a whole bunch of people that we had been crossing paths with across the country."

When the run ended, the five musicians left standing played their first official gig together at the Gold Hill Inn, performing as Elephant Revival Concept. After solidifying the group, the ensemble dropped "Concept" from the moniker. They started playing gigs around Colorado, released a few records and made strides in the national acoustic music circuit.

Elephant Revival's third album, 2013's *These Changing Skies*, peaked at #8 on *Billboard*'s Top Heatseekers chart.

Weaving a cohesive tapestry from disparate influences, Elephant Revival's music mesmerized with the evocation of a traditional folk group and the communal vim of a jam band. Every member contributed original songs, with many reflecting a proud social consciousness and deep commitment to certain ideals, such as responsible stewardship of the planet and its inhabitants.

"The more that we see that our music is resonating with folks, the more that there's a call to action," Rose said. "There are times to give back, to do good things. Part of being kind is trying to inspire people to be the best expression of themselves. It's humbling that we have a voice in our culture. It feels like we're of service, that's the bottom line." ●

BILL FRISELL }

ONE OF the most well-known and sought-after jazz musicians in the world grew up in Denver—Bill Frisell, a guitar great who graduated from Denver East High School in 1969.

"Everything was formed for me in Colorado—I have powerful memories of what happened during those years there," Frisell said. "From when I was very young, the whole music community embraced me, through the school system and all the musicians in town and the amazing teachers I had all along the way. I didn't realize how lucky I was to have had that at the time."

Frisell took up clarinet as a child and continued participating in school concerts and marching bands. But he had become interested in guitar for his personal enjoyment, playing in rock and R&B bands as a teenager.

"There was a talent show in high school, and these girls were doing a dance routine using a Wes Montgomery tune, 'Bumpin' on Sunset,' as their backup music," Frisell recalled. "The band director knew I played guitar. He said, 'Do you think you could learn this song so we could have live music?' I took home the record and it blew my mind. Luckily, I was at the point where I could figure it out where it was recognizable, and I played it at school and it was a big hit. That was a turning point—it led to other things."

Classmates in the Denver school system included Philip Bailey, Andrew Woolfolk and Larry Dunn, future members of Earth, Wind & Fire. "We all came up in school together starting in junior high," Frisell said. "We were in rival soul bands, but we were in concert band together. I'd taken a few lessons at the Denver Folklore Center, an extraordinary place. It was incredible what I would find out from just hanging out, standing around and finding out what I should be listening to."

Dale Bruning, a Denver-based guitarist and educator, advanced Frisell's preoccupation with jazz. Frisell attended the University of Northern Colorado, where he studied with Johnny Smith, one of the most singular musicians of his generation; Smith had lived in Colorado Springs since 1958.

"I met people who supported me in the idea of playing music. I would get so discouraged at times. Every time I was at that point, there was someone to lift me up. It could have gone the other way so easily—if someone had said, 'You suck,' that would have been it for me, broken me down."

Frisell moved to Boston in 1971 to attend the Berklee School of Music. By mid-decade, he had begun fusing jazz with his other musical interests, developing a niche through his unique exploration of variations in timbre, using an array of effects. He spent 1978 in Belgium to write music and then moved to New York City. He earned a reputation as ECM Records' in-house guitarist and as a member of John Zorn's Naked City group, one of the most extreme noise/rock outfits of the early 1990s. He collaborated with a wide variety of artists, not all of them jazz musicians. By the end of the 1990s, his aesthetic transcended the boundaries of any given performing situation.

Frisell moved to Seattle in 1989, where he continued to make his home, and garnered increasing notoriety as an impossible-to-categorize composer and bandleader, seamlessly navigating a variety of styles. In nine out of 10 years, Frisell held the No. 1 spot for guitar in the annual *DownBeat* Critics Poll.

In a career spanning more than 100 recordings, Frisell enjoyed his highest charting album when 2014's *Guitar in the Space Age!* reached #2 on the *Billboard* Jazz Albums chart. The recording paid joyous tribute to the guitar music

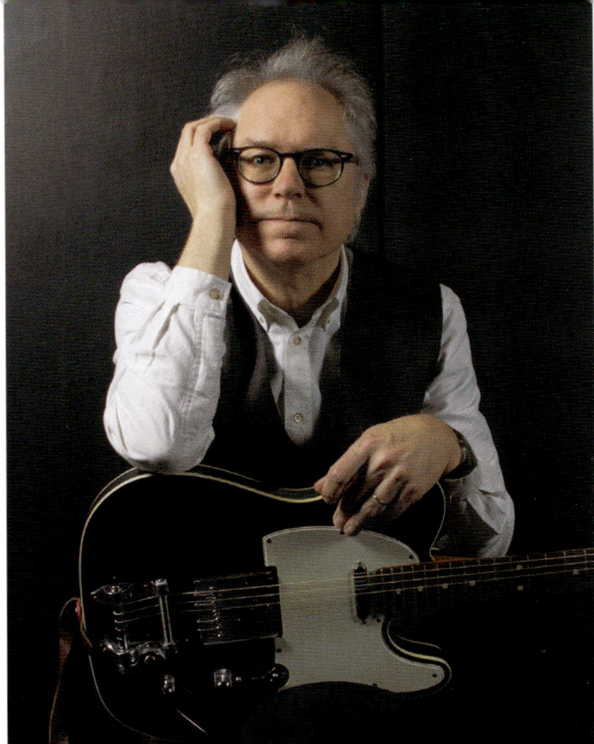

c. 2014

of the late 1950s and early 1960s initially inspired him.

"I was in Denver when I heard that music for the first time," Frisell recollected. "The Astronauts' 'Baja'—my friend across the street had one of their records. Junior Wells' 'Messing With the Kid'—I first heard at the Denver Folklore Center. The Beach Boys' 'Surfer Girl'—the first 45 I bought. I can still picture the label, what it felt like pulling the record out of the sleeve, almost smell it.

"Now I've been in music my whole life. Ultimately, it comes from within us—it's our imagination, what's in our minds. But in Colorado, there's something overwhelming in the air or the altitude. It formed the standard for what I hope for, about people being together." ●

RON MILES }

A MASTER cornetist, Ron Miles used jazz as a starting point for his original voice, but he helped elevate every style with which he was involved, from funk to sophisticated big-band charts to Hank Williams songs. A pillar of the Colorado jazz community, he found himself in high demand.

"People seek me out to play," Miles said. "I feel really fortunate."

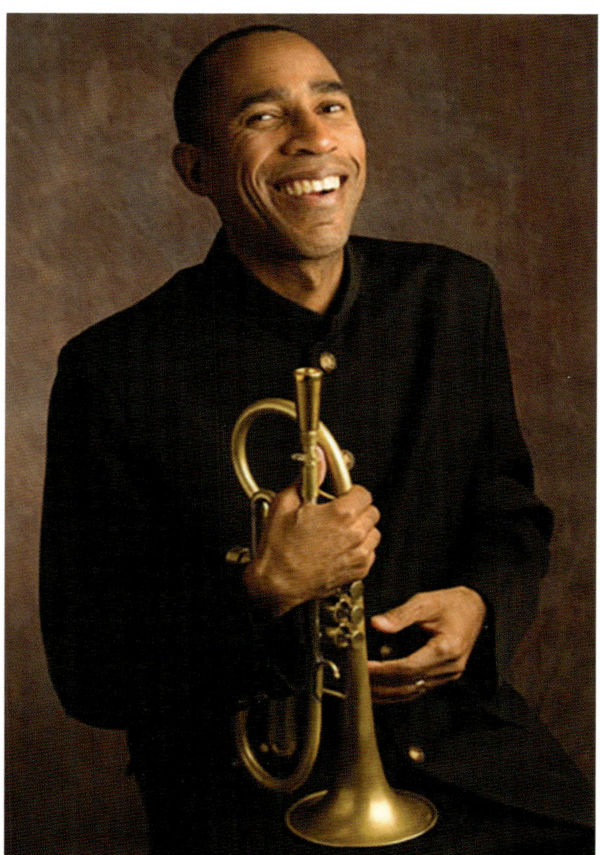

c. 2012

Miles began playing the trumpet at age 11, when his family moved to Denver. He attended Denver East High School.

"El Chapultapec, the Denver jazz club, had been an institution for decades, and hearing the many national acts who would pass through was a connection to the essence of jazz music," Miles said. "I would also attend the concerts Dick Gibson hosted at the Paramount Theatre, where he would bring in his favorite musicians to play. Clark Terry was one of the legendary figures who came through—I got a scholarship to go to his jazz camp in Emporia, Kansas."

Miles studied music at the University of Denver and started constructing a résumé with Boulder Creative Music Ensemble, a small, local avant-garde jazz group directed by saxophonist Fred Hess.

"I was 19, and it was important to be tuned into another tradition of music and play with people outside of academia who were a lot better than me," Miles said. "They were dedicated—we would play concerts where no one came and they would play like it was a full house. As time went on, we were able to hook up with people into a creative music scene that wasn't so style-specific, such as Bruce Odland, and that opened things up for all of us.

"That experience shaped my vision about being true to your music. It takes a while to figure it out, but you don't get to go backward, no matter how much you might like an older style of music. You have to find your own music, the music of your time."

Miles went on to the Manhattan School of Music.

"Being from Denver, you wonder how you stack up at a place like that. People liked what I did. That was the first time *The New York Times* wrote about me. I found that if you present authentic music, there will be a place for you."

Miles balanced his musical output with his career as an educator. A teacher at Denver's Metropolitan State College since 1998, he was the coordinator of the school's innovative jazz-studies program.

"I remember when I got lessons from Lester Bowie and Ornette Coleman—they didn't even charge me. Without saying anything, they let me know that that's what you do, you keep an eye out for the next group of folks. When I got a job at Metro, I said, 'I'm not charging anybody for a lesson ever again.' "

Miles appeared as a sideman on dozens of projects, for artists as diverse as bandleader Mercer Ellington, drummer Ginger Baker, clarinetist Don Byron and pianist Jason Moran. The singular, lonesome-sounding cornetist also led ensembles featuring Hess and drummer Bruno Carr, and he featured his compositions on a dozen recordings.

Since the mid-1990s, Miles had a running history with protean guitarist Bill Frisell, a fellow Denver native. Miles and New Orleans drummer Brian Blade played on *The Sweetest Punch,* Frisell's alternative album to Elvis Costello & Burt Bacharach's *Painted from Memory* CD. Teaming up with Frisell and Blade, Miles released two discs, the first time he'd recorded with the same group twice; *Circuit Rider* peaked at #46 on *Billboard*'s Jazz Albums chart in 2014.

Miles enjoyed what he got out of his life as a prominent musician in Denver, far from the New York City jazz scene.

"I've received a lot of support from a lot of angels to get well represented out in the world. Now we see a whole generation of musicians from Colorado. Because the scene's not so big, you've got to pair up with this creative punk scene, and that art-rock scene, and a soul and hip-hop scene until we start to see the commonality. From there, we can carve out our own niche without having to be pulled into any particular style. You just get together with people and figure out how to make music." ●

APPENDIX I

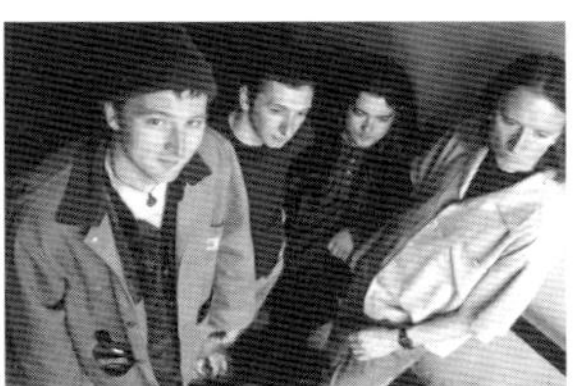

Acoustic Junction was signed by Capricorn Records after spending most of the 1990s touring all over the country. At the label's suggestion, the folk-rock band out of Boulder changed its name to Fool's Progress. The group folded in 2000; guitarist, vocalist and songwriter Reed Foehl went on to a solo career.

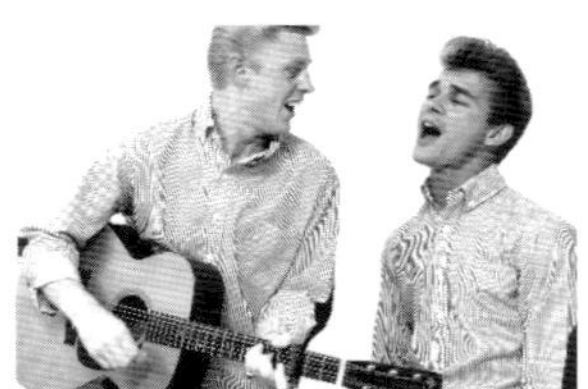

Denny & Jay (Rockwell and Cubbage), from Northern Colorado, were big stars locally—"H-U-R-T," released by Capitol Records, entered the charts on Denver's 950 KIMN in July 1964 and stayed there for six weeks, climbing as high as #2. But there was little interest in the youngsters outside of the Rocky Mountain region.

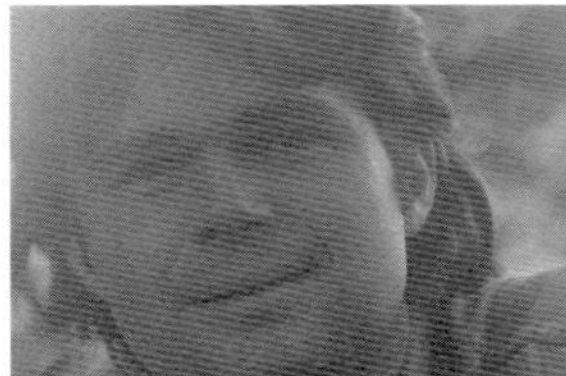

Tim Duffy was the creative force leading Orchestra of Clouds in the 1970s—his productions incorporated a dance troupe and clowns, galactic light shows and spaced-out monologues with his music. He then went the funk and R&B route, most notably with his All-Stars Soul Revue of versatile Colorado players.

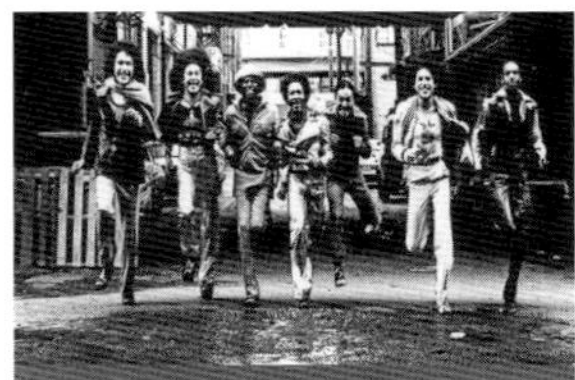

Freddi-Henchi & the Soulsetters, Colorado's premier party ensemble, held court at the Good Earth, a Boulder nightclub on the third floor of a building on what became the Pearl Street Mall. Guitarist Larry Wilkins, whose band King Louie & the Laymen was a 1960s Colorado frat-party favorite, later fronted Gangbusters.

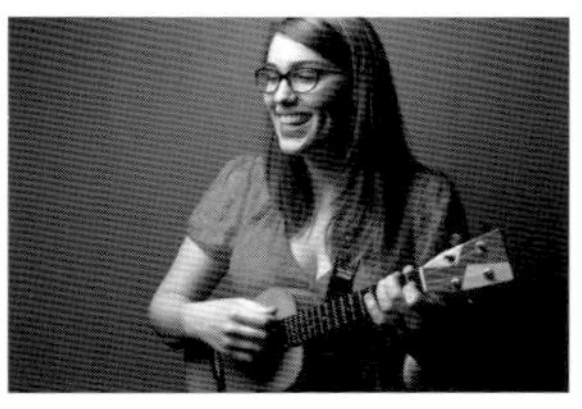

Danielle Ate the Sandwich, the stage name of Danielle Anderson, used simple observations and experiences to create her songs, which she usually played on ukulele and recorded in her tiny apartment kitchen. She posted her first YouTube video in 2007, became a darling of the website and played shows nationally.

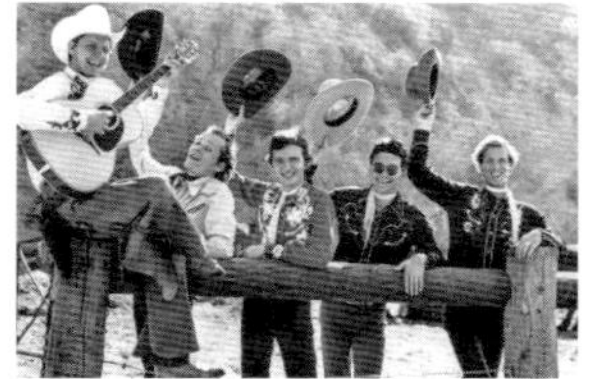

Dusty Drapes & the Dusters, a band of hippies who cut their long hair and played pure Western swing in the 1970s, signed with Columbia Records, but an album never came out. Country musician Junior Brown was an early member. Primary songwriter Dan McCorison eventually scored a solo deal with MCA.

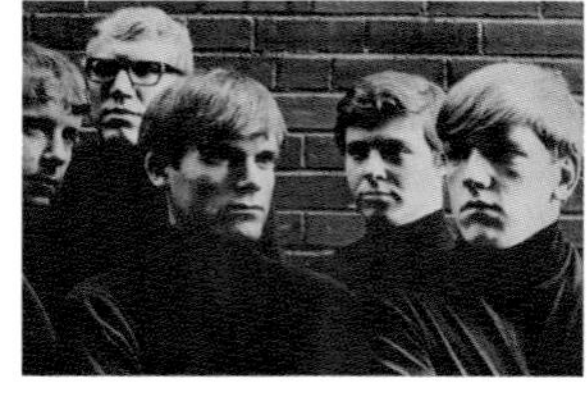

The Fogcutters, a University of Denver student band from 1965-1966, had a local hit, "Cry, Cry, Cry." A few members relocated to Los Angeles, changed their name to the Fantastic Zoo and recorded for Double Shot Records, backing labelmate Brenton Wood on his 1967 national hit, "The Oogum Boogum Song."

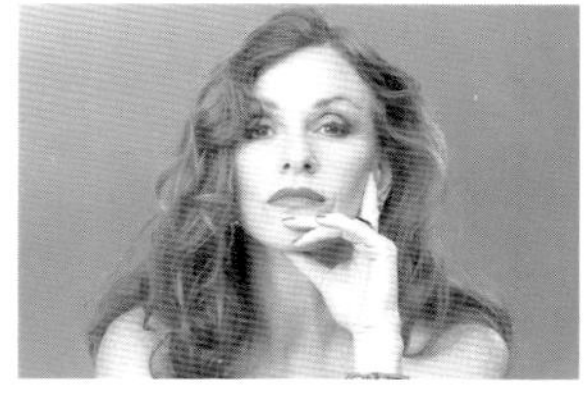

Lannie Garrett, Denver's most enduring chanteuse, treated fans to everything from big band shows to Patsy DeCline (her tongue-in-cheek take on country music). In 2006, she opened Lannie's Clocktower Cabaret, a nightclub in downtown Denver presenting her shows, national acts and Colorado entertainment.

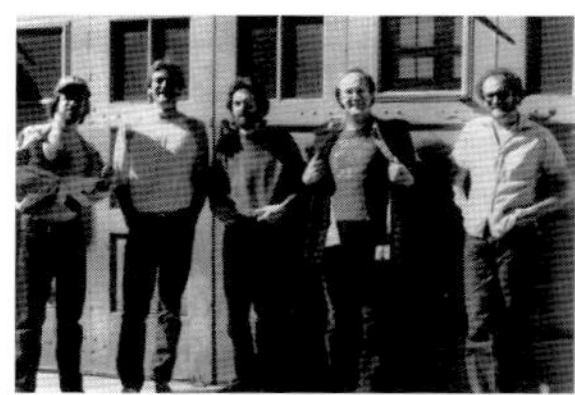

Gris Gris, led by singer and keyboardist Steve Conn, played "slightly twisted funky New Orleans dance music" in the early 1980s. Conn was a regular soloist at the Hotel Boulderado's mezzanine, and he served as *eTown*'s first musical director. He eventually moved to Nashville, where he made a career as a sideman.

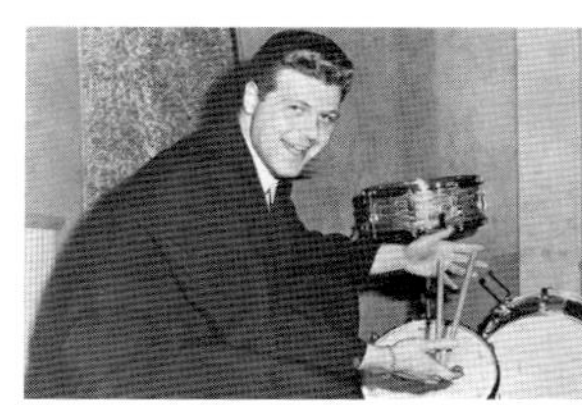

Ronny Kae was Denver-based Band Box Records' most visible local recording act during the 1960s. The drummer took the instrumental "Drums Fell off a Cliff" to #2 on radio station KIMN. Most Colorado artists in the late 1950s and early 1960s cut demo records at the Band Box recording studio on south Broadway.

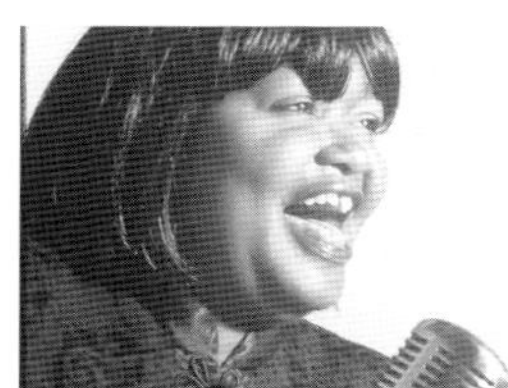

Hazel Miller came to be a Colorado institution belting out blues, gospel, jazz and pop at area clubs and theaters. She became a regular part of Big Head Todd & the Monsters' lineup and performed on the *eTown* radio broadcast heard on NPR. She also provided entertainment to U.S. military personnel serving overseas.

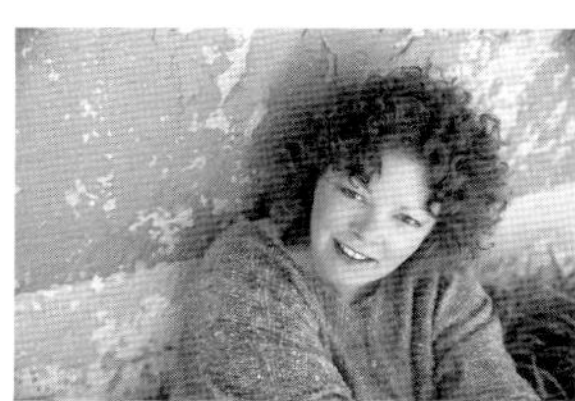

Mollie O'Brien, a nationally venerated interpretive singer of folk, blues and R&B, issued acclaimed albums with her brother, Tim O'Brien, and her husband, guitarist Rich Moore, and equally lauded solo releases. She had a regular stint with the Hopeful Gospel Quartet on "A Prairie Home Companion" in the early 2000s.

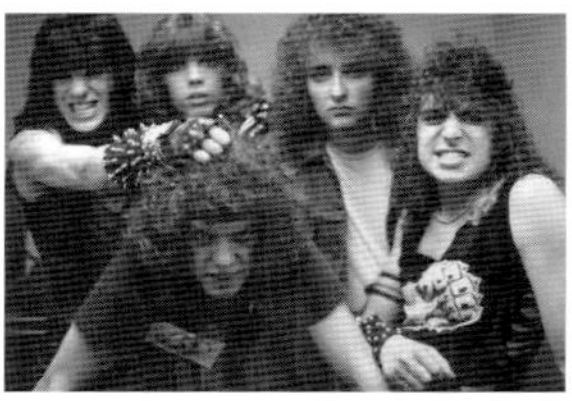

Jag Panzer, from Colorado Springs, formed in 1981 with a style influenced by New Wave of British Heavy Metal bands such as Judas Priest and Iron Maiden. The group's first album, *Ample Destruction*, eventually came to be considered a seminal underground metal album of the decade and was bootlegged repeatedly.

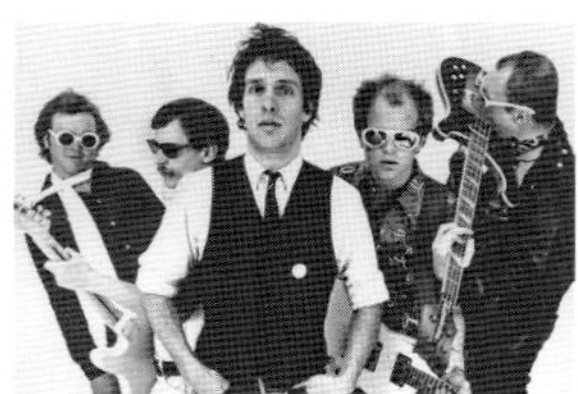

The Kamikaze Klones became new wave icons within the Colorado scene in the late 1970s and early 1980s, with legitimate hopes of a record deal that would make a sizable impact beyond the state. The Evergreen-bred band never got signed. The members of the Klones got together occasionally for reunion gigs.

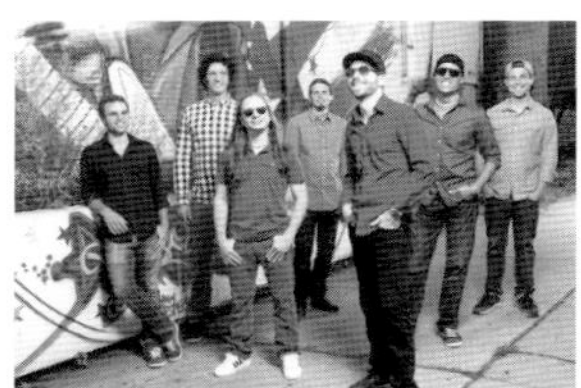

The Motet was founded in 1998 by drummer Dave Watts. The improvisational jazz and funk collective released seven albums and toured nationally, throwing dance parties at festivals such as Bonnaroo and Wakarusa. The group maintained a tradition of Halloween theme parties along Colorado's Front Range.

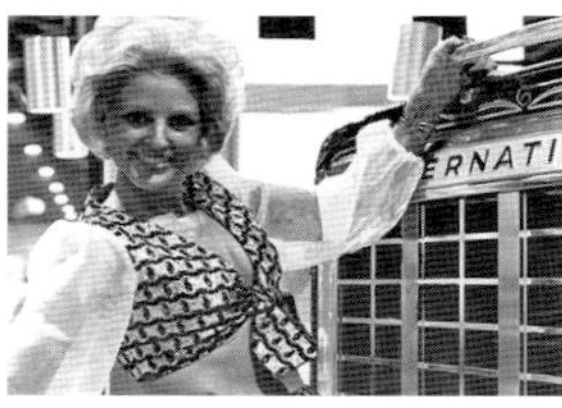

Bonnie Nelson, a country singer (also an accomplished horse rider and voted Miss Teen Colorado), was big on radio station KLAK in the 1970s; in time she moved to Nashville where she charted two minor records, "Don't Let It Go to Your Heart" (#83 in 1986) and "More Than Friendly Persuasion" (#84 in 1987).

APPENDIX I

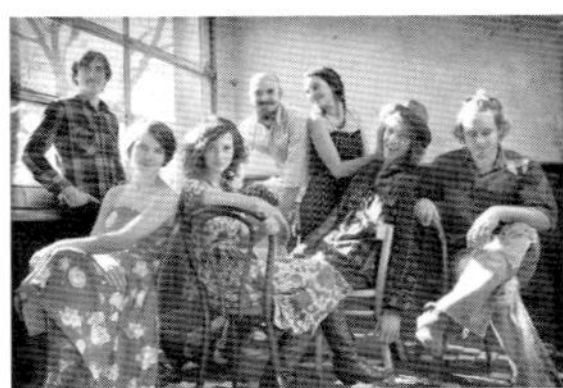

Paper Bird started as sidewalk buskers, performing its joyful blend of roots, folk and indie pop on the streets of Breckenridge. The septet was voted a "Top 10 Best Underground Band" by *The Denver Post* three years in a row, and Ballet Nouveau Colorado commissioned the act to score a ballet entitled "Carry On."

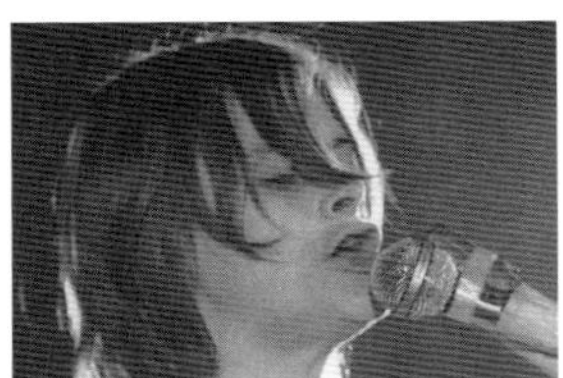

Judy Roderick, a University of Colorado student, signed a record deal with Vanguard in 1964, but her promising folk music got lost in the shuffle. She wed underground radio personality Bill Ashford, who supported her in fronting 60,000,000 Buffalo, a funky, bluesy Colorado rock band that broke up after one album.

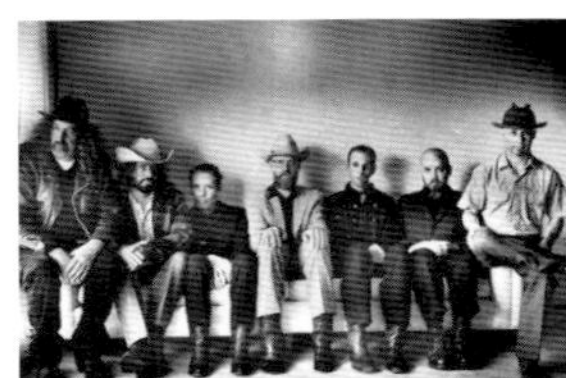

Slim Cessna's Auto Club formed in 1992 and pounded out a frenzied "country Gothic" hybrid linking rockabilly, country blues and punk rock. The group, praised by Jello Biafra as "the country band that plays the bar at the end of the world," recorded critically acclaimed albums on Biafra's Alternative Tentacles label.

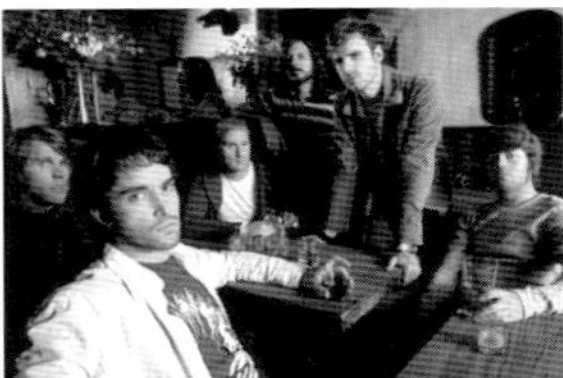

Vaux built a national following in the late 1990s through independent releases and van tours. The six-piece Denver post-hardcore band's Atlantic debut, *Beyond Virtue, Beyond Vice*, portended a whole new level of exposure, but Vaux severed ties with the major label. "Are You With Me" was an iTunes single of the week.

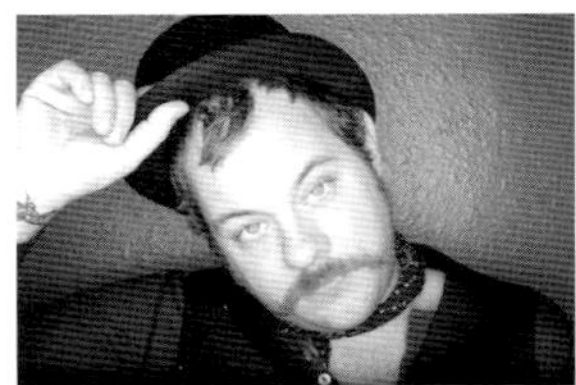

Nathaniel Rateliff started out in the band Born in the Flood before forming the Wheel and developing a dedicated following within the Denver music community. Recording under his own name, he toured internationally in support of his debut, *In Memory of Loss*, and his second record, *Falling Faster Than You Can Run.*

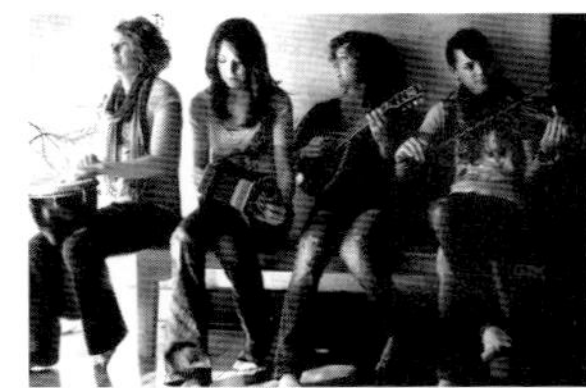

SHEL, a folk-pop band from Fort Collins, comprised four classically trained sisters who first appeared on the stage backing up their father, singer-songwriter Andrew Holbrook. The quartet had its brew of Celtic, folk and rock elements used in television shows, national ad campaigns and independent film.

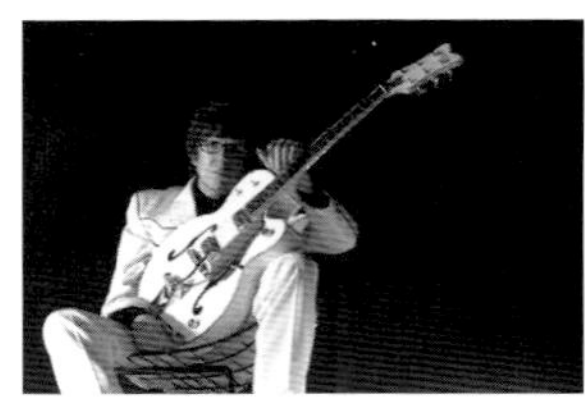

Kenny Vaughan joined a punk band in Denver, a cult favorite called the Jonny 3. Nashville called and offered him plenty of work, and the guitarist became a sought after sideman, recording with dozens of top artists including Lucinda Williams and Rodney Crowell along with a regular gig in Marty Stewart's band.

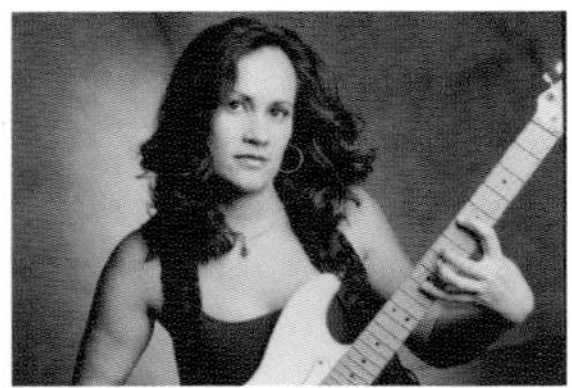

Wendy Woo was a mainstay of Colorado's music scene, known for using her guitar as a percussion instrument. Remaining an independent artist for eight albums, she lived in Boulder (where three newspapers named her "best local musician"), Denver (the alternative weekly *Westword* put her in its Hall of Fame) and Loveland.

APPENDIX II *They Also Served*

Morris Bernstein, a writer and producer born in the southern Colorado town of Capulin, founded Lute Records in the 1950s and claimed to have discovered Otis Redding.

Sam Bush, the founder and leader of New Grass Revival, was dubbed "the Mayor of Telluride" for performing every year at the Telluride Bluegrass Festival since 1975.

Eugene Chadbourne, former Shockabilly leader and free-jazz/country/rock innovator, grew up in Boulder; the prolific and innovative guitarist was a well-regarded eccentric.

Crooked Fingers, a North Carolina band led by Archers of Loaf lead singer Eric Bachmann, moved to Denver for a brief spell before he moved on to adventures elsewhere.

Dispatch, a jam band based in the Boston area, developed a following via word-of-mouth and file-sharing in the late 1990s; drummer Brad Corrigan grew up in Littleton.

Robben Ford, a touring guitarist with Joni Mitchell, George Harrison and the L.A. Express, lived in Boulder in the mid-1970s to study technique, composing and Buddhism.

Jon Ims, a singer-songwriter from Denver, was BMI's Songwriter of the Year for 1993. He also wrote the No. 1 country song "Falling Out of Love" recorded by Reba McEntire.

Sonny Landreth, the Louisiana slide guitar master who played with John Hiatt & the Goners, lived in Allenspark and then Estes Park in the late 1970s and early 1980s.

The Limeliters took their name from their early stomping grounds, the Limelight Club in Aspen; with lead singer Glenn Yarbrough they charted with "Dollar Down" in 1960.

Lyric, a "folky funk" duo, was managed by former Chicago drummer Danny Seraphine. "Would I Lie to You" grazed the adult contemporary charts in the late 1990s.

Dan McCrimmon, a fourth generation Coloradan, breathed life into western history through the folk circuit; he had teamed with Steven Fromholz to create the duo Frummox.

Ronnie Montrose grew up in Denver; he worked his way from session player (Van Morrison) to guitar hero (the Edgar Winter Group, Montrose, Gamma) to fusion virtuoso.

Tom Nix, a Colorado native, played throughout the Rocky Mountain region; he made the *Billboard* Country Singles charts in 1981 with "Home Along the Highway" (#79).

Nova, a curious mix of three Italians, one Englishman and a black bass player from Queens, settled in Boulder in 1977; the jazz-funk band then moved to L.A. to do an album.

Ophelia Swing Band, an endearingly ramshackle band with Dan Sadowsky, Tim O'Brien and Washboard Chaz, thrived playing acoustic swing and blues in the early 1970s.

The Photo Atlas, a dance-punk quartet from Denver, was named Spin.com's Artist of the Day, and the song "Red Orange Yellow" was featured in various video games.

The Pirate Signal, a Denver hip-hop duo composed of rapper-producer Yonnas Abraham and DJ A-What, headlined the Skull Candy Hip-Hop Tent on the 2008 Warped Tour.

Spike Robinson, a world-renowned saxophonist, lived in Boulder for years and was a fixture in area clubs before relocating to the United Kingdom, where he died in 2001.

Brent Rowan, a graduate of Arvada High School, became a premier session guitarist who supported Nashville's biggest stars, playing on more than 10,000 sessions.

The Rumble, one of a slew of Denver outfits featuring ace drummer Bob Rupp, won MTV's "Basement Tapes" competition in 1987. Rupp's Drums was his shop until 2003.

Runaway Express, easily Colorado's most prolific studio outfit, was fronted by Jim Ratts and his wife Salli. They won several local awards for their musical exploits.

Mitch Ryder, who gained fame fronting the Detroit Wheels, stopped performing in the 1970s and headed to Denver, working a day job for five years and writing songs at night.

Van Trevor recorded for Denver-based Bandbox Records in the early 1960s, making the country charts with "Born to Be in Love with You" (#22) and "Our Side" (#27).

Randy VanWarmer, born in Indian Hills, Colorado, signed with Bearsville and placed a huge pop hit in 1979, the delicate "Just When I Needed You Most"—#4 in *Billboard*.

APPENDIX III

The following artists also deserve recognition for their contributions to Colorado music:

A Shoreline Dream
Achilles & Frank
The Action Brass
Air Dubai
Armed Dwarf
The Auto-No
The Aviators
Bad Weather California
Baldo Rex
The Bedouins
The Beggars Opera Company
Bela Karoli
Big Gigantic
Biota
Black Irish
Blitz Girls
Joe Bonner
David Booker
Bop Street
Born in the Flood
Boulder Acoustic Society
The Brambles
Breathe Carolina
Antonio Brico
Bum Kon
The Cahoots
Bright Channel
Jamie Brockett
Dale Bruning
Joey Buffalo & the Sonics
Bum Kon
Cabaret Diosa
Cahoots
Calm
Candy Claws
The Captain & the Red Hot Flames
Cee Cee Carol
Cat-A-Tac
The Ceeds
Cells
Jon Chandler
Lee Chandler
Chaos Theory
The Chasers
Joseph Childress
Christie Front Drive
The Colorado Symphony Orchestra
John Common
The Contrasts
Ian Cooke
The Corvairs
Cowtown
Crank Call Love Affair
The Dalhart Imperials
Dakota Blonde
Dancing Assholes
The Daniels
The Dean Davis Company
Dead Silence
The Defex
Denver Joe
The Denver Symphony Orchestra
Dethcentrik
Dick & the Chicks
Michael Dinner
Rob Drabkin
Drop Dead, Gorgeous
Eighth Penny Matter
Electric Third Rail
The Elopers
The Esquires
The F.A.B. Company
The Fabulous Fremonts
The Fantabulous Jags
Fear Before the March of Flames
The Flameouts
Mary Flower
Eugene Fodor
Rebecca Folsom
Foreskin 500
Josephine Foster
Les Fradkin
Fresh Breath Committee
The Front
The Front Street Blues Band
Tony Furtado
The Galaxies
The Gamits
The Glass Menagerie
The Gluons
Great Caesar's Ghost
The Green Giants
The Guys
Hardwater
Hate Fuck Trio
Havok
Head for the Hills
Hearts of Palm
Fred Hess
The Higher Elevation
Warren Hill
Hillbilly Hellcats
Hit and Run
W.L. Horning
Hot IQs
Houses
Peanuts Hucko
The Hustlers
Idlewhile
The Immortal Nightflames
Instant Empire
The Instants
Blackie Jackson
The Jinns
Patti Jo & the Teardrops
Marty Jones
Jonny III
Karen Karsh
Kenny & the Kritix
Doug Kershaw
Kill Paradise
Randy King
King Louie & the Laymen
Clay Kirkland
Celeste Krenz
Art Lande
Achille Lauro
The Lawmen
Don Lewis
Willie Lewis
Little Fyodor
Little Women
Johnny Long
Ty Longley
Lord of Word & the Disciples of Bass
Love.45
Lynx
Mando & the Chili Peppers
ManeLine
Mike Marchant
René Marie
Matson Jones
Glenn Miller
Keith Miller
Chuck Mills & the Monarchs
The Minders
Monkey Siren
The Monocles
The Moonrakers
Max Morath
The Mother Folkers
Billy Murray
The Mutilators
New World Mutants
The Bruce Odland Big Band
Open Road
The Original Rabbits
Kat Orlando
Opie Gone Bad
Our Gang
Keith Oxman
Timothy P. & Rural Route 3
Patrick Park
Dexter Payne
Pearl
Planes Mistaken for Stars
Playalitical
The Poor
Princess Music
The Procussions
Propinquity
The Psychodelic Zombiez
The Queen City Jazz Band
Hugh Ragin
The Railbenders
Ralph & Clyde
Nelson Rangell
The Ravers
The Reals
Red Cloud West
The Reejers
Reverb & the Verse
Frankie Rino
The Rippingtons
Rivulets
The Road Runners
The Rockin' Rudolphs
Roper
The Rouge
Sage & Seer
Carla Sciaky

Scott Seskind
Sherri Jackson
Sick
Lee Sims & the Platte River Band
Sky King
Pete Smythe
Snake Rattle Rattle Snake
The Soul Survivors
The Soothsayers
Spoons
The Starlight Ramblers
Angie Stevens
The Sting Reys
Nina Storey
The Strolling Scones
SunshineWard
Super Band
Ralph Sutton
The Swayback
Sweet Water Well
Paul Taylor
Sally Taylor
3 The Hardway
Thinking Plague
Time
The Transistors
The Trolls
Eddie Turner
Joey Vain & Scissors
James Van Buren
Sally Van Meter
The Varve
Velvet Acid Christ
The Violators
The Visitors
Washboard Chaz
Ozie Waters
Dick Weissman
White Lightnin'
Bill White Acre
Paul Whiteman
Halden Wofford & the Hi-Beams
West Water Outlaws
White Trash
The Woodsman
Michael Woody & the Too High Band
Woven Hand
Yo, Flaco!
You Me & Apollo
Lionel Young Band
The Young Weasels
Dave Zobl
(Your favorite artist here)

BIBLIOGRAPHY

Most of the quotations in the various entries are words said directly to the author, in conversations and interviews, over the course of 26 years of reporting for *The Denver Post*, as the music director for radio station KCUV and as the director of the Colorado Music Hall of Fame. Other commentary generally relied on selected local writers whose pieces appeared in *The Denver Post*, *Rocky Mountain News*, *Boulder Daily Camera* and *Westword*. *Rolling Stone* magazine's writers got the Colorado crop of rock stars to reveal themselves in the mid-1970s. Rock 'n' roll researcher George Krieger's articles in *Colorado Heritage* and *Goldmine* were irreplaceable. *Billboard* Books and *Billboard* Publications were a choice source for clear, factual chart information, and Joel Whitburn's series took the guesswork out of tracking the rise and fall of the rock era's hits.

BOOKS

ALAN, CARTER. *U2: The Road to Pop.* Boston: Faber and Faber, Inc., 1992

BRONSON, FRED. *The Billboard Book of Number One Hits.* New York: Billboard Publications, Inc., 1988.

CLIFFORD, MIKE. *The Harmony Illustrated Encyclopedia of Rock.* New York: Harmony Books, 1986.

COLE, RICHARD WITH TRUBO, RICHARD. *Stairway To Heaven.* New York: Harper Collins, 1992.

CROSBY, DAVID, AND GOTTLIEB, CARL. *Long Time Gone.* New York: Doubleday, 1988.

DALTON, DAVID. *Mr. Mojo Risin'.* New York: St. Martin's Press, 1991.

DE LA PARRA, FITO. *Living the Blues.* Record Grafix, 1999.

DAVIS, STEPHEN. *Old Gods Almost Dead.* New York: Broadway Books, 2001.

FUDGER, DAVE, AND SILVERTON, PETE. *The Rock Diary.* New York: Proteus, 1983.

GUNN, JACKY, AND JENKINS, JIM. *Queen: As It Began.* New York: Hyperion, 1992.

HENDERSON, DAVID. *'Scuse Me While I Kiss The Sky.* New York: Doubleday, 1978.

HILDEBRAND, LEE. *Stars of Soul and Rhythm & Blues.* New York: Billboard Books, 1994.

HOPKINS, JERRY. *Hit & Run.* New York: Perigree, 1983.

JANCIK, WAYNE. *One-Hit Wonders.* New York: Billboard Publications, Inc., 1998.

JAVNA, JOHN, AND SHANNON, BOB. *Behind the Hits.* New York: Warner Books, 1986.

MARSH, DAVE. *The Heart of Rock & Soul.* New York: New American Library, 1989.

NEELY, KIM. *Five Against One.* New York: Penguin, 1998.

NORMAN, PHILIP. *Elton John.* New York: Harmony Books, 1991.

REES, DAFYDD & CRAMPTON, LUKE. *Encyclopedia of Rock Stars.* New York: DK Publishing, 1996.

SANCHEZ, TONY. *Up and Down with the Rolling Stones.* New York, William Morrow, 1979.

SANTELLI, ROBERT. *Aquarius Rising: The Rock Festival Years.* New York: Dell Publishing, 1980.

SHAPIRO, HARRY, AND GLEBEEK, CAESAR. *Electric Gypsy.* New York, St. Martin's Press, 1991.

SHELTON, ROBERT. *No Direction Home.* New York: Beech Tree Books/Morrow, 1986.

STAMBLER, IRWIN. *The Encyclopedia of Pop, Rock and Soul.* New York: St. Martin's Press, 1974.

WARD, ED, STOKES, GEOFFREY, AND TUCKER, KEN. *Rock of Ages.* New York: Summit Books, 1986.

WHITBURN, JOEL. *Top Pop Artists & Singles. Menomonee Falls,* Wisconsin: Record Research, 1979.

ZIMMER, DAVE, AND DILTZ, HENRY. *Crosby, Stills & Nash.* New York: St. Martin's Press, 1984.

MAGAZINES

ADAMS, SAM. *"Grooving His Game." Colorado AvidGolfer (October 2009)*

BERNSTEIN, JONATHAN. "Todd Snider Salutes Hard Working Americans in New Band." *Rolling Stone* (November 12, 2013).

CROWE, CAMERON. "Early Byrd Finds His Wings." *Rolling Stone* (October 21, 1976).

DEXTER, KERRY. "Following the Thread of Imperfection." *Dirty Linen* (February/March, 2003).

GAMBACCINI, PAUL. "Beethoven Rolls

Over Again." *Rolling Stone* (May 23, 1974).

HENKE, JAMES. "Dan Fogelberg has everything his own way." *Rolling Stone* (August 25, 1977).

HICKEY, NEIL. "Bob Dylan—whose songs so powerfully express a generation's conflicts—talks about his life and his music." *TV Guide* (September 11, 1976).

HOPKINS, JERRY. "Kiss Kiss Flutter Flutter Thank You Thank You." *Rolling Stone* (November 29, 1969).

KRIEGER, GEORGE W. "Astronauts to Zephyr: Colorado's music of the 1960s." *Colorado Heritage* (Winter 1997).

KRIEGER, GEORGE W. "Flash Cadillac (and the Continental Kids): America's Favorite Party Band. *Goldmine* (January 31, 1997).

O'REAR, CAINE. "Hard Working Americans: Freak Power." *American Songwriter* (January 20, 2014).

PARRISH, MICHAEL. "Out on a Limb." *Dirty Linen* (October/November 2002).

PAYNES, STEPH. "Spiro's List." *Musician* (August 1994).

RENSIN, DAVID. "Dan Fogelberg: Home Free at Last." *Rolling Stone* (March 13, 1975).

RUHLMANN, WILLIAM. "The Nitty Gritty on the Dirt Band: From One Unbroken Circle To Another." *Goldmine* (February 9, 1990).

SHERIDAN, JIM. "The Teaser Revealed—Tommy Bolin From The Archives." *Discoveries* (April 1997).

JUDITH SIMS. "The Eagles Take It Easy & Soar." *Rolling Stone* (August 17, 1972).

SOOCHER, STAN. "The Poco Reunion." *Musician* (February 1980).

THOMPSON, DAVE. "Ritchie Who?" *Goldmine* (October 9, 1998).

VORDA, ALAN. "Zephyr: A Volcano of Dreams." *Discoveries* (April 1991).

YOUNG, CHARLES M. "Tommy Bolin dead at 25 of overdose." *Rolling Stone* (January 13, 1977): 10, 14.

NEWSPAPERS

BACA, RICARDO. "The big Cheese." *The Denver Post,* March 21, 2003.

BACA, RICARDO. "Singles that changed the city." *The Denver Post*, July 6, 2008.

BACA, RICARDO. "Producer back on Denver scene." *The Denver Post*, April 24, 2009.

BACA, RICARDO. "Denver songwriter/producer Ryan Tedder is a one-man music industry." *The Denver Post,* October 25, 2009.

BRIGGS, BILL. "Singer who sued Jackson: 'Nobody will touch me.'" *The Denver Post*, May 17, 1994.

BROWN, MARK. "Ruling the Roost." *Rocky Mountain News*, August 10, 2002.

BROWN, MARK. "Soul in Motion." *Rocky Mountain News*, February 24, 2002.

CALLAHAN, PATRICIA AND O'GUIN, BECKY. "Phish fans confront the police." *The Denver Post*, August 6, 1996.

CARROLL, JANE. "At the Grammy circus with Rare Silk." *Boulder Camera*, March 4, 1984.

FERRIS, JEDD. "Todd Snider gets his jam band on with Hard Working Americans." *The Washington Post*, September 18, 2014.

GOLDSTEIN, A.J. "Forward." *Westword*, November 15-21, 2012.

GOLDSTEIN, A.M. "Ace Young, starring in 'Joseph,' credits Boulder upbringing for success." *Daily Camera*, April 17, 2015.

GRUNDY, GARETH. "John Grant: 'It was horrifying. I got out just in time.'" *The Guardian*, June 19, 2010.

HARDEN, MARK. "Bluesman not really all that old." *The Denver Post*, February 26, 1999.

HAUSE, BUTCH. "Katy Moffatt Back in Groove." *The Denver Post*, May 12, 1995.

HERRERA, DAVE. "A Mad and Faithful Tale." *Westword*, September 11-17, 2008.

KATZ, ALAN. "Judy Collins: Her Denver years marked beginning of folk music craze." *The Denver Post,* December 2, 1987.

KOHLHAASE, BILL. "Rob Mullins Leads Merry Band of Jazz Crusaders." *Los Angeles Times*, December 11, 1992.

KRECK, DICK. "Wild Wild Weekend." The *Denver Post*, June 25, 1989.

LEHNDORFF, JOHN. "Two decades on, there's a revival." *Boulder Daily Camera*, May 20, 1994.

LIPSHER, STEVE. "Untrussworthy: Bridge has a gap." *The Denver Post*, October 3, 1998.

LOFHOLM, NANCY. "Rock star Cocker lights up town with Christmas spirit." *The Denver Post*, December 24, 1999.

MCALLISTER, MARGIE. "Crosby preaches against drugs." *Boulder Daily Camera*, November 8, 1989.

MCQUAY, DAVID. "Subdudes have their act together." *The Denver Post*, November 26, 1989.

MEHLE, MICHAEL. "Local band casts simple 'Spell' on record deal." *Rocky Mountain News*, November 11, 1994.

MENCONI, DAVID. "Boulder's Hit Parade." *Boulder Daily Camera*, February 21, 1988.

MINICLIER, KIT. "His honor 'Rubber Duck' steps down." *Rocky Mountain News*, January 13, 1992.

MITCHELL, JUSTIN. "Guercio gives CU-Denver $200,000 in recording gear." *Rocky Mountain News*, September 26, 1986.

MOORE, JOHN. "16HP cooling their jets." *The Denver Post*, October 9, 2001.

MOORE, JOHN. "'The Book of Mormon': Colorado's kings of pop-culture subversion." *The Denver Post*, June 12, 2011.

MORRISON, BARRY. "Bear Can Bombs and The Beatles Just Won't Mix." *The Denver Post*, August 23, 1964.

OKSENHORN, STEWART. "Still Gritty after all these years." *Aspen Times*, July 20, 2013.

PAIGE, WOODY. "Fans everywhere can name his tune." *The Denver Post*, June 6, 1996.

PARELES, JON. "Go West, Young Band." *The New York Times*, February 6, 2013.

RASIZER, LEE. "Joined at the hip-hop." *Rocky Mountain News*, August 23, 2003.

REINER, ERIC L. "Hot Rize reunion rolls out bluegrass blitz." *The Denver Post*, March 6, 1996.

REINER, ERIC L. "Chuck Pyle melds music, poetry, humor." *The Denver Post*, January 21, 2000.

REINER, ERIC L. "The Zen Cowboy's om-age to the indie spirit." *The Denver Post*, January 27, 2006.

ROSEN, STEVE. "Bob Lind Bursts '60s Cocoon." *The Denver Post*, December 29, 1993.

ROSEN, STEVE. "Great Chemistry." *The Denver Post*, April 22, 1997.

SAUNDERS, BRET. "Year minus CD means no third Grammy for Reeves." *The Denver Post,* October 13, 2002.

SAUNDERS, BRET. "Reprising Johnny Smith's guitar magic." *The Denver Post*, February 26, 2003.

SAUNDERS, BRET. "Jazz: The many styles of Ron Miles." *The Denver Post*, March 6, 2011.

SHEELER, JIM. "Join The Club: Minds behind successful Boulder music venue are crazy like Foxes." *Boulder Daily Camera*, November 10, 1995.

STONEHOUSE, ANDY. "'Red Elvis' Dean Reed back in spotlight." *Boulder Daily Camera*, April 12, 2002.

PHOTOGRAPHIC CREDITS

COVER - Brian Brainerd (U2)
2 - Todd Caudle (U2)
8 - Curt Gunther (The Beatles)
11 - Michael Ochs Archives (Chuck Berry)
12 - Colorado Historical Society (Dean Reed)
13 - Colorado Historical Society (Dean Reed)
14 - Gary Stites collection (Gary Stites)
15 - George W. Krieger collection (Gary Stites)
16 - Elektra Records/Jim Marshall (Judy Collins)
17 - Judy Collins collection (Judy Collins)
18 - Judy Collins collection (Judy Collins)
19 - Tommy Facenda collection (Tommy Facenda)
20 - Randy Sparks collection (The New Christy Minstrels)
22 - Ashley Famous Agency (The Serendipity Singers)
23 - John Madden collection (The Serendipity Singers)
24 - Jim Gallagher collection (The Astronauts)
25 - George W. Krieger collection (The Astronauts)
26 - Jim Gallagher collection (The Astronauts)
27 - Curt Gunther (The Beatles)
28 - Nicholas DeSciose (The Beatles)
29 - Nicholas DeSciose (The Beatles)
30 - Jill Guerra collection (Bob Lind)
31 - Sam Fuller collection (The Rainy Daze)
32 - Sam Fuller collection (The Rainy Daze)
33 - Barry Fey collection (Canned Heat)
34 - United Artists Records (Canned Heat)
34 - George W. Krieger collection (Steve Alaimo)
35 - Columbia Records/Don Hunstein (Paul Revere & the Raiders)
36 - Atlantic Records (Led Zeppelin)
37 - Elektra Records (The Doors)
38 - Kenny Passarelli collection (Beast)
39 - Bret Saunders collection (Jimi Hendrix)
40 - Reprise Records (Jimi Hendrix)
41 - Nicholas DeSciose (The Rolling Stones)
42 - Dan Fong (The Rolling Stones)
43 - Probe/ABC Records (Zephyr)
44 - Dan Fong (Zephyr)
45 - Liberty Records (Sugarloaf)
46 - Bob Webber collection (Sugarloaf)
47 - Claridge Records (Sugarloaf)
48 - Chrysalis Records (Jethro Tull)
49 - Western History Collection/Denver Public Library (Jethro Tull)
50 - Joe Calvin collection (Grateful Dead)
53 - Henry Diltz (The Eagles)
54 - Atlantic Records (Manassas)
55 - Caribou Ranch collection (Stephen Stills)
56 - Beatrice Kemp collection (The Soul Survivors)
57 - Decca Records (Rick Nelson & the Stone Canyon Band)
58 - ABC/Dunhill Records (Jimmy Buffett)
59 - Rick Roberts collection (Rick Roberts)
60 - Tumbleweed Records (Danny Holien)
61 - Bill Szymczyk collection (Danny Holien)
62 - Daniel Mainzer (Joe Walsh)
63 - Dan Fong (Joe Walsh)
64 - Liberty Records (The Nitty Gritty Dirt Band)
65 - United Artists Records (The Nitty Gritty Dirt Band)
66 - Bill Warren (The Nitty Gritty Dirt Band)
67 - RCA Records (John Denver)
68 - RCA Records (John Denver)
69 - Karmen Dopslaff collection (John Denver)
70 - Asylum Records (Richie Furay)
71 - Kim Gottlieb-Walker (Richie Furay)
72 - Irving Azoff collection (REO Speedwagon)
73 - Bob Ferbrache (Queen)
73 - Dan Fong (Bob Seger)
74 - Harold Fielden collection (Flash Cadillac & the Continental Kids)
75 - Scott O'Malley collection (Flash Cadillac & the Continental Kids)
76 - Charlie Phillips collection (Flash Cadillac & the Continental Kids)
77 - Reprise Records (Emmylou Harris)
78 - Terry O'Neill/Getty Images (Elton John)
79 - Caribou Ranch collection (Elton John)
80 - Caribou Ranch collection (Chicago)
81 - Caribou Ranch collection (The Beach Boys)
82 - Warner Bros. Records (The Doobie Brothers)
83 - DiscReet/Warner Bros. Records (Ted Nugent)
84 - Epic Records (Michael Martin Murphey)
84 - Caribou Records (Gerard)
86 - MGM Records (C.W. McCall)
87 - Shad O'Shea collection (Shad O'Shea)
88 - Dan Fong (Katy Moffatt)
89 - Nick Andurlakis collection (Elvis Presley)
90 - Bill Warren (U2)
93 - Bob Ferbrache (Bob Dylan)
94 - Columbia Records (Billy Joel)
95 - Asylum Records/Ed Caraeff (Chris Hillman)
96 - A&M Records (Firefall)
97 - Atlantic Records (Firefall)
98 - Jock Bartley collection (Firefall)
99 - Bell Records (Gary Glitter)
100 - Bob Ferbrache (Tommy Bolin)
101 - Geffen Records (Tommy Bolin)
102 - Bobby Barth collection (Babyface)
103 - Larry Thompson collection (Stallion)
104 - Andy Katz (Dan Fogelberg)
105 - Full Moon/Epic Records (Dan Fogelberg)
106 - Jean Fogelberg collection (Dan Fogelberg)
107 - Capitol Records (Navarro)
108 - Ariola America Records (Mary MacGregor)
109 - EMI America Records (Michael Johnson)
110 - John McEuen collection (Steve Martin)
111 - Bob Ferbrache (Bruce Springsteen)
112 - Columbia Records (Philip Bailey)
113 - Columbia Records (Earth, Wind & Fire)
114 - Richie Furay collection (Poco)
115 - Sam Bush collection (Böenzee Cryque)
116 - Select Records (Chuck E. Weiss)
117 - Anton Corbijn (David Bowie)
118 - Warner Bros. Records (Van Halen)
118 - Michael Goldman (Heart)
119 - Enigma Records (Mojo Nixon)
119 - Columbia Records (Tim Goodman)
120 - Caribou Records (Carl Wilson)
120 - Michael Jensen collection (David Crosby)
121 - Asylum Records/George Gruel (Warren Zevon)
122 - Asylum Records/Gary Heery (Boulder)
123 - Warner Bros. Records (Gary Morris)
124 - GRP Records (Dave Grusin)
125 - Polygram Records (Rare Silk)
126 - RCA Records (The Nails)
127 - Greg Wigler (U2)
128 - Bill Warren (U2)
129 - Brian Brainerd (U2)
130 - Alternative Tentacles (Jello Biafra)
131 - Modern Records (Stevie Nicks)
132 - Urban Sound/Kurt Marcus (Chuck Pyle)
133 - RMC Records (Rob Mullins)
134 - Flying Fish Records/Steve Ramsey (Hot Rize)
135 - Scott O'Malley collection (Hot Rize)
136 - Mary Staley Pridgen (Telluride Bluegrass Festival)
139 - Mercury Records/Ross Halfin (Def Leppard)
140 - Atlantic Records/Steven Selikoff (Winger)
141 - Kip Winger collection (Winger)
142 - Bobbi Marcus collection (Chris Daniels)
143 - Chris Daniels collection (Chris Daniels)
145 - High Street Records (The Subdudes)
146 - RCA Records (Treat Her Right)
147 - Steve Taylor collection (Steve Taylor)
148 - Silver Wave Records (Wind Machine)
149 - Nova Records (Dotsero)
150 - Dan Fong (Willie Nelson)
151 - Andrew Novick collection (Warlock Pinchers)
152 - Profile Records (DJ Quik)
153 - Sharon Poteet (Jinx Jones)
153 - East West Records/James Calderero (En Vogue)
154 - MCA Records/Peter Darley Miller (Spinal Tap)
155 - Geffen Records/Gene Kirkland (Dizzy Reed)
155 - Geffen Records/Robert John (Guns N' Roses)
156 - Michael Goldman (Blues Traveler)
157 - A&M Records/Dennis Keeley (Blues Traveler)
158 - Michael Goldman (The Moody Blues)
160 - Epic Records/Gene Kirkland (Ozzy Osbourne)
160 - Capitol Records/Bill Bernstein (Paul McCartney)
161 - Jim Sheeler (James Brown)
161 - Life Records (Tag Team)
162 - Hollywood Record (The Fluid)
163 - Island Records/Michael Lavine (Spell)
164 - Epic Records/Lance Mercer (Pearl Jam)
165 - Epic Records (Michael Jackson)
166 - Sean Kelly collection (The Samples)
167 - W.A.R.? Records (The Samples)
168 - Giant Records (Big Head Todd & the Monsters)
169 - Rob Squires collection (Big Head Todd & the Monsters)
170 - Jim Mimna (Big Head Todd & the Monsters)
171 - RCA Records (Dave Matthews Band)
172 - Imprint Records (Gretchen Peters)
173 - Atlantic Records/Melanie Nissen (Jill Sobule)
174 - Decca Records (John Tesh)
175 - Domo Records (Kitaro)

176 - Michael Goldman (String Cheese Incident)
179 - Elektra Records (Phish)
180 - A&M Records/Ken Schles (Sixteen Horsepower)
181 - David Eugene Edwards collection (Sixteen Horsepower)
182 - Capricorn Records/Catherine Wessel (311)
183 - Gramavision Records/Michael Macioce (Medeski Martin & Wood)
184 - Paul Conley collection (Lothar & the Hand People)
185 - Astralwerks Records/Kevin Westenberg (Chemical Brothers)
186 - Interscope Records/Daniel Corrigan (All)
187 - Private-I/Mercury Records (Rick James)
188 - Sony Music (Joe Cocker)
189 - Atlantic Records/Eugene Gologursky (Ginger Baker)
190 - Capitol Records/Paul Drake (Jimmy Eat World)
190 - AP Photo/Ed Andrieski (Neil Diamond)
191 - spinART Records/Tamee Ealom (The Apples in Stereo)
193 - Chuck Morris Entertainment (Leftover Salmon)
194 - Melinda DiMauro (Five Iron Frenzy)
195 - Sarabellum Records (Five Iron Frenzy)
197 - AP Photo/Damian Dovarganes (Trey Parker & Matt Stone)
198 - SCI Fidelity Records (String Cheese Incident)
199 - SCI Fidelity Records (String Cheese Incident)
200 - Capricorn Records/Johnny Buzzerio (Widespread Panic)
201 - Frog Pad Records/Michael Weintrob (Yonder Mountain String Band)
202 - Blue Note Records/Clay Patrick McBride (Dianne Reeves)
203 - Motown Records/Kwaku Alston (India.Arie)
204 - Concord Music Group (Otis Taylor)
205 - Rounder Records (Corey Harris)
206 - Interscope Records/Anthony Mandler (Bubba Sparxxx)
206 - Eric Lars Bakke (Steve Herndon)
207 - Forefront Records (Stacie Orrico)
208 - Michael Goldman (Bassnectar)
211 - Epic Records (The Fray)
212 - Brandon Marshall (The Fray)
213 - Epic Records (The Fray)
214 - Kindercore Records (Dressy Bessy)
215 - Peak Records (Gerald Albright)
216 - Paul Schroder (Devotchka)
217 - Michael McGrath (Devotchka)
218 - Lindsay McWilliams (Rose Hill Drive)
219 - AP Photo/Branimir Kvartuc (Ace Young)
220 - Reprise Records/Pamela Littky (Single File)
221 - Caleb Chancey (Katie Herzig)
222 - Interscope Records (OneRepublic)
223 - Interscope Records (OneRepublic)
224 - Reuters (OneRepublic)
225 - Darren Mahuron/Summit Studios (Tickle Me Pink)
226 - Universal Republic Records (Flobots)
227 - AP Photo/Matt Sayles (Flobots)
228 - Atlantic Records/Pamela Littky (3OH!3)
230 - Krystie Blackburn (Pretty Lights)
231 - Krystie Blackburn (Pretty Lights)
232 - Nathan Meese collection (Meese)
233 - Matt Morris collection (Matt Morris)
234 - Relapse Records (Cephalic Carnage)
235 - Dualtone Records (The Lumineers)
236 - AP Images/Miles Chrisinger (The Lumineers)
237 - Fat Possum Records (Tennis)
238 - Tyler Ward Music (Tyler Ward)
238 - A&M/Octone Records/Steve Stanton (Churchill)
239 - Bella Union (John Grant)
240 - SCI Fidelity Records/C. Taylor Crothers (Keller Williams)
241 - George Boedecker collection (Hard Working Americans)
242 - Suitcase Town Music (Gregory Alan Isakov)
243 - Anne Staveley (Elephant Revival)
244 - Paul Moore (Bill Frisell)
245 - Bruce Forster (Ron Miles)
256 - Stephen Collector (Jock Bartley guitars)

EDITOR **JON RIZZI**
ART DIRECTOR **KATE GLASSNER BRAINERD**

The Colorado Music Hall of Fame, located at the Trading Post at Red Rocks Amphitheatre, is a non-profit organization founded in 2011 to inspire music fans in the power of Colorado music history. Through gala induction events, significant exhibitions profiling each enshrinee and impactful music education programs, the CMHOF honors those individuals who have made outstanding contributions, preserves and protects historical artifacts, and educates the public regarding everything that is worthwhile about music in Colorado.

For more information about this book and other Colorado Music Hall of Fame projects, please visit our website **www.cmhof.org**

ISBN: 978-0-9915668-1-5
PRINTED IN THE USA
Pioneer Press / Greeley, CO

ACKNOWLEDGMENTS

THIS BOOK was borne of two equal loves: my love for music and my love for Colorado.

I extend my deepest and sincere gratitude to my amazing publishing team—Jon Rizzi for bringing his special brand of editorial wit and intelligence, and Kate Glassner Brainerd for her design artistry and unflagging pursuit of excellence. I also bless my wife, Bridget, without whom I would have wound up like the lead character in the movie *High Fidelity*. Family and friends, too.

I especially appreciate chairman Chuck Morris and the Colorado Music Hall of Fame board of directors for their support. Special recognition goes to George Boedecker and Mick & Patty Matthews; this project simply would not exist without them.

All the writers and photographers represented here who offered the reality of the music in their own way have contributed greatly to our state's musical legacy.

Finally, to all the people who listen, talk and think about music every day and drive the Colorado music scene—my everlasting gratefulness.

Assembling the mass of material required for a book of this kind naturally calls for assistance and support from many organizations and individuals. Among too many to thank, I must at least mention:

Amy Abrams, Libby Anschutz, Gil Asakawa, Ricardo Baca, Larry Baird, Chas Barbour, Mike Barsch, Tim Benko, Mark Bliesener, Michael Boosler, Ron Bostwick, Tad Bowman, Alex Brahl, Brian Brainerd, Holli Branam, Mark Brown, Paul W. Brown, Kathie Broyles, Michael Burgermeister, Scott Campbell, Diane Carmen, Meredith Carson, Todd Caudle, Rich Clarkson, Doug Clifton, Kevin Clock, Steve Collector, Tim Cook, Kent Crawford, Duane Davis, Lori DeVey, Mike Dickson, Henry Diltz, Bob Dubac, Jon Eisenberg, Jay Elowsky, Paul Epstein, Brent Fedrizzi, Kevin Fitzgerald, Rickey Fitzsimmons, Aaron Friedman, Jon Frizzell, Bob Galinsky, David Gans, Rich Garcia, Chip Garofalo, Michelle Gibson, Michael Goldman, Asha Goodman, Ira Gordon, Erika Green, Max Gronenthal, Neil Guard, Will Guercio, David Hartley, Mark Hartley, Butch Hause, Tommy Hauser, John Hayes, Christian Hee, Dave Herrera, Richard Hesse, Candace Horgan, Bruce Hornsby, Geina Horton, Ariel Hyatt, Michael Jensen, Marty Jones, Doug Kaufmann, Jim Kauvar, Rick Kauvar, Kathryn Keller, David Kirby, Steve Knopper, Dick Kreck, Alf Kremer, George Krieger, Huey Lewis, Mark Lewis, Phil Lobel, Carrie Lombardi, Doug Looney, Tom Ludwig, Julie Luster-Leahy, David Mackay, John Macy, Sam Maddox, Jan Martin, Jim Mason, Nancy May, Dennis McNally, David McReynolds, Michael Mehle, Eric Melvin, David Menconi, Dick Merkle, Jerry Mills, Jason Minkler, Justin Mitchell, John Moore, Pam Moore, Jo Myers, Matt Need, Michael Ochs, Stan Oliner, Barry Ollman, Scott O'Malley, Phyllis Oyama, Woody Paige, Kenny Passarelli, Bal Patterson, Dave Plati, Larry Pogreba, Pat Porter, Richard Ray, Nancy Rebek, Randy Reed, Kent Rice, Dawn Richardson, Scott Roche, Pete Roos, Dave Rothstein, Leland Rucker, Mike Rudeen, Matt Rue, Bob Rupp, Erika Santucci, Sue Satriano, Bret Saunders, Danny Sax, Andy Schneidkraut, Brian Schwartz, Ted Scott, Jim Sheeler, Dan Sherman, Ray Skibitsky, Ed Smith, Larry Solters, Stan Soocher, George Sparks, Kevin Spellman, Jim Sprinkle, Dave Stidman, Don Strasberg, Carol Taylor, Devon Taylor, T. Taylor, David Thomas, Rob Thomas, Larry Thompson, Samantha Tillman, Scott Tobias, Andy Torri, Hal Totten, Brian Trembath, Harry Tuft, Eddie Turner, Lew Turner, Craig Umbaugh, Bruce Van Dyke, Tom Walker, Bill Warren, Bill Wedum, Kenny Weissberg, Dick Weissman, Jay Whearley, Sara Williams, Gretchen Willoughby, Mark Wolf, Mike Wolf, Marty Wolff, Don Woodard, Jay Young, Dolly Zander, Jacque Zaremba and Mark Zaremba.

—G. BROWN

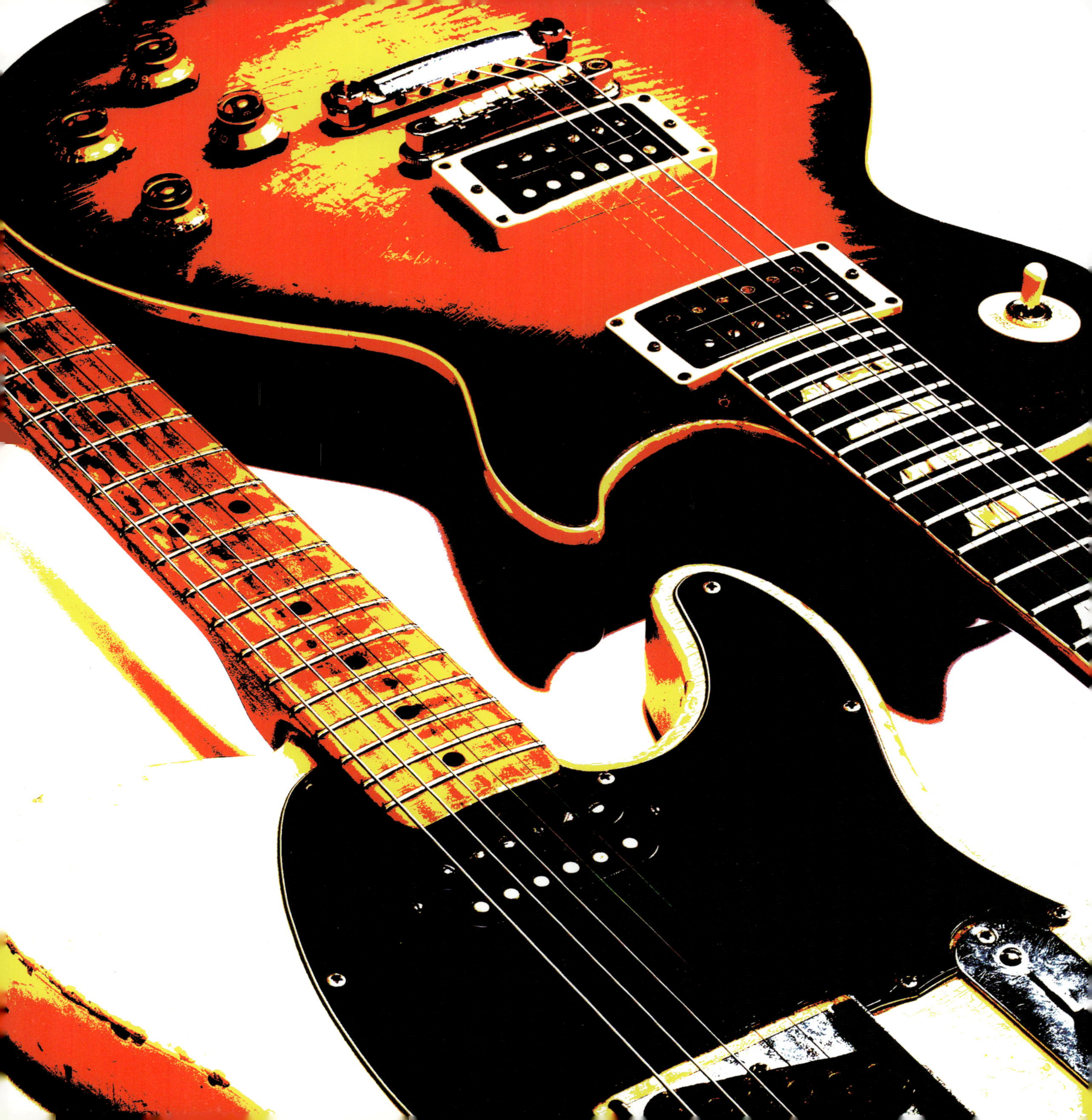